WEST ACADEMIC PUBLISHING'S EMERITUS ADVISORY BOARD

JESSE H. CHOPER
Professor of Law and Dean Emeritus
University of California, Berkeley

LARRY D. KRAMER
President, William and Flora Hewlett Foundation

GRANT S. NELSON
Professor of Law Emeritus, Pepperdine University
Professor of Law Emeritus, University of California, Los Angeles

JAMES J. WHITE
Robert A. Sullivan Emeritus Professor of Law
University of Michigan

WEST ACADEMIC PUBLISHING'S LAW SCHOOL ADVISORY BOARD

MARK C. ALEXANDER
Arthur J. Kania Dean and Professor of Law
Villanova University Charles Widger School of Law

JOSHUA DRESSLER
Distinguished University Professor Emeritus
Michael E. Moritz College of Law, The Ohio State University

MEREDITH J. DUNCAN
Professor of Law
University of Houston Law Center

RENÉE McDONALD HUTCHINS
Dean & Professor of Law
University of Maryland Carey School of Law

RENEE KNAKE JEFFERSON
Joanne and Larry Doherty Chair in Legal Ethics &
Professor of Law, University of Houston Law Center

ORIN S. KERR
William G. Simon Professor of Law
University of California, Berkeley

JONATHAN R. MACEY
Professor of Law,
Yale Law School

DEBORAH JONES MERRITT
Distinguished University Professor,
John Deaver Drinko/Baker & Hostetler Chair in Law Emerita
Michael E. Moritz College of Law, The Ohio State University

ARTHUR R. MILLER
University Professor and Chief Justice Warren E. Burger Professor of
Constitutional Law and the Courts, New York University

A. BENJAMIN SPENCER
Dean & Trustee Professor of Law
William & Mary Law School

PROFESSIONAL RESPONSIBILITY IN THE LIFE OF THE LAWYER

Third Edition

■ ■ ■

Alex B. Long
Williford Gragg Distinguished Professor of Law
University of Tennessee College of Law

Paula Schaefer
Art Stolnitz Distinguished Professor of Law
University of Tennessee College of Law

Cassandra Burke Robertson
John Deaver Drinko–BakerHostetler Professor of Law
and
Director, Center for Professional Ethics
Case Western Reserve University School of Law

AMERICAN CASEBOOK SERIES®

The publisher is not engaged in rendering legal or other professional advice, and this publication is not a substitute for the advice of an attorney. If you require legal or other expert advice, you should seek the services of a competent attorney or other professional.

American Casebook Series is a trademark registered in the U.S. Patent and Trademark Office.

© 2011 Thomson Reuters
© 2015 LEG, Inc. d/b/a West Academic
© 2024 LEG, Inc. d/b/a West Academic
    860 Blue Gentian Road, Suite 350
    Eagan, MN 55121
    1-877-888-1330

West, West Academic Publishing, and West Academic are trademarks of West Publishing Corporation, used under license.

Published in the United States of America

ISBN: 978-1-63659-834-5

To Jeremy and Abby

A.B.L.

To Ann Covington

P.S.

To Joan Burke and Thom Robertson

C.B.R.

PREFACE

This book is designed for the basic Professional Responsibility course taught in law school. A distinctive feature of *Professional Responsibility in the Life of the Lawyer* is its organization. Every new lawyer will go through various stages of a career. This book introduces students to the law and professional responsibilities applicable to lawyers in each stage.

Part 1 addresses one's entry into the legal profession. The first chapter provides an overview of a lawyer's professional responsibilities and prompts students to consider various aspects of professional identity. In the following chapters, the book explores the bar admission process, regulation of the legal profession, the unauthorized practice of law, and access to justice. Part 2 focuses on the rules regulating how an attorney attracts clients, from joining a law firm, to advertising and soliciting clients.

Part 3 focuses on the law and rules regulating the client-lawyer relationship, including the rules regarding the initial establishment of the relationship as well as the various duties (communication, competence, confidentiality, avoiding conflicts of interest, etc.) a lawyer owes to a client. This Part ends with chapters concerning the end of the attorney-client relationship and continuing obligations to former clients. Part 4 concentrates on professional conduct issues in particular areas of practice, including litigation, criminal law, transactional, and serving as a judge. Finally, Part 5 concludes with an exploration of issues lawyers should consider throughout their careers—well-being and legacy.

Professional Responsibility in the Life of the Lawyer, of course, covers the rules of professional conduct that are tested on the Multistate Professional Responsibility Exam (MPRE), which the vast majority of jurisdictions require for bar admission. But the book is not meant to merely be a march through relevant ethics rules. The book covers the relevant substantive law impacting lawyers, including fiduciary duties owed to clients (law that is not only the basis of liability to clients, but is also the basis of many professional conduct rules), the tort theory of legal malpractice, and the constitutional rules regarding lawyer advertising and solicitation of clients. In addition, the book asks students to think critically about what it means to be a lawyer. For example, the book incorporates lessons from the field of behavioral legal ethics, which considers the factors—often outside of a lawyer's conscious awareness—that may influence ethical (and unethical) decision making.

Finally, the book aims to help each student develop their own professional identity. As noted above, the first and last chapters of the book prompt students to think critically about aspects of professional identity, well-being, and legacy. Problems in every chapter place students in the role of a lawyer confronting professional conduct dilemmas. Through these hypotheticals, students are prompted to think about how they would proceed in line with not just their legal and ethical obligations, but also their own developing vision of what it means to be lawyer. Each chapter concludes with a "Profile of Attorney Professionalism," featuring attorneys who have demonstrated exceptional professionalism in practice and who serve as role models for other attorneys.

With this third edition of the book, original authors Professors Carl Pierce and Judy Cornett, who were responsible for the organizing principle of the book, are no longer contributing authors. But the remaining authors are grateful for Carl and Judy for bringing the book to life.

ALEX B. LONG
PAULA SCHAEFER
CASSANDRA BURKE ROBERTSON

February 2024

ACKNOWLEDGMENTS

The authors gratefully acknowledge the following for permission to reprint excerpts from the following materials:

Paula Schaefer, *Oral History of the Honorable Ann K. Covington*, American Bar Association Women Trailblazers in the Law Project (2010), reprinted with permission of Ann K. Covington and Paula Schaefer.

Benjamin H. Barton & Deborah L. Rhode, *Access to Justice and Routine Legal Services: New Technologies Meet Bar Regulators*, 70 HASTINGS L.J. 955 (2019), reprinted with permission of Benjamin H. Barton.

Margaret C. Benson, *Guardian Ad Litem: The Grinch Need Not Apply*, CHICAGO BAR JOURNAL (Oct. 2008), reprinted with permission of the Chicago Bar Association.

Alex B. Long, *What the Lawyer Well-Being Movement Could Learn from the Americans with Disabilities Act, Alex B. Long*, WILLIAM & MARY LAW REVIEW ONLINE, Vol. 63, No. 4 (2022), reprinted with permission of Alex B. Long.

Anonymous, *My Bar Admission Experience* (2023), reprinted with permission of Anonymous.

Joanna Litt, *'Big Law Killed My Husband': An Open Letter from a Sidley Partner's Widow*, THE AMERICAN LAWYER (Nov. 12, 2018), reprinted with permission from the 2018 edition of THE AMERICAN LAWYER © 2018 ALM Global Properties, LLC.

Candice Reed, LinkedIn Post, available at https://www.linkedin.com/posts/candicelreed_positivepsychology-attorneywellbeing-wellbeing-activity-7026598929899159552-7k1w?, reprinted with permission of Candice Reed.

A Passion for Justice: Sharon G. Lee, T LAW NEWS, A DIGITAL NEWSLETTER OF THE UNIVERSITY OF TENNESSEE COLLEGE OF LAW, (September 2023), reprinted with permission of the University of Tennessee College of Law.

Charles Swanson, Email to Friends Regarding the Passing of Pamela Reeves (September 10, 2020), reprinted with permission of Charles Swanson.

Summary of Contents

Preface V
Acknowledgments VII
Table of Cases XXV
Table of Statutes XXXI
Table of Rules XXXIII

PART 1. ENTERING THE PROFESSION

Chapter 1. Introduction: A Lawyer's Professional Responsibilities.... 3
A. Fiduciary Duty to Clients 4
B. Professional Conduct Rules 5
C. Developing a Professional Identity 7

Chapter 2. Admission to the Bar 13
A. Overview of Bar Admission Standards 14
B. The Character and Fitness Standard 16

Chapter 3. Regulation of the Legal Profession 35
A. Professional Discipline 35
B. Misconduct 37
C. Reporting Professional Misconduct 42
D. Imposing Disciplinary Sanctions 52
E. Other Consequences of Attorney Misconduct 55

Chapter 4. The Authorized and Unauthorized Practice of Law 57
A. Preventing the Unauthorized Practice of Law (UPL) 57
B. Multijurisdictional Practice (MJP) 64
C. Temporary Practice of Law in a State Where an Attorney Is Licensed 66
D. The Multi-State Practitioner, Disciplinary Authority, and Choice of Law 74

Chapter 5. Providing Access to Justice Through Pro Bono and Other Service 77
A. Law Student Pro Bono Service 78
B. Attorney Pro Bono Service 81
C. Conflicts of Interest and a Lawyer's Pro Bono Limited Scope Representations and Other Volunteer Activities 83
D. Court Appointments 83
E. Relying on Non-Lawyers and Improved Technology to Reduce the Access to Justice Gap 90

PART 2. ATTRACTING CLIENTS

Chapter 6. Practicing in a Law Firm 103
A. Practicing Law as a Member of a Law Firm 103
B. Discrimination, Diversity, and Inclusion in Law Firms 113
C. Leaving the Firm 117

Chapter 7. Advertising 125
A. The Constitutional Landscape 125
B. The Regulatory Landscape 136

Chapter 8. Solicitation 147
A. Live Person-to-Person Contact 148
B. Other Restrictions on Lawyer Solicitation 162

PART 3. THE CLIENT-LAWYER RELATIONSHIP

SECTION 1. ESTABLISHING THE CLIENT-LAWYER RELATIONSHIP 177

Chapter 9. Establishing a Client-Lawyer Relationship 179
A. Entering into a Client-Lawyer Relationship 179
B. Defining the Scope of Representation 185
C. Declining to Take a Case 193

Chapter 10. Billing the Client 197
A. Setting the Fee 197
B. Reasonableness of Fees and Other Charges 198
C. Other Prohibited Fee Arrangements 207
D. Sharing Fees with Other Lawyers 212

Chapter 11. Preventing Billing Fraud and Safekeeping Client Funds and Property 215
A. Billing Fraud 215
B. Trust Accounts and Other Requirements of Safekeeping Client Property 225

SECTION 2. COMMUNICATION AND DECISION-MAKING 229

Chapter 12. Communication and Decision-Making 231
A. An Overview of Communication and Decision-Making in an Agency Relationship 232
B. A Lawyer's Power to Obligate the Client in Dealings with Others 239
C. Identifying the Duly Authorized Constituents of an Organizational Client 241
D. Representing Clients with Disabilities, Diminished Capacity, or Communication Barriers 242

SUMMARY OF CONTENTS

SECTION 3. COMPETENCE AND DILIGENCE 249

Chapter 13. Competent and Diligent Representation of a Client 251
A. Rules of Professional Conduct 251
B. Civil Liability for Malpractice 253
C. Malpractice Insurance 270

SECTION 4. CONFIDENTIALITY 273

Chapter 14. Duty of Confidentiality 275
A. Protecting Confidential Information 275
B. Exceptions to the Lawyer's Duty of Confidentiality 281

Chapter 15. Attorney-Client Privilege, Work Product, and Competently Protecting Client Information 293
A. The Attorney-Client Privilege 293
B. Work Product Doctrine 302
C. Privilege and Work Product Exceptions and Waiver 304
D. Competently Protecting Confidential Client Information and Reducing the Risk of Privilege Waiver 314

SECTION 5. CONFLICTS OF INTEREST INVOLVING CURRENT CLIENTS 319

Chapter 16. Conflicts of Interest 321
A. General Principles 321
B. Directly Adverse Conflicts 322
C. Material Limitation Conflicts 325
D. Consent to Conflicts 330

Chapter 17. Conflicts of Interest Between Lawyer and Client 343
A. Business Transactions with Clients 344
B. Sex with Clients 351
C. Gifts from Clients 352
D. Agreements Regarding a Lawyer's Liability to a Client 353
E. Using Information to the Disadvantage of a Client 354
F. Financial Assistance and Gifts to Clients 354
G. Literary and Media Rights 355
H. Receiving Payment for the Representation from a Third-Party 356

SECTION 6. CONTINUING DUTIES TO FORMER CLIENTS 365

Chapter 18. Termination of the Client-Lawyer Relationship 367
A. Termination by the Client 367
B. Termination by the Lawyer 371
C. Protecting a Client's Interests and Resolving Fee Disputes upon Termination of the Relationship 380

Chapter 19. Conflicts of Interest Arising from Prior Representation 389
A. General Principles 389
B. Conflicts of Interest Between Current and Former Clients 391
C. Mobile Lawyers and Screening 398

PART 4. REPRESENTING CLIENTS

SECTION 1. LITIGATION PRACTICE 413

Chapter 20. Pre-Trial Advocacy 415
A. Informal Fact Investigation 415
B. Preparing Pleadings, Motions and Other Papers 417
C. Discovery 427

Chapter 21. Trial and Appellate Advocacy 441
A. Using Irrelevant or Inadmissible Information 441
B. Lawyer Acting as a Witness 442
C. Communicating with Jurors, the Judge, and Court Officers 442
D. Disruptive and Discriminatory Conduct 444
E. Truthfulness and Candor 445
F. Trial Publicity 455
G. Frivolous Appeals 456

Chapter 22. Criminal Prosecution Practice 461
A. The Investigative Function of Prosecutors 462
B. The Decision to Charge 469
C. Providing Exculpatory Evidence to the Defense 470
D. Trial Publicity 474
E. Remedying Wrongful Convictions 475

Chapter 23. Criminal Defense Practice 477
A. Constitutional Law: Ineffective Assistance of Counsel 477
B. Tort Law: Legal Malpractice 488
C. Rules of Professional Conduct 494

Chapter 24. Serving as a Judge 499
A. Becoming a Judge 500
B. Standards of Conduct for Judges 505
C. Regulating the Interaction Between Lawyers and Judges 508

SECTION 2. TRANSACTIONAL PRACTICE AND THE REPRESENTATION OF ORGANIZATIONAL CLIENTS 519

Chapter 25. Transactional Practice 521
A. Conflicts of Interest in Transactional Matters 521
B. Representing Clients in Non-Litigation Matters 523

Chapter 26. Representing Organizational Clients 539
A. Protecting Organizational Clients from Constituent Misconduct 540
B. Organizational Clients and Attorney-Client Privilege 545
C. Organizational Clients, Constituents, and Conflicts of Interest........... 555

PART 5. ATTORNEY WELL-BEING AND LEGACY

Chapter 27. Attorney Well-Being 561
A. The Attorney Well-Being Movement: An Issue of Attorney Ethics and Client Protection?... 562
B. When Should the Bar, Employers, and Colleagues Intervene to Address Concerns About Attorney Well-Being?..................................... 569
C. Thriving as Law Students and Lawyers: Making Choices and Developing Tools to Support Your Well-Being 581

Chapter 28. Reflections on a Rewarding Career as a Lawyer........... 591

INDEX 599

TABLE OF CONTENTS

PREFACE V

ACKNOWLEDGMENTS VII

TABLE OF CASES XXV

TABLE OF STATUTES XXXI

TABLE OF RULES.. XXXIII

PART 1. ENTERING THE PROFESSION

Chapter 1. Introduction: A Lawyer's Professional Responsibilities.... 3
A. Fiduciary Duty to Clients 4
B. Professional Conduct Rules 5
C. Developing a Professional Identity 7
    1. Lawyers as Public Citizens 7
    2. Lawyers as Leaders 8
    3. Lawyers as Caregivers 9
    4. Lawyers as Fallible Human Beings (and the Study of Behavioral Legal Ethics) 9

Chapter 2. Admission to the Bar.. 13
A. Overview of Bar Admission Standards 14
B. The Character and Fitness Standard 16
    In the Matter of the Bar Application of Tarra Denelle Simmons 16
    1. Criminal History 30
    2. Financial Responsibility 30
    3. Mental Health 31
    4. Substance Abuse 32
    5. Candor 32

Chapter 3. Regulation of the Legal Profession 35
A. Professional Discipline 35
B. Misconduct 37
    1. Attempting to Violate a Rule, Knowingly Assisting Another, or Using Another to Violate a Rule 38
    2. Committing a Criminal Act That Reflects Adversely on a Lawyer's Honesty, Trustworthiness, or Fitness as a Lawyer 38
    3. Engaging in Dishonest Conduct 39
    4. Engaging in Conduct Prejudicial to the Administration of Justice 40
    5. Engaging in Harassing or Discriminatory Conduct 41
C. Reporting Professional Misconduct... 42
    1. Knowledge 42

2. Substantial Question as to the Other Lawyer's Honesty, Trustworthiness, or Fitness 42
  3. Informing the Appropriate Authority 43
     In re James H. Himmel 44
     In re Riehlmann 48
D. Imposing Disciplinary Sanctions 52
   In re James H. Himmel 52
   In re Riehlmann 54
E. Other Consequences of Attorney Misconduct 55

Chapter 4. The Authorized and Unauthorized Practice of Law 57
A. Preventing the Unauthorized Practice of Law (UPL) 57
   1. Preventing UPL by Non-Lawyers 57
      Florida Bar v. Brumbaugh 59
   2. Assisting Others in the Unauthorized Practice of Law 63
   3. Permitting the Limited Practice of Law by Non-Lawyers ... 64
B. Multijurisdictional Practice (MJP) 64
   1. Licensure in Multiple Jurisdictions 64
   2. Special Rules Allowing an Attorney to Establish an Office in a State Where the Attorney Is Not Licensed 65
C. Temporary Practice of Law in a State Where an Attorney Is Licensed 66
   1. *Pro Hac Vice* Admission 66
   2. When Temporary Practice Amounts to the Unauthorized Practice of Law 67
      Birbrower, Montalbano, Condon & Frank, P.C. v. Superior Court 67
D. The Multi-State Practitioner, Disciplinary Authority, and Choice of Law 74

Chapter 5. Providing Access to Justice Through Pro Bono and Other Service 77
A. Law Student Pro Bono Service 78
   1. Promoting Law Student Pro Bono Service 78
   2. Pro Bono Bar Admission Requirement 79
      N.Y. Ct. Rules, § 520.16 Pro Bono Requirement for Bar Admission 79
B. Attorney Pro Bono Service 81
C. Conflicts of Interest and a Lawyer's Pro Bono Limited Scope Representations and Other Volunteer Activities 83
D. Court Appointments 83
   Hagopian v. Justice Administrative Commission 84
E. Relying on Non-Lawyers and Improved Technology to Reduce the Access to Justice Gap 90
   1. Relying on Non-Lawyers 91
      a. Court Navigators 91

  b. Limited License Legal Technicians (LLLTs) and Legal Paraprofessionals (LPs) 92
  c. Non-Lawyer Ownership of Law Firms 93
 2. TechnologiCal Innovation 94
  N.C. General Statutes § 84–2.2. Exemption and Additional Requirements for Web Site Providers 94
  Benjamin H. Barton & Deborah L. Rhode, *Access to Justice and Routine Legal Services: New Technologies Meet Bar Regulators* 95

PART 2. ATTRACTING CLIENTS

Chapter 6. Practicing in a Law Firm 103
A. Practicing Law as a Member of a Law Firm 103
 1. The Organizational Structure of Law Firms 104
 2. The Ethical Obligations of Partners, Managers, and Supervisory Lawyers 104
  a. Rule 5.1(a): Firm Lawyers with Managerial Authority 104
   In re Dickens 105
  b. Rule 5.1(b): Firm Lawyers with Supervisory Authority 109
  c. Rule 5.1(c): Responsibility for Another Lawyer's Violation of the Rules 109
  d. Rule 5.3: Responsibilities Regarding Non-Lawyer Assistants 110
 3. The Ethical Obligations of "Subordinate" Lawyers 110
  Kentucky Bar Ass'n v. Helmers 111
B. Discrimination, Diversity, and Inclusion in Law Firms 113
 1. Discrimination in Legal Practice 114
 2. Diversity and Inclusion Efforts in the Legal Profession 116
C. Leaving the Firm 117
 1. Soliciting Clients 117
  Tolson Firm, LLC v. Sistrunk 117
 2. Non-Compete Agreements 122

Chapter 7. Advertising 125
A. The Constitutional Landscape 125
 Dwyer v. Cappell 126
B. The Regulatory Landscape 136
 1. In General 136
 2. Online Marketing 137
  Hunter v. Virginia State Bar ex rel. Third District Committee 137
 3. Advertising Limited and Specialized Practices 143
 4. Law Firm Names 144
 5. Client Referrals 144
  a. Referrals in General 144
  b. Legal Services Plans and Lawyer Referral Services 145
  c. Reciprocal Referral Agreements 145

Chapter 8. Solicitation	**147**
A. Live Person-to-Person Contact	148
Ohralik v. Ohio State Bar Association	148
In re Primus	155
B. Other Restrictions on Lawyer Solicitation	162
Florida Bar v. Went for It, Inc.	162

PART 3. THE CLIENT-LAWYER RELATIONSHIP

SECTION 1. ESTABLISHING THE CLIENT-LAWYER RELATIONSHIP 177

Chapter 9. Establishing a Client-Lawyer Relationship	**179**
A. Entering into a Client-Lawyer Relationship	179
1. Agreeing to Represent Another	180
2. Duties to Prospective Clients	180
Togstad v. Vesely, Otto, Miller & Keefe	181
B. Defining the Scope of Representation	185
1. In General	185
2. Limiting the Scope of Representation	186
Nichols v. Keller	186
C. Declining to Take a Case	193
Chapter 10. Billing the Client	**197**
A. Setting the Fee	197
B. Reasonableness of Fees and Other Charges	198
1. Charging an Unreasonable Fee	198
In re Green	198
Heavener v. Meyers	201
In re Sulzer Hip Prosthesis and Knee Prosthesis Liability Litigation	203
2. Potential Consequences of Charging an Unreasonable Fee	207
C. Other Prohibited Fee Arrangements	207
1. Prohibited Contingent Fees	207
2. "Non-Refundable" General Retainers or Fees Paid in Advance	208
In re Disciplinary Action Against Hoffman	209
D. Sharing Fees with Other Lawyers	212
Chapter 11. Preventing Billing Fraud and Safekeeping Client Funds and Property	**215**
A. Billing Fraud	215
1. Pressure (and Incentives) to Overbill	216
2. Challenge of Accurate Time Tracking	217
3. Situational Factors That Contribute to Billing Fraud	218
4. Attorney Rationalizations for Overbilling	220
In re Wallace	221
B. Trust Accounts and Other Requirements of Safekeeping Client Property	225

TABLE OF CONTENTS

SECTION 2. COMMUNICATION AND DECISION-MAKING 229

Chapter 12. Communication and Decision-Making 231
A. An Overview of Communication and Decision-Making in an Agency Relationship 232
   1. Communication 232
   2. Allocation of Decision-Making Authority 233
      Olfe v. Gordon 235
   3. When Attorney and Client Disagree About a Decision 238
B. A Lawyer's Power to Obligate the Client in Dealings with Others 239
C. Identifying the Duly Authorized Constituents of an Organizational Client 241
D. Representing Clients with Disabilities, Diminished Capacity, or Communication Barriers 242
   1. In General 242
   2. Communication Barriers 244

SECTION 3. COMPETENCE AND DILIGENCE 249

Chapter 13. Competent and Diligent Representation of a Client 251
A. Rules of Professional Conduct 251
   1. Competence 251
   2. Diligence 252
B. Civil Liability for Malpractice 253
   1. Duty and Breach 253
      Rizzo v. Haines 253
      Wood v. McGrath, North, Mullin & Kratz, P.C. 257
      Simko v. Blake 261
   2. Causation and Damages 269
      Rizzo v. Haines 269
C. Malpractice Insurance 270
   1. Mandatory Professional Liability Insurance 270
   2. Filing Claims and Notifying Clients 271

SECTION 4. CONFIDENTIALITY 273

Chapter 14. Duty of Confidentiality 275
A. Protecting Confidential Information 275
   Perez v. Kirk & Carrigan 277
B. Exceptions to the Lawyer's Duty of Confidentiality 281
   1. Disclosure Reasonably Necessary to Prevent Death or Substantial Bodily Harm 281
   2. Disclosure Reasonably Necessary to Prevent or Rectify the Consequences of Client Crime or Fraud 282
   3. Disclosure Reasonably Necessary to Secure Legal Advice 284
   4. Disclosure Reasonably Necessary to Establish a Claim or Defense by the Lawyer 284

		5.	Disclosure Reasonably Necessary to Comply with Other Law or a Court Order 285

5. Disclosure Reasonably Necessary to Comply with Other Law or a Court Order 285
   People v. Belge 286
6. Disclosure Reasonably Necessary to Detect Conflicts of Interest 289

Chapter 15. Attorney-Client Privilege, Work Product, and Competently Protecting Client Information 293
A. The Attorney-Client Privilege 293
   Upjohn Company v. United States 295
B. Work Product Doctrine 302
C. Privilege and Work Product Exceptions and Waiver 304
   1. Exceptions and Waiver Through Intentional Conduct 304
      Lenz v. Universal Music Corp. 306
   2. Inadvertent Disclosure and Waiver 312
D. Competently Protecting Confidential Client Information and Reducing the Risk of Privilege Waiver 314

SECTION 5. CONFLICTS OF INTEREST INVOLVING CURRENT CLIENTS 319

Chapter 16. Conflicts of Interest 321
A. General Principles 321
B. Directly Adverse Conflicts 322
C. Material Limitation Conflicts 325
   People v. Jackson 327
D. Consent to Conflicts 330
   1. Generally 330
   2. Advance Conflict Waivers 331
      SuperCooler Technologies, Inc. v. Coca-Cola Co. 331

Chapter 17. Conflicts of Interest Between Lawyer and Client 343
A. Business Transactions with Clients 344
   Security Federal Sav. & Loan Ass'n v. Riviera, Ltd. 345
   Iowa Supreme Court Attorney Disciplinary Bd. v. Wintroub 348
B. Sex with Clients 351
C. Gifts from Clients 352
D. Agreements Regarding a Lawyer's Liability to a Client 353
E. Using Information to the Disadvantage of a Client 354
F. Financial Assistance and Gifts to Clients 354
G. Literary and Media Rights 355
H. Receiving Payment for the Representation from a Third-Party 356
   In the Matter of the Rules of Professional Conduct and Insurer Imposed Billing Rules and Procedures 357

SECTION 6. CONTINUING DUTIES TO FORMER CLIENTS 365

Chapter 18. Termination of the Client-Lawyer Relationship 367
A. Termination by the Client 367
   Hughes and Coleman, PLLC v. Chambers 367
B. Termination by the Lawyer 371
   1. Mandatory Withdrawal 372
   2. Permissive Withdrawal 373
      Kriegsman v. Kriegsman 373
      Cuadra v. Univision Communications, Inc. 375
C. Protecting a Client's Interests and Resolving Fee Disputes upon Termination of the Relationship 380
   1. Protecting a Client's Interests upon Termination 380
      Board of Professional Responsibility v. Prewitt 381
   2. Imposing Attorneys' Liens 383
   3. Returning Client Files 384
   4. Arbitrating Fee Disputes 385

Chapter 19. Conflicts of Interest Arising from Prior Representation 389
A. General Principles 389
B. Conflicts of Interest Between Current and Former Clients 391
   1. Material Adversity 391
   2. Substantially Related 392
      State ex rel. Wal-Mart Stores, Inc. v. Kortum 393
C. Mobile Lawyers and Screening 398
   Hodge v. Ufra-Sexton, LP 399

PART 4. REPRESENTING CLIENTS

SECTION 1. LITIGATION PRACTICE 413

Chapter 20. Pre-Trial Advocacy 415
A. Informal Fact Investigation 415
   1. Seeking Information from Individuals Represented by Counsel 416
   2. Communicating with Unrepresented Persons, Clarifying Your Partisan Role, and Refraining from Rendering Legal Advice to Unrepresented Persons 416
B. Preparing Pleadings, Motions and Other Papers 417
   1. Tort Liability Stemming from the Filing of Frivolous Claims and Motions 417
   2. Sanctions for Filing Frivolous Claims and Motions 419
      Garr v. U.S. Healthcare, Inc. 419
C. Discovery 427
   1. Preservation and Spoliation 428
      Zubulake v. UBS Warburg LLC ("Zubulake V") 428
   2. Manipulating Evidence 437

	3.	Frivolous Discovery Requests and Objections and Dilatory Tactics 438
	4.	Disclosure of a Client's Perjured Testimony During a Deposition 439
	5.	Protecting Privilege and Work Product and Addressing Inadvertent Disclosure 439

Chapter 21. Trial and Appellate Advocacy 441
A. Using Irrelevant or Inadmissible Information 441
B. Lawyer Acting as a Witness 442
C. Communicating with Jurors, the Judge, and Court Officers 442
D. Disruptive and Discriminatory Conduct 444
    1. Engaging in Conduct Intended to Disrupt a Tribunal 444
    2. Discriminatory Comments and Actions 444
E. Truthfulness and Candor 445
    1. Deception and Trickery at Trial 445
        United States v. Thoreen 446
    2. Candor Toward the Tribunal 450
        a. Disclosure of Adverse Legal Authority 450
        b. Disclosure of Adverse Facts 451
        c. Protecting the Tribunal Against Perjury and Other False Evidence 452
F. Trial Publicity 455
G. Frivolous Appeals 456

Chapter 22. Criminal Prosecution Practice 461
Berger v. United States 461
A. The Investigative Function of Prosecutors 462
    State of Minnesota v. Clark 462
B. The Decision to Charge 469
C. Providing Exculpatory Evidence to the Defense 470
    Brady v. Maryland 470
D. Trial Publicity 474
E. Remedying Wrongful Convictions 475

Chapter 23. Criminal Defense Practice 477
A. Constitutional Law: Ineffective Assistance of Counsel 477
    Strickland v. Washington 477
B. Tort Law: Legal Malpractice 488
    Barker v. Capotosto 488
C. Rules of Professional Conduct 494

Chapter 24. Serving as a Judge 499
A. Becoming a Judge 500
    1. The Judicial Selection Process 500
    2. Limitation on Campaign Activities and Free Speech Concerns 501
        Republican Party of Minnesota v. White 501

B.	Standards of Conduct for Judges		505
	1.	Assuring the Quality of Justice	506
	2.	Personal and Extrajudicial Activities	506
		a. Restrictions on Personal and Civic Activities	506
		b. Restrictions on Professional Engagements and Extrajudicial Moneymaking Activities	506
		c. Restrictions on Accepting Gifts and Loans	507
C.	Regulating the Interaction Between Lawyers and Judges		508
	1.	Motions for Recusal	508
		Cheney v. U.S. Dist. Court for Dist. of Columbia	508
		Caperton v. A.T. Massey Coal Co., Inc.	512
	2.	Interactions Between Lawyers and Judges	515
		a. Ex Parte Communication	515
		b. A Judge's Duty to Report Lawyer and Judicial Misconduct to Disciplinary Authorities	516
		c. A Lawyer's Duty to Report Judicial Misconduct to Disciplinary Authorities	516
		d. Avoiding Complicity in Judicial Misconduct	517

SECTION 2. TRANSACTIONAL PRACTICE AND THE REPRESENTATION OF ORGANIZATIONAL CLIENTS 519

Chapter 25. Transactional Practice 521
A. Conflicts of Interest in Transactional Matters 521
B. Representing Clients in Non-Litigation Matters 523
    1. Advising Clients 524
    2. Honesty in Negotiations and Other Interactions with Third Parties 526
        Wright v. Pennamped 526
    3. Tools Lawyers Can Use to Avoid Liability for Participating in Client Misconduct 532
    4. Lawyer Criminal and Civil Liability for Participating in Client Misconduct 533
        United States v. Collins 534

Chapter 26. Representing Organizational Clients 539
A. Protecting Organizational Clients from Constituent Misconduct 540
    1. Up-the-Ladder Reporting 541
    2. Loyal Disclosure 543
B. Organizational Clients and Attorney-Client Privilege 545
    1. Common Organizational Client Attorney-Client Privilege Issues 545
    2. Organizational Attorney-Client Privilege and Internal Investigations 548
        In re Grand Jury Subpoena: Under Seal 549
C. Organizational Clients, Constituents, and Conflicts of Interest 555

PART 5. ATTORNEY WELL-BEING AND LEGACY

Chapter 27. Attorney Well-Being 561
A. The Attorney Well-Being Movement: An Issue of Attorney Ethics and Client Protection? 562
    What the Lawyer Well-Being Movement Could Learn from the Americans with Disabilities Act 564
B. When Should the Bar, Employers, and Colleagues Intervene to Address Concerns About Attorney Well-Being? 569
    1. Bar Admission Hurdles for Applicants with Alcohol- and Drug-Related Incidents in Their Past 569
        My Bar Admission Experience 570
    2. Providing Resources and Support for Lawyers 574
    3. When Clients Are Harmed by an Attorney's Substance Abuse 575
        In the Matter of Justin K. Holstin, Respondent 575
    4. Identifying and Addressing the Warning Signs of an Attorney in Distress 577
        'Big Law Killed My Husband': An Open Letter from a Sidley Partner's Widow 577
C. Thriving as Law Students and Lawyers: Making Choices and Developing Tools to Support Your Well-Being 581
    1. Considerations in Selecting Your Employers Through the Years 581
    2. Your Mindset Matters: Frame Stressful Situations as Exciting and Embrace Your Ability to Grow 583
    3. Adopt a Gratitude Practice 585
    4. Integrate Mindfulness into Your Day 586
    5. Seek Confidential Professional Support When You Struggle 588

Chapter 28. Reflections on a Rewarding Career as a Lawyer 591
A Passion for Justice: Sharon G. Lee 592

INDEX 599

TABLE OF CASES

The principal cases are in bold type.

A.H. Robins Co., Inc., In re, 203
Abrams, In re, 38
Adams v. United States ex rel. McCann, 480
Akamai Technologies, Inc. v. Digital Island, Inc., 307
Allen, et al., In re, 552
Almeida, United States ex rel. v. Baldi, 471
Amendment to the Rules Regulating The Florida Bar, 454
Amendments, In re, 88
Anderson v. City of Bessemer City, 552
Anesthesia v. Wildmon, 118
Ang v. Martin, 489
Aramony, United States v., 553
Armor Screen Corp. v. Storm Catcher, Inc., 334
Arnold v. Kemp, 87
Asher, In re, 38
Atlanta Int. Ins. Co. v. Bell, 359
Attorney Grievance Com'n v. Kemp, 204
Attorney Grievance Com'n v. Smith, 63
Attorney Grievance Comm' v. Markey, 41
Attorney Grievance Comm'n of Maryland v. Cassilly, 475
Attorney Grievance Comm'n of Maryland v. Kimmel, 108
Attorney Grievance Comm'n of Md. v. Brady, 40
Attorney Grievance Comm'n of Md. V. Dore, 41
Attorney U v. Mississippi Bar, 42
Aubuchon, In re, 40
Augustson v. Linea Aerea Nacional-Chile S.A., 371
Autera v. Robinson, 255
B. Dahlenburg Bonar, P.S.C. v. Waite, Schneider, Bayless & Chesley Co., 369
Baker v. Beal, 264
Baker v. Fabian, Thielen & Thielen, 259
Baker v. Shapero, 368
Balla v. Gambro, 558

Bar Application of Tarra Denelle Simmons, In the Matter of the, 16
Bar Ass'n, State ex rel. v. Cox, 437
Barker v. Capotosto, 488
Bates v. State Bar of Arizona, 125, 130, 140, 145, 148, 163
Bayliss v. Williams, 346
Beal Bank SSB v. Arter & Hadden LLP, 233
Belge, People v., 286
Bell & Marra, PLLC v. Sullivan, 379
BellSouth Corp., In re, 334
Belsher, In re, 22
Berger v. United States, 461
Bevill, Bresler, In re, 554
Bigelow v. Virginia, 140
Birbrower, Montalbano, Condon & Frank, P.C. v. Superior Court, 67
Board of Professional Responsibility v. Prewitt, 381
Board of Trustees of the State University of New York v. Fox, 140
Bochetto v. Gibson, 456
Bolger v. Youngs Drug Products Corp., 140
Bordenkircher v. Hayes, 469
Bowen, In re, 354
Bowles v. United States, 448
Brady v. Maryland, 470
Brown v. Gatti, 456
Brown v. Hartlage, 501
Brown v. Legal Found. of Washington, 226
Bruning v. Law Offices of Ronald J. Palagi, 259, 260
Bryan Mfg. Co. v. Harris, 531
Burgin v. Godwin, 280
Burson, Petition of, 58
Cameron v. City of New York, 535
Cammer v. United States, 449
Campbell v. Bozeman Investors of Duluth, 371
Cantor, United States v., 43
Caperton v. A.T. Massey Coal Co., Inc., 512
Castillo, United States v., 535
Central Hudson Gas & Electric Corp. v. Public Service Comm'n of N.Y., 163

Central Hudson Gas & Electric Corp.
  v. Public Service Commission, 130
**Cheney v. U.S. Dist. Court for Dist.
  of Columbia, 508**
Christian v. Gordon, 203
Clackamas Gastroenterology Assocs.
  v. Wells, 114
Clark v. General Motors LLC, 207
Collins, United States v., 534
Committee on Legal Ethics of West
  Virginia State Bar v. Tatterson, 203
Compton v. Kittleson, 380
Connick v. Thompson, 473
Consolidation Coal Co. v. Bucyrus-
  Erie Co., 301, 545
Cooperman, In re, 209
Cooter & Gell v. Hartmarx Corp., 423,
  426
**Cuadra v. Univision
  Communications, Inc., 375**
Cushing, Matter of, 38
Cuti, United States v., 536
Cuyler v. Sullivan, 481, 487
Dickens, In re, 105
**Disciplinary Action Against
  Hoffman, In re, 209**
Disciplinary Proceeding Against
  Fossedal, In re, 22
Disciplinary Proceeding Against Hart,
  In re, 22
Disciplinary Proceeding Against
  McGrath, In re, 27
Diversified Industries, Inc. v.
  Meredith, 298
Duke v. State, 450
Dwyer v. Cappell, 126
Edenfield v. Fane, 130
EEOC v. Sidley Austin Brown &
  Wood, 114
Evans, United States v., 553
Falkowski v. Johnson, 441
Fine v. Communication Trends, 118
Fire Insurance Exchange v. Bell, 531
First Union Nat'l Bank v. Meyer,
  Faller, Weisman & Rosenberg, P.C.,
  369
FirsTier Bank, State ex rel. v.
  Buckley, 395
Fisher v. United States, 552
Flexible Manufacturing Systems, Inc.
  v. Super Prods. Corp., 457
Florida Bar v. Brumbaugh, 59
Florida Bar v. Martocci, 444, 445
Florida Bar v. Perlmutter, 40
Florida Bar v. Peterson, 443
Florida Bar v. Went for It, Inc., 162
Florida Bar, The v. American Legal
  and Business Forms, Inc., 60
Florida Bar, The v. Stupica, 60

Fonte, In re, 108
Ford, State v., 467
Ford, United States v., 448
Frank v. Bloom, 265
Franke, In re, 379
Freezer Servs., Inc., State ex rel. v.
  Mullen, 394
Friedman v. Dozroc, 417, 427
Friedman, In re, 40
FTC v. Cement Institute, 514
Gans v. Mundy, 255
Garaas, In re, 443
Garr v. U.S. Healthcare, Inc., 419
Geders v. United States, 480
Geisler, In re, 437
General Cigar Holdings, Inc. v.
  Altadis, S.A., 334
General Electric Co. v. Kirkpatrick,
  298
Gentile v. State Bar of Nevada, 168,
  455, 474
Giddings v. State, 463
Gideon v. Wainwright, 287
Giglio v. United States, 472
Gilbert v. Evan, 380
Ginsburg v. United States, 140
Goebel v. Lauderdale, 252
Goffer, United States v., 536
Golden, In re, 40
Goodstein, In re Application of, 33
Gouveia, United States v., 463
Grand Jury Proceedings, In re, 552
Grand Jury Subpoena Duces Tecum,
  553
Grand Jury Subpoena v. Under Seal,
  In re, 552
**Grand Jury Subpoena: Under
  Seal, In re, 549**
Grand Jury Subpoenas, In re, 546
Grand Jury, In re, 546
Grayson v. Wofsey, Rosen, Kweskin &
  Kuriansky, 259
Green, In re, 198
Grievance Administrator, Attorney
  Grievance Commission v. Cooper,
  209
Guenard v. Burke, 207
H.F. Ahmanson Co. v. Salomon
  Brothers, 392
**Hagopian v. Justice
  Administrative Commission, 84**
Hallauer, In re Guardianship of, 200
Hancock v. Bd. of Prof. Responsibility
  of Supreme Court of Tenn., 443
Hawkins v. Stables, 552
Heavener v. Meyers, 201
Hermann v. GutterGuard, Inc., 334
Hickman v. Taylor, 301, 303
Higgins v. Eichler, 546

Hilton v. Barnett Banks, Inc., 335
Hischke, State v., 453
Hishon v. King & Spalding, 114
Hodge v. Ufra-Sexton, LP, 399
Holloway v. Arkansas, 487
Hughes and Coleman, PLLC v. Chambers, 367
Hunt v. Blackburn, 293
Hunter v. Virginia State Bar ex rel. Third District Committee, 137
Hyland, Application of, 30
Ibanez v. Fla. Dep't of Bus. & Prof. Reg., Bd. of Accountancy, 134
Imbler v. Pachtman, 470
Iowa Supreme Court Attorney Disciplinary Bd. v. Wintroub, 348
Jackson, People v., 327
Jacobson v. Knepper & Moga, P.C., 113
James H. Himmel, In re, 44, 52
Janson v. LegalZoom.com, Inc., 62
Johnson, State v., 467
Jones, State v., 363, 379
Jones, United States v., 553
Justin K. Holstin, Respondent, In the Matter of, 575
Kaplan v. Pavalon & Gifford, 212
Kelley's Case, 111
Kellogg Brown & Root, Inc., In re, 546
Kentucky Bar Ass'n v. Helmers, 111
Keplinger, United States v., 553
Kirleis v. Dickie, McCamey & Chilcote, 114
Knight v. State, 479
Konigsberg v. State Bar, 19
Kriegsman v. Kriegsman, 373
Kulig, In re, 352
Kyles v. Whitley, 472
LaBach v. Hampton, 368
Laird v. Tatum, 502
Lawyers' Institute of San Diego, People ex rel. v. Merchants' Protective Corp., 69
Leary v. United States, 288
LeBlanc, In re, 517
Lefthand, State v., 467
Lennartson v. Anoka-Hennepin Indep. Sch. Dist. No. 11, 464
Lenz v. Universal Music Corp., 306
Lettley v. State, 487
Letts v. Icarian Development Co., S.A., 448
Levine v. Kling, 491
Lien v. Pitts, 237
Lipton v. Boesky, 263
Lisi v. Several Att'ys, 517

Lofton v. Fairmont Specialty Ins., Mgrs., 369
Lopez, United States v., 464
M.R., Matter of, 244
Mantia v. Hanson, 418
Mares v. Credit Bureau of Raton, 201
Marino v. Tagaris, 386
Mashaney v. Bd. of Indigents' Def. Servs., 491
Mason, In re, 40
Maxwell Schuman & Co. v. Edwards, 207
Maynard, People v., 444
McCarthy, State v., 467
McDermott, State v., 318
McDowell, State v., 453
McElroy v. Gaffney, 442
McGhee v. Pottawattamie Cnty., 470
McMann v. Richardson, 480
McVaney v. Baird, Holm, McEachen, 260
McWhirt v. Heavey, 259, 260
Meinhard v. Salmon, 346
Michael E. Tennenbaum, et al. v. Deloitte & Touche, 307
Michaels v. New Jersey, 470
Milavetz, Gallop & Milavetz, P.A. v. United States, 132
Miller, State v., 464
Minnesota, State of v. Clark, 462
Missouri Public Defender Commission, State ex rel. v. Waters, 495
Mooney v. Frazier, 270
Mooney v. Holohan, 471, 472
Mt. Hawley Insurance Company v. Felman Production, Inc., 317
NAACP v. Button, 158
Nagle v. Alspach, 457
Napue v. Illinois, 472
Nebarez v. Wal-Mart Stores, Inc., 393
Nevada Yellow Cab Corp. v. Eighth Judicial Dist. Court, 363
Nichols v. Keller, 186
Nix v. Whiteside, 452
Norton v. Tallahassee Mem'l Hosp., 334
Notice to Court Pursuant to Texas Disciplinary Rule of Professional Conduct 3.03 and Unopposed Motion to Withdraw as Counsel for Plaintiff, LBDS Holding Company, LLC v. ISOL Technology Inc. et al., 387
Ohralik v. Ohio State Bar Association, 148, 158
Olfe v. Gordon, 235
Parks v. Multimedia Technologies, 121

Pauline Weil, et al. v. Investment/Indicators, Research and Management, Inc., et al., 307
Peasley, In re, 40
Peel v. Attorney Registration and Disciplinary Commission, 143
Peoples Trust & Savings Bank v. Humphrey, 530
Perez v. Kirk & Carrigan, 277
Philadelphia v. Westinghouse Electric Corp., 298, 301
Phoenix Solutions, Inc. v. Wells Fargo Bank, N.A., et al., 307
Picker Int'l., Inc. v. Varian Assoc., Inc., 391
Pottorff v. Wal-Mart Stores, Inc., 393, 396
Powell v. Alabama, 480
Primus, In re, 155
Public Citizen Inc. v. La. Att'y Disciplinary Bd., 134
Pyle v. Kansas, 471
R.J. Reynolds Tobacco Co. v. FDA, 131
R.M.J., In re, 130
Ramirez v. Wal-Mart Stores, Inc., 393
Ramos v. Lamm, 201
Raskin v. Wyatt Co., 535
Rea, United States v., 535
Removal of a Chief Judge, In re, 505
Republican Party of Minnesota v. White, 501
Riehlmann, In re, 48, 54
Riek, In re, 473
Ring, People v., 69
Rizzo v. Haines, 253, 269
Robinson, In re, 107
Rorrer v. Cooke, 264
Rothman v. Fillette, 255
Ruden v. Jenk, 489
Rules of Professional Conduct and Insurer Imposed Billing Rules and Procedures, In the Matter of the, 357
Samaritan Foundation v. Goodfarb, 302
Sanborn v. State, 454
Sanderson v. Wal-Mart Stores, Inc., 393
Sather, People v., 200
Schenkel v. Monheit, 255
Schlumberger Techs., Inc. v. Wiley, 334
Schware v. Bd. of Bar Exam. of State of N.M., 14, 19
Scott v. Bodor, 528
Seat, Matter of, 41
Security Federal Sav. & Loan Ass'n v. Riviera, Ltd., 345

Shapero v. Kentucky Bar Association, 162, 166, 169
Shaw v. State, 491
Simko v. Blake, 261
Simmons, In re, 17
Simon v. G.D. Searle & Co., 546
Simon, United States ex rel. v. Murphy, 208
Sitton v. Print Direction, 118
Sitton, In re, 41
Smith v. Pennington, 118
Somuah v. Flachs, 370
Sperry, State v., 59
Spivak v. Sachs, 71
Spruance v. Commission On Judicial Qualifications, 506
Starcher, Matter of, 516
Stern v. County Court, 84
Stern, In re, 30
Strickland v. Washington, 477
Sulzer Hip Prosthesis and Knee Prosthesis Liability Litigation, In re, 203
SuperCooler Technologies, Inc. v. Coca-Cola Co., 331
Svoboda, United States v., 536
Tedder, United States v., 552
Tennessee Valley Authority v. Hill, 596
Thompson, United States ex rel. v. Dye, 471
Thomsen, In re, 445
Thoreen, United States v., 446
Togstad v. Vesely, Otto, Miller & Keefe, 181
Tolson Firm, LLC v. Sistrunk, 117
Trammel v. United States, 552
Tumey v. Ohio, 514
Turner v. Leathers, 346
United Transportation Union v. Michigan Bar, 158
Upjohn Company v. United States, 295, 552
Upjohn v. United States, 101 S. Ct. 677 (1981), 545
Verizon California, Inc. v. Ronald A. Katz Technology Licensing, 307
Vioxx Products Liability Litigation, In re, 546
Vista Mfg., Inc. v. Trac-4 Inc., 423, 426
Wallace, In re, 221
Wal-Mart Stores, Inc., State ex rel. v. Kortum, 393
Wilcox, United States ex rel. v. Johnson, 453
Wilkinson, In re, 63
Williamson v. John D. Quinn Const. Corp., 71
Williams-Yulee v. Florida Bar, 505

Wilson, People v., 200
Wimmershoff, In re, 200
Withrow v. Larkin, 512
Wood v. McGrath, North, 258
Wood v. McGrath, North, Mullin & Kratz, P.C., 257
Woodruff v. Tomlin, 265
Woods v. Covington Cnty. Bank, 334
Wright v. Apartment Investment and Management Co., 118
Wright v. Pennamped, 526
Wright v. Williams, 256
Young v. Acenbauch, 335
Youngblood, Petition of, 362
Zauderer v. Office of Disciplinary Counsel, 126, 129
Zeno, In re, 443
Zubulake v. UBS Warburg LLC ("Zubulake V"), 428

TABLE OF STATUTES

U.S. Const. Amend. 1 .... 125, 126, 130, 132, 134, 135, 137, 138, 140, 142, 143, 146, 150, 151, 158, 159, 167, 501
U.S. Const. Amend. 6 .... 463, 495
ALI Restatement (Second) of Torts, § 1 comment d, § 7(1) 491
ALI Restatement (Third) of Agency, § 1.01 233
ALI Restatement (Third) of Agency, § 2.01 233
ALI Restatement (Third) of Agency, § 2.02 233
ALI Restatement (Third) of Agency, § 8.11 232
ALI Restatement (Third) of the Law Governing Lawyers § 8 .... 282, 523, 533
ALI Restatement (Third) of the Law Governing Lawyers § 16 523
ALI Restatement (Third) of the Law Governing Lawyers § 20 232
ALI Restatement (Third) of the Law Governing Lawyers § 24(3) 244
ALI Restatement (Third) of the Law Governing Lawyers § 26 239
ALI Restatement (Third) of the Law Governing Lawyers § 27 240
ALI Restatement (Third) of the Law Governing Lawyers § 27 cmt. d, ill. 3 240
ALI Restatement (Third) of the Law Governing Lawyers § 31(2) 239
ALI Restatement (Third) of the Law Governing Lawyers § 31(3) 240
ALI Restatement (Third) of the Law Governing Lawyers § 49 275
ALI Restatement (Third) of the Law Governing Lawyers § 52(1) 523
ALI Restatement (Third) of the Law Governing Lawyers § 53 493
ALI Restatement (Third) of the Law Governing Lawyers § 56 533
ALI Restatement (Third) of the Law Governing Lawyers § 56 ..... 282, 523
ALI Restatement (Third) of the Law Governing Lawyers § 57 523
ALI Restatement (Third) of the Law Governing Lawyers § 68 276
ALI Restatement (Third) of the Law Governing Lawyers § 73 545
ALI Restatement (Third) of the Law Governing Lawyers § 73(4) 546
ALI Restatement (Third) of the Law Governing Lawyers § 95 534
ALI Restatement (Third) of the Law Governing Lawyers § 215 360
5 U.S.C.App. § 2 509
15 U.S.C. § 7701 161
17 U.S.C. § 107 306
18 U.S.C. § 401 448
18 U.S.C. § 3006A(g)(2)(A) 270
26 U.S.C. § 527 513
26 U.S.C. § 7602 297
28 U.S.C. § 455(a) 508, 509, 510
35 U.S.C. § 256 334
42 U.S.C. § 406(a)(2)(A) 206
42 U.S.C. § 1983 .... 129, 201, 470
42 U.S.C. § 1988(b) 201
42 U.S.C. §§ 12101–12213 24
42 U.S.C. § 12182(b)(2)(A)(ii) 245

TABLE OF RULES

ABA Model CJC Canon 1 505
ABA Model CJC Rule 1.1 505
ABA Model CJC Rule 1.2 505
ABA Model CJC Rule 1.3 505
ABA Model CJC Rule 2.3 506
ABA Model CJC Rule 2.5 506
ABA Model CJC Rule 2.11(A) 508, 511, 515
ABA Model CJC Rule 2.11(A)(5) ... 511, 512
ABA Model CJC Rules 3.1–3.4 506
ABA Model CJC Rule 3.6 506
ABA Model CJC Rules 3.8–3.12 507
ABA Model CJC Rule 3.13(A) 507
ABA Model CJC Rule 3.13(B) 507
ABA Model CJC Rule 3.14 507
ABA Model CJC Rule 3.15 507
ABA Model CJC Rule 4.1(A) 505
ABA Model CJC Rule 4.1A(1)–(12) 500
ABA Model CJC Rule 4.1(A)(8) 505
ABA Model CJC Rule 4.1(A)(11) 504
ABA Model CJC Rule 4.1(A)(12) 504
ABA Model CJC Rule 4.1(A)(13) 504
ABA Model CJC Rule 4.1(B) 500
ABA Model CJC Rule 4.2(B) 505
ABA Model CJC Rule 4.2(C) 500
ABA Model CJC Rule 4.2B 500
ABA Model Rule 1.0 .... 330, 337
ABA Model Rule 1.0(c) 103
ABA Model Rule 1.1 .... 252, 362, 415, 523
ABA Model Rule 1.2 ...... 234, 238, 239, 362
ABA Model Rule 1.2(a) 233
ABA Model Rule 1.2(b) 193
ABA Model Rule 1.2(d) 281, 524
ABA Model Rule 1.3 591
ABA Model Rule 1.4 234
ABA Model Rule 1.4(a) 232
ABA Model Rule 1.4(a)(5) 524, 525
ABA Model Rule 1.4(b) 233, 270
ABA Model Rule 1.5 360
ABA Model Rule 1.5(a) 198, 203
ABA Model Rule 1.5(b) 197
ABA Model Rule 1.5(c) 197
ABA Model Rule 1.5(d)(1) 207
ABA Model Rule 1.5(d)(2) 208
ABA Model Rule 1.5(e) 212
ABA Model Rule 1.6 ...... 277, 281, 285, 451
ABA Model Rule 1.6(a) 275, 276
ABA Model Rule 1.6(b) 281, 525
ABA Model Rule 1.6(b)(1) 281
ABA Model Rule 1.6(b)(2) 282, 283
ABA Model Rule 1.6(b)(3) 282, 532
ABA Model Rule 1.6(b)(4) 284
ABA Model Rule 1.6(b)(5) 284
ABA Model Rule 1.6(b)(6) 285
ABA Model Rule 1.6(b)(7) 290
ABA Model Rule 1.6(c) 439
ABA Model Rule 1.7 .... 83, 321, 322, 324, 325, 338, 522
ABA Model Rule 1.7(a) 322, 323
ABA Model Rule 1.7(a)(1) 326, 556
ABA Model Rule 1.7(a)(2) 325, 326, 468, 495, 556
ABA Model Rule 1.7(b) 330, 522
ABA Model Rule 1.7(b)(4) 232, 331
ABA Model Rule 1.8(e) 354
ABA Model Rule 1.8(f) 356, 357, 362
ABA Model Rule 1.8(g) 324
ABA Model Rule 1.8(h)(1) 353
ABA Model Rule 1.8(j) 344
ABA Model Rule 1.9 .... 83, 389, 409, 522
ABA Model Rule 1.9(a) 392, 556
ABA Model Rule 1.9(b) 399
ABA Model Rule 1.10 .... 83, 321, 322, 325, 398, 522
ABA Model Rule 1.10(a) 323, 324, 488
ABA Model Rule 1.10(c) 321
ABA Model Rule 1.11 488
ABA Model Rule 1.11(a)(2) 404
ABA Model Rule 1.12(c)(2) 404
ABA Model Rule 1.13 241
ABA Model Rule 1.13(a) 241, 540
ABA Model Rule 1.13(b) 541, 544
ABA Model Rule 1.13(c) 281, 541, 543, 544, 545
ABA Model Rule 1.13(d) 543
ABA Model Rule 1.13(g) 555
ABA Model Rule 1.15 225
ABA Model Rule 1.15(b) 225
ABA Model Rule 1.15(c) 225
ABA Model Rule 1.15(d) 226
ABA Model Rule 1.15(e) 226
ABA Model Rule 1.16 ...... 371, 386, 525
ABA Model Rule 1.16(a) 193, 372, 524, 541
ABA Model Rule 1.16(a)(1) 532
ABA Model Rule 1.16(b) 541
ABA Model Rule 1.16(b)(2) 532
ABA Model Rule 1.16(b)(4) 375
ABA Model Rule 1.16(b)(7) 375
ABA Model Rule 1.16(d) 380, 384
ABA Model Rule 2.1 .... 357, 523, 524

ABA Model Rule 3.1 419
ABA Model Rule 3.2 419
ABA Model Rule 3.3 .... 281, 439, 454, 544
ABA Model Rule 3.3(a) 450
ABA Model Rule 3.3(a)(1) 451
ABA Model Rule 3.3(a)(2) 450, 451
ABA Model Rule 3.3(a)(3) 452, 453, 454
ABA Model Rule 3.4 .... 427, 437, 438
ABA Model Rule 3.4(a) 428, 437
ABA Model Rule 3.4(b) 437
ABA Model Rule 3.4(c) 438
ABA Model Rule 3.4(d) 438
ABA Model Rule 3.4(e) 441, 442
ABA Model Rule 3.4(f) 416
ABA Model Rule 3.5 442
ABA Model Rule 3.5(d) 444
ABA Model Rule 3.6 456
ABA Model Rule 3.6(a) 455
ABA Model Rule 3.6(b) 455, 474
ABA Model Rule 3.8 461
ABA Model Rule 3.8(a) 469
ABA Model Rule 3.8(d) ... 472, 473, 475
ABA Model Rule 3.8(f) 456, 474
ABA Model Rule 3.8(g) 475
ABA Model Rule 3.8(h) 475
ABA Model Rule 3.9 455
ABA Model Rule 4.1 525
ABA Model Rule 4.1(b) .. 281, 524, 531, 533, 541
ABA Model Rule 4.2 .... 416, 468
ABA Model Rule 4.3 .... 416, 417
ABA Model Rule 4.4(b) 439
ABA Model Rule 5.1 574
ABA Model Rule 5.4 93
ABA Model Rule 5.5 58
ABA Model Rule 5.5(a) 63, 64
ABA Model Rule 5.5(b)(1) 64
ABA Model Rule 5.5(b)(2) 64
ABA Model Rule 5.5(d) 65
ABA Model Rule 5.7(a) 62
ABA Model Rule 6.1 81
ABA Model Rule 6.2 83
ABA Model Rule 6.2(b) 84
ABA Model Rule 6.2(c) 84
ABA Model Rule 7.1 136
ABA Model Rule 7.3 162
ABA Model Rule 8.1 .... 32, 281
ABA Model Rule 8.1(b) 32, 33
ABA Model Rule 8.3 281
ABA Model Rule 8.3(a) 42
ABA Model Rule 8.4(b) 38
ABA Model Rule 8.4(c) 446
ABA Model Rule 8.4(d) 40, 445
ABA Model Rule 8.4(g) ... 115, 444, 445
ABA Model Rule 8.5 74
ABA Model Rule 22 75

ABA Stds. for Crim. Justice § 1.3 462
ABA Stds. for Crim. Justice § 3–1.2 469
ABA Stds. for Crim. Justice § 3–1.6 469
ABA Stds. for Crim. Justice § 3–4.4 469
Fed.R.App.P. 38 .... 456, 457, 458
Fed.R.Civ.P. 11 .... 423, 458
Fed.R.Civ.P. 23.1 556
Fed.R.Civ.P. 26 316
Fed.R.Civ.P. 26(b) 307
Fed.R.Civ.P. 26(b)(3) 303
Fed.R.Civ.P. 26(b)(3)(A) 303
Fed.R.Civ.P. 26(b)(3)(B) 303
Fed.R.Civ.P. 26(b)(5)(A) 294
Fed.R.Civ.P. 26(b)(5)(B) 312, 313
Fed.R.Evid. 502 316
Fed.R.Evid. 701(b) 535
Fed.R.Evid. 702(a) 535
Fed.R.Evid. 704 535

Professional Responsibility in the Life of the Lawyer
Third Edition

PART 1

ENTERING THE PROFESSION

■ ■ ■

This book focuses on the rights and responsibilities of lawyers in connection with their practice of law. Part 1 of the book provides a foundation for a study of these rights and responsibilities, starting with issues that are most relevant to lawyers as they initially enter the profession.

Chapter 1 begins with some background about a lawyer's professional responsibilities, including the fiduciary duties a lawyer owes to a client. Chapter 2 addresses entry into the legal profession, including the rules and legal standards governing admission to the bar. Chapter 3 addresses how professional conduct rules are enforced, with a particular focus on the self-policing nature of the legal profession. Chapter 4 covers the rules regarding the unauthorized practice of law and the rules that govern a lawyer's ability to practice in multiple jurisdictions. Finally, Chapter 5 covers one of the special responsibilities an attorney assumes upon entering the profession: the duty to provide access to justice through pro bono and other services.

CHAPTER 1

INTRODUCTION: A LAWYER'S PROFESSIONAL RESPONSIBILITIES

■ ■ ■

Chapter Hypothetical. For more than a decade, you and your law firm have represented H.P. Simmons, a famous author known for her science fiction series *Immortal Beings*. After the final book in the series was published, H.P. announced that she was retiring from writing. *Immortal Beings* fans were devastated. Unbeknownst to these fans, H.P. recently released a new science fiction book, *The October Chronicles,* under the pen name Constance Fellows. You and two other lawyers at your law firm know about H.P.'s new book and pen name. You represented H.P. in negotiations with her new publisher, Little Blue Press.

A week ago, you were chatting with your spouse's best friend, Pat, at a dinner party. Pat always describes you as a "boring lawyer," so maybe you were showing off a little when you mentioned that your client H.P. Simmons just released a book under the pen name Constance Fellows. You immediately regretted the slip, and you swore Pat to secrecy. Pat assured you that your secret was safe as she pulled out her phone to order *The October Chronicles*.

This morning, you read a story in the *Sunday Times* reporting that H.P. Simmons has released a book under the pen name Constance Fellows. You feel certain that Pat is the source of the story and that the leak will soon be traced back to you.

This textbook prompts you to consider the issues you will face throughout your professional career. As a member of the legal profession, you will have numerous responsibilities and opportunities. You will represent clients who will trust you with some of the most important issues in their lives and businesses. You will also be a member of the bar, with the obligation to abide by the profession's conduct rules. Finally, you must decide what kind of person you will be in your personal and professional life. How will you treat others and contribute to your community? How will you balance the demands of being an attorney with obligations to your family, friends, and other interests?

Despite what you may have heard, the study of professional responsibility is not limited to the study of professional conduct rules. Professional responsibility is the study of every aspect of a lawyer's professional life: duties to clients, obligations as a member of the bar, and values that are essential to your professional identity. This textbook provides a framework that will help you understand your various duties and opportunities to succeed as a professional.

* * *

A. FIDUCIARY DUTY TO CLIENTS

Lawyers and clients are in a fiduciary relationship—a special relationship of trust and confidence. This means that when a lawyer agrees to represent a client in a matter, the lawyer must fulfill fiduciary duties of care and loyalty to the client. This is not something that lawyers and clients negotiate; the relationship is by definition fiduciary and comes with these responsibilities.

This text will often refer to the *Restatement (Third) of the Law Governing Lawyers* for a statement of the law of fiduciary duty. In practice, you would rely upon case law in the appropriate jurisdiction for a statement of the law.

The duty of care requires a lawyer to act with the competence and diligence normally exercised by lawyers under similar circumstances. *See Restatement (Third) of the Law Governing Lawyers* § 16(2). This is not a *reasonable person* standard, but a *reasonable lawyer* standard. Clients already expect a level of knowledge and skill based on the lawyer's training and study. In order to perform competently, a lawyer must also be mindful of the role that he or she is playing for the client. Advisor, negotiator, and courtroom advocate are just some of a lawyer's roles. The demands of each role are different and will be explored further throughout this book.

A lawyer's breach of the duty of care can give rise to liability for malpractice or professional negligence. *See id.* § 48. You will see examples of such cases in various chapters in this textbook.

The lawyer's other fiduciary duty to the client is the duty of loyalty. It requires the lawyer to protect client property and confidences, avoid prohibited conflicts of interests, and take no advantage arising from the attorney-client relationship. *See id.* § 16(3). In many jurisdictions, the breach of the duty of loyalty gives rise to a cause of action for breach of fiduciary duty. *See id.* § 49. You will also see cases involving these claims throughout the book.

As a lawyer, fiduciary duty to your client should be your touchstone. If you are in doubt about whether a course of conduct is right, you can often ask yourself if it is in your client's interest. Are you diligently working on your client's behalf? Are you providing the advice, advocacy, guidance, and representation your client deserves? Are you acting in your client's interest instead of in the interests of someone else or your own personal interests?

* * *

Problem 1.1. As you feared, the H.P. Simmons pen name leak was quickly traced to you. Your law firm released a statement publicly apologizing to H.P. Simmons and explaining that client confidentiality is of the utmost importance to the firm. *The October Chronicles* shot from number 4,709 to number 1 on the best-seller list within a week of the *Sunday Times* article. But that was no consolation to H.P. Simmons. In a subsequent article, H.P. was quoted as saying, "I certainly thought I could trust my lawyers with a secret. I am angry and devastated by this betrayal. I loved the freedom of releasing *The October Chronicles* without the pressure, hype, and expectation that always came with the release of an H.P. Simmons book. Now that has been taken from me."

Refer to the *Restatement (Third) of the Law Governing Lawyers* to determine the most appropriate cause of action for H.P. Simmons to assert in a lawsuit against you and your law firm. With citation to the pertinent section of the Restatement, explain what H.P would have to prove at trial to prevail on her claim.

* * *

B. PROFESSIONAL CONDUCT RULES

The next aspect of a lawyer's professional duty is the obligation to comply with professional conduct rules. These rules are adopted by the highest court of each state and by federal courts. In most jurisdictions, these rules are based to some extent upon the ABA's *Model Rules of Professional Conduct*. It is important to know that most jurisdictions adapt the rules (sometimes slightly and other times extensively), which results in widely varying versions of the rules in each jurisdiction. In this text, we will refer primarily to the *Model Rules* but we will sometimes reference variations on those rules adopted in specific jurisdictions.

A lawyer may be disciplined for violating a professional conduct rule. Discipline can range from a private reprimand to suspension or even disbarment. You will read cases throughout this textbook in which an attorney faced possible discipline for violating a professional conduct rule.

Civil liability is not a consequence of violating a professional conduct rule. However, the same conduct that is the subject of discipline may be the subject of a client's lawsuit. For example, if an attorney's lack of diligence results in the client's lawsuit being dismissed, the bar may discipline the attorney for violating Rule 1.3 (the rule requiring attorneys to be competent and diligent) and the client may sue the attorney for violating the attorney's duty of care.

Professional conduct rules generally fall within one of three categories. These categories are not clearly noted within the professional conduct rules. As a result, students sometimes perceive the rules as a mass of disconnected and meaningless obligations. Knowing the three categories can help you understand the purpose of a given rule so you can better understand what is necessary to comply with the rule's spirit—rather than merely following the technical letter of the rule. Understanding the categories can also help you see connections among the rules.

The first category contains rules that guide attorneys in fulfilling fiduciary obligations to their clients. Such rules address issues including competence, diligence, confidentiality, and avoiding conflicts of interest. As you know from reading Part A, attorneys owe fiduciary duties to their clients irrespective of the existence of these rules. But the professional conduct rules serve as an important reminder of these duties and a guide for fulfilling them. For example, it is an attorney's fiduciary duty to avoid conflicts of interest. Rule 1.7 provides that an attorney shall not represent a client if the representation is directly adverse to another client.

Rules in the second category describe limits of what lawyers can do on a client's behalf. The rules in this category address situations when a lawyer *may* or *must* take action that is contrary to a client's stated interests. Some of these rules are adopted by the bar as an expression of its values—such as rules that protect the integrity of the legal process or the rights of third parties. Other professional conduct rules in this category recognize ethical dilemmas that attorneys may face in practice and give the attorney discretion to make a personal judgment within the rule's parameters—such as rules that allow the disclosure of client confidences to protect a third party in defined circumstances. Still other rules in this category mirror other sources of law—a lawyer is legally and ethically prohibited from participating in a client's crime.

Finally, rules in the third category are aimed at promoting and preserving the integrity of the legal system and the legal profession. These rules cover topics such as attorney advertising, the duty to accept court appointments and provide pro bono service to those unable to pay, bar admission, disciplinary authority, and the obligation to report professional misconduct of another lawyer.

* * *

Problem 1.2. You receive a letter from Disciplinary Counsel of the State Board of Attorney Conduct. The letter explains that H.P. Simmons and several lawyers (including lawyers from your firm) reported that you violated the confidentiality rule of professional conduct by revealing information learned in the representation of your client. The letter asks you to respond in writing within fourteen days and explains that your response will be considered as Disciplinary Counsel determines whether to file a complaint for discipline.

Refer to the *Model Rules of Professional Conduct* to determine the specific provision you violated by disclosing your client's pen name. (The Table of Contents of the Model Rules will be helpful as you search for the rule addressing confidentiality.) Also, locate the professional conduct rule that requires a lawyer to report the professional misconduct of another lawyer. Must every rule violation be reported? Is the reporting obligation mandatory or permissive?

* * *

C. DEVELOPING A PROFESSIONAL IDENTITY

The American Bar Association law school accreditation standards require law schools to provide instruction in "professional identity formation." The ABA explains that this type of curriculum focuses on "what it means to be a lawyer and the special obligations lawyers have to their clients and society" and involves "an intentional exploration of the values, guiding principles, and well-being practices considered foundational to successful legal practice." ABA Law School Accreditation Standard 303(b), and Interpretation 303–5.

The following discussion considers some of the most important roles that lawyers play for their clients, communities, and selves. These roles are not separate from fulfilling professional conduct obligations, but are part and parcel of meeting those duties.

1. LAWYERS AS PUBLIC CITIZENS

In contrast to the life of a private citizen, a lawyer is a "public citizen." This role is described in the Preamble of the *Model Rules of Professional Conduct* as encompassing duties to improve the law and provide access to justice. As a public citizen, a lawyer is called upon to "further the public's understanding of and confidence in the rule of law and justice systems," because doing so is essential to a constitutional democracy. *Model Rules of Professional Conduct*, Preamble, Paragraph [6]. The Preamble emphasizes the lawyer's role in providing pro bono legal services and access to the legal system, stating, "[A]ll lawyers should devote professional time and resources and use civic influence to ensure equal access to our system of justice for all those who because of economic or social barriers cannot afford or secure adequate legal counsel." Model Rule 6.1 details the obligation to provide pro bono legal services, explaining that lawyers have a "professional responsibility to provide legal services to those unable to pay" and that lawyers should aspire to provide fifty hours of pro bono work each year.

Memphis attorney Buck Lewis explains that being a public citizen means that all lawyers, young and old and from all practice areas, are "supposed to be protecting the legal system and . . . [giving] our time and our talents and using this great education that we have for the public good." Mr. Lewis was a creative force behind TN Free Legal Answers, an online platform that pairs Tennessee attorney volunteers with income-eligible members of the public with legal problems. The result is a virtual legal advice clinic that has helped thousands of individuals. The online pro bono platform was so successful that it was subsequently adopted by the ABA, where it has been used nationally by thousands of attorneys and clients. Mr. Lewis explains that pro bono work is one of the biggest joys of being a lawyer, adding, "I don't want to live my professional life without having pro bono be a part of it, because that's what makes me happy and glad and joyful."

When asked what advice he would give about living a fulfilling life, Mr. Lewis said that even busy attorneys should make pro bono service a priority, because "if it's absent from your personal life and your professional life you're going to have a high risk of burning out." He concluded, "All the studies tell us that public service, and service to others, makes us happier and healthier and more successful."

2. LAWYERS AS LEADERS

Lawyers are constantly called upon to be leaders, in both their professional and personal lives. Understanding that there is an expectation that lawyers will step up and lead, law schools have begun developing curricula and programs to help law students develop leadership skills.

Law Professor Deborah Rhode was a trailblazer in recognizing the need to train lawyers as leaders. In their book, LEADERSHIP FOR LAWYERS, Deborah Rhode and Amanda Packel discuss learning strategies for lawyers who want to develop as leaders. They explain that prospective leaders need self-awareness of the positions they aspire to, the qualities they lack, and the obstacles they face. They explain that law students should "think deeply about their values, passions, and priorities, and what personal changes and sacrifices they are willing to make to realize their professional aspirations." They urge lawyers to evaluate throughout their careers how much time they spend on work that they find meaningful and adjust when necessary to better match their interests and talents. DEBORAH L. RHODE & AMANDA K. PACKEL, LEADERSHIP FOR LAWYERS 72 (2d ed. 2018).

3. LAWYERS AS CAREGIVERS

Research supports the idea that the most effective lawyers—just like the most successful healthcare providers—are excellent caregivers. The best doctors and nurses address not only the patient's medical needs, but also the related needs that help a patient get well again. In her article, *Lawyers as Caregivers*, Law Professor Paula Schaefer finds that a lawyer's clients have similar needs for lawyers to provide caregiving. These areas of care include: prompt communication, respectful interactions uninfluenced by bias and stereotypes, keeping confidences, and making a personal connection.

Numerous studies have found a positive correlation between a positive patient-doctor connection and better outcomes for patients. Such connections are made when doctors communicate with empathy, kindness, and interpersonal warmth. Research reveals that the doctor-patient interpersonal connection results in higher patient satisfaction, reduced risk of litigation, and improved adherence with treatment. Beyond that, a positive interpersonal connection between doctor and patient has also corresponded with improved health results. In one study, a group of patients had better health outcomes when their doctors followed a script that required five behaviors: (1) being warm and friendly; (2) engaging in active listening; (3) expressing empathy ("I can understand how difficult [your medical condition] must be for you."); (4) engaging in "20 seconds of thoughtful silence" as if pondering the treatment plan while taking the patient's pulse; and (5) expressing confidence and positive expectations. Paula Schaefer, *Lawyers as Caregivers*, 12 ST. MARY'S J. LEGAL MALPRACTICE & ETHICS, 331, 341–43 (2022).

Professor Schaefer suggests that lawyers can borrow from this caregiving research. Like patients, clients often feel anxiety, stress, fear, and helplessness. The research suggests that a lawyer's empathy, kindness, touch, encouragement, and humor—in other words, connectedness to the client—may positively impact these issues. These scripted interactions, which required five behaviors of doctors, led to measurably better outcomes for those patients. The difference for those patients was the connection the doctor made by spending time with the patient, being warm, actively listening, showing empathy, touching the patient, and expressing positive expectations. Lawyers can follow this same script, and it may very well result in the same positive outcomes for clients. *Id.* at 346.

4. LAWYERS AS FALLIBLE HUMAN BEINGS (AND THE STUDY OF BEHAVIORAL LEGAL ETHICS)

Even a lawyer with the best of intentions to act ethically is human, and therefore fallible. Research from psychology and other behavioral science fields explores how biases, heuristics, and situational factors can have an influence on ethical decision making. These factors often operate outside of a person's conscious awareness.

The field of behavioral legal ethics adds the perspective of this research to the study of legal ethics, providing attorneys with a new lens for understanding ethical decision making. This same research can also provide attorneys with tools for acting ethically. In short, behavioral legal ethics can help us understand why attorney misconduct occurs and what we can do about it.

For example, research on obedience and conformity can help new attorneys understand how they might be influenced by others (senior attorneys, colleagues, clients, etc.) to engage in unethical conduct. This research also provides insight into the circumstances that allow an individual to take a stand that is contrary to the position of the group or authority figure, such as when a competing authority figure is introduced into the mix (like a trusted colleague or a firm's ethics counsel).

As you study professional responsibility this semester, it will be tempting to think that you would never engage in the types of misconduct you read about in these cases. You might think that the lawyers who broke the rules either did not understand their obligations or chose to engage in misconduct out of greed or dishonesty. Throughout this textbook, we will prompt you to think about the other factors that may have been in play, how you could easily fall into a similar way of thinking, and steps you can take to avoid the same flawed decision-making in practice. The challenge is to leave this class understanding that you do not know everything and that you must be vigilant to avoid misconduct as an attorney.

Problem 1.3. Why do you suppose our hypothetical lawyer revealed confidential information about client H.P. Simmons? Do you think most attorneys understand the confidentiality obligation? Why would a lawyer who understands the law of confidentiality nonetheless "slip up" and how can you avoid such mistakes in practice?

Profile of Attorney Professionalism. It would be easy for a professional responsibility text to focus only on the negative. After all, many cases worthy of inclusion in a professional responsibility textbook involve a lawyer's lapse of professional judgment. In an effort to highlight positive role models, each chapter of this text will include a "Profile of Attorney Professionalism." These short profiles will feature attorneys who demonstrated exceptional professionalism in practice.

Before she became the first woman to serve on the Missouri Supreme Court, Ann Covington distinguished herself as a hard-working attorney who endeavored to provide exceptional service to her clients. She describes her early years in practice thus:

> I enjoyed [the practice of law] and it was extremely hard work. [I] have recognized . . . what a privilege it was to help people on a day-to-day basis, so to speak. Whereas, my practice later was more of a corporate representation, [when I first started practicing, the people who came to the office . . . placed] their business affairs or personal affairs in my hands. I felt terribly responsible for them. . . . One of the partners in [my firm], when I sometimes worried aloud about something, said: "Well, Ann, you didn't make these facts."
>
> Well, of course I didn't make the facts, but when [a client] would come and say, "Here's my situation," I felt responsible. Certainly in divorces, when children were involved, in contested custody matters—those were difficult. But, dissolution of partnerships could be almost as deadly as dissolutions of marriage. So, those things were a strain. And beyond that, the cases in juvenile court. We were all expected to accept appointments as guardians *ad litem* for children or in some cases for persons who were parents who were unable to pay. Termination of parental rights cases—those are heartbreaking. . . .
>
> I was very involved with many, many, many of my clients. [It was] gratifying to be able to help them. . . . Sometimes I felt pleasure when an opposing party would come to me and say: "You're quite the barracuda; I would never have guessed." But [it was also gratifying when a client came in with flowers for me or] said, "I made these cookies for you and your family." Those kinds of things . . . were so rewarding, and I cherish that time.

Paula Schaefer, *Oral History of the Honorable Ann K. Covington*, American Bar Association Women Trailblazers in the Law Project (2010).

CHAPTER 2

ADMISSION TO THE BAR

■ ■ ■

Chapter Hypothetical. You are a member of your state's Board of Law Examiners (BLE). In addition to overseeing the bar examination, the BLE makes determinations about whether a bar applicant has the qualifications to become a member of the bar. Under the state's supreme court bar admission rule, the BLE must determine if a bar applicant has "the reputation and character that in the opinion of the Board indicates no reasonable basis for substantial doubts that the applicant will adhere to the standards of conduct required of attorneys in this State." Each applicant completes a character and fitness application that asks questions concerning matters including: employment history; criminal record (broadly defined); driving infractions; financial history, including past due bills and bankruptcy; substance abuse and treatment; and mental health conditions and treatment. Sometimes the investigation reveals discrepancies or outright lies in the application.

When an application reveals a problem that concerns the BLE, the BLE issues a show cause order, requesting the applicant to present evidence establishing that the applicant meets the character standard. Following these hearings, the five BLE members vote on whether the applicant meets the standard. You find it challenging to decide whether an applicant's conduct is disqualifying. In cases of troubling past conduct, you struggle with the question of rehabilitation. Specifically, how does a person show that they have changed and how long must they maintain that change before they are trusted with a client's affairs and money?

During deliberations, you frequently remind your colleagues of the need to treat everyone the same. You fear that people of color and women are sometimes held to a different standard from other applicants with a similar record. You also think it is very hard to vote "no" on an applicant's admission because you know how much money they spent to earn a J.D.— and how much they are likely paying in student loans.

The problems in this Chapter require you to explain how you will vote on the fitness question for various bar applicants.

A. OVERVIEW OF BAR ADMISSION STANDARDS

Bar admission rules are set by the state's highest court pursuant to its authority to regulate the practice of law in the jurisdiction. The U.S. Supreme Court has explained that states can "require high standards of qualification, such as good moral character or proficiency in its law" for bar admission, but that "any qualification must have a rational connection with the applicant's fitness or capacity to practice law." *Schware v. Bd. of Bar Exam. of State of N.M.*, 353 U.S. 232, 239, 77 S. Ct. 752, 756, 1 L. Ed. 2d 796 (1957).

Typical admission standards require the applicant to: (1) have a J.D. degree from an accredited law school; (2) receive a passing score on the bar examination; and (3) have the character and fitness necessary for the practice of law. Each state's highest court is ultimately responsible for a state's bar admission standards, and typically delegates authority to a board of law examiners (or a similarly named body) that administers every aspect of bar admission—including the application, character and fitness investigation, and exam administration.

A great resource for understanding the admission requirements in each state is the Comprehensive Guide for Bar Admission Standards. The guide is updated each year by the National Conference of Bar Examiners (NCBE) and can be found on its website. Another good resource is the court rules of the state where you plan to be licensed. Typically, one court rule contains all of the bar admission standards. Finally, look at your state's board of law examiners website for application deadlines, fee schedules, and additional information. If you are not going to law school in the state where you will take the bar examination, pay special attention to the admission rules so you do not miss any deadlines.

In most states, the bar examination consists of the multi-state professional responsibility exam (MPRE), and a post-graduation, multi-day examination consisting of essay, multiple choice, and performance tests. Applicants who need testing accommodations should carefully research deadlines and application materials needed to receive an accommodation. Students sometimes miss these deadlines and then have to decide whether to delay taking the exam or take it without an accommodation.

The MPRE is a sixty question multiple choice test on professional responsibility topics. It is required in all but two U.S. jurisdictions (Wisconsin and Puerto Rico). While each jurisdiction has its own professional conduct rules, the MPRE uses the *Model Rules of Professional Conduct* as the governing authority. The NCBE prepares, administers, and grades the MPRE, but each state determines what score is needed to pass in the state. Most bar applicants take the MPRE while they are still in law school. Before you take the MPRE, check the admission rules in the state where you plan to be licensed to learn how long it will accept an MPRE score.

The more grueling part of the examination process is the two (or three) day exam administered in each state. (This is what most people refer to as the "bar exam," even though the MPRE is a bar admission exam). The vast majority of U.S. jurisdictions have adopted the Uniform Bar Exam (UBE), which consists of the multi-state essay exam (six thirty minute essays), the multi-state performance test (two ninety minute performance tests), and the multi-state bar exam (two hundred multiple choice questions). The UBE is developed by the NCBE. States grade the UBE and set their own passing scores. States also set a length of time that applicants can transfer a UBE score. Thus, a bar applicant could seek admission in more than one UBE jurisdiction without re-taking the bar exam. This portability of scores makes the UBE attractive to bar applicants.

As this book goes to press, the NCBE is planning to debut the NextGen bar exam in July 2026. Each jurisdiction will decide whether to adopt NextGen. Because the NCBE is planning to stop offering the UBE after February 2028, each jurisdiction will have to choose between creating its own exam or NextGen for the July 2028 exam and future administrations. In the years when the UBE and NextGen are administered concurrently, scores are expected to be portable between UBE and NextGen jurisdictions. You can learn more about the planned content of the exam on the NCBE's NextGen website.

Outside of transferring a UBE (or NextGen) score, there are other ways to seek admission without examination in a jurisdiction. In some states (but certainly not all), a bar applicant can seek admission without examination if certain requirements are met, such as practicing in another jurisdiction for five of the past seven years. You will hear this referred to as reciprocity or admission on motion. Recognizing the challenge of taking multiple bar exams, some states provide for temporary admission of military spouses.

Once an attorney is licensed in a state or the District of Columbia, the attorney may also seek admission to the bars of various federal courts. There is not a separate bar exam for this admission. But attorneys should be aware that these courts often have their own professional conduct rules that may be different from the rules in the state where the court is located. Attorneys can also be disciplined by the federal courts to which they are admitted.

* * *

B. THE CHARACTER AND FITNESS STANDARD

Problem 2.1. The executive director of the BLE forwarded the character and fitness application of Denise Lawson to members of the board who decided to issue a show cause order. At Denise's hearing, the Board heard the following evidence:

- Denise has struggled with alcohol and drug addiction throughout her teens and adult life. She has been fired from two jobs because she came to work under the influence of drugs and alcohol. She entered a residential treatment program three and a half years ago (just before law school) and has not used alcohol or drugs since.

- Denise filed for bankruptcy five years ago, when she lost a job and was unable to pay her bills. She has not had past due bills or financial difficulties since that bankruptcy. The lost job was one referenced above—related to her drug and alcohol abuse.

- Denise has excellent character references, including a current employer where she worked during law school and where she hopes to work if she is admitted to practice in the state.

Will you vote in favor of Denise's admission to the bar? Please consider the standard articulated in the *Simmons* case (below), as well as the discussion of conditional admission later in this chapter.

* * *

IN THE MATTER OF THE BAR APPLICATION OF TARRA DENELLE SIMMONS
414 P.3d 1111 (Wash. 2018)

YU, J.

Determining moral character as a credential for practicing law has a long and intriguing history.[1] While lawyers may have more work to do in regard to how the public perceives our contributions to society, the evaluation of a bar applicant's character is an important step toward building confidence in our legal profession and our system of justice.

At this point in time, every state bar has some form of certification of moral character as part of its admission process. Concerned with the morality of an applicant, the inquiry serves a legitimate interest in protecting the public and preserving a certain degree of professionalism. Nonetheless, we also know that throughout our history the standards used

---

[1] *See* Deborah L. Rhode, *Moral Character as a Professional Credential*, 94 YALE L.J. 491 (1985).

to assess moral character have shifted as society's norms and moral codes have changed. For example, categorical exclusions of women or rejection of applicants based on race, ethnicity, or sexual orientation were once generally accepted. But just as we have evolved in our understanding of humanity, we have also grown in our understanding of what makes a bar applicant a person of good moral character worthy of admission. Today, we affirm the principles that for purposes of bar admission, a moral character inquiry is determined on an individualized basis and that there is no categorical exclusion of an applicant who has a criminal or substance abuse history.

This case concerns a recent law school graduate's application to sit for the Washington State Bar Examination. Tarra Denelle Simmons has a challenging social history, including long-term substance abuse, multiple criminal convictions, and two bankruptcies. However, in the approximately five and a half years preceding her application to sit for the bar exam, Simmons successfully engaged in treatment for her substance abuse and childhood trauma. She has undisputedly maintained her sobriety since September 2011 and has not been accused of any criminal or unethical behavior since then.

Simmons was entirely candid about her past when she applied to sit for the summer 2017 bar exam, and she readily provided further information as requested by counsel for the Washington State Bar Association (WSBA). Bar counsel referred Simmons' application to the WSBA Character and Fitness Board (Board), which recommended by a vote of six to three that Simmons' application be denied. We then reviewed her application and the Board's recommendation, heard oral argument on November 16, 2017, and granted Simmons' application in a unanimous order later that day.[2] Order, *In re Simmons*, No. 201,671–5 (Wash. Nov. 16, 2017). We now explain the reasons for our decision.

BACKGROUND

Simmons was born to parents with substance abuse problems, and she grew up in poverty, surrounded by crime. She was the victim of many acts of sexual violence during her childhood and adolescence, and endured sporadic periods of homelessness beginning when she ran away at age 13. As a juvenile, Simmons was adjudicated for theft, possession of stolen property, and second degree assault.

Simmons struggled with addiction for years, and her adult history includes a 2001 conviction for second degree assault and five 2011 convictions for organized retail theft, unlawful possession of a firearm, and possession of controlled substances. As a result of her criminal convictions,

---

[2] Simmons partially waived her right to confidentiality in these proceedings. This opinion therefore contains personally identifying information and is not redacted. Her application file otherwise remains sealed. See Admission and Practice Rule (APR) 24.1(g).

Simmons' nursing license was placed on probationary status, she served a total of over three years in jail and prison, and she underwent two bankruptcies and a foreclosure on her home.

However, when Simmons was sent to prison in late 2011, she began engaging in meaningful treatment for her trauma and addiction for the first time. Since then, she has changed her life to a degree that can only be deemed remarkable, both in terms of the efforts she has put forth and the positive results she has achieved. Simmons has maintained her sobriety and conducted herself with complete openness and integrity over the past six years. She has been candid about her past, demonstrating sincere remorse and working diligently to make amends to her community as an outspoken advocate for civil legal aid with a focus on assisting formerly incarcerated individuals facing barriers to reentry.

Simmons attended the Seattle University School of Law and became the first student in her school's history to be awarded a two-year public interest fellowship from the Skadden Foundation. She graduated magna cum laude as a dean's medal recipient in May 2017, and letters from faculty and classmates further make it clear that Simmons was a substantial asset to the entire law school community. Letters from her supervisors and colleagues also unequivocally state that Simmons excelled and exhibited consistently ethical behavior in the five legal internships she completed during law school, in addition to the volunteer and advocacy work that she undertook for no course credit.

Despite Simmons' about-face life choices, her extensive criminal history and recent substance abuse nevertheless gave bar counsel reasonable grounds to refer the matter for further consideration. Thus, counsel for the WSBA sent Simmons' bar application to the Board for consideration of whether Simmons: 1) has demonstrated sufficient rehabilitation from her prior criminal conduct and addictions which contributed to that conduct, 2) now demonstrates that she conducts herself with a high degree of honesty, integrity and trustworthiness in her legal obligations, and 3) has the ability to conduct herself in a manner that engenders respect for the law and that adheres to the Washington Rules of Professional Conduct. In short, has she met her burden of proving that she currently has good moral character and fitness to practice law?

The Board held a hearing on April 14, 2017. Simmons testified on her own behalf and offered testimony supporting her application from three people: the youth policy director for the American Civil Liberties Union of Washington, a former litigator and administrative law judge, and a currently sitting superior court judge. Bar counsel presented no evidence and made no recommendation. The Board recommended to deny Simmons' application by a vote of six to three. Subsequently, Simmons asked this court to review her application and the Board's recommendation.

ISSUE

Has Simmons shown by clear and convincing evidence that she is currently of good moral character and possesses the requisite fitness to practice law?

STANDARD OF REVIEW

[The court explains that its review of the Board's recommendation is de novo].

ANALYSIS

Lawyers are "entrusted with anxious responsibilities" to safeguard their clients' money, their confidences, and, in some cases, their lives. *Schware v. Bd. of Bar Exam'rs,* 353 U.S. 232, 247, 77 S.Ct. 752, 1 L.Ed. 2d 796 (1957) (Frankfurter, J., concurring). To protect against abuses of trust, anyone who seeks a license to practice law in Washington "must be of good moral character and possess the requisite fitness to practice law."

However, while "good moral character" is essential for the ethical licensed practice of law, "[s]uch a vague qualification, which is easily adapted to fit personal views and predilections, can be a dangerous instrument for arbitrary and discriminatory denial of the right to practice law." *Konigsberg v. State Bar,* 353 U.S. 252, 263, 77 S.Ct. 722, 1 L.Ed. 2d 810 (1957). Therefore, in 2006, we revised the APRs and defined "good moral character" and "fitness to practice law" and provided detailed guidance on how to assess an applicant's character and fitness. APR 21, 22.

The current APRs provide for a preliminary review by bar counsel of all applications that indicate a possible character and fitness concern. APR 22.1(a)–(b). After gathering further information and conducting a review, bar counsel refers to the Board for further investigation and a hearing "any applicant about whom there is a substantial question whether the applicant possess[es] the requisite good moral character and fitness to practice law." APR 22.1(d). The Board will then conduct further inquiries, hold a hearing, and "[r]ecommend the approval or denial of an applicant's application." APR 23.1(a)(4). Where the Board recommends approval, the application is automatically reviewed by this court, which makes the final decision. APR 24.2(b)(1). If the Board recommends denial, the applicant may ask this court to review and decide the application. APR 24.2(b)(2). In this case, bar counsel referred Simmons' application to the Board, which recommended denial, and Simmons requested our review. We now apply the revised APRs for the first time in a published opinion.

A. The Board's analysis relating to character and fitness

The Board's determination of an applicant's character and fitness is governed by APR 20–24. The specific rules that are most relevant in this case are APR 20 and 21. As framed by the Board, the question posed was "whether, in light of Tarra Simmons' lengthy history of criminal and financial issues, she has proved to the Board by clear and convincing evidence that today she possess[es] the requisite good moral character and fitness to practice law in the State of Washington." Findings of Fact, Conclusions of Law, Analysis & Recommendation (Board Majority) at 2.

The Board entered in-depth findings of fact and conclusions of law. supporting its recommendation. While we have reviewed each of the findings and conclusions of law, our analysis in this opinion is more limited because the Board's recommendation, in most essential aspects, is correct and unchallenged by the parties. As the Board rightly noted, Simmons, the applicant, bears the burden of proving by clear and convincing evidence that she is currently of "good moral character" as that term is defined by APR 20(c), and that she is currently fit to practice law and meets all five essential eligibility requirements to do so in accordance with APR 20(d)–(e). APR 24.1(c).

The APRs define "good moral character" as "a record of conduct manifesting the qualities of honesty, fairness, candor, trustworthiness, observance of fiduciary responsibilities, adherence to the law, and a respect for the rights of other persons and the judicial process." APR 20(c).

"Fitness to practice law is a record of conduct that establishes that the applicant meets the essential eligibility requirements for the practice of law." APR 20(d). The "essential eligibility requirements" are:

(1) The ability to exercise good judgment and to conduct oneself with a high degree of honesty, integrity, and trustworthiness in financial dealings, legal obligations, professional relationships, and in one's professional business.

(2) The ability to conduct oneself in a manner that engenders respect for the law and adheres to the Washington Rules of Professional Conduct.

(3) The ability to diligently, reliably, and timely perform legal tasks and fulfill professional obligations to clients, lawyers, LLLTs, LPOs, courts, and others.

(4) The ability to competently undertake fundamental legal skills commensurate with the lawyer, LLLT, or LPO license applied for, such as legal reasoning and analysis, recollection of complex factual information and integration of such information with complex legal theories, problem solving, and recognition and resolution of ethical dilemmas; and

(5) The ability to communicate comprehensibly with clients, lawyers, LLLTs, LPOs, courts, and others, with or without the use of aids or devices.

APR 20(e).

The Board's determination of moral character and fitness is guided by 14 different factors enumerated in APR 21(a) as well as aggravating and mitigating factors enumerated in APR 21(b). As directed by APR 21, the Board appropriately considered Simmons' prior criminal conduct, her financial difficulties, and the probationary status of her nursing license. After considering all of these factors, the Board unanimously agreed that Simmons proved she met three of the five essential eligibility requirements: "[t]he ability to diligently, reliably, and timely perform legal tasks and fulfill professional obligations"; "[t]he ability to competently undertake fundamental legal skills"; and "[t]he ability to communicate comprehensibly." APR 20(e)(3)–(5).

However, the majority of the Board concluded that Simmons failed to meet two of these five essential eligibility requirements: "[t]he ability to exercise good judgment and to conduct oneself with a high degree of honesty, integrity, and trustworthiness in financial dealings, legal obligations, professional relationships, and in one's professional business" and "[t]he ability to conduct oneself in a manner that engenders respect for the law and adheres to the Washington Rules of Professional Conduct." APR 20(e)(1), (2); *see* APR 21(a)(1), (5), (7), (10), (12), (13). We disagree with the Board regarding these two essential eligibility requirements, and we therefore disagree with its ultimate recommendation in this case.

B. We disagree with the Board's assessment of Simmons' time in recovery and her attitude toward her prior conduct

The majority of the Board thought that Simmons had not yet spent enough time maintaining her sobriety and actively engaging in positive behaviors to establish a record of conduct consistent with good moral character and fitness to practice law. Second, the majority of the Board thought that "[s]ome of the attitudes she expressed in the record and at the hearing signal that her acquired fame has nurtured not integrity and honesty, but a sense of entitlement to privileges and recognition beyond the reach of others." Board Majority at 21. In light of the entire record presented, we do not agree.

1. Simmons has been in recovery for enough time to establish a record of conduct showing her good moral character and fitness to practice law

The "recency of the conduct," the "absence of recent misconduct," and the "length of time in which the applicant has been in recovery" are all mandatory factors for our consideration. *See* APR 21(b)(2), (9)(i), (ix). We do not take lightly the length of Simmons' criminal history and substance abuse as compared to the length of time in which she has maintained sobriety, refrained from misconduct, and worked actively to make amends for her past behavior. We are also mindful that "this court's ultimate responsibility in matters relating to admission of attorneys is to guard the public and its confidence in the judicial system." *In re Belsher*, 102 Wash. 2d 844, 850, 689 P.2d 1078 (1984). However, we ultimately conclude that Simmons' six-year record of complete sobriety, stable financial position, exemplary conduct, complete candor, and demonstrated ability to recognize and respond appropriately to situations that might lead to relapse is sufficient to persuade the court that she is highly likely to remain on her current path when she becomes a practicing attorney.

    a.   We decline to adopt a bright-line rule

The parties have debated the merits of a bright-line rule for determining sufficient rehabilitation or recovery (for example, creating a rebuttable presumption after a certain number of years without relapsing or engaging in any misconduct). Although we seek to provide guidance in this opinion, we decline to adopt a specific time period as evidence of complete rehabilitation for all applicants because of the individualized inquiry of character and fitness, and the complexity of recovery.

We acknowledge that the rules governing disbarment do have specific time-based restrictions. *E.g.*, APR 25.1(b) ("No petition for reinstatement shall be filed within a period of five years after disbarment."). However, the rules governing new applicants do not. This is not an oversight. It reflects the fact that although we are guided by the "common purpose" of protecting the public and the profession in both new applications and reinstatements, *Belsher*, 102 Wash.2d at 851, 689 P.2d 1078, a new applicant with prior criminal or substance abuse issues is very different from a reinstatement applicant who has previously been disbarred.

In reinstatement cases, it has already been conclusively proved that the applicants previously failed to fulfill their professional responsibilities so egregiously that this court could not allow them to continue practicing law for the safety of the public and the good of the profession. *See In re Disciplinary Proceeding Against Fossedal*, 189 Wash. 2d 222, 241, 399 P.3d 1169 (2017). We therefore do not allow previously disbarred attorneys to resume practicing law without proof "that they have overcome the weaknesses that produced the misconduct for which they were disbarred." *In re Disciplinary Proceeding Against Hart*, 118 Wash. 2d 280, 289, 822 P.2d 264 (1992).

New applicants, meanwhile, do not have previous lawful experience as independently practicing attorneys. *See Wright*, 102 Wash. 2d at 861, 690 P.2d 1134 (disapproving of the applicant's prior unauthorized practice of law). Thus, unlike a previous disbarment, prior misconduct by a new applicant rarely provides "conclusive evidence" that the applicant lacks good moral character and is not fit to practice law. *Belsher,* 102 Wash. 2d at 851, 689 P.2d 1078.

Moreover, in attorney discipline, and particularly in disbarment there is an aspect of holding an attorney accountable for misconduct, as well as protecting the public. The time restrictions on seeking reinstatement serve not only to protect the public but to hold the disbarred attorney accountable for abusing the trust of the legal profession and his or her former clients. *See Fossedal,* 189 Wash. 2d at 241, 399 P.3d 1169. New applicants have never held that trust. Therefore, instead of attempting to hold them accountable for their past misconduct ourselves, we consider the "sufficiency of punishment" they have already received as one of many factors when we evaluate their applications. APR 21(b)(9)(iii).

Because the WSBA simply does not have any directly comparable evidence by which to judge how new applicants will conduct themselves in the licensed practice of law, cases involving new bar applicants must be considered in an individualized manner. Specific time-based rules, or even flexible presumptions, are not appropriate, and we decline to adopt any at this time.

    b.   We follow evidence-based practices for evaluative purposes

Although we cannot adopt a generally applicable time-based rule, we are presented in this case with current, credible social science research of undisputed validity about the relationship between the duration of a person's sobriety and positive conduct and the person's reduced likelihood of relapsing or recidivating. This research reveals that 86 percent of addicts who maintain their sobriety for at least 5 years will never relapse, but that there is no further substantial decrease in the likelihood of relapse after 10 years have passed. Michael L. Dennis, Mark A. Foss & Christy K. Scott, *An Eight-Year Perspective on the Relationship between the Duration of Abstinence and Other Aspects of Recovery,* 31 EVAL. REV. 585, 604 (2007); *see also* John M. Nally, Susan Lockwood, Taiping Ho & Katie Knutson, *Post-Release Recidivism and Employment among Different Types of Released Offenders: A 5-Year follow-up Study in the United States,* 9 INTL'L J. CRIM. JUST. SCI. 16 (2014). Simmons has maintained her sobriety and exemplary conduct for over six years at this point. The research presented therefore indicates that she has reached the stage where her new positive behaviors are highly likely (in fact, about as likely as they ever will be) to represent lasting change, rather than the tenuous early stages of recovery. *Contra* Board Majority at 20–21 (describing Simmons' efforts thus far as "tender," "still fragile," and "still in their infancy").

. . .

We therefore do not view the recency of Simmons' prior misconduct as a negative factor, and we view favorably both her absence of recent misconduct and the length of time she has been in recovery given how far she has come to get to this point.

2. Simmons has demonstrated candor, insight, and respect for the law showing her good moral character and fitness to practice law

While the Board acknowledged that Simmons was completely candid and accepted full responsibility for her prior conduct, the Board was concerned that Simmons did not sufficiently understand the concerns raised by her prior misconduct and that her success has engendered in her an inappropriate sense of entitlement. These apprehensions raised questions for the Board about whether Simmons has a record demonstrating "respect for . . . the judicial process," whether she has shown the "ability to conduct [her]self in a manner that engenders respect for the law," and her "attitude toward the misconduct, including without limitation acceptance of responsibility and remorse." APR 20(c), (e)(2); APR 21(b)(9)(v). Considering the entire record, we find that Simmons is candid, sincere, and remorseful.

a. Simmons did not minimize her drug use

The Board found that Simmons "minimize[d] her historical drug activities" by failing to disclose in her initial bar application that she went through a six- to nine-month period of substance abuse in 2005, which resulted in brief inpatient treatment but no criminal charges or other direct, negative consequences. Board Majority at 17. The Board also felt that Simmons did not adequately acknowledge the concerns presented by a period beginning in 2009 during which she took opioid and amphetamine medications as prescribed by her doctors for chronic pain and mental health reasons. By 2011, Simmons was trading and selling those medications in exchange for methamphetamine. We agree with the Board that those periods of substance abuse are relevant concerns, but we do not agree that Simmons attempted to minimize or conceal them.

First, there was no question on the bar application that required Simmons to disclose her 2005 substance abuse. Indeed, it is doubtful that any question in the initial bar application lawfully *could* require such a disclosure given recent amendments to the APRs in accordance with the federal Americans with Disabilities Act of 1990, 42 U.S.C. §§ 12101–12213. See GR 9 Cover Sheet; U.S. Dep't of Justice, Office of Pub. Affairs, *Department of Justice Reaches Agreement with the Louisiana Supreme Court to Protect Bar Candidates with Disabilities* (Aug. 15, 2014), [https://perma.cc/6J7C-M9D4]. We must take an exclusively conduct-based approach to character and fitness review, and the existence of "drug or alcohol dependence, a health diagnosis, or treatment for either" cannot be an independent factor in the Board's consideration or our own, and the existence of any such condition cannot be a question on the bar application. APR 22.1(e).

Nevertheless, when bar counsel determined that such information was relevant in this case, Simmons readily provided her confidential medical records in response, and she spoke openly about her 2005 substance abuse at her hearing with the Board. The failure to voluntarily disclose information that, by federal law, cannot be requested without specific justification does not evince an attempt to conceal or minimize that information. We are therefore not concerned by the time and manner in which Simmons disclosed her 2005 substance abuse to bar counsel and the Board, and it is not a negative factor in our analysis.

Second, the Board was concerned by Simmons' candid admission that when she was taking addictive prescription medications, she was generally functional and did not recognize that she had a problem. Verbatim Report of Proceedings (VRP) (April 14, 2017) at 144–45, 156–57. However, she now realizes that she was addicted to those medications and knows that in the future, she cannot return to such addictive behaviors. *Id.* Given Simmons' current depth of insight, her prior lack of insight is not probative of her current moral character and fitness to practice law.[3]

b. Simmons' attitude is not inappropriate

The Board believed that Simmons demonstrated a "sense of entitlement to privileges and recognition beyond the reach of others" based on her inquiry as to whether her application needed to be referred to the Board and based on the public recognition that she has received for her remarkable success. We cannot agree with the Board's assessment.

We wholeheartedly agree that Simmons has *attained* privileges and recognition beyond the reach of others due to her hard work. For instance, she has the privilege of serving as cochair on the board of the Washington Statewide Reentry Council, and the recognition of graduating magna cum laude as a dean's medal recipient and the first Skadden fellow in her law school's history. Such things are indeed beyond the reach of most others. But Simmons did not attain her current privileges and recognitions through entitlement. She earned everything she has through dedication, talent, and a staggering amount of hard work. Simmons rightly takes pride in her extraordinary accomplishments, but there is no evidence that she expects special treatment.

---

[3] At oral argument, bar counsel contended that Simmons used the word "sorry" only once at her hearing before the Board, evincing a lack of remorse. Wash. Supreme Court oral argument, *In re Simmons*, No. 201,671-5 (Nov. 16, 2017), *audio recording by* TVW, Washington State's Public Affairs Network, http://www.tvw.org, at 44 min., 50 sec. We summarily reject the premise that this word count is an appropriate basis on which to evaluate Simmons' moral character. We therefore also decline to draw any inferences from the number of times that Simmons referred to her Skadden fellowship or the Skadden Foundation at her hearing. *Id.* at 27 min., 26 sec.

The Board was concerned because it thought that Simmons referred to the Board hearing as " 'unnecessary' " and that this statement indicated Simmons believed she was entitled to have her application granted without further inquiry. In her initial application to the WSBA, which was available to the Board but directed to bar counsel, Simmons stated in part:

"An unnecessary referral to the Character and Fitness Board would add little to assure the Washington Supreme Court of my current fitness and good character necessary to practice law, which is more than fully documented in this application and supporting materials . . . A referral to the Character and Fitness Board would be particularly harmful in my case because I have been awarded the Skadden Fellowship to serve the legal needs of a vulnerable population."

We do not view this as reflecting a belief by Simmons that the Board review process is unnecessary. Rather, Simmons' language in her application is consistent with her testimony to the Board that she was asking bar counsel to exercise its discretion to consider the record and the circumstances presented and decline to refer Simmons' application to the Board. . . .

Bar counsel apparently did not view Simmons' question about whether a referral was necessary as a negative factor at the time because it was not mentioned in counsel's referral memorandum to the Board. And when bar counsel decided a referral was needed, there is no evidence that Simmons complained or protested. Furthermore, at her hearing, Simmons "exhibited complete candor" and "was thorough and thoughtful in her presentation."

We also note that there is absolutely no published case law about how bar counsel decides whether a board referral is needed on the basis that there is "a substantial question whether the applicant possess[es] the requisite good moral character and fitness to practice law." APR 22.1(d); see TOM ANDREWS, ROB ARONSON, MARK FUCILE & ART LACHMAN, THE LAW OF LAWYERING IN WASHINGTON 2–20 (2012) (noting that without published opinions, bar applications remain "a guessing game for those who contemplate admission"). It may well have seemed obvious to experienced bar counsel and members of the Board that a character and fitness referral was inevitable in this case. However, it is not reasonable to assume that a first-time applicant should have the same perspective, even if the applicant received advice from a distinguished attorney when preparing her application, as Simmons did.

Asking whether a board referral was necessary under these circumstances does not evince "a sense of entitlement to privileges and recognition beyond the reach of others." It evinces the type of reasonable advocacy any litigator could ethically exercise on behalf of his or her clients, and likewise probably would exercise on his or her own behalf. It is entirely appropriate conduct for a person who wants to be a lawyer.

To the extent that the Board was also concerned that Simmons had developed an unwarranted sense of entitlement due to her "acquired fame," we do not share the Board's view. Board Majority at 21. Simmons' public recognition is not evidence that she is acting for her own gratification or to satisfy her own ego. The publicity that Simmons has received supports her continuing sobriety and exemplary conduct and is an important component of her career mission.

. . .

On the issue of Simmons' publicity and attitude toward her prior conduct, we also note a particularly relevant recommendation that the Board made in a previous case, which was not decided in a published opinion. There, the Board unanimously recommended to grant the application of the man who would become one of Simmons' attorneys in this case, Shon Hopwood.[4]

Unlike Simmons, Hopwood grew up in a relatively emotionally and financially stable family. He did not struggle with addiction or abuse, but he did struggle personally and financially. After his honorable discharge from the United States Navy, he participated in a string of armed bank robberies in Nebraska in his early 20s. He pleaded guilty to "five felony counts of bank robbery and one felony count of using a firearm during a crime of violence" and served a 10-year prison sentence. . . . After Hopwood completed his sentence and went on to excel in law school, this court granted his application to sit for the bar exam in 2014 in accordance with the Board's unanimous recommendation. His ethics and abilities as an attorney have never been questioned, and he is, by all accounts, a credit to the profession.

Both Hopwood and Simmons are living examples of a person's ability to change if he or she has the will and opportunity to do so. Both of their stories attracted media attention, and both of them openly and publicly shared their stories for the benefit of others. Both received extensive support for their applications from the public and from distinguished members of the legal community. The Board found them both to be candid and credible. There is no dispute that both Simmons and Hopwood generally present themselves in a professional and courteous manner, and there is no reason to believe that either one behaved uncharacteristically at the board hearing. Although every bar applicant is unique, we do not believe there is a sufficient basis on which to differentiate between

---

[4] We take judicial notice of the fact that Hopwood's story is well known within the legal community. *See, e.g.,* Tony Mauro, *Shon Hopwood's Amazing Legal Journey to be Featured on "60 Minutes,"* NAT'L L. J. Oct. 12, 2017, https://www.law.com/nationallawjournal/sites/nationallawjournal/2017/10/12/shon-hopwoods-amazing-legal-journey-to-be-featured-on-60-minutes/ [https://perma.cc/NFY2-EM9Y]. Furthermore, Hopwood waived his right to confidentiality in the Board's recommendation in his case, the WSBA did not oppose our considering it, and we have previously considered comparable evidence in disciplinary cases. *See In re Disciplinary Proceeding Against McGrath,* 178 Wash. 2d 280, 286, 308 P.3d 615 (2013).

Hopwood's and Simmons' respective attitudes toward their prior misconduct and the publicity they have received, except for their gender.[5]

We also give more weight to the testimony and letters supporting Simmons' application than the Board did. While it is true that many of Simmons' supporters had known her for three years or less at the time she applied, that is not at all relevant to the question of whether Simmons currently displays an unwarranted sense of entitlement. The people who testified and wrote in support of Simmons' application unquestionably interacted with her as she presents herself today. This support comes from an extraordinarily wide array of individuals, including a volunteer at the Mission Creek Corrections Center for Women who first met Simmons while she was incarcerated, Simmons' supervisors at the first places where she worked after her release from confinement (which were not high-profile settings but a fast food restaurant and a property management company), currently sitting Washington judges at both the trial and appellate levels, the dean of the Seattle University of School of Law and many law school faculty members, and respected practicing attorneys ranging from the elected King County prosecuting attorney to a staff attorney for the American Civil Liberties Union of Washington. It is undisputed by Simmons' many supporters that she consistently displays the utmost integrity, compassion, and dedication. We simply do not believe that so many people would put their own reputations at risk with no benefit to themselves to give their unequivocal support to a person who evinces an unwarranted sense of entitlement.

We conclude that the majority of the Board did not give sufficient weight to the level of personal insight Simmons has demonstrated, and that the Board erred in viewing Simmons' publicity and the pride she rightly takes in her accomplishments as negative factors. Simmons has shown she has "respect for . . . the judicial process" and the "ability to conduct [her]self in a manner that engenders respect for the law." We also do not view Simmons' "attitude toward the misconduct, including without limitation acceptance of responsibility and remorse" as a negative factor in this case. . . .

C. Simmons has met her burden of proof

We hold that Simmons has shown by clear and convincing evidence that she is currently of good moral character and she is fit to practice law.

---

[5] Much has been written about the difficult questions that arise when making the necessarily subjective determination that a person is or is not of good moral character and fit to practice law. *E.g.*, Jon Bauer, *The Character of the Questions and the Fitness of the Process: Mental Health, Bar Admissions and the Americans with Disabilities Act*, 49 U.C.L.A. L. REV. 93 (2001); Rhode, *supra*. While we disagree with the Board's recommendation in this case, we do *not* hold that it acted arbitrarily. . . . We therefore do not explore potential indicators of bias, and note only that it is extremely important for the WSBA and the courts to ensure that they are sufficiently informed to make subjective judgments about applicants with histories of substance abuse, criminal convictions, and financial problems.

Simmons has spent enough time in recovery, and she accepts full responsibility for her prior conduct. She has consistently demonstrated remorse, self-awareness, fortitude, and an unwavering dedication to earning and maintaining the respect of the profession. Her success during law school, both academically and in supervised internships, amply demonstrates she is worthy to sit for the bar. Indeed, given the substantial obstacles that she has overcome, her success is an even stronger indicator of her abilities than it would be for the average law student. As noted by Dean Annette E. Clark of the Seattle University School of Law, unlike Simmons, "[m]any of our law students have lived lives of privilege, and so when we attest to their character and fitness to practice law, it is under circumstances where they have not been tested in any meaningful sense by circumstances such as poverty, substance abuse, and domestic violence." Memorandum, Attach. B at 114. Simmons, meanwhile, has overcome all of those circumstances and more. Her remarkable achievements would simply not be possible without her extraordinary abilities and relentless hard work.

We grant Simmons' application to sit for the bar exam.

CONCLUSION

. . .

Simmons has proved by clear and convincing evidence that she is currently of good moral character and fit to practice law. We affirm this court's long history of recognizing that one's past does not dictate one's future. We therefore unanimously grant her application to sit for the bar exam.

* * *

Defining "Character and Fitness." How does Washington define the concept of "good moral character" and "fitness to practice law" for purposes of the bar admission process? Do the definitions provide bar examiners with sufficient guidance?

A History of Discrimination. The *Simmons* Court notes the risk of potentially discriminatory treatment of applicants as part of the admissions process. In the past, the character and fitness requirement was sometimes used to exclude individuals on the basis of race, sex, or political views. *See* Bruce A. Green & Rebecca Roiphe, *ABA Model Rule 8.4(g), Discriminatory Speech, and the First Amendment*, 50 HOFSTRA L. REV. 543, 572 (2022); Bobbi Jo Boyd, *Embracing Our Public Purpose: A Value-Based Lawyer-Licensing Model*, 48 U. MEM. L. REV. 351, 420 (2017).

* * *

1. CRIMINAL HISTORY

While state character and fitness applications vary, the NCBE shares a sample character and fitness application on its website. The NCBE reminds law students that this sample application should be used as only a guide. Review the sample application and note the questions that delve into an applicant's criminal history. Determine whether the application requires you to reveal: (1) matters that have been expunged from your record; (2) juvenile matters; and/or (3) matters in which you entered into a diversion agreement.

Problem 2.2. The BLE heard evidence in the following cases. How would you vote on these applicants? How does the *Simmons* decision guide your thinking on admitting these applicants?

- Steve Zorn has three convictions for drunk driving. One occurred ten years before he attended law school. One occurred just prior to going to law school and one occurred right after his first year of law school.

- Pamela Gruden is twenty-five years old. She has accumulated three speeding tickets in her life. The first occurred when she was 16, the second when she was in college, and the third during her second year of law school. In each case, she was driving 10–15 miles over the speed limit.

- While serving as treasurer of a law school student organization, Lora Spurrier stole $250 to help pay some overdue medical bills. She paid the money back shortly thereafter, but another student discovered her actions. Lora was never charged with a crime but she was found to have violated the school's honor code.

2. FINANCIAL RESPONSIBILITY

A lack of financial responsibility, as evidenced by unpaid and overdue financial obligations, can be a basis for denial of admission to the bar. One court explained the connection between financial responsibility and character and fitness as follows: "We believe that the applicant's failure to honor his financial obligations evidences a disregard of a legal obligation and reflects adversely on his fitness to practice law." *Application of Hyland*, 663 A.2d 1309, 1316 (Md. 1995). *See also In re Stern*, 943 A.2d 1247, 1258–59 (Md. 2008) (rejecting applicant's argument that his payment of past-due obligations is evidence of rehabilitation, noting that the applicant had allowed his debts to increase, had not addressed his financial obligations even though it appears he had the means to do so, and likely would not have addressed the financial obligations but for the exigency of the bar exam).

The NCBE sample character and fitness application also includes several questions that concern financial responsibility. Consider the sample application and determine if there are matters that you will have to disclose. Consider whether there are steps you can take while you are in law school to make bar admission officials comfortable with your admission despite past financial problems.

Problem 2.3. The BLE heard evidence in the following cases in which bar applicants had financial issues in their past. How would you vote on the character and fitness of these applicants? Can you point to language in the *Simmons* decision that guides you in analyzing the issue?

- Al Roane had three accounts (two credit cards and one account with a healthcare provider) that were substantially past due and were sent to collections agencies while Al was in law school. While applying for bar admission, Al paid off the past-due balances using money that was a gift from his mother. When asked why he had these unpaid accounts, Al explained that he was immature and did not realize the need to pay these bills. He says he has learned his lesson.

- Pamela Hill had a car repossessed by the lender when she failed to pay her auto loan two years before law school. She also has a credit card account with a balance that is 120 days past due. She testifies that she used the credit card for expenses when her student loans ran out in her 1L year. She has not had the financial means to pay off this past due bill but she will set up a payment plan as soon as she has a job. She wants to be allowed to take the bar exam so she can get a job that will allow her to pay this bill.

3. MENTAL HEALTH

Facing challenges that questions related to mental health violated the Americans with Disabilities Act, states have now narrowed the scope of character and fitness questions concerning mental health and treatment. Consider the NCBE sample character & fitness application and decide whether you think the current questions strike the right balance of protecting clients from attorneys whose mental health is likely to interfere with the practice of law and protecting bar applicants from discrimination.

Law students should always seek support, counseling, and treatment when necessary for their mental health. The fact that these questions are on the bar application sometimes scares law students and makes them hesitant to get help. But seeking help for mental health conditions will not prevent bar admission except in extreme cases. Please talk to your professional responsibility professor or dean of students if you do not know how to obtain services or are hesitant to seek help. They can discuss the issue with you and help you find resources.

Problem 2.4. Bar applicant Alejandra Merigo revealed in her application that during winter break of her 2L year, she received in-patient treatment and was prescribed medication to address severe depression, anxiety, and suicidal thoughts. There is no information in her application that indicates her condition has had an impact on her conduct at work, school, or elsewhere. Discuss whether it is appropriate for your state's character and fitness application to require an applicant to reveal this information. Discuss why you would (or would not) vote for the BLE to issue a show cause order to obtain additional information about Alejandra's condition.

4. SUBSTANCE ABUSE

Just like mental health concerns, law students who are struggling with substance abuse should obtain help to address the issue and not worry that doing so will prevent bar admission. It is more likely that not getting help will cause challenges in bar admission.

The *Simmons* case provides a useful discussion of length of rehabilitation and relapse and provides an example of someone admitted to the bar despite past substance abuse. For applicants that might not otherwise be admitted because of continuing substance abuse or a short period of rehabilitation, conditional admission rules can provide an avenue to bar admission. Such rules have been adopted in twenty-four states and allow admission subject to compliance—for a set period of time—with conditions such as random drug testing, counseling, participation in support groups, and supervision by a practice monitor. Conditional admission is discussed in greater depth in the Attorney Well-Being Chapter (Chapter 27).

5. CANDOR

Rule 8.1(b) requires more than truthful answers to questions posed by the bar admission officials. It requires the applicant to take the initiative to "disclose a material fact necessary to correct a misapprehension known by the person to have arisen in the matter," with Comment [1] explaining that this "requires correction of any prior misstatement in the matter that the applicant . . . may have made and the affirmative clarification of any misunderstanding on the part of the admissions . . . authority of which the person becomes aware."

As explained in Comment [1] to Rule 8.1, non-disclosure may provide grounds for denial of the application for admission and also, if discovered subsequent to admission to the bar, would provide grounds for imposition of professional discipline, which could include disbarment. Even if the undisclosed information would not warrant denial of your application to the bar, failure to respond truthfully to all requests for information could justify the rejection of your application. Courts emphasize candor in the admission process as relevant to determining character and fitness. *See, e.g., In re Application of Goodstein*, 1 N.E.3d 328, 332 (Ohio 2013) (noting the relevance of an applicant's "failure to provide complete and accurate information concerning the applicant's past.").

The duty of candor also applies to lawyers serving as a reference for a bar applicant. If an applicant's attorney reference is not honest in responding to a request for information, he or she can face professional discipline. It is important to distinguish the lawyer who is serving as a reference for a bar applicant and a lawyer who is representing or has represented a client in anticipation of or in connection with the client's application for admission to the bar. A lawyer representing a bar applicant is exempted from the affirmative disclosure requirements of Rule 8.1(b) if the information in question is protected by the lawyer's duty under Rule 1.6 not to reveal confidential information regarding a client.

Profile of Attorney Professionalism. After being admitted to the Washington bar, Tarra Simmons won a 2020 election to become a member of the Washington state legislature. She is the first person formerly convicted of a felony to hold that office. Following her election, Simmons explained, "I think the whole mission I have in life is to break down stigmas and barriers." She wants people who have had similar experiences "to have hope and opportunity when they come back from a mistake." Eoin Higgins, *Tarra Simmons Becomes First Person Formerly Convicted of a Felony Elected to Washington State Legislature*, TheAppeal.org (November 4, 2020).

CHAPTER 3

REGULATION OF THE LEGAL PROFESSION

■ ■ ■

Chapter Hypothetical. Rhett was a partner in the law firm of Palsgraf & Pennoyer, LLP. The firm discovered that over a four-year period, Rhett had deposited in his personal bank account fourteen checks from the same client totaling $30,000 that, pursuant to the firm's partnership agreement, should have been deposited in the firm's account.

This chapter focuses on the enforcement of the standards of professional conduct through the professional disciplinary process that exists in every state. Specifically, it focuses on how the rules of professional conduct are enforced, several commonly recognized forms of misconduct, and the professional obligation to hold other lawyers accountable for their serious misconduct. The chapter ends with an exploration of the different forms of professional discipline that may be imposed in the case of professional misconduct.

* * *

A. PROFESSIONAL DISCIPLINE

As Paragraph [10] of the Preamble to the *Model Rules of Professional Conduct* notes, the legal profession is largely self-governing. There are obviously legislative statutes of general applicability that might apply to lawyer conduct and even some statutes specifically regulating lawyer conduct. But the rules of professional conduct governing the conduct of lawyers are promulgated and enforced by members of the legal profession.

In 1908, the American Bar Association adopted the *Canons of Ethics*, its first set of rules of professional responsibility. The ABA replaced the Canons with the *Model Code of Professional Responsibility* in 1969. Following Watergate—a scandal that involved over thirty lawyers (including President Richard Nixon)—the ABA appointed a commission to revise the professional conduct code. The commission was chaired by attorney Robert Kutak and came to be known as the Kutak Commission. The Kutak Commission's work resulted in the *Model Rules of Professional Conduct*, which was adopted by the ABA in 1983. The *Model Rules* have been amended from time to time in the years that have followed, including a substantial amendment in 2002.

The highest court in each state retains the ultimate authority over the promulgation and enforcement of the rules of professional conduct within the state. As the name implies, the ABA's *Model Rules* are designed to be models for states to adopt. Nearly every state's highest court has based its professional conduct rules—at least in part—on the *Model Rules*. Thus, the professional conduct rules of a state will typically be numbered consistent with the *Model Rules* but may contain slightly different provisions from the *Model Rules*. These rules serve as the basis for the professional discipline system governing lawyers.

Additionally, the ABA has adopted the *Model Rules for Lawyer Disciplinary Enforcement*. These rules describe the disciplinary process, including the players in the disciplinary system (such as disciplinary counsel, hearing committees, and disciplinary board), available sanctions, and the procedure for disciplinary proceedings. These rules also address issues such as reciprocal discipline (discipline of an attorney in a jurisdiction based on discipline of the same attorney in another jurisdiction) and discipline when a lawyer has been found guilty of a serious crime. Like the *Model Rules of Professional Conduct*, the *Model Rules for Lawyer Disciplinary Enforcement* is often the framework for a state's rules governing lawyer disciplinary enforcement.

In most states, there is a disciplinary board that operates under the umbrella of the state's highest court and administers the lawyer disciplinary system. The board in a state receives and investigates complaints of lawyer misconduct. Disciplinary counsel for the board has subpoena power to compel the disclosure of evidence. If the board determines that probable cause exists to conclude that a lawyer has violated a rule of professional conduct, the board's disciplinary counsel will file formal disciplinary charges and prosecute the matter. At this point, the charges become public. The commentary to Rule 15 of the *Model Rules for Lawyer Disciplinary Enforcement* provide that "[l]iberal exchanges of non-privileged information should be encouraged." State rules of civil procedure do not apply to the ensuing discovery process (aside from the conduct of depositions).

A hearing panel, consisting primarily of lawyers but also some non-lawyers, conducts the hearing. Rule 18 of the ABA's *Model Rules for Lawyer Disciplinary Enforcement* explains that "[d]isciplinary proceedings are neither civil nor criminal but are sui generis." The proceedings themselves are governed by the rules of civil procedure and evidence. Both sides can present evidence, cross-examine witnesses, etc. The lawyer charged with misconduct is permitted to invoke the constitutional right against self-incrimination. The panel applies a "clear and convincing" standard of proof as opposed to the "proof beyond a reasonable doubt" or "preponderance of the evidence" standards typically applied in criminal or civil proceedings. The panel then typically submits a report summarizing its findings and recommended sanction to the disciplinary board.

The disciplinary board reviews the hearing panel's report and imposes discipline where warranted. Either side may seek review by the state's highest court, which may modify the sanction imposed. As discussed in Part D below, a court can choose from among a number of possible sanctions depending upon the seriousness of the violation.

While authors have identified numerous goals of the professional discipline process, courts routinely state that professional discipline serves to protect the public, deter similar misconduct, ensure the legal system's administration of justice, and preserve public confidence in the legal system's administration of justice. Punishment is generally not recognized as being one of the primary goals of lawyer discipline. *See* Mary Devlin, *The Development of Lawyer Disciplinary Procedures in the United States*, 7 GEO. J. LEGAL ETHICS 911, 934 (1994).

While the disciplinary system's purpose is to ensure compliance, the legal profession relies heavily on voluntary compliance with the rules in order to maintain the integrity of the profession. As Professor Neil Hamilton has explained, a professional lawyer is one who "[a]grees to comply with the ethics of duty—the minimum standards for the lawyer's professional skills and ethical conduct set by the Rules." Neil Hamilton, *Professionalism Clearly Defined*, 18 No. 4 PROF. LAW. 4, 6 (2008). Thus, Paragraph [16] of the Scope preceding the *Model Rules of Professional Conduct* provides that compliance with the rules of professional conduct "depends primarily upon understanding and voluntary compliance, secondarily upon reinforcement by peer and public opinion and finally, when necessary, upon enforcement through disciplinary proceedings."

* * *

B. MISCONDUCT

A lawyer who engages in professional misconduct is subject to professional discipline. Rule 8.4 of the *Model Rules of Professional Conduct*—simply entitled "Misconduct"—lists several forms of misconduct that threaten the integrity of the legal profession. The rule's first paragraph states that it is misconduct to violate a rule of professional conduct. Accordingly, the violation of any professional conduct rule can result in attorney discipline. In most disciplinary proceedings, an attorney is charged with various rule violations *and* the violation of Rule 8.4(a) (i.e., the attorney engaged in misconduct by violating the designated rules). The following sections explore what else—beyond a rule violation—constitutes misconduct under Rule 8.4.

1. ATTEMPTING TO VIOLATE A RULE, KNOWINGLY ASSISTING ANOTHER, OR USING ANOTHER TO VIOLATE A RULE

Rule 8.4(a) addresses attempts to violate the rules of professional conduct. For example, in *Matter of Cushing*, 646 N.E.2d 662 (Ind. 1995), an attorney attempted to file a pleading in California, even though he was not licensed to practice there. The court refused to accept the pleading for a variety of reasons. Had the lawyer been successful in filing the pleading, he would have violated the rule regarding the unauthorized practice of law in that jurisdiction. *See* Model Rule 5.5(a). But even though he was unsuccessful, he still *attempted* to violate the rule regarding the unauthorized practice of law, so he was found to have violated Rule 8.4(a)'s prohibition on attempting to violate a rule of professional conduct.

The rule also prohibits a lawyer from assisting or inducing another to violate the rules of professional conduct, such as where the lawyer tries to persuade another to lie to the court. *See In re Asher*, 772 A.2d 1161 (D.C. 2001). A lawyer may also not use another (typically a non-lawyer) to engage in conduct that the lawyer is prohibited from engaging in. *See In re Abrams*, 767 N.E.2d 15 (Mass. 2002) (imposing discipline where lawyer used a business associate to try to pay client to withdraw a disciplinary complaint).

2. COMMITTING A CRIMINAL ACT THAT REFLECTS ADVERSELY ON A LAWYER'S HONESTY, TRUSTWORTHINESS, OR FITNESS AS A LAWYER

Model Rule 8.4(b) prohibits a lawyer from committing a criminal act that reflects adversely on the lawyer's honesty, trustworthiness, or fitness as a lawyer in other respects. The rule applies not only to crimes committed in the lawyer's professional capacity but to crimes committed in the lawyer's personal capacity.

Comment [2] provides some clarification as to the scope of the rule. Based on this comment and the text of the rule, which of the following actions on the part of a lawyer should amount to a violation of Rule 8.4(b)?

(1) Driving with a suspended license;

(2) Leaving the scene of an accident;

(3) Driving while intoxicated;

(4) Willful neglect of an adult with severe mental and physical impairments by one entrusted with the care of the adult, a felony;

(5) Taking money from the account of a professional organization while serving in a non-lawyer capacity as the treasurer of the organization;

(6) Threatening another lawyer with a handgun during a deposition;

(7) Getting into a fight at a college football game with a fan of the opposing team; and

(8) Accumulating 50 unpaid parking citations.

* * *

Immediate Suspension for Serious Crimes. When a lawyer has been convicted of a "serious crime" or felony, many states provide that a court has the authority to suspend the lawyer from the practice of law pending formal disciplinary proceedings in order to protect the public. *See* Mass. Supreme Judicial Court Rule 4:01 § 12(4).

Problem 3.1: Refer back to the Chapter Hypothetical. Did Rhett violate Rule 8.4(b) when he deposited in his personal bank account fourteen checks from the same client totaling $30,000 that, pursuant to the firm's partnership agreement, should have been deposited in the firm's account?

* * *

3. ENGAGING IN DISHONEST CONDUCT

Model Rule 8.4(c) lists four types of conduct that a lawyer may not engage in: dishonesty, fraud, deceit, and misrepresentation. The rule is quite broad in scope. On its face, it does not even require that the lawyer *knowingly* engaged in dishonesty (although some courts have read such a requirement into the rule). As a result, the rule may apply in a host of situations.

Problem 3.2: The Palsgraf & Pennoyer firm eventually conducted an investigation into Rhett's conversion of funds, and the partners were shocked to learn that Rhett had engaged in some other forms of worrisome behavior. Should Rhett be subject to discipline for the following forms of misconduct under Rule 8.4(c)?

(a) Distributing to numerous people an email that he knew contained false information about an individual with whom he formerly had a romantic relationship in an attempt to shame the individual;

(b) Plagiarizing material from a legal site on the Internet for use in a court filing; or

(c) Secretly recording a phone conversation with an opposing lawyer (in a jurisdiction in which such conduct is not illegal).

* * *

4. ENGAGING IN CONDUCT PREJUDICIAL TO THE ADMINISTRATION OF JUSTICE

Rule 8.4(d) prohibits a lawyer from engaging in conduct prejudicial to the administration of justice. Neither the rule nor the comments provide further guidance as to what type of conduct qualifies as "conduct prejudicial to the administration of justice." The vast majority of disciplinary decisions under this rule involve misconduct in connection with a legal proceeding of some kind. Indeed, some courts interpret the rule to require that the misconduct in question have some bearing on the judicial process "in connection with an identifiable case or tribunal." *In re Mason*, 736 A.2d 1019, 1023 (D.C.1999). Conduct is only actionable under the majority approach where it "impedes or subverts the process of resolving disputes." *In re Friedman*, 23 P.3d 620, 628 (Alaska 2001).

For example, *In re Aubuchon*, 309 P.3d 886 (Ariz. 2013), involved a local prosecutor's office that had engaged in a series of "well-publicized disputes, lawsuits, investigations, and criminal prosecutions" concerning local judges. The chief prosecutor of the trial division, Aubuchon, filed a criminal complaint against Judge Donahoe charging Donahoe with bribing a public servant among other charges. She then moved for the judge to recuse himself from grand jury matters in light of the pending charges. The criminal charges were eventually dismissed, and disciplinary charges were brought against Aubuchon for having filed the criminal complaint without probable cause for the purpose of forcing the judge's recusal. The Arizona Supreme Court upheld the disciplinary panel's conclusion that Aubuchon prejudiced the administration of justice in violation of Arizona Rule 8.4(d). The court disbarred Aubuchon for this and other violations, citing the fact that she was a prosecutor as an aggravating factor when imposing the punishment.

Other examples might include threatening to retaliate against a witness if the witness testifies against the lawyer in a disciplinary hearing, *see Florida Bar v. Perlmutter*, 582 So.2d 616, 617 (Fla. 1991) (per curiam); knowingly presenting false testimony at trial, *see In re Peasley*, 90 P.3d 764, 772 (Ariz. 2004) (en banc); or engaging in abusive behavior during a deposition. *See In re Golden*, 496 S.E.2d 619 (S.C. 1998).

Other courts take a more expansive view of the rule. These courts tend to focus less on whether a lawyer's conduct interferes with the orderly operation of an existing proceeding and more on a broader conception of "the administration of justice." Courts adopting the broader, minority view of Rule 8.4(d) are likely to find a violation where a lawyer's conduct "reflects negatively on the legal profession and sets a bad example for the public at large." *Attorney Grievance Comm'n of Md. v. Brady*, 30 A.3d 902, 913 (Md.

Ct. App. 2011). The concern for these courts is that the lawyer's conduct undermines the public's trust in the legal profession or "engenders disrespect for the courts and for the legal profession." *Attorney Grievance Comm'n of Md. V. Dore*, 73 A.3d 161, 175–76 (Md. Ct. App. 2013). This might include conduct having no connection to the practice of law. *See Attorney Grievance Comm'n of Md. v. Markey*, 230 A.3d 942, 952–54 (Md. 2020) (finding government attorneys violated the rule by exchanging racist, homophobic, and misogynistic emails during work hours); *see also* Matter of Seat, 588 N.E.2d 1262, 1262–63 (Ind. 1992) (finding prosecutor who was arrested for driving under the influence violated the rule).

* * *

The two approaches. Assuming that no other rule of professional conduct applied, would a lawyer who provided advice to a Facebook friend about how to get away with shooting her ex-boyfriend be subject to discipline under Rule 8.4(d) under either of the approaches described above? *See In re Sitton*, 618 S.W.3d 288 (Tenn. 2021). As a future member of the legal profession, which do you think is the better approach?

* * *

5. ENGAGING IN HARASSING OR DISCRIMINATORY CONDUCT

Rule 8.4(g) prohibits a lawyer from engaging in conduct that the lawyer knows or reasonably should know is harassment or discrimination (on the basis of race, sex, and/or other characteristics) related to the practice of law. Numerous states have similar rules. Later chapters will revisit this rule in more detail when discussing law firm employment practices, formation of the attorney-client relationship, and trial practice. But for now, consider the potential reach of the rule.

Problem 3.3: In which of the following instances would a lawyer be subject to discipline under Rule 8.4(g)?

(a) While speaking at a bar association dinner, a lawyer makes an obviously racist statement.

(b) While presenting a continuing legal education course on hate speech, a lawyer summarizes the facts of a case involving slurs directed at LGBTQIA+ students.

(c) While serving as an adjunct professor at a law school, a lawyer makes several sexually suggestive statements to a student and engages in unwanted physical contact with that student.

* * *

C. REPORTING PROFESSIONAL MISCONDUCT

Law Professor Neil Hamilton has noted that part of being a professional means acceptance of the principle that "each lawyer agrees . . . to hold other lawyers accountable for meeting the minimum standards set forth in the Rules and to encourage them to realize core values and ideals of the profession." Neil Hamilton, *Professionalism Clearly Defined*, 18 No. 4 PROF. LAW. 4, 6 (2008). This principle underlies Rule 8.3(a)'s requirement that a lawyer report the serious misconduct of another lawyer to professional disciplinary authorities. There are several components to this rule.

1. KNOWLEDGE

Before a lawyer is subject to discipline for failing to report under Rule 8.3(a), the lawyer must first "know" of the other lawyer's violation of the rules. The *Model Rules* frequently refer to a lawyer's "knowledge." What constitutes "knowledge" for purposes of the rules? *See* Rule 1.0(f). Does this definition employ an objective conception of knowledge or a subjective one? With respect to the statement in Rule 1.0(f) that "knowledge may be inferred from circumstances," ABA Formal Ethics Opinion 04–433 states that "[m]ost cases and ethics opinions conclude that 'knowledge' is determined by an objective standard." Or, as the Mississippi Supreme Court put it:

> The supporting evidence must be such that a reasonable lawyer under the circumstances would have formed a firm opinion that the conduct in question had more likely than not occurred and that the conduct, if it did occur, raises a substantial question as to the purported offender's honesty, trustworthiness or fitness to practice law in other respects.

Attorney U v. Mississippi Bar, 678 So.2d 963, 972 (Miss. 1996). Some authorities also express the idea that "[s]tudious ignorance of readily accessible facts is . . . the functional equivalent of knowledge." N.Y.C. Ass'n of the Bar Comm. on Prof'l & Jud. Ethics, Formal Op. 003 (1990).

2. SUBSTANTIAL QUESTION AS TO THE OTHER LAWYER'S HONESTY, TRUSTWORTHINESS, OR FITNESS

The second threshold for required action under Rule 8.3(a) is that the other lawyer's violation of a rule must raise a substantial question as to the other lawyer's honesty, trustworthiness, or fitness as a lawyer in other respects. Not every violation of the Model Rules of Professional Responsibility raises a substantial question about a lawyer's honesty, trustworthiness, and fitness as a lawyer in other respects. Which ones do? *See* Comment [3] to Rule 8.3 for more guidance.

3. INFORMING THE APPROPRIATE AUTHORITY

Once these thresholds are met, the rule requires that a lawyer "inform the appropriate professional authority." Thus, the reporting obligation is mandatory in a jurisdiction that has adopted this model rule. *But see* Georgia R. Prof'l Conduct, R. 8.3(a) (stating that a lawyer "should" inform the appropriate authority). As discussed, each state has its own professional disciplinary authority that investigates complaints of misconduct. Typically, this is the appropriate professional authority to whom a lawyer must report.

Rule 8.3(a) does not specify *when* a report of misconduct must be made. Opinions often say something along the lines of that a lawyer must report "within a reasonable time under the circumstances." *United States v. Cantor*, 897 F.Supp. 110 (S.D.N.Y. 1995). A comment to the Massachusetts version of Rule 8.3(a) provides:

> [i]n most situations, a lawyer may defer making a report under this Rule until the matter has been concluded, but the report should be made as soon as practicable thereafter. An immediate report is ethically compelled, however, when a client or third person will likely be injured by a delay in reporting, such as where the lawyer has knowledge that another lawyer has embezzled client or fiduciary funds and delay may impair the ability to recover the funds.

MASS. R. OF PROF'L CONDUCT 8.3 cmt. 3A.

Note also the exception to Rule 8.3(a)'s reporting requirement where the information about the other lawyer's misconduct is "gained by a lawyer or judge while participating in an approved lawyers' assistance program."

* * *

Problem 3.4. When the partners at Palsgraf & Pennoyer confronted Rhett about his conversion of funds and other misconduct, Rhett explained that his family had been suffering some financial woes as a result of a family member's medical problems. He volunteered to repay the firm and offered to resign. The firm's management committee, consisting of several partners, refused Rhett's resignation offer and permitted him to stay on. The committee concluded that Rhett was under significant financial and emotional pressure when he deposited the checks and engaged in the other forms of misconduct, and that his actions were an aberration and were unlikely to be repeated. Therefore, they concluded Rhett's actions did not raise a serious question as to his fitness to practice law and did not report his actions to the appropriate disciplinary authorities. Are the individual partners on the management committee subject to professional discipline under Rule 8.3(a)?

IN RE JAMES H. HIMMEL
533 N.E.2d 790 (Ill. 1988)

JUSTICE STAMOS delivered the opinion of the court:

[On January 22, 1986, the Administrator of the Attorney Registration and Disciplinary Commission (the Commission) filed a complaint with the Hearing Board, alleging that respondent James H. Himmel violated the Illinois Rules of Professional Conduct by failing to disclose to the Commission information concerning attorney misconduct. The Hearing Board found that respondent had violated the relevant rule of professional conduct and recommended that respondent be reprimanded.

Himmel was retained by his client, Tammy Forsberg, to help recover the proceeds of a settlement she believed had been converted by her former attorney, John R. Casey. Himmel investigated the matter and discovered that Casey had misappropriated the settlement funds.]

In April 1983, respondent drafted an agreement in which Casey would pay Forsberg $75,000 in settlement of any claim she might have against him for the misappropriated funds. By the terms of the agreement, Forsberg agreed not to initiate any criminal, civil, or attorney disciplinary action against Casey. This agreement was executed on April 11, 1983. Respondent stood to gain $17,000 or more if Casey honored the agreement. In February 1985, respondent filed suit against Casey for breaching the agreement, and a $100,000 judgment was entered against Casey. If Casey had satisfied the judgment, respondent's share would have been approximately $25,588.

The [disciplinary] complaint stated that at no time did respondent inform the Commission of Casey's misconduct. According to the Administrator, respondent's first contact with the Commission was in response to the Commission's inquiry regarding the lawsuit against Casey. [Casey was eventually disbarred.]

. . . Before retaining respondent, Forsberg collected $5,000 from Casey. After being retained, respondent made inquiries regarding Casey's conversion, contacting the insurance company that issued the settlement check, its attorney, Forsberg, her mother, her fiancé and Casey. Forsberg told respondent that she simply wanted her money back and specifically instructed respondent to take no other action. Because of respondent's efforts, Forsberg collected another $10,400 from Casey. Respondent received no fee in this case.

The Hearing Board found that respondent received unprivileged information that Casey converted Forsberg's funds, and that respondent failed to relate the information to the Commission in violation of [Illinois' version of Rule 8.3(a)]. The Hearing Board noted, however, that respondent had been practicing law for 11 years, had no prior record of any complaints, obtained as good a result as could be expected in the case, and requested no fee for recovering the $23,233.34. Accordingly, the Hearing Board recommended a private reprimand.

Upon the Administrator's exceptions to the Hearing Board's recommendation, the Review Board reviewed the matter. The Review Board's report stated that the client had contacted the Commission prior to retaining respondent and, therefore, the Commission did have knowledge of the alleged misconduct. Further, the Review Board noted that respondent respected the client's wishes regarding not pursuing a claim with the Commission. Accordingly, the Review Board recommended that the complaint be dismissed.

The Administrator now raises three issues for review: (1) whether the Review Board erred in concluding that respondent's client had informed the Commission of misconduct by her former attorney; (2) whether the Review Board erred in concluding that respondent had not violated [Illinois' version of Rule 8.3(a)]; and (3) whether the proven misconduct warrants at least a censure.

As to the first issue, the Administrator contends . . . that even if Forsberg had reported Casey's misconduct to the Commission, such an action would not have relieved respondent of his duty to report under [Illinois' version of Rule 8.3(a)]. Additionally, the Administrator argues that no evidence exists to prove that respondent failed to report because he assumed that Forsberg had already reported the matter.

. . .

We begin our analysis by examining whether a client's complaint of attorney misconduct to the Commission can be a defense to an attorney's failure to report the same misconduct. Respondent offers no authority for such a defense and our research has disclosed none. Common sense would dictate that if a lawyer has a duty under the Code, the actions of a client would not relieve the attorney of his own duty. Accordingly, while the parties dispute whether or not respondent's client informed the Commission, that question is irrelevant to our inquiry in this case. We have held that the canons of ethics in the Code constitute a safe guide for professional conduct, and attorneys may be disciplined for not observing them. The question is, then, whether or not respondent violated the Code, not whether Forsberg informed the Commission of Casey's misconduct.

As to respondent's argument that he did not report Casey's misconduct because his client directed him not to do so, we again note respondent's failure to suggest any legal support for such a defense. A lawyer, as an officer of the court, is duty-bound to uphold the rules in the Code. The title of [the relevant rule] reflects this obligation: "A lawyer should assist in maintaining the integrity and competence of the legal profession." A lawyer may not choose to circumvent the rules by simply asserting that his client asked him to do so.

As to the second issue, the Administrator argues that the Review Board erred in concluding that respondent did not violate [Illinois' version of Rule 8.3(a)]. The Administrator urges acceptance of the Hearing Board's finding that respondent had unprivileged knowledge of Casey's conversion of client funds, and that respondent failed to disclose that information to the Commission. The Administrator states that respondent's knowledge of Casey's conversion of client funds was knowledge of illegal conduct involving moral turpitude. . . . Further, the Administrator argues that the information respondent received was not privileged. . . . Therefore, the Administrator concludes, respondent violated his ethical duty to report misconduct under [Illinois' version of Rule 8.3(a)]. According to the Administrator, failure to disclose the information deprived the Commission of evidence of serious misconduct, evidence that would have assisted in the Commission's investigation of Casey.

Respondent contends that the information was privileged information received from his client, Forsberg, and therefore he was under no obligation to disclose the matter to the Commission. Respondent argues that his failure to report Casey's misconduct was motivated by his respect for his client's wishes, not by his desire for financial gain. To support this assertion, respondent notes that his fee agreement with Forsberg was contingent upon her first receiving all the money Casey originally owed her. Further, respondent states that he has received no fee for his representation of Forsberg.

Our analysis of this issue begins with a reading of the applicable disciplinary rules. [Illinois' version of Rule 8.3(a)] states: "A lawyer possessing unprivileged knowledge of a violation of [the rules regarding dishonest conduct] shall report such knowledge to a tribunal or other authority empowered to investigate or act upon such violation."

. . .

We agree with the Administrator's argument that the communication regarding Casey's conduct [was not privileged]. The record does not suggest that this information was communicated by Forsberg to the respondent in confidence. We have held that information voluntarily disclosed by a client to an attorney, in the presence of third parties who are not agents of the client or attorney, is not privileged information. . . . In this case, Forsberg discussed the matter with respondent at various times while her mother and her fiancé were present. Consequently, unless the mother and fiancé were agents of respondent's client, the information communicated was not privileged. Moreover, we have also stated that matters intended by a client for disclosure by the client's attorney to third parties, who are not agents of either the client or the attorney, are not privileged. The record shows that respondent, with Forsberg's consent, discussed Casey's conversion of her funds with the insurance company involved, the insurance company's lawyer, and with Casey himself. Thus, . . . the information was not privileged.

Though respondent repeatedly asserts that his failure to report was motivated not by financial gain but by the request of his client, we do not deem such an argument relevant in this case. This court has stated that discipline may be appropriate even if no dishonest motive for the misconduct exists. . . . In addition, we have held that client approval of an attorney's action does not immunize an attorney from disciplinary action. . . . We have already dealt with, and dismissed, respondent's assertion that his conduct is acceptable because he was acting pursuant to his client's directions.

Respondent does not argue that Casey's conversion of Forsberg's funds was not . . . conduct involving dishonesty, fraud, deceit, or misrepresentation under [Illinois' version of Rule 8.4(c)]. . . . We conclude, then, that respondent possessed unprivileged knowledge of Casey's conversion of client funds . . . and that respondent failed in his duty to report such misconduct to the Commission. Because no defense exists, we agree with the Hearing Board's finding that respondent has violated [Illinois' version of Rule 8.3(a)] and must be disciplined. . . .

* * *

The Duty to Report vs. the Duty of Confidentiality. *Himmel* was decided under the older Model Code standard as it existed in Illinois at the time. At the time, a lawyer's duty of confidentiality extended only to communications subject to the attorney-client privilege or other "secrets." Today, a lawyer's duty of confidentiality is broader and extends to any information relating to the representation of a client, regardless of whether it is privileged or a "secret." *See* Rule 1.6(a). (A future chapter will explore this concept in much greater detail.) Under this more modern version of the rule, Himmel would have owed his client a duty of confidentiality with respect to the conversation he and his client had, even though the conversation was in the presence of others. So, which of a lawyer's duties prevails in this situation: the duty to report misconduct or the duty of confidentiality? *See* Rule 8.3(c); *see also id.* Comment [2].

***Himmel* and Ethical Fading.** In the year following the highly-publicized *Himmel* decision, the number of attorney reports of misconduct to the Illinois Attorney Registration and Disciplinary Commission increased dramatically—from 154 to 922. *See* Paula Schaefer, *Behavioral Legal Ethics Lessons for Corporate Counsel*, 69 CASE WESTERN RESERVE L. REV. 975, 1003 (2019). Professor Schaefer explains that "ethical fading" occurs when a person stops recognizing the ethical dimension of a decision.

For an attorney who is aware of another attorney's misconduct, ethical fading explains why that attorney may fail to see his or her own ethical obligation in the situation, namely, the obligation to report the misconduct. Publicity about the consequences of failing to make such a report counters ethical fading and reminds attorneys of the ethical dimension of the situation for themselves. In a sense, this text book is intended to counter ethical fading.

* * *

IN RE RIEHLMANN
891 So.2d 1239 (La. 2005)

This disciplinary matter arises from formal charges filed by the Office of Disciplinary Counsel ("ODC") against respondent, Michael G. Riehlmann, an attorney licensed to practice law in Louisiana.

. . .

Respondent is a criminal defense attorney who was formerly employed as an Assistant District Attorney in the Orleans Parish District Attorney's Office. One evening in April 1994, respondent met his close friend and law school classmate, Gerry Deegan, at a bar near the Orleans Parish Criminal District Court. . . . During their conversation in the bar, Mr. Deegan told respondent that he had that day learned he was dying of colon cancer. In the same conversation, Mr. Deegan confided to respondent that he had suppressed exculpatory blood evidence in a criminal case he prosecuted while at the District Attorney's Office. Respondent recalls that he was "surprised" and "shocked" by his friend's revelation, and that he urged Mr. Deegan to "remedy" the situation. It is undisputed that respondent did not report Mr. Deegan's disclosure to anyone at the time it was made. Mr. Deegan died in July 1994, having done nothing to "remedy" the situation of which he had spoken in the bar.

Nearly five years after Mr. Deegan's death, one of the defendants whom he had prosecuted in a 1985 armed robbery case was set to be executed by lethal injection on May 20, 1999. In April 1999, the lawyers for the defendant, John Thompson, discovered a crime lab report which contained the results of tests performed on a piece of pants leg and a tennis shoe that were stained with the perpetrator's blood during a scuffle with the victim of the robbery attempt. The crime lab report concluded that the robber had Type "B" blood. Because Mr. Thompson has Type "O" blood, the crime lab report proved he could not have committed the robbery; nevertheless, neither the crime lab report nor the blood-stained physical evidence had been disclosed to Mr. Thompson's defense counsel prior to or during trial. Respondent claims that when he heard about the inquiry of Mr. Thompson's lawyers, he immediately realized that this was the case to which Mr. Deegan had referred in their April 1994 conversation in the bar. On April 27, 1999, respondent executed an affidavit for Mr. Thompson in which he attested that during the 1994 conversation, "the late Gerry Deegan said to me that he had intentionally suppressed blood evidence in the armed robbery trial of John Thompson that in some way exculpated the defendant."

In May 1999, respondent reported Mr. Deegan's misconduct to the ODC. In June 1999, respondent testified in a hearing on a motion for new trial in Mr. Thompson's armed robbery case. During the hearing, respondent testified that Mr. Deegan had told him that he "suppressed exculpatory evidence that was blood evidence, that seems to have excluded Mr. Thompson as the perpetrator of an armed robbery." Respondent also admitted that he "should have reported" Mr. Deegan's misconduct, and that while he ultimately did so, "I should have reported it sooner, I guess."

On September 30, 1999, respondent gave a sworn statement to the ODC in which he was asked why he did not report Mr. Deegan's disclosure to anyone at the time it was made. Respondent replied:

> I think that under ordinary circumstances, I would have. I really honestly think I'm a very good person. And I think I do the right thing whenever I'm given the opportunity to choose. This was unquestionably the most difficult time of my life. Gerry, who was like a brother to me, was dying. And that was, to say distracting would be quite an understatement. I'd also left my wife just a few months before, with three kids, and was under the care of a psychiatrist, taking antidepressants. My youngest son was then about two and had just recently undergone open-heart surgery. I had a lot on my plate at the time. A great deal of it of my own making; there's no question about it. But, nonetheless, I was very, very distracted, and I simply did not give it the important consideration that it deserved. But it was a very trying time for me. **And that's the only explanation I have, because, otherwise, I would have reported it immediately had I been in a better frame of mind.** [emphasis added]

. . .

On January 2, 2001, the ODC filed one count of formal charges against respondent, alleging that his failure to report his unprivileged knowledge of Mr. Deegan's prosecutorial misconduct violated Rule[ ] 8.3(a) (reporting professional misconduct) . . . .

The [disciplinary] board concluded that a reasonable lawyer under the circumstances would have formed a firm opinion that Mr. Deegan had wrongfully failed to disclose the blood evidence, and that respondent did in fact form such an opinion because he advised Mr. Deegan that what he (Deegan) did was "not right" and that he (Deegan) had to "rectify" the situation. Accordingly, the board found respondent had sufficient knowledge of misconduct by Mr. Deegan to trigger a duty to report the misconduct to the disciplinary authorities.

The board then turned to a discussion of whether respondent's failure to report Mr. Deegan's misconduct for more than five years after learning of it constituted a failure to report under Rule 8.3(a). The board acknowledged that Rule 8.3(a) does not provide any specific time limit or period within which the misconduct must be reported. Nevertheless, the board reasoned that Rule 8.3(a) serves no useful purpose unless it is read to require reporting to an appropriate authority within a reasonable time under the circumstances. Therefore, absent special circumstances, the board determined that a lawyer must report his knowledge of misconduct "promptly." Applying these principles to the instant case, the board determined respondent's disclosure in 1999 of misconduct he discovered in 1994 was not timely and did not satisfy the requirements of Rule 8.3(a).

. . .

The board found respondent knowingly violated a duty owed to the profession, and that his actions resulted in both actual and potential injury to Mr. Thompson. The board noted that if respondent had taken further action in 1994, when Mr. Deegan made his confession, Mr. Thompson's innocence in connection with the armed robbery charge may have been established sooner. The board also observed that negative publicity attached to respondent's actions, thereby causing harm to the legal profession. The board determined the baseline sanction for respondent's conduct is a suspension from the practice of law.

. . .

Considering the prior jurisprudence, the board determined that some period of suspension is appropriate for respondent's conduct. In light of the significant mitigating factors in this matter, the board recommended that respondent be suspended from the practice of law for six months. One board member dissented and would recommend a suspension of at least one year and one day.

DISCUSSION

In this matter we are presented for the first time with an opportunity to delineate the scope of an attorney's duty under Rule 8.3 to report the professional misconduct of a fellow member of the bar. . . .

[I]t is clear that absolute certainty of ethical misconduct is not required before the reporting requirement is triggered. The lawyer is not required to conduct an investigation and make a definitive decision that a violation has occurred before reporting; that responsibility belongs to the disciplinary system and this court. On the other hand, knowledge requires more than a mere suspicion of ethical misconduct. We hold that a lawyer will be found to have knowledge of reportable misconduct, and thus reporting is required, where the supporting evidence is such that a reasonable lawyer under the circumstances would form a firm belief that the conduct in question had more likely than not occurred. . . .

. . .

Applying the principles set forth above to the conduct of respondent in the instant case, we find the ODC proved by clear and convincing evidence that respondent violated Rule 8.3(a). First, we find that respondent should have known that a reportable event occurred at the time of his 1994 barroom conversation with Mr. Deegan. . . . Regardless of the actual words Mr. Deegan said that night, and whether they were or were not "equivocal," respondent understood from the conversation that Mr. Deegan had done something wrong. Respondent admitted as much in his affidavit, during the hearing on the motion for new trial in the criminal case, during his sworn statement to the ODC, and during his testimony at the formal hearing. Indeed, during the sworn statement respondent conceded that he would have reported the matter "immediately" were it not for the personal problems he was then experiencing. Respondent also testified that he was surprised and shocked by his friend's revelation, and that he told him to remedy the situation. There would have been no reason for respondent to react in the manner he did had he not formed a firm opinion that the conduct in question more likely than not occurred. . . .

We also find that respondent failed to promptly report Mr. Deegan's misconduct to the disciplinary authorities. As respondent himself acknowledged, he should have reported Mr. Deegan's statements sooner than he did. There was no reason for respondent to have waited five years to tell the ODC about what his friend had done.

In his answer to the formal charges, respondent asserts that he did comply with the reporting requirement of Rule 8.3(a) because he promptly reported Mr. Deegan's misconduct to the District Attorney and the Criminal District Court through the attorneys for the criminal defendant, John Thompson. Respondent has misinterpreted Rule 8.3(a) in this regard. . . . It is undisputed that respondent did not report to the appropriate entity, the ODC, until 1999. That report came too late to be construed as "prompt."

. . .

Reporting another lawyer's misconduct to disciplinary authorities is an important duty of every lawyer. Lawyers are in the best position to observe professional misconduct and to assist the profession in sanctioning it. While a Louisiana lawyer is subject to discipline for not reporting misconduct, it is our hope that lawyers will comply with their reporting obligation primarily because they are ethical people who want to serve their clients and the public well. Moreover, the lawyer's duty to report professional misconduct is the foundation for the claim that we can be trusted to regulate ourselves as a profession. If we fail in our duty, we forfeit that trust and have no right to enjoy the privilege of self-regulation or the confidence and respect of the public.

* * *

Resisting the Duty to Report. The general consensus is that lawyers are often reluctant to comply with their obligation to report the misconduct of other lawyers. *See, e.g.*, John S. Dzienkowski, *Ethical Decisionmaking and the Design of Rules of Ethics*, 42 HOFSTRA L. REV. 55, 80 (2013). What accounts for this reluctance?

* * *

D. IMPOSING DISCIPLINARY SANCTIONS

The ABA *Standards for Imposing Lawyer Sanctions* contain a hierarchy of possible sanctions for misconduct. These include admonition (or non-public reprimand); reprimand (or public censure); interim suspension; suspension; disbarment; and the catch-all "other sanctions and remedies," which could include restitution and/or the requirement that the lawyer attend continuing legal education courses. *See* Standards 2.2–2.8. In imposing sanctions, a court is directed to consider the duty violated, the lawyer's mental state, the potential or actual injury caused by the lawyer's misconduct, and any aggravating or mitigating circumstances. *See* Standard 3.0. Certain duties (like the duty to maintain client confidences) are sufficiently weighty that when a lawyer intentionally violates the duty with the intent to benefit himself, disbarment or suspension is the presumptive punishment, at least when harm results to the client. *See* Standard 4.21. In contrast, when a lawyer *negligently* reveals information relating to representation of a client not otherwise lawfully permitted to be disclosed and this disclosure causes injury or potential injury to a client, the *Standards* suggest that reprimand should be the presumptive sanction. *See* Standard 4.23.

The *Standards for Imposing Lawyer Sanctions* list several aggravating factors, the existence of which might justify a heightened sanction. These include prior disciplinary offenses, dishonest conduct, and a refusal to acknowledge wrongdoing. The *Standards* also list a number of mitigating factors, including absence of a prior disciplinary record, personal or emotional problems, and remorse.

IN RE JAMES H. HIMMEL
533 N.E.2d 790 (Ill. 1988)

[Authors' Note: See *supra* for the court's discussion of Mr. Himmel's misconduct.]

The third issue concerns the appropriate quantum of discipline to be imposed in this case. The Administrator contends that respondent's misconduct warrants at least a censure, although the Hearing Board recommended a private reprimand and the Review Board recommended dismissal of the matter entirely. In support of the request for a greater quantum of discipline, the Administrator cites to the purposes of attorney discipline, which include maintaining the integrity of the legal profession and safeguarding the administration of justice. The Administrator argues that these purposes will not be served unless respondent is publicly disciplined so that the profession will be on notice that a violation of [Illinois' version of Rule 8.3(a)] will not be tolerated. The Administrator argues that a more severe sanction is necessary because respondent deprived the Commission of evidence of another attorney's conversion and thereby interfered with the Commission's investigative function....

. . .

In evaluating the proper quantum of discipline to impose, we note that it is this court's responsibility to determine appropriate sanctions in attorney disciplinary cases.... We have stated that while recommendations of the Boards are to be considered, this court ultimately bears responsibility for deciding an appropriate sanction.... [W]hen determining the nature and extent of discipline to be imposed, the respondent's actions must be viewed in relationship "to the underlying purposes of our disciplinary process, which purposes are to maintain the integrity of the legal profession, to protect the administration of justice from reproach, and to safeguard the public...."

Bearing these principles in mind, we agree with the Administrator that public discipline is necessary in this case to carry out the purposes of attorney discipline.... Though we agree with the Hearing Board's assessment that respondent violated [Illinois' version of Rule 8.3(a)], we do not agree that the facts warrant only a private reprimand....

This failure to report resulted in interference with the Commission's investigation of Casey, and thus with the administration of justice. Perhaps some members of the public would have been spared from Casey's misconduct had respondent reported the information as soon as he knew of Casey's conversions of client funds. We are particularly disturbed by the fact that respondent chose to draft a settlement agreement with Casey rather than report his misconduct.... Both respondent and his client stood to gain financially by agreeing not to prosecute or report Casey for conversion. According to the settlement agreement, respondent would have received $17,000 or more as his fee. If Casey had satisfied the judgment entered against him for failure to honor the settlement agreement, respondent would have collected approximately $25,588.

We have held ... that fairness dictates consideration of mitigating factors in disciplinary cases. Therefore, we do consider the fact that Forsberg recovered $10,400 through respondent's services, that respondent has practiced law for 11 years with no record of complaints, and that he requested no fee for minimum collection of Forsberg's funds. However, these considerations do not outweigh the serious nature of respondent's failure to report Casey, the resulting interference with the Commission's investigation of Casey, and respondent's ill-advised choice to settle with Casey rather than report his misconduct.

Accordingly, it is ordered that respondent be suspended from the practice of law for one year.

Respondent suspended.

IN RE RIEHLMANN
891 So.2d 1239 (La. 2005)

[Authors' Note: See *supra* for the court's discussion of Mr. Riehlmann's misconduct.]

Having found professional misconduct, we now turn to a discussion of an appropriate sanction. In considering that issue, we are mindful that the purpose of disciplinary proceedings is not primarily to punish the lawyer, but rather to maintain the appropriate standards of professional conduct, to preserve the integrity of the legal profession, and to deter other lawyers from engaging in violations of the standards of the profession. . . .

Respondent's actions violated the general duty imposed upon attorneys to maintain and preserve the integrity of the bar. . . . [However], we find that the respondent's conduct was merely negligent. Accordingly, Standard 7.3 of the ABA's *Standards for Imposing Lawyer Sanctions* provides that the appropriate baseline sanction is a reprimand.

The only aggravating factor present in this case is respondent's substantial experience in the practice of law. As for mitigating factors, we adopt those recognized by the disciplinary board, placing particular emphasis on the absence of any dishonest or selfish motive on respondent's part. Notwithstanding these factors, however, respondent's failure to report Mr. Deegan's bad acts necessitates that some sanction be imposed. Respondent's knowledge of Mr. Deegan's conduct was sufficient to impose on him an obligation to promptly report Mr. Deegan to the ODC. Having failed in that obligation, respondent is himself subject to punishment. Under all of the circumstances presented, we conclude that a public reprimand is the appropriate sanction.

* * *

Aggravating and Mitigating Factors. Should the fact that a lawyer was relatively inexperienced qualify as a mitigating factor in a disciplinary proceeding? Should the fact that a lawyer had a substance abuse problem at the relevant time qualify as an aggravating factor or a mitigating factor?

Disbarment. Standard 2.2 of the ABA *Standards for Imposing Lawyer Sanctions* provides that "[w]here disbarment is not permanent, procedures should be established for a lawyer who has been disbarred to apply for readmission...." Are there circumstances under which disbarment should be permanent?

Discipline in *Himmel* and *Riehlmann*. Do you agree with the sanctions imposed in the *Himmel* and *Riehlmann* cases?

Problem 3.5: What sort of professional discipline should be imposed in Rhett's case (a) against Rhett and (b) the partners on the management committee?

* * *

E. OTHER CONSEQUENCES OF ATTORNEY MISCONDUCT

Of course, attorney discipline—the focus of this chapter—is just one aspect of the study of professional conduct. As noted in Chapter 1, attorneys also face the prospect of civil liability to clients for professional negligence, breach of fiduciary duty, and/or breach of contract. It follows that when an attorney breaches an obligation to a client (such as the duty of competence or to protect client confidences), the attorney could face both civil liability (for violating a duty owed to the client) and professional discipline (for violating the associated rule of professional conduct). Throughout this textbook, you will see examples of both types of cases.

It should be noted that lawyers are not insulated from other forms of liability simply because the lawyer was acting on behalf of a client. This includes criminal liability. Section 8 of the *Restatement* provides that "a lawyer is guilty of a crime committed in the course of a representation 'to the same extent and on the same basis as would a nonlawyer acting similarly'," but also that "[t]he traditional and appropriate activities of a lawyer in representing a client in accordance with the requirements of the applicable lawyer code" are relevant considerations in determining criminal liability. In addition to the general body of criminal law, there are a few criminal statutes that specifically address lawyers. *See* N.Y. Jud. Law § 487 (making it a misdemeanor for a lawyer to engage in "any deceit or collusion, or consent[ ] to any deceit or collusion, with intent to deceive the court or any party"). We will address the prospect of criminal liability later in this textbook.

Profile of Attorney Professionalism. The American legal profession has seen numerous codes of professional conduct. In 1887, Alabama's state bar association became the first to adopt an official code of professional ethics. The Alabama bar's code was influenced heavily by George Sharswood's *Essay on Professional Ethics*. Sharswood was a law professor and dean at the University of Pennsylvania who eventually became Chief Justice of the Pennsylvania Supreme Court. As described by legal historian Carol Rice Andrews, "Sharswood structured his essay around three fundamental obligations: '[f]idelity to the court, fidelity to the client, [and] fidelity to the claims of truth and honor." Carol Rice Andrews, *Ethical Limits on Litigation Advocacy: A Historical Perspective*, 63 CASE WESTERN L. REV. 381, 409 (2012). "[A]lthough Sharswood believed that the lawyer should act with zeal on behalf of his client, he also believed that this obligation was tempered by the lawyer's obligations of fidelity to the court and to the truth." *Id.* at 411.

The ABA drew upon Alabama's code when it eventually adopted its 1908 *Canons of Ethics*. In 1969, the ABA put forth its *Model Code of Professional Responsibility*, which was later replaced by the 1983 *Model Rules of Professional Conduct*. The *Model Rules* were then substantially amended in 2002 as part of the ABA's Ethics 2000 initiative, and then again (although less substantially) in 2013 as part of the ABA's Ethics 20/20 initiative. Today, nearly every state uses the ABA's *Model Rules* as the model for their rules of professional conduct. The views of the legal profession have evolved over time. But Justice Sharswood's *Essay* played an important role in the development of professional values and continues to influence the profession's thinking on those values.

CHAPTER 4

THE AUTHORIZED AND UNAUTHORIZED PRACTICE OF LAW

■ ■ ■

Chapter Hypothetical. Tony is licensed to practice law in New Dakota. His practice consists mostly of environmental law, but he also occasionally does some debt-collection work. Tony's mother-in-law, Vera, lives in Old Dakota. She called to ask for Tony's help about a judgment that had been entered against her by her condominium association for her failure to pay homeowner's dues. Vera hoped that Tony might be able to negotiate terms for a reduced payment amount, as well as a payment schedule. Tony said he would see what he could do.

Only lawyers are permitted to engage in the practice of law. But defining "the practice of law" has sometimes proven to be difficult. And while lawyers may engage in the practice of law, they are not authorized to practice law in every jurisdiction simply by virtue of being a lawyer. There are complex rules regarding a lawyer's ability to engage in the practice of law in multiple jurisdictions. This chapter explores the rules regarding the unauthorized practice of law as they apply to non-lawyers and lawyers.

* * *

A. PREVENTING THE UNAUTHORIZED PRACTICE OF LAW (UPL)

1. PREVENTING UPL BY NON-LAWYERS

Engaging in the unauthorized practice of law is a crime. In some jurisdictions, there may be meaningful penalties associated with the unauthorized practice of law. *See* Mo. Rev. Stat § 484.020 (providing for treble the amount charged for services by one who engages in the unauthorized practice of law). State supreme courts have the authority to regulate the practice of law within a state. Therefore, courts may define for themselves what qualifies as "the practice of law." At the same time, state legislatures also frequently define what qualifies as the practice of law as part of statutes prohibiting the unauthorized practice of law.

Courts frequently note that it "is neither necessary nor desirable to attempt the formulation of a single specific definition of what constitutes the practice of law." *Petition of Burson*, 909 S.W.2d 768, 775 (Tenn. 1995). But definitions of the practice of law typically reference at least one of three main concepts. First, it is common for the "practice of law" to be defined in reference to the tasks or the functions that lawyers typically perform:

> "Practice of law" means the appearance as an advocate in a representative capacity or the drawing of papers, pleadings or documents or the performance of any act in such capacity in connection with proceedings pending or prospective before any court, commissioner, referee or any body, board, committee or commission constituted by law or having authority to settle controversies, or the soliciting of clients directly or indirectly to provide such services.

Tenn. Code Ann. § 23–3–101(2). Second, it is also common to define the concept with reference to providing legal advice. N.C. Gen. Stat. § 84–2.1(a) (defining the "practice of law" to include giving advice or opinion upon the legal rights of any person, firm, or corporation). Many definitions incorporate both concepts. *See id.*

Third, and perhaps the idea referenced most frequently, the practice of law is defined as involving the exercise of "professional judgment." Courts often note that "the practice of law relates to the rendition of services for others that call for the professional judgment of a lawyer. The essence of the professional judgment of the lawyer is [the] educated ability to relate the general body and philosophy of law to a specific legal problem of a client." *Burson*, 909 S.W.2d at 775. Where this type of professional judgment is not required, a non-lawyer may undertake the activity. This squares with the traditional justification for restricting the practice of law to lawyers: the need to protect the public from the rendition of legal services by unqualified individuals. *See* ABA Model Rule 5.5, Comment [2].

Individuals who are not licensed to practice law may represent themselves in legal proceedings, even when doing so would otherwise amount to the practice of law; this is not the *unauthorized* practice of law. Except in certain designated administrative proceedings (e.g., unemployment benefit hearings), a corporation is not permitted to represent itself in a legal proceeding. The corporation must be represented by a lawyer.

* * *

Problem 4.1. Tony communicated with Laura, the lawyer for the homeowner's association, informing Laura that he was representing his mother-in-law and instructing Laura to direct all future communications to him. The two lawyers engaged in discussions regarding Vera's assets and ability to pay and how the relevant Old Dakota collections statute would apply in Vera's case. Eventually, Tony made a settlement offer, which Laura accepted on behalf of the association. Did Tony engage in the practice of law?

* * *

FLORIDA BAR V. BRUMBAUGH
355 So.2d 1186 (Fla. 1978)

PER CURIAM.

The Florida Bar has filed a petition charging Marilyn Brumbaugh with engaging in the unauthorized practice of law, and seeking a permanent injunction prohibiting her from further engaging in these allegedly unlawful acts. . . .

Respondent, Marilyn Brumbaugh, is not and has never been a member of the Florida Bar, and is, therefore, not licensed to practice law within this state. She has advertised in various local newspapers as "Marilyn's Secretarial Service" offering to perform typing services for "Do-It-Yourself" divorces, wills, resumes, and bankruptcies. The Florida Bar charges that she performed unauthorized legal services by preparing for her customers those legal documents necessary in an uncontested dissolution of marriage proceeding and by advising her customers as to the costs involved and the procedures which should be followed in order to obtain a dissolution of marriage. For this service, Ms. Brumbaugh charges a fee of $50.

. . . In *State v. Sperry*, 140 So.2d 587, 595 (Fla.1962), we noted:

> The reason for prohibiting the practice of law by those who have not been examined and found qualified to practice is frequently misunderstood. It is not done to aid or protect the members of the legal profession either in creating or maintaining a monopoly or closed shop. It is done to protect the public from being advised and represented in legal matters by unqualified persons over whom the judicial department can exercise little, if any, control in the matter of infractions of the code of conduct which, in the public interest, lawyers are bound to observe.

. . .

With regard to the charges made against Marilyn Brumbaugh, this Court appointed a referee to receive evidence and to make findings of fact, conclusions of law, and recommendations as to the disposition of the case. The referee found that respondent, under the guise of a "secretarial" or "typing" service prepares, for a fee, all papers deemed by her to be needed for the pleading, filing, and securing of a dissolution of marriage, as well as detailed instructions as to how the suit should be filed, notice served, hearings set, trial conducted, and the final decree secured. The referee also found that in one instance, respondent prepared a quit claim deed in reference to the marital property of the parties. The referee determined that respondent's contention that she merely operates a typing service is rebutted by numerous facts in evidence. Ms. Brumbaugh has no blank forms either to sell or to fill out. Rather, she types up the documents for her customers after they have asked her to prepare a petition or an entire set of dissolution of marriage papers. Prior to typing up the papers, respondent asks her customers whether custody, child support, or alimony is involved. Respondent has four sets of dissolution of marriage papers, and she chooses which set is appropriate for the particular customer. She then types out those papers, filling in the blank spaces with the appropriate information. Respondent instructs her customers how the papers are to be signed, where they are to be filed, and how the customer should arrange for a final hearing. . . .

The Florida Bar argues that the above activities of respondent violate the rulings of this Court in *The Florida Bar v. American Legal and Business Forms, Inc.*, 274 So.2d 225 (Fla. 1973), and *The Florida Bar v. Stupica*, 300 So.2d 683 (Fla. 1974). In those decisions we held that it is lawful to sell to the public printed legal forms, provided they do not carry with them what purports to be instructions on how to fill out such forms or how to use them. We stated that legal advice is inextricably involved in the filling out and advice as to how to use such legal forms, and therein lies the danger of injury or damage to the public if not properly performed in accordance with law. . . . Other states have [held] that the sale of legal forms with instructions for their use does not constitute unauthorized practice of law. However, these courts have prohibited all personal contact between the service providing such forms and the customer, in the nature of consultation, explanation, recommendation, advice, or other assistance in selecting particular forms, in filling out any part of the forms, suggesting or advising how the forms should be used in solving the particular problems.

Although persons not licensed as attorneys are prohibited from practicing law within this state, it is somewhat difficult to define exactly what constitutes the practice of law in all instances. This Court has previously stated that:

> . . . if the giving of such advice and performance of such services affect important rights of a person under the law, and if the reasonable protection of the rights and property of those advised and served requires that the persons giving such advice possess legal skill and a knowledge of the law greater than that possessed by the average citizen, then the giving of such advice and the

performance of such services by one for another as a course of conduct constitute the practice of law.

Sperry, supra, 140 So.2d at 591.

. . .

. . . The tendency of persons seeking legal assistance to place their trust in the individual purporting to have expertise in the area necessitates this Court's regulation of such attorney-client relationships, so as to require that persons giving such advice have at least a minimal amount of legal training and experience. Although Marilyn Brumbaugh never held herself out as an attorney, it is clear that her clients placed some reliance upon her to properly prepare the necessary legal forms for their dissolution proceedings. To this extent we believe that Ms. Brumbaugh overstepped proper bounds and engaged in the unauthorized practice of law. We hold that Ms. Brumbaugh, and others in similar situations, may sell printed material purporting to explain legal practice and procedure to the public in general and she may sell sample legal forms. . . . Further, we hold that it is not improper for Marilyn Brumbaugh to engage in a secretarial service, typing such forms for her clients, provided that she only copy the information given to her in writing by her clients. In addition, Ms. Brumbaugh may advertise her business activities of providing secretarial and notary services and selling legal forms and general printed information. However, Marilyn Brumbaugh must not, in conjunction with her business, engage in advising clients as to the various remedies available to them, or otherwise assist them in preparing those forms necessary for a dissolution proceeding. More specifically, Marilyn Brumbaugh may not make inquiries nor answer questions from her clients as to the particular forms which might be necessary, how best to fill out such forms, where to properly file such forms, and how to present necessary evidence at the court hearings. Our specific holding with regard to the dissolution of marriage also applies to other unauthorized legal assistance such as the preparation of wills or real estate transaction documents. While Marilyn Brumbaugh may legally sell forms in these areas, and type up instruments which have been completed by clients, she must not engage in personal legal assistance in conjunction with her business activities, including the correction.

* * *

Application of *Brumbaugh* to LegalZoom. *Brumbaugh* is the leading case involving non-lawyers engaging in the practice of law. Despite its age, courts have referenced the decision in deciding whether non-lawyer legal service providers like LegalZoom are engaged in the unauthorized practice of law. LegalZoom's website offers blank legal forms that customers may download, print, and fill in themselves. In addition, LegalZoom's website provides a fully-automated online questionnaire that customers complete when seeking to form a limited liability company, prepare a will, or obtain other legal documents. This information provided by the customer is entered into a template that contains standardized language created by attorneys. LegalZoom then sends the unsigned document to the customer. LegalZoom has faced numerous UPL claims over the years, and courts have reached different conclusions on the issue. *See* Terry Carter, *LegalZoom Business Model OK'd by South Carolina Supreme Court*, ABA JOURNAL, April 5, 2014; *Janson v. LegalZoom.com, Inc.*, 802 F. Supp. 2d 1053 (W.D. Mo. 2011) (concluding LegalZoom engaged in UPL). North Carolina actually enacted legislation that attempts to define permissible activities on the part of companies like LegalZoom. *See* N.C. Gen. Stat. § 84–2.2.

Other Applications. Artificial Intelligence (AI) refers to the capacity of a machine to mimic intelligent human behavior. AI technology is now being used in contract drafting, contract review, title management, and legal research, among other areas of the legal field. The question that arises is whether this form of technology exercises the type of professional judgment that typically defines the practice of law. Given the difficulty many individuals experience in being able to afford legal services, there is also the normative question of whether the legal profession should loosen its restrictions on UPL in order to allow for greater access to justice through the use of technology. *See generally* Benjamin H. Barton, *Glass Half-Full: The Decline and Rebirth of the Legal Profession* 85–90 (2015).

Law-Related Services. Innovative law firms are always seeking ways to better serve clients while expanding their market share. One way some firms have accomplished these goals is through the offering of law-related services. Rule 5.7(b) defines law-related services (also sometimes known as "ancillary services") as "services that might reasonably be performed in conjunction with and in substance are related to the provision of legal services, and that are not prohibited as unauthorized practice of law when provided by a nonlawyer." Examples include providing title insurance, financial planning, and legislative lobbying. Even though a lawyer who provides such services may not be engaged in the practice of law, the lawyer is still subject to the rules of professional conduct if (1) the lawyer provides the services in circumstances that are not distinct from the lawyer's provision of legal services to the client, or (2) an entity controlled by the lawyer (individually or with others) "fails to take reasonable measures to assure that a person obtaining the law-related services knows that the services are not legal services and that the protections of the client-lawyer relationship do not exist." Model Rule 5.7(a).

* * *

2. ASSISTING OTHERS IN THE UNAUTHORIZED PRACTICE OF LAW

Model Rule 5.5(a) prohibits a lawyer from assisting another in the unauthorized practice of law. This rule does not prohibit lawyers from delegating functions to legal assistants and other non-lawyers, "so long as the lawyer supervises the delegated work and retains responsibility for their work." *Id.* Comment [2]. One clear example of a violation of this rule would be a lawyer who permits a non-lawyer assistant, without supervision, to engage in actions—such as settling claims, advising clients, or drafting pleadings—that amount to the practice of law. *See Attorney Grievance Com'n v. Smith*, 116 A.3d 977 (Md. 2015).

A lawyer who employs or oversees a law student must take steps to ensure that the student is not engaged in the unauthorized practice of law. Law students who work as law clerks in the summer, during the regular school year, or in legal clinics, frequently engage in activity that comes right up to the line of "practicing law." In some cases, students may actually engage in the practice of law. In the case of students enrolled in a law school's legal clinic, this does not amount to the unauthorized practice of law. State statutes prohibiting the unauthorized practice of law frequently contain an exception for law school legal clinics. *See, e.g.*, N.C. Gen. Stat. § 84–8(1). In addition, some jurisdictions have established legal intern license programs, which permit law students to engage in the limited practice of law under the supervision of a licensed attorney. *See, e.g.*, Idaho Bar Commission Rule 221. Where neither type of provision is applicable, a lawyer employing a law student must supervise any work delegated to the student and retain responsibility for that work. *See* Model Rule 5.1, Comment [1]; *id.* Rule 5.3, Comment [1]. The failure to do so may lead to professional discipline or potential tort liability. *See In re Wilkinson*, 805 So.2d 142 (La. 2002) (imposing discipline against attorney for his failure to properly supervise a law clerk in his office who provided incorrect legal advice to a client).

* * *

Problem 4.2. Assume that Tony's mother-in-law, Vera, decides she wants to go to court over the condominium association's claims and represent herself. If Tony does not appear on her behalf but provides her with advice and assistance concerning the matter, would he be assisting his mother-in-law in the unauthorized practice of law? *See* ABA Formal Opinion 07–446 (2007).

3. PERMITTING THE LIMITED PRACTICE OF LAW BY NON-LAWYERS

In recent years, a number of jurisdictions have experimented with permitting non-lawyers to engage in some limited forms of the practice of law. The most obvious comparison is to a nurse practitioner in the medical field. The trend has its roots in the fact that many individuals cannot afford to hire a lawyer for even basic legal services.

For example, in Arizona, a Legal Paraprofessional is a professional with specific education and experience who is licensed to provide legal services in limited practice areas, including family law and criminal law where no jail time is involved. A licensed Legal Paraprofessional is authorized to provide certain legal services without the supervision of an attorney, including drafting, signing, and filing legal documents; providing advice, opinions, or recommendations about possible legal rights, remedies, defenses, options, or strategies; appearing before a court or tribunal; and negotiating on behalf of a client. One can become a Legal Paraprofessional by completing a designated course of study and passing an examination. *See* Arizona Code of Judicial Administration § 7–210.

* * *

B. MULTIJURISDICTIONAL PRACTICE (MJP)

In modern practice in the United States, many attorneys are licensed in multiple states. Absent a professional conduct rule or law to the contrary, a lawyer who has an office or other "systematic or continuous presence" in a state must be licensed to practice there. Model Rule 5.5(b)(1). Further, even without an office in a state, a lawyer who wants to represent to the public that he or she is admitted to practice law in the jurisdiction must also be licensed there. Model Rule 5.5(b)(2). A lawyer who engages in the practice of law in violation of another jurisdiction's admissions rule is subject to professional discipline. Model Rule 5.5(a).

Beyond being licensed in a state, a lawyer must also be admitted to practice in the federal courts where the lawyer wishes to appear on behalf of a client. Federal courts have their own admission rules. Attorneys should be aware that federal courts also adopt professional conduct rules and may discipline attorneys for violating those rules.

1. LICENSURE IN MULTIPLE JURISDICTIONS

The Uniform Bar Examination (UBE) and soon, the NextGen bar exam, allow bar applicants to transfer their scores when seeking admission in another UBE or NextGen jurisdiction within a designated period of time. While an applicant must still proceed through the normal bar application process, the applicant is relieved of the need to take a new exam when applying for admission in a UBE or NextGen state.

Most states also permit a lawyer admitted in another jurisdiction to apply for admission by motion without having to take a new bar exam. States that allow for admission by motion ordinarily require a lawyer to have practiced in the other jurisdiction for a number of years before being eligible. Five years is common.

* * *

Problem 4.3. After he finished law school seven years ago, Tony took and passed the New Dakota bar exam so he could practice there. He's been licensed in New Dakota ever since. New Dakota is not a UBE or NextGen state. Tony is now thinking about moving to West Dakota and practicing there. Does Tony need to be licensed in West Dakota even though he passed the New Dakota bar exam? Does he need to take the West Dakota bar exam?

* * *

2. SPECIAL RULES ALLOWING AN ATTORNEY TO ESTABLISH AN OFFICE IN A STATE WHERE THE ATTORNEY IS NOT LICENSED

Model Rule 5.5(d) permits a lawyer admitted in another U.S. jurisdiction or in a foreign jurisdiction to provide legal services through an office or other systematic and continuous presence in a jurisdiction where the lawyer is acting as in-house counsel. The rule also permits a lawyer licensed in another jurisdiction to provide legal services in a different jurisdiction when the lawyer is providing services authorized by federal law or other law in the jurisdiction.

A number of states have also adopted "practice pending admission" rules. These rules create a limited window whereby a lawyer who is licensed in another jurisdiction can practice on a temporary basis in another jurisdiction while waiting on admission in the other jurisdiction. Typically, the lawyer who seeks to practice pending admission must be supervised by or associate with another lawyer licensed in the jurisdiction. *See* Ohio S. Ct. R. for the Gov't of the Bar, R. I § 19.

* * *

Problem 4.4. Tony is thinking about going ahead and moving to West Dakota and practicing there before being admitted. West Dakota's practice pending admission rule is identical to Ohio's. Read Ohio's rule listed above.

(a) What advice would you give Tony concerning his plan?

(b) Could a recent law school graduate also take advantage of this rule?

* * *

C. TEMPORARY PRACTICE OF LAW IN A STATE WHERE AN ATTORNEY IS LICENSED

An attorney licensed in a state may sometimes be asked to provide legal services that have a connection to another jurisdiction. For example, the lawyer's client may ask the lawyer for advice about the law of another state. Or the lawyer's client may be sued in another state and ask the lawyer to represent the client there. A client who is a resident of another state might also contact the lawyer seeking legal advice or preparation of a contract or legal document.

1. *PRO HAC VICE* ADMISSION

Rule 5.5(c) explicitly notes *pro hac vice* ("for this occasion") admission is one means by which a lawyer may temporarily practice in a jurisdiction. Although such *pro hac vice* motions are routinely granted, there are some competing policy concerns. On the one hand, clients will often want to use lawyers with whom they have previously worked, and it might impose a hardship on a client to be denied its lawyer of choice in a given matter. On the other hand, there is the concern that out-of-state lawyers, unfamiliar with the law in the other jurisdiction, will stumble into ethical difficulties.

Under the ABA's Model Rule on *Pro Hac Vice* Admission, the lawyer seeking such admission must "become familiar with the rules of professional conduct, rules of discipline, contempt and sanctions orders, local court rules, court policies and procedures." In addition, the party being represented by the lawyer practicing on a *pro hac vice* basis must also be represented by an in-state lawyer who serves as counsel of record and actively participates in the representation. As the report accompanying the Rule notes, "[t]hroughout the litigation, local counsel must remain responsible to the client and for the conduct of the proceeding. This includes advising the client of the lawyer's professional judgment when it differs from that of the out-of-state lawyer on contemplated actions." Some states require that both the in-state and out-of-state lawyer sign all the pleadings, motions, briefs, and other papers and that the in-state lawyer personally appear for all court proceedings, unless excused by the court in which the case is pending.

As explained in one state ethics opinion,

[T]ypical acts required of local counsel, such as moving of admission *pro hac vice* or the signing of pleadings, always carry with them affirmative ethical obligations. For example, in this, as in all circumstances, the signing of pleadings by an attorney constitutes a good faith representation regarding the pleadings and the conduct of the discovery procedure of which the pleadings are a part. There is nothing in the role of local counsel that changes this basic ethical responsibility. Local counsel, if he or she signs the pleadings, must be familiar with them and investigate them to the extent required by this good faith requirement.

State Bar of Georgia, Formal Advisory Op. 05–10 (2006). Local counsel may also be subject to discipline for the out-of-state lawyer's misconduct "when the local counsel knows of the abuse and ratifies it by his or her conduct." *Id.*

2. WHEN TEMPORARY PRACTICE AMOUNTS TO THE UNAUTHORIZED PRACTICE OF LAW

Pro hac vice admission is an option for a lawyer who needs to represent a client in some type of litigation matter. But *pro hac vice* admission is not typically an option for business lawyers, whose day-to-day practice may involve providing advice concerning non-litigation matters. A lawyer who practices law in a jurisdiction in which the lawyer is not admitted to practice may be engaged in the unauthorized practice of law. The next decision, which sent shock waves through the bar when it was decided, addresses the situation in which an out-of-state attorney represents a client in a transaction related to a state in which the attorney is not licensed. Even practicing law in another jurisdiction on a temporary basis may raise UPL issues.

BIRBROWER, MONTALBANO, CONDON & FRANK, P.C. v. SUPERIOR COURT
949 P.2d 1 (Cal. 1998)

CHIN, JUSTICE.

Business and Professions Code section 6125 states: "No person shall practice law in California unless the person is an active member of the State Bar." We must decide whether an out-of-state law firm, not licensed to practice law in this state, violated section 6125 when it performed legal services in California for a California-based client under a fee agreement stipulating that California law would govern all matters in the representation.

I. BACKGROUND

The facts with respect to the unauthorized practice of law question are essentially undisputed. Birbrower is a professional law corporation incorporated in New York, with its principal place of business in New York. During 1992 and 1993, Birbrower attorneys, defendants Kevin F. Hobbs and Thomas A. Condon (Hobbs and Condon), performed substantial work in California relating to the law firm's representation of ESQ. Neither Hobbs nor Condon has ever been licensed to practice law in California. None of Birbrower's attorneys were [sic] licensed to practice law in California during Birbrower's ESQ representation.

ESQ is a California corporation with its principal place of business in Santa Clara County. In July 1992, the parties negotiated and executed the fee agreement in New York, providing that Birbrower would perform legal services for ESQ, including "All matters pertaining to the investigation of and prosecution of all claims and causes of action against Tandem Computers Incorporated (Tandem)." [As part of the same agreement, ESQ-NY, a New York affiliate of ESQ, also retained Birbrower. Birbrower had provided legal services for ESQ-NY for several years prior to this agreement, including in connection with the agreement with Tandem at issue.] The "claims and causes of action" against Tandem, a Delaware corporation with its principal place of business in Santa Clara County, California, related to a software development and marketing contract between Tandem and ESQ dated March 16, 1990 (Tandem Agreement). The Tandem Agreement stated that "The internal laws of the State of California (irrespective of its choice of law principles) shall govern the validity of this Agreement, the construction of its terms, and the interpretation and enforcement of the rights and duties of the parties hereto." Birbrower asserts, and ESQ disputes, that ESQ knew Birbrower was not licensed to practice law in California.

While representing ESQ, Hobbs and Condon traveled to California on several occasions. In August 1992, they met in California with ESQ and its accountants. During these meetings, Hobbs and Condon discussed various matters related to ESQ's dispute with Tandem and strategy for resolving the dispute. They made recommendations and gave advice. During this California trip, Hobbs and Condon also met with Tandem representatives on four or five occasions during a two-day period. . . .

Around March or April 1993, Hobbs, Condon, and another Birbrower attorney visited California to interview potential arbitrators and to meet again with ESQ and its accountants. Birbrower had previously filed a demand for arbitration against Tandem with the San Francisco offices of the American Arbitration Association (AAA). In August 1993, Hobbs returned to California to assist ESQ in settling the Tandem matter. While in California, Hobbs met with ESQ and its accountants to discuss a proposed settlement agreement Tandem authored. Hobbs also met with Tandem representatives to discuss possible changes in the proposed agreement. Hobbs gave ESQ legal advice during this trip, including his opinion that ESQ should not settle with Tandem on the terms proposed.

ESQ eventually settled the Tandem dispute, and the matter never went to arbitration. . . .

In January 1994, ESQ sued Birbrower for legal malpractice and related claims. . . . Birbrower . . . filed a counterclaim, which included a claim for attorney fees for the work it performed in both California and New York. . . . ESQ moved for summary judgment and/or adjudication on the first through fourth causes of action of Birbrower's counterclaim . . . . ESQ argued that by practicing law without a license in California and by failing to associate legal counsel while doing so, Birbrower violated section 6125, rendering the fee agreement unenforceable. . . . [The trial court and the Court of Appeal held that Birbrower violated section 6125 and that the fee agreement was therefore unenforceable.]

We granted review to determine whether Birbrower's actions and services performed while representing ESQ in California constituted the unauthorized practice of law under section 6125. . . .

II. DISCUSSION

A. The Unauthorized Practice of Law

The California Legislature enacted section 6125 in 1927 as part of the State Bar Act (the Act), a comprehensive scheme regulating the practice of law in the state. Since the Act's passage, the general rule has been that, although persons may represent themselves and their own interests regardless of State Bar membership, no one but an active member of the State Bar may practice law for another person in California. The prohibition against unauthorized law practice is within the state's police power and is designed to ensure that those performing legal services do so competently.

A violation of section 6125 is a misdemeanor. (§ 6126). . . .

Although the Act did not define the term "practice law," case law explained it as " 'the doing and performing services in a court of justice in any matter depending therein throughout its various stages and in conformity with the adopted rules of procedure.' " *People ex rel. Lawyers' Institute of San Diego v. Merchants' Protective Corp.* 189 Cal. 531, 535, 209 P. 363 (1922) . *Merchants* included in its definition legal advice and legal instrument and contract preparation, whether or not these subjects were rendered in the course of litigation. *Ibid.; see People v. Ring* 70 P.2d 281, 26 Cal. App. 2d. Supp. 768, 772–773 (1937) (holding that single incident of practicing law in state without a license violates § 6125). . . .

In addition to not defining the term "practice law," the Act also did not define the meaning of "in California." In today's legal practice, questions often arise concerning whether the phrase refers to the nature of the legal services, or restricts the Act's application to those out-of-state attorneys who are physically present in the state.

Section 6125 has generated numerous opinions on the meaning of "practice law" but none on the meaning of "in California." In our view, the practice of law "in California" entails sufficient contact with the California client to render the nature of the legal service a clear legal representation. In addition to a quantitative analysis, we must consider the nature of the unlicensed lawyer's activities in the state. Mere fortuitous or attenuated contacts will not sustain a finding that the unlicensed lawyer practiced law "in California." The primary inquiry is whether the unlicensed lawyer engaged in sufficient activities in the state, or created a continuing relationship with the California client that included legal duties and obligations.

Our definition does not necessarily depend on or require the unlicensed lawyer's physical presence in the state. Physical presence here is one factor we may consider in deciding whether the unlicensed lawyer has violated section 6125, but it is by no means exclusive. For example, one may practice law in the state in violation of section 6125 although not physically present here by advising a California client on California law in connection with a California legal dispute by telephone, fax, computer, or other modern technological means. Conversely, although we decline to provide a comprehensive list of what activities constitute sufficient contact with the state, we do reject the notion that a person automatically practices law "in California" whenever that person practices California law anywhere, or "virtually" enters the state by telephone, fax, e-mail, or satellite. . . .

Exceptions to section 6125 do exist, but are generally limited to allowing out-of-state attorneys to make brief appearances before a state court or tribunal. They are narrowly drawn and strictly interpreted. For example, an out-of-state attorney not licensed to practice in California may be permitted, by consent of a trial judge, to appear in California in a particular pending action.

In addition, with the permission of the California court in which a particular cause is pending, out-of-state counsel may appear before a court as counsel *pro hac vice*. . . . The out-of-state attorney must also associate an active member of the California Bar as attorney of record and is subject to the Rules of Professional Conduct of the State Bar. . . .

The Act does not regulate practice before United States courts. . . .

B. The Present Case

The undisputed facts here show that . . . our "sufficient contact" definition of "practice law in California" . . . would [not] excuse Birbrower's extensive practice in this state. Nor would any of the limited statutory exceptions to section 6125 apply to Birbrower's California practice. As the Court of Appeal observed, Birbrower engaged in unauthorized law practice in California on more than a limited basis, and no firm attorney engaged in that practice was an active member of the California State Bar.... [I]n 1992 and 1993, Birbrower attorneys traveled to California to discuss with ESQ and others various matters pertaining to the dispute between ESQ and Tandem. Hobbs and Condon discussed strategy for resolving the dispute and advised ESQ on this strategy. Furthermore, during California meetings with Tandem representatives in August 1992, Hobbs demanded Tandem pay $15 million, and Condon told Tandem he believed damages in the matter would exceed that amount if the parties proceeded to litigation. Also in California, Hobbs met with ESQ for the stated purpose of helping to reach a settlement agreement and to discuss the agreement that was eventually proposed. Birbrower attorneys also traveled to California to initiate arbitration proceedings before the matter was settled. As the Court of Appeal concluded, "... the Birbrower firm's in-state activities clearly constituted the practice of law" in California.

...

California is not alone in regulating who practices law in its jurisdiction. Many states have substantially similar statutes that serve to protect their citizens from unlicensed attorneys who engage in unauthorized legal practice. Like section 6125, these other state statutes protect local citizens "against the dangers of legal representation and advice given by persons not trained, examined and licensed for such work, whether they be laymen or lawyers from other jurisdictions." *Spivak v. Sachs* (1965) 16 N.Y.2d 163, 263 N.Y.S.2d 953, 956, 211 N.E.2d 329, 331. Whether an attorney is duly admitted in another state and is, in fact, competent to practice in California is irrelevant in the face of section 6125's language and purpose.... [A] decision to except out-of-state attorneys licensed in their own jurisdictions from section 6125 is more appropriately left to the California Legislature.

Assuming that section 6125 does apply to out-of-state attorneys not licensed here, Birbrower alternatively asks us to create an exception to section 6125 for work incidental to private arbitration or other alternative dispute resolution proceedings. Birbrower points to fundamental differences between private arbitration and legal proceedings, including procedural differences relating to discovery, rules of evidence, compulsory process, cross-examination of witnesses, and other areas. As Birbrower observes, in light of these differences, at least one court has decided that an out-of-state attorney could recover fees for services rendered in an arbitration proceeding. *See Williamson v. John D. Quinn Const. Corp.* (S.D.N.Y. 1982) 537 F. Supp. 613, 616 (*Williamson*).

...

We decline Birbrower's invitation to craft an arbitration exception to section 6125's prohibition of the unlicensed practice of law in this state. Any exception for arbitration is best left to the Legislature, which has the authority to determine qualifications for admission to the State Bar and to decide what constitutes the practice of law. Even though the Legislature has spoken with respect to international arbitration and conciliation, it has not enacted a similar rule for private arbitration proceedings. . . .

Finally, Birbrower urges us to adopt an exception to section 6125 based on the unique circumstances of this case. Birbrower notes that "Multistate relationships are a common part of today's society and are to be dealt with in commonsense fashion." In many situations, strict adherence to rules prohibiting the unauthorized practice of law by out-of-state attorneys would be " 'grossly impractical and inefficient.' "

Although . . . we recognize the need to acknowledge and, in certain cases, accommodate the multistate nature of law practice, the facts here show that Birbrower's extensive activities within California amounted to considerably more than any of our state's recognized exceptions to section 6125 would allow. Accordingly, we reject Birbrower's suggestion that we except the firm from section 6125's rule under the circumstances here.

C. Compensation for Legal Services

Because Birbrower violated section 6125 when it engaged in the unlawful practice of law in California, the Court of Appeal found its fee agreement with ESQ unenforceable in its entirety. Without crediting Birbrower for some services performed in New York, for which fees were generated under the fee agreement, the court reasoned that the agreement was void and unenforceable because it included payment for services rendered to a California client in the state by an unlicensed out-of-state lawyer. . . . The Court of Appeal let stand, however, the trial court's decision to allow Birbrower to pursue its fifth cause of action in *quantum meruit*.

It is a general rule that an attorney is barred from recovering compensation for services rendered in another state where the attorney was not admitted to the bar.

. . . Because Birbrower practiced substantial law in this state in violation of section 6125, it cannot receive compensation under the fee agreement for any of the services it performed in California. Enforcing the fee agreement in its entirety would include payment for the unauthorized practice of law in California and would allow Birbrower to enforce an illegal contract.

Birbrower asserts that even if we agree with the Court of Appeal and find that none of the above exceptions allowing fees for unauthorized California services apply to the firm, it should be permitted to recover fees for those limited services it performed exclusively in New York under the agreement. . . .

We agree with Birbrower that it may be able to recover fees under the fee agreement for the limited legal services it performed for ESQ in New York to the extent they did not constitute practicing law in California, even though those services were performed for a California client. Because section 6125 applies to the practice of law in California, it does not, in general, regulate law practice in other states.

* * *

The ABA's Response to *Birbrower*. The logic of *Birbrower* obviously would have heavy implications for lawyers who represent businesses with locations in multiple jurisdictions. Partly in response to *Birbrower*, the ABA amended Model Rule 5.5 to explicitly permit the temporary practice of law in a jurisdiction in a broad set of circumstances enumerated in subsections (c)(3) and (4). As you read the rule, consider how the rule would have applied had the rule been adopted at the time of *Birbrower*.

* * *

Problem 4.5. When Tony was discussing Vera's case with Laura, he and Laura exchanged numerous emails. Tony sent all of his emails from his office in New Dakota to Laura in her office in Old Dakota. After the two lawyers agreed on a settlement, Laura noticed Tony's New Dakota address on an email. She asked Tony if he was licensed to practice in Old Dakota. Tony responded that he was not but that if any further action was required or if the settlement fell through that he would hire local counsel. Assuming Tony was engaged in the practice of law, was he engaged in the practice of law *in* Old Dakota?

Problem 4.6. Assume for purposes of this problem that Tony was engaged in the practice of law in Old Dakota. Assume further that Old Dakota has adopted Model Rule 5.5(c)(2) & (c)(4). Would those rules authorize Tony to represent Vera in Old Dakota on a temporary basis, or was he engaged in the unauthorized practice of law in Old Dakota?

Remote Practice. In 2020, during the pandemic, the ABA provided clarification on a related scenario. If a lawyer is licensed in, say, Ohio and practices the law of Ohio for clients located in Ohio, is the lawyer engaged in UPL if the lawyer is physically located in, say, Michigan? According to ABA Formal Op. No. 495, the answer is "no." As long as a local jurisdiction does not define this as the unauthorized practice of law, this type of remote practice does not amount to a violation of Rule 5.5.

* * *

D. THE MULTI-STATE PRACTITIONER, DISCIPLINARY AUTHORITY, AND CHOICE OF LAW

What happens if a lawyer is licensed in two states that have different ethics rules relating to a lawyer's conduct in a given situation? Which rule must the lawyer follow? What happens if a lawyer licensed in one state, while lawfully practicing in another state, commits an act that is unethical under one state's law but not the other? Even if the act is unethical under the law of both states, which state has the power to discipline the lawyer? ABA Model Rule 8.5 addresses these issues.

* * *

Problem 4.7. Miguel is licensed in both New Dakota and East Dakota. Miguel and Briana jointly represent a client in a matter before a tribunal in New Dakota. During the course of representation, Miguel learns that Briana has committed a fraud upon the court. New Dakota's rules of professional conduct require a lawyer to report another lawyer's serious misconduct to disciplinary authorities even if the client does not consent to the disclosure. In contrast, East Dakota follows Model Rule 8.3, which excuses a lawyer from the duty to report if the client refuses to consent to the disclosure. Which state's rule of professional conduct determines Miguel's reporting obligation?

Problem 4.8. Tony pays for an advertisement to run on a television station in East Dakota. Tony is only licensed in New Dakota, but his office is located close to the New Dakota/East Dakota border, so he hopes to attract some clients from both states but provide the services from his New Dakota office. Assume that the advertisement is determined to be false or misleading in violation of the ethical rules in place in both New Dakota and East Dakota and that both states have adopted Model Rule 8.5.

(a) In which jurisdiction(s) is Tony subject to discipline?

(b) If the rules regarding lawyer advertising differ between the states, which rule should a disciplinary authority in New Dakota apply?

* * *

In a 2023 ethics opinion, the ABA provided lawyers with guidance concerning the application of Rule 8.5. One question that had arisen is how one determines where the "predominant effect" of a lawyer's conduct occurs under Rule 8.5(b)(2). According to the opinion, among the factors to consider are where the transaction occurs, the location of the lawyer's principal office, where the lawyer is admitted, and the jurisdiction with the greatest interest in the lawyer's conduct. *See* ABA Formal Op. No. 504 (2023).

If a lawyer is disciplined in a jurisdiction with authority to do so, should all jurisdictions in which the lawyer is licensed be required to impose the same discipline? Rule 22, Paragraph [D] of the ABA *Model Rules for Lawyer Disciplinary Enforcement* adopts a rule of "reciprocal discipline." The rule provides that all jurisdictions in which the offending lawyer is licensed should treat a determination of misconduct by another jurisdiction as conclusive and should impose the identical discipline, unless: the procedure used in the jurisdiction imposing discipline "was so lacking in notice or opportunity to be heard as to constitute a deprivation of due process;" the proof accepted as establishing the misconduct was so infirm "as to give rise to the clear conviction that the court could not, consistent with its duty, accept as final the conclusion on that subject;" or "the discipline imposed would result in grave injustice . . . or be offensive to the public policy of the jurisdiction."

Profile of Attorney Professionalism. Macon Bolling Allen is believed to be the first African-American to practice law in the United States. Allen passed the Maine bar exam in 1844. He moved to Boston after having difficulty finding clients in Maine and was admitted to the bar in Massachusetts. In 1845, Allen tried a case before a jury, making him the first Black lawyer to argue a jury trial. He later became a Justice of the Peace. Following the end of the Civil War, Allen moved to South Carolina and established the law firm of Whipper, Elliott, and Allen, believed to be the first all African-American law firm in the country. In 1873, Allen was selected by the South Carolina legislature to be a criminal court judge in Charleston. He went on to become a probate judge before eventually retiring.

CHAPTER 5

PROVIDING ACCESS TO JUSTICE THROUGH PRO BONO AND OTHER SERVICE

■ ■ ■

Chapter Hypothetical. Like many states, your state's supreme court has an Access Justice Commission. The court is concerned that numerous citizens of the state need but are unable to pay for basic civil legal services. These individuals need legal advice and representation for matters related to child support, employment, housing, simple contract disputes, healthcare benefits, orders of protection, and other issues. Without a lawyer, these individuals often represent themselves, burdening the courts and compromising their legal rights. In other cases, those who cannot afford a lawyer simply forgo the court system.

You have accepted the court's invitation to serve on the ten-person Access to Justice Commission. The questions in this chapter ask for your views as a member of the Commission.

Access to justice is a pressing problem. The Washington Supreme Court summarized the problem:

> Our adversarial civil legal system is complex. It is unaffordable not only to low income people but . . . moderate income people as well (defined as families with incomes between 200% and 400% of the Federal Poverty Level). One example of the need for this rule is in the area of family relations which are governed by a myriad of statutes. Decisions relating to changes in family status (divorce, child residential placement, child support, etc.) fall within the exclusive province of our court system. Legal practice is required to conform to specific statewide and local procedures, and practitioners are required to use standard forms developed at both the statewide and local levels. Every day across this state, thousands of unrepresented (pro se) individuals seek to resolve important legal matters in our courts. Many of these are low income people who seek but cannot obtain help from an overtaxed, underfunded civil legal aid system. Many others are moderate income people for whom existing market rates for legal services

are cost-prohibitive and who, unfortunately, must search for alternatives in the unregulated marketplace.

In the Matter of the Adoption of New APR 28—Limited Practice Rule for Limited License Legal Technicians (2012).

A task force of the New York Bar reached similar conclusions. It found that New Yorkers lacked legal assistance in:

- 99% of tenants in eviction cases in New York City and 98% of tenants in New York State;
- 97% of parents in child support proceedings in New York City and 95% of parents in New York State; and
- 44% of homeowners in foreclosure cases in New York State.

Task Force to Expand Access to Civil Legal Services in New York (2010).

The Preamble to the *Model Rules of Professional Conduct* explains the attorney's obligation in this regard, describing lawyers as having "special responsibility for the quality of justice." Model Rules Preamble, Paragraph [1]. To improve access to justice, the Preamble urges lawyers to care for those who cannot afford legal assistance by devoting "professional time and resources and us[ing] civic influence to ensure equal access to our system of justice...." *Id.* at Paragraph [6].

The profession faces challenges in putting these principles into practice. Legal educators and the bar must decide how best to inculcate a spirit of volunteerism in the next generation of lawyers. State courts and rule committees must endeavor to draft rules that encourage pro bono service and remove barriers to access to justice. Organizations that provide legal services to the poor must develop new programs that facilitate attorneys getting involved and making a difference. This chapter addresses these and other challenges faced by the profession as we work to provide access to justice.

* * *

A. LAW STUDENT PRO BONO SERVICE

1. PROMOTING LAW STUDENT PRO BONO SERVICE

In its accreditation standards, the American Bar Association requires that a law school's curriculum provide substantial opportunities for students to participate in pro bono legal services. ABA Standards for Approval of Law Schools, Standard 303(b)(2). In its interpretation of the rule, the ABA explains that schools are encouraged to promote pro bono services consistent with Rule 6.1 priorities (primarily providing pro bono services for persons of limited means and organizations that serve them). The interpretation further encourages law schools to provide students with opportunities to provide at least fifty hours of pro bono services over their law school career. ABA Standards for Approval of Law Schools, Interpretation 303–3. Both the Standard and Interpretation acknowledge that pro bono opportunities in law school also may include the provision of law-related public services, such as: (1) working to help groups protect and secure legal rights; (2) assisting charitable, religious, and other groups that are unable to afford legal representation; and (3) participating in groups that educate the public about the law. ABA Standards for Approval of Law Schools, Standard 303(b)(2) and Interpretation 303–4.

U.S. law schools have adopted a variety of approaches to giving students opportunities to perform pro bono services. An Internet search reveals a good variety of programs instituted by law schools around the country. Programs range from walk-in clinics—in which students answer legal questions from members of the community—to programs that serve a specific group, like veterans or immigrant families. (You will have an opportunity to research these programs in Problem 5.1.) Some law schools have hired full time staff to coordinate pro bono programs, while other schools' programs are run primarily through student organizations and faculty volunteers.

Law schools have reached different conclusions about whether pro bono service should be a graduation requirement or should be encouraged but not required. For example, Tulane University School of Law requires students to perform at least thirty hours of law-related, uncompensated pro bono service under an attorney's supervision. In another example, at the University of Tennessee College of Law, student pro bono service is not required, but students with exceptional pro bono service receive special recognition at commencement.

2. PRO BONO BAR ADMISSION REQUIREMENT

In 2012, New York became the first state to adopt a rule that makes pro bono service a prerequisite to bar admission. Because the rule requires fifty hours of service prior to applying for bar admission, most applicants will perform this service during law school. Supporters of the proposal assert that the requirement will fill a need for legal services and provide real legal experience that prepares students for practice. Critics have concerns about forcing unwilling persons to perform legal services, both from the standpoint of the bar applicant (who has no choice in the matter) and of the client (who may be provided substandard legal services).

N.Y. CT. RULES, § 520.16
PRO BONO REQUIREMENT FOR BAR ADMISSION

(a) Fifty-hour pro bono requirement. Every applicant admitted to the New York State bar on or after January 1, 2015, other than applicants for admission without examination pursuant to section 520.10 of this Part, shall complete at least 50 hours of qualifying pro bono service prior to filing an application for admission with the appropriate Appellate Division department of the Supreme Court.

(b) Pro bono service defined. For purposes of this section, pro bono service is supervised pre-admission law-related work that:

(1) assists in the provision of legal services without charge for

(i) persons of limited means;

(ii) not-for-profit organizations; or

(iii) individuals, groups or organizations seeking to secure or promote access to justice, including, but not limited to, the protection of civil rights, civil liberties or public rights;

(2) assists in the provision of legal assistance in public service for a judicial, legislative, executive or other governmental entity; or

(3) provides legal services pursuant to subdivisions two and three of section 484 of the Judiciary Law, or pursuant to equivalent legal authority in the jurisdiction where the services are performed.

(c) Supervision required. All qualifying pre-admission pro bono work must be performed under the supervision of:

(1) a member of a law school faculty, including adjunct faculty, or an instructor employed by a law school;

(2) an attorney admitted to practice and in good standing in the jurisdiction where the work is performed; or

(3) in the case of a clerkship or externship in a court system, by a judge or attorney employed by the court system.

(d) Location of pro bono service. The 50 hours of pro bono service, or any portion thereof, may be completed in any state or territory of the United States, the District of Columbia, or any foreign country.

(e) Timing of pro bono service. The 50 hours of pro bono service may be performed at any time after the commencement of the applicant's legal studies and prior to filing an application for admission to the New York State bar.

(f) Proof required. Every applicant for admission shall file with the appropriate Appellate Division department an Affidavit of Compliance with the Pro Bono Requirement, describing the nature and dates of pro bono service and the number of hours completed. The Affidavit of Compliance shall include a certification by the supervising attorney or judge confirming the applicant's pro bono activities. For each position used to satisfy the 50-hour requirement, the applicant shall file a separate Affidavit of Compliance.

(g) Prohibition on political activities. An applicant may not satisfy any part of the 50-hour requirement by participating in partisan political activities.

* * *

Problem 5.1. Your state's Access to Justice Commission has voted in favor of proposing a bar admission pro bono requirement. You have agreed to take the lead drafting the proposed rule. Which aspects of the New York rule will you incorporate into your rule? How will your proposal differ from the New York rule?

* * *

B. ATTORNEY PRO BONO SERVICE

Rule 6.1 provides that it is a lawyer's professional responsibility to provide legal representation to individuals unable to pay and that each lawyer should aspire to provide at least fifty hours of pro bono services each year. The rule creates a hierarchy of preferred services, stating that a "substantial majority" of the lawyer's pro bono services should be provided to individuals of limited means (or to organizations in order to meet the legal needs of individuals of limited means). Model Rule 6.1(a). Beyond that, subpart (b) guides lawyers in additional services that they may provide to fulfill their fifty-hour requirement, including providing substantially reduced fee representations to persons of limited means and participating in activities to improve the law. Model Rule 6.1(b). The comments provide some direction about who qualifies as a "person of limited means" under the rule. *See* Model Rule 6.1, Comment [3].

While many states do not set a goal for the number of pro bono hours an attorney should perform, twenty-nine states set a specific goal. Of these, most include a fifty-hour requirement like Model Rule 6.1. Other jurisdictions set a lower goal (twenty hours in Mississippi and Florida), while others set a higher goal (eighty hours in Oregon). Eight states suggest a specific financial contribution attorneys should make to support the provision of legal services to the poor.

A growing number of states encourage pro bono service by asking attorneys to report their pro bono hours (and sometimes also the amount of money donated to support legal aid organizations). Such reporting typically occurs when attorneys pay annual bar dues. Currently, eight states have adopted a mandatory reporting system. Even though pro bono service is not mandatory in these states, attorneys are required to answer questions about how many hours of service they provided. Twelve states have adopted a permissive reporting scheme. Attorneys are asked for the information about pro bono hours, but are not required to provide it. The theory is that even though pro bono service is not mandatory, knowing that they will be asked about their service may prompt attorneys to seek out pro bono opportunities.

Giving attorneys continuing legal education (CLE) credit for time spent representing clients on a pro bono basis is another tool states use to encourage pro bono service. Currently, ten states have such rules. For example, in Arizona, attorneys can earn up to five of their fifteen required CLE credits through pro bono service each year. Under Arizona's rule, one credit hour of CLE is awarded for every five hours of pro bono service. In another example, Delaware allows attorneys to earn up to six hours of CLE credit every two years by performing pro bono work, earning one hour of credit for every six hours of pro bono work.

Another avenue for increasing pro bono services is to increase the pool of attorneys able to provide those services. In thirty-eight jurisdictions, retired attorneys who are no longer active members of the bar are permitted to provide pro bono services under so called "emeritus attorney" professional conduct rules. Other rules allow in-house attorneys (practicing under a limited license because they did not take the bar exam in that state) to provide pro bono services in the state. *See, e.g.,* Tennessee Rules of Prof'l Conduct, R. 5.5(e) (allowing in-house attorneys licensed in another jurisdiction to perform defined pro bono services in Tennessee); 22 N.Y.C.R.R. § 522.8 (permitting registered in-house attorneys licensed in another jurisdiction to perform defined pro bono services in New York).

Finally, states can make it easier for attorneys to perform pro bono service by relaxing the conflict of interest rules for "limited scope" pro bono representations. This issue is addressed more fully in Part C, below.

* * *

Problem 5.2. As a member of the Access to Justice Commission, which of the above methods of encouraging pro bono service would you like to see incorporated into your state's professional conduct rules? Why do you think these methods are effective methods to encourage pro bono service?

Intrinsic Motivations for Pro Bono Service. While the legal profession tends to focus on pro bono service as a professional obligation, research shows that providing services to underserved populations increases one's sense of happiness and well-being. *See* Mark L. Jones, *Grabbing the Bull by the Horns: Jurisprudential, Ethical, and Other Lessons for Lawyers and Law Students in the Immigration Labyrinth and Beyond*, 45 U. ARK. LITTLE ROCK L. REV. 381, 465 (2023).

* * *

C. CONFLICTS OF INTEREST AND A LAWYER'S PRO BONO LIMITED SCOPE REPRESENTATIONS AND OTHER VOLUNTEER ACTIVITIES

In later chapters, you will learn that a lawyer cannot represent a client when the lawyer or the lawyer's firm has a conflict of interest. Model Rules 6.3, 6.4, and 6.5 add a twist to the conflict of interest analysis for lawyers who are members of legal services organizations, engaged in law reform activities, or participants in limited legal services programs. Use these rules to answer the following questions.

* * *

Problem 5.3. You are asked to serve on the Board of Directors for the local Legal Aid organization. The partners in your firm are concerned that your membership on the board will create a conflict of interest for the firm. Legal Aid lawyers frequently represent tenants in eviction proceedings filed by the firm for an important client. Would your membership on the Board of Directors create a conflict of interest that would prevent the firm from representing the client in future cases adverse to Legal Aid clients?

Problem 5.4. Your local bar association hosts a Saturday morning walk-in legal clinic for low-income individuals. Attorneys meet the clients in person and provide legal advice during the clinic. Participants understand that there will not be a continuing attorney-client relationship, unless the attorney and client agree otherwise. You would like to volunteer as an attorney for the walk-in clinic. Do you need to check for conflicts of interest between your law firm's clients and the individuals seeking advice at the clinic? If you recognize a conflict between an individual seeking advice at the clinic and a firm client, may you nonetheless provide advice to the individual on this one-time basis?

* * *

D. COURT APPOINTMENTS

Courts often appoint attorneys to represent individuals in criminal and sometimes even civil matters. Rule 6.2 provides that an attorney should generally accept such appointments absent good cause.

One good cause noted in Rule 6.2 is that the representation is likely to result in violation of professional conduct rules. Obviously, if the representation would create a conflict of interest, this is a proper basis to seek relief from the appointment. *See* Model Rules 1.7, 1.9, and 1.10. Attorneys also sometimes worry that their representation of an appointed client may violate the competence obligation of a fiduciary as found in Rule 1.1. Courts generally dismiss these concerns, though, and expect attorneys to do the research and work necessary to perform competently. *See, e.g.,*

Stern v. County Court, 773 P.2d 1074, 1080 (Colo. 1989) (agreeing with the trial court's determination that, even if attorney was not competent to handle the criminal appointment, attorney was "very capable" of becoming competent).

An attorney may also want to avoid an appointment for a client that is unpopular or whose conduct or cause is troubling to the lawyer. For example, a lawyer may find it difficult to represent a person accused of abusing a child. Rule 6.2(c) provides that if the lawyer finds the client or cause "so repugnant" that the lawyer's ability to represent the client is likely to be impaired, this is good cause to avoid the appointment. Nonetheless, comments to the rules remind attorneys that it is their duty to accept a "fair share of unpopular matters or indigent or unpopular clients." Model Rule 6.2, Comment [1].

While attorneys are often paid for their work on court-appointed cases, sometimes they are asked to accept a representation pro bono. In other cases, appointed attorneys may receive pay that is substantially below market rates for paying clients. While most attorneys recognize the importance of pro bono service, they can face a financial strain when they are appointed to work on a significant case or several small cases for which they will receive little or no pay. Rule 6.2(b) provides that "unreasonable financial burden" is good cause to request relief from a court appointment. This issue was addressed in the following case.

HAGOPIAN V. JUSTICE ADMINISTRATIVE COMMISSION
18 So.3d 625 (Fla. Dist. Ct. App. 2009)

WALLACE, JUDGE.

I. THE FACTS

A. Introduction

In an effort to combat gang activity in Manatee County, the Statewide Prosecutor began charging persons alleged to be gang members with the offense of racketeering. Terry Green was one of the persons so charged. In 2008, an information was filed in the Manatee County Circuit Court charging Mr. Green and eleven codefendants with one count of racketeering and one count of conspiracy to commit racketeering. The circuit court appointed the public defender to represent one of Mr. Green's codefendants and appointed the five Manatee County attorneys whose names appeared on the registry list maintained by the clerk of the circuit court to represent five more of the codefendants. The circuit court could not appoint the Office of Criminal Conflict and Civil Regional Counsel to represent Mr. Green or any of his codefendants because of a conflict of interest. As a result of the shortage of available attorneys to represent the remaining defendants in Mr. Green's case and similar cases, the circuit court created an "Involuntary Appointment List" and began appointing attorneys whose names were placed on the Involuntary Appointment List to represent Mr. Green and other codefendants. The first two attorneys involuntarily appointed to represent Mr. Green were granted leave to withdraw because they lacked the requisite experience. The circuit court then appointed Mr. Hagopian, a sole practitioner, from the Involuntary Appointment List to represent Mr. Green. Mr. Hagopian moved to withdraw from Mr. Green's case, but the circuit court denied his motion. Mr. Hagopian now seeks review by certiorari of the order denying his motion to withdraw.

B. Chapter 2007-62

[The court describes the flat fee schedule for appointed counsel in the matter, explaining that it "obviously provides minimal compensation in cases that prove to be complicated or time-consuming for appointed counsel."]

. . .

G. The Order Appointing Mr. Hagopian and His Objection

On July 22, 2008, the circuit court entered an order in the *Brown* case appointing Mr. Hagopian to represent Mr. Green.

. . .

Mr. Hagopian promptly filed a motion to withdraw and requested a hearing. In his motion, Mr. Hagopian asserted four grounds for relief. First, the compensation available under section 27.5304 would be insufficient to compensate him for the work necessary to provide effective representation to Mr. Green. Second, the inadequacy of the compensation would inevitably give rise to a conflict of interest between Mr. Hagopian and the client and deprive Mr. Green of his right to conflict-free counsel. Third, the vast scope of the work necessary to handle the case would cause Mr. Hagopian to be unable to properly represent his existing clients, render him unable to accept new business, and ultimately lead to the ruin of his law practice. Fourth, the involuntary appointment would deprive Mr. Hagopian of his constitutional rights to due process of law, the right to contract, and the rights of association and free speech.

II. THE HEARING ON THE MOTION TO WITHDRAW

The circuit court promptly conducted an evidentiary hearing on Mr. Hagopian's motion to withdraw. In addition to Mr. Hagopian, three witnesses testified at the hearing: (1) Walt Smith, the trial court administrator of the Twelfth Judicial Circuit; (2) Mark Lipinski, an attorney board-certified in criminal law who practiced in Manatee County; and (3) Joseph Campoli, an attorney appointed from the Involuntary Appointment List to represent one of the defendants in the *Agustin* case.

[The court's discussion of the witnesses other than Mr. Hagopian is omitted.]

[At the hearing, Mr. Hagopian testified that he] was admitted to The Florida Bar in 1993. The circuit court described Mr. Hagopian as "a former prosecutor who is now a prominent and successful solo practitioner. His Bradenton practice is about equally divided between civil and criminal cases[,] and his entire office staff consists of one secretary." Mr. Hagopian estimated his monthly overhead at $12,000.

Although Mr. Hagopian had not defended a RICO prosecution previously, he did not dispute his competency to handle such a case. Instead, as the circuit court noted, his objections to the appointment were "financial and ethical." Mr. Hagopian explained the vast scope of the State's case against Mr. Green with reference to a thirty-four-page discovery exhibit that he had received from the Statewide Prosecutor's Office:

> That is a listing ... of 382 witnesses; 216 law enforcement witnesses, 178 from Manatee County Sheriff, 36 from the Bradenton Police Department, one from [the Florida Department of Law Enforcement], one from the Palmetto Police Department, 155 so-called civilian witnesses, 11 codefendants. If my addition is correct, that's 382 witnesses that are listed on the discovery exhibit. There are also 176 separate law enforcement police reports listed in that discovery exhibit. There are nine predicate acts listed for my client alone, Mr. Green, and there are a total of [11] codefendants.

Based on the complexity of the case, Mr. Hagopian estimated that it would take a minimum of 500 hours to investigate and prepare the case. This estimate did not include trial time. He expected that a trial could consume an additional two to six weeks. In addition to the demands that the case would place on his time, Mr. Hagopian anticipated that it would be necessary for him to hire an additional secretary to handle the administrative details of the case. However, under the JAC contract, attorneys may not be reimbursed for staff time devoted to a case.

Mr. Hagopian testified in detail about the impact that a case of this magnitude would have on his solo law practice. First, the demands of the case on his time would be so great that he believed he would be unable to effectively represent his existing clients. This would require him to seek to withdraw from matters he had already accepted and to return some retainers. Second, Mr. Hagopian also expected that the demands of the case would make it impossible for him to accept any new business for a substantial period of time. As a result, Mr. Hagopian explained, "If I were forced against my will to properly defend this individual, it could possibly shut my practice down."

Mr. Hagopian testified concerning his fee arrangements if he were to handle a similar matter for a private client: "I wouldn't even touch this case for anything less than $100,000 down, up-front, plus a trial fee of at least $50,000, plus depending on how much more I dig into it, another [$]50 to 100,000 for the work done." In response to a question from the circuit court, Mr. Hagopian testified that no attorney competent to defend the case would be willing to do the work for $75 per hour or even $110 per hour. After considering all of the circumstances-including the JAC's payment policies and practices-Mr. Hagopian concluded: "[T]here's just no way that I could possibly do this."

. . .

III. THE ORDER UNDER REVIEW

At the conclusion of the hearing on Mr. Hagopian's motion to withdraw, the circuit court entered a fourteen-page, single-spaced order [denying Mr. Hagopian's motion]. . . . Although we quash the circuit court's order, we praise the circuit court for its careful and thoughtful approach to this very difficult matter. The circuit court's conscientious handling of Mr. Hagopian's motion to withdraw has made this court's task much easier. [Court's detailed discussion of the order is omitted, as are a summary of the parties' arguments and a general discussion of the law.]

VII. DISCUSSION

[Court's detailed discussion of the nature of this prosecution omitted.]

In considering the circuit court's denial of the motion to withdraw, we must put aside nostalgic conceptions of the practice of law in order to make a realistic assessment of what the involuntary appointment to Mr. Green's case actually meant for Mr. Hagopian and his solo law practice. For many people, lawyers and nonlawyers alike, the appointment of a lawyer from the private bar to represent an unpopular defendant accused of a serious crime brings to mind the image of Atticus Finch, the hero of Harper Lee's Pulitzer Prize-winning novel, *To Kill a Mockingbird*. Atticus Finch defended Tom Robinson, an indigent man charged with rape, "without mention of a fee, perpetuating in the eyes of readers everywhere the noble image of the lawyer dedicated to justice with no thought of . . . 'lucre.'" *Arnold v. Kemp,* 306 Ark. 294, 813 S.W.2d 770, 780 (1991) (Newbern, J., concurring). But the practice of law has changed drastically since the 1930s when the fictional Atticus Finch practiced law.

A number of factors have combined to increase the burden of involuntary appointments to criminal cases on members of the private bar in the modern era. First, the practice of criminal law has become increasingly complex and specialized. *See* Christopher D. Atwell, Comment, *Constitutional Challenges to Court Appointment: Increasing Recognition of an Unfair Burden,* 44 Sw. L.J. 1229, 1242–43 (1990). Second, as the practice of law has changed, costs for personnel, libraries, equipment, and general overhead have increased significantly. *See id.* at 1243. Lawyers have also become expected to use computer-assisted legal research to ensure that their research is complete and up-to-date, but the costs of this service can be significant. *See* Michael Whiteman, *The Impact of the Internet and Other Electronic Sources on an Attorney's Duty of Competence under the Rules of Professional Conduct,* 11 Alb. L.J. Sci. & Tech. 89, 103 (2000) (concluding that computer-assisted legal research "has become recognized as a standard research technique among judges, lawyers[,] and law students, with price being perhaps the only thing holding back all attorneys from utilizing it in their research"). The lawyer's need to generate fees to pay these costs makes it more difficult to undertake appointed work for a reduced fee or for no fee at all. Third, competition among lawyers for business has become intense. *See* Atwell, 44 Sw. L.J. at 1243. Such competition makes it more difficult for a lawyer with a small office to undertake appointed work and continue to sustain his or her law practice.

These factors formed the backdrop for the testimony in the circuit court. . . . After a thorough consideration of the record in this extraordinary case, we conclude that Mr. Hagopian established two grounds under rule 4–6.2 supporting his withdrawal from further representation of Mr. Green. The three grounds described in the rule constitute a nonexclusive list of "circumstances that would justify 'good cause' to avoid court-ordered appointments." *In re Amendments,* 573 So.2d at 806. First, under rule 4–6.2(a), a lawyer may seek to avoid appointment by a court to represent a person when "representing the client is likely to result in violation of the Rules of Professional Conduct or of the law." . . . .

. . .

Here, the undisputed evidence established that the involuntary appointment to Mr. Green's case would make it impossible for Mr. Hagopian to handle the legal business of his existing clients and provide them with competent representation. Such derelictions by Mr. Hagopian would result in the violation of rules 4–1.1, 4–1.2(a), 4–1.3, and 4–1.4. Under these circumstances, Mr. Hagopian established good cause for moving to withdraw from Mr. Green's case. *See In re Amendments,* 573 So.2d at 806; ABA Formal Op. 06–441 at 4–5.

Second, under rule 4–6.2(b), a lawyer may seek to avoid an appointment by a court to represent a person when "representing the client is likely to result in an unreasonable financial burden on the lawyer." Here, the undisputed evidence established that the extraordinary time and effort that would be required to represent Mr. Green effectively-together with the minimal and uncertain compensation offered-threatened Mr. Hagopian with the ruin of his successful solo law practice. By any standard, the involuntary appointment to Mr. Green's defense was an unreasonable financial burden for Mr. Hagopian.

. . .

To be sure, under the circuit court's order, Mr. Hagopian was to be compensated at a higher rate for indigent defense than section 27.5304(12)(d) authorized—$110 per hour instead of $75 per hour. Still, the $110 hourly rate was substantially below the market rate for a successful lawyer such as Mr. Hagopian. Moreover, the $110 per-hour rate would not make up for losses resulting from time and resources devoted to the representation for which no compensation would be paid.

Furthermore, a focus on the enhanced hourly rate proposed by the circuit court overlooks the cost to Mr. Hagopian of the preclusion of other employment caused by the involuntary appointment. Generally speaking, payment at a below-market hourly rate for the defense of an indigent accused will be adequate in a routine felony prosecution. A criminal defense attorney can accept a routine case for a reduced fee and fit it into the balance of his or her practice. But the vast scope of Mr. Green's case threatened to overwhelm Mr. Hagopian's small office, requiring him to devote substantially all of his productive time to the case for an extended period. Under these circumstances, the hourly rate of $110 is inadequate because it does not replace income lost due to Mr. Hagopian's inability to handle the business of private clients who pay the market rate for his services.

When a lawyer is required to work exclusively on a single client's business for an extended period of time, work for existing clients must generally be postponed or referred to other attorneys. While the lawyer is working exclusively on one client's affairs, it is difficult-if not impossible-to accept new business. For such work on behalf of a single client performed on a "crash basis," the lawyer ought to receive a premium above his or her normal fee to compensate for the disruption to the lawyer's practice. [citations omitted]. The circumstances of the involuntary appointment of Mr. Hagopian to Mr. Green's case turn basic law office economics on its head by requiring Mr. Hagopian to work for one client on a "crash basis" at a rate substantially below the market rate for similar services.

For these reasons, Mr. Hagopian established grounds for withdrawal from further representation of Mr. Green under rule 4–6.2. The circuit court departed from the essential requirements of the law in denying Mr. Hagopian's motion to withdraw.

Before concluding, we address two matters pertinent to the limits of our decision. First, we emphasize the extraordinary nature of this case. Our decision to grant the petition and quash the circuit court's order is based on the undisputed evidence presented in the circuit court concerning the unusual complexity of the RICO prosecution against Mr. Green and the ruinous effect the involuntary appointment will have on Mr. Hagopian's solo law practice. Our decision should not be read as granting lawyers a free pass to avoid unwanted appointments to represent indigent persons in more conventional prosecutions.

. . .

[W]e understand that our decision does not resolve the problem presented by this case. Mr. Green needs a lawyer, and he will not have the benefit of Mr. Hagopian's services. However, the only matter before us is whether the circuit court departed from the essential requirements of the law in denying Mr. Hagopian's motion to withdraw. We hold that it did, and we grant Mr. Hagopian's petition for writ of certiorari.

Unfortunately, no member of the criminal defense bar has volunteered to represent Mr. Green in the circuit court. At the conclusion of the hearing in the court below, the circuit judge remarked on the difficulties he had encountered in finding counsel for Mr. Green and expressed his hope that Mr. Green would soon have a lawyer. We appreciate the substantial efforts the circuit judge has made in this regard, and we share the concern he has expressed about finding counsel for Mr. Green.

VIII. CONCLUSION

For the reasons stated above, we grant the petition and quash the circuit court's order denying Mr. Hagopian's motion to withdraw.

* * *

E. RELYING ON NON-LAWYERS AND IMPROVED TECHNOLOGY TO REDUCE THE ACCESS TO JUSTICE GAP

New York Court of Appeals Chief Judge Jonathan Lippman said in 2014, "Even with whatever success we've had with public funding of legal services and pro bono work by lawyers, there is still a gaping hole in our system of providing legal services to the poor and people of limited means." *See* Robert Ambrogi, *Washington State Moves Around UPL, Using Legal Technicians to Help Close the Justice Gap*, ABA Journal (Jan. 1, 2015). One possible approach to increasing access to justice for those unable to afford a lawyer is to increase the involvement of non-lawyers in the legal process. Another might be to loosen the definition of the "practice of law," or to otherwise allow entrepreneurs to take advantage of technological advances and develop innovative ways of providing limited legal services. The following sections explore these possibilities.

1. RELYING ON NON-LAWYERS

In 2014, the ABA Task Force on the Future of Legal Education called on states to license "persons other than holders of a JD to deliver limited legal services." Since then, several jurisdictions have experimented with permitting non-lawyers to provide assistance in legal matters to individuals who might not otherwise receive any type of assistance. Jurisdictions have taken different approaches in this area.

a. Court Navigators

New York's Court Navigator Program began in 2014. The program provides assistance for unrepresented parties in landlord-tenant and consumer debt proceedings. The program's website describes the role that non-lawyer "Court Navigators" play in such proceedings:

> Specially trained and supervised non-lawyers, called Court Navigators, provide general information, written materials, and one-on-one assistance to eligible unrepresented litigants. In addition, Court Navigators provide moral support to litigants, help them access and complete court forms, assist them with keeping paperwork in order, in accessing interpreters and other services, explain what to expect and what the roles of each person is in the courtroom. Court Navigators are also permitted to accompany unrepresented litigants into the courtroom in the Bronx, New York, Kings, and Queens County Housing Court and Bronx Civil Court. While these Court Navigators cannot address the court on their own, they are able to respond to factual questions asked by the judge.

Court Navigators are prohibited from providing legal information and legal advice to the individuals they assist.

Similar programs now exist in numerous states. Like New York's program, most operate in a single locale or courthouse. According to one study, "[v]ery few programs have formal authorization to deploy legal navigators in the court, such as judicial order, regulation or statute." Mary E. McClymont, *Nonlawyer Navigators in State Courts: An Emerging Consensus* 14 (2019). Instead, they have been organized by a host of entities, ranging from state access to justice commissions to nonprofit organizations to concerned judges and court staff. Volunteers include college students, AmeriCorps members, and retirees.

* * *

Problem 5.5. As a member of your state's Access to Justice Commission, would you be in favor of a proposal to create a Legal Navigator program? Consider the following questions:

(a) Do you have concerns with allowing court navigators like those in New York to provide these sorts of services?

(b) Do these sorts of programs go far enough in terms of the services provided?

(c) What sort of training or education should court navigators have?

* * *

b. Limited License Legal Technicians (LLLTs) and Legal Paraprofessionals (LPs)

<u>Washington's Limited License Legal Technician Program</u>

Washington launched its LLLT program—the first of its kind in the U.S.—in 2015. Non-lawyer LLLTs could become licensed in the area of family law to "help clients prepare and review legal documents and forms; advise them on other documents they may need; explain legal procedures and proceedings, including procedures for service of process and filing of legal documents; and gather relevant facts and explain their significance." Ambrogi, *supra*. To become licensed as an LLLT, an applicant was required to have at least an associate's degree, complete 45 credit hours of specially-designed course work (including civil procedure, legal research and writing, professional responsibility, etc.), and complete 3,000 hours of substantive legal work under the supervision of an attorney. LLLTs were subject to a licensing and regulatory framework similar to that of lawyers.

But in 2020, the Washington Supreme Court voted to sunset the program. Part of the justification for the decision was the lack of interest. At the time, there were only 39 licensed LLLTs in the state. *See* Lyle Moran, *How the Washington Supreme Court's LLLT Program Met its Demise*, ABA Journal (July 9, 2020). Critics of the court's decision to sunset the program charged that the program was poorly promoted and that the licensing requirements were unduly burdensome. *See* Lacy Ashworth, *Nonlawyers in the Legal Profession: Lessons from the Sunsetting of Washington's LLLT Program*, 74 ARK. L. REV. 689, 726 (2022).

<u>Arizona's Legal Paraprofessionals Program</u>

According to a 2019 report by the Arizona Supreme Court Task Force on the Delivery of Legal Services, the access to justice gap in Arizona is particularly acute. In response, the Arizona Supreme Court approved a new LP program in February 2021. To become an LP, one must satisfy an educational requirement and pass an examination in one of the four designated practice areas: family law; limited jurisdiction civil cases; limited jurisdiction criminal cases where no jail time is involved; and state administrative law (where the administrative agency allows). The services an LP can provide are more extensive than those that LLLTs in

Washington had been authorized to perform. An Arizona LP can prepare and sign legal documents; provide specific advice, opinions, or recommendations about possible legal rights, remedies, defenses, options, or strategies; draft and file documents, including initiating and responding to actions, related motions, discovery, interim and final orders, and modification of orders, and arrange for service of legal documents; appear before a court or tribunal on behalf of a party, including mediation, arbitration, and settlement conferences where not prohibited by the rules and procedures of the forum; and negotiate legal rights or responsibilities for a specific person or entity. *See* Ariz. Code Jud. Admin. § 7–210(f).

Other states with similar programs include Utah,[1] Oregon,[2] and Minnesota.[3]

* * *

Problem 5.6. As a member of your state's Access to Justice Commission, would you be in favor of a proposal to create some type of LLLT or LP program? Consider the following questions:

(a) Should non-lawyers be permitted to provide the sorts of services that Arizona LPs provide? Or should only lawyers be permitted to perform these services?

(b) Assuming that a jurisdiction decides to adopt a program like those in Washington or Arizona, what kinds of services should the non-lawyers be permitted to provide?

(c) What sort of training or education should LLLTs or LPs have?

(d) Do you think there are enough people who would like to become an LLLT or LP to justify creating and sustaining such programs?

* * *

c. Non-Lawyer Ownership of Law Firms

Another suggestion for increasing access to justice is to permit non-lawyer ownership of law firms. While the ABA amended the rules to specifically address the provision of law-related services by lawyers, it has been unwilling to amend the rule to permit non-lawyer ownership of law firms. Rule 5.4 explicitly prohibits lawyers from sharing legal fees with non-lawyers (with limited exceptions) and forming partnerships involving the practice of law with non-lawyers. The concern underlying the rule is

---

[1] *See* Rule 14–802 of the Rules Governing the Utah State Bar.

[2] *See* Supreme Court of Oregon, Rules for Licensing Paralegals, https://www.osbar.org/lp.

[3] *See* Minnesota Supreme Court, Order Amending Rules Governing Legal Paraprofessional Pilot Project, https://www.ble.mn.gov/wp-content/uploads/2021/12/Administrative-Order-Amending-Rules-Governing-Legal-Paraprofessional-Pilot-Project.pdf.

"that if nonlawyers, who are not bound by the Rules of Professional Conduct, have a financial interest in a lawyer's profits, they might prioritize profit over the duties the lawyer owes to clients and adversely influence a lawyer's conduct." Stephen P. Younger, *The Pitfalls and False Promises of Nonlawyer Ownership of Law Firms*, 132 YALE L. FORUM 259, 261–62 (2022). The main arguments in favor of loosening the restrictions of Rule 5.4 and permitting some form of fee-sharing with non-lawyers or non-lawyer ownership of law firms are "(1) that nonlawyers will increase innovation in the practice of law and delivery of legal services; and (2) that this innovation will increase access to justice by expanding the amount and availability of low-cost legal services that will be available to indigent populations." *Id.* at 275.

Some states have already amended their versions of Rule 5.4 in line with these sort of proposals. In August 2020, the Arizona Bar eliminated its version of Rule 5.4 to allow for the licensing of Alternate Business Structures that are partially owned by non-lawyers but that provide legal services. In February 2021, California amended its version of Rule 5.4 to facilitate greater cooperation (and fee-sharing) with non-profit organizations. The new rule allows a law firm to share or pay a non-court-awarded legal fee with a non-profit organization where the fee arises from a settlement or other resolution of a matter that the non-profit "employed, retained, recommended, or facilitated employment of the lawyer or law firm in the matter provided."

* * *

2. TECHNOLOGICAL INNOVATION

N.C. GENERAL STATUTES § 84–2.2.
EXEMPTION AND ADDITIONAL REQUIREMENTS FOR WEB SITE PROVIDERS

(a) The practice of law, including the giving of legal advice, as defined by G.S. 84–2.1 does not include the operation of a Web site by a provider that offers consumers access to interactive software that generates a legal document based on the consumer's answers to questions presented by the software, provided that all of the following are satisfied:

(1) The consumer is provided a means to see the blank template or the final, completed document before finalizing a purchase of that document.

(2) An attorney licensed to practice law in the State of North Carolina has reviewed each blank template offered to North Carolina consumers, including each and every potential part thereof that may appear in the completed document. The name and address of each reviewing attorney

must be kept on file by the provider and provided to the consumer upon written request.

(3) The provider must communicate to the consumer that the forms or templates are not a substitute for the advice or services of an attorney.

(4) The provider discloses its legal name and physical location and address to the consumer.

(5) The provider does not disclaim any warranties or liability and does not limit the recovery of damages or other remedies by the consumer.

(6) The provider does not require the consumer to agree to jurisdiction or venue in any state other than North Carolina for the resolution of disputes between the provider and the consumer.

(7) The provider must have a consumer satisfaction process. All consumer concerns involving the unauthorized practice of law made to the provider shall be referred to the North Carolina State Bar. The consumer satisfaction process must be conspicuously displayed on the provider's Web site.

(b) A Web site provider subject to this section shall register with the North Carolina State Bar prior to commencing operation in the State and shall renew its registration with the State Bar annually. The State Bar may not refuse registration.

(c) Each Web site provider subject to this section shall pay an initial registration fee in an amount not to exceed one hundred dollars ($100.00) and an annual renewal fee in an amount not to exceed fifty dollars ($50.00). (2016–60, s. 2.).

* * *

BENJAMIN H. BARTON & DEBORAH L. RHODE, *ACCESS TO JUSTICE AND ROUTINE LEGAL SERVICES: NEW TECHNOLOGIES MEET BAR REGULATORS*
70 HASTINGS L.J. 955 (2019)

We are in the early stages of a technological revolution in legal services. Technology is displacing lawyers in a wide array of tasks such as document drafting, review, and assembly, and is also reshaping the way that lawyers find clients and deliver assistance. For most consumers, these are welcome developments. Such innovations generally reduce costs and increase both accessibility and efficiency. The potential gains are particularly great for low-and middle-income consumers, who cannot afford to address a vast array of basic, often urgent, legal needs. Yet for lawyers, the consequences of technology have been more mixed. Many feel that their professional independence and livelihoods are threatened by the growth of online forms, computerized algorithms, and price competition with internet providers. Responding to these concerns, bar regulators have often fought back through ethics rulings that attempt to rein in organizations such as LegalZoom, Rocket Lawyer, and Avvo Legal Services.

. . .

Technology has ... created new ways of retaining [attorneys]. LegalZoom and Rocket Lawyer both sell monthly plans for legal advice from attorneys. It's Over Easy is a website that offers couples several packages of divorce services. The basic plan offers downloadable forms and spousal support calculators, and more expensive plans serve papers and offer telephone and email consultations. The TIME's UP Legal Defense Fund, handled by the National Women's Law Center, is an online matching service that pairs lawyers with individuals seeking assistance for sexual harassment and discrimination. Avvo Legal Services is also a matching program that s[ells] basic legal services such as divorces, wills, and incorporations for a flat fee. At first glance, this may not appear all that innovative. Low, flat fees for routine services are the hallmark of LegalZoom and Rocket Lawyer. Avvo Legal Services' innovation was that the customers hire a licensed lawyer to do the work, rather than proceeding through a computer-driven forms program.

. . .

One key benefit of new technologies is that they enhance providers' ability to differentiate their offerings. So, if customers want a true do-it-yourself experience of legal services, they can buy a form through LegalZoom and fill it out themselves. If they want somewhat more guidance, they can opt for an interactive program that asks questions and then generates completed forms. If a LegalZoom or Rocket Lawyer client wants some legal advice to go with their forms they can pay for the subscription service, and an It's Over Easy client can buy a more expensive package.

If consumers want to pay a flat fee for more traditional legal services, however, there were few options before the launch of Avvo Legal Services. Avvo hoped that its matching service would demystify the process and help lawyers and clients find each other with minimal transaction costs and a fixed price point that works for both.

There are some further upsides for consumers from this tech explosion. First, when a service or product is commoditized and sold on the Internet, the price of that service tends to drop, sometimes dramatically. This is of particular benefit in the legal services market for low- and middle-income Americans, which, as noted earlier, is characterized by pervasive unmet needs. Second, the Internet offers greater transparency and information in a market that has lacked both for years. One reason that consumers traditionally relied so heavily on the recommendations of friends or family in hiring lawyers was that it was difficult to find more credible information concerning quality. Bar-run referral services did not rate lawyers. Nor did bar regulatory authorities disclose lawyer disciplinary and malpractice records in a form accessible to consumers. One of Avvo's greatest contributions to the market for legal services is its national data bank on lawyer disciplinary actions, as well as its platform for client reviews and its own quality rating.

The impact of these technologies on lawyers is more mixed. Some experts, including Great Britain's leading authority Richard Susskind, believe that technologies will eventually displace attorneys in any context where services can be routinized and commodified. Other commentators are less pessimistic. They believe that technology has the potential to bring new consumers into the market by making services more accessible and affordable. In their view, a growing market and more demand for services would compensate for the inevitable fall in prices. Many commentators similarly argue that technological innovation and standardization can help lawyers increase profits by reducing costs. A wide array of research indicates that solo and small practitioners are spending too much time on running their businesses and seeking clients. Technology can help streamline these processes as well as relieve lawyers from some of the most routine, mind-numbing aspects of legal practice.

The rank and file of the profession, however, has not always been eager to embrace these opportunities. At first, this allowed early non-lawyer adopters to capitalize on technological innovations without attracting competition or regulatory attention. For example, bar regulators did not get around to trying to stem LegalZoom until 2007, long after the company was already well known and hard to dislodge. This late start may help explain why the organized bar has largely failed in its efforts to curtail LegalZoom's online forms business.

By contrast, bar regulators immediately sought to ban lawyers from participating in the new Avvo Legal Services Plan, which is part of why they succeeded in killing it. By Summer 2018, ethics committees in Illinois, Indiana, New Jersey, New York, Ohio, Pennsylvania, South Carolina, Utah, and Virginia had all issued opinions condemning certain aspects of the plan. The collective weight of these opinions helped convince Avvo's new parent company to terminate its Legal Services Plan. There was an irony to this result—bar regulators have been unable to restrict many of the technological innovations that are in direct competition with lawyers, including computerized forms and free legal advice. Instead, regulatory authorities are attempting to curtail a technology that seeks to bring consumers and lawyers together (albeit at a much lower price), which could benefit under-employed tech-savvy practitioners.

* * *

Pros and Cons. As a member of your state's Access to Justice Commission, would you oppose the adoption of a statute like North Carolina's? What would be your suggestion regarding the Commission's ultimate position when it comes to relying upon technology to close the access to justice gap? Consider the following questions:

(a) If the services provided by LegalZoom, Rocket Lawyer, etc. do not amount to the practice of law, they come right up to that line. Do you have concerns with permitting these sorts of entities provide the services they do?

(b) Do the potential benefits in terms of expanding access to justice outweigh any potential concerns you might have?

(c) How sympathetic are you to the concerns of some lawyers that technological innovations may cut into their profits? How valid are those concerns?

Profile of Attorney Professionalism. Bill Colby was a young attorney when he accepted a pro bono case that would change the law, his clients' lives, and his own life.

It was 1987 when a partner in Bill Colby's law firm asked him to consider representing the Cruzan family in a dispute with the State of Missouri. In 1983, the Cruzans' daughter, Nancy, had been in a car accident that left her in a coma. Shortly after the accident—and before anyone understood the extent of Nancy's injuries—the Cruzans agreed to a medical procedure to insert a feeding tube. Later, doctors determined that Nancy had no hope of recovery and diagnosed her condition as a "persistent vegetative state." Once they understood that Nancy would never recover, the family asked for the feeding tube to be removed. The family agonized over the decision, but felt certain it would be Nancy's wish. The state-run hospital refused to remove Nancy's feeding tube without a court order. Unable to afford a lawyer, the Cruzans searched for an attorney willing to handle the case free of charge.

When he agreed to accept the case, Bill Colby expected he would be handling a one-day trial in probate court in southwestern Missouri. Instead, for four years, he represented the Cruzan family in numerous courts, including the U.S. Supreme Court.

In his book *Long Goodbye: The Deaths of Nancy Cruzan*, Bill Colby tells the story of the Cruzan family's case. He describes the long hours he worked on the case, the weight of being at the center of politically charged litigation, and the professional and personal relationship he developed with the Cruzan family. Though he was not paid for his work, Bill Colby grew as a lawyer during the case, shaped the law concerning a patient's right to die in the United States, and zealously represented the Cruzan family. WILLIAM H. COLBY, LONG GOODBYE: THE DEATHS OF NANCY CRUZAN (2002).

PART 2

ATTRACTING CLIENTS

■ ■ ■

Lawyers need clients. Most new lawyers will go to work as an employee for a firm or organization that provides its newer lawyers with clients. This relationship imposes various responsibilities on both sides. Chapter 6 addresses the rights and responsibilities of lawyer in relation to other individuals within a law office. Some new lawyers will choose to hang out their own shingle and start a solo or small firm private practice. To do this, they will need to attract clients. Even lawyers who work in larger firms are often expected to develop a client base. So, Chapters 7 and 8 focus on the legal rules regarding lawyer advertising and solicitation of clients.

CHAPTER 6

PRACTICING IN A LAW FIRM

∎ ∎ ∎

Chapter Hypothetical. The law firm of Palsgraf & Pennoyer has over 200 attorneys, with offices in several different cities. The firm has different practice groups (business, litigation, etc.), headed up by a partner who serves as the leader of the practice group. A management committee, which consists of several firm partners, has primary authority for the administration of the firm, including setting firm policies. The firm is currently dealing with several personnel issues involving some of its attorneys and support staff.

While some lawyers will set up their own shops after being admitted to the practice of law in a jurisdiction, the vast majority will go to work for an employer. Although the *Model Rules* use the terms "firm" or "law firm" to describe the typical legal employer, the Terminology section makes clear that those terms cover not just traditional law firms but other types of law offices as well, including the office of a prosecutor or public defender, "a legal service organization or the legal department of a corporation or other organization." Model Rule 1.0(c). Every lawyer in a firm—whether a first-year associate, a managing partner, or the owner of the firm—has rights and responsibilities in relation to other individuals within the firm. This chapter examines some of those rights and responsibilities.

* * *

A. PRACTICING LAW AS A MEMBER OF A LAW FIRM

One's rights and responsibilities as a member of a firm may depend on the role that one plays within the firm. The responsibilities of a partner or person in a similar managerial role may be different than those of an associate or other non-manager. The following section explores how one's role within a law office may shape one's ethical obligations.

1. THE ORGANIZATIONAL STRUCTURE OF LAW FIRMS

Within a traditional law firm, the management of the firm is left to the partners. However, partners are not necessarily all created equal. Many firms have created a distinction between equity partners (or profit-sharing partners) and non-equity partners (or income partners), who are paid a salary from the firm's profits instead of sharing in the firm's profits. Non-equity partners frequently do not participate in the governance of the firm. Robert W. Hillman, *Law, Culture, and the Lore of Partnership: Of Entrepreneurs, Accountability, and the Evolving Status of Partners*, 40 WAKE FOREST L. REV. 793, 821 (2005). Many firms delegate the management of the firm's business to an individual or group of individuals, who may have few, if any, other duties within the firm. Elizabeth Chambliss, *The Nirvana Fallacy in Law Firm Regulation Debates*, 33 FORDHAM URB. L.J. 119, 127 (2005).

A second category of lawyer in a traditional law firm is the associate. Law firm associates are, of course, employees of the firm. But again, as a practical matter, there may be important distinctions among associates. For example, associates on the cusp of partnership may have supervisory authority over other associates in a given matter. A third category of law firm lawyer in a traditional law firm is the lawyer who is "of counsel." This term can potentially apply to a variety of lawyers, including a lawyer who practices in association with a firm but on a part-time basis, a retired partner, or a firm lawyer who occupies a position in between that of partner and associate with no expectation of one day becoming partner. But, as ABA Formal Ethics Opinion 90–357 explains, the "core characteristic" of an "of counsel" relationship with a firm is a " 'close, regular, personal relationship'; but a relationship which is neither that of a partner (or its equivalent, a principal of a professional corporation), with the shared liability and/or managerial responsibility implied by that term; nor, on the other hand, the status ordinarily conveyed by the term 'associate,' which is to say a junior non-partner lawyer, regularly employed by the firm."

2. THE ETHICAL OBLIGATIONS OF PARTNERS, MANAGERS, AND SUPERVISORY LAWYERS

a. Rule 5.1(a): Firm Lawyers with Managerial Authority

Rule 5.1(a) envisions a situation in which law firm partners in a traditional law firm and those with comparable managerial authority in other organizations will establish "ethical infrastructures" that will, among other things, help other firm lawyers resolve any ethical dilemmas they may come across. Ted Schneyer, *Professional Discipline for Law Firms?*, 77 CORNELL L. REV. 1, 10 (1991). According to Professor Schneyer, "a law firm's organization, policies, and operating procedures ... may have at least as much to do with causing and avoiding unjustified harm as do the individual values and practice skills of [the firm's] lawyers." *Id.* Thus, Comment [2] to Model Rule 5.1 provides that a lawyer with managerial authority over the professional work of a firm must make "reasonable efforts to establish internal policies and procedures designed to provide reasonable assurance that all lawyers in the firm will conform to the Rules of Professional Conduct." Comment [3] lists a number of examples of the types of internal policies and procedures that a firm might utilize to help ensure that its lawyers are practicing in an ethical manner, including systems designed to check for conflicts of interest.

The following case provides an example of some of the potential dangers of not having an effective ethical infrastructure in place.

IN RE DICKENS
174 A.3d 283 (D.C. 2017)

REID, SENIOR JUDGE:

This attorney disciplinary case involves the main partner in a small law firm, respondent Deborah Luxenberg, and an attorney, respondent Dorrance Dickens, who started at the firm as a law clerk but became an associate and eventually a partner. Disciplinary Counsel charged Ms. Luxenberg with several violations of the District of Columbia Rules of Professional Conduct after Mr. Dickens allegedly stole at least $1,434,298.50 from three estates, including that of Ms. Luxenberg's client, Michelle Seltzer. Following his theft, Mr. Dickens fled to an island outside of the United States.

. . .

In 1998, the firm incorporated in Maryland as Luxenberg and Johnson, and in 2003, when Mr. Dickens became a partner, the firm changed its name to Luxenberg, Johnson and Dickens. The firm had no partnership agreement but Ms. Luxenberg always retained a 52% interest in the firm. Ms. Luxenberg's practice has been devoted to family matters such as divorce and custody. Although she has never been the managing partner of the firm, she decided which clients the firm would represent and who would handle the client matters. Mr. Johnson also had a family law practice, and he took on cases in other areas of the law.

. . .

In early 2007, Ms. Luxenberg and Mr. Johnson decided to move the main office of the firm from the District of Columbia to Maryland, and to maintain satellite offices in the District and Virginia. By this time Mr. Johnson's law practice was limited and his time centered on administration of the firm. Even though he was not a member of the Virginia Bar and Ms. Luxenberg had knowledge of that fact, Mr. Dickens worked out of the

Virginia office that the firm leased in February 2007; the lease was signed by Mr. Dickens but the firm paid the rent for several months before delegating that responsibility to Mr. Dickens.

The management of the small firm was not rigorous after the 2007 move of the main office to Maryland and Mr. Dickens' relocation to the Virginia office. Although the firm appears to have some policies and procedures to ensure compliance with ethical obligations, these were either loosely followed or not enforced with respect to matters handled by Mr. Dickens. Generally, the firm held biweekly staff meetings during which open cases were reviewed; however, Mr. Dickens' attendance at these meetings decreased significantly, his participation by phone was sporadic, and there were occasions on which he simply could not be reached. Moreover, despite the firm's record-keeping policies, Mr. Dickens failed to execute retainer agreements with clients that he represented, maintain proper billing records, and save electronic client documents to the firm's computer server. Even when the firm discovered that Mr. Dickens had clients for whom the main office had no records, or when the firm received checks, sometimes for substantial amounts of money, without documentation ... the firm made little or no effort to ensure that Mr. Dickens followed its policies and procedures, as well as the ethical rules of the legal profession.

[Sometime in early 2009, Mr. Dickens advised Ms. Luxenberg that he planned to leave the firm to spend time on other interests, but that he could still handle some legal matters. Over the course of the next two years, Dickens was in and out of contact with the firm and its clients. During this time, he also allegedly stole the money in question. Disciplinary counsel charged Luxenberg with numerous rule violations, including a violation of Rule 5.1(a).]

With respect to Rule 5.1(a), Ms. Luxenberg first contends that "Disciplinary Counsel failed to prove by clear and convincing evidence that [Ms.] Luxenberg had sufficient managerial authority within her [f]irm to place her in charge of putting in place policies and procedures to ensure that [Mr.] Dickens, a named partner in the [f]irm, complied with the Rules of Professional Conduct." Disciplinary Counsel supports the finding of the Hearing Committee and the Board that Rule 5.1(a) applies to Ms. Luxenberg and that she violated that rule. Specifically, Disciplinary Counsel maintains that Ms. Luxenberg had managerial authority within the firm because "the Board noted [her] roles as founder, decision-maker, and business-generator, her controlling interest and her husband's low practice profile," all of which "established her as a partner and lawyer with managerial authority in the firm, even if she called her husband 'managing partner.'"

The plain words of Rule 5.1(a) assign "partners" and lawyers who have "managerial authority in a law firm" the responsibility of making "reasonable efforts to ensure" that the firm's lawyers "conform to the Rules of Professional Conduct." District of Columbia Rules of Professional Conduct, Rule 5.1(a), and Comment [1]. Rule 5.1(a) of the American Bar Association (ABA) *Model Rules of Professional Conduct* is virtually the same as the District's Rule 5.1(a), and Comment [1] to the rule states that "Paragraph (a) applies to lawyers who have managerial authority over the professional work of a firm." However, the comment further specifies that "[t]his includes members of a partnership." ABA *Model Rules of Professional Conduct*, Rule 5.1(a), and Comment [1]; *see also* Center for Professional Responsibility, ABA, *Annotated Model Rules of Professional Conduct*, 443 (5th ed. 2003).

Ms. Luxenberg argues that "there are no cases [in this jurisdiction] in which this [c]ourt sanctioned a partner under Rule 5.1(a) for the actions of *another partner*" (emphasis in original). She maintains that our "cases discussing Rule 5.1 deal exclusively with situations in which the respondent has supervisory control within the firm or over the offending attorney." She specifically cites *In re Robinson*, 74 A.3d 688 (D.C. 2013), a case involving a partner who hired his son-in-law, also an attorney, to supervise the firm's escrow account; this court agreed with the Board's finding that the partner "fail[ed] to ensure firm compliance with the Rules of Professional Conduct" because he ignored warning signs and "was on notice that matters relating to the trust account were awry" due to two overdrafts on the account. . . .

In the factual context of this case, however, we agree with the Board that Rule 5.1(a) applies to Ms. Luxenberg. The Hearing Committee found that she was the majority owner (52%) of Luxenberg, Johnson & Dickens, and she generally made the decisions as to what clients the firm would represent and who would handle the client matters. Indeed, she identified and introduced Mr. Dickens to Ms. Seltzer as the firm lawyer who would handle Ms. Seltzer's 2004 request, and later her 2009 request.

Despite Ms. Luxenberg's effort to distance herself from Mr. Dickens with respect to Ms. Seltzer's trusts and estates matter, it is clear that Mr. Dickens considered himself a member of the Luxenberg firm; indeed, he clearly identified himself in the 2009 trust document as "Dorrance D. Dickens, trustee, of Luxenberg, Johnson and Dickens, P.C." Ms. Luxenberg's actions also reflected her belief that Mr. Dickens was still a member of the Luxenberg firm; she sent communications to him at the firm's Virginia satellite office, and continued efforts to reach Mr. Dickens through the administrator of the firm's Virginia office. Moreover, Ms. Luxenberg had made clear to Mr. Dickens in 2009, in writing, that she would continue to be "involved" in the Seltzer matter. In short, the record contains substantial evidence that even though Ms. Luxenberg did not have the title of managing partner, she was a "partner" with "managerial authority" during the time the firm handled Ms. Seltzer's trusts and estates matter; therefore, she fell under the coverage of Rule 5.1(a).

While the firm had some policies and practices that would assure its lawyers conformed to the Rules of Professional Conduct, Ms. Luxenberg did not make "reasonable efforts" to make certain these policies and procedures actually were in effect and followed. Notably, she took no action when Mr. Dickens began to and continued to miss firm meetings during which firm client matters were reviewed, and despite the firm's policy that all client records should be sent to the firm's main files, she did not make "reasonable efforts" to ensure Mr. Dickens' compliance with the policy after he did not respond to repeated requests for the Seltzer documents, or to Ms. Luxenberg's admonition about the missing documents in a tense phone call around September 2009, prior to the execution of the 2009 trust document.

... Ms. Luxenberg "was on notice that matters relating to [Ms. Seltzer's] trust ... were awry." *In re Robinson*, 74 A.3d at 696. Ms. Luxenberg may have "assume[d]" that Mr. Dickens would follow the Rules of Professional Conduct, Rule 5.1(a), Comment [3], but she did not make "reasonable efforts" to ensure that Mr. Dickens' behavior conformed to the Rules of Professional Conduct. Since the firm was very small initially, informal enforcement of policies and procedures and "occasional admonition ordinarily might be sufficient," Rule 5.1(a), Comment [3]. However, as we asserted in *In re Robinson*, once warning signs appeared, suggesting clear problems regarding ethical behavior, informal enforcement and occasional admonition no longer sufficed.

Similar conclusions were reached in *Attorney Grievance Comm'n of Maryland v. Kimmel*, 405 Md. 647, 955 A.2d 269 (Md. 2008) and *In re Fonte*, 75 A.D.3d 199, 905 N.Y.S.2d 173 (2010). In *Kimmel*, ... [we] pointed out that periodic review ordinarily is sufficient for a small firm with experienced attorneys, but that "other or different circumstances may indicate the need for 'more elaborate' supervisory measures." One of the differences is the "[p]hysical isolation of an attorney from peers," necessitating "a heightened need to adapt supervisory strategies [or periodic review] to ensure compliance with the Rules."

Here, as of 2007, not only was Mr. Dickens in a new office in a jurisdiction where he was not licensed to practice law, Virginia, but he also decreased his attendance at meetings in the firm's Maryland office, a jurisdiction in which he was also not licensed to practice law. He was no longer in the same office with his mentors and partners. Particularly when warning signs appeared that things definitely were not in order with respect to Mr. Dickens' work on the Seltzer trusts and estates matter, as a partner with managerial authority over the Seltzer matter, Ms. Luxenberg should have instituted periodic reviews and intervened to make certain that Mr. Dickens was doing the Seltzer work in a timely manner and was conforming to the Rules of Professional Conduct in his handling of the Seltzer trust assets. As the court said in *In re Fonte, supra*, "[i]n the face of . . . warning [signs], [especially of improper handling of trust assets], greater oversight and immediate intervention was warranted." In sum, the record contains substantial evidence to support the Board's finding and conclusion that Ms. Luxenberg violated Rule 5.1(a).

[Based on this and other rule violations, Luxenberg was suspended from the practice of law for six months.]

* * *

b. Rule 5.1(b): Firm Lawyers with Supervisory Authority

Read Rule 5.1(b) and then consider the following problem:

Problem 6.1. Bob is a senior associate at the firm, and Carol is a newer associate. Bob has been assigned responsibility for supervising the work of Carol on a particular matter.

(a) Bob gave Carol instructions about how to proceed on the matter but has not responded to any of her emails asking for clarification. Is Bob subject to discipline even though he is not a partner at the firm?

(b) When Bob finally checks in with Carol, he learns that several firm partners have dumped a number of big assignments on Carol. As a result of her caseload, Carol is not able to devote sufficient time to the matter on which she is working with Bob. What, if anything, is Bob's responsibility under Rule 5.1(b)? *See* ABA Formal Op. No. 06–441.

* * *

c. Rule 5.1(c): Responsibility for Another Lawyer's Violation of the Rules

Under Rule 5.1(c), a lawyer may face discipline, in part, based on the actions of another lawyer. Read the Rule and Comments [4] and [5] and then consider the following problem:

Problem 6.2. Deborah is a partner at the firm and Dorrance is a senior associate. Deborah does mostly estate planning for wealthy clients, and Dorrance does much of his work under Deborah's supervision.

(a) Dorrance's behavior grew somewhat erratic over the course of several months. He was frequently out of the office and unreachable by phone. He seemed evasive about the status of several client matters. Any attorney in Deborah's position who was properly supervising Dorrance would have been able to tell that Dorrance was engaged in some type of impropriety regarding his client's estates. But Deborah says she never actually knew until Dorrance disappeared with a large sum of money that he had stolen from his clients. Is Deborah subject to discipline under Rule 5.1(c)(2)?

(b) Several clients who were the victims of Dorrance's crimes reached out to Deborah to inquire about apparent financial irregularities associated with trusts in their name. By this point, Deborah was generally aware of what Dorrance had done, but the clients were not. In an effort to buy more time to figure out the extent of Dorrance's crimes, Deborah told the clients that she was sure there was a reasonable explanation for the irregularities and that she would look into it. Is Deborah subject to discipline under Rule 5.1(c)(1)?

* * *

d. Rule 5.3: Responsibilities Regarding Non-Lawyer Assistants

Rule 5.3 largely tracks Rule 5.1. But, instead of applying to a lawyer's responsibilities regarding other lawyers in the firm, Rule 5.3 applies to a lawyer's responsibilities regarding non-lawyers associated with the firm. Read the rule and its comments and then consider the following problem:

Problem 6.3. Charles is of counsel at Palsgraf & Pennoyer. He recently accepted an executive position with the state bar that requires him to travel a good bit. He knew he would be gone for two weeks on various trips, so he instructed the paralegal he works with, Carlie, to help with his ongoing medical malpractice matters. With Charles' knowledge, Carlie drafted demand letters to defendants, negotiated settlements with insurance carriers, communicated with and advised clients, and dealt with medical providers. Is Charles subject to discipline under Rule 5.3?

* * *

3. THE ETHICAL OBLIGATIONS OF "SUBORDINATE" LAWYERS

Rule 5.2 addresses the responsibilities of "subordinate" lawyers. The rule does at least two important things. First, Rule 5.2(a) makes clear that a lawyer who acts under the direction of another lawyer remains subject to discipline if the action amounts to a violation of the rule. In other words, a subordinate lawyer generally cannot avoid professional discipline by simply claiming, "I just did what I was told." Second, Rule 5.2(b) provides a limited exception for a subordinate lawyer who acts in accordance with a supervisor's reasonable resolution of an arguable question of professional duty. However, there are few reported decisions in which subordinate attorneys have successfully asserted Rule 5.2(b)'s safe harbor. *See, e.g., In re Kelley's Case,* 627 A.2d 597, 600 (N.H. 1993) (rejecting associate's Rule 5.2(b) defense in conflict of interest case because "there could have been no 'reasonable' resolution of an 'arguable' question of duty"); *see also* DOUGLAS R. RICHMOND, PROFESSIONAL RESPONSIBILITIES OF LAW FIRM ASSOCIATES 199 (2007) (detailing cases).

The most common type of disciplinary case involving Rule 5.2 is the situation in which a subordinate lawyer receives inadequate supervision and fails to act competently in representing a client. Courts have generally not been receptive to the idea that Rule 5.2(b)'s safe harbor shields the lawyer from professional discipline in such cases. Another situation that arises under Rule 5.2 is when a subordinate lawyer is aware of misconduct on the part of other lawyers in the firm and either remains silent about it or perhaps even participates in the misconduct. The following case is an extreme example of this scenario.

KENTUCKY BAR ASS'N V. HELMERS
353 S.W.3d 599 (Ky. 2011)

[David L. Helmers worked for the law firm of Gallion, Baker, and Bray as a clerk during law school and subsequently as an associate. He worked almost exclusively on researching potential claims for injuries arising from the use of the diet drug Fen-Phen. The firm filed a class action on behalf of plaintiffs who alleged they were injured by Fen-Phen against the defendant American Home Products (AHP). This case is referred to as the *Guard* case. As a result of a settlement of the *Guard* case, AHP awarded $200,000,000 to the plaintiffs. How the settlement award would be allocated among the various plaintiffs was the responsibility of their attorneys, including Helmers. One of Helmers' supervisors, Gallion, instructed Helmers to meet with some of the plaintiffs regarding the settlement.]

When meeting with the individual clients, Respondent presented a proposed settlement amount, and led the client to believe that the settlement award offer came straight from AHP. He did not inform them that their attorneys (including himself) had decided how much their individual monetary award would be, that the individual client's case was just one of 440 cases that had been settled for an aggregate sum of $200,000,000.00 . . . or that $7,500,000 of the settlement fund was being held to indemnify AHP against certain other claims.

Furthermore, Respondent had been instructed by the other attorneys to offer each client an amount substantially below the amount assigned to that client in the predetermined allocations that AHP had approved. If the client refused the initial offer, he or she was presented with a larger offer at a later date. This continued until the client agreed to the settlement, and simulated from the client's perspective, an actual settlement negotiation with AHP. The clients were never informed by Respondent that they could entirely refuse the offer and were not provided copies of the documents they signed. Additionally, Respondent told many of the clients that if they spoke to others about their settlement award, they could face a penalty assessment of $100,000.

Apparently, Gallion had misinformed [his partner] Mills about the true terms of the settlement, and in early 2002, Mills discovered that the total settlement award was $200,000,000 and not $150,000,000 as Gallion had told him. To assuage Mills, Gallion instructed Respondent to make a second distribution of settlement money to the clients. Respondent set up meetings with the clients he had previously met with and presented them a letter stating that the trial court had authorized a second distribution. This letter also revealed to clients for the first time that an unspecified amount was being held in escrow to indemnify certain third parties, if necessary. Respondent also asked if the plaintiffs would object if some of the undistributed award money was given to charity. A donation to the "Kentucky Fund for Healthy Living, Inc." in the amount of $20,000,000 was made. [The paid Board of Directors for this organization included Gallion and two of the other partners in the firm. Gallion and another partner in the firm, Cunningham, were eventually sentenced to 20 years in prison for diverting funds from the settlement.]

Because of their actions in the *Guard* case, most of the attorneys with whom Respondent worked have been disbarred. [Helmers was charged with, among other violations of the rules, violating Kentucky's version of Rule 5.2(a) "by violating Rules of Professional Conduct in part at the direction of Gallion" and two other lawyers.]

Respondent has not filed a notice with this Court to review the Board's decision, and we do not elect to review the decision of the Board under SCR 3.370(8). We have, however, taken note of the mitigating circumstances that prompted the Trial Commissioner to recommend a lesser punishment. We are aware that Respondent has had no other disciplinary issues raised against him. We are aware that Respondent was a young law student when he first began working for Gallion, and that Gallion was then a well-regarded and reputable attorney. We are aware that as a new attorney working with Gallion, Cunningham, and Mills, Respondent was inexperienced, impressionable, and may have been influenced, and perhaps even led astray, by those more seasoned lawyers. But, we cannot ignore the fact it takes no technical expertise or experience in the settling of class action lawsuits, or any sophisticated understanding of the rules of ethics to know that Respondent's course of conduct, personally and directly deceiving his clients, some of whom had been egregiously injured, was wrong. That he did so at the direction of his employer does not permit us to overlook the serious deficiency in character revealed by the facts before us.

In light of the serious ethical violations committed by Respondent, permanent disbarment from the practice of law in Kentucky is reasonable. The decision of the Board is hereby adopted under SCR 3.370(10).

* * *

Behavioral Legal Ethics and *Helmers*. If Helmers knew that his conduct was so obviously wrong, why did he do it? Most professional misconduct is not nearly as egregious, but there are numerous examples of lawyers turning a blind eye to or participating in what they had to have known was professional misconduct on the part of their colleagues. Using social psychology, Law Professor Andrew Perlman has argued that as a result of Rule 5.2(b)'s "safe harbor," subordinate lawyers are in an opportune situation to ignore their own reasoned analysis and accept the instruction of a superior attorney. Factors such as hierarchal pressure and superior experience of a senior attorney, the threat of losing a job if instructions are not followed, and the mantra of "zealous representation" on behalf of clients all encourage (or at least justify) a subordinate lawyer to follow a questionable course of action while erroneously expecting shelter under Rule 5.2(b). Andrew M. Perlman, *Unethical Obedience by Subordinate Attorneys: Lessons from Social Psychology*, 36 HOFSTRA L. REV. 451 (2007).

Wrongful Discharge Claims. Sometimes a subordinate lawyer declines to go along with another lawyer's unethical course of action. In others, the subordinate lawyer may raise concerns about the conduct internally within the firm or make a report to disciplinary authorities pursuant to Rule 8.3(a) about the other lawyer's misconduct. In doing so, the subordinate runs the risk that the other lawyer or the firm will retaliate against the subordinate lawyer. Under the at-will employment rule, employers are generally free to fire their employees for any reason. However, nearly every jurisdiction has recognized an exception to the rule in the form of a tort claim of wrongful (or retaliatory) discharge where the firing threatens some important public policy. The majority of courts have been willing to recognize such claims brought by lawyers who are fired after complying with their ethical obligations under Rule 8.3(a). *See* Alex B. Long, *Retaliatory Discharge and the Ethical Rules Governing Attorneys*, 79 U. COLO. L. REV. 1043, 1048 (2008). *But see, e.g., Jacobson v. Knepper & Moga, P.C.*, 706 N.E.2d 491 (Ill. 1998) (refusing to recognize claim).

* * *

B. DISCRIMINATION, DIVERSITY, AND INCLUSION IN LAW FIRMS

According to the National Association for Law Placement (NALP), women and people of color have made "incremental progress in representation at major U.S. law firms." NALP, *2021 Report on Diversity in U.S. Law Firms*. But there remain significant areas of underrepresentation. For example, while representation of associates of color rose to around 27% in 2021, the percentage of Black or African-American associates was only slightly above 5%. Women made up close to 26% of all firm partners, and people of color made up close to 11%. Various factors account for the relative lack of diversity within law firms. The following section explores the legal profession's efforts to address these issues.

1. DISCRIMINATION IN LEGAL PRACTICE

Discrimination in hiring and promotion practices may account for some of the lack of diversity in law firms. There are numerous instances of lawyers bringing employment discrimination lawsuits against law firms under Title VII or other federal or state discrimination statutes. In *Hishon v. King & Spalding*, 467 U.S. 69 (1984), the Supreme Court held that Title VII applied to the claim of an associate who alleged that she had been discriminated against on the basis of sex when her law firm failed to invite her to become a partner. As her employer, the firm was prohibited under Title VII from discriminating against the plaintiff with respect to the terms, conditions, or privileges of employment. Consideration for partnership was such a term, condition, or privilege of her employment contract with the firm.

The *Hishon* court emphasized that while Title VII regulates the employer-employee relationship, it does not regulate the relationship between partners in an organization. Therefore, generally speaking, a partner in a law firm does not have a claim under Title VII or other discrimination statutes. However, in *Clackamas Gastroenterology Assocs. v. Wells*, 538 U.S. 440 (2003), the Supreme Court held that the fact that an individual is designated a partner or shareholder does not necessarily mean that the individual cannot be considered an "employee" for purposes of a statutory discrimination claim. Instead, the fundamental question is whether the individual is subject to the right of control by the employer. Many law firms rely on multi-tiered partnership structures in which non-equity partners sometimes lack management and decision-making authority. As a result, some law firm partners have argued (with varying degrees of success) that they were really employees for purposes of Title VII and related statutory discrimination laws. *See EEOC v. Sidley Austin Brown & Wood*, 315 F.3d 696 (7th Cir. 2002); *Kirleis v. Dickie, McCamey & Chilcote*, 2009 WL 3602008 (W.D. Pa., Oct. 28, 2009).

Employment discrimination in law firms may take many forms, ranging from the failure to provide reasonable accommodations for lawyers with disabilities, to the creation of a hostile work environment on the basis of race or sex, to the perpetuation of stereotypical or hostile attitudes toward working mothers. For example, there have been numerous lawsuits by lawyers alleging that their firms began giving them less frequent and less desirable work assignments based on the firms' assumptions that "women place family responsibilities above professional commitments." David B. Wilkins & G. Mitu Gulati, *Why Are There So Few Black Lawyers in Corporate Law Firms? An Institutional Analysis*, 84 CALIF. L. REV. 493, 557–58 (1996). In general, lawyers alleging employment discrimination have had mixed success when suing their firms. *See* Nancy Levit, *Lawyers Suing Law Firms: The Limits on Attorney Employment Discrimination Claims and the Prospects for Creating Happy Lawyers*, 73 U. PITT. L. REV. 65 (2011).

The rules of professional conduct in a jurisdiction may also address employment discrimination in the legal profession. ABA Model Rule 8.4(g) explains that it is professional misconduct for a lawyer to engage in conduct that the lawyer knows or reasonably should know is harassment or discrimination on the basis of race, sex, and other protected characteristics in conduct related to the practice of law. A comment explains that the phrase "conduct related to the practice of law" includes "operating or managing a law firm or law practice." *Id.*, cmt. [4]. Therefore, the rule reaches employment discrimination in law firms. A few states have adopted Rule 8.4(g), and numerous states have similar rules that might potentially reach employment discrimination. *See* Maine Rules of Prof'l Conduct R. 8.4(g).

A few states have rules of professional conduct that specifically prohibit lawyers from engaging in discrimination in the employment context. *See* Alex B. Long, *Employment Discrimination in the Legal Profession: A Question of Ethics?*, 2016 U. ILL. L. REV. 445, 459 (2016). For example, Rule 8.4(g) of the Vermont Rules of Professional Conduct provides that it is professional misconduct for a lawyer to "discriminate against any individual because of his or her race, color, religion, ancestry, national origin, sex, sexual orientation, place of birth or age, or against a qualified handicapped individual, in *hiring, promoting or otherwise determining the conditions of employment of that individual.*" (Emphasis added.) While there are numerous instances of professional discipline involving discriminatory behavior on the part of lawyers in the course of representing clients, there are few reported disciplinary decisions to date involving employment discrimination by one lawyer against another. *See* Alex B. Long, *Employment Discrimination in the Legal Profession: A Question of Ethics?*, 2016 U. ILL. L. REV. 445, 459 (2016).

Problem 6.4. The management committee of the Palsgraf & Pennoyer firm received several internal complaints of inappropriate behavior on the part of Arnie, a partner, and Bobby, an associate. Read Model Rule 8.4(g) and Comments [3] and [4], and then consider the following questions:

(a) Over a period of six months, Arnie made two racist statements in the presence of Clarise, a Black associate who did some of her work under Arnie's supervision. One of the statements was a racial slur describing a witness in a case, and the other involved an offensive stereotype describing the same individual. Clarise would likely not have a claim against the firm based on Arnie's statements under Title VII, in part, because the comments were not severe or pervasive enough to create a hostile work environment for Clarise. Is Arnie nonetheless subject to discipline under Rule 8.4(g)?

(b) Bobby is an associate who, over the course of several months, has directed numerous crude and sexually explicit statements toward Donna, another associate, while suggesting the two begin a sexual relationship. Donna complained to firm management about the behavior, but the firm failed to adequately address her concerns, and Bobby's behavior continued. As a result, Donna experiences what would qualify as a hostile work environment and would potentially have a Title VII claim against the firm for its failure to address Bobby's behavior.

(i) Is Bobby subject to discipline under Rule 8.4(g)?

(ii) Is the firm or any of its partners subject to professional discipline?

* * *

2. DIVERSITY AND INCLUSION EFFORTS IN THE LEGAL PROFESSION

The rules of professional conduct may also address attempts to increase diversity and inclusivity within law firms. Rule 8.4(g) addresses employment discrimination. But the rule also speaks to law firms' efforts to increase diversity. A comment to Rule 8.4 clarifies that the rule permits lawyers to "engage in conduct undertaken to promote diversity and inclusion without violating this Rule by, for example, implementing initiatives aimed at recruiting, hiring, retaining and advancing diverse employees or sponsoring diverse law student organizations."

Hiring practices may contribute to diversity within an organization and help shape the organization's culture, but retention practices are generally recognized as being more important in terms of changing a firm's culture. *See* Alex B. Long, *Reasonable Accommodation as Professional Responsibility, Reasonable Accommodation as Professionalism*, 47 U.C. DAVIS L. REV. 1753, 1798 (2014). One key obstacle to retention and career development for female lawyers and lawyers of color is the "the lack of reliable mentors to whom they can relate." *See* Alex B. Long, *Employment*

Discrimination in the Legal Profession: A Question of Ethics?, 2016 U. ILL. L. REV. 445, 450 (2016). Mentoring programs are widely recognized as one of the most effective means of retaining qualified lawyers. Rule 5.1 encourages law firm partners to develop mentoring programs and engage in hands-on supervision in order to fulfill their supervisory responsibilities. Therefore, Rule 5.1 may serve as a means of increasing diversity and inclusivity.

* * *

C. LEAVING THE FIRM

Sometimes when a lawyer leaves a firm, the split is amicable. In other instances, there may be some animosity. The two sides may disagree as to who will continue to represent a client. A firm might also wish to place some limits on the departing lawyer's ability to compete with the firm in the future. This section looks at some of the special rules that apply when a lawyer leaves a law firm.

* * *

1. SOLICITING CLIENTS

One common scenario involves a lawyer who leaves a firm and seeks to bring along firm clients to join the lawyer at a new firm. A lawyer who solicits existing clients to join the lawyer may face potential claims of breach of fiduciary duty or interference with contract, as well as possible disciplinary charges. The following case involves this scenario.

TOLSON FIRM, LLC v. SISTRUNK
789 S.E.2d 265 (Ga. Ct. App. 2016)

BOGGS, JUDGE.

This case involves a dispute between law partners, Hezekiah Sistrunk, Jr., and Jane Sams, a general partnership, d/b/a Cochran, Cherry, Givens, Smith, Sistrunk & Sams, P.C. a/k/a The Cochran Firm, Atlanta (collectively "the Cochran Firm" or "the plaintiffs") and a former associate attorney, Audrey Tolson, and her law firm, the Tolson Firm, LLC (collectively "Tolson" or "the defendants"), following Tolson's departure from the Cochran Firm. The plaintiffs allege that Tolson took eight cases with her when she terminated her employment with the Cochran Firm and that five of the cases subsequently settled for a cumulative sum of almost three million dollars.

The defendants assert on appeal that the trial court erred by denying summary judgment in their favor on the Cochran Firm's claims for breach of duty of loyalty [and] tortious interference with contract. . . .

. . .

Audrey Tolson's Liability for Breach of Loyalty or Fiduciary Duty. It is well-established that "a cause of action against an [at-will] employee for breach of loyalty must be based upon a fiduciary duty owed by the employee and must rise and fall with any claim for breach of fiduciary duty." (Footnote omitted.) *Physician Specialists in Anesthesia v. Wildmon,* 238 Ga. App. 730, 735, 521 S.E.2d 358 (1999).

> A fiduciary or confidential relationship arises where one party is so situated as to exercise a controlling influence over the will, conduct, and interest of another or where, from a similar relationship of mutual confidence, the law requires the utmost good faith, such as the relationship between partners, principal and agent, etc. OCGA § 23-2-58. Such relationship may be created by law, contract, or the facts of a particular case. Moreover, since "a confidential relationship may be found whenever one party is justified in reposing confidence in another, the existence of a confidential or fiduciary relationship is generally a factual matter for the jury to resolve."

(Citations and punctuation omitted.) *Wright v. Apartment Investment and Management Co.,* 315 Ga. App. 587, 592 (2)(a), 726 S.E.2d 779 (2012).

In this case, the Cochran Firm asserts Audrey Tolson owed a fiduciary duty based upon her status as its agent. In support of this assertion, a partner submitted an affidavit averring that: Audrey Tolson was the "primary point of contact at the Firm for many cases, including the ones at issue in this litigation"; that she had authority to enter into client engagement agreements on behalf of the law firm without prior approval; that she had authority to accept or reject cases; and solicited business on the law firm's behalf. This evidence creates a genuine issue of material fact as to whether Audrey Tolson was a fiduciary owing a duty of loyalty.

> The relation of principal and agent is a fiduciary one, and the latter cannot make advantage and profit for himself out of the relationship, or out of knowledge thus obtained, to the injury of his principal; and the agency being established, the agent will be held to be a trustee as to any profits, advantages, rights, or privileges under any contract made and obtained within the scope and reason of such agency. . . .

(Citations and punctuation omitted.) *Smith v. Pennington,* 192 Ga. 478, 481, 15 S.E.2d 727 (1941). Accordingly, we have held that an agent "cannot engage in acts in direct competition with the employer's business before the employment relationship ends," *Fine v. Communication Trends,* 305 Ga. App. 298, 309, 699 S.E.2d 623 (2010) or "solicit customers for a rival business before the end of his employment." *Sitton v. Print Direction,* 312 Ga. App. 365, 372–373, 718 S.E.2d 532 (2011). With regard to a departing attorney's solicitation of an employer's clients, the *Restatement (Third)* provides consistent authority:

> Absent an agreement with the firm providing a more permissive rule, a lawyer leaving a law firm may solicit firm clients:
>
> (a) prior to leaving the firm:
>
> (i) only with respect to firm clients on whose matters the lawyer is actively and substantially working; and
>
> (ii) only after the lawyer has adequately and timely informed the firm of the lawyer's intent to contact firm clients for that purpose; and
>
> (b) after ceasing employment in the firm, to the same extent as any other nonfirm lawyer.

Restatement (Third) of Laws, The Law Governing Lawyers § 9 (3) (2000).

. . . [G]enuine issues of material fact exist as to whether [Tolson] acted in direct competition with the Cochran Firm and solicited existing clients before her employment ended. Audrey Tolson testified that she told the Cochran Firm's office manager at the end of the day on Friday, May 6, "that [she] was leaving." She explained that she did not tell the office manager where she would be going because "I didn't know where I was going to go, so . . . I didn't tell her that. I just told her that I was leaving." She told no one else at the Cochran Firm that Friday that she intended to leave, and she did not take any personal items from her office home with her other than possibly her laptop.

The office manager testified that Audrey Tolson told her on Friday "that she made up her mind that she was going to go," but asked her to not tell anyone. Tolson testified, "I don't know that I . . . told her one way or the other. I didn't—I don't think she asked me if she could tell anybody, but I don't think I told her not to tell anybody."

The following Monday, Audrey Tolson did not report for work and sent an email to a managing partner stating, in part:

> Because I won't be accepting a partnership in another big plaintiffs['] firm like I anticipated, I will be taking 7 of my clients with me, per the clients['] request. Just so you know, I have only notified a small number of my clients. All of the ones I notified are either cases that I brought in or that I have done most or all of the work on and am their primary point of contact with the firm. . . . I made sure that they were aware that, per the bar association rules, they have the right to choose whether they want to stay with the firm or go with me, and that I would be good with either decision. I did not attempt to persuade any of my clients to go with

me and I hope that you or no one in the office would attempt to dissuade those who have decided to do so.... I am leaving 20+ cases behind and would like to submit a joint letter so that the rest of my clients are aware of my departure and won't hold me responsible in their cases going forward and won't think I abandoned their case without any notice.... The clients in the following cases have authorized me to pick up their files from the office.... I told all of the clients I spoke to that, given our history, I didn't think they would need to sign anything and that it would probably be okay with you for me [to] send a letter indicating that I have picked the original files up so that they would not have to incur copying cost. I hope I didn't speak out of turn, but I did not want to give the perception that there was any "in fighting" at the Cochran Firm.

Audrey Tolson testified that she did not contact any clients about her impending departure until the Sunday after she spoke with the office manager and that she did so only by telephone.

The Cochran Firm points to the following evidence to show that Audrey Tolson breached her duty of loyalty: the May 9 resignation email in which she admitted soliciting clients before formally terminating her employment; a client's testimony that Audrey Tolson told him in a personal meeting at the Cochran Firm no later than May 9th that she would be leaving the firm and that he could decide between her and the firm for continued representation; and the affidavit testimony of a client's daughter who witnessed Audrey Tolson tell her mother on Saturday, May 7 that she was leaving the Cochran Firm, that she wanted to take over the case, and "that it would be easier to leave the case with her, since she had performed the majority of the work on the file."

The above-referenced evidence shows a genuine issue of material fact as to whether Audrey Tolson's employment ended on Friday, May 6 or Monday, May 9. Accordingly, her solicitation of Cochran Firm clients over the intervening weekend may or may not have violated her fiduciary duty and duty of loyalty.

Nothing in State Bar Formal Advisory Opinion 97–3 persuades us to reach a different result. It provides, in relevant part:

With respect to the timing of the disclosure of the attorney's departure to the client, the ultimate consideration is the client's best interest. To the extent practical, a joint notification by the law firm and the departing attorney to the affected clients of the change is the preferred course of action for safeguarding the client's best interests. However, the appropriate timing of a notification to the client is determined on a case by case basis. Depending on the nature of the departing attorney's work for the client, the client may need advance notification of the departure to make a determination as to future representation.

The departing attorney may also owe certain duties to the firm which may require that the departing attorney should advise the firm of the attorney's intention to leave the firm and the attorney's intention to notify clients of his or her impending departure, prior to informing the clients of the situation. Specifically, the departing attorney should not engage in professional conduct which involves "dishonesty, fraud, deceit, or willful misrepresentation" with respect to the attorney's dealings with the firm as set forth in Standard 4.

In conclusion, as long as the departing attorney complies with the Standards governing advertisements, solicitation, and general professional conduct, the attorney may ethically contact those clients with whom the attorney had significant contact or active representation at the former law firm, so as to advise the clients of the attorney's departure as well as the client's right to select his or her legal counsel. Legal issues which may arise from a particular set of facts involving a departing attorney including, but not limited to, contract or tortious interference with contract, are beyond the scope of this formal advisory opinion.

(Emphasis supplied.)

. . .

Interference with Contract. . . .

"In order for a defendant to be liable for tortious interference with contractual relations, one must be a stranger to both the contract and the business relationship giving rise to and underpinning the contract." *Parks v. Multimedia Technologies*, 239 Ga. App. 282, 291 (3)(f), 520 S.E.2d 517 (1999). As Audrey Tolson was not a stranger to the business relationship between the Cochran Firm and its former clients, the trial court erred by failing to grant summary judgment in her favor on this portion of the Cochran Firm's complaint.

* * *

The Interference Claim in *Tolson*. *Tolson* may not have been a "stranger" to the contracts between the firms and clients while she was still employed, but did she become one once she quit the firm? At that point, what would it take for her solicitation of existing firm clients to become tortious?

The Ethics of Soliciting Firm Clients. Model Rule 7.3, which is covered in a later chapter, addresses the solicitation of clients and may place limits on the ability of a departing lawyer to solicit firm clients. The

Georgia ethics opinions referenced in *Tolson* highlights potential ethical concerns in these situations. ABA Formal Opinion 99–414 explains that a departing lawyer who is responsible for the client's representation or who plays a principal role in the law firm's delivery of legal services in a current matter has an ethical *duty* to notify a client of the lawyer's impending departure. According to the opinion, the duty to notify a client of the lawyer's impending departure is shared by the firm and the departing lawyer, and arises from the duty under Rule 1.4 to communicate with a client about matters that may affect the status of the client's matter.

Soliciting vs. Notifying Clients. Both the ABA opinion and *Tolson* attempt to draw a line between notification of impending departure while still employed (permissible) and solicitation of clients while still employed (impermissible). Is there a clear difference between these actions?

Whose Client? The *Restatement (Third) of the Law Governing Lawyers* provides that with reference to a departing lawyer's duties to a firm, a client is the client of the firm. *Restatement* § 9 Comment [i].

Problem 6.5. Unhappy with the culture of the Palsgraf & Pennoyer firm, Clarise and Donna decide to leave and start their own firm. Prior to leaving, the two associates notify each current client for whom they play a principal role in the firm's delivery of legal services of their intent to leave. They correctly inform these clients that it is up to the clients to decide who they wish to represent them in the future, be it Palsgraf & Pennoyer, Clarise and Donna, or someone else. When several clients ask what their hourly rates will be, Clarise and Donna truthfully respond that they will charge less than they do at Palsgraf & Pennoyer. After leaving the firm, Clarise and Donna sent a letter to other clients for whom they did work while at the firm, announcing the creation of the new firm and offering to provide "quality legal services at a reasonable rate should the need ever arise."

(a) Are Clarise and Donna subject to liability on a breach of fiduciary duty theory while still employed by the firm?

(b) Are they subject to liability on an interference theory for their actions after leaving the firm?

* * *

2. NON-COMPETE AGREEMENTS

In order to prevent a departing lawyer from "stealing" a firm's clients, it might be tempting for a law firm to enter into non-compete agreements with its lawyers that limit their ability to solicit or represent firm clients upon departure. These types of agreements are fairly common in other settings. However, Rule 5.6(a) prevents a firm from doing this on the theory that such agreements unfairly limit the ability of clients to choose their lawyers. As a result, courts in most jurisdictions have refused to enforce non-compete agreements between lawyers in violation of Rule 5.6(a) on the grounds that those agreements offend public policy.

Profile of Attorney Professionalism. Sandra Day received her law degree from Stanford in 1952, where she finished third in her class. She was a member of the Stanford Law Review and graduated Order of the Coif. Yet, she had difficulty finding a job after graduation: "I called at least 40 of those firms asking for an interview, and not one of them would give me an interview. I was a woman, and they said, 'We don't hire women,' and that was a shock to me. It was a total shock. It shouldn't have been. I should have known better. I should have followed what was going on, but I hadn't. And it just came as a real shock because I had done well in law school, and it never entered my mind that I couldn't even get an interview." At one point, she was offered a job as a legal secretary. *'Out Of Order' At The Court: O'Connor On Being The First Female Justice*, NPR (March 5, 2013).

Six months after law school, Day married her husband, John O'Connor, with whom she had three children. Despite the initial barriers to employment she experienced, over the course of her legal career, she served as a deputy county attorney, a solo practitioner, and assistant state attorney general. Later, she was appointed to the Arizona Supreme Court. In 1981, President Ronald Reagan appointed Sandra Day O'Connor as an Associate Justice of the Supreme Court. She retired from the Court in 2006.

CHAPTER 7

ADVERTISING

■ ■ ■

Chapter Hypothetical. In response to concerns within the organized bar about the prevalence of lawyer advertisements in the state, the New Dakota Supreme Court recently amended its advertising rules for lawyers. Among other things, the new rules (a) prohibit endorsements by a celebrity or public figure; (b) require that if a paid endorsement is used in an advertisement, the ad must disclose that the endorser is being paid or otherwise compensated for the appearance or endorsement; and (c) prohibit the portrayal of a client by a non-client, the re-enactment of any events or scenes, or pictures or persons that are not actual or authentic, without a disclosure that such depiction is a dramatization. The rest of New Dakota's advertising rules track those found in the ABA's *Model Rules of Professional Conduct*.

Lawyer Stephen A. Brill is now facing several disciplinary complaints related to a television ad and information appearing on one of his social media accounts.

A. THE CONSTITUTIONAL LANDSCAPE

Obviously, attempts to restrict what lawyers may include in their advertisements raise free speech concerns. The U.S. Supreme Court was first presented with a challenge to restrictions on lawyer advertising in *Bates v. State Bar of Arizona*, 433 U.S. 350 (1977). *Bates* involved a blanket ban on lawyer advertisements. Arizona offered a host of justifications for the ban, including the arguments that lawyer advertisements damage the dignity of the legal profession, are inherently misleading, and tend to stir up litigation. The Court held that states cannot prohibit truthful, nondeceptive advertising of the availability of, and fees for, routine legal services. In the process, the Court rejected Arizona's proffered justifications for its blanket ban, finding that advertising by lawyers is not inevitably misleading and that "the postulated connection between advertising and the erosion of true professionalism to be severely strained." *Id.* at 368. Moreover, the Court cited some of the benefits of lawyer advertisements, including the fact that they may enable consumers to locate a suitable lawyer.

Less than a decade later, the Court decided *Zauderer v. Office of Disciplinary Counsel*, 471 U.S. 626 (1985). There, the Court was confronted with the question of whether a state may, consistent with the First Amendment, prohibit a lawyer from running newspaper advertisements containing nondeceptive illustrations. The Court concluded that the State of Ohio had failed to identify a substantial state interest that justified the restriction on speech. The Court rejected Ohio's argument that it had a substantial governmental interest in preserving the dignity of the profession that was advanced by the restriction on the inclusion of illustrations. In addition, the Court rejected the idea that a blanket ban on illustrations was justified simply because *some* illustrations might be deceptive or manipulative.

In *Zauderer*, the Court also considered whether it was permissible for the state to discipline a lawyer for failing to disclose certain information regarding fee arrangements in an advertisement. Specifically, the ad in question informed consumers that the law firm in question represented clients on a contingent fee basis, so "[i]f there is no recovery, no legal fees are owed by our clients." *Id.* at 631. However, the ad failed to inform consumers that there were some expenses they would be required to bear, regardless of whether they won or lost. The Court concluded that requiring attorneys to include this information in their ads was reasonably related to the goal of preventing deceptive advertising and was therefore constitutionally permissible.

The Court has also considered several cases involving lawyer solicitation of individual clients, a subject addressed in the next chapter. But *Bates* and *Zauderer* provide much of the constitutional backdrop concerning the ability of states to regulate lawyer advertisements. The ABA's *Model Rules of Professional Conduct* regarding advertising, which are covered in Part B of this chapter, take one approach to regulating such ads. Concerned over the proliferation of lawyer advertisements, several states have gone even further in their attempts to regulate lawyer advertisements.

DWYER V. CAPPELL
762 F.3d 275 (3d Cir. 2014)

AMBRO, CIRCUIT JUDGE:

Attorney Andrew Dwyer, lauded by New Jersey judges in separate judicial opinions, published on his law firm's website those complimentary remarks. One of the judges objected to this, and ultimately the New Jersey Supreme Court adopted an attorney-conduct guideline that bans advertising with quotations from judicial opinions unless the opinions appear in full. Is the guideline an unconstitutional infringement on speech as applied to the advertisements of Mr. Dwyer and his firm? We believe it is and thus reverse the contrary decision of the District Court.

I. FACTS AND PROCEDURAL HISTORY

In 2007, Dwyer launched a website, www.thedwyerlawfirm.com. Its home page greeted potential clients with the following prominently displayed advertisement:

"Are You Thinking Of Suing Your Employer?"

"Mr. Dwyer is, I think, an exceptional lawyer, one of the most exceptional lawyers I've had the pleasure of appearing before me. He is tenacious, professional in his presentation to the Court, a bit too exuberant at times, certainly passionate about his position, but no one can fault his zeal and his loyalty to his client, and no one can question his intellect. . . ."

—Hon. Jose L. Fuentes, J.S.C.

"The inescapable conclusion is . . . that plaintiffs achieved a spectacular result when the file was in the hands of Mr. Dwyer. . . . Mr. Dwyer was a fierce, if sometimes not disinterested advocate for his clients, and through an offensive and defensive motion practice and through other discovery methods molded the case to the point where it could be successfully resolved."

—Hon. William L. Wertheimer, J.S.C.

The excerpts are from unpublished (though presumably public) judicial opinions concerning fee applications in employment discrimination cases brought under the New Jersey Law Against Discrimination. They were made in the context of the statute's fee-shifting provisions, which require judges to assess the abilities and legal services of plaintiffs' attorneys.

By letter to Dwyer in April 2008, Judge Wertheimer requested that his quoted comments be removed from the website. The Judge explained that, although he did "not have reason to doubt the accuracy of the verbiage," he "would not care for potential clients [of Dwyer] to believe that it is a blanket endorsement" of him. Dwyer refused to take the excerpt down because he did not believe the language was false or misleading. Subsequently, Judge Wertheimer's letter and Dwyer's response were forwarded to the New Jersey Bar's Committee on Attorney Advertising (the "Committee"), whose members are the defendants-appellees before us.

In February 2009, after several meetings and after receiving submissions from Dwyer, the Committee published a Notice to the Bar soliciting comments on a proposed attorney advertising guideline (the "Proposed Guideline"). It provided that "[a]n attorney or law firm may not include, on a website or other advertisement, a quotation from a judge or court opinion (oral or written) regarding the attorney's abilities or legal services." Dwyer submitted a comment in which he argued that the Proposed Guideline was an unconstitutional ban on speech. In addition, while the Proposed Guideline was pending, Dwyer added to [his] website a third excerpt from an unpublished opinion concerning a fee application in a suit under the New Jersey Conscientious Employee Protection Act:

> "Based upon my observations of [Dwyer] in court there's no question in my mind that he is in the upper echelon of employment lawyers in this state...."
>
> —**Hon. Douglas H. Hurd, J.S.C.**

Three years later, in May 2012, the New Jersey Supreme Court approved an amended version of the Proposed Guideline, now called Guideline 3. It differs from the Proposed Guideline in one respect: whereas the Proposed Guideline simply banned advertising with quotes from judges or judicial opinions, Guideline 3 bans those ads but allows attorneys to advertise with the full text of judicial opinions. In its final form, Guideline 3 provides:

> *Attorney Advertisements: Use of Quotations or Excerpts From Judicial Opinions About the Legal Abilities of an Attorney*
>
> An attorney or law firm may not include, on a website or other advertisement, a quotation or excerpt from a court opinion (oral or written) about the attorney's abilities or legal services. An attorney may, however, present the full text of opinions, including those that discuss the attorney's legal abilities, on a website or other advertisement.

The official comment to Guideline 3 demonstrates that it was promulgated to target Dwyer's website specifically:

> This Guideline arises from the review by the Committee on Attorney Advertising of an attorney's website that included two quotations from judges about the attorney's legal abilities. The quotations were from unpublished opinions of the judges on fee applications and the judges' names and titles were included in the advertisement.
>
> [Rule of Professional Conduct] 7.1(a) prohibits misleading statements. When a judge discusses an attorney's legal abilities in an opinion, such as in a fee-shifting or division-of-fee case, the judge is setting forth findings of fact and conclusions of law pertinent to the decision in the matter. The judge is not personally endorsing the attorney or making a public statement about the attorney for advertising purposes. In fact, judges are expressly prohibited from endorsing attorneys or providing testimonials regarding attorneys. The Committee finds that such quotations or

excerpts, when taken out of the context of the judicial opinion and used by an attorney for the purpose of soliciting clients, are prohibited judicial endorsements or testimonials. As such, these quotations or excerpts from a judicial opinion in attorney advertising are inherently misleading in violation of [Rule of Professional Conduct] 7.1(a).

The day before Guideline 3 went into effect Dwyer filed this action in the District of New Jersey seeking injunctive and declaratory relief under 42 U.S.C. § 1983. He simultaneously moved for a temporary restraining order and preliminary injunction to enjoin enforcement of the Guideline. The District Court denied the request for a temporary restraining order and set a full briefing schedule for the preliminary injunction motion. The parties then filed cross-motions for summary judgment, which the District Court considered concurrently with the motion for a preliminary injunction.

During discovery, Dwyer deposed Carol Johnston, the designated agent for the Committee. Ms. Johnston testified that the excerpts on Dwyer's website violated Guideline 3. She claimed that, even if the quotations include hyperlinks to the full text of the judicial opinions, they would still violate the Guideline. She also testified that, although the Committee had no evidence demonstrating that the excerpts misled potential clients, based on "common sense" it had concluded that excerpts from judicial opinions regarding attorneys' abilities are inherently misleading. Aside from Judge Wertheimer, there have been no complaints about Mr. Dwyer's website, and no one has claimed being misled by the judicial excerpts.

The District Court granted the Committee's summary judgment motion, denied Dwyer's motion for summary judgment, and denied as moot his motion for a preliminary injunction. It explained that "[t]he core of the parties' dispute is the legal issue of whether Guideline 3 is most appropriately characterized as a 'restriction' on speech, or whether it instead is a regulatory requirement of 'additional disclosure.' " The Court concluded that "because [Guideline 3] requires full disclosure of a judicial opinion," it is "not a ban on speech but is instead a disclosure requirement." Moreover, it held that a judicial quotation's potential to mislead is "self-evident" because, "[w]ithout the surrounding context of a full opinion, judicial quotations relating to an attorney's abilities could easily be misconstrued as improper judicial endorsement of an attorney, thereby threatening the integrity of the judicial system."

The District Court applied the test for disclosure requirements set in *Zauderer v. Office of Disciplinary Counsel of Supreme Court of Ohio*, 471 U.S. 626, 651, 105 S. Ct. 2265, 85 L.Ed.2d 652 (1985). Under that standard, it determined that the Guideline was "reasonably related to the [S]tate's interest in preventing the deception of consumers" and was not "unduly burdensome." Thus, it upheld the Guideline as constitutional. *Id.* In a footnote, the Court noted that, even if Guideline 3 were a restriction on speech subject to the more rigorous intermediate scrutiny under *Central Hudson Gas & Electric Corp. v. Public Service Commission,* 447 U.S. 557, 563–64 (1980)—under which the regulation must " 'directly advanc[e]' a substantial governmental interest and be 'n[o] more extensive than is necessary to serve that interest,' "—it would still be constitutional. Dwyer appeals these decisions as applied to him and his firm.

. . .

III. DISCUSSION

A. Restrictions on Speech and Disclosure Requirements. The First Amendment states that "Congress shall make no law . . . abridging the freedom of speech," U.S. Const. amend. I, and applies to the States through the Due Process Clause of the Fourteenth Amendment. The parties agree that our case involves only commercial speech. It is by now well settled that "commercial speech is entitled to the protection of the First Amendment, albeit to protection somewhat less extensive than that afforded noncommercial speech." *Zauderer,* 471 U.S. at 637, 105 S. Ct. 2265 (internal quotation marks omitted). Similarly, though there was once a time when attorney advertising could be proscribed without justification, it is now settled that such advertising is "a form of commercial speech, protected by the First Amendment, and . . . 'may not be subjected to blanket suppression.' " *In re R.M.J.,* 455 U.S. 191, 199 (1982) (quoting *Bates v. Arizona,* 433 U.S. 350, 383 (1977)). " '[T]he party seeking to uphold a restriction on commercial speech carries the burden of justifying it.' " *Edenfield v. Fane,* 507 U.S. 761, 770 (1993).

As the District Court noted, this case concerns two possible tracks of analysis, only one of which can apply: restrictions on speech and disclosure requirements. The Committee maintains that Guideline 3 is a disclosure requirement targeting misleading advertising and hence subject only to *Zauderer* scrutiny. Dwyer contends that Guideline 3 is a restriction on non-misleading speech that should instead be reviewed under *Central Hudson* intermediate scrutiny.

There are material differences between "outright prohibitions" on speech, where the State attempts to "prevent attorneys from conveying information to the public," and "disclosure requirements," which seek only to require them to "provide somewhat more information than they might otherwise be inclined to present." *Zauderer,* 471 U.S. at 650. Recognizing these differences, the Supreme Court has created different frameworks once it is determined whether a regulation is a restriction or a disclosure requirement.

For restrictions, there are three general categories of commercial speech: non-misleading, potentially misleading, and misleading. The more misleading the advertisement, the more constitutional leeway is granted [to] the States in restricting it. In this context, "[c]ommercial speech that is not false, deceptive, or misleading" may only be restricted if the regulation withstands intermediate scrutiny under *Central Hudson*. States may prohibit potentially misleading ads, but only if the information cannot be presented in a way that is not deceptive (such as through adding a disclosure requirement). Advertising that is inherently misleading or has proven to be misleading in practice "may be prohibited entirely."

As noted, disclosure requirements receive less rigorous scrutiny than restrictions on speech. *See Zauderer,* 471 U.S. at 651; *see also R.J. Reynolds Tobacco Co. v. FDA,* 696 F.3d 1205, 1212 (D.C. Cir. 2012) (characterizing *Zauderer* scrutiny of disclosure requirements as "akin to rational-basis review"). In the attorney advertising context, the Supreme Court has consistently preferred disclosure over prohibition. It recognized in *Bates* that, "because the public lacks sophistication concerning legal services," advertising by attorneys poses special risks of deception. 433 U.S. at 383. Because of this risk, "some limited supplementation, by way of warning or disclaimer[1] or the like, might be required," even where an advertisement contains only truthful information about the availability and terms of legal services, "so as to assure that the consumer is not misled." *Id.* at 384; *see also id.* at 375 ("[T]he preferred remedy is more disclosure, rather than less."). Subsequently, in *R.M.J.* the Court noted that where an attorney advertisement is potentially misleading, "the remedy in the first instance is not necessarily a prohibition but preferably a requirement of disclaimers or explanation." 455 U.S. at 203. *Bates* and *R.M.J.* demonstrate that, when it comes to attorney advertising, the State may compel supplemental disclosures to clarify truthful but potentially misleading advertisements. However, in neither case did the Court set a standard for evaluating these disclosures.

That void was filled by *Zauderer*. There an attorney advertised to putative clients that "cases are handled on a contingent fee basis of the amount recovered. If there is no recovery, no legal fees are owed by our clients." 471 U.S. at 631, 105 S. Ct. 2265. The advertisement failed to comply with a state disclosure requirement mandating that any advertisement for contingent fee representation warn that, while potential contingent-fee clients would not be responsible for legal fees, they may still be responsible for court costs. *Id.* at 633, 105 S. Ct. 2265. Zauderer was

---

[1] Though we typically think of a disclaimer as a "statement that one is not responsible for or involved with something," BLACK'S LAW DICTIONARY 562 (10th ed.2014), and a disclosure as "a revelation of facts," *id.*, they may meld. For example, to require that lawyers' advertisements state that what a judge wrote "is not an endorsement" is both a disclaimer of an endorsement and a disclosure of supplemental information. Thus, courts sometimes use the terms interchangeably.

subsequently brought up on disciplinary charges for, among other things, failing to include the disclosure.

The Supreme Court rejected Zauderer's argument that the state disclosure requirement violated his free speech rights. *Id.* at 650–53, 105 S. Ct. 2265. It explained that where the State requires an advertiser to "include in his advertising purely factual and uncontroversial information about the terms under which his services will be available," the "constitutionally protected interest in *not* providing any particular factual information in [the advertisement] is minimal." *Id.* at 651, 105 S. Ct. 2265 (emphasis in original). The Court was quick to note, however, that this did not mean "that disclosure requirements do not implicate the advertiser's First Amendment rights at all." *Id.* at 651. It therefore set out the now-prevailing standard for assessing their constitutional validity: disclosure requirements are permissible so long as they are "reasonably related to the State's interest in preventing deception of consumers," with the understanding that "unjustified or unduly burdensome disclosure requirements might offend the First Amendment by chilling protected commercial speech."

Applying this new standard to Zauderer's case, the Court held that the State's requirement "easily pass[ed] muster...." Absent the disclosure, it was "hardly a speculative" assumption that a substantial number of laypersons not aware of the distinction between "fees" and "costs" would be left with the impression that a loss in court would be entirely free of charge. *Id.* Although the State produced no evidence that consumers were deceived, the Court explained that "[w]hen the possibility of deception is as self-evident as it is in this case, we need not require the State to conduct a survey of the . . . public before it [may] determine that the [advertisement] had a tendency to mislead." In this rule-of-reason context, the disclosure requirement did not abridge Zauderer's freedom of speech.

The Supreme Court reaffirmed the *Zauderer* framework for analyzing disclosure requirements in *Milavetz, Gallop & Milavetz, P.A. v. United States*, 559 U.S. 229, 249 (2010). There attorneys brought a First Amendment challenge to a requirement that professionals assisting consumers with bankruptcy must state in their ads that "[w]e are a debt relief agency. We help people file for bankruptcy relief under the Bankruptcy Code." The attorneys contended that *Central Hudson* intermediate scrutiny should apply. The Court rejected this argument and instead upheld the requirement under *Zauderer*. It explained that *Zauderer* applied because the provision in question was "directed at misleading commercial speech" and "impose[d] a disclosure requirement rather than an affirmative limitation on speech." The takeaway: there exist different frameworks for analyzing restrictions on speech and disclosure requirements.

Guideline 3 bears characteristics of both categories. Yet we need not decide whether it is a restriction on speech or a disclosure requirement. This is because the Guideline is not reasonably related to preventing consumer deception and is unduly burdensome. Hence, it is unconstitutional under even the less-stringent *Zauderer* standard of scrutiny.

B. Guideline 3 Cannot Survive *Zauderer* Scrutiny. The Committee hyperbolizes that the excerpts prohibited by Guideline 3 are inherently misleading because laypersons reading such quotes would understand them to be judicial endorsements. Even were we to assume that excerpts of judicial opinions are potentially misleading to some persons, the Committee fails to explain how Dwyer's providing a complete judicial opinion somehow dispels this assumed threat of deception.[2]

A disclosure requirement is "reasonably related to the State's interest in preventing deception of consumers" where it could plausibly dispel the misleading nature of the advertisement to those who read it. *Zauderer*, 471 U.S. at 651. In *Zauderer*, the requirement succinctly highlighted the latent ambiguity in the advertisement by requiring a disclosure that, although consumers would not owe legal fees, they could still potentially owe court costs. Similarly, in *Milavetz*, the required disclosure clarified to consumers that an advertisement for bankruptcy "relief" was hiding the possibility that this relief could itself be costly. In each case there was a reasonable argument that the disclosure remedied the potentially misleading advertisement.

In contrast, Guideline 3 does not require disclosing anything that could reasonably remedy conceivable consumer deception stemming from Dwyer's advertisement. Providing a full judicial opinion does not reveal to a potential client that an excerpt of the same opinion is not an endorsement. Indeed, providing the full opinion may add only greater confusion. A reasonable attempt at a disclosure requirement might mandate a statement such as "This is an excerpt of a judicial opinion from a specific legal dispute. It is not an endorsement of my abilities." Such a statement or its analogue would, we believe, likely suffice under *Zauderer*. Guideline 3 does not.

---

[2] As to whether judicial opinion excerpts on Dwyer's website actually have the potential to mislead, we note that the Committee has produced no evidence this is so, instead relying on "common sense." While it is the law that "[w]hen the possibility of deception is . . . self-evident" a state is not required to produce evidence to justify its imposition of a disclosure requirement, "we cannot allow rote invocation of the words 'potentially misleading' to supplant the . . . burden to demonstrate that the harms it recites are real and that its restriction will in fact alleviate them to a material degree." Unlike the advertisements targeted by the disclosure requirements in *Zauderer* and *Milavetz*, which had the obvious propensity to deceive laypersons, the deceptiveness of accurately transcribed statements made by judges in judicial opinion excerpts is far from "self-evident."

Even more supportive of Dwyer's position is that Guideline 3 is unduly burdensome. The Supreme Court recognized in *Zauderer* that "unduly burdensome disclosure requirements might offend the First Amendment by chilling protected commercial speech." 471 U.S. at 651. While the Court did not explain in what circumstances a disclosure requirement could be "unduly burdensome," it later clarified that this condition exists where the required disclosure is so lengthy that it "effectively rules out" advertising by the desired means.

Ibanez thus becomes instructive. [*Ibanez v. Fla. Dep't of Bus. & Prof. Reg., Bd. of Accountancy*, 512 U.S. 136, 142, 114 S. Ct. 2084, 129 L.Ed.2d 118 (1994).] There, a Florida attorney who was also a certified financial planner ("CFP") listed her CFP credential next to her name in advertisements in the yellow pages, on her business card, and on her law office stationery. In a subsequent disciplinary proceeding, the State Board of Accountants argued that, if Ibanez wanted to list herself as a CFP, Florida law required that she would have to provide a disclosure. It required, "in the immediate proximity" of the CFP designation, Ibanez to:

> [1] state that the recognizing agency [here the Certified Financial Planner Board of Standards] is not affiliated with or sanctioned by the state or federal government . . . [and] [2] set out the recognizing agency's requirements for recognition, including, but not limited to, education, experience, and testing.

The Supreme Court rejected the requirement as unduly burdensome because "[t]he detail required . . . effectively rule[d] out notation of the [CFP] designation on a business card or letterhead, or in a yellow pages listing."[3]

Post-*Ibanez* the Fifth Circuit Court similarly struck down an attorney disclosure requirement as unduly burdensome. *See Public Citizen Inc. v. La. Att'y Disciplinary Bd.*, 632 F.3d 212, 228–29 (5th Cir. 2011). The case involved a Louisiana requirement that attorneys disclose substantial information in any televised advertisement:

> [A]n attorney [television] advertisement must include, both written in a large font *and* spoken slowly, at least all of the following information: (1) the lawyer's name and office location; (2) a client's responsibility for costs; (3) all jurisdictions in which the lawyer is licensed; (4) the use of simulated scenes or pictures or actors portraying clients; and (5) the use of a spokesperson, whether the spokesperson is a lawyer, and whether the spokesperson is paid.

---

[3] The Court also found the requirement unjustified because the alleged harm was "purely hypothetical."

This requirement, the Court held, "effectively rule[d] out" attorneys' abilities "to employ short advertisements of any kind" and was therefore overly burdensome.

Guideline 3 effectively rules out the possibility that Dwyer can advertise with even an accurately quoted excerpt of a judicial statement about his abilities. To comply with Guideline 3, he must advertise with a full-length judicial opinion if he wants to use any portion of that opinion on the website. Even a hyperlink to unquoted portions of the opinion fails the Guideline. This requirement is far more onerous than the disclosures invalidated in *Ibanez* and *Public Citizen* and necessarily prevents any form of advertisement with simply a judicial excerpt. The only realistic medium for quoting a full judicial opinion in an advertisement is, ironically, a website, with its theoretically endless capacity. However, even on Dwyer's own website providing a full-text judicial opinion is so cumbersome that it effectively nullifies the advertisement.

While the intention behind Guideline 3 may be to make it so burdensome to quote judicial opinions that attorneys will cease doing so, that type of restriction—an outright ban on advertising with judicial excerpts—would properly be analyzed under the heightened *Central Hudson* standard of scrutiny. Although such a ban would fail as applied to Dwyer given our holding under the less stringent *Zauderer* standard, we need not decide whether such a ban would be valid in other cases. Because Guideline 3 effectively precludes advertising with accurate excerpts from judicial opinions on Dwyer's website, it is unduly burdensome.

Guideline 3 as applied to Dwyer's accurate quotes from judicial opinions thus violates his First Amendment right to advertise his commercial services. Requiring Dwyer to reprint in full on his firm's website the opinions noted above is not reasonably related to preventing consumer deception. To the extent the excerpts of these opinions could possibly mislead the public, that potential deception is not clarified by Guideline 3. In any event, what is required by the Guideline overly burdens Dwyer's right to advertise. We thus reverse the order of the District Court and remand the case.

* * *

Problem 7.1. The Law Office of Stephen A. Brill recently ran a television ad in which a local sports figure recommended Brill's services. (Brill paid the figure a small sum of money to appear in the ad.) Brill also ran another that featured Brill in a cape, flying (in a simulated manner) over the city to visit a client. At the end of the ad, an animated dog named Sparky turns to the camera and says, "Brill is the best!" One of Brill's competitors filed a complaint with the New Dakota Board of Professional Responsibility about the ads. Brill has challenged the constitutionality of New Dakota's new advertising rules as applied to his ads. Taking into account the rules described in *Zauderer, Central Hudson,* and *Dwyer,* be prepared to explain the arguments both sides might make concerning the constitutionality of each of the following rules from New Dakota:

(a) the rule prohibiting endorsements by a celebrity or public figure;

(b) the rule requiring that if a paid endorsement is used in advertisement, the ad must disclose that the endorser is being paid or otherwise compensated for the appearance or endorsement; and

(c) the rule prohibiting a portrayal of a client by a non-client, the re-enactment of any events or scenes, or pictures or persons, which are not actual or authentic, without a disclosure that such depiction is a dramatization.

* * *

B. THE REGULATORY LANDSCAPE

1. IN GENERAL

While some states have promulgated somewhat detailed rules of professional conduct regarding advertising, the *Model Rules* take a somewhat minimalist approach. Use Model Rule 7.1 and Comments [1]–[3] to answer the problem below.

* * *

Problem 7.2. Would Brill be subject to discipline if, instead, New Dakota had simply adopted Model Rule 7.1?

False or Misleading Communications. A lawyer has handled only one criminal case—a case in which she was appointed to defend an individual charged with criminal contempt of court for allegedly violating a protective order to stay away from his girlfriend. After the girlfriend failed to appear at two consecutive hearings, the case against the lawyer's client was dismissed with prejudice. Would the lawyer be subject to discipline under Rule 7.1 if the lawyer now advertises that she has never lost a criminal case?

Comparisons with Other Lawyers. What, if anything, will a lawyer have to be able to prove in order to avoid professional discipline under Rule 7.1 before the lawyer can advertise that "my fee rates are very reasonable"? Is a lawyer subject to discipline for claiming in an ad to be "the toughest lawyer around"?

Problem 7.3. Over the past four years, Stephen A. Brill has represented three clients who recovered in excess of $1,000,000 in personal injury actions. Most of Brill's clients recovered significantly less during that timeframe. May Brill include in a TV ad the statement "Three $1,000,000 recoveries for clients in the past four years!"? What if he added the statement "Results obtained vary from case to case and no specific recovery can be guaranteed"?

* * *

2. ONLINE MARKETING

Attorney websites are generally viewed as advertising, since they constitute unambiguous self-promotion. But what about websites that include substantive legal analysis? This has become a controversial issue for blogs maintained by lawyers and law firms. Most bloggers argue that blogs embody primarily political speech, as opposed to commercial speech, and are therefore fully protected by the First Amendment. However, even the substantive legal analysis usually has marketing purpose. The following case addresses where to draw the line between political speech and commercial speech when the attorney may have more than one motivation for sharing information.

* * *

HUNTER V. VIRGINIA STATE BAR EX REL. THIRD DISTRICT COMMITTEE
744 S.E.2d 611 (Va. 2013)

Opinion by JUSTICE CLEO E. POWELL.

In this appeal of right by an attorney from a Virginia State Bar ("VSB") disciplinary proceeding before a three judge panel appointed pursuant to Code § 54.1–3935, we consider whether an attorney's blog posts are commercial speech . . . and whether the panel ordered the attorney to post a disclaimer that is insufficient under Rule 7.2(a)(3) of the Virginia Rules of Professional Conduct.

I. FACTS AND PROCEEDINGS

Horace Frazier Hunter, an attorney with the law firm of Hunter & Lipton, PC, authors a trademarked blog titled "This Week in Richmond Criminal Defense," which is accessible from his law firm's website, www.hunterlipton.com. This blog, which is not interactive, contains posts discussing a myriad of legal issues and cases, although the overwhelming majority are posts about cases in which Hunter obtained favorable results for his clients. Nowhere in these posts or on his website did Hunter include disclaimers.

On March 24, 2011, the VSB charged Hunter with violating [Virginia's advertising rules] by his posts on this blog. Specifically, the VSB argued that he violated Rules 7.1 and 7.2 because his blog posts discussing his criminal cases were inherently misleading as they lacked disclaimers. . . .

In a hearing on October 18, 2011, the VSB presented evidence of Hunter's alleged violations. The VSB also entered [into evidence] all of the blog posts Hunter had posted on his blog to date. At that time, none of the posts entered contained disclaimers. Of these thirty unique posts, only five discussed legal, policy issues. The remaining twenty-five discussed cases. Hunter represented the defendant in twenty-two of these cases and identified that fact in the posts. In nineteen of these twenty-two posts, Hunter also specifically named his law firm. One of these posts described a case where a family hired Hunter to represent them in a wrongful death suit and the remaining twenty-one of these posts described criminal cases. In every criminal case described, Hunter's clients were either found not guilty, plea bargained to an agreed upon disposition, or had their charges reduced or dismissed.

At the hearing, Hunter testified that he has many reasons for writing his blog—including marketing, creation of a community presence for his firm, combatting any public perception that defendants charged with crimes are guilty until proven innocent, and showing commitment to criminal law. Hunter stated that he had offered to post a disclaimer on his blog, but the offered disclaimer was not satisfactory to the VSB. Hunter admitted that he only blogged about his cases that he won. . . .

Following the hearing, the VSB held that . . . Hunter's website contained legal advertising . . . based on its factual finding that "[t]he postings of [Hunter's] case wins on his webpage advertise[d] cumulative case results." Moreover, the VSB found that at least one purpose of the website was commercial. The VSB further held that he violated Rule 7.2 by "disseminating case results in advertising without the required disclaimer" because the one that he proposed to the VSB was insufficient. The VSB imposed a public admonition with terms including a requirement that he remove case-specific content for which he has not received consent and post a disclaimer that complies with Rule 7.2(a)(3) on all case-related posts.

Hunter appealed to a three judge panel of the circuit court and the court heard argument. . . . The court held VSB's interpretation of Rules 7.1 and 7.2 do not violate the First Amendment and that the record contained substantial evidence to support the VSB's determination that Hunter had violated those rules. The court imposed a public admonition and required Hunter to post the following disclaimer: "Case results depend upon a variety of factors unique to each case. Case results do not guarantee or predict a similar result in any future case." This appeal followed.

II. ANALYSIS

A. *Whether "[t]he Ruling of the Circuit Court finding a violation of Rules 7.1(a)(4) and 7.2(a)(3) conflicts with the First Amendment to the Constitution of the United States."*

Rule 7.1(a)(4), which is the specific portion of the Rule that the VSB argued that Hunter violated, states:

(a) A lawyer shall not, on behalf of the lawyer or any other lawyer affiliated with the lawyer or the firm, use or participate in the use of any form of public communication if such communication contains a false, fraudulent, misleading, or deceptive statement or claim. For example, a communication violates this Rule if it:

. . .

(4) is likely to create an unjustified expectation about results the lawyer can achieve, or states or implies that the lawyer can achieve results by means that violate the Rules of Professional Conduct or other law.

The VSB also argues that Hunter violated the following subsection of Rule 7.2(a)(3):

(a) Subject to the requirements of Rules 7.1 and 7.3, a lawyer may advertise services through written, recorded, or electronic communications, including public media. In the determination of whether an advertisement violates this Rule, the advertisement shall be considered in its entirety, including any qualifying statements or disclaimers contained therein. Notwithstanding the requirements of Rule 7.1, an advertisement violates this Rule if it:

. . .

(3) advertises specific or cumulative case results, without a disclaimer that (i) puts the case results in a context that is not misleading; (ii) states that case results depend upon a variety of factors unique to each case; and (iii) further states that case results do not guarantee or predict a similar result in any future case undertaken by the lawyer. The disclaimer shall precede the communication of the case results. When the communication is in writing, the disclaimer shall be in bold type face and uppercase letters in a font size that is at least as large as the largest text used to advertise the specific or cumulative case results and in the same color and against the same colored background as the text used to advertise the specific or cumulative case results.

In response to these allegations, Hunter contends that speech concerning the judicial system is "quintessentially 'political speech' " which is within the marketplace of ideas. . . .

The VSB responds that Hunter's blog posts are inherently misleading commercial speech.

Turning to Hunter's argument that his blog posts are political, rather than commercial, speech, we note that "[t]he existence of 'commercial activity, in itself, is no justification for narrowing the protection of expression secured by the First Amendment.'" *Bigelow v. Virginia*, 421 U.S. 809, 818 (1975) (quoting *Ginsburg v. United States*, 383 U.S. 463, 474 (1966)). However, when speech that is both commercial and political is combined, the resulting speech is not automatically entitled to the level of protections afforded political speech. *Board of Trustees of the State University of New York v. Fox*, 492 U.S. 469, 474 (1989).

While it is settled that attorney advertising is commercial speech, *Bates v. State Bar of Arizona*, 433 U.S. 350, 363–64 (1977), *Bates* and its progeny were decided in the era of traditional media. In recent years, however, advertising has taken to new forms such as websites, blogs, and other social media forums, like Facebook and Twitter.

Thus, we must examine Hunter's speech to determine whether it is commercial speech, specifically, lawyer advertising.

> Advertising, like all public expression, may be subject to reasonable regulation that serves a legitimate public interest. To the extent that commercial activity is subject to regulation, the relationship of speech to that activity may be one factor, among others, to be considered in weighing the First Amendment interest against the governmental interest alleged. Advertising is not thereby stripped of all First Amendment protection. The relationship of speech to the marketplace of products or of services does not make it valueless in the marketplace of ideas.

Bigelow, 421 U.S. at 826 (internal citations omitted). Simply because the speech is an advertisement, references a specific product, or is economically motivated does not necessarily mean that it is commercial speech. *Bolger v. Youngs Drug Products Corp.*, 463 U.S. 60, 67 (1983). "The combination of *all* these characteristics, however, provides strong support for the . . . conclusion that [some blog posts] are properly characterized as commercial speech" even though they also discuss issues important to the public. *Id.* at 67–68 (emphasis in original).

Certainly, not all advertising is necessarily commercial, *e.g.*, public service announcements. However, all commercial speech is necessarily advertising. *See* WEBSTER'S THIRD NEW INTERNATIONAL DICTIONARY 31 (1993) (defining "advertisement" as "a calling attention to or making known[;] an informing or notifying[;] a calling to public attention[;] a statement calling attention to something[;] a public notice; esp[ecially] a paid notice or announcement published in some public print (as a newspaper, periodical, poster, or handbill) or broadcast over radio or television"). Indeed, the Supreme Court of the United States has said that "[t]he diverse motives, means, and messages of advertising may make speech 'commercial' in widely varying degrees." *Bigelow*, 421 U.S. at 826.

Here, Hunter's blog posts, while containing some political commentary, are commercial speech. Hunter has admitted that his motivation for the blog is at least in part economic. The posts are an advertisement in that they predominately describe cases where he has received a favorable result for his client. He unquestionably references a specific product, *i.e.*, his lawyering skills, as twenty-two of his twenty-five case-related posts describe cases that he has successfully handled. Indeed, in nineteen of these posts, he specifically named his law firm in addition to naming himself as counsel.

Moreover, the blog is on his law firm's commercial website rather than an independent site dedicated to the blog. *See* Howard J. Bashman, "How Appealing Blog" (Feb. 11, 2013, 9:40 AM), http://howappealing.law.com (an independent blog by a Pennsylvania appellate attorney that is accessible through Law.com at http://legalblogwatch.typepad.com/). The website uses the same frame for the pages openly soliciting clients as it does for the blog, including the firm name, a photograph of Hunter and his law partner, and a "contact us" form. The home page of the website on which Hunter posted his blog states only:

Do you need Richmond attorneys?

Hunter & Lipton, CP [sic] is a law practice in Richmond, Virginia specializing in litigation matters from administrative agency hearings to serious criminal cases. As experienced Richmond attorneys, we bring a genuine desire to help those who find themselves in difficult situations. Our partnership was founded on the idea that everyone, no matter what the circumstance, deserves a zealous advocate to fight on his or her behalf.

People make mistakes, and may even find themselves in situations not of their own making. And for these people, the system can be extraordinarily unforgiving and unjust-but you do not have to face this system alone.

If you find yourself in a difficult legal situation, the Richmond attorneys of Hunter & Lipton, LLP would consider it a privilege to represent you. Please contact our office with any questions or to schedule a consultation.

This non-interactive blog does not allow for discourse about the cases, as non-commercial commentary often would by allowing readers to post comments. *See, e.g.,* Law.com Legal Blog Watch, http://legalblogwatch.typepad.com/; Above the Law, http://abovethelaw.com/. *See also* JUNE LESTER & WALLACE C. KOEHLER, JR., FUNDAMENTALS OF INFORMATION

STUDIES 102 (2d ed.2007) (observing that "[i]n contrast to the interaction possible in some other forms of web-published information, blog readers are most frequently permitted to leave comments and create threads of discussion"). Instead, in furtherance of his commercial pursuit, Hunter invites the reader to "contact us" the same way one seeking legal representation would contact the firm through the website.

Thus, the inclusion of five generalized, legal posts and three discussions about cases that he did not handle on his non-interactive blog, no more transform[s] Hunter's otherwise self-promotional blog posts into political speech, "than opening sales presentations with a prayer or a Pledge of Allegiance would convert them into religious or political speech." *Fox*, 492 U.S. at 474–75. Indeed, unlike situations and topics where the subject matter is inherently, inextricably intertwined, Hunter chose to comingle sporadic political statements within his self-promoting blog posts in an attempt to camouflage the true commercial nature of his blog. "Advertisers should not be permitted to immunize false or misleading product information from government regulation simply by including references to public issues." *Bolger*, 463 U.S. at 68. When considered as a whole, the economically motivated blog overtly proposes a commercial transaction that is an advertisement of a specific product.

Having determined that Hunter's blog posts discussing his cases are commercial speech, we must determine whether the expression is protected by the First Amendment. [Applying the *Central Hudson* test, the court found that the blog posts had the potential to be misleading. The court then concluded that "the VSB has a substantial governmental interest in protecting the public from an attorney's self-promoting representations that could lead the public to mistakenly believe that they are guaranteed to obtain the same positive results if they were to hire Hunter" and "the disclaimer requirement directly advanced that interest." Accordingly, as applied to Hunter's post, the restrictions were permissible.]

* * *

Social Media as Advertising. Model Rule 7.2(a) generally permits lawyers to "communicate information regarding the lawyer's services through any media," and makes all such communication subject to Rule 7.1's prohibition on "false and misleading communication." This broad approach contrasts to the former version of the rule, which more directly regulated "advertising." Some states still regulate advertising directly. In such states, it can be difficult to determine what communications qualify as advertisements. Under what circumstances would a lawyer's Facebook page or TikTok account be subject to the rules regarding advertising? Imagine, for example, a lawyer posts on her Facebook page, "Great day in court today. Won the slip and fall case!" Should this be treated as an advertisement for purposes of the rules? What other information would you need to know? *See generally* California Ethics Opinion No. 2012–186 (discussing application of ethics rule to lawyers' use of social media).

Problem 7.4. While the Board was investigating the complaint against Brill, it also learned that Brill has a Facebook page on which he lists his firm name, office address, etc. The only posts that appear are posts in which Brill describes his recent courtroom successes or professional activities. Some of the statements on the page are arguably false and misleading. Would Brill be subject to discipline under Rule 7.1 for making a false or misleading communication concerning the lawyer's services under Rule 7.1? Would Brill's Facebook page qualify as an "advertisement" in those jurisdictions that still use this terminology?

* * *

3. ADVERTISING LIMITED AND SPECIALIZED PRACTICES

In *Peel v. Attorney Registration and Disciplinary Commission*, 496 U.S. 91 (1990), the U.S. Supreme Court held that a state cannot prohibit attorneys from making truthful, nondeceptive statements regarding their specialization and qualifications. In that case, Peel's letterhead contained the following:

> Gary E. Peel
> Certified Civil Trial Specialist
> By the National Board of Trial Advocacy
> Licensed: Illinois, Missouri, Arizona.

Because each piece of information conveyed by the letterhead was true and verifiable, the Court held that it was protected by the First Amendment. However, the Court also left the door open for the states to require attorneys to provide consumers more information: "To the extent that potentially misleading statements of private certification or specialization could confuse consumers, a State might consider screening certifying organizations or requiring a disclaimer about the certifying organization or the standards of a specialty." *Id.* at 110.

Claiming "Specialist" Status. Comment [9] to Rule 7.2 permits a lawyer to advertise that the lawyer is a specialist in a particular area so long as the self-labeling is not misleading. But Rule 7.2(c) says a lawyer may not imply that she is *"certified* as a specialist in a particular field" unless the lawyer has actually been certified by an approved organization (emphasis added). Is a prospective client likely to see any meaningful difference between these two claims?

* * *

4. LAW FIRM NAMES

Problem 7.5. Based on your reading of Rules 7.1 and 7.2, with particular attention to Comment [5] to Rule 7.1, which of the following law firm names would be permissible?

(A) Sonya Goodman & Associates. [Assume that Sonya Goodman is the only lawyer in the firm but has several paralegals working for her.]

(B) The Best Law Firm. [Assume no one in the firm has Best as a last name.]

(C) The Social Security Law Office. [Assume the firm handles social security cases.]

(D) None of the above.

Problem 7.6. Allen and Bailey practice together as partners. Their firm is named Allen & Bailey. Conner desires to share office space and office expenses with Allen and Bailey but does not desire to become a partner in the firm. Further, Allen and Bailey will occasionally associate with Conner on certain cases, and Conner will occasionally associate with Allen and Bailey. Because they are practicing out of the same office, they want to put a sign on the door that includes all three names. Can they do this without violating Rule 7.1? Can they refer to themselves as "An Association of Attorneys"?

Free Speech and Firm Names. Based on your reading of *Dwyer v. Cappell, supra,* could a state constitutionally prohibit a law firm from naming itself "The Ethics Rule Breaker Law Firm"? Why or why not?

* * *

5. CLIENT REFERRALS

Model Rule 7.2 permits a lawyer to pay the costs associated with advertising. However, it places limits on the ability of a lawyer to pay others to recommend the lawyer's services. The rule also addresses other forms of referral, including referral agreements and legal services plans.

a. Referrals in General

Problem 7.7. Pat represented Shonna in a matter. Shonna was so pleased with the job Pat did that she referred several of her friends to Pat. In return, the next time Pat did legal work for Shonna, he reduced his regular fee in appreciation. Is Pat subject to discipline? Could Pat give a $10 gift certificate to a local restaurant in appreciation for her referrals?

b. Legal Services Plans and Lawyer Referral Services

A Michigan ethics opinion described the nature of legal services plans:

> Most for-profit prepaid legal service plans are owned and operated by plan sponsors which, for a modest monthly charge, offer subscribers certain "covered" legal services for no additional cost and other specified services at reduced fees. The covered legal services are provided by participating lawyers and usually include such services as unlimited telephone consultations and letter writing, and the preparation of simple wills. The reduced fee services usually cover court representation at a fixed hourly rate and contingency fee arrangements, both for less than fees customarily charged by lawyers for similar services. Certain matters are explicitly excluded, such as matters where the interests of two plan members are in direct conflict, suits against the plan's sponsor and complex matters.

State Bar of Michigan Standing Committee on Professional and Judicial Ethics Op. No. RI 223 (1995).

In contrast, a lawyer referral service is "an organization that holds itself out to the public as a lawyer referral service" and, presumably, provides "unbiased referrals to lawyers with appropriate experience" in the relevant subject area. Model Rule 7.2, Comment [6]. Model Rule 7.2 permits a lawyer to participate in a legal services plan or not-for-profit lawyer referral service, or to pay the usual charges with such organizations. However, the lawyer must act reasonably to ensure that the lawyer's activities are compatible with the lawyer's professional obligations, including the duty to maintain decisional independence, loyalty, and competence.

c. Reciprocal Referral Agreements

Problem 7.8. Pat and Mike were old law school buddies who are each now solo practitioners. Pat practices criminal law and Mike practices family law. While reminiscing about old times, Pat said to Mike, "You're a heck of a lawyer. If I ever have a client who needs a divorce, I'm going to refer him to you. Will you do the same if one of your clients ever has a drunk driving case?" Mike said, "It's a deal, buddy." If Pat and Mike carry out this agreement, are they subject to discipline?

Profile of Attorney Professionalism. As mentioned in the introductory text to this chapter, one of the leading cases involving attorney advertising is *Bates v. State Bar of Arizona*, 433 U.S. 350 (1977). The attorneys whose conduct was at issue in that case were John Bates and Van O'Steen.

After starting their own firm a few years after graduating from Arizona State University College of Law, the attorneys decided that they needed to advertise to attract business. They ran an advertisement in the *Arizona Republic* that stated that they were offering "legal services at very reasonable fees." The advertisement went on to list prices for routine legal services, like non-contested divorces. David L. Hudson, Jr., *Attorney Advertising and Free Speech, Bates v. State Bar of Arizona (1977)*, Free Speech Center at Middle Tennessee State University (December 15, 2023), available at https://firstamendment.mtsu.edu/article/bates-v-state-bar-of-arizona/.

Arizona disciplinary authorities charged the attorneys with violating Arizona's rule of professional conduct prohibiting a lawyer from advertising legal services. They were found to have violated the rule. With the help of William Canby, their former constitutional law professor, they appealed to the Arizona Supreme Court, asserting that Arizona's attorney advertising prohibition violated the First Amendment. *Id.*

After losing before the Arizona Supreme Court, their case was heard by the United States Supreme Court. In a 5–4 decision, the Supreme Court held that Arizona's rule offended the First Amendment. The Arizona Bar defended its ban on several grounds, including the adverse effects that advertising might have on professionalism. Writing for the majority, Justice Blackmun rejected these arguments, finding "the postulated connection between advertising and the erosion of true professionalism to be severely strained." While recognizing potential dangers associated with lawyer advertising, Blackmun also noted the potential benefits in terms of improving access to justice:

> As the bar acknowledges, "the middle 70% of our population is not being reached or served adequately by the legal profession." ABA, *Revised Handbook on Prepaid Legal Services* 2 (1972). Among the reasons for this underutilization is fear of the cost, and an inability to locate a suitable lawyer.... The disciplinary rule at issue likely has served to burden access to legal services, particularly for the not-quite-poor and the unknowledgeable. A rule allowing restrained advertising would be in accord with the bar's obligation to "facilitate the process of intelligent selection of lawyers, and to assist in making legal services fully available."

Bates, 433 U.S. at 376–77.

CHAPTER 8

SOLICITATION

■ ■ ■

Chapter Hypothetical. The State of New Dakota recently enacted new rules of professional conduct regarding the solicitation of clients. According to the report of the state bar committee that drafted them, the rules were designed to protect consumers "against inappropriate solicitations or potentially misleading ads, as well as overly aggressive marketing," and to "benefit the bar by ensuring that the image of the legal profession is maintained at the highest possible level." The report cited several examples of what it viewed as overly aggressive advertising occurring in other states, but no evidence of similar marketing occurring in New Dakota. The new rules imposed a 30-day moratorium on the solicitation of clients with potential personal injury or wrongful death claims. The rule also prohibited lawyers who represented defendants or potential defendants in such instances from contacting injured parties or their representatives about the possibility of settlement for the same time period. The state that borders New Dakota—Old Dakota—has instead adopted ABA Model Rule 7.3 in its entirety.

A few months ago, there was a terrible airplane crash near the border of New Dakota and Old Dakota. Over 100 passengers (all of whom were from New Dakota or Old Dakota) were killed. Hundreds of local residents also suffered property damage from falling debris from the crash. Malcolm, a lawyer licensed in both states, now faces professional discipline for his solicitation of prospective clients in connection with the crash.

Although advertising involves the active pursuit of clients, it is typically regarded as a less aggressive and less threatening means of pursuing clients than the "solicitation" examined in this chapter. Model Rule 7.3 regulates lawyer solicitation of clients. Rule 7.3(a) defines a solicitation in terms of "a communication initiated by or on behalf of a lawyer or law firm that is directed *to a specific person* the lawyer knows or reasonably should know needs legal services *in a particular matter* and that offers to provide, or reasonably can be understood as offering to provide, legal services for that matter." (Emphasis added.) First, the chapter considers the rules of professional conduct regarding solicitation by live person-to-person contact and the constitutional rules that limit the ability of jurisdictions to restrict such forms of solicitation. The chapter then explores other, theoretically less intrusive forms of lawyer solicitation and the rules that govern them.

* * *

A. LIVE PERSON-TO-PERSON CONTACT

OHRALIK V. OHIO STATE BAR ASSOCIATION
436 U.S. 447 (1978)

MR. JUSTICE POWELL delivered the opinion of the Court.

In *Bates v. State Bar of Arizona*, 433 U.S. 350 (1977), this Court held that truthful advertising of "routine" legal services is protected by the First and Fourteenth Amendments against blanket prohibition by a State. The Court expressly reserved the question of the permissible scope of regulation of "in-person solicitation of clients. . . ." Today we . . . hold that the State—or the Bar acting with state authorization—constitutionally may discipline a lawyer for soliciting clients in person, for pecuniary gain, under circumstances likely to pose dangers that the State has a right to prevent.

I

Appellant, a member of the Ohio Bar, . . . learned . . . about an automobile accident . . . in which Carol McClintock, a young woman with whom appellant was casually acquainted, had been injured. Appellant made a telephone call to Ms. McClintock's parents, who informed him that their daughter was in the hospital. Appellant suggested that he might visit Carol in the hospital. Mrs. McClintock assented to the idea, but requested that appellant first stop by at her home.

During appellant's visit with the McClintocks, they explained that their daughter had been driving the family automobile on a local road when she was hit by an uninsured motorist. Both Carol and her passenger, Wanda Lou Holbert, were injured and hospitalized. In response to the McClintocks' expression of apprehension that they might be sued by Holbert, appellant explained that Ohio's guest statute would preclude such a suit. When appellant suggested to the McClintocks that they hire a lawyer, Mrs. McClintock retorted that such a decision would be up to Carol, who was 18 years old and would be the beneficiary of a successful claim.

Appellant proceeded to the hospital, where he found Carol lying in traction in her room. After a brief conversation about her condition, appellant told Carol he would represent her and asked her to sign an agreement. Carol said she would have to discuss the matter with her parents. She did not sign the agreement, but asked appellant to have her parents come to see her. Appellant also attempted to see Wanda Lou

Holbert, but learned that she had just been released from the hospital. . . . He then departed for another visit with the McClintocks.

On his way, appellant detoured to the scene of the accident, where he took a set of photographs. He also picked up a tape recorder, which he concealed under his raincoat before arriving at the McClintocks' residence. Once there, he re-examined their automobile insurance policy, discussed with them the law applicable to passengers, and explained the consequences of the fact that the driver who struck Carol's car was an uninsured motorist. Appellant discovered that the McClintocks' insurance policy would provide benefits of up to $12,500 each for Carol and Wanda Lou under an uninsured-motorist clause. Mrs. McClintock acknowledged that both Carol and Wanda Lou could sue for their injuries, but recounted to appellant that "Wanda swore up and down she would not do it." . . . The McClintocks also told appellant that Carol had phoned to say that appellant could "go ahead" with her representation. Two days later, appellant returned to Carol's hospital room to have her sign a contract, which provided that he would receive one-third of her recovery.

In the meantime, appellant obtained Wanda Lou's name and address from the McClintocks after telling them he wanted to ask her some questions about the accident. He then visited Wanda Lou at her home, without having been invited. He again concealed his tape recorder and recorded most of the conversation with Wanda Lou. After a brief, unproductive inquiry about the facts of the accident, appellant told Wanda Lou that he was representing Carol and that he had a "little tip" for Wanda Lou: the McClintocks' insurance policy contained an uninsured-motorist clause which might provide her with a recovery of up to $12,500. The young woman, who was 18 years of age and not a high school graduate at the time, replied to appellant's query about whether she was going to file a claim by stating that she really did not understand what was going on. Appellant offered to represent her, also, for a contingent fee of one-third of any recovery, and Wanda Lou stated "O.K."[1]

Wanda's mother attempted to repudiate her daughter's oral assent the following day, when appellant called on the telephone to speak to Wanda. Mrs. Holbert informed appellant that she and her daughter did not want to sue anyone or to have appellant represent them, and that if they decided to sue, they would consult their own lawyer. Appellant insisted that Wanda had entered into a binding agreement. A month later Wanda confirmed in writing that she wanted neither to sue nor to be represented by appellant. She requested that appellant notify the insurance company that he was not

---

[1] Appellant told Wanda that she should indicate assent by stating "O.K.," which she did. Appellant later testified: "I would say that most of my clients have essentially that much of a communication. . . . I think most of my clients, that's the way I practice law." . . . In explaining the contingent-fee arrangement, appellant told Wanda Lou that his representation would not "cost [her] anything" because she would receive two-thirds of the recovery if appellant were successful in representing her but would not "have to pay [him] anything" otherwise.

her lawyer, as the company would not release a check to her until he did so.[2] Carol also eventually discharged appellant. Although another lawyer represented her in concluding a settlement with the insurance company, she paid appellant one-third of her recovery[3] in settlement of his lawsuit against her for breach of contract.

Both Carol McClintock and Wanda Lou Holbert filed [disciplinary] complaints against appellant.... After a hearing, the Board found that appellant had violated Disciplinary Rules 2–103(A) and 2–104(A) of the Ohio Code of Professional Responsibility.[4] The Board rejected appellant's defense that his conduct was protected under the First and Fourteenth Amendments. The Supreme Court of Ohio adopted the findings of the Board, reiterated that appellant's conduct was not constitutionally protected, and increased the sanction of a public reprimand recommended by the Board to indefinite suspension.

... We now affirm the judgment of the Supreme Court of Ohio.

II

The solicitation of business by a lawyer through direct, in-person communication with the prospective client has long been viewed as inconsistent with the profession's ideal of the attorney-client relationship and as posing a significant potential for harm to the prospective client. It has been proscribed by the organized Bar for many years. Last Term the Court ruled that the justifications for prohibiting truthful, "restrained" advertising concerning "the availability and terms of routine legal services" are insufficient to override society's interest, safeguarded by the First and Fourteenth Amendments, in assuring the free flow of commercial information. *Bates*, 433 U.S. at 384.... The balance struck in *Bates* does not predetermine the outcome in this case. The entitlement of in-person solicitation of clients to the protection of the First Amendment differs from that of the kind of advertising approved in *Bates*, as does the strength of the State's countervailing interest in prohibition.

A

Appellant contends that his solicitation of the two young women as clients is indistinguishable, for purposes of constitutional analysis, from

---

[2] Before appellant would "disavow further interest and claim" in Wanda Lou's recovery, he insisted by letter that she first pay him the sum of $2,466.66, which represented one-third of his "conservative" estimate of the worth of her claim.

[3] Carol recovered the full $12,500 and paid appellant $4,166.66. She testified that she paid the second lawyer $900 as compensation for his services.

[4] DR 2–103(A) of the Ohio Code (1970) provides: "A lawyer shall not recommend employment, as a private practitioner, of himself, his partner, or associate to a non-lawyer who has not sought his advice regarding employment of a lawyer." DR 2–104(A) (1970) provides in relevant part: "A lawyer who has given unsolicited advice to a layman that he should obtain counsel or take legal action shall not accept employment resulting from that advice, except that: (1) A lawyer may accept employment by a close friend, relative, former client (if the advice is germane to the former employment), or one whom the lawyer reasonably believes to be a client."

the advertisement in *Bates*. Like that advertisement, his meetings with the prospective clients apprised them of their legal rights and of the availability of a lawyer to pursue their claims. According to appellant, such conduct is "presumptively an exercise of his free speech rights" which cannot be curtailed in the absence of proof that it actually caused a specific harm that the State has a compelling interest in preventing. But in-person solicitation of professional employment by a lawyer does not stand on a par with truthful advertising about the availability and terms of routine legal services. . . .

In-person solicitation by a lawyer of remunerative employment is a business transaction in which speech is an essential but subordinate component. While this does not remove the speech from the protection of the First Amendment, . . . it lowers the level of appropriate judicial scrutiny.

As applied in this case, the Disciplinary Rules are said to have limited the communication of two kinds of information. First, appellant's solicitation imparted to Carol McClintock and Wanda Lou Holbert certain information about his availability and the terms of his proposed legal services. In this respect, in-person solicitation serves much the same function as the advertisement at issue in *Bates*. But there are significant differences as well. Unlike a public advertisement, which simply provides information and leaves the recipient free to act upon it or not, in-person solicitation may exert pressure and often demands an immediate response, without providing an opportunity for comparison or reflection. The aim and effect of in-person solicitation may be to provide a one-sided presentation and to encourage speedy and perhaps uninformed decisionmaking; there is no opportunity for intervention or counter-education by agencies of the Bar, supervisory authorities, or persons close to the solicited individual. . . . In-person solicitation . . . actually may disserve the individual and societal interest, identified in *Bates*, in facilitating "informed and reliable decisionmaking." . . .

It also is argued that in-person solicitation may provide the solicited individual with information about his or her legal rights and remedies. In this case, appellant gave Wanda Lou a "tip" about the prospect of recovery based on the uninsured-motorist clause in the McClintocks' insurance policy, and he explained that clause and Ohio's guest statute to Carol McClintock's parents. But neither of the Disciplinary Rules here at issue prohibited appellant from communicating information to these young women about their legal rights and the prospects of obtaining a monetary recovery, or from recommending that they obtain counsel. DR 2–104(A) merely prohibited him from using the information as bait with which to obtain an agreement to represent them for a fee. The Rule does not prohibit a lawyer from giving unsolicited legal advice; it proscribes the acceptance of employment resulting from such advice.

... While entitled to some constitutional protection, appellant's conduct is subject to regulation in furtherance of important state interests.

B

The state interests implicated in this case are particularly strong. In addition to its general interest in protecting consumers and regulating commercial transactions, the State bears a special responsibility for maintaining standards among members of the licensed professions. "The interest of the States in regulating lawyers is especially great since lawyers are essential to the primary governmental function of administering justice, and have historically been 'officers of the courts.'" While lawyers act in part as "self-employed businessmen," they also act "as trusted agents of their clients, and as assistants to the court in search of a just solution to disputes."

... The substantive evils of solicitation have been stated over the years in sweeping terms: stirring up litigation, assertion of fraudulent claims, debasing the legal profession, and potential harm to the solicited client in the form of overreaching, overcharging, underrepresentation, and misrepresentation. The American Bar Association, as amicus curiae, defends the rule against solicitation primarily on three broad grounds: It is said that the prohibitions embodied in DR 2–103(A) and 2–104(A) serve to reduce the likelihood of overreaching and the exertion of undue influence on lay persons, to protect the privacy of individuals, and to avoid situations where the lawyer's exercise of judgment on behalf of the client will be clouded by his own pecuniary self-interest.

... [A]ppellant has conceded that the State has a legitimate and indeed "compelling" interest in preventing those aspects of solicitation that involve fraud, undue influence, intimidation, overreaching, and other forms of "vexatious conduct." We agree that protection of the public from these aspects of solicitation is a legitimate and important state interest.

III

Appellant's concession that strong state interests justify regulation to prevent the evils he enumerates would end this case but for his insistence that none of those evils was found to be present in his acts of solicitation. He challenges what he characterizes as the "indiscriminate application" of the Rules to him and thus attacks the validity of DR 2–103(A) and DR 2–104(A) not facially, but as applied to his acts of solicitation. And because no allegations or findings were made of the specific wrongs appellant concedes would justify disciplinary action, appellant ... argues that we must decide whether a State may discipline him for solicitation per se without offending the First and Fourteenth Amendments.

... [A]ppellant errs in assuming that the constitutional validity of the judgment below depends on proof that his conduct constituted actual overreaching or inflicted some specific injury on Wanda Holbert or Carol McClintock. His assumption flows from the premise that nothing less than actual proved harm to the solicited individual would be a sufficiently important state interest to justify disciplining the attorney who solicits employment in person for pecuniary gain.

Appellant's argument misconceives the nature of the State's interest. The Rules prohibiting solicitation are prophylactic measures whose objective is the prevention of harm before it occurs. The Rules were applied in this case to discipline a lawyer for soliciting employment for pecuniary gain under circumstances likely to result in the adverse consequences the State seeks to avert. In such a situation, which is inherently conducive to overreaching and other forms of misconduct, the State has a strong interest in adopting and enforcing rules of conduct designed to protect the public from harmful solicitation by lawyers whom it has licensed.

The State's perception of the potential for harm in circumstances such as those presented in this case is well founded. The detrimental aspects of face-to-face selling even of ordinary consumer products have been recognized and addressed by the Federal Trade Commission, and it hardly need be said that the potential for overreaching is significantly greater when a lawyer, a professional trained in the art of persuasion, personally solicits an unsophisticated, injured, or distressed lay person.[5] Such an individual may place his trust in a lawyer, regardless of the latter's qualifications or the individual's actual need for legal representation, simply in response to persuasion under circumstances conducive to uninformed acquiescence. Although it is argued that personal solicitation is valuable because it may apprise a victim of misfortune of his legal rights, the very plight of that person not only makes him more vulnerable to influence but also may make advice all the more intrusive. Thus, under these adverse conditions the overtures of an uninvited lawyer may distress the solicited individual simply because of their obtrusiveness and the invasion of the individual's privacy, even when no other harm materializes. Under such circumstances, it is not unreasonable for the State to presume that in-person solicitation by lawyers more often than not will be injurious to the person solicited.

The efficacy of the State's effort to prevent such harm to prospective clients would be substantially diminished if, having proved a solicitation in circumstances like those of this case, the State were required in addition to prove actual injury. Unlike the advertising in *Bates*, in-person

---

[5] Most lay persons are unfamiliar with the law, with how legal services normally are procured, and with typical arrangements between lawyer and client. To be sure, the same might be said about the lay person who seeks out a lawyer for the first time. But the critical distinction is that in the latter situation the prospective client has made an initial choice of a lawyer at least for purposes of a consultation; has chosen the time to seek legal advice; has had a prior opportunity to confer with family, friends, or a public or private referral agency; and has chosen whether to consult with the lawyer alone or accompanied.

solicitation is not visible or otherwise open to public scrutiny. Often there is no witness other than the lawyer and the lay person whom he has solicited, rendering it difficult or impossible to obtain reliable proof of what actually took place. This would be especially true if the lay person were so distressed at the time of the solicitation that he could not recall specific details at a later date. If appellant's view were sustained, in-person solicitation would be virtually immune to effective oversight and regulation by the State or by the legal profession, in contravention of the State's strong interest in regulating members of the Bar in an effective, objective, and self-enforcing manner. It therefore is not unreasonable, or violative of the Constitution, for a State to respond with what in effect is a prophylactic rule.

On the basis of the undisputed facts of record, we conclude that the Disciplinary Rules constitutionally could be applied to appellant. He approached two young accident victims at a time when they were especially incapable of making informed judgments or of assessing and protecting their own interests. He solicited Carol McClintock in a hospital room where she lay in traction and sought out Wanda Lou Holbert on the day she came home from the hospital, knowing from his prior inquiries that she had just been released. Appellant urged his services upon the young women and used the information he had obtained from the McClintocks, and the fact of his agreement with Carol, to induce Wanda to say "O.K." in response to his solicitation. He employed a concealed tape recorder, seemingly to [e]nsure that he would have evidence of Wanda's oral assent to the representation. He emphasized that his fee would come out of the recovery, thereby tempting the young women with what sounded like a cost-free and therefore irresistible offer. He refused to withdraw when Mrs. Holbert requested him to do so only a day after the initial meeting between appellant and Wanda Lou and continued to represent himself to the insurance company as Wanda Holbert's lawyer.

The court below did not hold that these or other facts were proof of actual harm to Wanda Holbert or Carol McClintock but . . . the absence of explicit proof or findings of harm or injury is immaterial. The facts in this case present a striking example of the potential for overreaching that is inherent in a lawyer's in-person solicitation of professional employment. They also demonstrate the need for prophylactic regulation in furtherance of the State's interest in protecting the lay public. We hold that the application of DR 2–103(A) and 2–104(A) to appellant does not offend the Constitution.

. . .

* * *

Live Person-to-Person Contact. Take a look at Model Rule 7.3(b), which regulates live person-to-person solicitation of clients. If the *Ohralik* case occurred today, would Ohralik have been subject to professional discipline if, instead of visiting Carol at the hospital, he had called her on the telephone and offered to represent her? What are the justifications for distinguishing between live person-to-person solicitation and non-live person-to-person solicitation?

Rule 7.3's Exceptions. Relying on *Ohralik*, Rule 7.3 generally prohibits live person-to-person solicitation. However, Rule 7.3(b) does allow lawyers to engage in real-time solicitation with respect to three categories of people. Review the exceptions in Rule 7.3(b) where live person-to-person solicitation is permitted. Why is such solicitation permitted in these cases?

Runners and Cappers. Imagine that instead of personally visiting Carol, Ohralik hired a non-lawyer to approach Carol in the hospital and make the same sales pitch that Ohralik made in the actual case. (Such individuals are sometimes referred to as "runners" or "cappers.") Would he still have been subject to discipline? *See* Rules 7.2(b) and 8.4(a).

Problem 8.1. Sensing an opportunity for new business following the plane crash, lawyer Malcolm decided to engage in some solicitation of potential clients. Malcolm obtained the cell phone numbers of some of the families of the crash victims as well as the numbers for several of the property owners who suffered property damage as a result of the crash. Malcolm texted these individuals within a week of the crash and expressed his condolences while also offering his legal services in connection with the crash. Read Model Rule 7.3(b) and its comments. Is Malcolm subject to professional discipline for engaging in improper non-live person-to-person solicitation?

* * *

IN RE PRIMUS
436 U.S. 412 (1978)

MR. JUSTICE POWELL delivered the opinion of the Court.

We consider on this appeal whether a State may punish a member of its Bar who, seeking to further political and ideological goals through associational activity, including litigation, advises a lay person of her legal rights and discloses in a subsequent letter that free legal assistance is available from a nonprofit organization with which the lawyer and her associates are affiliated. . . .

I

Appellant, Edna Smith Primus, is a lawyer practicing in Columbia, S.C. During the period in question, she was . . . an officer of and cooperating lawyer with the Columbia branch of the American Civil Liberties Union (ACLU). She received no compensation for her work on behalf of the ACLU, but was paid a retainer as a legal consultant for the South Carolina Council on Human Relations (Council), a nonprofit organization with offices in Columbia.

During the summer of 1973, local and national newspapers reported that pregnant mothers on public assistance in Aiken County, S.C., were being sterilized or threatened with sterilization as a condition of the continued receipt of medical assistance under the Medicaid program. Concerned by this development, Gary Allen, an Aiken businessman and officer of a local organization serving indigents, called the Council requesting that one of its representatives come to Aiken to address some of the women who had been sterilized. At the Council's behest, appellant, who had not known Allen previously, called him and arranged a meeting in his office in July 1973. Among those attending was Mary Etta Williams, who had been sterilized by Dr. Clovis H. Pierce after the birth of her third child. Williams and her grandmother attended the meeting because Allen, an old family friend, had invited them and because Williams wanted "[t]o see what it was all about. . . ." At the meeting, appellant advised those present, including Williams and the other women who had been sterilized by Dr. Pierce, of their legal rights and suggested the possibility of a lawsuit.

Early in August 1973 the ACLU informed appellant that it was willing to provide representation for Aiken mothers who had been sterilized. Appellant testified that after being advised by Allen that Williams wished to institute suit against Dr. Pierce, she decided to inform Williams of the ACLU's offer of free legal representation. Shortly after receiving appellant's letter[1] . . . Williams visited Dr. Pierce to discuss the progress of

---

[1] . . . [T]he letter stated:

August 30, 1973

Mrs. Marietta Williams
347 Sumter Street
Aiken, South Carolina 29801

Dear Mrs. Williams:

You will probably remember me from talking with you at Mr. Allen's office in July about the sterilization performed on you. The American Civil Liberties Union would like to file a lawsuit on your behalf for money against the doctor who performed the operation. We will be coming to Aiken in the near future and would like to explain what is involved so you can understand what is going on.

Now I have a question to ask of you. Would you object to talking to a women's magazine about the situation in Aiken? The magazine is doing a feature story on the whole sterilization problem and wants to talk to you and others in South Carolina. If you don't mind doing this, call me *collect* at 254–8151 on Friday before 5:00, if you receive this letter in time. Or call me on Tuesday morning (after Labor Day) *collect*.

I want to assure you that this interview is being done to show what is happening to women against their wishes, and is not being done to harm you in any way. But I want you to decide, so call me collect and let me know of your decision. This practice must stop.

About the lawsuit, if you are interested, let me know, and I'll let you know when we will come down to talk to you about it. We will be coming to talk to Mrs. Waters at the same time; she has already asked the American Civil Liberties Union to file a suit on her behalf.

her third child, who was ill. At the doctor's office, she encountered his lawyer and at the latter's request signed a release of liability in the doctor's favor. Williams showed appellant's letter to the doctor and his lawyer, and they retained a copy. She then called appellant from the doctor's office and announced her intention not to sue. There was no further communication between appellant and Williams.

[In a disciplinary complaint, appellant was charged with engaging in] "solicitation in violation of the Canons of Ethics" by sending the August 30, 1973, letter to Williams... Appellant ... asserted, inter alia, that her conduct was protected by the First and Fourteenth Amendments....

... The panel filed a report recommending that appellant be found guilty of soliciting a client on behalf of the ACLU, in violation of Disciplinary Rules (DR) 2–103(D)(5)(a) and (c) and 2–104(A)(5) of the Supreme Court of South Carolina,[2] and that a private reprimand be issued. It noted that "[t]he evidence is inconclusive as to whether [appellant] solicited Mrs. Williams on her own behalf, but she did solicit Mrs. Williams on behalf of the ACLU, which would benefit financially in the event of successful prosecution of the suit for money damages."...

... [T]he Supreme Court of South Carolina entered an order which ... increased the sanction, sua sponte, to a public reprimand.

... We now reverse.

Sincerely,
s/ Edna Smith
Edna Smith
Attorney-at-law

[2] [DR 2–103(D)(5)(a) and (c) provided as follows:]

(D) A lawyer shall not knowingly assist a person or organization that recommends, furnishes, or pays for legal services to promote the use of his services or those of his partners or associates. However, he may cooperate in a dignified manner with the legal service activities of any of the following, provided that his independent professional judgment is exercised in behalf of his client without interference or control by any organization or other person:

(5) Any other non-profit organization that recommends, furnishes, or pays for legal services to its members or beneficiaries, but only in those instances and to the extent that controlling constitutional interpretation at the time of the rendition of the services requires the allowance of such legal service activities, and only if the following conditions, unless prohibited by such interpretation, are met:

(a) The primary purposes of such organization do not include the rendition of legal services ... [and]

(c) Such organization does not derive a financial benefit from the rendition of legal services by the lawyer.

[DR 2–104(A)(5) provided as follows:]

(A) A lawyer who has given unsolicited advice to a layman that he should obtain counsel or take legal action shall not accept employment resulting from that advice, except that:

(5) If success in asserting rights or defenses of his client in litigation in the nature of a class action is dependent upon the joinder of others, a lawyer may accept, but shall not seek, employment from those contacted for the purpose of obtaining their joinder.

II

This appeal concerns the tension between contending values of considerable moment to the legal profession and to society. Relying upon *NAACP v. Button*, 371 U.S. 415 (1963), and its progeny, appellant maintains that her activity involved constitutionally protected expression and association. In her view, South Carolina has not shown that the discipline meted out to her advances a subordinating state interest in a manner that avoids unnecessary abridgment of First Amendment freedoms. . . .

[W]e decide today in *Ohralik v. Ohio State Bar Assn.*, 436 U.S. 447, that the States may vindicate legitimate regulatory interests through proscription, in certain circumstances, of in-person solicitation by lawyers who seek to communicate purely commercial offers of legal assistance to lay persons.

Unlike the situation in *Ohralik*, however, appellant's act of solicitation took the form of a letter to a woman with whom appellant had discussed the possibility of seeking redress for an allegedly unconstitutional sterilization. This was not in-person solicitation for pecuniary gain. Appellant was communicating an offer of free assistance by attorneys associated with the ACLU, not an offer predicated on entitlement to a share of any monetary recovery. And her actions were undertaken to express personal political beliefs and to advance the civil-liberties objectives of the ACLU, rather than to derive financial gain. The question presented in this case is whether, in light of the values protected by the First and Fourteenth Amendments, these differences materially affect the scope of state regulation of the conduct of lawyers.

III

. . . [In *Button* this Court held] "that the activities of the NAACP, its affiliates and legal staff shown on this record are modes of expression and association protected by the First and Fourteenth Amendments which Virginia may not prohibit, under its power to regulate the legal profession, as improper solicitation of legal business violative of [state law] and the Canons of Professional Ethics." 371 U.S. at 428–29. The solicitation of prospective litigants, many of whom were not members of the NAACP or the Conference, for the purpose of furthering the civil-rights objectives of the organization and its members was held to come within the right " 'to engage in association for the advancement of beliefs and ideas.' " *Id.* at 430. . . .

Subsequent decisions have interpreted *Button* as establishing the principle that "collective activity undertaken to obtain meaningful access to the courts is a fundamental right within the protection of the First Amendment." *United Transportation Union v. Michigan Bar*, 401 U.S. 576, 585 (1971). . . .

IV

We turn now to the question whether appellant's conduct implicates interests of free expression and association sufficient to justify the level of protection recognized in *Button* and subsequent cases. . . .

. . . [T]he record does not support the state court's effort to draw a meaningful distinction between the ACLU and the NAACP. . . . For the ACLU, as for the NAACP, "litigation is not a technique of resolving private differences"; it is "a form of political expression" and "political association." [*Button*,] 371 U.S. at 429, 431.

. . . Appellant's letter of August 30, 1973, to Mrs. Williams thus comes within the generous zone of First Amendment protection reserved for associational freedoms. . . .

V

South Carolina's action in punishing appellant for soliciting a prospective litigant by mail, on behalf of the ACLU, must withstand the "exacting scrutiny applicable to limitations on core First Amendment rights. . . ." South Carolina must demonstrate "a subordinating interest which is compelling," and that the means employed in furtherance of that interest are "closely drawn to avoid unnecessary abridgment of associational freedoms."

Appellee contends that the disciplinary action taken in this case is part of a regulatory program aimed at the prevention of undue influence, overreaching, misrepresentation, invasion of privacy, conflict of interest, lay interference, and other evils that are thought to inhere generally in solicitation by lawyers of prospective clients, and to be present on the record before us. We do not dispute the importance of these interests. This Court's decision in *Button* makes clear, however, that "[b]road prophylactic rules in the area of free expression are suspect," and that "[p]recision of regulation must be the touchstone in an area so closely touching our most precious freedoms." 371 U.S. at 438. . . .

A

The Disciplinary Rules in question sweep broadly. Under DR 2–103(D)(5), a lawyer employed by the ACLU or a similar organization may never give unsolicited advice to a lay person that he retain the organization's free services, and it would seem that one who merely assists or maintains a cooperative relationship with the organization also must suppress the giving of such advice if he or anyone associated with the organization will be involved in the ultimate litigation. . . . Moreover, the Disciplinary Rules in question permit punishment for mere solicitation unaccompanied by proof of any of the substantive evils that appellee maintains were present in this case. In sum, the Rules in their present form have a distinct potential for dampening the kind of "cooperative activity that would make advocacy of litigation meaningful," as well as for permitting discretionary enforcement against unpopular causes.

B

. . . Where political expression or association is at issue, this Court has not tolerated the degree of imprecision that often characterizes government regulation of the conduct of commercial affairs. The approach we adopt today in *Ohralik*, 436 U.S. 447, that the State may proscribe in-person solicitation for pecuniary gain under circumstances likely to result in adverse consequences, cannot be applied to appellant's activity on behalf of the ACLU. Although a showing of potential danger may suffice in the former context, appellant may not be disciplined unless her activity in fact involved the type of misconduct at which South Carolina's broad prohibition is said to be directed.

The record does not support appellee's contention that undue influence, overreaching, misrepresentation, or invasion of privacy actually occurred in this case. Appellant's letter of August 30, 1973, followed up the earlier meeting—one concededly protected by the First and Fourteenth Amendments—by notifying Williams that the ACLU would be interested in supporting possible litigation. The letter imparted additional information material to making an informed decision about whether to authorize litigation, and permitted Williams an opportunity, which she exercised, for arriving at a deliberate decision. The letter was not facially misleading; indeed, it offered "to explain what is involved so you can understand what is going on." The transmittal of this letter—as contrasted with in-person solicitation—involved no appreciable invasion of privacy; nor did it afford any significant opportunity for overreaching or coercion. Moreover, the fact that there was a written communication lessens substantially the difficulty of policing solicitation practices that do offend valid rules of professional conduct. *See Ohralik*, 436 U.S. at 466–67. . . .

At bottom, the case against appellant rests on the proposition that a State may regulate in a prophylactic fashion all solicitation activities of lawyers because there may be some potential for overreaching, conflict of interest, or other substantive evils whenever a lawyer gives unsolicited advice and communicates an offer of representation to a layman. . . . In the context of political expression and association, however, a State must regulate with significantly greater precision.

VI

The State is free to fashion reasonable restrictions with respect to the time, place, and manner of solicitation by members of its Bar. . . . The State's special interest in regulating members whose profession it licenses, and who serve as officers of its courts, amply justifies the application of narrowly drawn rules to proscribe solicitation that in fact is misleading, overbearing, or involves other features of deception or improper influence.

As we decide today in *Ohralik*, a State also may forbid in-person solicitation for pecuniary gain under circumstances likely to result in these evils. And a State may insist that lawyers not solicit on behalf of lay organizations that exert control over the actual conduct of any ensuing litigation. . . . Accordingly, nothing in this opinion should be read to foreclose carefully tailored regulation that does not abridge unnecessarily the associational freedom of nonprofit organizations, or their members, having characteristics like those of the NAACP or the ACLU.

. . . The judgment of the Supreme Court of South Carolina is Reversed.

MR. JUSTICE BRENNAN took no part in the consideration or decision of this case.

* * *

Rule 7.3's Exceptions. Obviously relying on the distinction drawn by the Court in *Primus*, Rule 7.3(b) limits its prohibition on marketing activities to those motivated by "the lawyer's pecuniary gain." Why is live person-to-person solicitation permitted in these cases but not in case like *Ohralik*?

Dissenting and Concurring Opinions. Justice Rehnquist dissented in *Primus*. He questioned whether there was any principled distinction between the actions of the lawyers in *Primus* and *Ohralik* and suggested that even a lawyer who works for the ACLU or similar organization might be tempted to place the organization's political goals over those of the best interests of an individual client. For his part, Justice Marshall concurred in the outcomes in *Primus* and *Ohralik*, but wrote separately to emphasize his concern that unduly restrictive solicitation rules might deprive the consumers of legal services of important information. Did the Court draw the appropriate line in these cases in terms of a lawyer's pecuniary motive? Does Rule 7.3?

The CAN-SPAM Act. In addition to the disciplinary rules governing solicitation of clients, there are state and federal laws that may apply. For instance, the federal CAN-SPAM Act, 15 U.S.C. § 7701 *et seq.*, imposes specific requirements on those who send emails for the purpose of advertising or promoting a commercial product or service. These requirements include, among others, that the email not be deceptive or misleading, that it provides recipients with the ability to opt out of future mailings, and that the email is clearly and conspicuously identified as an advertisement or solicitation.

* * *

B. OTHER RESTRICTIONS ON LAWYER SOLICITATION

Model Rule 7.3 places some restrictions on even non-live person-to-person solicitation. In *Shapero v. Kentucky Bar Association*, 486 U.S. 466 (1988), the Court held that states cannot ban targeted direct mail solicitation of persons known to need legal services, as long as the letters are not false or deceptive. In *Shapero*, a lawyer was disciplined for targeting persons facing foreclosure by mailing a letter offering a free consultation. In holding that Kentucky's blanket ban on targeted direct mail solicitation offended the First Amendment, the Court rejected the assertion that this case was simply "*Ohralik* in writing," *id.* at 475, and noted that solicitation letters are closer to the *Bates* pole than to the *Ohralik* pole on the marketing continuum: "A letter, like a printed advertisement (but unlike a lawyer), can readily be put in a drawer to be considered later, ignored, or discarded." *Id.* at 467.

After almost two decades of invalidating state prohibitions on various forms of lawyer marketing, in 1995, the Court finally upheld a state regulation of targeted direct mail solicitation.

FLORIDA BAR V. WENT FOR IT, INC.
515 U.S. 618 (1995)

JUSTICE O'CONNOR delivered the opinion of the Court.

Rules of the Florida Bar prohibit personal injury lawyers from sending targeted direct-mail solicitations to victims and their relatives for 30 days following an accident or disaster. This case asks us to consider whether such rules violate the First and Fourteenth Amendments of the Constitution. We hold that in the circumstances presented here, they do not.

I

In 1989, the Florida Bar completed a 2-year study of the effects of lawyer advertising on public opinion. After conducting hearings, commissioning surveys, and reviewing extensive public commentary, the Bar determined that several changes to its advertising rules were in order.... Two of these amendments are at issue in this case. Rule 4–7.4(b)(1) provides that "[a] lawyer shall not send, or knowingly permit to be sent, ... a written communication to a prospective client for the purpose of obtaining professional employment if: (A) the written communication concerns an action for personal injury or wrongful death or otherwise relates to an accident or disaster involving the person to whom the communication is addressed or a relative of that person, unless the accident or disaster occurred more than 30 days prior to the mailing of the communication." Rule 4–7.8(a) states that "[a] lawyer shall not accept referrals from a lawyer referral service unless the service: (1) engages in no communication with the public and in no direct contact with prospective clients in a manner that would violate the Rules of Professional Conduct if the communication or contact were made by the lawyer." Together, these rules create a brief 30-day blackout period after an accident during which lawyers may not, directly or indirectly, single out accident victims or their relatives in order to solicit their business.

In March 1992, G. Stewart McHenry and his wholly owned lawyer referral service, Went For It, Inc., filed this action for declaratory and injunctive relief in the United States District Court for the Middle District of Florida challenging Rules 4.7–4(b)(1) and 4.7–8 as violative of the First and Fourteenth Amendments to the Constitution. McHenry alleged that he routinely sent targeted solicitations to accident victims or their survivors within 30 days after accidents and that he wished to continue doing so in the future. Went For It, Inc. represented that it wished to contact accident victims or their survivors within 30 days of accidents and to refer potential clients to participating Florida lawyers. In October 1992, McHenry was disbarred for reasons unrelated to this suit. . . .

The District Court . . . entered summary judgment for the plaintiffs, . . . relying on *Bates v. State Bar of Arizona*, 433 U.S. 350 (1977), and subsequent cases. The Eleventh Circuit affirmed on similar grounds. . . . We granted certiorari . . . and now reverse.

II

A

Constitutional protection for attorney advertising, and for commercial speech generally, is of recent vintage. . . .

In *Bates v. State Bar of Arizona, supra*, the Court struck a ban on price advertising for what it deemed "routine" legal services. . . . Expressing confidence that legal advertising would only be practicable for such simple, standardized services, the Court rejected the State's proffered justifications for regulation.

Nearly two decades of cases have built upon the foundation laid by *Bates*. It is now well established that lawyer advertising is commercial speech and, as such, is accorded a measure of First Amendment protection. Such First Amendment protection, of course, is not absolute. We have always been careful to distinguish commercial speech from speech at the First Amendment's core. . . . [W]e engage in "intermediate" scrutiny of restrictions on commercial speech, analyzing them under the framework set forth in *Central Hudson Gas & Electric Corp. v. Public Service Comm'n of N.Y.*, 447 U.S. 557 (1980). Under *Central Hudson*, the government may freely regulate commercial speech that concerns unlawful activity or is misleading. . . . Commercial speech that falls into neither of those categories, like the advertising at issue here, may be regulated if the government satisfies a test consisting of three related prongs: first, the government must assert a substantial interest in support of its regulation; second, the government must demonstrate that the restriction on commercial speech directly and materially advances that interest; and third, the regulation must be " 'narrowly drawn' "....

B

"Unlike rational basis review, the *Central Hudson* standard does not permit us to supplant the precise interests put forward by the State with other suppositions".... The Florida Bar asserts that it has a substantial interest in protecting the privacy and tranquility of personal injury victims and their loved ones against intrusive, unsolicited contact by lawyers.... This interest obviously factors into the Bar's paramount (and repeatedly professed) objective of curbing activities that "negatively affec[t] the administration of justice."... Because direct mail solicitations in the wake of accidents are perceived by the public as intrusive, the Bar argues, the reputation of the legal profession in the eyes of Floridians has suffered commensurately.... The regulation, then, is an effort to protect the flagging reputations of Florida lawyers by preventing them from engaging in conduct that, the Bar maintains, " 'is universally regarded as deplorable and beneath common decency because of its intrusion upon the special vulnerability and private grief of victims or their families.' "

... We have little trouble crediting the Bar's interest as substantial. On various occasions we have accepted the proposition that "States have a compelling interest in the practice of professions within their boundaries, and ... as part of their power to protect the public health, safety, and other valid interests they have broad power to establish standards for licensing practitioners and regulating the practice of professions." Our precedents also leave no room for doubt that "the protection of potential clients' privacy is a substantial state interest."

... Under *Central Hudson*'s second prong, the State must demonstrate that the challenged regulation "advances the Government's interest 'in a direct and material way.' " That burden, we have explained, " 'is not satisfied by mere speculation and conjecture; rather, a governmental body seeking to sustain a restriction on commercial speech must demonstrate that the harms it recites are real and that its restriction will in fact alleviate them to a material degree.' " In *Edenfield*, the Court invalidated a Florida ban on in-person solicitation by certified public accountants (CPAs). We observed that the State Board of Accountancy had "present[ed] no studies that suggest personal solicitation of prospective business clients by CPAs creates the dangers of fraud, overreaching, or compromised independence that the Board claims to fear." Moreover, "[t]he record [did] not disclose any anecdotal evidence ... that validate[d] the Board's suppositions." . . . In fact, we concluded that the only evidence in the record tended to "contradic[t] rather than strengthe[n] the Board's submissions."

. . . The direct-mail solicitation regulation before us does not suffer from such infirmities. The Florida Bar submitted a 106-page summary of its 2-year study of lawyer advertising and solicitation to the District Court. That summary contains data—both statistical and anecdotal—supporting the Bar's contentions that the Florida public views direct-mail solicitations in the immediate wake of accidents as an intrusion on privacy that reflects poorly upon the profession. As of June 1989, lawyers mailed 700,000 direct solicitations in Florida annually, 40% of which were aimed at accident victims or their survivors. . . . A survey of Florida adults commissioned by the Bar indicated that Floridians "have negative feelings about those attorneys who use direct mail advertising." . . . Fifty-four percent of the general population surveyed said that contacting persons concerning accidents or similar events is a violation of privacy. . . . A random sampling of persons who received direct-mail advertising from lawyers in 1987 revealed that 45% believed that direct-mail solicitation is "designed to take advantage of gullible or unstable people"; 34% found such tactics "annoying or irritating"; 26% found it "an invasion of your privacy"; and 24% reported that it "made you angry." . . . Significantly, 27% of direct-mail recipients reported that their regard for the legal profession and for the judicial process as a whole was "lower" as a result of receiving the direct mail. . . .

The anecdotal record mustered by the Bar is noteworthy for its breadth and detail. With titles like "Scavenger Lawyers" (*The Miami Herald*, Sept. 29, 1987) and "Solicitors Out of Bounds" (*St. Petersburg Times*, Oct. 26, 1987), newspaper editorial pages in Florida have burgeoned with criticism of Florida lawyers who send targeted direct mail to victims shortly after accidents. . . . The study summary also includes page upon page of excerpts from complaints of direct-mail recipients. For example, a Florida citizen described how he was " 'appalled and angered by the brazen attempt' " of a law firm to solicit him by letter shortly after he was injured and his fiancee was killed in an auto accident. . . . Another found it " 'despicable and inexcusable' " that a Pensacola lawyer wrote to his mother three days after his father's funeral. . . . Another described how she was " 'astounded' " and then " 'very angry' " when she received a solicitation following a minor accident. . . . Still another described as " 'beyond comprehension' " a letter his nephew's family received the day of the nephew's funeral. . . . One citizen wrote, " 'I consider the unsolicited contact from you after my child's accident to be of the rankest form of ambulance chasing and in incredibly poor taste. . . . I cannot begin to express with my limited vocabulary the utter contempt in which I hold you and your kind.' " . . .

In light of this showing—which respondents at no time refuted . . .— we conclude that the Bar has satisfied the second prong of the *Central Hudson* test. . . . After scouring the record, we are satisfied that the ban on direct-mail solicitation in the immediate aftermath of accidents, unlike the rule at issue in *Edenfield*, targets a concrete, nonspeculative harm.

In reaching a contrary conclusion, the Court of Appeals determined that this case was governed squarely by *Shapero v. Kentucky Bar Assn.*, 486 U.S. 466 (1988). Making no mention of the Bar's study, the court concluded that " 'a targeted letter [does not] invade the recipient's privacy any more than does a substantively identical letter mailed at large. The invasion, if any, occurs when the lawyer discovers the recipient's legal affairs, not when he confronts the recipient with the discovery.' " . . .

While some of *Shapero*'s language might be read to support the Court of Appeals' interpretation, *Shapero* differs in several fundamental respects from the case before us. First and foremost, *Shapero*'s treatment of privacy was casual. Contrary to the dissent's suggestions, . . . the State in *Shapero* did not seek to justify its regulation as a measure undertaken to prevent lawyers' invasions of privacy interests. . . . Rather, the State focused exclusively on the special dangers of overreaching inhering in targeted solicitations. . . . Second, in contrast to this case, *Shapero* dealt with a broad ban on all direct-mail solicitations, whatever the time frame and whoever the recipient. Finally, the State in *Shapero* assembled no evidence attempting to demonstrate any actual harm caused by targeted direct mail. The Court rejected the State's effort to justify a prophylactic ban on the basis of blanket, untested assertions of undue influence and overreaching. . . .

We find the Court's perfunctory treatment of privacy in *Shapero* to be of little utility in assessing this ban on targeted solicitation of victims in the immediate aftermath of accidents. While it is undoubtedly true that many people find the image of lawyers sifting through accident and police reports in pursuit of prospective clients unpalatable and invasive, this case targets a different kind of intrusion. The Florida Bar has argued, and the record reflects, that a principal purpose of the ban is "protecting the personal privacy and tranquility of [Florida's] citizens from crass commercial intrusion by attorneys upon their personal grief in times of trauma." . . . The intrusion targeted by the Bar's regulation stems not from the fact that a lawyer has learned about an accident or disaster (as the Court of Appeals notes, in many instances a lawyer need only read the newspaper to glean this information), but from the lawyer's confrontation of victims or relatives with such information, while wounds are still open, in order to solicit their business. In this respect, an untargeted letter mailed to society at large is different in kind from a targeted solicitation; the untargeted letter involves no willful or knowing affront to or invasion of the tranquility of bereaved or injured individuals and simply does not cause the same kind of reputational harm to the profession unearthed by the Florida Bar's study. . . .

The harm targeted by the Florida Bar cannot be eliminated by the targeted letter's brief journey to the trash can. The purpose of the 30-day targeted direct-mail ban is to forestall the outrage and irritation with the state-licensed legal profession that the practice of direct solicitation only days after accidents has engendered. The Bar is concerned not with citizens' "offense" in the abstract, ... but with the demonstrable detrimental effects that such "offense" has on the profession it regulates.[1] Moreover, the harm posited by the Bar is as much a function of simple receipt of targeted solicitations within days of accidents as it is a function of the letters' contents. Throwing the letter away shortly after opening it may minimize the latter intrusion, but it does little to combat the former....

Passing to *Central Hudson*'s third prong, we examine the relationship between the Florida Bar's interests and the means chosen to serve them. [With respect to this prong, the Court employs an intermediate test that is less stringent than the "least restrictive means" test but more stringent than rational basis review.]

Respondents levy a great deal of criticism, echoed in the dissent ... at the scope of the Bar's restriction on targeted mail. "[B]y prohibiting written communications to all people, whatever their state of mind," respondents charge, the rule "keeps useful information from those accident victims who are ready, willing and able to utilize a lawyer's advice." This criticism may be parsed into two components. First, the rule does not distinguish between victims in terms of the severity of their injuries. According to respondents, the rule is unconstitutionally overinclusive insofar as it bans targeted mailings even to citizens whose injuries or grief are relatively minor.... Second, the rule may prevent citizens from learning about their legal options, particularly at a time when other actors—opposing counsel and insurance adjusters—may be clamoring for victims' attentions. Any benefit arising from the Bar's regulation, respondents implicitly contend, is outweighed by these costs.

We are not persuaded by respondents' allegations of constitutional infirmity. We find little deficiency in the ban's failure to distinguish among injured Floridians by the severity of their pain or the intensity of their grief. Indeed, it is hard to imagine the contours of a regulation that might satisfy respondents on this score. Rather than drawing difficult lines on the basis that some injuries are "severe" and some situations appropriate (and others, presumably, inappropriate) for grief, anger, or emotion, the Florida Bar has crafted a ban applicable to all postaccident or disaster solicitations

---

[1] Missing this nuance altogether, the dissent asserts apocalyptically that we are "unsettl[ing] leading First Amendment precedents".... We do no such thing. There is an obvious difference between situations in which the Government acts in its own interests, or on behalf of entities it regulates, and situations in which the Government is motivated primarily by paternalism....

for a brief 30-day period.... The Bar's rule is reasonably well-tailored to its stated objective of eliminating targeted mailings whose type and timing are a source of distress to Floridians, distress that has caused many of them to lose respect for the legal profession.

Respondents' second point would have force if the Bar's rule were not limited to a brief period and if there were not many other ways for injured Floridians to learn about the availability of legal representation during that time. Our lawyer advertising cases have afforded lawyers a great deal of leeway to devise innovative ways to attract new business. Florida permits lawyers to advertise on prime-time television and radio as well as in newspapers and other media. They may rent space on billboards. They may send untargeted letters to the general population, or to discrete segments thereof. There are, of course, pages upon pages devoted to lawyers in the Yellow Pages of Florida telephone directories. These listings are organized alphabetically and by area of specialty.... These ample alternative channels for receipt of information about the availability of legal representation during the 30-day period following accidents may explain why, despite the ample evidence, testimony, and commentary submitted by those favoring (as well as opposing) unrestricted direct-mail solicitation, respondents have not pointed to—and we have not independently found—a single example of an individual case in which immediate solicitation helped to avoid, or failure to solicit within 30 days brought about, the harms that concern the dissent.... In fact, the record contains considerable empirical survey information suggesting that Floridians have little difficulty finding lawyers when they need one.... Finding no basis to question the commonsense conclusion that the many alternative channels for communicating necessary information about attorneys are sufficient, we see no defect in Florida's regulation.

III

Speech by professionals obviously has many dimensions. There are circumstances in which we will accord speech by attorneys on public issues and matters of legal representation the strongest protection our Constitution has to offer. *See, e.g., Gentile v. State Bar of Nevada*, 501 U.S. 1030 (1991). This case, however, concerns pure[ly] commercial advertising, for which we have always reserved a lesser degree of protection under the First Amendment. Particularly because the standards and conduct of state-licensed lawyers have traditionally been subject to extensive regulation by the States, it is all the more appropriate that we limit our scrutiny of state regulations to a level commensurate with the " 'subordinate position' " of commercial speech in the scale of First Amendment values.

We believe that the Florida Bar's 30-day restriction on targeted direct-mail solicitation of accident victims and their relatives withstands scrutiny under the three-part *Central Hudson* test that we have devised for this context. The Bar has substantial interest both in protecting injured Floridians from invasive conduct by lawyers and in preventing the erosion of confidence in the profession that such repeated invasions have engendered. The Bar's proffered study, unrebutted by respondents below, provides evidence indicating that the harms it targets are far from illusory. The palliative [solution] devised by the Bar to address these harms is narrow both in scope and in duration. The Constitution, in our view, requires nothing more.

The judgment of the Court of Appeals, accordingly, is reversed.

JUSTICE KENNEDY, with whom JUSTICE STEVENS, JUSTICE SOUTER, and JUSTICE GINSBURG join, dissenting.

. . .

Although I agree with the Court that the case can be resolved by following the three-part inquiry we have identified to assess restrictions on commercial speech, . . . [i]t would oversimplify to say that what we consider here is commercial speech and nothing more, for in many instances the banned communications may be vital to the recipients' right to petition the courts for redress of grievances. . . .

As the Court notes, the first of the *Central Hudson* factors to be considered is whether the interest the State pursues in enacting the speech restriction is a substantial one. . . . The State says two different interests meet this standard. The first is the interest "in protecting the personal privacy and tranquility" of the victim and his or her family. As the Court notes, that interest has recognition in our decisions as a general matter; but it does not follow that the privacy interest in the cases the majority cites is applicable here. The problem the Court confronts, and cannot overcome, is our recent decision in *Shapero v. Kentucky Bar Assn.*, 486 U.S. 466 (1988). In assessing the importance of the interest in that solicitation case, we made an explicit distinction between direct in-person solicitations and direct mail solicitations. *Shapero*, like this case, involved a direct mail solicitation, and there the State recited its fears of "overreaching and undue influence." . . . We found, however, no such dangers presented by direct mail advertising. We reasoned that "[a] letter, like a printed advertisement (but unlike a lawyer), can readily be put in a drawer to be considered later, ignored, or discarded." . . .

To avoid the controlling effect of *Shapero* in the case before us, the Court seeks to declare that a different privacy interest is implicated. As it sees the matter, the substantial concern is that victims or their families will be offended by receiving a solicitation during their grief and trauma. But we do not allow restrictions on speech to be justified on the ground that the expression might offend the listener. . . .

. . .

In the face of these difficulties of logic and precedent, the State and the opinion of the Court turn to a second interest: protecting the reputation and dignity of the legal profession. The argument is, it seems fair to say, that all are demeaned by the crass behavior of a few. The argument takes a further step in the amicus brief filed by the Association of Trial Lawyers of America. There it is said that disrespect for the profession from this sort of solicitation (but presumably from no other sort of solicitation) results in lower jury verdicts. In a sense, of course, these arguments are circular. While disrespect will arise from an unethical or improper practice, the majority begs a most critical question by assuming that direct mail solicitations constitute such a practice. The fact is, however, that direct solicitation may serve vital purposes and promote the administration of justice, and to the extent the bar seeks to protect lawyers' reputations by preventing them from engaging in speech some deem offensive, the State is doing nothing more (as amicus the Association of Trial Lawyers of America is at least candid enough to admit) than manipulating the public's opinion by suppressing speech that informs us how the legal system works. The disrespect argument thus proceeds from the very assumption it tries to prove, which is to say that solicitations within 30 days serve no legitimate purpose. This, of course, is censorship pure and simple; and censorship is antithetical to the first principles of free expression.

II

Even were the interests asserted substantial, the regulation here fails the second part of the *Central Hudson* test, which requires that the dangers the State seeks to eliminate be real and that a speech restriction or ban advance that asserted State interest in a direct and material way.... Here, what the State has offered falls well short of demonstrating that the harms it is trying to redress are real, let alone that the regulation directly and materially advances the State's interests. The parties and the Court have [relied upon] a document prepared by the Florida Bar, one of the adverse parties, and submitted to the District Court in this case.... This document includes no actual surveys, few indications of sample size or selection procedures, no explanations of methodology, and no discussion of excluded results. There is no description of the statistical universe or scientific framework that permits any productive use of the information.... The most generous reading of this document permits identification of 34 pages on which direct mail solicitation is arguably discussed. Of these, only two are even a synopsis of a study of the attitudes of Floridians towards such solicitations. The bulk of the remaining pages include comments by lawyers about direct mail (some of them favorable), excerpts from citizen complaints about such solicitation, and a few excerpts from newspaper articles on the topic. Our cases require something more than a few pages of self-serving and unsupported statements by the State to demonstrate that a regulation directly and materially advances the elimination of a real harm when the State seeks to suppress truthful and nondeceptive speech....

III

... Were it appropriate to reach the third part of the *Central Hudson* test, it would be clear that the relationship between the Bar's interests and the means chosen to serve them is not a reasonable fit. The Bar's rule creates a flat ban that prohibits far more speech than necessary to serve the purported state interest. Even assuming that interest were legitimate, there is a wild disproportion between the harm supposed and the speech ban enforced....

... The only seeming justification for the State's restriction is the one the Court itself offers, which is that attorneys can and do resort to other ways of communicating important legal information to potential clients. Quite aside from the latent protectionism for the established bar that the argument discloses, it fails for the more fundamental reason that it concedes the necessity for the very representation the attorneys solicit and the State seeks to ban. The accident victims who are prejudiced to vindicate the State's purported desire for more dignity in the legal profession will be the very persons who most need legal advice, for they are the victims who, because they lack education, linguistic ability, or familiarity with the legal system, are unable to seek out legal services....

... The State's restriction deprives accident victims of information which may be critical to their right to make a claim for compensation for injuries. The telephone book and general advertisements may serve this purpose in part; but the direct solicitation ban will fall on those who most need legal representation: for those with minor injuries, the victims too ill-informed to know an attorney may be interested in their cases; for those with serious injuries, the victims too ill-informed to know that time is of the essence if counsel is to assemble evidence and warn them not to enter into settlement negotiations or evidentiary discussions with investigators for opposing parties.... A solicitation letter is not a contract. Nothing in the record shows that these communications do not at the least serve the purpose of informing the prospective client that he or she has a number of different attorneys from whom to choose, so that the decision to select counsel, after an interview with one or more interested attorneys, can be deliberate and informed....

IV

It is most ironic that, for the first time since *Bates v. State Bar of Arizona*, the Court now orders a major retreat from the constitutional guarantees for commercial speech in order to shield its own profession from public criticism.... There is no authority for the proposition that the Constitution permits the State to promote the public image of the legal profession by suppressing information about the profession's business aspects. If public respect for the profession erodes because solicitation distorts the idea of the law as most lawyers see it, it must be remembered that real progress begins with more rational speech, not less. . . .

. . . By validating Florida's rule, today's majority is complicit in the Bar's censorship. For these reasons, I dissent from the opinion of the Court and from its judgment.

* * *

Post-*Went for It*. Following *Went for It*, a number of jurisdictions adopted similar blackout periods. Conn. Rules of Prof'l Conduct R. 7.3(c)(4) (imposing a forty-day moratorium on soliciting clients for "an action for personal injury or wrongful death or otherwise relates to an accident or disaster involving the person to whom the solicitation is addressed or a relative of that person"); Ga. Rules of Prof'l Conduct R. 7.3(a)(3) (imposing a thirty-day moratorium on "written communication concern[ing] an action for personal injury or wrongful death"); Tenn. Rules of Prof'l Conduct R. 7.3(d)(3) (imposing a thirty-day moratorium on the solicitation of potential clients if "the communication concerns an action for personal injury, divorce or legal separation, worker's compensation, wrongful death, or otherwise relates to an accident, filing of divorce or legal separation, or disaster involving the person to whom the communication is addressed or a member of that person's family").

Problem 8.2. In addition to sending text messages to potential clients concerning the plane crash, Malcolm decided to reach out to potential clients in other ways.

(a) Malcolm followed up his text messages with letters mailed to the home addresses of the family members of victims and property owners whose property had been damaged, offering his services. Is Malcolm subject to discipline in Old Dakota (which has adopted Model Rule 7.3) for sending these letters?

(b) Malcolm also decided to engage in some digital marketing in connection with the crash. Specifically, he contracted with a digital marketing company that helped identify relevant internet search terms. When a user used one of those terms while conducting a search connected to the crash, truthful information about Malcolm's practice and his willingness to represent clients in connection with the crash would appear as one of the "sponsored" ads in the list of search results. Has Malcolm engaged in prohibited solicitation in violation of Model Rule 7.3 by utilizing this type of marketing?

(c) When the New Dakota Board of Professional Responsibility found out about Malcolm's text messages and letters, it brought him up on disciplinary charges for violating the thirty-day moratorium. (Refer back to the language of the moratorium and the history surrounding its adoption.) Malcolm decides to challenge the constitutionality of the moratorium. In light of *Went for It*, can the moratorium withstand a constitutional challenge?

Problem 8.3. You are a member of a committee in Old Dakota that is considering adopting a 30-day blackout period on solicitation in certain situations like those adopted by other states. Would you be in favor of such rules? If so, which ones?

Profile of Attorney Professionalism. Edna Smith Primus was the lawyer whose actions were at issue in the *Primus* case included in this chapter. Primus, "the daughter of a sharecropper," was the "first [B]lack woman to graduate from the law school of the University of South Carolina" in 1972 and was only the third Black woman to be admitted to the South Carolina Bar. *Supreme Court Clears Black Woman Attorney*, JET, Sept. 14, 1978, at 6. Roughly a year after receiving her law degree, Primus became involved in the events that led to the Supreme Court decision that bears her name. Primus, a frequent advocate for the underrepresented, was an attorney with the South Carolina Council on Human Relations (SCCHR), a group that "played a key role in fostering better living and social conditions for African-Americans and promoting racial harmony within South Carolina and the South generally." *Records of the South Carolina Council on Human Relations,* South Carolina Library, The University of South Carolina, *available at* http://library.sc.edu/socar/mnscrpts/scchr.html. Primus also served as a legal services attorney in the city of Columbia and served in the role of managing attorney of that office for many years.

Edna Primus sought to advance the rights of women and minorities throughout her long legal career. Her professional life serves as an example of principled and persistent advocacy that highlights the important role of lawyers as active members in their communities.

PART 3

THE CLIENT-LAWYER RELATIONSHIP

■ ■ ■

Now that you have attracted a prospective client, you are ready to form an attorney-client relationship and then commence your representation of the client. In Part 3, we examine the attorney-client relationship.

Section 1 of Part 3 focuses on the formation of the attorney-client relationship, with chapters focusing on the agreement between the lawyer and client about the scope of the representation to be provided by the lawyer, the fee to be paid by the client, and the related duty of safekeeping client funds and property. In this section we will also introduce the lawyer's duties to prospective clients.

Subsequent sections focus on fiduciary obligations and professional conduct duties in an ongoing attorney-client relationship—communication and decision-making in Section 2; competence and diligence in Section 3; confidentiality and privilege in Section 4; and the obligation to avoid conflicts of interest in Section 5. Finally in Section 6, we examine the termination of the attorney-client relationship and the duties lawyers owe to their former clients.

SECTION 1

ESTABLISHING THE CLIENT-LAWYER RELATIONSHIP

■ ■ ■

This section includes three chapters that focus on the formation of the attorney-client relationship, including payment for the lawyer's services. Chapter 9 covers the legal rules that determine when an attorney-client relationship has been entered, the duties a lawyer owes to prospective clients (including those the lawyer decides not to represent), and how the parties may limit the scope of the lawyer's representation of a client. Chapter 10 focuses on the fees a lawyer may permissibly charge a client for providing legal services. Chapter 11 then examines the lawyer's legal and ethical obligation to avoid billing fraud, as well as a lawyer's duty to safeguard client funds and property entrusted to the lawyer.

CHAPTER 9

ESTABLISHING A CLIENT-LAWYER RELATIONSHIP

■ ■ ■

Chapter Hypothetical. Darren, a lawyer in the law firm of Palsgraf & Pennoyer LLP, is facing two legal malpractice claims and two disciplinary complaints stemming from two separate incidents. The first involves Darren's failure to file a lawsuit prior to the expiration of the statute of limitations. The second involves Darren's alleged failure to protect a client's interests during a divorce proceeding. In addition, a third prospective client, who holds some controversial views, has approached Darren about possible representation.

Assuming that the advertising or solicitation efforts of a lawyer in private practice have been successful in attracting a prospective client, there remains the final step of entering into a client-attorney relationship. As discussed in Chapter 1, a lawyer assumes various common law and ethical duties by entering into a client-attorney relationship. This includes a duty to competently and diligently pursue the client's interests. Therefore, it is essential that the parties understand the scope of the lawyer's anticipated representation.

* * *

A. ENTERING INTO A CLIENT-LAWYER RELATIONSHIP

The *Model Rules of Professional Conduct* do not specify when a client-lawyer relationship is formed. Instead, one must look to substantive law. Once such a relationship is formed, a lawyer assumes a fiduciary duty towards the client. But even if a lawyer and a prospective client do not enter into a formal client-lawyer relationship, the lawyer may owe certain duties to the individual.

* * *

1. AGREEING TO REPRESENT ANOTHER

Section 14 of the *Restatement (Third) of the Law Governing Lawyers* summarizes the substantive law regarding when a client-lawyer relationship is formed. One obvious situation is when there is mutual assent. But § 14(b) lists another way such a relationship can be formed. Read this section and then answer the question in the problem that follows:

Problem 9.1. Darren's profile on the Palsgraf & Pennoyer website lists personal injury law as one of Darren's practice areas. Elizabeth reviews the website and calls Darren's office. She tells Darren's assistant that she was hurt when she fell in a store about a year ago and would like Darren to represent her in a personal injury action. Darren's assistant tells Elizabeth to bring in any medical bills or other relevant information she might have. She also arranges a medical examination for Elizabeth with the store's insurance company. However, Darren's assistant does not tell Elizabeth that Darren would then decide whether to take the case. Elizabeth delivers the requested information to Darren's office the next day. Due to an oversight, Darren does not communicate with Elizabeth for thirty days, and then eventually tells Elizabeth that he does not wish to take the case. By then, the statute of limitations had run on Elizabeth's claims. Could a jury applying the test from the *Restatement* find that an attorney-client relationship existed between Darren and Elizabeth prior to Darren's communication declining representation?

The Duty to Assess the Facts. Note that a lawyer has a duty to inquire into, and assess the facts and circumstances of, a possible representation before entering into the client-lawyer relationship in order to make sure that the lawyer can ethically represent the client. *See* Model Rule 1.16, Comment [1].

* * *

2. DUTIES TO PROSPECTIVE CLIENTS

Even if a prospective client and a lawyer do not form a client-lawyer relationship, the lawyer owes various legal and professional duties to the prospective client. Section 15 of the *Restatement (Third) of the Law Governing Lawyers* defines the concept of a "prospective client" and articulates the legal duties owed by a lawyer to a prospective client. Model Rule 1.18(a) and Comment [2] define the concept for purposes of the professional conduct rules.

As you read the following case, consider whether the plaintiff, Mrs. Togstad, would qualify as a prospective client under the *Restatement* and *Model Rules* approaches.

* * *

TOGSTAD V. VESELY, OTTO, MILLER & KEEFE
291 N.W.2d 686 (Minn. 1980) (en banc)

PER CURIAM.

This is an appeal by the defendants from a judgment of the Hennepin County District Court involving an action for legal malpractice. The jury found that the defendant attorney Jerre Miller was negligent and that, as a direct result of such negligence, plaintiff John Togstad sustained damages in the amount of $610,500 and his wife, plaintiff Joan Togstad, in the amount of $39,000. Defendants (Miller and his law firm) appeal to this court from the denial of their motion for judgment notwithstanding the verdict or, alternatively, for a new trial. We affirm.

[The Court explains that as a result of alleged medical malpractice by a hospital and a physician, Mr. Togstad was left paralyzed on his right side and unable to speak.]

About 14 months after her husband's hospitalization began, plaintiff Joan Togstad met with attorney Jerre Miller regarding her husband's condition. Neither she nor her husband was personally acquainted with Miller or his law firm prior to that time. John Togstad's former work supervisor, Ted Bucholz, made the appointment and accompanied Mrs. Togstad to Miller's office. Bucholz was present when Mrs. Togstad and Miller discussed the case.

Mrs. Togstad testified that she told Miller "everything that happened at the hospital".... She stated that she "believed" she had told Miller "about the procedure and what was undertaken, what was done, and what happened." She brought no records with her. Miller took notes and asked questions during the meeting, which lasted 45 minutes to an hour. At its conclusion, according to Mrs. Togstad, Miller said that "he did not think we had a legal case, however, he was going to discuss this with his partner." She understood that if Miller changed his mind after talking to his partner, he would call her. Mrs. Togstad "gave it" a few days and, since she did not hear from Miller, decided "that they had come to the conclusion that there wasn't a case." No fee arrangements were discussed, no medical authorizations were requested, nor was Mrs. Togstad billed for the interview.

Mrs. Togstad denied that Miller had told her his firm did not have expertise in the medical malpractice field, urged her to see another attorney, or related to her that the statute of limitations for medical malpractice actions was two years. She did not consult another attorney until one year after she talked to Miller. Mrs. Togstad indicated that she did not confer with another attorney earlier because of her reliance on Miller's "legal advice" that they "did not have a case."

On cross-examination, Mrs. Togstad was asked whether she went to Miller's office "to see if he would take the case of [her] husband . . . ." She replied, "Well, I guess it was to go for legal advice, what to do, where shall we go from here? That is what we went for." Again, in response to defense counsel's questions, Mrs. Togstad testified as follows:

> Q. And it was clear to you, was it not, that what was taking place was a preliminary discussion between a prospective client and lawyer as to whether or not they wanted to enter into an attorney-client relationship?
>
> A. I am not sure how to answer that. It was for legal advice as to what to do.
>
> Q. And Mr. Miller was discussing with you your problem and indicating whether he, as a lawyer, wished to take the case, isn't that true?
>
> A. Yes.

On re-direct examination, Mrs. Togstad acknowledged that when she left Miller's office she understood that she had been given a "qualified, quality legal opinion that [she and her husband] did not have a [medical] malpractice case."

Miller's testimony was different in some respects from that of Mrs. Togstad. Like Mrs. Togstad, Miller testified that Mr. Bucholz arranged and was present at the meeting, which lasted about 45 minutes. According to Miller, Mrs. Togstad described the hospital incident, including the conduct of the nurses. He asked her questions, to which she responded. Miller testified that "[t]he only thing I told [Mrs. Togstad] after we had pretty much finished the conversation was that there was nothing related in her factual circumstances that told me that she had a case that our firm would be interested in undertaking."

Miller also claimed he related to Mrs. Togstad "that because of the grievous nature of the injuries sustained by her husband, that this was only my opinion and she was encouraged to ask another attorney if she wished for another opinion" and "she ought to do so promptly." He testified that he informed Mrs. Togstad that his firm "was not engaged as experts" in the area of medical malpractice, and that they associated with the Charles Hvass firm in cases of that nature. Miller stated that at the end of the conference he told Mrs. Togstad that he would consult with Charles Hvass and if Hvass's opinion differed from his, Miller would so inform her. Miller recollected that he called Hvass a "couple days" later and discussed the case with him. It was Miller's impression that Hvass thought there was no liability for [medical] malpractice in the case. Consequently, Miller did not communicate with Mrs. Togstad further.

On cross-examination, Miller testified as follows:

Q. Now, so there is no misunderstanding, and I am reading from your deposition, you understood that she was consulting with you as a lawyer, isn't that correct?

A. That's correct.

Q. That she was seeking legal advice from a professional attorney licensed to practice in this state and in this community?

A. I think you and I did have another interpretation or use of the term "advice". She was there to see whether or not she had a case and whether the firm would accept it.

Q. We have two aspects; number one, your legal opinion concerning liability of a case for [medical] malpractice; number two, whether there was or wasn't liability, whether you would accept it, your firm, two separate elements, right?

A. I would say so. . . . Certainly, she was seeking my opinion as an attorney in the sense of whether or not there was a case that the firm would be interested in undertaking.

Kenneth Green, a Minneapolis attorney, was called as an expert by plaintiffs. He stated that in rendering legal advice regarding a claim of medical malpractice, the "minimum" an attorney should do would be to request medical authorizations from the client, review the hospital records, and consult with an expert in the field. John McNulty, a Minneapolis attorney, and Charles Hvass testified as experts on behalf of the defendants. McNulty stated that when an attorney is consulted as to whether he will take a case, the lawyer's only responsibility in refusing it is to so inform the party. He testified, however, that when a lawyer is asked his legal opinion on the merits of a medical malpractice claim, community standards require that the attorney check hospital records and consult with an expert before rendering his opinion.

Hvass stated that he had no recollection of Miller's calling him in October 1972 relative to the Togstad matter. He testified that:

> . . . [W]hen a person comes in to me about a medical malpractice action, based upon what the individual has told me, I have to make a decision as to whether or not there probably is or probably is not, based upon that information, medical malpractice. And if, in my judgment, based upon what the client has told me, there is not medical malpractice, I will so inform the client.

Hvass stated, however, that he would never render a "categorical" opinion. In addition, Hvass acknowledged that if he were consulted for a "legal opinion" regarding medical malpractice and 14 months had expired since the incident in question, "ordinary care and diligence" would require him to inform the party of the two-year statute of limitations applicable to that type of action.

This case was submitted to the jury by way of a special verdict form. The jury found that Dr. Blake and the hospital were negligent and that Dr. Blake's negligence (but not the hospital's) was a direct cause of the injuries sustained by John Togstad; that there was an attorney-client contractual relationship between Mrs. Togstad and Miller; that Miller was negligent in rendering advice regarding the possible claims of Mr. and Mrs. Togstad; that, but for Miller's negligence, plaintiffs would have been successful in the prosecution of a legal action against Dr. Blake; and that neither Mr. nor Mrs. Togstad was negligent in pursuing their claims against Dr. Blake. The jury awarded damages to Mr. Togstad of $610,500 and to Mrs. Togstad of $39,000....

... The thrust of Mrs. Togstad's testimony is that she went to Miller for legal advice, was told there wasn't a case, and relied upon this advice in failing to pursue the claim for medical malpractice. In addition, according to Mrs. Togstad, Miller did not qualify his legal opinion by urging her to seek advice from another attorney, nor did Miller inform her that he lacked expertise in the medical malpractice area. Assuming this testimony is true, ... we believe a jury could properly find that Mrs. Togstad sought and received legal advice from Miller under circumstances which made it reasonably foreseeable to Miller that Mrs. Togstad would be injured if the advice were negligently given. Thus, under either a tort or contract analysis, there is sufficient evidence in the record to support the existence of an attorney-client relationship.

... [D]efendants [also] assert that a new trial should be awarded on the ground that the trial court erred by refusing to instruct the jury that Miller's failure to inform Mrs. Togstad of the two-year statute of limitations for medical malpractice could not constitute negligence....

... [T]here is adequate evidence supporting the claim that Miller was also negligent in failing to advise Mrs. Togstad of the two-year medical malpractice limitations period and thus the trial court acted properly in refusing to instruct the jury in the manner urged by defendants. One of defendants' expert witnesses, Charles Hvass, testified:

Q. Now, Mr. Hvass, where you are consulted for a legal opinion and advice concerning malpractice and 14 months have elapsed (since the incident in question), wouldn't you hold yourself out as competent to give a legal opinion and advice to these people concerning their rights, wouldn't ordinary care and diligence require that you inform them that there is a two-year statute of limitations within which they have to act or lose their rights?

A. Yes. I believe I would have advised someone of the two-year period of limitation, yes.

Consequently, based on the testimony of Mrs. Togstad, *i.e.*, that she requested and received legal advice from Miller concerning the [medical] malpractice claim, and the above testimony of Hvass, we must reject the defendants' contention, as it was reasonable for a jury to determine that Miller acted negligently in failing to inform Mrs. Togstad of the applicable limitations period.

... Based on the foregoing, we hold that the jury's findings are adequately supported by the record. Accordingly, we uphold the trial court's denial of defendants' motion for judgment notwithstanding the jury verdict....

* * *

Duties Owed to Prospective Clients. Section 15 of the *Restatement (Third) of the Law Governing Lawyers* explains that a lawyer owes a prospective client the common-law duties of reasonable care, confidentiality, loyalty, and protection of property entrusted to the lawyer. Identify how Model Rule 1.18 (including the comments to that rule) addresses these issues.

* * *

How Can a Lawyer Avoid Owing a Duty of Reasonable Care to Someone Interested in Becoming a Client? If a person interested in becoming a client makes contact with a lawyer, how can the lawyer avoid owing that person a duty of reasonable care if the lawyer is not interested in taking on the person as a client? For example, in the *Togstad* case, what are the things that lawyer Miller could have done to avoid Mr. and Mrs. Togstad bringing a successful claim for legal malpractice against him and his firm? The following problem addresses this issue—steps to take to avoid obligations to prospective clients—in the context of a law firm website.

Problem 9.2. Palsgraf & Pennoyer LLP's website has a link entitled "Contact Us." When a visitor clicks on this link, a screen comes up that asks, "Think you might need a lawyer?" There is a box on the screen in which the visitor is invited to briefly describe the nature of the visitor's legal issue and to leave a name, phone number, and email. Look at Comments [2]–[4] to Rule 1.18. What advice would you give to the firm concerning its website? *See* ABA Formal Opinion No. 10–457 (2010).

* * *

B. DEFINING THE SCOPE OF REPRESENTATION

1. IN GENERAL

Upon entering into a client-lawyer relationship, most lawyers will send an engagement letter that clarifies the scope of that representation, i.e., exactly what it is the lawyer is expected to do. The engagement letter should define the matter on which the lawyer has been retained with particularity and clearly define the lawyer's obligations regarding the matter. Rule 1.5(b) explains the extent of a lawyer's duty to communicate the scope of the representation to the client. (The next chapter will address the fees a lawyer may charge in detail, but Rule 1.5(b) also generally requires that the lawyer communicate the basis or rate of the fee and expenses to a client.)

* * *

2. LIMITING THE SCOPE OF REPRESENTATION

Sometimes a lawyer and client may wish to limit the scope of the lawyer's representation. For example, maybe the client has limited goals. Maybe there are particular actions the lawyer refuses to take on behalf of the client. Or maybe the client cannot afford the full menu of services the lawyer would ordinarily provide in the situation. Model Rule 1.2(c) provides that a lawyer may limit the scope of the representation if the limitation is reasonable under the circumstances and the client gives informed consent. As the next case illustrates, the failure to effectively communicate with a client concerning the scope of representation may have other consequence aside from professional discipline.

* * *

NICHOLS V. KELLER
19 Cal.Rptr.2d 601 (Ct. App. 1993)

MARTIN, ACTING PRESIDING JUSTICE.

Plaintiff appeals from summary judgments in a legal malpractice action arising from an industrial accident.

In December 1987, Zurn Industries employed the 46-year-old plaintiff at a cogeneration plant construction project in Crow's Landing, Stanislaus County. Zurn was a subcontractor and Kiewit Industrial was the general contractor on the project. Plaintiff had been a union boilermaker for over 24 years. On December 7, plaintiff commenced work on the exterior of a large boiler [when he was injured on the job].

On February 24, 1988, plaintiff and his wife met with defendant E. Paul Fulfer, an attorney with the defendant firm of Fulfer & Fulfer, to discuss plaintiff's accident and legal rights and remedies. At the conclusion of the meeting, defendant Fulfer had plaintiff sign a workers' compensation application for adjudication of claim. Fulfer executed the form as "applicant's attorney" and filed the application on plaintiff's behalf with the Stockton office of the Division of Industrial Accidents/California

Department of Industrial Relations.... Defendant Fulfer then associated defendant Edward Keller, an attorney with defendant firm of LaCoste, Keller, Mello & Land, to prosecute the workers' compensation claim. Fulfer signed a formal pleading bearing the caption "association of attorneys" on January 20, 1989.

Defendant Keller met with plaintiff on March 28, 1988, and said he would represent plaintiff in his pending workers' compensation matter against Zurn Industries and Aetna Casualty and Surety Company. Defendant Keller continued to represent plaintiff in the workers' compensation proceeding until July 1989.

Sometime in 1989, plaintiff and his wife traveled from their home in Nevada to a workers' compensation medical appointment in the San Francisco area. On their return trip, they visited the Boilermakers Union Hall in Pittsburg, California. Plaintiff and his wife spoke with union employees Jim Wilson and Greg Bingham regarding plaintiff's accident at the cogeneration plant. They suggested plaintiff meet with another attorney and scheduled an appointment with James Butler of the law offices of William L. Veen in San Francisco.

On July 7, 1989, plaintiff and his wife met with attorney Butler. According to plaintiff, "At this meeting I learned for the first time that a third-party claim could and very likely should have been brought in regards to my industrial injury in December 1987, and that my wife and I may have a legal claim against Edward C. Keller and Elbert Paul Fulfer, attorneys, who had failed to advise or inform us of these facts."

On March 21, 1990, plaintiff filed a complaint for damages in Stanislaus County Superior Court. Plaintiff named attorneys Keller, Fulfer, and their respective law firms as defendants. He alleged causes of action for legal malpractice [involving Fulfer's failure to advise plaintiff concerning the availability of a third-party claim and the applicable statute of limitations].

On December 17, 1990, defendant Fulfer and his law firm filed a motion for summary judgment. Defendants alleged ... the attorney-client relationship, if any, which existed between defendant Fulfer and plaintiff was limited solely to the subject matter of plaintiff's workers' compensation claim....

On January 31, 1991, the court filed a minute order granting defendants' motions for summary judgment.... "Defendant Keller's motion for summary judgment is granted.... [I]t is undisputed that the representation was undertaken for the limited purpose of the workman's compensation claim. Furthermore, an attorney's obligation does not include a duty to advise on all possible alternatives no matter how remote or tenuous...."

On April 4, 1991, plaintiff filed a notice of appeal.

DISCUSSION

I. DID DEFENDANTS OWE PLAINTIFF A DUTY TO ADVISE HIM OF THE POSSIBILITY OF A THIRD-PARTY CIVIL LAWSUIT AND THE APPLICABLE STATUTE OF LIMITATIONS?

Plaintiff contends: "[A]n attorney does have a duty to provide sound advice in furtherance of the client's best interests. Mr. Nichols, a man of limited education ... went to respondents seeking legal advice and representation from members of the Bar of California regarding any and all legal remedies he might be eligible for arising from his work injury. Respondents' failure to advise appellant that he may have a third party claim; respondents' failure to advise appellant regarding the applicable statute of limitations; and respondents' failure to refer appellant to an attorney experienced in third party actions was a breach of that duty. . . ."

Actionable legal malpractice is compounded of the same basic elements as other kinds of actionable negligence: duty, breach of duty, causation, and damage. . . . An attorney, by accepting employment to give legal advice or render legal services, impliedly agrees to use ordinary judgment, care, skill, and diligence in the performance of the tasks he or she undertakes.

The question of the existence of a legal duty of care in a given factual situation presents a question of law which is to be determined by the courts alone. . . . Absent the existence of a duty by the professional to the claimant, there can be no breach and no negligence.

One legal scholar has noted:

> An attorney advising or representing an injured employee concerning workers' compensation benefits must consider whether the employee should also pursue a lawsuit for civil damages against (1) a third party ... or (2) the employee's employer or coworker, or the employer's workers' compensation insurer. . . . For comparable injuries, damages recoveries often greatly exceed workers' compensation recoveries.

> The compensation attorney should either personally conduct a skilled and careful inquiry into the prospects for obtaining damages for the client that would exceed recoverable workers' compensation benefits or refer the client to an attorney who is competent to determine the prospects for such a recovery. . . .

> A workers' compensation attorney's failure to file and pursue a timely lawsuit for civil damages, or to refer the client to another lawyer for that purpose, can be the basis for a legal malpractice action. . . .

Often, it is prudent to initiate both a compensation claim and a civil action, and to pursue both until it is determined that one of them will provide a full recovery. . . .

Peyrat, *Cal. Workers' Damages Practice* (Cont. Ed. Bar 1985) § 1.4, pp. 4–5.

A significant area of exposure for the workers' compensation attorney concerns that attorney's responsibility for counseling regarding a potential third-party action. One of an attorney's basic functions is to advise. Liability can exist because the attorney failed to provide advice. Not only should an attorney furnish advice when requested, but he or she should also volunteer opinions when necessary to further the client's objectives. The attorney need not advise and caution of every possible alternative, but only of those that may result in adverse consequences if not considered. Generally speaking, a workers' compensation attorney should be able to limit the retention to the compensation claim if the client is cautioned (1) there may be other remedies which the attorney will not investigate and (2) other counsel should be consulted on such matters. However, even when a retention is expressly limited, the attorney may still have a duty to alert the client to legal problems which are reasonably apparent, even though they fall outside the scope of the retention. The rationale is that, as between the lay client and the attorney, the latter is more qualified to recognize and analyze the client's legal needs. The attorney need not represent the client on such matters. Nevertheless, the attorney should inform the client of the limitations of the attorney's representation and of the possible need for other counsel. MALLEN & SMITH, LEGAL MALPRACTICE (3d ed. 1989) §§ 19.5, 19.28, pp. 159–62, 229–33. . . .

In their motions for summary judgment, defendant attorneys maintained they agreed to undertake only a limited employment. Attorney Fulfer asserted he agreed to represent plaintiff in the workers' compensation matter only and, even then, for two specific purposes: (1) to file a workers' compensation application on plaintiff's behalf and (2) to refer plaintiff to defendant Keller, so the latter could actually prosecute the workers' compensation claim on plaintiff's behalf. Attorney Keller argued the attorney-client relationship between the plaintiff and himself was solely for the purpose of representation in the workers' compensation claim. Keller claimed he owed only a duty to prosecute that claim and not to prosecute any possible third-party claim or to advise plaintiff as to the prosecution of such a claim. Defendants reiterate these positions on appeal.

In his opposition to the motions for summary judgment, plaintiff attached the declaration of attorney Yale Jones, a certified specialist in workers' compensation law. Jones declared attorney Fulfer acted below the standard of care of an attorney in the Stockton area by failing to (1) advise plaintiff of the different remedies available through the Workers'

Compensation Appeal Board and through a civil action; (2) advise plaintiff of the statute of limitations applicable to plaintiff's third-party action; (3) advise plaintiff to consult another attorney concerning any available rights and remedies plaintiff might have against third parties; and (4) provide plaintiff with written advice regarding which rights defendant Fulfer would protect or which needed to be reviewed by other competent attorneys and what would happen in the event plaintiff did not protect those rights. Attorney Jones also declared defendant Keller acted below the standard of care for the same reasons.

. . . The lower court's minute order concluded: "[I]t is undisputed that the representation was undertaken for the limited purpose of the workman's compensation claim. Furthermore, an attorney's obligation does not include a duty to advise on all possible alternatives no matter how remote or tenuous. . . ."

It seems to us the foreseeability factor compels a finding of duty in cases of this type. A trained attorney is more qualified to recognize and analyze legal needs than a lay client, and, at least in part, this is the reason a party seeks out and retains an attorney to represent and advise him or her in legal matters. MALLEN & SMITH, LEGAL MALPRACTICE, *supra*, §§ 19.5, 19.28, pp. 159–62, 229–33. . . .

. . . In the context of personal injury consultations between lawyer and layperson, it is reasonably foreseeable the latter will offer a selective or incomplete recitation of the facts underlying the claim; request legal assistance by employing such everyday terms as "workers' compensation," "disability," and "unemployment"; and rely upon the consulting lawyer to describe the array of legal remedies available, alert the layperson to any apparent legal problems, and, if appropriate, indicate limitations on the retention of counsel and the need for other counsel. In the event the lawyer fails to so advise the layperson, it is also reasonably foreseeable the layperson will fail to ask relevant questions regarding the existence of other remedies and be deprived of relief through a combination of ignorance and lack or failure of understanding. And, if counsel elects to limit or prescribe his representation of the client, *i.e.*, to a workers' compensation claim only without reference or regard to any third party or collateral claims which the client might pursue if adequately advised, then counsel must make such limitations in representation very clear to his client. Thus, a lawyer who signs an application for adjudication of a workers' compensation claim and a lawyer who accepts a referral to prosecute the claim owe the claimant a duty of care to advise on available remedies, including third-party actions. . . .

. . . The lower court erroneously granted summary judgment on the duty element of legal negligence and reversal is required. . . .

* * *

Problem 9.3. Darren met with a prospective client named Agnes about the possibility of representing her in connection with her divorce. Agnes explained that she and her husband had already gone through mediation and agreed upon a settlement and distribution of the marital assets. Agnes explained that she did not want to renegotiate the agreement and that she did not need Darren to review all of the financial documents involved; she simply wanted to make sure that the agreement was clear enough so that there would not be any interpretation issues that might result in future litigation. "I'm sick of the whole thing and I just want to be done with it," an obviously distraught Agnes told Darren. Read Model Rule 1.2(c) and Comments [6]–[8]. Would Agnes' proposed limitation on the scope of representation be reasonable under Rule 1.2(c)?

Problem 9.4. Darren documented his agreement with Agnes in a letter:

Dear Agnes:

This letter will confirm that you have retained my law firm for the purpose of reviewing a Property Settlement Agreement that was the product of divorce mediation.

This letter will further confirm that I have not conducted any discovery in this matter on your behalf. I have not reviewed income tax returns or other financial documentation to confirm or verify your husband's income for the past several years. I have no information concerning the gross and net values of the property you and your husband own.

Based upon the fact that I have not had an opportunity to conduct full and complete discovery in this matter, including but not limited to appraisals of real estate and business interests, depositions and interrogatories, I am not in a position to advise you as to whether or not the Agreement is fair and equitable and whether or not you should execute the Agreement as prepared. In sum, I am not in a position to make a recommendation or determination that the Property Settlement Agreement as prepared represents a fair and reasonable compromise of the issues concerning equitable distribution, or whether the amount of alimony and/or child support that you will receive under the terms of the Agreement is an amount that would be awarded to you if, in fact, this matter proceeded to trial.

After reviewing the Agreement with you, I am satisfied that you understand the terms and conditions of the Agreement; that you feel that you are receiving a fair and equitable amount of the assets that were acquired during the marriage; and that the amount of support that is provided in the Agreement will, in fact, provide you with an income that will allow you to maintain a respectable lifestyle.

I will use my best efforts to review the Agreement for clarity and precision in an attempt to reduce the potential for future litigation.

The rest of the agreement discussed the firm's fee and other billing matters and requested that Agnes confirm her agreement with the arrangement in writing, which she did.

Agnes entered into the Property Settlement Agreement. Several months later, she learned that her husband had hidden substantial assets from her during the mediation. A simple review of the couple's tax returns and other financial records by a reasonably competent attorney would have revealed these assets. As a result, she sought to have the Agreement set aside. In addition, she sued Darren and Palsgraf & Pennoyer LLP for malpractice for failing to protect her interests, and also filed a disciplinary complaint against them in connection with Darren's representation of her in the matter.

(a) Read Model Rule 1.0(e). Did Darren obtain Agnes's informed consent as necessary under Rule 1.2(c) when limiting the scope of representation?

(b) In light of the decision in *Nichols*, is Agnes likely to be able to establish that Darren breached his duty of care for purposes of her legal malpractice claim?

* * *

Enhancing Access to Justice by Providing Limited Scope Representation. Traditionally, the legal profession was hesitant to permit lawyers to provide anything less than the full slate of services foreseeably necessary for the client's representation. But limited scope representation may be a way for clients with limited financial means to obtain legal representation.

> A lawyer who provides a client with some, but not all, of the work normally involved in litigation is said to be providing "unbundled" legal services. By this unbundling, a person who cannot afford full representation can receive at least some legal assistance. In certain circumstances, it may be preferable for a lay person to have limited legal services rather than no services at all.

Ethics Op. of the Colorado Bar Ass'n, Formal Op. 101 (1998).

Nonprofit & Court-Annexed Limited Legal Services Programs. As part of the effort to expand access to justice for those unable to afford full legal representation, legal service organizations, other non-profit organizations, and some courts have established programs—variously called legal-advice hotlines, advice-only clinics, or pro se counseling programs—through which volunteer lawyers provide limited short-term legal services to clients as permitted by Rule 1.2(c). One deterrent to lawyer participation in these types of programs is the possibility that representation of a client in one of these programs might result in a conflict of interest with an existing or former client. To address these concerns, Model Rule 6.5 relaxes the conflict of interest rules for lawyers who provide services as part of this type of program.

* * *

C. DECLINING TO TAKE A CASE

The client-lawyer relationship is contractual in nature. Therefore, both sides are generally free to enter into a relationship or decline to do so. There may be some instances in which a lawyer is required to decline representation. For example, Model Rule 1.16(a) prohibits a lawyer from representing a client where the representation would result in a violation of the rules of professional conduct or other law, or where "the lawyer's physical or mental condition materially impairs the lawyer's ability to represent the client. . . ." Obvious examples would include where the lawyer lacks the competence to represent a client or has a conflict of interest.

A lawyer might choose to decline to represent a client for other reasons. Sometimes a client or his cause might be repugnant to a lawyer. Model Rule 1.2(b) tries to alleviate concerns over the representation of repugnant clients or causes by noting that a lawyer's representation of a client "does not constitute an endorsement of the client's political, economic, social or moral views or activities." At the same time, one leading legal ethicist has argued that "[i]t is proper . . . to publicly challenge lawyers to justify their representation of particular clients." Monroe H. Freedman, *Response, The Lawyer's Moral Obligation of Justification*, 74 TEX. L. REV. 111, 112 (1995).

As discussed in an earlier chapter, Model Rule 8.4(g) prohibits discrimination on the basis of race, sex, and other characteristics in conduct related to the practice of law. When the rule was being considered, there was concern that the rule might impact lawyers' longstanding freedom to choose which clients they wished to represent. Read the rule and then consider the following problem:

Problem 9.5. A religious organization has approached Darren about the possibility of entering into a client-lawyer relationship. The organization wishes to mount a First Amendment challenge to a local ordinance that requires all schools to provide gender-neutral restrooms and locker room facilities.

(a) Would Darren be subject to discipline if he agreed to represent this organization and argue its position in court?

(b) Would Darren be subject to discipline if he declined to represent the organization based on his opposition to the organization's views?

* * *

Agreeing to Represent a Controversial Client. EC 2–27 of the old Model Code declared that "[h]istory is replete with instances of distinguished and sacrificial services by lawyers who have represented unpopular clients and causes." Perhaps the best-known literary example of an exemplary lawyer is Atticus Finch in *To Kill a Mockingbird*. What sort of client or cause would you find repugnant enough to cause you to decline representation?

Profile of Attorney Professionalism. Perhaps the most famous real-life example of a lawyer representing an unpopular client or cause is John Adams' representation of the British soldiers accused of murder in the Boston Massacre in 1770. Boston radicals used the incident to whip up public anger toward the British Crown. At the time, Adams was a 34-year-old lawyer who was asked to represent the soldiers when no one else would. "Although he realized he would be vilified by the town's inhabitants and the press, thus jeopardizing his thriving legal practice, Adams ... immediately agreed to do so, firm in his belief that all persons accused of a crime were entitled to an effective legal defense." John F. Tobin, *The Boston Massacre Trials*, N.Y. STATE BAR JOURNAL 12 (July/August 2013). Adams was indeed vilified: "Within days of agreeing to defend Preston and the soldiers, rocks were thrown through the windows of Adams's home and he was jeered by passersby on the streets." *Id.* Adams was accused of having been bribed to take the case. DAVID MCCULLOUGH, JOHN ADAMS 68 (2001). Ultimately, the commanding officer and six of the soldiers involved were acquitted. Two other soldiers were convicted of manslaughter.

The local paper criticized Adams for representing the soldiers, and Adams claimed to have lost more than half of his practice as a result of his representation. *Id.* at 68. However, Adams' career, of course, survived. Over time, his public standing actually improved as a result of his actions. Looking back on his life's accomplishments, Adams remarked:

> The part I took in defense of Captain Preston and the soldiers procured me anxiety and obloquy enough. It was, however, . . . one of the best pieces of service I ever rendered my country. Judgment of death against those soldiers would have been as foul a stain upon this country as the executions of the Quakers or witches

anciently. As the evidence was, the verdict of the jury was exactly right.

Tobin, supra at 17.

CHAPTER 10

BILLING THE CLIENT

■ ■ ■

Chapter Hypothetical. Katherine hired Lynn, an experienced lawyer, to represent her in a probate matter. Katherine's husband, Robert, had died without a will. The couple had several children, and Robert had several other living relatives. Under the relevant intestacy statute, Katherine was entitled to one-third of Robert's estate. Katherine and Lynn agreed to a contingency fee arrangement under which Lynn would receive one-third of the proceeds from the estate that Katherine received. Around the same time, Mary hired Lynn to represent her on a contingent fee basis in a domestic relations matter, while another client, Nora, agreed to hire Lynn on a flat fee basis to represent her in her divorce.

There are many kinds of fee agreements that a lawyer and client may enter into. The easiest to understand are hourly fees (*e.g.*, $250/hour) and flat fees for completion of a task (*e.g.*, $5,000 to handle a divorce). In contrast, with contingent fees, a lawyer's fee is contingent upon the client recovering; if the client recovers nothing, the lawyer recovers nothing. Contingent fees exist, in part, to enable individuals to receive legal services who otherwise could not afford to pay a fee. The material in this chapter covers the various rules pertaining to attorney-client fee agreements and the billing practices of attorneys.

* * *

A. SETTING THE FEE

Model Rules 1.5(b) and 1.5(c) contain some specific procedural requirements concerning fee agreements. Take a look at the rules and then consider the problem that follows. As you read Rule 1.5(c), ask yourself why the rule singles out contingent fees for special treatment.

* * *

Problem 10.1. Lynn and Katherine orally agreed to the one-third contingency fee arrangement one week after Lynn initially agreed to represent Katherine in the probate matter involving Robert's estate. During this same conversation, Lynn told Katherine that Katherine would be responsible for any expenses Lynn incurred as part of the representation. Has Lynn complied with the requirements of Rule 1.5(b) and (c)?

* * *

B. REASONABLENESS OF FEES AND OTHER CHARGES

1. CHARGING AN UNREASONABLE FEE

Model Rule 1.5(a) prohibits a lawyer from making an agreement for, charging, or collecting an unreasonable fee or an unreasonable amount for expenses. The rule lists several factors to consider in determining whether a fee is reasonable. As you read the cases that follow, consider how those factors apply.

* * *

IN RE GREEN
11 P.3d 1078 (Colo. 2000)

A tile contractor hired Green in 1991 to sue a homeowner and her husband for failure to pay for the contractor's installation of ceramic tile in their house. Green filed an action in Douglas County District Court on behalf of the contractor against the homeowners for breach of contract and to foreclose a mechanics' lien in the amount of $7,422.33. The defendants counterclaimed, asserting that the contractor breached implied warranties of fitness for a particular purpose and merchantability. The contract between the tile contractor and the homeowners entitled the party who prevailed at trial to attorney's fees and costs. Green and his client agreed that if the client prevailed, then Green would accept as his fee whatever amount the court awarded. Otherwise, the client would owe Green nothing.

[The judge awarded Green's client damages in the amount of $7,422.33, plus costs, interest, and attorney's fees. Green requested attorney's fees for the trial in the amount of $29,554.80, which he calculated by multiplying his hourly rate of $165 by the 179.12 hours he claimed to have worked on the case. The defendants appealed the verdict, and Green's client prevailed. By the conclusion of the appeal, Green claimed to have expended 618.13 hours of time and that his hourly fee rate was $165, amounting to $101,991.45 in attorney's fees. Subtracting the amount of fees he had previously claimed for the trial ($29,554.80), Green asked for $72,436.65 in attorney's fees for his work on the appeal. After some complicated procedural history, the trial judge ultimately awarded Green $16,500 for his work at trial and held that it lacked jurisdiction to set an amount for the work performed during the appeal. Disciplinary counsel brought a complaint against Green, charging him with violating Colo. RPC 1.5(a) (charging an excessive fee).]

The hearing board found, by clear and convincing evidence, that Green violated Colo. RPC 1.5(a), stating that particularly in light of the fee's amount in relation to the recovery, the fee was "outrageous on its face" and "grossly unreasonable." . . .

Arguably, the $69,000 Green charged for the appeal is unreasonable per se because of the relatively small judgment of $7,400 involved. However, the issue is more complex. For instance, the attorney for the homeowners, who represented the losing party on all of the critical issues on appeal, testified that his attorney's fees for the appeal "were in the $30,000 to $40,000 range."

Green's affidavit setting forth his time entries for work performed on the appeal contains unreasonable charges. There are charges reflecting time Green spent on tasks that could have been done by a non-lawyer at a significantly lower rate than $165 per hour. For example, there are multiple entries reflecting the faxing of documents to the client and opposing counsel, entries for calls made to the court of appeals clerk's office, and the delivery of documents to opposing counsel. Colo. RPC 1.5(a)(1) indicates that one factor in determining the reasonableness of a fee is "the novelty and difficulty of the questions involved, and the skill requisite to perform the legal service properly." Under this principle, charging an attorney's hourly rate for clerical services that are generally performed by a non-lawyer, and thus for which an attorney's professional skill and knowledge add no value to the service, is unreasonable as a matter of law.

In addition, some entries for time spent on legal work are excessive. For example, there is an entry for receiving and reviewing the court of appeals decision and faxing it to the client. The court of appeals' opinion is twelve pages long. Green represents that he spent 6.0 hours performing these services. At $165 per hour, Green therefore charged $990 for reviewing and faxing a twelve-page decision. This is an unreasonable charge as a matter of law for one of two alternative reasons. If the time was spent merely in "reviewing," in other words reading the appellate opinion with minimal additional legal analysis or research involved, it was an excessive and inefficient use of the attorney's time and it is unreasonable to charge for the lawyer's own inefficiencies:

> In short, the determination of what fees are reasonable involves more than simply multiplying the number of hours spent on a given case times a specific rate. An attorney must use judgment and discretion in rendering a bill. This includes recognizing the limits of one's own capacity and one's own inefficiencies. There is no reason or excuse for charging a client . . . for one's own inefficiencies.

In re Guardianship of Hallauer, 44 Wash. App. 795, 723 P.2d 1161, 1166 (1986).

If, on the other hand, his time involved more extensive work, then the billing statement is so vague that it fails reasonably to identify the nature of the services performed. Either of these two bases is a sufficient rationale to conclude that this charge was unreasonable.

Thus, our review of the entire record, and specifically Green's affidavit for fees charged for the appeal, supports the hearing board's conclusion to the extent that it determined that Green charged an unreasonable fee on the appeal in violation of Colo. RPC 1.5(a). . . .

Having concluded that Green charged an unreasonable fee in violation of Colo. RPC 1.5(a), we now address the appropriate level of discipline. Under the American Bar Association *Standards for Imposing Lawyer Sanctions*, public censure "is generally appropriate when a lawyer negligently engages in conduct that is a violation of a duty owed to the profession, and causes injury or potential injury to a client, the public, or the legal system." ABA *Standards for Imposing Lawyer Sanctions* at 7.3 (1991 & Supp. 1992) (hereinafter ABA *Standards*). "Charging a client an unreasonable or excessive fee is a violation of a duty owed as a professional." *People v. Sather*, 936 P.2d 576, 579 (Colo. 1997). On the other hand, "[s]uspension is generally appropriate when a lawyer knowingly engages in conduct that is a violation of a duty owed to the profession, and causes injury or potential injury to a client, the public, or the legal system." ABA *Standards*, *supra*, at 7.2.

The commentary to standard 7.3 states, "Courts typically impose reprimands when lawyers engage in a single instance of charging an excessive or improper fee." We have recently found a public censure appropriate when a lawyer charges an excessive fee. *See In re Wimmershoff*, 3 P.3d 417, 421 (Colo. 2000); *see also People v. Wilson*, 953 P.2d 1292, 1294 (Colo. 1998). We therefore begin with the presumption that a public censure is the appropriate level of discipline.

The hearing board found the existence of a mitigating factor and several aggravating factors. The only mitigating factor found by the hearing board was that Green had cooperated in these proceedings. *See* ABA *Standards*, *supra*, 9.32(e). Aggravating factors included the presence of a prior disciplinary offense, *see id.* at 9.22(a); that Green had a dishonest or selfish motive, *see id.* at 9.22(b); that there was a pattern of misconduct, *see id.* at 9.22(c); that the misconduct involved multiple offenses, *see id.* at 9.22(d); that Green refused to acknowledge the wrongful nature of his conduct, *see id.* at 9.22(g); and that Green has substantial experience in the practice of law, *see id.* at 9.22(i). As a result of our having dismissed all but the single violation of charging an unreasonable fee, the aggravating factors of a pattern of misconduct and the presence of multiple offenses no longer apply.

In our analysis, Green's prior discipline is not a significant factor. He received a letter of admonition twelve years ago for making false accusations against a judge. . . . [T]he hearing board acknowledged that this admonition was remote in time. This mitigates the fact of prior discipline. *See id.* at 9.32(m). Considering the seriousness of the misconduct, together with the aggravating and mitigating factors, we conclude that a public censure is an adequate and appropriate sanction. . . .

* * *

HEAVENER V. MEYERS
158 F. Supp. 2d 1278 (E.D. Okla. 2001)

As the prevailing party in this civil rights case brought under 42 U.S.C. § 1983, Plaintiff is entitled to seek reimbursement for his reasonable attorney's fees. 42 U.S.C. § 1988(b). A fee request under § 1988(b) places the burden on Plaintiff to establish two elements: (1) that he was the "prevailing party" in the litigation; and (2) that his request is "reasonable." As there is no question about Plaintiff's prevailing party status, the lone inquiry in this case is whether Plaintiff has established that his fee request is "reasonable."

"The most useful starting point for determining the amount of a reasonable fee is the number of hours reasonably expended on the litigation multiplied by a reasonable hourly rate." *Ramos v. Lamm*, 713 F.2d 546, 552 (10th Cir. 1983) (quoting *Hensley*, 461 U.S. at 433, 103 S. Ct. 1933). This resulting "lodestar" figure—the product of reasonable hours times a reasonable rate—is presumed to be a reasonable fee. With respect to a determination of the reasonable number of hours, the court must carefully scrutinize the reported hours to determine if they can reasonably be charged to Defendant. It is incumbent upon Plaintiff to "prove and establish the reasonableness of each dollar, each hour, above zero." *Mares v. Credit Bureau of Raton*, 801 F.2d 1197, 1210 (10th Cir. 1986). Plaintiff's counsel has the obligation to keep "meticulous, contemporaneous time records" to enable the court to determine an appropriate fee. *Ramos*, 713 F.2d at 553. . . .

Counsel is further obligated to "make a good-faith effort to exclude from a fee request hours that are excessive, redundant, or otherwise unnecessary, just as a lawyer in private practice ethically is obligated to exclude such hours from his fee submission." *Hensley*, 461 U.S. at 434, 103 S. Ct. 1933.

Counsel's invoice contains numerous entries which reflect the unreasonableness of the requested hours. Two examples highlight the court's concerns. First, the invoice reflects five separate entries, totaling 19 hours, related to research on the issue of Eleventh Amendment immunity raised by the State of Oklahoma in a motion to dismiss. Plaintiff initially sued Meyers, in his individual and official capacities, and the State of Oklahoma, ex rel Oklahoma Highway Patrol ("the State"). In response to the State's motion to dismiss, Plaintiff voluntarily dismissed Meyers, in his official capacity, and the State. This dismissal was filed after nineteen hours of research by Messer on the State's Eleventh Amendment defense. These hours are clearly excessive in the specific context of the Eleventh Amendment defense raised by the State and, moreover, are indicative of a systematic practice of excessive billing by counsel attributable, in large part, to counsel's inexperience. The Eleventh Amendment immunity generally afforded the state and its officers, sued in their official capacity, is well-established. Absent a waiver, or congressional authorization of the suit, the Eleventh Amendment bars damages suits against States and state officials in federal court, whether the claims are federal claims or pendent state claims. It is beyond reason to assign nineteen hours of research to an issue which is so well-established in the area of civil rights litigation in general, and section 1983 claims in particular. Excessive hours in the context of this simple, well-defined issue is indicative of counsel's overall excessive billing practices and their use of this litigation as an "educational forum" for excessive force claims brought under section 1983 and Oklahoma's common law.

The second category of excessiveness exhibited by counsel in their fee application involves counsel's billing for "discussion" time. No less than 49 entries in counsel's invoice contain billings for "discussion" with co-counsel. This is duplicative work which is not compensable and will not be condoned by the court. . . . While certain complex litigation may require a combined effort by counsel, this factually limited excessive force case, with well-established legal standards, is not one which requires joint effort on specific tasks. The court's criticism in this respect is not directed to the use of two attorneys to litigate the matter. Having made that decision, however, counsel are not free to charge twice for essentially the same work performed outside the hearing and trial context. If counsel chooses to employ a senior partner/associate type of working relationship on a particular case, they should keep in mind that this court will not compensate them for duplicative work. Counsel should take all necessary steps to assure that the lines of responsibility are clearly delineated and that duplication of effort is eliminated. Counsel in this case have failed to do so. Their invoice is clear evidence of their abuse. These records reflect that counsel undertook to bill twice for essentially the same task, one direct (the actual research, drafting, or preparation) and one indirect (telling co-counsel or "discussing" what one has learned or done). This practice is reflective of the unreasonableness of counsel's fee request.

In addition to the specific billing practices outlined above which highlight the unreasonableness of Plaintiff's request for fees, the court notes that the simplicity of this case does not justify the expenditure of 555.27 hours of attorney and paralegal time. This was a simple, straightforward Fourth Amendment excessive force claim brought against a single Highway Patrol Officer under section 1983, with pendent state claims for assault, battery, and intentional infliction of severe emotional distress. The facts giving rise to the claim were based on a single, isolated event involving Plaintiff and Meyers. Contrary to counsel's opinion otherwise, no novel factual or legal issues were involved. Only four depositions were taken. Several discovery disputes did arise and motions to compel were filed. In addition, the parties filed several motions *in limine* regarding evidentiary issues. No dispositive motions were filed by either Plaintiff or Meyers. Under this scenario—a simple civil rights claim with moderate discovery and evidentiary issues—the request for compensation based on 555.27 hours is clearly excessive.

* * *

IN RE SULZER HIP PROSTHESIS AND KNEE PROSTHESIS LIABILITY LITIGATION
290 F. Supp. 2d 840 (N.D. Ohio 2003)

[Following settlement of a class action, the court exercised the authority granted to it by the terms of the settlement to resolve a dispute concerning the reasonableness of the attorneys' fees.]

Any analysis of a fee agreement between an attorney and his client begins with the general rule that an attorney may not charge "in excess of a reasonable fee." . . . ABA Model Rule 1.5(a) ("[a] Lawyer's fee shall be reasonable"); *In re A.H. Robins Co., Inc.*, 86 F.3d at 373 ("the law of this circuit has long been clear that federal district courts have inherent power and an obligation to limit attorneys' fees to a reasonable amount"). Furthermore, it has "long . . . been established" that "contingency fee arrangements are subject to [this] reasonableness standard." *Christian v. Gordon*, 2001 WL 883551 at *3 (Terr. V.I. June 20, 2001).

With respect to contingency fee arrangements, in particular, the Sixth Circuit Court of Appeals has noted that [the rules of professional conduct] are "based largely upon Canon 13 of the old ABA Canons of Professional Ethics, adopted in 1908." This Canon provided that a "contract for a contingent fee . . . should be reasonable under all the circumstances of the case, *including the risk and uncertainty of the compensation*, but should always be subject to the supervision of a court, as to its reasonableness." *Id.* (emphasis added). This Canon highlights the obvious but critical characteristic of a contingent fee arrangement—the presence of risk. That is why the attorney's fee is called "contingent." *See Committee on Legal*

Ethics of West Virginia State Bar v. Tatterson, 177 W.Va. 356, 352 S.E.2d 107, 113–14 (1986) ("Courts generally have insisted that a contingent fee be truly contingent. The typically elevated contingent fee reflecting the risk to the attorney of receiving no fee will usually be permitted only if the representation indeed involves a significant degree of risk."). And the reasonableness of an attorney's contingent fee depends directly on whether (or to what extent) real risk is present: "[w]hen there is virtually no risk and no uncertainty, contingent fees represent an improper measure of professional compensation." *Attorney Grievance Com'n v. Kemp*, 303 Md. 664, 496 A.2d 672, 678 (1985) (quoting Formal Op. 76–1 from the Ethics Committee of the Maryland State Bar Association). . . .

Several cases reveal these rules in practical application. One such case is a hypothetical posed in the *Restatement* § 35 Comment [c], illus. 1, at 259. As summarized by Professor Geoffrey Hazard, "if a lawyer helps a client recover the proceeds of a [$15,000] life insurance policy, knowing that there are no grounds for the insurer to contest payment, and the company pays the entire amount upon demand, a 'standard' one-third 'contingent' fee [of $5,000] would clearly be unreasonable." *The Law of Lawyering* § 8.6 at 8–16 (citing the *Restatement*). . . .

[T]he parties in this case agreed in principle in August of 2001 to settle their dispute. The primary open questions which remained after that date were the level of funding and the precise sources of those funds. On February 1, 2002, the parties announced that they had resolved these issues and had signed a "Memorandum of Understanding," which was essentially the outline of a full settlement agreement. In other words, as of February 1, 2002, the parties had agreed upon the critical terms necessary to end their dispute, including the amount of payment to plaintiff class members, and the fact of this settlement was widely broadcast. After February 2, 2002, then, an attorney who was retained by a class member in this case knew or should have known that there was, at the very least, a markedly decreased risk of nonrecovery by his client. . . .

The practical reality in this case is that, after February 2, 2002, an attorney's representation of a plaintiff class member did not involve a significant degree of risk that his client would not recover. A lawyer who entered into an attorney-client relationship with a plaintiff in this case after that date knew it was extremely unlikely that he would ever have to draft any documents, conduct any discovery, make any court appearances, file any pleadings, undertake any legal research, correspond with any defendant, or negotiate with any party. After February 2, 2002, an attorney knew that the only effort required to ensure his client received benefits was to: (1) monitor the case to determine whether the Court approved the Settlement Agreement at the Final Fairness Hearing; (2) watch to see if the defendants elected to withdraw from the settlement, based on opt-outs; and (3) timely and properly fill out the claims forms and submit them to the Claims Administrator. None of this effort is substantial or requires special expertise. . . .

Despite having reason to know that there was a low degree of risk and a small amount of effort required to recover benefits for their clients, about 40 attorneys who signed contingent fee agreements with plaintiffs in this case after February 2, 2002, have insisted on receiving their full contingent fee. . . .

In the absence of any real risk, an attorney's purportedly contingent fee which is grossly disproportionate to the amount of work required is [unreasonable within the meaning of the rules of professional conduct]. . . . This Court easily concludes that, by insisting on receipt of their full contingent fee, these attorneys are charging an unreasonable and clearly excessive fee. These attorneys knew or should have known, before they entered into their contingent fee agreements with their clients, that the contingency factor was negligible, their effort would not bear a reasonable relationship to the size of their client's recovery, and the fee agreement would work to yield them a windfall. Moreover, their insistence on receiving the full contingent fee amount may well amount to a breach of their fiduciary relationship with their own clients. . . .

Put in the simplest terms possible: these attorneys are being greedy. They have insisted on receiving excessive compensation at the expense of their own clients. They have received far more in fees than is fair to compensate them for the amount of effort they spent and the amount of risk they took. They have violated the terms and the intent of the settlement agreement in this case, by which they are bound. And they have probably violated the rules of ethics as well. . . .

Accordingly, the Court will exercise its continuing jurisdiction over this case, the settlement trust, and the attorneys who appear before it, as follows. *At this juncture*, the Court will not refer for an ethics inquiry any of the attorneys who fall into the circumstances discussed. Rather, the Court hereby orders all attorneys representing plaintiffs in this case to ensure their actions comport with this opinion. Specifically, *any* contingent fee agreement between an attorney and a plaintiff class member in this case, which was completed *after February 2, 2002,* and was intended to allow the attorney to recover contingent fees in this case, is neither ethical nor permissible, and may not be enforced. **No person may take any steps to enforce any such agreement, and any attorney who has obtained contingent fees pursuant to such a contract shall return those fees to the plaintiff class member.** . . .

* * *

Problem 10.2. When Katherine hired Lynn to assist with Robert's estate, she was unsure as to the total value of the estate. But she provided

Lynn with a list of stocks that Robert owned and told Lynn that Robert kept some valuables in a safe (although she didn't know exactly what was in the safe). The list that Katherine provided to Lynn described stock that Robert owned in ten different large corporations. When they opened Robert's safe, they saw that the valuables in the safe were likely only worth a few thousand dollars. Eventually, Lynn was able to determine the value of Robert's estate to be $1.8 million. Most of the value of the estate derived from the stock Robert had owned. Lynn spent approximately 50 hours on the matter, with her work split evenly between researching the value of the estate and filing the necessary paperwork in probate court. After the matter was resolved and Katherine had received her $600,000 from the estate, Lynn sent Katherine a bill for $200,000 (or one-third of $600,000), plus the expenses she incurred. Katherine now believes that this amount is unreasonable and says she will not pay Lynn. Lynn tells Katherine that Katherine was lucky to have hired Lynn since Lynn is, in her own words, "the best probate lawyer around." Has Lynn attempted to charge an unreasonable fee in violation of Rule 1.5(a)? What other information might you like to know before deciding?

Statutory Caps on Fees. There may also be statutory constraints on contingent fees. For example, federal law limits the fee for claimants' attorneys in Social Security cases to 25% of any back pay award. 42 U.S.C. § 406(a)(2)(A). Some states, likewise, impose statutory limits on attorney fees. *See, e.g.*, Tenn. Code Ann. § 29–26–120 (placing cap on attorney fee in medical malpractice cases of 33 1/3% of total recovery).

Reasonable Fees for Expenses. Comment [1] to Rule 1.5 addresses the cost of services performed in-house or other out-of-pocket expenses incurred in the course of representation. With regard to things like copying costs, a firm may charge "a reasonable amount to which the client has agreed in advance or by charging an amount that reasonably reflects the cost incurred" by the firm. At the same time, ABA Formal Ethics Opinion 93–379 warns that "in the absence of an agreement to the contrary, it is impermissible for a lawyer to create an additional source of profit for the law firm beyond that which is contained in the provision of professional services themselves. The lawyer's stock in trade is the sale of legal services, not photocopy paper, tuna fish sandwiches, computer time or messenger services."

Problem 10.3. For which of the following expenses could Lynn ethically charge her clients without first seeking client approval?

(a) Overtime pay for an assistant who helps Lynn to meet a filing deadline.

(b) A subscription to a database on probate law in order for Lynn to get up to speed on recent developments in probate law.

(c) The costs of storage of a client's files.

* * *

2. POTENTIAL CONSEQUENCES OF CHARGING AN UNREASONABLE FEE

One obvious consequence of attempting to collect an unreasonable fee is professional discipline. Another potential consequence is that a court will find the fee agreement to offend public policy to the point that the agreement is unenforceable. In addition to the contract defense of unconscionability, a contract that offends public policy may be also unenforceable as a matter of contract law. *Restatement (Second) of Contracts* § 178 (1979). While there is some dispute as to whether a fee agreement that violates a rule of professional conduct for lawyers offends public policy for purposes of this contract defense, courts often find fee agreements that violate some portion of Rule 1.5 to offend public policy. *See, e.g., Maxwell Schuman & Co. v. Edwards*, 663 S.E.2d 329, 333 (N.C. Ct. App. 2008); Alex B. Long, *Fee Agreements That Offend Public Policy*, 61 S.C. L. REV. 287 (2009).

This, in turn, leads to the question of what payment, if any, the attorney is entitled to receive. Where a contract is unenforceable on public policy grounds, the offending party may not recover on the contract, and the general contract rule is that *quantum meruit* recovery is also not permitted lest courts encourage future wrongdoing of a similar nature. *See* Long, *supra* at 295. However, in the case of lawyer-client fee agreements, section 39 of the *Restatement (Third) of the Law Governing Lawyers* articulates a general rule permitting *quantum meruit* recovery where a fee agreement is unenforceable. *See, e.g., Clark v. General Motors LLC*, 161 F. Supp. 3d 752 (W.D. Mo. 2015) (holding that attorneys attempted to charge an unreasonable fee but nonetheless permitting attorneys to recover for the reasonable value of the services).

Problem 10.4. Assume for purposes of this problem that Lynn is determined to have charged an unreasonable fee in violation of Rule 1.5(a) in her representation of Katherine. In your opinion, should she be allowed to recover for the reasonable value of her services rendered?

* * *

C. OTHER PROHIBITED FEE ARRANGEMENTS

1. PROHIBITED CONTINGENT FEES

Model Rule 1.5(d)(1) places limits on the ability of lawyers to charge a contingent fee in some domestic relations matters. The public policy underlying the rule is one of encouraging reconciliation "by removing any incentive to the attorney to press forward with the divorce." *Guenard v.*

Burke, 443 N.E.2d 892, 895 (Mass. 1982). Courts typically declare fee agreements that violate Rule 1.5(d)(1) to be unenforceable as against public policy but permit a lawyer to recover the reasonable value of services rendered. *See, e.g., Maxwell Schuman & Co.*, 663 S.E.2d at 333. Should such recovery in *quantum meruit* be the norm in these cases?

Model Rule 1.5(d)(2) prohibits a lawyer from charging a contingent fee for representing a defendant in a criminal case. The rule is often justified on conflict of interest grounds: a lawyer who only receives a fee if a client is found not guilty may have an incentive to push the client to reject a reasonable plea deal. *See United States ex rel. Simon v. Murphy*, 349 F. Supp. 818, 823–24 (E.D. Pa. 1972).

Problem 10.5. Mary retained Lynn's services because Mary's ex-husband had failed to make court-ordered child support payments over the past six months. Mary and Lynn entered into a contingency fee agreement, under which Lynn's fee will be 10% of whatever portion of the balance owed by the ex-husband that Lynn is able to collect on Mary's behalf. Read Model Rule 1.5(d)(1) carefully. Is Lynn subject to discipline?

* * *

2. "NON-REFUNDABLE" GENERAL RETAINERS OR FEES PAID IN ADVANCE

Lawyers sometimes assert that fees paid in advance are "non-refundable," but that is rarely the case and can create disciplinary problems for the attorney.

As a threshold matter, it is helpful to know that the word "retainer" is often used loosely by attorneys to mean different things. A retainer (also known as a "general retainer") can mean a fee paid to ensure a lawyer's availability during a specified time for a specified matter, apart from any other compensation for services. This type of retainer is not used very frequently. Such general retainer fees are considered earned upon receipt because the payment is not for future services but for the lawyer's agreement to be available. In a 2023 formal ethics opinion, the ABA explained that although general retainers are sometimes thought to be synonymous with "nonrefundable," that is actually incorrect. Even though a general retainer is earned on receipt, it might have to be refunded if it is determined to be unreasonable or unearned if the lawyer does not make himself or herself available to handle the subject matter. *See* ABA Comm. on Ethics & Prof'l Responsibility, Formal Op. 505, at 3 (2023).

Lawyers also sometimes use the word retainer to mean an advanced fee paid in contemplation of future legal services. For the sake of clarity, this book will call this an "advanced fee." The lawyer does not earn the advanced fee until the work is performed, so the money still belongs to the client and must be deposited in a trust account (discussed in the next chapter). Once the work is completed, the lawyer can pay herself out of the advanced fee at the agreed upon rate—whether that is payment for time billed or at a flat or fixed rate for handling the matter.

Attorneys sometimes attempt to call an advanced fee "nonrefundable" but that does not make it so. For example, in one case, a lawyer charged a flat fee of $5,000 to handle a probate matter and included the following phrase in the fee agreement: "This is the minimum fee no matter how much or how little work I do in this investigatory stage . . . and will remain the minimum fee and is not refundable even if you decide prior to my completion of the investigation that you wish to discontinue the use of my services for any reason whatsoever." *In re Cooperman*, 611 N.Y.S.2d 465 (1994).

Most courts and ethics opinions have concluded that such provisions are unenforceable because they may amount to charging an unreasonable fee (under Rule 1.5), are inconsistent with the obligation to return unearned fees when a representation is terminated (under Rule 1.16), and attempt to chill the unfettered right of a client to discharge an attorney. *See id.*; *Grievance Administrator, Attorney Grievance Commission v. Cooper*, 757 N.W.2d 867 (Mich. 2008); ABA Comm. on Ethics & Prof'l Responsibility, Formal Op. 505, at 3 (2023). Some jurisdictions permit lawyers to label an advance fee or general retainer "non-refundable" so long as the fee is reasonable, and the lawyer remains available to do the work for which the advanced fee or general retainer was charged. *See, e.g.*, Tenn. R.P.C. 1.5(f), Comment [4][a]. Consider the following decision.

IN RE DISCIPLINARY ACTION AGAINST HOFFMAN
834 N.W.2d 636 (N.D. 2013)

In July 2010, Wetmore retained Hoffman to represent him in a criminal matter involving several felony charges, and the two executed a written contract for legal services. The agreement provided that in exchange for a "minimum fee" of $30,000, Hoffman would defend the charges to dismissal, sentence or deferred imposition of sentence, including a jury trial if necessary. The agreement also stated "[t]here is no refund of the minimum fee." Wetmore paid Hoffman $30,000 and an additional $1,000 for an advance payment of expenses, as required in the contract. Hoffman placed the $30,000 in his operating account.

According to the evidence at the hearing, Hoffman had conferences with Wetmore on July 16, August 4, and August 27, 2010; he wrote the prosecuting attorney a letter on August 27, 2010, and received a fax from Wetmore on September 8, 2010; he began preparing for a preliminary hearing on September 16, 2010; he appeared at a 45-minute preliminary hearing in the case on September 21, 2010; he had a two-hour meeting with

Wetmore after the preliminary hearing; and Wetmore terminated his employment on September 22, 2010. After terminating Hoffman's employment, Wetmore asked him to return the "unearned portion" of the $30,000 payment, but Hoffman refused.

In August 2011, Disciplinary Counsel petitioned for discipline against Hoffman regarding his employment contract with Wetmore, alleging violations of N.D.R. Prof. Conduct 1.5(a), Fees . . . and N.D.R. Prof. Conduct 1.16(e), Declining or Terminating Representation. . . .

We . . . consider whether the amount provided for and charged in the agreement was reasonable under N.D.R. Prof. Conduct 1.5. The record shows Hoffman was taking over a serious felony case from another attorney, and Hoffman testified he was concerned Wetmore was changing attorneys to obtain a continuance of the preliminary hearing. On July 7, 2010, Wetmore signed Hoffman's fee contract and employed Hoffman to defend him on four counts of gross sexual imposition. In testimony before the Hearing Panel, Wetmore acknowledged that he had discussed the written contract with Hoffman before signing it. Hoffman testified that he went over the contract in detail because of the "red flags" presented by Wetmore, in that Wetmore was firing another attorney for whom Hoffman had respect, that there was a long history with the case, that it would be a difficult case, and that Wetmore had a tendency to repeat himself in their meetings and not stay focused. Hoffman also testified that Wetmore was talking about hiring numerous experts and demanding Hoffman talk to them at very early stages of the proceedings. Hoffman testified that he felt the need to protect himself. Further, Hoffman was aware that Wetmore had fired a lawyer just before the first scheduled preliminary hearing, that there would be another preliminary hearing scheduled, and Hoffman was concerned Wetmore would again switch lawyers before the next hearing. Hoffman also testified that he wanted to be compensated for his availability, for the time and responsibility he invested, and for the risk he assumed in the early stages of a serious case involving multiple felonies.

Under the facts and circumstances of this case, we conclude that the $30,000 "minimum fee" initially charged in the legal services contract was reasonable under the factors in Rule 1.5(a). We reject the Hearing Panel's recommendation to find violations of N.D.R. Prof. Conduct 1.5(a) and 1.15(a) and (c), because we conclude that the "minimum fee" charged by Hoffman in the initial agreement retaining his services was reasonable under the facts and circumstances. . . .

Although we conclude that Hoffman did not violate N.D.R. Prof. Conduct Rule[ ] 1.5(a) . . .by entering into the minimum fee agreement, we still must examine the lawyer's obligations under N.D.R. Prof. Conduct 1.16(e), when the lawyer's services are terminated.

Rule 1.16(e), N.D.R. Prof. Conduct, describes steps a lawyer must take when the representation of the client is terminated:

> Upon termination of representation, a lawyer shall take steps to the extent reasonably practicable to protect a client's interests, such as giving reasonable notice to the client, allowing time for employment of other counsel, surrendering papers and property to which the client is entitled *and refunding any advance payment of fee or expense that has not been earned or incurred*. The lawyer may retain papers relating to the client only to the extent permitted by Rule 1.19.

(Emphasis added.) . . .

Our recent cases have been clear that, upon a lawyer's termination of representation, a lawyer must refund any advance payment of fee or expense not earned or incurred, particularly in cases where the attorney did not complete the contemplated work for which the attorney was retained. Our decisions have not been as clear regarding the lawyer's obligation to refund "nonrefundable" fees, where a client purportedly breaches a contract for legal services and where the lawyer is appropriately performing services as anticipated under the contract. . . .

Courts have discussed that while nonrefundable retainers may be permitted, there is also a general reasonableness standard, including a requirement that the total fee charged must be "reasonable." Thus, even when a fee agreement is designated "nonrefundable" and is reasonable at the time of entering the agreement, an attorney may be required to refund any advanced fee that has not been earned under Rule 1.16, incorporating the concept that the "total" fee must still be reasonable. . . .

We conclude that Hoffman violated N.D.R. Prof. Conduct 1.16(e) in failing to refund any fees after Wetmore terminated his services at a time when all or substantially all of the services contemplated under the contract had not been performed. [The court concluded that professional discipline was not appropriate because the law regarding non-refundable fees in North Dakota was not clear at the time. But the court nonetheless concluded that Hoffman was required to refund Wetmore some of the unearned fee.]

In this case, the Hearing Panel, in considering the factors under Rule 1.5, found that Hoffman had represented Wetmore for about two and one-half months, expended 25.8 hours on the case, and was also working on other cases during this time. Hoffman testified that he had turned away other work, but the value of that work is not clear. Hoffman correctly argues that he is not limited to only consideration of an hourly fee in determining what would constitute "reasonable" fees under N.D.R. Prof. Conduct 1.5. However, under these facts and circumstances, while a lawyer is not necessarily limited to an hourly rate for compensation, we do not disagree with the Hearing Panel's findings that the work done under the agreement before Hoffman's termination had a value of $4,540. We conclude that Hoffman is entitled to compensation for that work but must refund $25,460 to Wetmore with interest under N.D.R. Prof. Conduct 1.16(e).

* * *

Problem 10.6. Nora and Lynn agreed that Lynn's fee to represent Nora in her divorce would be $10,000, payable in advance, and that the fee was nonrefundable. The day after entering into the agreement and before Lynn did any work on the matter or incurred any other detriment, Nora changed her mind, fired Lynn, and hired a new lawyer. Lynn, citing the fee agreement, refused to refund Nora's money. Is Lynn subject to discipline? If so, on what grounds?

* * *

D. SHARING FEES WITH OTHER LAWYERS

As ABA Formal Opinion No. 487 (2019) explains, Model Rule 1.5(e) "is designed to regulate fee-sharing between lawyers in different firms who handle a case simultaneously." Under the rule, the fee may be divided either in proportion to the work that each lawyer performs or in some other agreed-upon manner where both lawyers assume joint responsibility for the matter. "Joint responsibility" in this context "entails financial and ethical responsibility for the representation as if the counsel were associated in a partnership." *Id.* This portion rule is implicated where a lawyer refers a matter to another lawyer who will try the client's case.

Note the numerous requirements of Rule 1.5(e). These requirements exist in order to cut down on the potential for disagreement among the lawyers as well as the potential for client surprise. Section 47, Comment [i], of the *Restatement (Third) of the Law Governing Lawyers* takes the position that a fee agreement that fails to comply with Rule 1.5(e) is unenforceable against a client. It may also be unenforceable as between the two lawyers involved. *Kaplan v. Pavalon & Gifford,* 12 F.3d 87 (7th Cir. 1993).

Profile of Attorney Professionalism. Stephen Jones hired lawyer Michael Liner to assist him in receiving social security disability benefits. Because many such individuals are unable to pay their attorney's fees upfront, the Social Security Administration is supposed to withhold attorney's fees as part of an award and release them to the attorney. However, in Jones' case, the Social Security Administration accidentally released the fees directly to Jones. Liner, who has a disability himself, assumed he would never collect his fees in this case. However, Jones approached Liner and offered to pay the agreed-upon fee. Instead, Jones and Liner agreed that Jones would donate money from the fee award to different charities over the course of eighteen months. The two men established a non-profit organization, The Stephen Project, to help collect donations for these different charities. For more information, see https://linerlegal.com/thestephenproject/.

CHAPTER 11

PREVENTING BILLING FRAUD AND SAFEKEEPING CLIENT FUNDS AND PROPERTY

■ ■ ■

Chapter Hypothetical I. Rachelle is an associate at a large firm. All firm associates are expected to bill at least 2,000 hours per year. Anyone above that level is eligible for an annual bonus that is typically in the range of $10,000–$20,000. Rachelle is in the employment law section, which has had a slow year. In May, she only billed 120 hours, which put her significantly behind in meeting the 2,000-hour target. In July, at her annual evaluation, her section leader expressed concern about Rachelle's low billable hours, suggested that she seek projects in other sections when work is slow, and concluded with "We do not want to have to let you go." Rachelle took that to mean that the firm would fire her if she did not start billing more time. Rachelle had pretty good months in August and September, but it still was not enough to put her on track for meeting 2,000 hours. She knew she would need high billables in the final three months of the year, but that was going to be challenging because she was planning to get married and take a honeymoon in December—which meant being away from the office for ten days.

A. BILLING FRAUD

A lawyer engages in billing fraud by submitting a bill to a client for work the attorney did not complete. The bill is fraudulent because the attorney is requesting payment that he or she is not entitled to receive. And as discussed below, the conduct is equally problematic even if an attorney submits false time entries to the firm and a senior attorney is the one who sends the bill to the client.

While billing fraud sounds sinister, many attorneys likely engage in this misconduct without giving it much thought. They almost certainly do not think they are committing fraud. This section is aimed at raising awareness concerning the pressures, situations, and rationalizations that lead attorneys to overbill their clients so that students can recognize these issues in practice.

1. PRESSURE (AND INCENTIVES) TO OVERBILL

Most attorneys in private practice bill their clients for time expended working on the client's matter. As a result, time billed is often an important (if not the most important) way that firms measure the contributions of attorneys. Ann-Marie Slaughter put it this way: "Nothing captures the belief that more time equals more value better than the cult of billable hours afflicting large law firms across the country." Anne-Marie Slaughter, *Why Women Still Can't Have It All*, THE ATLANTIC, at 21 (July/August 2012). Eli Wald explains that the modern elite law firm is characterized by well-credentialed lawyers working around the clock in pursuit of their clients' interests. Eli Wald, *Glass Ceilings and Dead Ends: Professional Ideologies, Gender Stereotypes, and the Future of Women Lawyers at Large Law Firms*, 78 FORDHAM L. REV. 2245, 2271 (2010).

In a large U.S. law firm, the minimum (or target) billable hours for an associate is in the vicinity 2,000 per year. If an attorney works five days a week for fifty weeks of the year, the math works out to a minimum requirement of billing eight hours a day. It takes far more than eight hours in the office to bill eight hours of time. A typical attorney will work ten to twelve hours a day—including many weekends—to bill the minimum of 2,000 hours a year. But even if the billable hour target is less than 2,000 hours, it can be incredibly challenging to meet that target if the attorney does not have a steady stream of work and is not committed to putting work above other personal needs.

Problem 11.1. By the end of November, Rachelle calculates that she is 273 hours away from meeting her 2,000 billable hours target. She has never billed that many hours in a month (her high was 210 in a month when she was in trial), but she thinks it is possible. She does the math and learns that she will need to bill around 9 hours a day, every day of the month. If she does not work during her scheduled wedding and honeymoon, she will have to bill 13 hours a day for the rest of the month. She decides that she will not work on her wedding or the day before her wedding, but the rest of the month she will need to work (even if it is while she is sitting on the beach with her new husband). Luckily, she has been working on a big case for the business litigation section that is a few months away from trial. She is highlighting key testimony from depositions that the trial team may use at trial. She can access that deposition database while on her honeymoon and keep busy with that. She decides she can make up any lost time when she gets back.

What factors are motivating or pressuring Rachelle to bill 273 hours in December? Does the goal of billing a certain number of hours per month create a risk that she will overbill her clients—including doing work less efficiently or doing work that does not actually need to be done? Do senior attorneys in the firm bear responsibility for this risk? If so, how can they lessen the risk that associates will overbill?

* * *

2. CHALLENGE OF ACCURATE TIME TRACKING

The process of keeping track of time spent on a client's matter can be difficult. Most attorneys who bill time track their work in six-minute increments. Accurately capturing the work accomplished in six-minute blocks of time can be challenging. Even the best-intentioned attorney who plans to keep notes of times when they start and stop working on a matter will sometimes realize that they have gone several hours without noting their time. Some attorneys find tracking time so challenging that they do not keep good records; with no contemporaneous notes, their only remaining option is to estimate the time they worked on different matters. This estimation can sometimes be to the client's benefit, but there are also times when it is to the client's detriment. Some attorneys delay days and even weeks in tracking their time—often only entering time for client matters as often as the firm requires.

Technology can help attorneys track time. An internet search for "attorney billing software" results in numerous entries for products with a variety of features aimed at making time-tracking simpler. This timekeeping software can help attorneys more accurately capture time and efficiently record descriptions of the work completed. But the software only works if the attorney is diligent in using it.

Another challenge to accurate time tracking is multi-tasking. An attorney cannot bill clients for time spent checking social media, looking at e-mail, chatting with a friend, grabbing coffee, or any of the dozens of non-work related things most of us do on any given day. Too much time spent on distractions from work will cut into billable hours, but billing clients for time doing these things is billing fraud. Speaking of multi-tasking, it is also fraudulent to bill two clients for the same time—such as billing one client for travel while simultaneously billing another client for work done during the travel. *See* A.B.A. Formal Ethics Opinion 93–379 (1993).

Pursuant to Rule 5.1, attorneys with management responsibility in a law firm should provide instruction on proper billing practices, adopt procedures that encourage accurate billing (such as requirements that billing entries be made contemporaneously rather than monthly), and invest in resources like billing software that facilitate proper billing.

Problem 11.2. Rachelle knows that she needs to bill at least nine hours a day in December to reach 2,000 billable hours for the year. On December 1, she is in the office from 8:00 a.m. to 6:00 p.m., and works on the deposition project for most of the day, other than a short break to grab lunch (which she ate at her desk) and to return phone calls and emails on a couple of other matters. As Rachelle sits down to work on the depositions in her home office at 9:00 p.m., she realizes that she has not tracked her time throughout the day, so she makes some notes in the firm's billing software. She bills "0.1" hours for each of the returned phone calls and emails, which totals a half hour. She estimates that it only took her a half hour to get lunch, so she enters a single entry of 9 hours for reviewing depositions for the upcoming trial. That means she has billed 9.5 for the day and she plans to work for another hour before she goes to bed, bringing her daily total to 10.5. Would Rachelle's clients be frustrated to learn about her method for tracking her time? Does it matter if her clients are businesses or people?

* * *

3. SITUATIONAL FACTORS THAT CONTRIBUTE TO BILLING FRAUD

Even individuals with the best of intentions to act ethically can be negatively influenced by features of a situation. Tigran Eldred explains that the body of research on "situationism" considers the "tremendous yet subtle power that situational variables can have on how people think and behave." Tigran W. Eldred, *Insights from Psychology: Teaching Behavioral Legal Ethics as a Core Element of Professional Responsibility*, 2016 MICH. ST. L. REV. 757, 773 (2016).

In the context of attorney billing, situational factors may influence an attorney to overbill. One factor is the conduct of the attorney's fellow lawyers. If an attorney's peers tend to bill 180 hours or more every month and are not careful in contemporaneously tracking their time—perhaps estimating it at the end of the day—that will have an influence on the attorney. The pressure to conform to the conduct of others is well-documented. Another situational factor is the opportunity that is created by the setting in which attorneys work. Because of the type of work attorneys do—much of it completed in solitude without oversight by or understanding of the client—attorneys have the opportunity to falsely bill clients, sometimes with little chance that the client will recognize the inflated or false entries. Attorneys may even catch themselves thinking that there is no way the client will know how long a task actually took. (You should recognize such thoughts as a bad sign.)

Still another factor that may influence junior attorneys is the separation between the task of tracking time and the result of clients being harmed by paying for work that was done unnecessarily or not done at all. When those clients are businesses and not people, it can be even easier to believe that no one is being hurt. Because the associate is often not the person who sends the bill, and may not even interact with the person who pays it, it can be easy to believe that the junior attorney is not harming anyone through her billing methods.

Consider how these situational factors and others played a role in the billing fraud described in the following affidavit from a former partner in a large law firm. Also consider the actions of the associate he describes in this affidavit and why that associate decided to participate in the conduct.

AFFIDAVIT OF CARLOS SPINELLI-NOSEDA

1. I am an attorney-at-law in the State of New York. I submit this affidavit to notify the Departmental Disciplinary Committee (the "Committee") that I intend to resign as an attorney and counselor-at-law in the State of New York, pursuant to 22 N.Y.C.R.R. Section 603.11(b).

2. I was admitted to practice as an attorney in the State of New York by the Appellate Division, Second Department on March 15, 1995, under the name Carlos Javier Spinelli-Noseda. I practiced law in the State of New York until I resigned from my partnership at Sullivan & Cromwell LLP (the "Firm") on March 16, 2008. I have an unblemished disciplinary record. During the entire period of my practice, I maintained an office for the practice of law in the First Department at 125 Broad Street, New York, New York, 10004.

3. I resigned my law partnership, and now seek to resign from the Bar, because I engaged in improper billing for expenses to clients and the Firm from approximately July 1998 (when I was an associate at the Firm) to February 2008. Most of this intentional misappropriation of client and Firm funds occurred between September 2000 and January 2008. I estimate that the total amount of my own falsified expenses over the years exceeded $500,000, of which approximately 2/3 were client-related.

4. I am working with the Firm to quantify the precise amounts involved and to make appropriate restitution.

5. With respect to clients, my misconduct involved billing non-client, personal expenses to clients. My expense reports falsely labeled various travel and entertainment expenses as client-related when, in fact, they were personal. These expenses occurred both in the United States and internationally. From time to time, although clients permitted me to fly first-class on long-distance international flights, I would purchase an economy or business class ticket, invoice the client for the first-class fare that I had not actually paid and retain the difference for myself personally. I believe a total of five clients were affected by my misconduct. My clients were unaware that my billing for these expenses was not legitimate.

6. With respect to the Firm, I would submit expenses for my personal meals, travel and lodging as if they were business-development expenses and, from time to time, would list the names of business colleagues who were not actually present at these events and collect reimbursement from

the Firm for expenses that the Firm would not have paid had it known the truth.

7. From time to time, I also submitted, without the Firm's knowledge or authorization, false expenses for domestic and international airfare and meals that I did not actually undertake at all. From time to time, I also intentionally submitted illegitimate and inflated expenses for a non-New York-based Firm associate (whom I understand is no longer at the Firm). When I was paid for these inflated expenses, I passed along a portion of the proceeds received to the associate.

8. In March 2008, aware that the Firm might audit my expenses, I informed the Firm of my misappropriation of client and Firm funds. In a letter dated March 20, 2008, I reported my misconduct to the Committee, and I understand that the Firm also notified the Committee. I am aware that the Committee has commenced an investigation into my misconduct. I acknowledge that my actions violated the New York Lawyer's Code of Professional Responsibility, notably, DR 1–102(A)(4) inasmuch as my conduct constituted dishonesty, fraud, deceit and misrepresentation, and DR 1-102(A)(7) inasmuch as my conduct adversely reflects on my fitness and integrity as lawyer.

9. I acknowledge that, if charges were brought against me based upon the misconduct as set forth above, I could not successfully defend myself on the merits.

10. My resignation from the Bar is freely and voluntarily rendered, and is not the product of coercion or duress. I am fully aware of the implications of my resignation from the Bar under the circumstances outlined above.

Carlos Spinelli-Noseda

For commentary on Mr. Spinelli-Noseda's resignation from the bar and links to the affidavit, see Anthony Lynn, *Ex-Sullivan Partner Resigns Bar Over $500,000 in False Billings*, NEW YORK LAW JOURNAL, ALM | Law.com (Sept. 24, 2008); Debra Cassens Weiss, *Ex-Partner at S&C Gives up Law License over $500K in False Expenses*, ABAJournal.com (Sept. 24, 2008).

* * *

4. ATTORNEY RATIONALIZATIONS FOR OVERBILLING

Finally, another factor that contributes to billing fraud is rationalization. Rationalizations are stories we tell ourselves justifying why our dishonest conduct is not harmful or is otherwise acceptable under the circumstances. In the context of overbilling, a lawyer may think her sloppy billing methods are acceptable because they are the same as those used by other attorneys in the firm. In overbilling a bit from time to time, a lawyer might reason that there are probably times that the lawyer has underbilled the client, so it all comes out about even in the end. When a client is a faceless business, it can be easy to rationalize that no one is really getting hurt by a slightly inflated bill. Lawyers will often minimize the harm inflicted, and reason that any liberties taken in billing were necessary so that the attorney could hit a billable target, stay employed, make partner, or meet expectations of senior attorneys or colleagues.

Tigran Eldred explains that rationalization allows an attorney to explain away ethical lapses and maintain a positive self-image. Tigran Eldred, *Insights from Psychology, supra* at p. 791. Knowing the role of rationalization in billing misconduct, you can watch for moments when you think this way. Consider whether rationalization played a role in the following case and in the next problem.

* * *

IN RE WALLACE
232 So.3d 1216 (La. 2017)

The following facts are not in dispute, having been stipulated to by the parties. By way of background, respondent joined the law firm of Liskow & Lewis ("the firm") as an associate attorney in 1998. After his promotion to shareholder in 2005, respondent served as the firm's hiring partner and head of recruiting. He also chaired the firm's diversity committee as the firm's first minority recruiting and retention partner. In 2012, respondent was elected to the firm's board of directors and served as the board's junior director through April 2015.

As a member of the firm, respondent generally billed on an hourly basis but sometimes worked on cases on a contingency basis. The firm's policy set hourly billing targets for shareholders at 1,800 billable hours annually. These billing targets were one of several factors taken into consideration for annual salary increases, discretionary bonuses, and promotion within the firm.

In November 2015, the firm's compensation committee noted that respondent's "fee bill credit," which is a measure of collections attributable to an attorney's recorded billable time, seemed low. Therefore, the committee inquired into the status of certain files for which respondent had recorded significant billable time. This inquiry led to the discovery that, between 2012 and 2015, respondent had recorded billing entries on a contingency fee case that had been dismissed in October 2012. Because this particular case was an unsuccessful contingency fee matter, the falsely billed hours were not billed to the client or submitted to any court for approval. The committee found two other files containing entries that had not been billed to clients.

The firm presented these preliminary findings to respondent on November 9, 2015. At that meeting, respondent acknowledged and apologized for his misconduct and assured the firm that his actions had not impacted any of the firm's clients. Respondent informed the firm about other files in which he had recorded false or inflated time or in which he created false receivables that were never billed to clients. With respondent's assistance and cooperation, the firm conducted a full investigation in order to assess whether his conduct had impacted any of the firm's clients. Upon completion of the investigation, the firm confirmed that respondent's conduct did not adversely impact any clients.

The firm identified seven files containing, in part, false entries or receivables. Regarding the contingency fee file that was dismissed in October 2012, the firm discovered false entries totaling 52.25 hours in 2012, false entries totaling 385 hours in 2013, false entries totaling 270 hours in 2014, and false entries totaling 376 hours in 2015. In three other cases, respondent recorded false and inflated entries totaling $91,544.50; he then prepared and reported the bills to the firm's accounting office, but the bills were never sent to the clients. In three additional cases, respondent recorded false and inflated entries that were written off without the preparation of bills and were not billed to the clients. In total, respondent submitted 428 entries that the firm classified as "certainly false" and an additional 220 entries that the firm classified as "reasonably certain" to be "false or inflated."

Between 2012 and 2014, respondent received merit bonuses totaling $85,000. The firm concluded that respondent would most likely have received some or all of these merit bonuses even without the false inflation of his billable hours.

Respondent indicated he engaged in this misconduct because he was concerned that his accurate billable hours, when coupled with an insufficient book of business, were not commensurate with his leadership position in the firm. He denied that he engaged in the misconduct out of a desire for discretionary bonuses or any other monetary gain.

On November 22, 2015, respondent voluntarily submitted his letter of resignation to the firm, effective November 30, 2015. He also voluntarily renounced his entire termination bonus, which totaled approximately $85,000, owed to him for his share of the firm's accounts receivable. The firm determined that this renunciation likely exceeded any losses the firm incurred as a result of respondent's conduct.

Respondent self-reported his misconduct to the ODC on November 25, 2015. The firm reported its findings to the ODC on December 4, 2015.

. . .

In March 2016, the ODC filed formal charges against respondent, alleging that his conduct violated Rules 8.4(a) (violation of the Rules of Professional Conduct) and 8.4(c) (engaging in conduct involving dishonesty, fraud, deceit, or misrepresentation) of the Rules of Professional Conduct. Respondent, through counsel, answered the formal charges and admitted his misconduct but asserted that numerous mitigating factors were present.

Prior to a formal hearing in this matter, respondent and the ODC filed a joint stipulation of facts, wherein respondent admitted to the facts as set forth above. Respondent also stipulated to violating the Rules of Professional Conduct as alleged in the formal charges. The parties further stipulated to the presence of several aggravating and mitigating factors. In aggravation, they stipulated to a dishonest or selfish motive, a pattern of misconduct, and substantial experience in the practice of law (admitted 1998). In mitigation, they stipulated to the absence of a prior disciplinary record, timely good faith effort to make restitution or to rectify the consequences of the misconduct, full and free disclosure to the disciplinary board and a cooperative attitude toward the proceedings, character or reputation, and remorse.

. . .

The record supports a finding that respondent intentionally violated duties owed to the public and the legal profession. His actions had the potential to cause significant harm, however, there is no evidence that any client harm actually occurred. Likewise, it appears little or no actual harm was suffered by respondent's law firm. The record supports the aggravating and mitigating factors as stipulated to by the parties.

Turning to the issue of an appropriate sanction, we find that respondent's conduct involved a long and repetitive pattern of dishonesty. As such, the lengthy thirty-month suspension sought by the ODC is clearly appropriate. However, there are significant mitigating circumstances present, including respondent's voluntary resignation from the firm and his renunciation of his entire termination bonus. These factors, coupled with the lack of harm to respondent's clients and the firm, justify the deferral of all but twelve months of the suspension.

Accordingly, under the circumstances of this case, we will suspend respondent from the practice of law for thirty months, with all but twelve months deferred, retroactive to January 8, 2016, the date of respondent's interim suspension.

* * *

Problem 11.3. In late January, Rachelle was called into a meeting with the head of her section and the attorney whose case is about to go to trial—the case Rachelle supported with work in the deposition database. The attorneys told Rachelle that they were concerned that she had made some false time entries in her December billing. The total hours caught the eye of the section head. Rachelle had never billed anything close to the 270 hours that she billed in December. The section leader was especially surprised given that Rachelle had gotten married and went on a honeymoon. That lead to a conversation with the attorney whose case was going to trial. She, too, was surprised at the number of hours Rachelle had billed the client doing work in the deposition database. The database created a record of each attorney's access and length of time working in the database. When those records were compared with Rachelle's time entries, there was an obvious mismatch of many more hours billed than time working in the database. When confronted with this evidence, Rachelle admitted that she had overbilled the client in the month of December, but she expected to make it up by under-billing that client in January. She also explained that she had feared losing her job, and that is why she worked so hard to bill enough hours to meet her 2,000 hour target.

What consequences should Rachelle face in the firm? Should her misconduct be reported to the bar? If so, what level of discipline is appropriate?

* * *

The "Fraud Triangle." In 1973, criminologist Donald R. Cressey introduced the idea of the "fraud triangle" to explain how and why one in a position of trust betrays that trust and commits fraud. The three points of the triangle involve (1) pressure (a personal financial problem that the individual does not believe can be shared with others), (2) opportunity (a lack of internal measures to detect financial irregularities), and (3) rationalization (which involves the ability to justify one's actions and conclude that the benefits of committing fraud outweigh the risks). Does Cressey's theory explain attorney billing fraud? Would you add additional factors based on the readings in this chapter?

* * *

Chapter Hypothetical II. J.J. had worked at a mid-sized firm for five years (practicing in the area of family law) when he decided to leave the firm to start his own practice. When he was at the mid-sized firm, J.J. relied on the senior partners and administrative staff to manage bank accounts and the firm's books. Now that he is on his own, he knows he needs to learn how to handle these matters on his own.

B. TRUST ACCOUNTS AND OTHER REQUIREMENTS OF SAFEKEEPING CLIENT PROPERTY

Model Rule 1.15 addresses a lawyer's duty to keep a client's property safe when holding property for a client. The rule requires that the client's funds be held separate from the lawyer's funds in an account maintained in the state of the lawyer's office. This account is known as a "trust account." The rule specifically prohibits the lawyer from depositing the lawyer's funds into the account, other than to pay a bank service charge on the account. Model Rule 1.15(b). The rule recognizes that a lawyer may be asked to hold client property other than money. In that case, the property should be kept in a safe location, separate from the lawyer's own property. The rule further provides that records for the trust account must be maintained for five years after termination of the representation.

Comment [1] notes the need to keep books and records in accordance with generally accepted accounting principles and to comply with any recordkeeping rules established in the state. The same comment refers the reader to the ABA's Model Rule on Financial Recordkeeping, which provides additional guidance on complying with the requirements of Rule 1.15. The Financial Recordkeeping Model Rule requires the lawyer to maintain detailed financial records, including "receipt and disbursement journals," "ledger records for all trust accounts," "copies of retainer and compensation agreements with clients," "copies of bills . . . to clients," and "checkbook registers." With respect to trust accounts required by Rule 1.15, the Financial Recordkeeping Model Rule provides that "only a lawyer admitted to practice law in this jurisdiction shall be an authorized signatory on the account."

When Should Lawyers Deposit Funds in a Trust Account? There are a few common situations in which a lawyer will hold funds on behalf of a client. First, the client may be asked to provide an advance on fees and expenses (often called a "special retainer" or "retainer") before the lawyer performs work on behalf of the client. Once the lawyer has earned the fees and the client has approved the bill, then the funds become the lawyer's property and should be moved out of the client trust account. In contrast to holding unearned fees, if an attorney has earned fees from a client, those fees should be deposited in the attorney's operating account. This situation is described in Model Rule 1.15(c).

A second common scenario for using a trust account occurs when the lawyer negotiates a settlement on the client's behalf. Typically, the opposing party will write a check to the lawyer, who then deposits it in the client trust account. Again, some portion of the settlement may accrue to the attorney (for example, if the attorney and client had agreed on a contingency fee) or to a third party (as payment of litigation expenses or court costs). The lawyer will typically provide the client with an accounting and will transfer funds out of the trust account once the settlement check has cleared. Finally, the lawyer may hold funds as the administrator of a client's estate or as part of an escrow arrangement for a business or real estate transaction. In all of these situations, a lawyer who holds client funds or property acts as a fiduciary with regard to those funds and must comply with the state rules on safekeeping client property. The obligation to notify the client (and any third party) of receipt of funds and distribute those funds is addressed in Rule 1.15(d).

Finally, a lawyer may have possession of funds about which there is a dispute as to ownership. That dispute could involve the client, a third party, and even the lawyer. Model Rule 1.15(e) requires the money to be held in trust until the dispute is resolved, but that any undisputed amount must be distributed.

IOLTA Trust Accounts. Some states require (and others permit) attorneys to use an "IOLTA" trust account for client funds held for a short period of time. IOLTA stands for Interest on Lawyers' Trust Account. When an IOLTA account is used, the interest paid on the account is pooled to fund legal aid for low-income state residents in civil matters. If each client's funds were held in a separate account, any interest earned would normally be less that the administrative fees associated with the account. However, by allowing clients' funds to be pooled together, the interest earned in the aggregate can be significant. IOLTA accounts survived a constitutional "takings" challenge in *Brown v. Legal Found. of Washington*, 538 U.S. 216 (2003). The Supreme Court concluded that using the money for public purposes would indeed be an unconstitutional taking but held that no damages would be due when clients suffered no loss of funds. That is, as long as administrative expenses would outweigh the interest payable to any individual client, the client had suffered no compensable loss, and the state need not disgorge the interest payments.

Failure to Properly Safeguard Funds and Property. Failing to properly account for a client's funds or other property is one of the most common bases of attorney discipline. Because the duty to keep accurate records falls upon the attorney, violations are generally easy to prove. The more difficult question in cases involving violations of Rule 1.15 is the proper sanction.

Problem 11.4. J.J. is practicing in the state where your law school is located. Using professional conduct rules and other resources made available by bar disciplinary authorities (such as ethics opinions or handbooks) or the state's highest court (such as court rules or opinions), help J.J. answer the following questions:

- Is J.J. required to have an IOLTA account? Are there other requirements for attorney trust accounts (such as overdraft notification to bar disciplinary authorities)?

- What guidance does the state provide regarding when client funds should be deposited in a separate trust account versus when client funds should be deposited in a pooled trust account (like an IOLTA account)?

- How long is J.J. required to keep financial records?

- Does the state provide any guidance about accepting credit card payments from clients?

Profile of Attorney Professionalism. Walter Dellinger was a dedicated attorney to those in need, providing pro bono representation that will have a profound effect for years to come. Dellinger changed the face of public service and access to justice.

Dellinger has zealously represented the rights of others. He successfully protected same-sex relationships in the failed attempt to criminalize private consensual acts of same-sex couples and another attempt to constitutionally prohibit same-sex marriage.

However, Dellinger's representation in *Brown v. Legal Foundation of Washington* will stand as his most memorable and impactful case, changing the lives of low-income individuals and their ability to receive access to justice. In 2003, Dellinger was approached by the justices of the Washington Supreme Court to defend the IOLTA program that provides legal aid funding to low-income individuals. As an attorney devoted to public service, Dellinger gave a resounding yes, agreeing to represent the case on a pro bono basis. Two clients whose money was placed in an IOLTA trust account filed suit arguing the IOLTA program was an unconstitutional taking of client funds.

Dellinger saved the IOLTA program by convincing the Supreme Court that there was nothing to "take" from the client funds because without the IOLTA program, there would be no net interest earnings. Dellinger knew of the impact the program has on low-income individuals, and without his representation in this case, thousands of individuals would be without legal aid today.

David Lash, *Walter Dellinger's Little-Known, Outsize Impact On Legal Aid*, LAW 360 (Feb. 18, 2022, 6:04 PM).

SECTION 2

COMMUNICATION AND DECISION-MAKING

■ ■ ■

This section focuses on communication and decision-making in the attorney-client relationship. During the representation of a client, there are numerous actions that the lawyer must take on the client's behalf—from calling opposing counsel to sending a courier to the courthouse to file a motion. But which actions are so significant that the lawyer must communicate with the client about them and when must the lawyer defer to the client's decision about how to proceed? These issues are considered in the following chapter. The chapter also discusses the lawyer's communications and decision-making in the context of representing organizational clients and clients with diminished capacity.

CHAPTER 12

COMMUNICATION AND DECISION-MAKING

■ ■ ■

Chapter Hypothetical. Giancarlo (who uses they/them pronouns) is an attorney representing Cass County in a high-profile case pending before the State Supreme Court. Giancarlo filed a motion to recuse a Justice in the case. In the motion, Giancarlo asserted that the named Justice's partiality might reasonably be questioned due to public comments she made before she was appointed to the state's high court.

Prior to filing the recusal motion, Giancarlo did not consult with the Cass County Council to discuss the plan or seek permission. But that was not unusual. By their count, Giancarlo had filed at least twenty motions during the twenty-eight months the case had been working its way through lower courts. Giancarlo frequently talked to the Cass County Law Director about the status of the litigation and sometimes gave a report in a closed door session of a County Council meeting when the Law Director suggested it. But Giancarlo never asked the Law Director or the Cass County Council for input concerning whether to file a specific motion.

Cass County Council members first learned about the motion to recuse when every local news outlet reported on it. The media reports typically focused on the political affiliation of the Justice before her elevation to the State Supreme Court. The Justice, Governor (who appointed her), and many Cass County Council members are all members of the same political party. Following the media stories, some Cass County voters expressed their anger—mostly on social media—that the County was seeking recusal of the Justice.

Several Council members told the media that they were angry that they had not been consulted in advance of Giancarlo filing the motion. Councilwoman Mary Hanks said, "This is a colossal big deal. We were not informed about this. This is wrong. I am extremely upset." Councilman Walter Hadley said that he did not believe it was proper to seek the Justice's recusal and that the County Council should have been alerted to "something of this magnitude." The Cass County Law Director said, "While the County does not micromanage outside attorneys in litigation, the Cass County Council should have been consulted on an issue like this."

Giancarlo defended their decision to file the recusal motion without consulting with the Cass County Council. "It was a decision by me, the attorney who was hired to win the lawsuit for the County. I did what I thought was necessary in order to meet the client's objective in the case," they said.

In the course of a client's matter, hundreds of decisions must be made. The lawyer must decide when to communicate information to the client, when the lawyer can make a decision without consultation, and when the lawyer must consult with the client before taking action. If the lawyer and client disagree about a decision, the lawyer must have an understanding of the principles that govern resolution of that conflict.

The following materials introduce the ethical and legal dimensions of these issues. First, we consider when an attorney has an obligation to communicate information to a client during a matter. Then, we look specifically to the allocation of decision-making authority between lawyer and client. Navigating these issues is surprisingly complicated, but the law of agency is instructive and will be referred to throughout this chapter.

* * *

A. AN OVERVIEW OF COMMUNICATION AND DECISION-MAKING IN AN AGENCY RELATIONSHIP

1. COMMUNICATION

The attorney-client relationship is an agency relationship. As in any agency relationship, the agent (here the attorney) has an obligation to communicate information to the principal (here the client). *See Restatement (Third) of Agency*, § 8.11; *Restatement (Third) of the Law Governing Lawyers* § 20.

Professional conduct rules provide guidance about this communication obligation. Model Rule 1.4(a) describes five scenarios when an attorney has an obligation to communicate with a client. First, when a decision requires the client's informed consent, the lawyer must promptly communicate with the client. In order to obtain informed consent, a lawyer must provide information about material risks of a course of conduct, as well as alternatives available to that course of conduct. (Waiving a conflict of interest is one example of a scenario that requires a client's informed consent. *See* Model Rule 1.7(b)(4). We will consider waiver of conflicts of interest in later chapters).

Rule 1.4(a) continues that a lawyer must "reasonably consult" the client about the means the lawyer uses to accomplish the client's objectives. Next, the rule provides that the lawyer must keep the client "reasonably informed" about the status of the mater. Further, when a client requests information about the matter, the attorney must respond promptly.

Finally, a lawyer has an obligation to inform the client of any legal or professional conduct limitations on the lawyer's ability to comply with the client's expectations in the matter.

Model Rule 1.4(b) provides that the lawyer must "explain a matter to the extent necessary to permit the client to make informed decisions" in the matter. Comment 5 provides further guidance, explaining the client needs sufficient information to make decisions about the objectives of the representation and means by which they are accomplished. In a sense, part b of Rule 1.4 is intended to remind lawyers that the client is the principal, and thus the decision-maker, in the attorney-client relationship. In that relationship the attorney's role is to explain things so that the client can make decisions about the representation.

Thus, the attorney is encouraged, and indeed required, to communicate with the client throughout the matter. Rule 1.4 provides some guidance about the allocation of decision-making authority between attorney and client. Further guidance is provided in Rule 1.2, discussed in the next section.

* * *

Communicating About Malpractice. Imagine that a lawyer negligently fails to file a claim on a client's behalf within the applicable statute of limitations. Must the lawyer communicate this fact to the client? *See* Beal Bank SSB v. Arter & Hadden LLP, 42 Cal. 4th 503 (2007); Benjamin P. Cooper, *The Lawyer's Duty to Inform His Client of His Own Malpractice*, 61 BAYLOR L. REV. 174 (2009).

* * *

2. ALLOCATION OF DECISION-MAKING AUTHORITY

As the principal in the attorney-client agency relationship, the client is in control and gives authority to the attorney. *Restatement (Third) of Agency*, § 1.01 (explaining that the fiduciary agency relationship arises when the agent assents to acting on the principal's behalf and subject to the principal's control). Actual authority can be expressly given ("Defend me in this litigation."). *Id.* at §§ 2.01, 2.02. Actual authority may also be implied from the client's request and includes the acts necessary and incidental to achieving the client's objectives. *Id.*

These agency principles are also embodied in professional conduct rules. Model Rule 1.2(a) provides a lawyer must abide by the client's decision about the objectives of a matter. Next, it refers lawyers to the communication obligation in Rule 1.4 and states that the lawyer must consult with the client about the means by which the client's objectives are to be pursued. The rule notes that a lawyer can take actions that are impliedly authorized to carry out the representation. The rule concludes by explaining that some decisions are reserved for the client. Specifically, a lawyer is to abide by the client's decision whether to settle a matter and, in a criminal case, whether to enter a plea, waive jury trial, and testify.

These legal and professional conduct principles should guide the lawyer throughout the representation. The client is in charge. The lawyer has been given actual authority (both express and implied) to make many decisions on the client's behalf, but the lawyer must also reasonably consult with the client along the way. Some decisions are so insignificant that the lawyer need not consult the client. Other decisions obviously require consultation. The difficult part is determining when the client expects or reasonably could expect communication. The following problem asks you to decide how a lawyer should navigate these questions.

Problem 12.1. In our hypothetical, Giancarlo has been representing Cass County in litigation for twenty-eight months. During that time, Giancarlo has made hundreds of large and small decisions in the matter. For each of the following decisions (or in the language of the rule, decisions about the "means" of carrying out the representation), explain whether Giancarlo should or should not have discussed the decision with the client prior to taking the action.

As you work through each decision, articulate your criteria for which decisions should be discussed and which need not be discussed with the client. Cite language in the comments or text of Rule 1.2 and 1.4 if they influence your analysis. If you need additional information to decide, list the information that you would need.

   a. The decision to hire a courier (at a cost of $20 per hour) to hand-deliver highly confidential documents to an expert witness in the case.

   b. The decision to subpoena a third-party witness for deposition in the case.

   c. The decision to file a motion for summary judgment that could dispose of the entire case.

   d. The decision to file post-trial motions to preserve issues for appeal.

   e. The decision to seek recusal of a State Supreme Court Justice.

* * *

The following case involves an issue of client authority over the objectives and attorney communication in a matter.

OLFE V. GORDON
93 Wis.2d 173, 286 N.W.2d 573 (1980)

CALLOW, JUSTICE.

Early in 1971 Olfe, a widow about sixty-two years of age, was approached by Elmer J. Demman (Demman) who proposed buying Olfe's three-family house and the land upon which it was situated for the purpose of constructing an office building. A verbal agreement was reached between Olfe and Demman in which Demman was to purchase the property for $87,000. Olfe, after meeting with Demman and his attorney, decided she needed an attorney. Olfe consulted Gordon, telling him that she wanted a first mortgage. Olfe testified that when she left the office Gordon "was going to go ahead with getting the documents ready to sign for a first mortgage." On two subsequent occasions, Olfe testified she had contact with Gordon during which she was told that work was proceeding on obtaining a first mortgage for her.

On September 15, 1971, Olfe, Gordon, Demman, and Attorney C. J. Schloemer met with Demman's attorney at his office. Gordon told Olfe he brought Schloemer, his law partner, to the meeting because Schloemer "was well versed" in real estate matters. The first offer Demman's attorney presented to Schloemer was unacceptable, and a second offer to purchase was prepared and presented to Schloemer who reviewed the document and handed it to Gordon. Gordon looked at the document and asked Olfe to sign it. Prior to signing the offer to purchase, Olfe asked: " 'This isn't a second mortgage, is it?' " Gordon gave no answer and Schloemer said: "It is second only to cost of construction." Olfe signed the offer to purchase. She testified she understood Schloemer's remark to mean "that a second mortgage was only on the new building that was going to go up and that the land and the home on it was still under first mortgage." Olfe testified she did not read the document because "I'm not very good at legal terms and that is the reason I hired an attorney to represent me to read it and to see that I was signing for a first mortgage."

Olfe received about $22,500 of the purchase price on November 4, 1971, the date of the closing. The balance of about $64,500 was to be paid in two equal installments during the two succeeding years. No subsequent payments were ever made to Olfe prior to a foreclosure proceeding which was commenced by Continental Savings and Loan, the holder of the first mortgage. It was at this time that Olfe discovered she had only a second mortgage on the entire property. A judgment of foreclosure was entered. Schloemer later negotiated on Olfe's behalf a sale of her second mortgage interest to Continental Savings and Loan for $37,500.

Olfe commenced this action against Gordon and his professional liability insurer to recover the difference between the unpaid principal balance on the mortgage note and the amount which she had received from

Continental Savings and Loan. Her complaint alleged she hired Gordon to protect and represent her interest and that "she wanted a first mortgage on said premises if the said purchaser was unable to pay the entire sum of the sale price at the closing." . . .

Olfe's appeal presents two issues: (1) Is expert testimony required to establish the standard of care on the part of an attorney in a malpractice action; and if so, is such testimony required to establish negligence on the part of Gordon? (2) Does the record contain sufficient credible evidence, when taken in the light most favorable to Olfe, to warrant sending the case to the jury?

. . . Olfe's first two allegations, that Gordon failed to provide in the offer to purchase that Olfe's security interest would be a first mortgage and that he failed to draft or cause to be drafted a mortgage that would be senior to any other Demman would obtain on the premises of sale, are contentions that Gordon is liable for damages caused by his negligent disregard of Olfe's instructions. The legal theory on which these allegations are premised is well established: "It has generally been recognized that an attorney may be liable for all losses caused by his failure to follow with reasonable promptness and care the explicit instructions of his client. Moreover, an attorney's honest belief that the instructions were not in the best interests of his client provides no defense to a suit for malpractice." The attorney-client relationship in such contexts is one of agent to principal, and as an agent the attorney "must act in conformity with his authority and instructions and is responsible to his principal if he violates this duty." While actions for disregard of instructions can be based upon fiduciary and contractual principles, the principal's cause of action for an agent's breach of duty may also lie in tort. "[I]f a paid agent does something wrongful, either knowing it to be wrong, or acting negligently, the principal may have either an action of tort or an action of contract." . . . Expert testimony is not required to show that the agent (attorney) has violated his duty.

Olfe does not allege that she was harmed by a lack of legal expertise on the part of Gordon. She does not assert that Gordon failed to comply with statutes prescribing the necessary formalities concerning the documents' validity. Rather, she seeks to hold Gordon liable for his failure to effectuate her intent, even though the documents he prepared were not legally invalid. While preparation of an offer to purchase and preparation of a mortgage involve "special knowledge or skill or experience on subjects which are not within the realm of the ordinary experience of mankind, and which require special learning, study, or experience," proof of negligence in failing to follow specific instructions concerning the nature and purpose of the documents desired does not require expert testimony. This case is controlled by the law of agency, and the attorney-client relationship does not alter Gordon's alleged relationship to Olfe as an agent to his principal.

As such, duties of care owed Olfe by Gordon are established not by the legal profession's standards but by the law of agency. A jury is competent to understand and apply the standards of care to which agents are held. This case falls within the exception to the rule that expert testimony is necessary to establish the negligence of attorneys. Here Olfe concedes that the documents drafted by Gordon were valid instruments but argues they failed to effectuate her intent and were inconsistent with her specific instructions. We conclude that expert testimony was not required to establish the applicable standard of care and Gordon's alleged departure from that standard in order to have a jury determine the merits of Olfe's allegations that Gordon was negligent in that he failed to properly draft documents consistent with Olfe's instructions. . . .

To establish a prima facie case subjecting an agent to liability in tort, the principal must show a duty of care owed by the agent to the principal, a breach of that duty, and injury to the principal as a proximate result of the breach. In contending that Olfe's proof does not establish a prima facie case, Gordon asserts that his alleged breach of the duty to obey the instructions of his principal was not the cause of Olfe's injury. Gordon relies on the following statement from *Lien v. Pitts*, 46 Wis.2d 35, 46, 174 N.W.2d 462, 468 (1970): " 'It is a rule of long-standing that the signing of an instrument raises a strong presumption that its contents are understood by the signer, and such presumption is not overcome by his statements that he did not understand the nature of the instrument which he signed.' "

. . .

Olfe, however, seeks recovery from her agent, employed to protect her interests, and in so doing she does not rely solely on her statement that she did not understand the contents of the instruments. She testified she asked, " 'This isn't a second mortgage, is it?' " Gordon gave no answer, and Schloemer said, "It is second only to cost of construction." In our view, Gordon's silence and Schloemer's answer could reasonably be viewed by one or more jurors as misinforming Olfe or insufficiently informing her, as she alleges. These responses could be viewed as having the effect of reinforcing Olfe's perception of the standing of the mortgage.

Moreover, Gordon's argument overlooks Olfe's contention that the reason she employed Gordon was that she desired her security interest in the property sold to Demman to be legally protected. Had Olfe desired to make the sale in an informal manner and take as security Demman's assertion that he would pay her, there would have been no need to employ Gordon to prepare an offer to purchase and a mortgage. Olfe cannot be barred from recovery merely because she concluded Gordon had properly performed the services for which he was employed.

* * *

3. WHEN ATTORNEY AND CLIENT DISAGREE ABOUT A DECISION

Comments to Model Rule 1.2 discuss the allocation of authority between attorney and client when they disagree about the *means* to be utilized in representation. Comment 2 provides that clients normally defer to lawyers on such issues, "particularly with respect to technical, legal, and tactical matters." In contrast, the comment notes that lawyers usually defer to clients on the expense to be incurred and the impact on third parties. The comment provides that "other law" may address how such disputes should be resolved, but that ultimately a fundamental disagreement can be resolved by the lawyer's withdrawal or the client's discharge of the lawyer.

The law of agency provides that when attorney and client disagree about a decision, resolution of the dispute is relatively easy—much easier than suggested by comment 2 to Model Rule 1.2. Attorneys cannot budge on decisions that run afoul of the law or professional conduct obligations. And they certainly can make the case that they are in the best position to determine if a tactical decision—such as whether to file a motion—is wise. But as long as the decision is legal and consistent with professional conduct rules, the choice is the client's. The client is the principal in the agency relationship. Even if the lawyer arguably had authority to make the decision, the client can take that authority away. This is a basic tenet of the law of agency. The lawyer could, of course, withdraw from the representation in order to avoid carrying out that decision. But if the lawyer is to continue representing the client, the lawyer must abide by the client's instructions.

Problem 12.2. Assume for purposes of this problem that Giancarlo asked for a closed door session with the Cass County Council prior to filing the motion to recuse the State Supreme Court Justice. In that session, Giancarlo explained that based on their research of prior State Supreme Court decisions: (1) seeking recusal of this Justice could make a win more likely, and (2) if the Justice hears the case, defeat is almost certain given the makeup of the court. Giancarlo explained that they have a solid argument—on the law and on the facts—for seeking the Justice's recusal given specific statements she has made that indicate how she would rule in just such a case.

Do you think the council will be influenced by Giancarlo's reasons for seeking recusal? If the Council votes against filing the motion, what should Giancarlo do next? If Giancarlo insists on filing the motion, what avenues are available to the Council?

* * *

B. A LAWYER'S POWER TO OBLIGATE THE CLIENT IN DEALINGS WITH OTHERS

When will a client be bound by the actions of a lawyer, such as settling a case, waiving a defense, or retaining a lawyer from another firm to consult on the client's matter? Does the client have a cause of action against the lawyer if the lawyer took action not authorized by the client? The law of agency answers these questions.

A client will be bound by a lawyer's actions if the lawyer has either actual authority or apparent authority to bind the client. Both are discussed below. These concepts are also important for determining a lawyer's liability to a client. If the lawyer took action on behalf of the client even though the lawyer did not have the express or implied authority to do so, then the lawyer will face liability to the client for exceeding actual authority.

Actual Authority: Section 26 of the *Restatement (Third) of the Law Governing Lawyers* explains that a lawyer has *actual authority* on behalf of a client in proceedings before a tribunal or in dealings with third parties when the client has expressly or impliedly authorized the act or ratifies the act after learning what the lawyer has done, or if the lawyer has irrevocable authority conferred by law to do or refrain from doing the act in question. Model Rule 1.2 also addresses issues of actual authority. The rule directs lawyers to abide by the client's decisions about the objectives of the representation. Stated another way, the lawyer has express authority to achieve the client's stated objectives, such as "I want a first mortgage" or "I want you to help me get a divorce." Model Rule 1.2 also explains a lawyer's implied authority: "A lawyer may take such actions on behalf of the client as is impliedly authorized to carry out the representation."

If the lawyer has actual authority to act on behalf of the client, the lawyer has both the power and the right to obligate the client. The client is obligated by the lawyer's action, and assuming the lawyer was not negligent, the client has no claim against the lawyer for adverse consequences resulting from the lawyer's actions.

Model Rule 1.2 notes that certain decisions are reserved for the client. The rule provides that a lawyer is to abide by the client's decision whether to settle a matter and, in a criminal case, whether to enter a plea, waive jury trial, and testify. Section 22 of the *Restatement (Third) of the Law Governing Lawyers* provides a similar list. In the language of agency, lawyers are treated as not having actual authority to make these decisions absent express direction from the client.

Actual authority can be revoked by the client. Section 31(2) of the *Restatement (Third) of the Law Governing Lawyers* identifies five events that will terminate, or revoke, the lawyer's actual authority to act on behalf of the client. They are (1) discharge of the lawyer by the client, (2) withdrawal of the lawyer from the representation, (3) death of the client or in the case of a corporation or similar organization, loss of its legal capacity to function as such, (4) death, incapacity, disbarment, or suspension of the lawyer, or a court order requiring the lawyer to terminate the client's representation, or (5) completion of the representation. Consistent with the law of agency, this list should also include a communication from the client to the lawyer revoking the client's prior grant of authority to the lawyer. A client can terminate a lawyer's actual authority to take action on behalf of the client without discharging the lawyer. All it takes is a message delivered to the lawyer.

Apparent Authority: Even in the absence of actual authority, a lawyer may have *apparent authority*. Section 27 of the *Restatement (Third) of the Law Governing Lawyers* specifies that a lawyer's act is considered to be that of the client "if the tribunal or third person reasonably assumes that the lawyer is authorized to do the act on the basis of the client's (and not the lawyer's) manifestations of such authorization." A lawyer's apparent authority ends only when the third party or court knows or has reason to know that the lawyer no longer has actual authority. *See Restatement (Third) of the Law Governing Lawyers* § 31(3) ("A lawyer's apparent authority to act for a client with respect to another person ends when the other person knows or should know of facts from which it can be reasonably inferred that the lawyer lacks actual authority. . . .)." If the lawyer acts within the scope of the apparent but not actual authority, the client will be obligated but probably will not be happy. The client will be able to hold the lawyer liable for the adverse consequences because the lawyer exceeded actual authority.

* * *

Problem 12.3. Assume now that Giancarlo represents Cass County in a different civil action that is still pending in the trial court. In that case, the court orders counsel either to appear at a pretrial conference with authority to settle the case or to arrange for the presence of an authorized person. Cass County has not been informed of the order and has not authorized Giancarlo to approve a settlement. Giancarlo, without disclosing that lack of authority, attends the conference and agrees to a settlement they think will be acceptable to Cass County. Is the settlement enforceable? What are Cass County's available remedies if it does not like the settlement and wishes to continue the litigation? *See Restatement (Third) of the Law Governing Lawyers* § 27 Comment d, ill. 3.

* * *

C. IDENTIFYING THE DULY AUTHORIZED CONSTITUENTS OF AN ORGANIZATIONAL CLIENT

Model Rule 1.13 addresses the representation of organizational clients. Rule 1.13(a) provides that a lawyer employed by an organization represents the organization "acting through its duly authorized constituents." Comment 1 explains that an organizational client is a legal entity, but that it can only act through its officers, directors, employees, shareholders, and other constituents. The entity is the client. Absent a separate agreement, the constituents are not clients.

The reference to "duly authorized constituents" is necessarily vague to cover all possible organizations and all their possible constituents who are authorized to act. Comment 1 to Rule 1.13 provides that Rule 1.13 is applicable to unincorporated associations, such as partnerships, and that the catchall reference to "other constituents" was meant to embrace persons whose status in an unincorporated organization was equivalent to that of officers, directors, employees, etc.

Professional conduct rules reference the various powers of an organization's duly authorized constituents. First, only a duly authorized constituent of the organization can enter into a legally binding client-lawyer relationship. Second, only a duly authorized constituent can make a decisions concerning the organization's representation that must or may be made by the client. Third, the lawyer must direct such communication concerning the organization's representation as is required by Rule 1.4 to a duly authorized constituent and must not reveal information relating to the organization's representation to a person who is not a duly authorized constituent. Finally, as will be explored in greater depth in a later chapter, there are situations in which a lawyer for an organization will be required by Rule 1.13 to consult with the constituents who possess "the highest authority" to act on behalf of the organization and to act in the best interests of the organization even when the authorized constituents want to take action that will create liability for or to the organization.

In many situations, a lawyer will have no doubt about the identity of an organizational client's authorized constituents. The associate general counsel, senior vice president, or other executive who hired the lawyer may be the lawyer's point of contact and primary decision maker in the representation. Other times, a lawyer may face uncertainty about whether someone else in the organization is the authorized constituent for purposes of making an important decision in the representation. Consider the following problem based on our chapter hypothetical.

Problem 12.4. As part of the representation of Cass County, Giancarlo frequently talked to the Cass County Law Director about the status of the litigation and sometimes gave a report in a closed door session of a County Council meeting when the Law Director suggested it. Is the

Cass County Law Director an authorized constituent of Cass County for purposes of this litigation? Are there certain decisions for which the Cass County Council should be consulted rather than the Law Director? How should Giancarlo decide?

* * *

D. REPRESENTING CLIENTS WITH DISABILITIES, DIMINISHED CAPACITY, OR COMMUNICATION BARRIERS

1. IN GENERAL

Model Rule 1.14 articulates a special rule involving communication and decision-making in the case of the representation of a client with "diminished capacity." The rule defines this concept in terms of "a client's capacity to make adequately considered decisions in connection with a representation." There is much room for disagreement about the extent of the capacity of some clients to make adequately considered decisions in connection with the client's representation and how that affects the responsibilities of the lawyer to communicate with the client and to involve the client in decisions affecting the client's interest. The legal profession, however, has also recognized that some clients' capacity to make adequately considered decisions concerning their representation can be diminished due to legal incompetency, mental health issues, or other reasons. How does such impairment affect the lawyer's responsibilities concerning communication with the client and the respective roles of lawyer, client, and others in decision-making concerning the impaired client's representation?

Use the rule and its comments to answer the following problem.

* * *

Problem 12.5. Melissa is eighteen years old. She has Down's Syndrome. When she was a child, her parents divorced, and her mother, Helen, was granted custody. As Melissa approached age 18, she expressed a desire to live with her father. Because Helen wanted Melissa to continue to live with her, she instituted an action seeking guardianship of Melissa once she became an adult. Melissa's father is contesting Helen's action and wants to be appointed guardian. Pursuant to a state court rule, the trial court appointed Paul to act as Melissa's attorney in the matter. Paul spoke with several experts who had dealt with Melissa, and they offered conflicting opinions as to whether Melissa was competent to make decisions about where to live and which parent should be her guardian. Melissa has made it clear to Paul that she wishes to live with her father, but Paul has serious doubts as to whether Melissa fully understands what is at stake and whether living with her father is truly in Melissa's best interests. He is conflicted about what he should do at the scheduled hearing, so he comes to you for advice as to his ethical obligations. What advice do you have for him?

* * *

The Uncertain Contours of Rule 1.14. Numerous commentators have expressed concern over the failure of Rule 1.14 to create clear standards for attorneys to follow. For example, Rule 1.14(a) requires that the "lawyer shall, as far as reasonably possible, maintain a normal client-lawyer relationship with the client" even when the client has diminished capacity "to make adequately considered decisions in connection with a representation." What specifically should the lawyer do to comply with this rule? Comment [2] counsels that the lawyer should "treat the client with attention and respect" and states that "[e]ven if the person has a legal representative, the lawyer should as far as possible accord the represented person the status of client, particularly in maintaining communication." However, Comment [4] suggests that "[i]f a legal representative has already been appointed for the client, the lawyer should ordinarily look to the representative for decisions on behalf of the client." Are these two comments reconcilable? Section 24(2) of the *Restatement* fleshes out the lawyer's responsibility toward a client with diminished capacity by stating, "A lawyer ... must ... pursue the lawyer's reasonable view of the client's objectives or interests as the client would define them if able to make adequately considered decisions on the matter, even if the client ... gives contrary instructions." Is this directive more satisfactory than the requirements of Model Rule 1.14? If a lawyer acted contrary to her client's instructions on the ground that the client had diminished capacity, would the client have a cause of action for legal malpractice, or a basis for a disciplinary complaint, against the lawyer?

Determining "Diminished Capacity." How can a lawyer determine that a client has diminished capacity? Comment [6] advises that "[i]n appropriate circumstances, the lawyer may seek guidance from an appropriate diagnostician." But Rule 1.14(c) cautions that "[i]nformation relating to the representation of a client with diminished capacity is protected by Rule 1.6." How then would the lawyer seek guidance from an appropriate diagnostician? And what would constitute "appropriate circumstances" for seeking such guidance? Comment [6] lists a number of factors the lawyer may consider in deciding to seek such guidance. Do these factors provide a sufficient foundation upon which to make a decision to seek diagnostic guidance?

Guardian Ad Litem vs. Appointed Counsel. In some instances, a court will appoint a guardian ad litem for a child or other person lacking the capacity to make decisions. In others, the child or other person may be represented by counsel, appointed or otherwise. One court has explained the difference between the two roles:

> A court-appointed counsel's services are to the child. Counsel acts as an independent legal advocate for the best interests of the child and takes an active part in the hearing, ranging from subpoenaing and cross-examining witnesses to appealing the decision, if warranted. If the purpose of the appointment is for legal advocacy, then counsel would be appointed. A court-appointed guardian ad litem's services are to the court on behalf of the child. The GAL acts as an independent fact finder, investigator and evaluator as to what furthers the best interests of the child. The GAL submits a written report to the court and is available to testify. If the purpose of the appointment is for independent investigation and fact finding, then a GAL would be appointed. The GAL can be an attorney, a social worker, a mental health professional or other appropriate person. These rules are not intended to expand the circumstances when such appointments are to be made; neither are these appointments to be made routinely.

In the Matter of M.R., 638 A.2d 1274 (N.J. 1994).

Section 24(3) of the *Restatement (Third) of the Law Governing Lawyers* spells out two circumstances in which the lawyer is not required to respect the decisions of the client's guardian or other legal representative: (1) when the lawyer represents the client in a matter against the interests of that person or (2) when that person instructs the lawyer to act in a manner that the lawyer knows will violate that person's duties toward the client. Should the *Model Rules of Professional Conduct* be amended to add such a provision?

* * *

2. COMMUNICATION BARRIERS

In order for a client to make informed decisions concerning the representation, the client must be able to communicate effectively with the lawyer. A lawyer's ethical obligations of competence and effective communication do not cease simply because there is a communication barrier that makes effective communication difficult. ABA Formal Opinion 500 (2021) explains that the duty of communication is not excused in this situation.

The opinion explains that the ethical duties of competence and communication "establish a baseline for a lawyer's duties when there is a barrier to communication because the lawyer and the client do not share a common language, or when a client is a person with a non-cognitive physical condition that affects how the lawyer communicates with a client, such as a hearing or speech disability." The opinion then explains that in cases when lawyer and client cannot communicate with reasonable efficacy, the lawyer must take steps to employ an appropriate interpreter or use a language translation device. The opinion provides that "once it is reasonably apparent that, without an interpreter, translator, or an appropriate assistive or language-translation device, there cannot be a reliably understandable reciprocal exchange of information between the lawyer and the client, the lawyer must take steps to help the client understand the need for and purpose of an interpreter or translator, and, when reasonably necessary, take steps to secure such services."

The opinion also notes that "the duty of competence requires close attention to social and cultural differences that can affect a client's understanding of legal advice, legal concepts, and other aspects of the representation." Cultural differences may impact how a client gathers and processes information. Therefore, effective communication may require

> (i) identifying these differences; (ii) seeking to understand them and how they bear upon the representation; (iii) paying attention to implicit bias and other cognitive biases that can distort understanding; (iv) adapting the framing of questions to help elicit information relating to the representation in context-sensitive ways; (v) explaining the matter in multiple ways to promote better client insight and comprehension; (vi) "allow[ing] for additional time for client meetings and ask[ing] confirming questions to assure that information is being exchanged accurately and completely"; and (vii) conducting additional research or drawing upon the expertise of others when that is necessary to ensure effective communication and mutual understanding.

* * *

Legal Obligations. Law offices are covered as places of public accommodation under Title III of the Americans with Disabilities Act (ADA). The ADA requires such entities "to take such steps as may be necessary to ensure that no individual with a disability is . . . denied services . . . because of the absence of auxiliary aids and services," such as qualified interpreters. 42 U.S.C. § 12182(b)(2)(A)(ii).

Profile of Attorney Professionalism.

> Georgia, a 94-year-old nursing home resident, is a widow with two senior-citizen-aged children. She worked for years as a hotel maid, laboring hard for the monthly social security benefits that are her only income. She owns no home, no pension, no bank accounts.

Suffering from Alzheimer's and a host of physical problems, she spends her days sitting in a wheelchair looking at the television.

Georgia was born in the same year that the income tax, stainless steel, and assembly line were introduced in America. No longer able to feed or care for herself, she needed someone to make decisions for her and to ensure that she has the best quality of life possible, so her son Alfred filed a petition to be appointed guardian.

But Probate Judge Mary Ellen Coghlan needed to know if Alfred's appointment would be in his mother's best interests. Could he take care of her? Would he? Because neither Georgia nor her family could afford to pay an attorney, Judge Coghlan appointed Chicago Volunteer Legal Services as guardian ad litem (GAL). Volunteer Eve Epstein agreed to take the case.

. . .

Eve traveled to Georgia's south side nursing home and visited with her in her room. After noting that Georgia was neat and clean and that her room looked tidy, she tried to engage her in conversation, without much luck. Eve spoke with the nursing home staff who confirmed that Alfred was a frequent and kind visitor. Eve also spoke with Georgia's daughter who resides in an assisted living program due to her own medical problems. She wanted her brother to be guardian of their mother. After a thorough investigation, Eve recommended that Alfred be appointed guardian and Judge Coghlan made the appointment.

A few days later, Alfred sent Eve a letter. "Miss Epstein, I would like to thank you for all the help I received from you. I know I could never pay you for your time, so I just wanted to thank you with all my heart. Maybe you could get a cup of coffee to go with your lunch." He'd enclosed a $10 bill with the letter.

. . .

Kim Halvorsen, an associate at Clifford Law Offices, is GAL for 55-year old Michael, who has dementia and lives in a nursing home. His wife and his mother both wanted to be his guardian and both wanted the other woman out of his life. When the wife was given limited guardianship, the mother was given visitation rights. Unfortunately, the women frequently tried to visit at the same time and got into fights. When one altercation turned physical and the police had to escort them from the home, staff threatened to ban them both. Kim went to court and got a specific visitation schedule to keep the two women apart. They still fight and both call Kim regularly complaining about the other. Kim has her work cut out for her as she tries to do what is best for Michael.

Kim got the case because Clifford Law Offices adopted the Adult GAL Program as its firm-wide pro bono program, and committed to handle two cases per attorney per year. Managing partner, Thomas K. Prindable, who took the firm's first case himself, admires the work of the Probate Court and the work that GALs perform. "When you go in these Probate courtrooms it makes your heart just open up. There are wonderful people working very hard to ensure that the weakest members of our society are protected. It's an honor to be part of that."

Margaret C. Benson, *Guardian Ad Litem: The Grinch Need Not Apply*, CHICAGO BAR JOURNAL (Oct. 2008). Reprinted with permission of the Chicago Bar Association.

SECTION 3

COMPETENCE AND DILIGENCE

■ ■ ■

In this section, we focus on that duty of care to clients. This duty is typically discussed in terms of the lawyer's duty to competently and diligently represent the client. Chapter 13 addresses this duty as well as the extent to which a lawyer's failure to perform duties to her client may subject the lawyer to discipline or civil liability.

CHAPTER 13

COMPETENT AND DILIGENT REPRESENTATION OF A CLIENT

■ ■ ■

Chapter Hypothetical. Miranda is a solo practitioner who has been in practice for three years. As a solo practitioner, Miranda has a heavy caseload. Most of her work involves personal injury cases, but she recently agreed to represent Jill, who was being sued for trademark infringement and related claims. Unfortunately, the representation did not go well, and Jill has now filed a disciplinary complaint and sued Miranda for malpractice.

Lawyers cannot guarantee that the work they perform on behalf of a client will produce the outcome the client wants. All the lawyer can do is work competently with the law and facts to make it as likely as reasonably possible that the client's objectives for the representation will be accomplished. These materials introduce you to some of the legal and professional responsibility issues that arise when clients are dissatisfied with their lawyer's performance, including the possibility of a legal malpractice action.

* * *

A. RULES OF PROFESSIONAL CONDUCT

1. COMPETENCE

Model Rule 1.1 lists four components of competence. The first two—legal knowledge and skill—can be acquired through legal education and experience. Comment [1] to Rule 1.1 states that representation in some matters may require only the "proficiency . . . of a general practitioner," while in others, "[e]xpertise in a particular field of law may be required." How will you know the required level of expertise that is necessary in a given case? Does criminal defense require expertise? Criminal defense in a capital case? Comment [2] notes that competence in a given matter may be achieved either through "necessary study" or through "association of a lawyer of established competence." Do these two means of acquiring competence correspond to the situations in which generalized knowledge vs. specialized knowledge is required? Note also that Rule 1.1 imposes an ongoing duty upon all lawyers to keep up to date with changes in the law and its practice "including the benefits and risks associated with relevant technology." *Id.* Comment [8].

The third and fourth components of competence—thoroughness and preparation—would seem to depend on simple hard work at least as much as study and experience. Note that Comment [5] explains that thoroughness and preparation include adequate investigation into both the factual and legal elements of a problem. *See, e.g., Goebel v. Lauderdale*, 214 Cal. App.3d 1502 (1989) (involving lawyers who provided advice to clients that would have violated state penal code); Lawrence Duncan MacLachlan, *Gandy Dancers on the Web: How the Internet Has Raised the Bar on Lawyers' Professional Responsibility to Research and Know the Law*, 13 GEO. J. LEGAL ETHICS 607 (2000).

Problem 13.1. Prior to her representation of Jill, Miranda had never done work in the trademark area. Miranda's only prior knowledge of trademark law came from having taken Intellectual Property in her second year of law school. (She made a C+ in the class.) Putting aside for now the question of whether Miranda competently represented Jill, was Miranda competent to take on the representation in the first place? *See* Rule 1.1, Comments [1]–[4]; *see also* Rule 1.16, Comment [1].

Problem 13.2. Miranda eventually moved for summary judgment on Jill's behalf. Among the cases cited in her brief were two cases that did not exist. It turns out that Miranda had relied on a new generative Artificial Intelligence (AI) tool called ProTalk to draft the brief and that ProTalk fabricated the two cases when drafting the brief. When the judge in the case confronted Miranda about the fictitious cases, Miranda admitted her use of AI. She explained that she used ProTalk in order to meet the filing deadline and that she just assumed that ProTalk functioned like common, reliable legal search engines. With reference to the language of Model Rule 1.1 and its comments, explain how Miranda violated her duty of competence.

* * *

2. DILIGENCE

Model Rule 1.3 provides that in the representation, a lawyer must act with diligence and promptness. Comment [1] to Rule 1.3 provides that a lawyer must act with "commitment and dedication to the interests of the client and with zeal in advocacy upon the client's behalf." However, the comment also warns that this duty "does not require the use of offensive tactics or preclude the treating of all persons involved in the legal process with courtesy and respect." Is the balance between "zeal" and "courtesy and respect" a difficult one to maintain? Comment [3] warns against procrastination, noting that the "client's interests can often be adversely affected by the passage of time" and that "delay can cause a client needless anxiety and undermine confidence in the lawyer's trustworthiness." The comment identifies heavy caseloads as one possible cause of such delay.

* * *

B. CIVIL LIABILITY FOR MALPRACTICE

A legal malpractice claim is a claim of professional negligence. As such, a plaintiff must establish all of the elements of the standard tort action for negligence: duty, breach, causation (both causation in fact and proximate cause), and damages.

1. DUTY AND BREACH

A lawyer generally owes a duty to a client to "exercise the competence and diligence normally exercised by lawyers in similar circumstances." *Restatement (Third) of the Law Governing Lawyers* § 52(1). A lawyer typically only owes a duty to a client; a lawyer does not owe any duty of care to a third party. Possible exceptions to that general rule include where the client has invited a third party to rely upon the lawyer's services, or where a third party is the intended beneficiary of the representation (such as in the case of a will).

Professional negligence claims raise some challenging issues in terms of the duty and breach elements. For example, Paragraph [20] of the Scope preceding the *Model Rules* advises that the "[v]iolation of a Rule should not itself give rise to a cause of action against a lawyer," because, in part, the rules "are designed ... to provide a structure for regulating conduct through disciplinary agencies." *See also Restatement (Third) of the Law Governing Lawyers* § 52(2)(a). The violation of a disciplinary rule is not negligence *per se*, as that term is used in tort law. Paragraph [20] also goes on to provide that violation of a rule should not "create any presumption in such a case that a legal duty has been breached."

The following cases explore some other special rules regarding duty and breach that may apply in a legal malpractice action.

RIZZO V. HAINES
555 A.2d 58 (Pa. 1989)

STOUT, JUSTICE.

Barton A. Haines, Esquire, appeals from the order of the Superior Court ... affirming in part, and reversing and remanding in part, the judgment order of the Court of Common Pleas of Philadelphia County that held that he negligently, and in bad faith, conducted settlement negotiations for his client Frank L. Rizzo. . . . We affirm.

On September 20, 1968, Rizzo, while stopped in a vehicle at an intersection, was rear-ended by a City of Philadelphia police vehicle. At the time, Rizzo was an off-duty police officer for the City of Philadelphia. Rizzo's soft-tissue neck, back, and arm injuries, sustained in the accident, eventually worsened, and he came under the supervision of Henry T. Wycis, M.D. After three surgical procedures . . . he became permanently partially paralyzed. . . .

Rizzo originally retained Anthony J. Caiazzo, Esquire, to institute a suit against the City of Philadelphia [hereinafter "City" case]. Later he retained the law firm of Richter, Syken, Ross & Levant, which assigned the case to Haines, an associate with the firm. The relationship between Haines and the Richter firm deteriorated, and Haines left the firm. He copied the Rizzo file and took it and the client, who by this time had become a personal friend, with him. Frank and Lena Rizzo, under Haines' counsel, instituted a medical malpractice action against Dr. Wycis and the hospital where the surgeries were performed [hereinafter "Wycis" case]. The instant action arises from Haines' representation of Rizzo in these two lawsuits.

Haines did not pursue consolidation of the two cases. Rather, after a failed attempt on the part of the City to join Dr. Wycis' estate, the City case was listed for a jury trial before the Honorable Merna B. Marshall. [During settlement discussions with the City, Haines initially demanded $1.2 million and then raised the amount to $2 million. The attorney for the City responded by saying that he could offer more than $550,000 and asked Haines, "What do you really want?" Haines replied "$2 million." Haines never told Rizzo that the City was willing to offer more than $550,000, and Rizzo had not instructed Haines to raise the demand to $2 million. Rizzo had told that Haines that he was willing to settle for between $700,000 and $750,000.] The jury returned a verdict in favor of Mr. Rizzo for $450,000.

Throughout the course of the City case, Haines repeatedly led the Rizzos to believe that the Wycis case had a recovery value of between $800,000 and $1 million. The record reveals, however, that there was insufficient evidence of Dr. Wycis' malpractice to justify this figure. Furthermore, the doctor's professional liability insurance coverage was only $100,000. In addition, there was insufficient evidence that the hospital was negligent either in extending staff privileges to Dr. Wycis or in caring for Rizzo. On January 23, 1978, the Wycis case was dismissed on a summary judgment motion . . . on the basis that, *inter alia*, the recovery in the City suit had fully compensated Rizzo for his injuries.

The Rizzos instituted the instant malpractice action against Haines alleging, *inter alia*, professional negligence in settling the City case. . . . The case was tried without a jury. . . . On January 18, 1984, the judge found for the Rizzos. He awarded $300,000 compensatory damage for negligent settlement.... Judge Kremer denied the post-trial motions.... The Superior Court affirmed....

In *Schenkel v. Monheit*, 266 Pa. Super. 396, 405 A.2d 493 (1979), the Superior Court held that an allegedly aggrieved client must establish three elements in order to recover for legal malpractice. They are:

1. The employment of the attorney or other basis for duty;

2. The failure of the attorney to exercise ordinary skill and knowledge; and

3. That such negligence was the proximate cause of damage to the plaintiff.

We believe that the necessity for an attorney's use of ordinary skill and knowledge extends to the conduct of settlement negotiations. As this Court stated in *Rothman v. Fillette*, 503 Pa. 259, 469 A.2d 543 (1983), in addition to the fact that settlement is the faster way to get money into the hands of the victims of tortious conduct,

> [v]oluntary settlement of civil controversies is in high judicial favor. Judges and lawyers alike strive assiduously to promote amicable adjustments of matters in dispute, as for the most wholesome of reasons they certainly should. When the effort is successful, the parties avoid the expense and delay incidental to litigation of the issues; the court is spared the burdens of a trial and the preparation and proceedings that must forerun it.

Id. at 267, 469 A.2d at 546 (footnote omitted) (quoting *Autera v. Robinson*, 419 F.2d 1197, 1199 (D.C. Cir. 1969)). We recognize that a disappointed client may be inclined to subject his or her attorney to the standard that only hindsight may provide, and as a general policy there should be judicial reluctance to relitigate suits in the guise of legal malpractice. Nevertheless, as stated in *Gans v. Mundy*, 762 F.2d 338 (3d Cir. 1985):

> [A]n attorney's considered decision involving at a minimum the requisite exercise of 'ordinary skill and capacity,' and which is an 'informed judgment,' does not constitute malpractice.

Id. at 341. Therefore, an attorney may not shield himself from liability in failing to exercise the requisite degree of professional skill in settling the case by asserting that he was merely following a certain strategy or exercising professional judgment. Rather, the importance of settlement to the client and society mandates that an attorney utilize ordinary skill and knowledge.

Consistent with ordinary skill and knowledge, it was incumbent upon Haines, as a matter of law, to communicate all settlement offers to his client. This rule derives from the settled principle that an attorney must have express authority from the client to settle the case. Since the client's choice to accept or reject a settlement offer must be an informed one, we further believe that Haines was also under a duty to investigate the offers that were proposed by the City. Thus, contrary to Haines' assertion, the duty imposed by the trial court was not simply that he elicit his opponent's maximum settlement authority in the form of an offer. Rather, it was a duty to take reasonable steps to investigate the inquiries or offers that the City extended.

. . .

. . . Haines clearly breached this duty to investigate settlement offers by failing to respond to Moran's comment at trial that he could get more than $550,000. Despite the comment, he took no steps to ascertain how much "more" the City was willing to pay. He also breached the duty to communicate this settlement offer to his client. Since the other elements of attorney malpractice have been met, we hold that breach of these duties is sufficient to support a malpractice action.

Concerning the necessity for expert testimony to establish the standard of care, . . . this Court [has previously] noted the general rule that expert testimony is essential where it would help the finder of fact understand an issue that is beyond the knowledge of the average person. Clearly, where the issues are not beyond such knowledge, the appropriate standard of care can be established without expert testimony. Where the issue is simple, and the lack of skill obvious, the ordinary experience and comprehension of lay persons can establish the standard of care.

Instantly, the Rizzos presented the expert testimony of M. Mark Mendel, Esquire. The trial court concluded that this expert made inaccurate factual assumptions in reaching some of his opinions, and therefore did not rely on this expert in reaching its conclusion that Haines violated the standard of care that he owed his clients. Nevertheless, we agree with the trial court that breach of the duty to investigate, and to inform one's client of, settlement offers does not require expert testimony. See Joos, supra, 94 Mich. App. at 423, 288 N.W.2d at 445 ("It is well within the ordinary knowledge and experience of a layman jury to recognize that . . . the failure of an attorney to disclose [settlement offers] is a breach of the professional standard of care."). See also Wright v. Williams, 47 Cal. App.3d. 802, 810, 121 Cal. Rptr. 194, 200 (1975) ("In some circumstances, the failure of attorney performance may be so clear that the trier of fact may find professional negligence unaided by the testimony of experts."). Instantly, there was sufficient nonexpert testimony to support the finding that Haines breached the standard of care by failing to investigate and inform his client of the City's settlement offer.

* * *

WOOD v. MCGRATH, NORTH, MULLIN & KRATZ, P.C.
589 N.W.2d 103 (Neb. 1999)

CONNOLLY, J.

We granted the appellant, Beverly J. Wood's petition for further review of the Nebraska Court of Appeals' decision. The Court of Appeals concluded that as a matter of law, Timothy J. Pugh, an attorney with the appellee, the law firm of McGrath, North, Mullin & Kratz, P.C. (McGrath), did not breach the standard of care or commit legal malpractice by failing to inform Wood that the law relating to two issues relevant to a divorce settlement was unsettled and that the settlement resolved those issues against her. We reverse the Court of Appeals' decision and conclude that the doctrine of judgmental immunity does not apply to an attorney's failure to inform a client of unsettled legal issues relevant to a settlement agreement.

BACKGROUND

Wood brought a legal malpractice action against McGrath, alleging that Pugh had negligently represented her in a dissolution action. The underlying dissolution action was concluded by settlement and decree. In her petition against McGrath, Wood alleged that Pugh allowed her to accept less than her share of the marital estate and was negligent by, inter alia, failing to inform her that (1) the settlement reflected a distribution which excluded all rights to then unvested stock options which her husband held through his employment at Werner Enterprises, Inc.; (2) the state of the law indicated that a trial court could likely include all such stock options within the marital estate; (3) the settlement reflected a distribution which excluded approximately $210,489 from the marital estate to account for potential capital gains tax on the stock that the couple owned; and (4) the state of the law indicated that a trial court could likely value the Werner stock without deducting any potential capital gains tax.

At trial, Wood testified that Pugh told her the settlement awarded her forty percent of the marital estate and that when she asked if that was appropriate, she said Pugh told her a judge would award her anywhere from 35 to 50 percent—that she could do better or worse than the settlement by going to trial. However, Wood testified that Pugh never discussed the different terms of the settlement, never mentioned any alternatives to settling, never provided any reasons to reject the settlement, and never discussed the potential outcome of a trial. She stated that she would not have signed the agreement if Pugh had told her that a trial court might include the unvested stock options as part of the marital estate and that a trial court might prohibit the deduction of potential capital gains tax when valuing the stock, contrary to what the settlement proposed.

Two attorneys testified as expert witnesses for Wood. David Domina stated that when a property settlement raises the issue of unvested stock options, the decision is the client's whether to pursue the issue to trial or to nonetheless settle the issue and that a lawyer breaches the applicable standard of care by failing to inform the client of the existence of the issue and the related law. Domina testified that when a settlement agreement deducts potential capital gains taxes from the value of a marital estate, a lawyer breaches the applicable standard of care by failing to inform a client of the effect of the deduction and the related law. Paul Galter testified that, given the terms of the settlement agreement presented to Wood, Pugh breached the standard of care because Pugh did not give Wood sufficient information on the unvested stock options and capital gains tax issues. Galter stated that Pugh had a duty to tell Wood that the agreement raised the issues; to explain their effects to Wood; and to explain what the relevant law on the issues was, including what courts in other jurisdictions had held, before permitting her to sign the agreement.

At the close of Wood's evidence, McGrath moved for a directed verdict, which the court sustained on the issues of the stock valuation and the exclusion of unvested stock options.

On appeal, Wood asserted, inter alia, that the trial court erred in granting McGrath's directed verdict, arguing that Pugh breached the standard of care by failing to properly advise her in regard to the settlement agreement.

The Court of Appeals noted that the law on both the inclusion of unvested stock options in the marital estate and the consideration of potential capital gains taxes in valuing the estate were unsettled in Nebraska at the time the parties entered into the agreement. *Wood v. McGrath,* North, 7 Neb. App. 262, 581 N.W.2d 107 (1998). Accordingly, the court held that the judgmental immunity rule applied and concluded that Pugh's acts and omissions relating to the issues were not negligent as a matter of law. The court then stated that "Pugh, upon exercise of informed judgment, was not obligated to give additional advice regarding the unsettled nature of relevant legal principles." *Id.* at 282, 581 N.W.2d at 121.

ASSIGNMENT OF ERROR

In her petition for further review, Wood asserts that the Court of Appeals erred in affirming the trial court's judgment.

ANALYSIS

Wood argues that the doctrine of judgmental immunity does not apply to Pugh's failure to inform her of the law relating to the unvested stock options and capital gains tax deduction issues; that the settlement resolved those issues against her; and that given the body of law on the issues at the time, a trial judge might have resolved those issues in her favor. McGrath notes that the law regarding those issues was unsettled in Nebraska when Pugh represented Wood and argues that the doctrine of judgmental immunity applies to an attorney's decision regarding unsettled law, citing *Baker v. Fabian, Thielen & Thielen*, 254 Neb. 697, 578 N.W.2d 446 (1998). McGrath thus contends that when presenting a client with a settlement, an attorney has no duty to inform a client of possible options when the law relating to a relevant issue is unsettled.

In *Baker, supra*, this court held that an attorney is not liable for an error in judgment on a point of law which has not been settled by this court and on which reasonable doubt may be entertained by well-informed lawyers. Thus, an attorney's judgment or recommendation on an unsettled point of law is immune from suit, and the attorney has no duty to accurately predict the future course of unsettled law. This immunity rule encourages practicing attorneys in this state to predict, in a professional manner, the outcome of legal issues relevant to their clients' cases. See Canon 7, EC 7–3 and 7–5, of the Code of Professional Responsibility. However, Pugh's recommendations (or lack thereof) on the unvested stock options and capital gains tax issues are not before us. Rather, the issue is whether the doctrine of judgmental immunity applies to Pugh's failure to inform Wood that the law relating to unvested stock options and potential capital gains tax issues, while unsettled in Nebraska, were settled in other jurisdictions in a manner which would have been favorable to Wood. The question of whether an attorney owes a duty to inform a client of the unsettled nature of relevant law was not addressed in *Baker*. Thus, we must determine whether to extend the *Baker* judgmental immunity rule to an attorney's failure to inform a client of unsettled legal issues relevant to a settlement agreement.

"[W]e insist that lawyers . . . advise clients with respect to settlements with the same skill, knowledge, and diligence with which they pursue all other legal tasks." *Bruning v. Law Offices of Ronald J. Palagi*, 250 Neb. 677, 689, 551 N.W.2d 266, 272 (1996) (citing *Grayson v. Wofsey, Rosen, Kweskin & Kuriansky*, 231 Conn. 168, 646 A.2d 195 (1994)). See also *McWhirt v. Heavey*, 250 Neb. 536, 550 N.W.2d 327 (1996). We declined in *McWhirt* " 'to adopt a rule that insulates attorneys from exposure to malpractice claims arising from their negligence in settled cases if the attorney's conduct has damaged the client.' " We decline to adopt such a rule now.

The decision to settle a controversy is the client's. See Canon 7, EC 7–7. If a client is to meaningfully make that decision, he or she needs to have the information necessary to assess the risks and benefits of either settling or proceeding to trial. "A lawyer should exert his or her best efforts to ensure that decisions of a client are made only after the client has been informed of relevant considerations." Canon 7, EC 7–8. The desire is [to ensure] that a client's decision to settle is an informed one.

The attorney's research efforts may not resolve doubts or may lead to the conclusion that only hindsight or future judicial decisions will provide accurate answers. The attorney's responsibilities to the client may not be satisfied concerning a material issue simply by determining that a proposition is doubtful or by unilaterally deciding the issue. Where there are reasonable alternatives, the attorney should inform the client that the issue is uncertain, unsettled or debatable and allow the client to make the decision. RONALD E. MALLEN & JEFFREY M. SMITH, LEGAL MALPRACTICE § 17.15 at 531–32 (4th ed. 1996).

Additionally, an allegation that an attorney is negligent by failing to inform a client of an unsettled legal issue relevant to a settlement does not demand that an attorney accurately predict the future course of unsettled law. Thus, an allegation that an attorney did not properly inform a client of relevant unsettled legal issues does not provide the same need for immunity from suit as does an attorney's judgment or recommendation in an area of unsettled law.

Ultimately, we cannot support what would be the clear result of extending the judgmental immunity rule in the instant case. If we conclude that the judgmental immunity rule applies to an attorney's failure to inform a client of unsettled legal issues relevant to a settlement, an attorney could forgo conducting research or providing a client with information on a relevant legal issue once he or she determined that the legal issue at hand was unsettled in this state. We fail to see how this result promotes the settlement of disputes in a client's best interests.

We conclude that the doctrine of judgmental immunity does not apply to an attorney's failure to inform a client of unsettled legal issues relevant to a settlement. Our conclusion makes no judgment as to whether Pugh was negligent. It imposes no additional duty as a matter of law to research or inform a client on unsettled legal matters. Rather, it simply directs that consistent with *Bruning v. Law Offices of Ronald J. Palagi*, 250 Neb. 677, 551 N.W.2d 266 (1996); *McWhirt v. Heavey*, 250 Neb. 536, 550 N.W.2d 327 (1996); and *McVaney v. Baird, Holm, McEachen*, 237 Neb. 451, 466 N.W.2d 499 (1991), whether an attorney is negligent for such a failure is determined by whether the attorney exercised the same skill, knowledge, and diligence as attorneys of ordinary skill and capacity commonly possess and exercise in the performance of all other legal tasks. At the same time, an attorney's ultimate recommendation in an area of unsettled law is immune from suit. *Baker v. Fabian, Thielen & Thielen, supra.* Such a result gives the client the benefit of both professional advice and the information necessary to make an informed decision whether to settle a dispute.

CONCLUSION

The Court of Appeals erred in concluding that Pugh was not negligent as a matter of law in failing to inform Wood of the unsettled nature of the law regarding whether unvested stock options were part of the marital estate and whether the marital estate's unvested stock options should have been valued without deducting potential capital gains tax. Accordingly, we reverse the Court of Appeals' decision and remand the cause to the Court of Appeals with directions to remand the cause to the district court for a new trial.

* * *

The Scope of the "Informed Judgment" or "Judgmental Immunity" Rule. Assume that there is a split of authority at the time a lawyer decides to file an action. The lawyer proceeds on the assumption that the law is in her client's favor, but is unaware of the contrary decisional law. Eventually, the court rules against the lawyer's position. Does the rule from *Wood* protect the lawyer from a malpractice claim?

Problem 13.3. Identify the alleged act(s) of negligence related to Miranda's handling of the summary judgment motion that Jill could assert in her malpractice claim against Miranda. How will her lawyer go about establishing that Miranda failed to meet the applicable standard of care? Is she likely to be successful in establishing this element of the claim?

* * *

SIMKO V. BLAKE
532 N.W.2d 842 (Mich. 1994)

Plaintiffs Arthur Louis Simko, Margaret Simko, and Tara Marie Simko filed suit against defendant Marvin Blake, an attorney, alleging that the defendant committed professional malpractice in failing to adequately represent Arthur Simko in a prosecution of possessing over 650 grams of cocaine, M.C.L. § 333.7401(2)(a)(i); M.S.A. § 14.15(7401)(2)(a)(i), and possession of a firearm in the commission or attempt to commit a felony, M.C.L. § 750.227b; M.S.A. § 28.424(2). Although the defendant was convicted and the conviction eventually was reversed by the Court of Appeals, Mr. Simko spent more than two years in prison.

In the underlying criminal case, on the night of March 6, 1987, a state police officer observed a speeding car traveling with its lights flashing in an apparent effort to attract the officer's attention. The car exited the highway and stopped to wait for the police car. The driver of the vehicle alighted from his car and told the police that the passenger, Arthur Simko, needed medical attention.

Plaintiff appeared flushed, was perspiring, and his breathing was labored. The officer summoned an ambulance. While waiting for the ambulance to arrive, the officer discovered what appeared to be drug paraphernalia on the floor of the car. A further search of the car revealed a cup containing cocaine residue, a bullet in plaintiff's pocket, a pistol in the glove compartment, a pistol in the trunk, several rounds of ammunition, and 988 grams of a substance containing cocaine.

Arthur Simko was represented by Marvin Blake. At the close of the prosecution's case, and again at the close of defendant's case, Mr. Blake moved for a directed verdict on the ground that the evidence was insufficient to convict plaintiff. The trial judge denied both motions. Mr. Simko was ultimately found guilty by the jury and sentenced to mandatory sentences of life without parole plus two years.

Arthur Simko then retained another attorney and appealed his conviction. The Court of Appeals reversed; however, by that time, he had already served two years of his prison sentence.

At the time plaintiff filed his appeal, he also filed a legal malpractice action against defendant. Arthur Simko alleged that the defendant failed to properly investigate his case and failed to properly prepare to defend him. Specifically, Mr. Simko alleged that Mr. Blake did not produce any witnesses in his defense besides Mr. Simko himself, failed to produce plaintiff's personal physician who had been treating him for a pinched nerve and who prescribed medication that would have offered an explanation of his medical condition at the time of arrest, and failed to provide Mr. Simko with the name and location of the hotel where Mr. Simko had spent the day before he was arrested that may have protected him from impeachment.*

The malpractice action was dismissed by the trial court when it granted defendant's motion for summary disposition. The trial court stated:

> The proximate cause of his conviction was the trial court's error in denying the motion for directed verdict in favor of the defendant in the underlying case.
>
> The Court of Appeals, in holding that a directed verdict should have been granted indirectly not only stated that the trial court here erred but that the jury erred as well.
>
> By holding that the standard was satisfied for the granting of a motion for directed verdict, in effect, the Court of Appeals held

---

* Author's note: The police were in possession of the name and address of a hotel in Florida at which Simko had spent the previous day. At trial, Simko's testimony was impeached because he could not remember the name of the hotel.

that a reasonable well-instructed jury could not convict based upon the evidence presented during the course of the trial.

The jury in the underlying case by virtue of the Court of Appeals decision acted unreasonably in light of evidence presented for the jury to consider.

As a result, the defendant Blake cannot possibly be held responsible for the acts of an unreasonable jury.

The Court of Appeals affirmed, stating that,

[b]y challenging the sufficiency of the evidence against Simko, Blake raised a complete and ultimately successful defense to both charges.... Blake was not Simko's insurer against all possible misfortune.... His duty was to raise an adequate defense to the criminal charges, not to protect Simko from judge and jury. [201 Mich. App. 191, 195, 506 N.W.2d 258 (1993).]

We affirm the decision of the Court of Appeals and hold that Marvin Blake fulfilled his duty to Arthur Simko.

II

We hold that defendant's motion for summary disposition was properly granted by the trial court because the plaintiffs failed to state a claim upon which relief can be granted. Plaintiffs' complaint and pleadings failed to state a breach of duty.

Pursuant to MCR 2.116(C)(8), a motion for summary disposition is granted if the claim is so clearly unenforceable as a matter of law that no factual development could possibly justify recovery. A motion [for] summary disposition is tested on the pleadings alone, and all factual allegations contained in the complaint must be accepted as true.

III

In order to state an action for legal malpractice, the plaintiff has the burden of adequately alleging the following elements:

(1) the existence of an attorney-client relationship;

(2) negligence in the legal representation of the plaintiff;

(3) that the negligence was a proximate cause of an injury; and

(4) the fact and extent of the injury alleged.

[The parties admitted that an attorney-client relationship existed.] Thus, the issue is not whether a duty existed, but rather the extent of that duty once invoked.

It is well established that "[a]n attorney is obligated to use reasonable skill, care, discretion and judgment in representing a client." *Lipton v. Boesky*, 110 Mich. App. 589, 594, 313 N.W.2d 163 (1981). Further, according to SJI2d 30.01, all attorneys have a duty to behave as would an attorney "of ordinary learning, judgment or skill . . . under the same or similar circumstances. . . ."

An attorney has the duty to fashion such a strategy so that it is consistent with prevailing Michigan law. However, an attorney does not have a duty to insure or guarantee the most favorable outcome possible. An attorney is never bound to exercise extraordinary diligence, or act beyond the knowledge, skill, and ability ordinarily possessed by members of the legal profession.

To require attorneys, or other professionals, to act over and beyond average skill, learning, and ability, would be an unreasonable burden on the profession and the legal system. As the Court of Appeals stated:

> There is no motion that can be filed, no amount of research in preparation, no level of skill, nor degree of perfection that could anticipate every error or completely shield a client from the occasional aberrant ruling of a fallible judge or an intransigent jury. To impose a duty on attorneys to do more than that which is legally adequate to fully vindicate a client's rights would require our legal system, already overburdened, to digest unnecessarily inordinate quantities of additional motions and evidence that, in most cases, will prove to be superfluous. And, *because no amount of work can guarantee a favorable result, attorneys would never know when the work they do is sufficiently more than adequate to be enough to protect not only their clients from error, but themselves from liability.* [201 Mich. App. at 194, 506 N.W.2d 258 (emphasis added).]

Lastly, mere errors in judgment by a lawyer are generally not grounds for a malpractice action where the attorney acts in good faith and exercises reasonable care, skill, and diligence. *Baker v. Beal*, 225 N.W.2d 106, 112 (Iowa 1975). Where an attorney acts in good faith and in honest belief that his acts and omissions are well founded in law and are in the best interest of his client, he is not answerable for mere errors in judgment. *Rorrer v. Cooke*, 313 N.C. 338, 340–342, 329 S.E.2d 355 (1985). . . . MALLEN & SMITH, LEGAL MALPRACTICE (3d ed.), §§ 14.12 to 14.17, pp. 836–53:

> [T]here can be no liability for acts and omissions by an attorney in the conduct of litigation which are based on an honest exercise of professional judgment. This is a sound rule. Otherwise every losing litigant would be able to sue his attorney if he could find another attorney who was willing to second guess the decisions of the first attorney with the advantage of hindsight. . . . To hold that an attorney may not be held liable for the choice of trial tactics and the conduct of a case based on professional judgment is not to say, however, that an attorney may not be held liable for

any of his actions in relation to a trial. He is still bound to exercise a reasonable degree of skill and care in all his professional undertakings. [*Woodruff v. Tomlin*, 616 F.2d 924, 930 (C.A. 6 1980) (citations omitted).]

IV

We find that the defendant acted as would an attorney of ordinary learning, judgment, or skill under the same or similar circumstances, and his alleged acts and omissions were a matter of trial tactics based on reasonable professional judgment.

From October 12 through October 15, 1987, Mr. Simko's trial was held in the Recorder's Court for the City of Detroit, before the Honorable Craig S. Strong. Mr. Simko was the only witness to testify. Dr. Karbal and Mrs. Simko were not called as witnesses because Mr. Blake did not feel that they would be beneficial to the defense's case. Following the prosecution's presentation of the case, and again after the defense rested, Mr. Blake moved for a directed verdict of acquittal. Both motions were denied by Judge Strong. On October 15, 1987, Mr. Simko was convicted by the jury as charged.

We find, as a matter of law, that the plaintiffs' allegations could not support a breach of duty because they are based on mere errors of professional judgment and not breaches of reasonable care. Plaintiffs' allegations of breach of duty are contained in ¶¶ 10(a)–(k) of plaintiffs' complaint. The only specific allegations that could have altered the outcome of Mr. Simko's trial are contained in ¶¶ 10(d)–(i). Plaintiffs alleged that defendant should have called other witnesses besides Mr. Simko, including Mr. Simko's physician, Dr. Michael Karbal, and Mr. Simko's wife, Margaret Simko. In addition, ¶ 10(i) alleges that Mr. Blake failed to ascertain the name and location of the hotel where Mr. Simko had allegedly spent the day before he was arrested.

First, it is a tactical decision whether to call particular witnesses, as long as the attorney acts with full knowledge of the law and in good faith. *Woodruff, supra* at 933. *Woodruff* held that a charge of malpractice on the basis of an attorney's decision to not cross-examine an expert witness did not constitute malpractice. Similarly, in *Frank v. Bloom*, 634 F.2d 1245, 1256–57 (C.A. 10 1980), the court stated that it will afford latitude to the attorney when making tactical strategies:

[I]t is the duty of the attorney who is a professional to determine trial strategy. If the client had the last word on this, the client could be his or her own lawyer.

Here, plaintiffs are alleging that defendant was negligent in not calling Dr. Karbal and Mrs. Simko. This, however, is a tactical decision that this Court may not question. Perhaps defendant made an error of judgment in deciding not to call particular witnesses, and perhaps another attorney would have made a different decision; however, tactical decisions do not constitute grounds for a legal malpractice action. *Woodruff, supra.* Plaintiffs' claim that certain witnesses should have been called is nothing but an assertion that another lawyer might have conducted the trial differently, a matter of professional opinion that does not allege violation of the duty to perform as a reasonably competent criminal defense lawyer.

Second, the failure to ascertain the name and location of the hotel where a client was located at a particular time does not constitute negligence. There is no duty to infallibly protect a client from impeachment. This would be an impossible standard for defense counsel to meet and would violate and extend beyond the well-established reasonable care standard.

V

We conclude that there was no legal basis for holding that Mr. Blake's actions constituted negligence, or otherwise constitute malpractice. When an attorney fashions a trial strategy consistent with the governing principles of law and reasonable professional judgment, the attorney's conduct is legally adequate. Accordingly, we affirm the decision of the Court of Appeals and hold that the defendant fulfilled his duty to his client.

LEVIN, JUSTICE (dissenting).

I

The majority states:

[A]ttorneys must only act as would an attorney of ordinary learning, judgment, or skill under the same or similar circumstances.

. . .

I agree that a lawyer need "only act" as would a lawyer of ordinary learning, judgment, diligence, or skill under the same or similar circumstances. But he must *so act*. If the majority were to allow this case to come to trial, the evidence were to show, and a trier of fact were to find, that a lawyer of ordinary learning, judgment, diligence, or skill, under the same or similar circumstances, would have avoided errors that Blake allegedly committed, then Blake is, or should be, subject to liability for damage found to have resulted from conviction of an offense subjecting Simko to a sentence of life in prison and actual incarceration for over two years.

. . .

The majority also states that "mere errors in judgment by a lawyer are *generally* not grounds for a malpractice action where the attorney acts in good faith and exercises reasonable care, skill, and diligence." (Emphasis added.) It is implicit in the formulation adopted by the majority, requiring a lawyer to act as would a lawyer of "ordinary learning, *judgment*, or skill," that errors of judgment may constitute negligence. Whether an error of judgment, or a "mere" error of judgment, constitutes negligence depends on whether a lawyer of ordinary learning, judgment, diligence, or skill would have avoided the error or "mere" error of judgment. That "generally" is a question of fact for the trier of fact to decide.

. . .

Blake's motion for summary disposition was filed on the basis that the Simkos "failed to state a claim on which relief can be granted." In finding facts on this second appellate review, the majority ignores that only the pleadings may be considered by the circuit court and the appellate courts in ruling on such a motion.

The majority finds, as a matter of fact or law, that the "alleged acts and omissions were trial tactics based on good faith and reasonable professional judgment." The complaint particularized concerning the errors claimed by Simko. In response to the motion for summary disposition, the Simkos filed an affidavit of a lawyer stating that in his opinion Blake had erred. Blake did not file an affidavit in support of the motion for summary disposition, probably because no such support is required or permitted. Nevertheless the majority finds, as a matter of fact or law, that Blake acted in good faith and exercised reasonable professional judgment.

The majority finds, as a matter of fact or law, that certain witnesses were not called because Blake "did not feel that they would be beneficial to the defense's case."

Because Blake did not file an affidavit in support of his motion for summary disposition, and, even if he had, it could not properly have been considered in deciding the motion, there is no record support for fact finding by the majority.

Because there is no factual record, the majority does not have a basis for asserting that the witnesses were not called because Blake "did not feel that they would be beneficial to defense's case." Since there is no record, we do not know whether either or both witnesses were interviewed by Blake, and what might have occurred during any such interview. The silent record no more justifies a finding that Blake had a reason for not calling the witnesses, than it would a finding that he simply neglected or overlooked calling them. A silent record supports no finding of fact at all.

* * *

Trial Tactics and the "Error in Judgment" Rule. Relying on a Sixth Circuit opinion (*Woodruff*), *Simko* held that if the failure to call a witness was error, it was a "mere error in judgment" and such errors "are generally not grounds for a malpractice action where the attorney acts in good faith and exercises reasonable care, skill, and diligence." Are *Simko* and *Woodruff* "merely" applications of the "error in judgment" rule from *Wood* to trial tactics or are the courts applying a different standard altogether? Are a lawyer's decisions (or tactics) at trial so unique or special that they should not be the basis for malpractice liability?

Comparing the *Simko* Test to the *Restatement* Test. By applying the error in judgment rule, the *Simko* court was able to conclude that the plaintiff's allegation of courtroom negligence was legally deficient. No testimony was heard; the court simply determined that the alleged conduct—which was required to be taken in the light most favorable to the plaintiff—could not amount to professional negligence. Suppose instead that the *Simko* court had applied the professional negligence test provided by the *Restatement (Third) of the Law Governing Lawyers*. A court applying this *Restatement* test would have to concede that the facts alleged were sufficient to state a claim that Blake breached the standard of care (*i.e.*, failed to act with the competence and diligence normally exercised by lawyers in similar circumstances). A factfinder should be allowed to hear the evidence—including testimony of an expert witness who filed an affidavit opposing dismissal—and be allowed to decide whether Blake's conduct in the litigation failed to meet the standard of care. The *Simko* test immunizes courtroom mistakes, while the *Restatement* tests allows a jury to decide if the attorney failed to act as a reasonable attorney would have acted.

Problem 13.4. After Miranda's motion for summary judgment was denied, the case proceeded to trial. At the original trial in the trademark case, Miranda failed to call an expert witness who could testify on Jill's behalf as to how the trademarks at issue were dissimilar. Assume that the trial court follows the rule from *Simko* regarding attorney malpractice claims involving trial tactics. In which of the following situations would the rule from *Simko* not bar Jill's malpractice claim?

(a) Jill has an expert witness who will testify that any reasonable attorney in Miranda's position would have called an expert witness at trial.

(b) The reason why Miranda failed to introduce any expert testimony was because she failed to research the potential uses of expert witnesses in trademark infringement cases and, therefore, did not appreciate the role an expert might play at trial.

* * *

2. CAUSATION AND DAMAGES

RIZZO V. HAINES
555 A.2d 58 (Pa. 1989)

[The portion of the court's opinion involving breach of the lawyer's duty to Rizzo appears *supra*.]

[I]n order for one to prevail on a claim of legal malpractice, one must establish that the party against whom the initial claim was asserted, in this case the City, would have reached agreement upon a settlement in an ascertainable amount. . . . Mr. Moran testified that, at trial, he had the authority to settle the case for $750,000. . . . Instantly, firm settlement offers were communicated to Haines, and the attorney making the offers had the authority to settle. In addition, Haines was authorized to settle at about $750,000. Thus, we are unpersuaded by Haines' assertion that the damages were uncertain. The trial court awarded $300,000 in compensatory damages based on the difference between Rizzo's actual recovery and what he would have recovered except for Haines' negligence. We believe that this calculation was proper.

* * *

Establishing Causation in Legal Malpractice Actions. As is the case with most negligence claims, a plaintiff alleging legal malpractice must establish that the defendant's negligence was both a factual and proximate cause of the plaintiff's damages.

How is a legal malpractice plaintiff supposed to prove that the lawyer's negligence was a cause in fact of the plaintiff's damages? A proximate cause? Where the allegation of malpractice involves conduct related to civil litigation, there generally must be a "trial within a trial"—a trial within the broader legal malpractice trial in which the plaintiff's underlying case is tried as it should have been, absent the alleged negligence. If this trial establishes that the plaintiff would not have obtained a better result even in the absence of the lawyer's negligence, the malpractice case is over. What if the alleged malpractice occurs in the transactional setting? For example, how could a plaintiff establish that a lawyer's negligence in negotiating a contract resulted in unfavorable terms for the plaintiff without asking a jury to engage in guesswork?

Malpractice Claims Involving Criminal Defense. A later chapter will explore the legal standard that applies when a criminal defendant brings a malpractice claim against the defendant's lawyer based on the lawyer's negligent handling of the criminal matter. *See Restatement (Third) of the Law Governing Lawyers* § 53 Comment [d].

Public Defender Immunity. Lawyers who are employed by the Federal Public Defender's Office enjoy statutory immunity from malpractice liability. 18 U.S.C. § 3006A(g)(2)(A). Should lawyers who are *appointed* by a court to represent indigent criminal defendants enjoy immunity from malpractice liability? The majority of courts to consider the issue have said no. *Cf. Mooney v. Frazier*, 693 S.E.2d 333 (W. Va. 2010) (rejecting majority rule).

* * *

C. MALPRACTICE INSURANCE

Law students probably don't give much thought to malpractice insurance, but for lawyers it is a very important topic. As you read the following materials, ask yourself whether malpractice insurance coverage should be voluntary or mandatory.

1. MANDATORY PROFESSIONAL LIABILITY INSURANCE

One issue related to malpractice insurance is whether a lawyer should be required to carry such insurance and, if not, whether the lawyer must disclose this fact to a client. There are several possible approaches to this issue. Oregon is the only state that makes malpractice insurance mandatory. Roughly half of the states require lawyers to disclose the fact that they do not carry malpractice insurance. Benjamin P. Cooper, *Attorney Self-Disclosure*, 79 U. CIN. L. REV. 697, 712 (2010). A few states require lawyers to inform their clients directly of the fact that they do not maintain malpractice insurance above a certain level. *See, e.g.*, Ohio Code of Professional Responsibility DR 1–104. In keeping with the ABA Model Court Rule on Insurance Disclosure, a greater number require only that a lawyer disclose on their annual registration statements to the state bar whether they maintain malpractice insurance. A number of states have rejected proposals that would have required disclosure in some form. Susan Saab Fortney, *Law as Profession: Examining the Role of Accountability*, 40 FORDHAM URB. L.J. 177, 195–96 (2012).

Recall from Chapter 12 that a lawyer has a duty under Model Rule 1.4(b) to "explain a matter to the extent reasonably necessary to permit the client to make informed decisions regarding the representation." Does this rule impose upon a lawyer a duty to inform a client about the lawyer's failure to carry malpractice insurance?

* * *

2. FILING CLAIMS AND NOTIFYING CLIENTS

The ABA notes, "All insurance policies include language requiring the insured to give prompt notice to the insurance company of a malpractice claim or suit. This requirement enables the insurer to defend the claim or, when possible, to mitigate or avoid a loss." AMERICAN BAR ASSOCIATION STANDING COMMITTEE ON LAWYERS' PROFESSIONAL LIABILITY, SELECTING LEGAL MALPRACTICE INSURANCE 9 (2003). But must a lawyer inform the client about her malpractice? According to the ABA committee, the lawyer must "inform[ ] the client of any errors committed by the attorney that may result in harm to the client's interest." The committee warns that "[f]ailure to disclose errors may result in disciplinary proceedings and a possible loss of the attorney's license." The committee based its opinion on the lawyer's duty to "keep a client informed about the status of a matter to the extent necessary to permit the client to make informed decisions." What decisions might a client have to make as a result of the lawyer's malpractice in his or her case?

A lawyer's failure to notify a client about a possible mistake may also make the client that much angrier if and when the client learns of the mistake. The failure to inform a client of the lawyer's possible malpractice might also toll the statute of limitations. Thus, the committee concludes, "The bottom line is that it is in the attorney's and the client's best interest [for the attorney] to disclose any errors to the client as soon as possible."

Profile of Attorney Professionalism. Memphis attorney Lucian Pera, a self-described "legal ethics geek," represents lawyers and law firms in matters ranging from malpractice to professional discipline. He also regularly advises law firms on issues of loss prevention. Lucian explains, "Basically, any time a lawyer or law firm has any kind of ethics problem, or claim, or similar issue, I can get called in to help."

Why does a lawyer need a legal ethics expert? Lucian notes the growing complexity and sophistication of the law governing the practice of law and its importance to lawyers. He explains, "[T]hose of us who practice in the ethics area, either just for our own law firms, or for other clients, tend to be the holders of lots of specialized, 'geeky' knowledge—knowledge most other lawyers are very comfortable not knowing and relying on us for." Lucian regularly writes articles and gives seminars on ethics and loss prevention issues. He says this is useful to "sensitize lawyers to the fact that there is actually specialized knowledge about ethics and loss prevention that can be very useful when a lawyer is in a pinch."

It is not always easy for lawyers to decide to hire another lawyer. Lucian says that lawyers can be slow to ask for help, but they are happy when they make the call. "I enjoy this work because I can do for lawyers, using my ethics 'geek' knowledge and experience, just what we lawyers do for clients—I help solve lawyers' problems so that they can get back to representing their own clients. You would be amazed how happy lawyers can be after they realize they can get this kind of help."

For five years, Lucian was a member of the ABA Ethics 2000 Commission that studied and revised the *Model Rules of Professional Conduct*. Lucian notes that most states adopted the Ethics 2000 rule amendments within five years and explains that this brought much greater uniformity to the law of attorney ethics. "That's an incredibly good development, because the practice of law, even in the smallest states and the most isolated towns, involves lawyers working across jurisdictional lines more than ever before. For example, the conflict of interest rules are today more uniform, across more American jurisdictions, than ever before in history. Ethics 2000 is responsible for that, and it was great to be a part of that."

Lucian stays in touch with clients and friends by sending a card every January to celebrate Elvis Presley's birthday. Each card features a photo of The King provided by *The Commercial Appeal*, the daily newspaper in Memphis. Lucian has represented the newspaper for years. Lucian says that sending the card "combines my long-time work with *The Commercial Appeal*, a native Memphian's love of Elvis, and a mission to share with folks outside Memphis a little bit of history from The Cultural Center of The Universe."

SECTION 4

CONFIDENTIALITY

∎ ∎ ∎

This Section introduces the law and rules that address a lawyer's obligation to keep client confidences and to protect privileged and work product protected information when requested in litigation. Chapter 14 addresses the lawyer's duty to refrain from disclosing information relating to the client's representation, as well as exceptions that permit disclosure. Chapter 15 addresses the attorney-client privilege and the work-product doctrine.

CHAPTER 14

DUTY OF CONFIDENTIALITY

■ ■ ■

Chapter Hypothetical. Cynthia Burns is a long-time friend who knows you handle family law issues in your law practice. One night, she calls you at home and says she wants you to be her lawyer because she wants a divorce. She says her husband has been unfaithful, and she cannot tolerate being married to him anymore. You agree to represent her and within the week, you file a petition for divorce in the appropriate court. You are worried about your client's mental and physical health. She says she is not sleeping or eating well because she is so stressed about the end of her marriage.

A. PROTECTING CONFIDENTIAL INFORMATION

As a fiduciary, lawyers owe their clients a duty of confidentiality. Unauthorized disclosure of client confidences is a breach of that duty and can result in liability for the lawyer. Such a disclosure is the subject of the case *Perez v. Kirk and Carrigan*, excerpted below. *See also Restatement (Third) of the Law Governing Lawyers* § 49 (2000).

Beyond civil liability, a lawyer can be disciplined for disclosing client confidences. This is the subject of Model Rule 1.6(a). The rule provides that an attorney must not reveal "information relating to the representation of the client" unless the client consents, the disclosure is impliedly authorized to carry out the representation, or an exception applies. Though the confidentiality exceptions vary from state to state, most jurisdictions have adopted a professional conduct rule substantially similar to Rule 1.6(a). This means that in most jurisdictions, attorneys must not reveal any information learned in the representation of the client. The information that must be kept confidential can come from the client or from some other source. Not only is "embarrassing" information covered by the rule, but all information no matter how seemingly mundane. Even if the client revealed the same information to a third party, the lawyer cannot reveal that information absent the client's consent, implied authorization, or an exception.

While some believe this rule is broader than necessary to protect clients, the rule has the advantage of simplicity. Except to the extent necessary to carry out the representation, a lawyer should not tell anyone about the lawyer's clients, their problems, or the work the lawyer is doing on their behalf.

It is worth noting the distinction between the attorney-client privilege and the attorney's ethical and fiduciary duty of confidentiality. The attorney-client privilege allows attorney and client to refuse to testify regarding (or produce a document reflecting) a communication made in confidence between attorney and client for the purpose of obtaining or providing legal advice. *Restatement (Third) of the Law Governing Lawyers* § 68 (2000). Some attorneys incorrectly believe that only privileged information must be kept confidential. But this is incorrect; whether privileged or not privileged, if information is learned through the lawyer's representation of the client, the lawyer may not reveal it absent authorization or exception. The attorney-client privilege and work product doctrine will be discussed in detail in Chapter 15.

Subpart (c) of Model Rule 1.6 addresses an attorney's obligation to competently protect confidential client information. Because this duty also touches upon special issues related to protecting privilege and work product, it will be discussed in Chapter 15.

* * *

Problem 14.1. While you are representing your friend Cynthia Burns in her divorce, you run into a mutual friend Ross Conner. Ross asks if you sense that Cynthia has been worried about something lately. He says he saw her the other day and she seemed depressed. Separately consider each of the following possible responses to Ross's question. Analyze whether one or more of these responses would violate your obligation under Rule 1.6(a).

(1) "Cynthia hired me to file a petition for divorce on her behalf. I can't really say anything else about the situation."

(2) "Cynthia learned recently that her husband cheated on her. I think that is probably why she seems depressed."

(3) "I'm really worried about her, too! She told me that she has not been sleeping or eating. What can we do to cheer her up?"

Problem 14.2. Suppose for purposes of this question only that you turned down the opportunity to represent Cynthia in her divorce, but only after she mentioned her husband's infidelity. If you are not (and never were) Cynthia's lawyer, do you have an obligation to keep the information about her cheating husband confidential? Refer to Model Rule 1.18 in your analysis.

Problem 14.3. As you represent Cynthia in the divorce proceedings, what categories of information do you believe you are impliedly authorized to reveal to your opposing counsel? Can you reveal information about

Cynthia's case to a partner or associate in your law firm consistent with your obligation under Rule 1.6(a)? Consider Comment 5 to Rule 1.6 as you answer both questions in this problem.

Problem 14.4. If you reveal confidential information to mutual friend Ross Conner concerning Cynthia, does Cynthia have a valid cause of action against you for breach of fiduciary duty? Consider the following case.

* * *

PEREZ V. KIRK & CARRIGAN
822 S.W.2d 261 (Tex. Ct. App. 1991)

DORSEY, JUSTICE.

Ruben Perez appeals a summary judgment rendered against him on his causes of action against the law firm of Kirk & Carrigan, and against Dana Kirk and Steve Carrigan individually (henceforth all three will be collectively referred to as "Kirk & Carrigan"). We reverse the summary judgment and remand this case for trial.

The present suit arises from a school bus accident on September 21, 1989, in Alton, Texas. Ruben Perez was employed by Valley Coca-Cola Bottling Company as a truck driver. On the morning of the accident, Perez attempted to stop his truck at a stop sign along his route, but the truck's brakes failed to stop the truck, which collided with the school bus. The loaded bus was knocked into a pond and 21 children died. Perez suffered injuries from the collision and was taken to a local hospital to be treated.

The day after the accident, Kirk & Carrigan, lawyers who had been hired to represent Valley Coca-Cola Bottling Company, visited Perez in the hospital for the purpose of taking his statement. Perez claims that the lawyers told him that they were his lawyers too and that anything he told them would be kept confidential. With this understanding, Perez gave them a sworn statement concerning the accident[1]. However, after taking Perez' statement, Kirk & Carrigan had no further contact with him. Instead, Kirk & Carrigan made arrangements for criminal defense attorney Joseph Connors to represent Perez. Connors was paid by National

---

[1] Among other things, Perez generally stated that he had a previous accident while driving a Coke truck in 1987 for which he was given a citation, that he had a speeding violation in 1988, that he had not filled out a daily checklist to show that he had checked the brakes on the morning of the accident, that he had never before experienced problems with the brakes on his truck and that they were working just before the accident, that he tried to apply the brakes to stop the truck, but that the brakes for the trailer were not working at all to stop the truck (the truck had two sets of brakes: the ones for the cab worked; the ones for the trailer did not and the greater weight of the trailer had the effect of pushing the entire truck, even though the cab brakes were working), that Perez did not have enough time to apply the emergency brakes, and that there was nothing the managers or supervisors at Valley Coca-Cola could have done to prevent the accident.

Union Fire Insurance Company which covered both Valley Coca-Cola and Perez for liability in connection with the accident.

Sometime after Connors began representing Perez, Kirk & Carrigan, without telling either Perez or Connors, turned Perez' statement over to the Hidalgo County District Attorney's Office. Kirk & Carrigan contend that Perez' statement was provided in a good faith attempt to fully comply with a request of the district attorney's office and under threat of subpoena if they did not voluntarily comply. Partly on the basis of this statement, the district attorney was able to obtain a grand jury indictment of Perez for involuntary manslaughter for his actions in connection with the accident.[2]

Ruben Perez filed the present suit . . . assert[ing] numerous causes of action against Kirk & Carrigan for breach of fiduciary duty, negligent and intentional infliction of emotional distress, violation of the Texas Deceptive Trade Practices-Consumer Protection Act [the "DTPA"] and conspiracy to violate . . . the Texas Insurance Code. . . . Perez complained generally by his petition that Kirk & Carrigan had caused him to suffer public humiliation and emotional distress by turning over his supposedly confidential statement to the district attorney. In addition to the turnover of this statement, Perez alleged generally that Kirk & Carrigan, Valley Coca-Cola, and National Union engaged in an overall plan to shift the blame for the accident away from them and onto Perez, by concealing information tending to show that Valley Coca-Cola's faulty maintenance of the brakes on the truck was the real cause of the accident.

Kirk & Carrigan moved for summary judgment on all of the claims made against them by Perez, on the grounds that no attorney-client or other fiduciary relationship existed, that even if a fiduciary relationship did exist no damages resulted from the asserted breach, that all of Perez' claims basically allege groundless prosecution and therefore constitute an invalid claim for malicious prosecution, that Perez was not a consumer under the DTPA, and that Perez failed to state a cause of action for conspiracy to violate the Texas Insurance Code. . . .

By his sole point of error, Perez complains simply that the trial court erred in granting Kirk & Carrigan's motion for summary judgment. The movant for summary judgment has the burden of showing that there is no genuine issue of material fact and that he is entitled to judgment as a matter of law. In deciding whether there is a disputed material fact issue precluding a summary judgment, evidence favorable to the non-movant will be taken as true, every reasonable inference must be indulged in the non-movant's favor, and any doubts must be resolved in his favor. . . .

---

[2] By his summary judgment affidavit offered in support of Perez, Joseph Connors stated that, in his professional opinion as a board certified criminal law specialist, if he had known that the statement had been provided and had been able to have Perez explain his lack of training or knowledge about the brake system to the grand jury, Perez would not have been indicted for manslaughter. . . .

Breach of Fiduciary Duty

With regard to Perez' cause of action for breach of the fiduciary duty of good faith and fair dealing, Kirk and Carrigan contend that no attorney-client relationship existed and no fiduciary duty arose, because Perez never sought legal advice from them.

An agreement to form an attorney-client relationship may be implied from the conduct of the parties. Moreover, the relationship does not depend upon the payment of a fee, but may exist as a result of rendering services gratuitously.[3]

In the present case, viewing the summary judgment evidence in the light most favorable to Perez, Kirk & Carrigan told him that, in addition to representing Valley Coca Cola, they were also Perez' lawyers and that they were going to help him. Perez did not challenge this assertion, and he cooperated with the lawyers in giving his statement to them, even though he did not offer, nor was he asked, to pay the lawyers' fees. We hold that this was sufficient to imply the creation of an attorney-client relationship at the time Perez gave his statement to Kirk & Carrigan.

The existence of this relationship encouraged Perez to trust Kirk & Carrigan and gave rise to a corresponding duty on the part of the attorneys not to violate this position of trust. Accordingly, the relation between attorney and client is highly fiduciary in nature, and their dealings with each other are subject to the same scrutiny as a transaction between trustee and beneficiary. Specifically, the relationship between attorney and client has been described as one of uberrima fides, which means, "most abundant good faith," requiring absolute and perfect candor, openness and honesty, and the absence of any concealment or deception. In addition, because of the openness and candor within this relationship, certain communications between attorney and client are privileged from disclosure in either civil or criminal proceedings under the provisions of Tex. R. Civ. Evid. 503 and Tex. R. Crim. Evid. 503, respectively....

Kirk & Carrigan seek to avoid this claim of breach, on the ground that the attorney-client privilege did not apply to the present statement, because unnecessary third parties were present at the time it was given.... However, whether or not the Rule 503 attorney-client privilege extended to Perez' statement, Kirk & Carrigan initially obtained the statement from Perez on the understanding that it would be kept confidential. Thus, regardless of whether from an evidentiary standpoint the privilege attached, Kirk & Carrigan breached their fiduciary duty to Perez either by wrongfully disclosing a privileged statement or by wrongfully representing that an unprivileged statement would be kept

---

[3] An attorney's fiduciary responsibilities may arise even during preliminary consultations regarding the attorney's possible retention if the attorney enters into discussion of the client's legal problems with a view toward undertaking representation.

confidential. Either characterization shows a clear lack of honesty toward, and a deception of, Perez by his own attorneys regarding the degree of confidentiality with which they intended to treat the statement.

This type of deceitful and fraudulent conduct within the attorney-client relationship has been treated as a tortious breach of duty in other contexts. *See Burgin v. Godwin*, 167 S.W.2d 614 (Tex. Civ. App.—Amarillo 1942, writ ref'd w.o.m.). . . .

In *Burgin*, for instance, the attorneys had a written agreement with their client for compensation, which the parties subsequently modified by an oral agreement. The attorneys later attempted to avoid the oral modification by asserting the statute of frauds. In holding that the attorneys were not entitled to the protections of the statute of frauds, the Amarillo Court of Appeals reasoned that the attorneys were under a duty to act with the most scrupulous fidelity and reveal to their client the exact status brought about by the contractual relationship and the need to reduce the oral modification to writing. . . .

Similarly, in the present case, the attorneys were at least under a fiduciary duty not to misrepresent to Perez that his conversations with them were confidential. Kirk & Carrigan should not now be able to assert the lack of attorney-client privilege (as the attorneys in *Burgin* were not allowed to assert the statute of frauds) to excuse the harm caused by their own misrepresentation to Perez. We hold that it was error for the trial court to grant summary judgment on the ground that Kirk & Carrigan did not owe or breach a fiduciary duty to Perez.

In addition, however, even assuming a breach of fiduciary duty, Kirk & Carrigan also contend that summary judgment may be sustained on the ground that Perez could show no damages resulting from the breach. Kirk & Carrigan contend that their dissemination of Perez' statement could not have caused him any damages in the way of emotional distress, because the statement merely revealed Perez' own version of what happened. We do not agree. Mental anguish consists of the emotional response of the plaintiff caused by the tortfeasor's conduct. It includes, among other things, the mental sensation of pain resulting from public humiliation.

Regardless of the fact that Perez himself made the present statement, he did not necessarily intend it to be a public response as Kirk & Carrigan contend, but only a private and confidential discussion with his attorneys. Perez alleged that the publicity caused by his indictment, resulting from the revelation of the statement to the district attorney in breach of that confidentiality, caused him to suffer emotional distress and mental anguish. We hold that Perez has made a valid claim for such damages. . . .

In conclusion, for the reasons stated above, we sustain Perez' point of error. We REVERSE the summary judgment rendered against Perez and REMAND this case for trial.

* * *

B. EXCEPTIONS TO THE LAWYER'S DUTY OF CONFIDENTIALITY

The confidentiality exceptions found in Model Rule 1.6(b) reflect situations in which the bar has determined a lawyer may disclose confidential information even though the client would prefer otherwise. Because these exceptions are contrary to the client's stated interests, the *Model Rules* refer to these exceptions as "Disclosure Adverse to Client." *See* Heading to Model Rule 1.6, Comments 6–17. The exceptions reflect a policy decision that the defined interests of a third party or the lawyer's own interests outweigh the client's interest in confidentiality. Today, Model Rule 1.6(b) contains seven exceptions when disclosure is permitted.

Many states' confidentiality exceptions differ from Model Rule 1.(6)(b). Some examples of these differences are highlighted throughout this chapter. In practice, it is important to consult the jurisdiction's rule to determine whether a lawyer is prohibited, permitted, or required to disclose client confidences in a given situation. Relying on your memory of Model Rule 1.6's exceptions may get you into trouble.

This chapter focuses on the confidentiality exceptions contained in Model Rule 1.6(b). Other professional conduct rules (addressed throughout this textbook) cross-reference Rule 1.6(b), permitting disclosure of client confidences in a given situation if permitted by Rule 1.6(b). *See* Model Rule 1.6(b), cmt. 17, citing Rules 1.2(d), 4.1(b), 8.1 and 8.3. Other rules permit the disclosure of confidences under the circumstances defined by the rule and without reference to Rule 1.6(b). *See* Model Rule 3.3 (concerning disclosure of a client's criminal or fraudulent conduct in a legal proceeding to the tribunal) and Model Rule 1.13(c) (concerning disclosure of organizational client's agent's misconduct to protect the organization from substantial injury).

1. DISCLOSURE REASONABLY NECESSARY TO PREVENT DEATH OR SUBSTANTIAL BODILY HARM

Model Rule 1.6(b)(1) permits, but does not require, the lawyer to disclose client confidences to the extent the lawyer reasonably believes necessary to prevent "reasonably certain death or substantial bodily harm." There are a number of possible alternative approaches with respect to this exception. In some jurisdictions, the exception is stated in mandatory, rather than permissive, terms. Thus, a lawyer *must* disclose information to the extent reasonably necessary to prevent reasonably certain death or substantial bodily harm. *See, e.g.*, Illinois Rules of Professional Conduct 1.6(b). Prior to its amendment in 2002, the ABA Model Rule permitted a lawyer to disclose information relating to the representation to the extent the lawyer reasonably believes necessary to prevent *the client* from committing *a criminal act* the lawyer believes is likely to result in *imminent* death or substantial bodily harm.

* * *

Problem 14.5. While you are representing Cynthia Burns in her divorce, she comes to your office and shows you a gun. She tells you she purchased it so she can "kill her cheating husband." What steps, if any, should you take prior to disclosing Cynthia's plan? If you determine that Cynthia is serious, would you disclose her plan to someone? If yes, to whom would you make your disclosure? Do comments 6, 16, and 17 help you answer these questions?

* * *

2. DISCLOSURE REASONABLY NECESSARY TO PREVENT OR RECTIFY THE CONSEQUENCES OF CLIENT CRIME OR FRAUD

The focus of subparts 2 and 3 of Model Rule 1.6(b) is on preventing or mitigating the financial consequences of client crime or fraud. The rule requires that the client used the lawyer's services in furtherance of the crime or fraud. A crime is conduct for which there is a criminal penalty. In its simplest terms, fraud is lying to someone to obtain their money. Fraud can be the basis of civil or criminal liability.

An attorney who believes his or her services are being used to perpetrate a crime or fraud should be concerned about the prospect of liability—not only for the client but also for the lawyer. Generally, a lawyer is not insulated from civil or criminal liability simply because she was acting on a client's behalf. *Restatement (Third) of the Law Governing Lawyers* §§ 8, 56 (2000). Thus, it is in the client's interest and the lawyer's that the client ceases the misconduct. The lawyer's ability to disclose client fraud may be significant in this circumstance. A client inclined to ignore the lawyer's advice to stop engaging in misconduct may be persuaded if the client understands the lawyer has the power to reveal the misconduct.

As is the case with the exception permitting disclosure to prevent death or substantial bodily harm, jurisdictions have taken different approaches with respect to the exception contained in Model Rule 1.6(b)(2) and (3). Below is a representative sample:

- Indiana: "may" reveal "to the extent the lawyer reasonably believes necessary . . . to prevent the client from committing any criminal act . . ."

- Texas: "may" reveal "when the lawyer has reason to believe it is necessary to do so in order to prevent the client from committing a criminal or fraudulent act."

- Alaska: "may" reveal "to the extent the lawyer reasonably believes necessary to prevent a client from committing a criminal or fraudulent act that the lawyer believes is likely to result in . . . substantial injury to the financial interests or property of another."

- Wisconsin: "shall" reveal "to the extent the lawyer reasonably believes necessary to prevent the client from committing a criminal or fraudulent act that the lawyer reasonably believes is likely to result in death or substantial bodily harm or in substantial injury to the financial interest or property of another."

- New Jersey: "shall" reveal "to the proper authorities as soon as, and to the extent, the lawyer reasonably believes necessary to prevent the client or another person, from committing a criminal, illegal, or fraudulent act that the lawyer reasonably believes is likely to result in . . . substantial injury to the financial interests or property of another."

- Florida: "shall" reveal "to the extent the lawyer reasonably believes necessary to prevent a client from committing a crime."

* * *

Problem 14.6. You just worked with Cynthia Burns to complete a draft of answers to interrogatories. As she talks to you about edits to the draft interrogatories, she mentions that she has found a clever way to hide assets from her soon-to-be ex-husband. She has invested about $10,000 in Bitcoin over the past year. You know that Cynthia's failure to disclose that investment will amount to falsely answering one of the interrogatories and will ultimately defraud her husband out of marital assets.

Outline a script for what you will say to Cynthia to dissuade her from lying about the $10,000 in assets. In addition to Rule 1.6(b)(2), do any other professional conduct rules (or civil procedure rules) apply in this situation?

Problem 14.7. During the course of your representation of Cynthia Burns in her divorce, she casually mentions an unrelated real estate venture. Cynthia admits that she has put in place a scheme to defraud investors of substantial sums of money. You counsel Cynthia that her conduct will harm the investors, and you explain the civil and criminal consequences of her conduct. You urge her to take corrective action, but Cynthia laughs and says, "I'll take my chances." Under Model Rule

1.6(b)(2) or (3), may you disclose confidential information to protect the investors from financial harm?

* * *

3. DISCLOSURE REASONABLY NECESSARY TO SECURE LEGAL ADVICE

Rule 1.6(b)(4) allows a lawyer to disclose confidential client information in order to obtain legal advice about the lawyer's compliance with professional conduct rules. This rule encourages attorneys to seek help in determining how to fulfill their professional conduct obligations.

* * *

Problem 14.8. You have completed some research and believe you may face professional discipline (and perhaps other consequences) if you participate in Cynthia Burns' plan to hide her Bitcoin investment (referenced in Problem 14.6). You want to get a second opinion about how you should handle the situation. Who might you consult in order to determine your professional conduct obligations? What can you reveal in that conversation?

* * *

4. DISCLOSURE REASONABLY NECESSARY TO ESTABLISH A CLAIM OR DEFENSE BY THE LAWYER

Rule 1.6(b)(5) allows a lawyer to disclose confidences to the extent necessary: (1) for the lawyer to state a claim or defense in a "controversy" with the client; (2) for the lawyer to defend against a "criminal charge or civil claim" based upon conduct in which client was involved; or (3) for the lawyer "to respond to allegations in any proceeding" related to the lawyer's representation of the client. The first category covers disclosure in a lawyer's lawsuit against a client for an unpaid fee, as well disclosure to defend against a client's malpractice claim. The second category encompasses the lawyer's ability to defend against a civil lawsuit filed by a third party claiming, for example, that lawyer and client defrauded the third party. This second category also allows the lawyer to disclose confidences to the extent necessary to defend against a criminal charge arising out of the lawyer's representation of the client. Finally, the third category allows a lawyer to disclose client confidences to respond to a proceeding such as an ethics complaint against the lawyer.

In this age of online customer reviews, can a lawyer defend against a negative client review on a website like Yelp? Consider Rule 1.6(b)(5) and comments 10, 11, 16, and 17 as you consider this issue in the context of Problem 14.9.

Problem 14.9. After the conclusion of Cynthia Burns' divorce, your assistant alerts you to a negative, anonymous review on Yelp. You read the review and immediately realize the review was posted by Cynthia Burns. Cynthia's post reads:

This attorney cost me a fortune in my divorce! The ironic thing is that we were friends when I hired her, but we aren't friends anymore. If you want to have two coins to rub together at the end of your divorce, I highly recommend getting a different lawyer!

You immediately respond with the following post:

I want my clients to be happy with my representation, but I refuse to lie and cheat for them. The client who wrote this review wanted to hide a $10,000 Bitcoin investment from her husband. I won't be a party to fraud! I convinced her that she had to tell the truth when we answered interrogatories about her assets. Sorry that this client doesn't have her 10,000 Bitcoins to rub together, but I refuse to lie for any client.

Have you violated Rule 1.6 or was your disclosure consistent with Rule 1.6(b)(5)? Do comments 10, 11, 16, and 17 help or hurt an argument that your disclosure is appropriate? Draft a new response to the Yelp review that you are certain does not violate Model Rule 1.6.

* * *

5. DISCLOSURE REASONABLY NECESSARY TO COMPLY WITH OTHER LAW OR A COURT ORDER

Rule 1.6(b)(6) permits an attorney to disclose confidential client information to the extent necessary to comply with "other law" or "a court order." The "court order" exception may arise in litigation (in discovery or at trial) when an attorney asserts that certain information is protected, but the court nonetheless orders the disclosure of the information. Comment 15 explains that a lawyer "should assert on behalf of the client all nonfrivolous claims that [an order to compel disclosure of information] is not authorized by other law or that the information sought is protected against disclosure by the attorney-client privilege or other applicable law." The comment concludes that if ultimately compelled to disclose information, the lawyer should consult with the client about a possible appeal and if review is not sought, the lawyer may reveal the information consistent with the court's order.

The "other law" exception is addressed in Comment 12. It provides that the question of whether other law trumps the confidentiality rule is "a question of law beyond the scope of these Rules." Thus, if an attorney learns information in the representation of a client (such as information about child abuse) and the attorney's research reveals a legal obligation to reveal that information (such as a statute requiring persons to report child abuse to a state agency), the attorney must conduct additional research to determine which obligation prevails. The answer can vary from jurisdiction to jurisdiction. The following case from Onondaga County, New York, resolves the question of whether New York public health laws supersede a New York attorney's duty of confidentiality to his client.

* * *

PEOPLE V. BELGE
372 N.Y.S.2d 798 (Onondaga Co. Ct. 1975)

ORMAND N. GALE, JUDGE.

In the summer of 1973 Robert F. Garrow, Jr. stood charged in Hamilton County with the crime of murder. The Defendant was assigned two attorneys, Frank H. Armani and Francis R. Belge. A defense of insanity had been interposed by counsel for Mr. Garrow. During the course of the discussions between Garrow and his two counsel, three other murders were admitted by Garrow, one being in Onondaga County. On or about September of 1973 Mr. Belge conducted his own investigation based upon what his client had told him and with the assistance of a friend the location of the body of Alicia Hauck was found in Oakwood Cemetery in Syracuse. Mr. Belge personally inspected the body and was satisfied, presumably, that this was the Alicia Hauck that his client had told him that he murdered.

This discovery was not disclosed to the authorities, but became public during the trial of Mr. Garrow in June of 1974, when to affirmatively establish the defense of insanity, these three other murders were brought before the jury by the defense in the Hamilton County trial. Public indignation reached the fever pitch; statements were made by the District Attorney of Onondaga County relative to the situation and he caused the Grand Jury of Onondaga County, then sitting, to conduct a thorough investigation. As a result of this investigation Frank Armani was No Billed by the Grand Jury but Indictment No. 75–55 was returned as against Francis R. Belge, Esq., accusing him of having violated § 4200(1) of the Public Health Law, which, in essence, requires that a decent burial be accorded the dead, and § 4143 of the Public Health Law, which, in essence, requires anyone knowing of the death of a person without medical attendance, to report the same to the proper authorities. Defense counsel moves for a dismissal of the Indictment on the grounds that a confidential, privileged communication existed between him and Mr. Garrow, which should excuse the attorney from making full disclosure to the authorities.

The National Association of Criminal Defense Lawyers, as Amicus Curiae . . . succinctly state the issue in the following language:

> If this indictment stands, "The attorney-client privilege will be effectively destroyed. No defendant will be able to freely discuss the facts of his case with his attorney. No attorney will be able to listen to those facts without being faced with the Hobson's choice of violating the law or violating his professional code of Ethics."

. . . .

In the most recent issue of the New York State Bar Journal (June 1975) there is an article by Jack B. Weinstein, entitled "Educating Ethical Lawyers." In a sub-caption to this article is the following language which is pertinent: "The most difficult ethical dilemmas result from the frequent conflicts between the obligation to one's client and those to the legal system and to society. It is in this area that legal education has its greatest responsibility, and can have its greatest effects." In the course of his article Mr. Weinstein states that there are three major types of pressure facing a practicing lawyer. He uses the following language to describe these:

> First, there are those that originate in the attorney's search for his own well-being. Second, pressures arise from the attorney's obligation to his client. Third, the lawyer has certain obligations to the courts, the legal system, and society in general.

Our system of criminal justice is an adversary system and the interests of the state are not absolute, or even paramount. "The dignity of the individual is respected to the point that even when the citizen is known by the state to have committed a heinous offense, the individual is nevertheless accorded such rights as counsel, trial by jury, due process, and the privilege against self-incrimination."[4]

A trial is in part a search for truth, but it is only partly a search for truth. The mantle of innocence is flung over the defendant to such an extent that he is safeguarded by rules of evidence which frequently keep out absolute truth, much to the chagrin of juries. Nevertheless, this has been a part of our system since our laws were taken from the laws of England and over these many years has been found to best protect a balance between the rights of the individual and the rights of society.

The concept of the right to counsel has again been with us for a long time, but since the decision of *Gideon v. Wainwright*, 372 U.S. 335, it has been extended more and more so that at the present time a defendant is entitled to have counsel at a parole hearing or a probation violation hearing.

---

[4] Criminal Law Bulletin (Dec. 1974). Article by Monroe H. Freedman.

The effectiveness of counsel is only as great as the confidentiality of its client-attorney relationship. If the lawyer cannot get all the facts about the case, he can only give his client half of a defense. This, of necessity, involves the client telling his attorney everything remotely connected with the crime.

Apparently, in the instant case, after analyzing all the evidence, and after hearing of the bizarre episodes in the life of their client, they decided that the only possibility of salvation was in a defense of insanity. For the client to disclose not only everything about this particular crime but also everything about other crimes which might have a bearing upon his defense, requires the strictest confidence in, and on the part of, the attorney.

When the facts of the other homicides became public, as a result of the defendant's testimony to substantiate his claim of insanity, "Members of the public were shocked at the apparent callousness of these lawyers, whose conduct was seen as typifying the unhealthy lack of concern of most lawyers with the public interest and with simple decency." A hue and cry went up from the press and other news media suggesting that the attorneys should be found guilty of such crimes as obstruction of justice or becoming an accomplice after the fact. From a layman's standpoint, this certainly was a logical conclusion. However, the constitution of the United States of America attempts to preserve the dignity of the individual and to do that guarantees him the services of an attorney who will bring to the bar and to the bench every conceivable protection from the inroads of the state against such rights as are vested in the constitution for one accused of crime. Among those substantial constitutional rights is that a defendant does not have to incriminate himself. His attorneys were bound to uphold that concept and maintain what has been called a sacred trust of confidentiality.

The following language from the brief of the Amicus Curiae further points up the statements just made:

> The client's Fifth Amendment rights cannot be violated by his attorney. There is no viable distinction between the personal papers and criminal evidence in the hands or mind of the client. Because the discovery of the body of Alicia Hauck would have presented "a significant link in a chain of evidence tending to establish his guilt" (Leary v. United States, 395 U.S. 6 (1969)), Garrow was constitutionally exempt from any statutory requirement to disclose the location of the body. And Attorney Belge, as Garrow's attorney, was not only equally exempt, but under a positive stricture precluding such disclosure. Garrow, although constitutionally privileged against a requirement of compulsory disclosure, was free to make such a revelation if he chose to do so. Attorney Belge was affirmatively required to

withhold disclosure. The criminal defendant's self-incrimination rights become completely nugatory if compulsory disclosure can be exacted through his attorney.

In the case at bar we must weigh the importance of the general privilege of confidentiality in the performance of the defendant's duties as an attorney, against the inroads of such a privilege, on the fair administration of criminal justice as well as the heart tearing that went on in the victim's family by reason of their uncertainty as to the whereabouts of Alicia Hauck. In this type situation the Court must balance the rights of the individual against the rights of society as a whole. There is no question but Attorney Belge's failure to bring to the attention of the authorities the whereabouts of Alicia Hauck when he first verified it, prevented bringing Garrow to the immediate bar of justice for this particular murder. This was in a sense, obstruction of justice. This duty, I am sure, loomed large in the mind of Attorney Belge. However, against this was the Fifth Amendment right of his client, Garrow, not to incriminate himself. If the Grand Jury had returned an indictment charging Mr. Belge with obstruction of justice under a proper statute, the work of this Court would have been much more difficult than it is.

There must always be a conflict between the obstruction of the administration of criminal justice and the preservation of the right against self-incrimination which permeates the mind of the attorney as the alter ego of his client. But that is not the situation before this Court. We have the Fifth Amendment right, derived from the constitution, on the one hand, as against the trivia of a pseudo-criminal statute on the other, which has seldom been brought into play. Clearly the latter is completely out of focus when placed alongside the client-attorney privilege. An examination of the Grand Jury testimony sheds little light on their reasoning. The testimony of Mr. Armani added nothing new to the facts as already presented to the Grand Jury. He and Mr. Belge were co-counsel. Both were answerable to the Canons of professional ethics. The Grand Jury chose to indict one and not the other. It appears as if that body were grasping at straws.

It is the decision of this Court that Francis R. Belge conducted himself as an officer of the Court with all the zeal at his command to protect the constitutional rights of his client. Both on the grounds of a privileged communication and in the interests of justice the Indictment is dismissed.

* * *

6. DISCLOSURE REASONABLY NECESSARY TO DETECT CONFLICTS OF INTEREST

When a lawyer considers moving to a new firm and when groups of lawyers consider merging two firms, it is necessary to know whether the change will create a conflict of interest. For example, assume that lawyer

Sue has practiced law for many years at a small law firm. Sue would like to join a new law firm, but Sue and the new firm want to know if the move will create a conflict of interest.

Rule 1.6(b)(7) allows lawyers in Sue's situation to reveal information necessary to detect and resolve conflicts of interest. The rule prohibits revealing information that would compromise the attorney-client privilege or otherwise prejudice a client. Conflicts of interest will be addressed further in Chapters 16, 17, and 19.

Profile of Attorney Professionalism. Jamie Kunz and Dale Coventry knew that their client Andrew Wilson killed a security guard in a Chicago McDonald's in 1982. But Wilson was never charged with the crime. Instead, an innocent man, Alton Logan, was convicted and sentenced to life in prison.

Attorneys Kunz and Coventry knew that prosecutors had the wrong man in 1982. They describe Wilson as "kind of gleeful" when he told them that he was the one who killed the McDonald's security guard but that Logan had been charged with the crime. Kunz and Coventry even watched parts of the Logan trial. They did not want to see an innocent man go to jail, but they knew they had a legal and ethical obligation not to disclose their client's confession to the crime.

In a 2008 interview, Coventry explained "Well, the vast majority of the public apparently believes [we should have disclosed that the wrong man was in prison], but if you check with attorneys or ethics committees or . . . anybody who knows the rules of conduct for attorneys, it's very, very clear- it's not morally clear-but we're in a position to where we have to maintain client confidentiality, just as a priest would or a doctor would. It's just a requirement of the law. The system wouldn't work without it," Coventry said. Coventry and Kunz explained that they researched the issue and sought legal advice, and ultimately determined that they could not disclose their client's information. They concluded that even if they disclosed the information, it would likely be inadmissible in court because their disclosure would have violated the attorney-client privilege.

When asked if they were silent to avoid disbarment, Coventry answered, "I don't think I considered [disbarment] as much as I considered my responsibility to my client. I was very concerned to protect him."

Coventry and Kunz recognized they could reveal Wilson's confession if they had his permission. They asked Wilson if he would agree that they could disclose he was the shooter after Wilson's death. He agreed. So, when Wilson died in 2007, Coventry and Kunz disclosed that Wilson had been the shooter. Their disclosure eventually lead to Alton Logan's release from prison in 2008. He had served twenty-six years behind bars for a crime he did not commit. *26-Year Secret Kept Innocent Man in Prison*, 60 Minutes, available at http://www.cbsnews.com/news/26-year-secret-kept-innocent-man-in-prison/1/.

While many have criticized Coventry and Kunz for their silence, they acted consistent with their legal and professional conduct obligations under Illinois law. There is also a story of professionalism in attorneys who work to change the law or attorney conduct rules to address an injustice. We find examples of this in Massachusetts and Alaska. The high courts of both states have adopted rules permitting attorneys to disclose confidential client information to the extent necessary to prevent the wrongful execution or incarceration of another.

CHAPTER 15

ATTORNEY-CLIENT PRIVILEGE, WORK PRODUCT, AND COMPETENTLY PROTECTING CLIENT INFORMATION

■ ■ ■

Chapter Hypothetical. You represent Convinsio Corporation in litigation with its competitor Kinsera Inc. Both companies are in the business of providing web-based marketing services for nonprofit corporations. In January of this year, Kinsera filed a complaint in federal court alleging claims against Convinsio for copyright infringement. Kinsera alleges that in April and May of last year, Convinsio improperly accessed Kinsera's password-protected website and copied Kinsera's proprietary and copyrighted computer program codes, which it then improperly used to develop its own website. Convinsio denies these allegations. The case has now entered the discovery phase.

A. THE ATTORNEY-CLIENT PRIVILEGE

In litigation, lawyer and client cannot be compelled to testify or otherwise provide information regarding their communications made in confidence for the purpose of obtaining or providing legal assistance. This is the attorney-client privilege. The purpose of the attorney-client privilege is to encourage open, unguarded communication between attorney and client, so that the client is more likely to receive appropriate legal advice. *See Hunt v. Blackburn*, 128 U.S. 464, 470, 9 S. Ct. 125, 127 (1888) (explaining that attorney-client privilege "is founded upon the necessity, in the interest and administration of justice, of the aid of persons having knowledge of the law and skilled in its practice, which assistance can only be safely and readily availed of when free from the consequences or the apprehension of disclosure.").

It may be helpful to consider an example. Suppose a client e-mails his attorney with a question about whether the client has a cause of action for employment discrimination. The e-mail is protected by the attorney-client privilege because it reflects a confidential communication between attorney and client for the purpose of seeking legal advice. The attorney's confidential response to the client—analyzing the client's chance of prevailing in an employment discrimination suit—is also privileged.

In order to invoke the attorney-client privilege, the attorney must object when the information is requested in litigation, such as in a written discovery request, in a deposition, or at trial. For example, suppose that opposing counsel makes a request for production of documents that seeks: "All e-mail communications between Plaintiff and Plaintiff's attorney from June 1 to the present." The law of attorney-client privilege provides the basis for counsel to refuse the request. The attorney would object in writing ("Plaintiff objects to producing the requested information because it is protected by the attorney-client privilege"), refuse to produce the information, and describe the withheld documents on a "privilege log" (required by Federal Rule of Civil Procedure 26(b)(5)(A) and state court rules of civil procedure).

The privilege protects from disclosure the attorney-client communication, but that does not mean facts can be hidden from an opponent by communicating them to an attorney. For example, suppose a client's confidential e-mail to her attorney states, "I ran the red light, but I still think the accident happened because the defendant was speeding. Do you think I can win anyway?" While the e-mail between attorney and client is privileged, the fact that the client ran the red light is not. Because of privilege, the defendant cannot obtain the e-mail in discovery or ask the client, "What did you tell your attorney about the accident?" However, the defendant is entitled to ask the plaintiff (in an interrogatory, deposition, or on the witness stand at trial), "Did you run the red light?" There is no basis to object that the information is privileged simply because it was communicated to an attorney.

At first blush, the attorney's duty of confidentiality and the attorney-client privilege may appear to be similar, but they are different in several important ways. First, the source of law for each is distinct. An attorney has a legal duty of confidentiality because of the fiduciary relationship between attorney and client. This duty is also a professional conduct obligation embodied in Model Rule 1.6. The attorney-client privilege is an evidentiary privilege that is embodied in rules of evidence, statutes, and/or case law depending on the jurisdiction. In federal court, Federal Rule of Evidence 501 provides that privilege is "governed by the principles of the common law as they may be interpreted by courts of the United States in light of reason and experience." This evidentiary rule also provides that if the state law applies in the case, then state privilege law applies. As a result, federal courts look to state privilege law to resolve privilege issues in cases filed in federal court based on diversity jurisdiction.

Second, more information is encompassed within the confidentiality obligation than within attorney-client privilege. Under Rule 1.6, a lawyer must keep in confidence *all information* learned in the representation of a client. This includes privileged information (such as a client's e-mail to her lawyer seeking legal advice about an issue) and non-privileged information (such as the client's name, the type of lawsuit the lawyer filed on the client's behalf, information the client's friend told the lawyer, and information the client told the lawyer in the presence of a third party). As a result, an attorney can violate the duty of confidentiality by disclosing even non-privileged information. Recall the hypotheticals about client Cynthia Burns' divorce in the previous chapter. Suppose that Cynthia's attorney discloses to a friend, "Cynthia's divorce is getting messy. Her husband claims in a court filing that she is a heroin addict." The attorney has not disclosed privileged information, but the attorney has violated the confidentiality obligation.

Third, the contexts in which the issues of confidentiality and privilege arise are different. The confidentiality duty obligates a lawyer to not discuss with third parties any information learned while representing clients, absent client consent or an exception. In contrast, the attorney-client privilege is invoked in litigation. It is the basis for an attorney objecting to any question (in discovery or at trial) seeking information about confidential communications between client and attorney for the purpose of giving or receiving legal advice.

Finally, consequences of disclosure are distinct. If an attorney violates the confidentiality obligation, the attorney may be disciplined by the bar and may be sued by the client for violating fiduciary duty. When privileged information is disclosed to a third party by an attorney or client, a court may be asked to determine whether the disclosure waived the privilege. If the court finds privilege was waived, the information may be offered as evidence at trial. The issue of privilege waiver will be discussed further later in this chapter.

The attorney-client privilege extends to organizational clients, such as corporations. Federal courts disagreed about which employees' communications with counsel were covered by the privilege until the U.S. Supreme Court addressed the issue in the following case.

UPJOHN COMPANY V. UNITED STATES
449 U.S. 383 (1981)

JUSTICE REHNQUIST delivered the opinion of the Court.

We granted certiorari in this case to address important questions concerning the scope of the attorney-client privilege in the corporate context and the applicability of the work-product doctrine in proceedings to enforce tax summonses.... With respect to the privilege question the parties and various amici have described our task as one of choosing between two "tests" which have gained adherents in the courts of appeals.

We are acutely aware, however, that we sit to decide concrete cases and not abstract propositions of law. We decline to lay down a broad rule or series of rules to govern all conceivable future questions in this area, even were we able to do so. We can and do, however, conclude that the attorney-client privilege protects the communications involved in this case from compelled disclosure and that the work-product doctrine does apply in tax summons enforcement proceedings.

I

Petitioner Upjohn Co. manufactures and sells pharmaceuticals here and abroad. In January 1976, independent accountants conducting an audit of one of Upjohn's foreign subsidiaries discovered that the subsidiary made payments to or for the benefit of foreign government officials in order to secure government business. The accountants so informed petitioner, Mr. Gerard Thomas, Upjohn's Vice President, Secretary, and General Counsel. Thomas is a member of the Michigan and New York Bars, and has been Upjohn's General Counsel for 20 years. He consulted with outside counsel and R.T. Parfet, Jr., Upjohn's Chairman of the Board. It was decided that the company would conduct an internal investigation of what were termed "questionable payments." As part of this investigation the attorneys prepared a letter containing a questionnaire which was sent to "All Foreign General and Area Managers" over the Chairman's signature. The letter began by noting recent disclosures that several American companies made "possibly illegal" payments to foreign government officials and emphasized that the management needed full information concerning any such payments made by Upjohn. The letter indicated that the Chairman had asked Thomas, identified as "the company's General Counsel," "to conduct an investigation for the purpose of determining the nature and magnitude of any payments made by the Upjohn Company or any of its subsidiaries to any employee or official of a foreign government." The questionnaire sought detailed information concerning such payments. Managers were instructed to treat the investigation as "highly confidential" and not to discuss it with anyone other than Upjohn employees who might be helpful in providing the requested information. Responses were to be sent directly to Thomas. Thomas and outside counsel also interviewed the recipients of the questionnaire and some 33 other Upjohn officers or employees as part of the investigation.

On March 26, 1976, the company voluntarily submitted a preliminary report to the Securities and Exchange Commission on Form 8–K disclosing certain questionable payments. A copy of the report was simultaneously submitted to the Internal Revenue Service, which immediately began an investigation to determine the tax consequences of the payments. Special agents conducting the investigation were given lists by Upjohn of all those interviewed and all who had responded to the questionnaire. On November

23, 1976, the Service issued a summons pursuant to 26 U.S.C. § 7602 demanding production of:

> All files relative to the investigation conducted under the supervision of Gerard Thomas to identify payments to employees of foreign governments and any political contributions made by the Upjohn Company or any of its affiliates since January 1, 1971 and to determine whether any funds of the Upjohn Company had been improperly accounted for on the corporate books during the same period.
>
> The records should include but not be limited to written questionnaires sent to managers of the Upjohn Company's foreign affiliates, and memorandums or notes of the interviews conducted in the United States and abroad with officers and employees of the Upjohn Company and its subsidiaries.

... The company declined to produce the documents specified in the second paragraph on the grounds that they were protected from disclosure by the attorney-client privilege and constituted the work product of attorneys prepared in anticipation of litigation. On August 31, 1977, the United States filed a petition seeking enforcement of the summons ... in the United States District Court for the Western District of Michigan. That court ... concluded that the summons should be enforced. Petitioners appealed to the Court of Appeals for the Sixth Circuit which ... agreed that the privilege did not apply "[t]o the extent that the communications were made by officers and agents not responsible for directing Upjohn's actions in response to legal advice ... for the simple reason that the communications were not the 'client's.' " ... Noting that Upjohn's counsel had interviewed officials such as the Chairman and President, the Court of Appeals remanded to the District Court so that a determination of who was within the "control group" could be made. In a concluding footnote the court stated that the work-product doctrine "is not applicable to administrative summonses issued under 26 U.S.C. § 7602." ...

II

Federal Rule of Evidence 501 provides that "the privilege of a witness ... shall be governed by the principles of the common law as they may be interpreted by the courts of the United States in light of reason and experience." The attorney-client privilege is the oldest of the privileges for confidential communications known to the common law. 8 J. WIGMORE, EVIDENCE § 2290 (McNaughton rev. 1961). Its purpose is to encourage full and frank communication between attorneys and their clients and thereby promote broader public interests in the observance of law and administration of justice. The privilege recognizes that sound legal advice or advocacy serves public ends and that such advice or advocacy depends upon the lawyer's being fully informed by the client.... Admittedly complications in the application of the privilege arise when the client is a corporation, which in theory is an artificial creature of the law, and not an individual; but this Court has assumed that the privilege applies when the client is a corporation . . ., and the Government does not contest the general proposition.

The Court of Appeals, however, considered the application of the privilege in the corporate context to present a "different problem," since the client was an inanimate entity and "only the senior management, guiding and integrating the several operations, . . . can be said to possess an identity analogous to the corporation as a whole." . . . The first case to articulate the so-called "control group test" adopted by the court below, *Philadelphia v. Westinghouse Electric Corp.*, 210 F. Supp. 483, 485 (E.D. Pa.), *petition for mandamus and prohibition denied sub nom. General Electric Co. v. Kirkpatrick*, 312 F.2d 742 (C.A. 3 1962), *cert. denied*, 372 U.S. 943 (1963), reflected a similar conceptual approach:

> Keeping in mind that the question is, "Is it the corporation which is seeking the lawyer's advice when the asserted privileged communication is made?", the most satisfactory solution, I think, is that if the employee making the communication, of whatever rank he may be, is in a position to control or even to take a substantial part in a decision about any action which the corporation may take upon the advice of the attorney, . . . then, in effect, *he is (or personifies) the corporation* when he makes his disclosure to the lawyer and the privilege would apply. (Emphasis supplied.)

Such a view, we think, overlooks the fact that the privilege exists to protect not only the giving of professional advice to those who can act on it but also the giving of information to the lawyer to enable him to give sound and informed advice. . . .

In the case of the individual client the provider of information and the person who acts on the lawyer's advice are one and the same. In the corporate context, however, it will frequently be employees beyond the control group as defined by the court below—"officers and agents . . . responsible for directing [the company's] actions in response to legal advice"—who will possess the information needed by the corporation's lawyers. Middle-level—and indeed lower-level—employees can, by actions within the scope of their employment, embroil the corporation in serious legal difficulties, and it is only natural that these employees would have the relevant information needed by corporate counsel if he is adequately to advise the client with respect to such actual or potential difficulties. This fact was noted in *Diversified Industries, Inc. v. Meredith*, 572 F.2d 596, 608–09 (C.A. 8 1978) (en banc):

In a corporation, it may be necessary to glean information relevant to a legal problem from middle management or non-management personnel as well as from top executives. The attorney dealing with a complex legal problem "is thus faced with a 'Hobson's choice.' If he interviews employees not having 'the very highest authority,' their communications to him will not be privileged. If, on the other hand, he interviews only those employees with the 'very highest authority,' he may find it extremely difficult, if not impossible, to determine what happened."

. . .

The control group test adopted by the court below thus frustrates the very purpose of the privilege by discouraging the communication of relevant information by employees of the client to attorneys seeking to render legal advice to the client corporation. The attorney's advice will also frequently be more significant to noncontrol group members than to those who officially sanction the advice, and the control group test makes it more difficult to convey full and frank legal advice to the employees who will put into effect the client corporation's policy.

The narrow scope given the attorney-client privilege by the court below not only makes it difficult for corporate attorneys to formulate sound advice when their client is faced with a specific legal problem but also threatens to limit the valuable efforts of corporate counsel to ensure their client's compliance with the law. In light of the vast and complicated array of regulatory legislation confronting the modern corporation, corporations, unlike most individuals, "constantly go to lawyers to find out how to obey the law," . . . particularly since compliance with the law in this area is hardly an instinctive matter. . . .[1] The test adopted by the court below is difficult to apply in practice, though no abstractly formulated and unvarying "test" will necessarily enable courts to decide questions such as this with mathematical precision. But if the purpose of the attorney-client privilege is to be served, the attorney and client must be able to predict with some degree of certainty whether particular discussions will be protected. An uncertain privilege, or one which purports to be certain but results in widely varying applications by the courts, is little better than no privilege at all. The very terms of the test adopted by the court below suggest the unpredictability of its application. The test restricts the availability of the privilege to those officers who play a "substantial role"

---

[1] The Government argues that the risk of civil or criminal liability suffices to ensure that corporations will seek legal advice in the absence of the protection of the privilege. This response ignores the fact that the depth and quality of any investigations to ensure compliance with the law would suffer, even were they undertaken. The response also proves too much, since it applies to all communications covered by the privilege: an individual trying to comply with the law or faced with a legal problem also has strong incentive to disclose information to his lawyer, yet the common law has recognized the value of the privilege in further facilitating communications.

in deciding and directing a corporation's legal response. Disparate decisions in cases applying this test illustrate its unpredictability.

The communications at issue were made by Upjohn employees[2] to counsel for Upjohn acting as such, at the direction of corporate superiors in order to secure legal advice from counsel.... Information, not available from upper-echelon management, was needed to supply a basis for legal advice concerning compliance with securities and tax laws, foreign laws, currency regulations, duties to shareholders, and potential litigation in each of these areas. The communications concerned matters within the scope of the employees' corporate duties, and the employees themselves were sufficiently aware that they were being questioned in order that the corporation could obtain legal advice. The questionnaire identified Thomas as "the company's General Counsel" and referred in its opening sentence to the possible illegality of payments such as the ones on which information was sought.... A statement of policy accompanying the questionnaire clearly indicated the legal implications of the investigation.... This statement was issued to Upjohn employees worldwide, so that even those interviewees not receiving a questionnaire were aware of the legal implications of the interviews. Pursuant to explicit instructions from the Chairman of the Board, the communications were considered "highly confidential" when made ... and have been kept confidential by the company. Consistent with the underlying purposes of the attorney-client privilege, these communications must be protected against compelled disclosure.

The Court of Appeals declined to extend the attorney-client privilege beyond the limits of the control group test for fear that doing so would entail severe burdens on discovery and create a broad "zone of silence" over corporate affairs. Application of the attorney-client privilege to communications such as those involved here, however, puts the adversary in no worse position than if the communications had never taken place. The privilege only protects disclosure of communications; it does not protect disclosure of the underlying facts by those who communicated with the attorney:

> [T]he protection of the privilege extends only to *communications* and not to facts. A fact is one thing and a communication concerning that fact is an entirely different thing. The client cannot be compelled to answer the question, "What did you say or write to the attorney?" but may not refuse to disclose any relevant

---

[2] Seven of the eighty-six employees interviewed by counsel had terminated their employment with Upjohn at the time of the interview.... Petitioners argue that the privilege should nonetheless apply to communications by these former employees concerning activities during their period of employment. Neither the District Court nor the Court of Appeals had occasion to address this issue, and we decline to decide it without the benefit of treatment below.

fact within his knowledge merely because he incorporated a statement of such fact into his communication to his attorney.

Philadelphia v. Westinghouse Electric Corp., 205 F. Supp. 830, 831.... Here the Government was free to question the employees who communicated with Thomas and outside counsel. Upjohn has provided the IRS with a list of such employees, and the IRS has already interviewed some 25 of them. While it would probably be more convenient for the Government to secure the results of petitioner's internal investigation by simply subpoenaing the questionnaires and notes taken by petitioner's attorneys, such considerations of convenience do not overcome the policies served by the attorney-client privilege. As Justice Jackson noted in his concurring opinion in *Hickman v. Taylor*, [329 U.S. 495, 516 (1947)]: "Discovery was hardly intended to enable a learned profession to perform its functions . . . on wits borrowed from the adversary."

[W]e conclude that the narrow "control group test" sanctioned by the Court of Appeals, in this case cannot, consistent with "the principles of the common law as . . . interpreted . . . in the light of reason and experience," Fed. Rule Evid. 501, govern the development of the law in this area.... Accordingly, the judgment of the Court of Appeals is reversed, and the case remanded for further proceedings.

[Concurring in part and concurring in the judgment, CHIEF JUSTICE BURGER joined in Part I of the Court's opinion but objected to the Court's refusal to "articulate a standard that will govern similar cases and afford guidance to corporations, counsel advising them, and federal courts."]

* * *

When state law (rather than federal law) is applicable, the contours of the organizational client's attorney-client privilege may be defined differently. For example, Illinois courts apply the control group test. *Consolidation Coal Co. v. Bucyrus-Erie Co.*, 432 N.E.2d 250, 257–58 (Ill. 1982) (holding that the control group test is applicable in the corporate client context and elaborating on which individuals should be considered members of the control group). In Arizona, the communications encompassed within the organizational client's attorney-client privilege are described in the following excerpt:

> All communications initiated by the employee and made in confidence to counsel, in which the communicating employee is directly seeking legal advice [on behalf of the corporation] are privileged. In contrast, where an investigation is initiated by the corporation, factual communications from the corporate employees to corporate counsel are within the corporation's privilege only if they concern the employee's own conduct within the scope of his or her employment and are made to assist counsel

in assessing or responding to the legal consequences of that conduct for the corporate client.

Samaritan Foundation v. Goodfarb, 862 P.2d 870 (Ariz. 1993) (en banc).

Additional issues related to organizational clients and privilege are considered in a future chapter.

* * *

Problem 15.1. Kinsera's First Request for Production of Documents to Convinsio contains the following request: "Produce all communications sent from Convinsio employees or received by Convinsio employees that refer or relate to the Kinsera website during the time period of April 1 to May 31" of last year. During your review of Convinsio's documents during this time period, you found a number of documents that you know you must produce in response to this request. You also found the following documents that you think may be protected by the attorney-client privilege. Analyze whether each document is or is not protected by the attorney-client privilege.

    a. In a May 5 email, Convinsio's marketing director, Rhonda Harvey, tells attorney Henry Lee that Convinsio is creating a new website that contains similar elements to that found on Kinsera's website. Rhonda wants Henry to provide advice about whether Convinsio is doing anything that violates copyright law or any other law.

    b. In another May 5 email, Henry Lee responds to Rhonda Harvey's email and tells her he'll need additional information to answer her question. He asks her some questions about the new website that Convinsio is developing and how it is similar to Kinsera's website.

    c. Rhonda Harvey's handwritten notes (dated May 5), outline a telephone conversation between Rhonda Harvey and Henry Lee concerning steps Convinsio should take to avoid infringing Kinsera's copyright as Convinsio develops its new website.

Problem 15.2. What should you do to protect the attorney-client privilege when you respond to Kinsera's First Request for Production of Documents to Convinsio?

* * *

B. WORK PRODUCT DOCTRINE

Work product doctrine (also known as "work product protection") is a body of law that protects information prepared for trial or in anticipation of litigation by a party or a party's agent. The purpose of the doctrine is to allow parties to prepare for litigation without fear that an opponent will gain access to that work. Even though many attorneys would say they *always* anticipate litigation, work product doctrine only applies to work product that was prepared for pending or threatened litigation. There must be a nexus between the litigation (or the imminent litigation) and the preparation of work product. An example of work product is an attorney's notes from interviews with witnesses who may have knowledge about the facts of a lawsuit the attorney is planning to file.

The law of work product allows a party to refuse to produce that information to an opponent in discovery or at trial. In federal court, the authority for work product protection is found in Federal Rule of Civil Procedure 26(b)(3) and (4) and case law, including the still-important case *Hickman v. Taylor*, 329 U.S. 495 (1947). In that case, the U.S. Supreme Court first articulated the work product doctrine.

In a case pending in federal court, federal work product doctrine applies even if state law applies to the underlying claim. (Recall that this is different from the law of attorney-client privilege.) For cases pending in state court, state law defines work product protection.

Like attorney-client privilege, an attorney must object to producing work product if it is requested in discovery or of a witness at trial. Unlike privileged information, though, there are some circumstances in which a party may be allowed access to an opponent's work product. Under Federal Rule of Civil Procedure 26(b)(3)(A), a party may obtain an opponent's work product if it is otherwise within the scope of discovery and the party "has substantial need for the materials to prepare its case and cannot, without undue hardship, obtain their substantial equivalent by other means." The law provides greater protection for work product that includes an attorney's opinions and mental impressions. Under Federal Rule of Civil Procedure 26(b)(3)(B), a court that allows discovery of work product must protect against disclosure "the mental impressions, conclusions, opinions, or legal theories of a party's attorney or other representative concerning the litigation."

* * *

Problem 15.3. The litigation between Kinsera and Convinsio has received a bit of media attention. In an apparent effort to persuade clients that Convinsio is the "bad guy" in the dispute, Kinsera posted the following information on the home page of its website. (The post is in an area available to the public and not password-protected).

Copyright Infringement Litigation

We know our clients have heard reports about our copyright infringement lawsuit against Convinsio. We want to assure you that we will prevail in this litigation.

In November, a former Convinsio employee alerted Kinsera of Convinsio's illegal conduct. He told us that a few months earlier, Convinsio executives directed employees to improperly access Kinsera's website with a password that was improperly and illegally obtained. With access to this password-protected area, Convinsio was able to use Kinsera's copyright-protected computer code to create a new Convinsio website. When this Convinsio employee complained to his superiors about their illegal conduct, he was fired. He then bravely contacted Kinsera and agreed to sign an affidavit under penalty of perjury detailing Convinsio's illegal conduct. With this and other information uncovered in our investigation, we know we will win our lawsuit against Convinsio.

After you saw this information on Kinsera's website, you served Kinsera with Convinsio's Second Request for Production of Documents seeking a copy of the affidavit. Kinsera refused to provide the affidavit, objecting that it is protected by the work product doctrine. The issue of work product waiver will be addressed in the following Part C. But as a threshold matter (without reference to the issue of waiver), analyze whether the affidavit appears to constitute work product protected from disclosure in litigation.

* * *

C. PRIVILEGE AND WORK PRODUCT EXCEPTIONS AND WAIVER

1. EXCEPTIONS AND WAIVER THROUGH INTENTIONAL CONDUCT

The law recognizes a number of exceptions to the attorney-client privilege. The attorney-client privilege cannot be invoked to prohibit a lawyer from disclosing information necessary to resolve a fee dispute with the client or to defend the lawyer against a charge of misconduct in representing the client. The law also recognizes exceptions to the privilege in defined circumstances when an attorney-client communication is relevant to: (1) a dispute concerning a client-decedent's disposition of property; (2) a claimed breach of a client-fiduciary's duties to beneficiaries of a trust; (3) a claimed breach of an organizational client's manager's fiduciary duties. In all three of these situations, it is in the interest of the ultimate beneficiary of the attorney-client relationship for the otherwise privileged communications to be disclosed.

There is a "crime-fraud" exception to both the attorney-client privilege and work product protection. If the client consulted the lawyer for assistance in committing a crime or fraud that was ultimately accomplished, the privilege or work product protection does not apply.

The attorney-client privilege and work product protection can be waived by the client's (or the client's authorized agent's) intentional conduct. Waiver can occur when the client agrees to waive privilege or work-product protection. Privilege and work product can also be waived by putting the content of privileged or work product protected communications at issue in litigation. This arises when a client asserts that she relied upon the advice of counsel as a defense in a criminal or civil case. Such "at issue" waiver can also occur when the client claims the lawyer's assistance was ineffective or negligent. Privilege and work product can also be waived by allowing a witness to employ the material while testifying or in preparing to testify. An attorney's failure to object when privileged or work product protected information is requested in litigation is also a means by which the privilege can be waived.

Finally, intentional disclosure of privileged information (to a third party) or of work product (if the disclosure increases the likelihood of access by an adverse party) can result in a court ruling that the privilege is waived. In the age of electronic communication, it is easier than ever for clients to voluntarily disclose privileged information to third parties. Disclosure can be as simple as forwarding an attorney's e-mail to a friend or posting an attorney's legal advice or work product on Facebook or a blog. If opposing counsel learns about such a disclosure (by reading it on Facebook, for example) he or she will likely request that the court find the privilege waived. In the case of intentional disclosures, the court may find that the privilege is waived for all related communications on the same subject matter. These issues are addressed in the following case.

* * *

LENZ v. UNIVERSAL MUSIC CORP.
2010 WL 4286329 (N.D. Cal. 2010)

ORDER GRANTING IN PART AND DENYING IN PART DEFENDANTS' MOTION TO COMPEL PRODUCTION OF PRIVILEGED DOCUMENTS AND TESTIMONY

PATRICIA V. TRUMBULL, UNITED STATES MAGISTRATE JUDGE.

INTRODUCTION

Defendant Universal Music Corporation, Universal Music Publishing, Inc. and Universal Music Publishing Group (collectively "defendants") move to compel production of documents and testimony withheld on the basis of waived claim of attorney-client privilege. Plaintiff Stephanie Lenz opposes the motion. Having reviewed the papers and considered the arguments of counsel, defendants' motion to compel is granted in part and denied in part.

BACKGROUND

Plaintiff Lenz alleges that defendant Universal improperly notified the video-sharing website, YouTube, that the 29 second video of her young toddler dancing to Prince's musical composition "Let's Go Crazy" was an unauthorized use. Universal administers the copyrights for a number of Prince's musical compositions, including "Let's Go Crazy." As a result of the June 4, 2007 notice from Universal, YouTube removed the video from its website until Lenz later sent two counter-notices demanding that her video be restored. YouTube restored her video to its website a few weeks afterwards.

Plaintiff Lenz alleges that defendant Universal knew or should have known that it was a self-evident non-infringing fair use under 17 U.S.C. Section 107. Plaintiff Lenz also alleges that she has incurred substantial and irreparable injury, including "harm to her free speech rights under the First Amendment," and to her "sense of freedom to express herself."

During the pendency of this action, defendant Universal notes that Lenz has made repeated disclosures to third parties regarding her confidential communications with legal counsel and has referenced "multiple subjects related to this litigation and [her] allegations before the court." Specifically, it notes that the multiple disclosures by plaintiff Lenz have related to the actual motive for pursuing the action, discussions regarding certain legal strategies, "core allegations" in the action, and have occurred in e-mails, electronic chats with online friends, and on her personal blog located at www.piggyhawk.wordpress.com. For example, plaintiff has stated that the action provides a forum for her lawyers at Electronic Frontier Foundation to "get [ ] their teeth into UMG [Universal Music Group]" for sending takedown notices.

In light of the above, defendant Universal moves [to] compel plaintiff (1) to produce all responsive documents withheld on the basis of a claim of attorney-client privilege, where plaintiff has waived the privilege as to the subject matter of the communications by breaching the confidentiality of communications with her counsel; and (2) to compel plaintiff to testify further at deposition regarding such matters.

LEGAL STANDARD

"Parties may obtain discovery regarding any nonprivileged matter that is relevant to any party's claim or defense...." Fed. R. Civ. P. 26(b). "For good cause, the court may order discovery of any matter relevant to the subject matter involved in the action." *Id.* "Relevant information need not be admissible at the trial if the discovery appears reasonably calculated to lead to the discovery of admissible evidence." *Id.*

"The scope of discovery permissible under Rule 26 should be liberally construed; the rule contemplates discovery into any matter that bears on or that reasonably could lead to other matter that could bear on any issue that is or may be raised in a case." *Phoenix Solutions, Inc. v. Wells Fargo Bank, N.A., et al.,* 254 F.R.D. 568, 575 (N.D. Cal. 2008). Permissible discovery, however, may be limited by relevant privileges, including the attorney-client privilege. *Id.* "As a general matter, '[a] party is not entitled to discovery of information protected by the attorney-client privilege.' " *Id.* "Because the attorney-client privilege is in derogation of the search for truth, it is 'narrowly and strictly construed.' " *Verizon California, Inc. v. Ronald A. Katz Technology Licensing,* 266 F.Supp.2d 1144, 1147 (C.D. Cal. 2003) (internal citations omitted).

The party asserting the attorney-client privilege bears the burden of proving that it applies. *Pauline Weil, et al. v. Investment/Indicators, Research and Management, Inc., et al.,* 647 F.2d 18, 25 (9th Cir. 1981) (internal citations omitted). "One of the elements that the asserting party must prove is that it has not waived the privilege." *Id.*

"The disclosure of confidential information resulting in the waiver of the attorney-client privilege constitutes waiver of privilege as to communications relating to the subject matter that has been put at issue." *Phoenix Solutions, Inc. v. Wells Fargo Bank, N.A., et al.,* 254 F.R.D. at 575. "The privilege which protects attorney-client communications may not be used both as a sword and a shield." *Akamai Technologies, Inc. v. Digital Island, Inc.,* 2002 WL 1285126 at *8 (N.D. Cal. 2002).

"The doctrine of waiver of attorney-client privilege is rooted in notions of fundamental fairness." *Michael E. Tennenbaum, et al. v. Deloitte & Touche,* 77 F.3d 337, 340 (9th Cir. 1996). "Its principal purpose is to protect against the unfairness that would result from a privilege holder selectively disclosing privileged communications to an adversary, revealing those that support the cause while claiming the shelter of the privilege to avoid disclosing those that are less favorable." *Id.* at 340–41.

"[I]t has been widely held that voluntary disclosure of the content of a privileged attorney communication constitutes waiver of the privilege as to all other such communications on the same subject." *Pauline Weil, et al. v. Investment/Indicators, Research and Management, Inc., et al, supra,* 647 F.2d at 24.

DISCUSSION

I. Communications By Plaintiff

The following three categories of communications are at issue: (1) communications regarding plaintiff's motivation for pursuing the action; (2) communications regarding specific legal strategies; and (3) communications regarding the substance of plaintiff's factual allegations.

At plaintiff Lenz's deposition, her counsel stated at the outset, that with respect to communications plaintiff had had with the Electronic Frontier Foundation, she would only be allowed to authenticate what she had previously written, to verify the date, time, place, and person she communicated with, and to clarify her understanding of her own words. Plaintiff's counsel instructed her not to answer any questions outside these parameters.

A. Communications Regarding Plaintiff's Motivation for Pursuing the Action

Plaintiff Lenz asserts that she is pursuing the action to vindicate her First Amendment right of free expression. However, defendant Universal contends that plaintiff's communications with third parties suggest alternative motives for pursuing the action.

On June 14, 2007, plaintiff sent the following e-mail:

> They [EFF] are very, very interested in the case. I imagine so. I've never heard of anything like it. She [EFF lawyer Marcia Hoffman] said that Universal Music Group is creating a trend of just going all over the web claiming copyright infringement left and right & that they're breaking laws & such to do it. So EFF is pretty well salivating over getting their teeth into UMG yet again.

In another e-mail to her mother on that same day, plaintiff stated that she couldn't "say much," but that EFF was planning a "publicity blitz and/or a lawsuit against Universal." She further stated that EFF would be funding this endeavor and that "[a]ny lawyer fees would come out of the settlement."

In her blog, plaintiff posted the following:

> Today, I got an e-mail from someone at EFF. He asked some questions, asked to see the correspondence from YouTube, asked to see the video, etc. I forwarded everything to him and explained that I'm sensitive to copyright issues and have some knowledge on the topic. . . . The letter [from EFF] seemed to have the tone of "this sounds familiar and is something we're interested in talking about."

Plaintiff Lenz contends that the waiver doctrine is rooted in principles of fairness, and that the court should scrutinize the basis for defendant Universal's waiver argument and whether any prejudice results from the lack of any further discovery. *See, e.g.,* Opp. at 6–7. (Comments 1–3).

Here, plaintiff has voluntarily waived the privilege as to communications with her attorney regarding the possible motives for bringing the action. Plaintiff's communications with third parties relate to the actual substance of her conversations with her attorney. Therefore, in the interests of fundamental fairness, defendant Universal shall obtain further discovery regarding communications involving this subject matter. Accordingly, defendant Universal's motion to compel further discovery regarding plaintiff's communications with her attorneys as to her motives for bringing the action is granted.

B. Communications Regarding Legal Strategies

Plaintiff also made disclosures to third parties regarding specific legal strategies.

In a Gmail Chat, plaintiff disclosed to her friend her communications with EFF regarding re-pleading the complaint:

> [W]e're going back to the same judge with more facts, more case law and strengthening the federal aspect. We're dropping the state charge, which was that they violated the contract w/ YouTube . . . this way their threat of [h]itting me with a SLAPP suit ('pay our lawyers') is dust . . . b/c the SLAPP statute is a state thing, not a federal [thing]. If I make no state claim, they can't respond with the SLAPP allegation . . . thing is, they're fighting YouTube over the federal thing right now too . . . so in my case it's like "pick a federal law you're accusing me of breaking" it's lose-lose for them on [DMCA] front but they can't admit publicly that they're filing DMCA notices b/c that would obliterate the YouTube fight they're having . . . I told [EFF counsel] Corynne [McSherry] that since pursuing the federal portion of the case achieves the ends I have in mind, that's fine to drop the state portion (that they filed a false DMCA notice, tha[t] they're accusing me of copyright

infringement and that a ruling in our case could clarify a cloudy decision known as "Rossi")

Plaintiff relayed the same conversation in another Gmail Chat with another friend that same day.

Plaintiff also revealed EFF's legal strategy relating to the timing of filing the lawsuit. As noted above, on June 14, 2007, she revealed to her mother that she and EFF were communicating about a "publicity blitz" for her case. Apparently, additional correspondence reveals efforts by plaintiff and EFF to coordinate the filing of the complaint and the re-posting of the video on YouTube.

On June 21, 2007, plaintiff informed her chat friend that EFF was ready to file her complaint at that time. She stated "they [the lawyers] said I can blog it [the case] discretely but I've decided it's less hassle just to point on Monday and [watch] the hit counter on my video go ding ding ding. It should be reinstated by YouTube . . . ."

On July 18, 2007, plaintiff had another chat with a friend:

me [plaintiff]: hey, EFF may file my suit today

Erin [plaintiff's friend]: oh? That's good, yes?

Me [plaintiff]: yeah[,] it was held up b/c were waiting for YouTube to restore the video, which they never did.

See, e.g., Opp. at 7–8. (Comments 4–6).

As discussed above, plaintiff has voluntarily waived privilege here. Contrary to plaintiff's assertion that her communications were analogous to her having merely disclosed that she had spoken to an attorney and that EFF was taking the case, plaintiff disclosed the actual substance of her communications with her attorney. Nonetheless, her communications regarding certain specific legal strategies, including whether to drop the state law claim for interference, whether she had potential exposure to a SLAPP suit, and her discussions regarding the timing of the filing of the lawsuit are not relevant. Plaintiff's communications with her attorney regarding the "clarification about the *Rossi* decision," however, are relevant. Accordingly, defendant Universal's motion to compel further discovery regarding plaintiff's communications with her attorney as to the specific legal strategies identified above is granted in part and denied in part.

C. Communications Regarding Plaintiff's Factual Allegations

In conversations with third parties, plaintiff further disclosed communications she had with her attorneys regarding certain factual allegations.

On April 16, 2008, plaintiff stated in a Gmail Chat with her friend the following:

> [Y]ou'll love the brief my lawyer wrote up, once it's a finished public document . . . She's really going after UMPG & now Prince is the villain as well. Our lawsuit was filed before we knew he had a hand in it. Now she's kind of hinting that they're doing this b/c Prince bullied them into it and that there's been ample public proof that he wants everyone targeted, no matter whether they're actually guilty of anything. It's delicious.

Several months later, plaintiff stated that:

> [Plaintiff] I asked [EFF counsel Corynne McSherry] if she though[t] they [Universal] were holding out to the last minute to settle & she thinks that b/c it's Prince, they have to fight . . .
>
> [Plaintiff's Friend:] You think Prince is forcing them to fight it out instead of trying to settle?
>
> [Plaintiff:] I think that's what Corynne thinks.

In another communication, plaintiff stated:

> [Reporter from "Zerogossip.com"]: You contacted the Electronic Frontier Foundation. What are you hoping for?
>
> [Plaintiff]: When I contacted EFF, I did so at the suggestion of a friend of mine who's a lawyer in Canada. I wanted to know my rights, how to protect myself in case UPMG sued me and in what way (if any) I had infringed copyright. In discussing the situation with one of the EFF lawyers, we came to the conclusion that I did not infringe the copyright and eventually we decided to file this lawsuit.

On June 12, 2007, plaintiff responded on her blog to a reader, who asked about a fair use defense. Plaintiff wrote: "You're right Richard. Mine's not a 'fair use' case at all. Nor is it a parody. It's something different. I've never heard of anything like it, which is why I contacted EFF." At plaintiff's deposition, she stated that "[a]t the time it may have been my opinion. It may have been I was misunderstanding what I'd been told by counsel."

As before, the court finds that plaintiff has voluntarily waived the privilege here. In the interests of fundamental fairness, defendant Universal shall obtain further discovery regarding plaintiff's communications with her attorney on this subject matter as well. Accordingly, defendant Universal's motion to compel further discovery regarding plaintiff's communications with her attorney as to the specific factual allegations set forth above is granted.

CONCLUSION

For the foregoing reasons, defendants' motion to compel is granted in part and denied in part. Plaintiff Lenz shall produce further responsive documents no later than November 8, 2010. Defendant Universal may depose plaintiff on the subject matters set forth above for no more than 2 hours and the deposition shall be held no later than December 1, 2010.

IT IS SO ORDERED.

* * *

Problem 15.4. Refer to the facts in Problem 15.3. Assume that the affidavit is otherwise protected by the work product doctrine. Analyze whether Kinsera waived work product protection by disclosing information about the affidavit on its website.

* * *

2. INADVERTENT DISCLOSURE AND WAIVER

In the age of electronic communication, inadvertent disclosure of privileged and work product protected information is a common occurrence. The most common inadvertent disclosure scenario occurs in litigation during discovery. One party requests that the other produce documents relevant to the case. The responding party objects to producing privileged and work product protected documents, but accidentally includes one or more privileged and work product protected documents in its document production. This is a common mistake given the volume of documents that attorneys must review in a document production. It is impossible to detect and correctly code all of the privileged documents with 100% accuracy. Inadvertent disclosure can also happen outside of discovery, such as when a lawyer mistakenly sends an e-mail intended for a client to opposing counsel.

Privilege is not necessarily waived by an inadvertent disclosure. Federal courts follow Federal Rule of Evidence 502(b) to determine if such a disclosure results in waiver. The rule provides that the disclosure of a privileged or work product protected document does not result in waiver if: (1) the disclosure was "inadvertent"; (2) the privilege holder took "reasonable steps" to prevent disclosure; and (3) the privilege holder "promptly took reasonable steps to rectify the error," including following Federal Rule of Civil Procedure 26(b)(5)(B). In state court, the issue of privilege waiver may be resolved by reference to case law or a rule of evidence, typically containing a test similar to Federal Rule of Evidence 502(b).

Professional conduct authorities in most jurisdictions require recipients of an inadvertent disclosure to at least notify the sending attorney. Professional conduct rules in approximately thirty states follow

Model Rule 4.4(b), which provides that if a receiving attorney knows (or reasonably should know) that a document was inadvertently sent, then the receiving attorney shall promptly notify the sender. Some states have adopted professional conduct rules that require even more of the recipient than notice, such as retrieving the document if it was already disseminated, returning it to the sending attorney, and using the document only if a waiver ruling is obtained from the court. *See, e.g.,* Tennessee Rules of Professional Conduct 4.4(b). In other states, case law or ethics opinions address the receiving attorney's obligation upon receipt of an inadvertent disclosure.

Despite such authority in most jurisdictions, sending attorneys often learn of their own inadvertent disclosures at a deposition when opposing counsel hands a privileged document to the witness. Perhaps receiving attorneys rationalize that notice was not necessary because (in their opinion) the disclosure was not "inadvertent."

When sending attorneys learn that they inadvertently disclosed a privileged document, they may be able to use a rule of civil procedure to protect the content of the document from further use and disclosure pending a ruling on waiver. In federal court, Federal Rule of Civil Procedure 26(b)(5)(B) provides that a party may assert a claim of privilege or work product for documents it has already produced in discovery. Once the receiving party has been alerted to this claim it: (1) must promptly return, sequester, or destroy the information; (2) must not use or disclose the information until the claim is resolved; (3) must take steps to retrieve the information (if it had already been disclosed prior to receiving notice); and (4) may present the information to the court for a determination of the issue. Similar rules of procedure have been adopted in some state courts.

The bottom line is that inadvertent disclosure and waiver is a complicated issue today. Because the issue of waiver turns on the facts of each case, parties often file opposing briefs arguing about the Rule 502(b) factors: whether the disclosure was inadvertent, whether the sending party took reasonable steps to prevent the disclosure, and whether the sending party took reasonable steps to rectify the error. It is difficult to predict whether a court will find privilege waived under the facts of any given case given the subjective standard embodied in Rule 502(b). These disputes can jeopardize the attorney-client privilege and increase the costs of litigation. As a result, parties are increasingly employing "clawback" agreements and court orders to address the issue of inadvertent disclosure and privilege waiver. Such agreements are considered in the following section.

* * *

Problem 15.5. When you responded to Kinsera's discovery requests in Problem 15.1, you objected on Convinsio's behalf to producing Rhonda Harvey's handwritten notes on the grounds that they are protected by the attorney-client privilege. You even listed the document on the privilege log that you provided to opposing counsel. Nonetheless, your paralegal has just alerted you that a copy of the notes was apparently produced to Kinsera two months ago. You and your paralegal have no idea how this happened.

Do you think Kinsera's attorney had an obligation under Rule 4.4(b) to inform you of the disclosure? What are the possible consequences of counsel's failure to do so?

What steps should you take in order to seek the return of the notes and to prevent their use in the pending litigation? Analyze whether the court will find that you waived the attorney-client privilege given the circumstances of your disclosure. (For purposes of this latter question, assume that the parties do not have a clawback agreement or order in the case. Clawback provisions will be discussed in the following part.)

* * *

D. COMPETENTLY PROTECTING CONFIDENTIAL CLIENT INFORMATION AND REDUCING THE RISK OF PRIVILEGE WAIVER

Protecting confidential client information is more difficult today than ever before. To provide some perspective, consider an attorney's practice fifty years ago. Lawyers and clients communicated primarily in person, by phone, and by letter. Lawyers dictated pleadings, contracts, and correspondence to secretaries who prepared the documents on typewriters. The client's file was kept in a manila folder, housed in a file cabinet in the lawyer's office. In the present-day law practice, lawyers and clients use technology to communicate, creating a trail of electronic communications every day. Lawyers draft and edit correspondence and documents for clients using various computers, tablets, and phones. Client information is not only found in a physical file cabinet, but on numerous devices, programs, platforms, and in the cloud. A client's confidences can be accessed by a hacker, compromised through a computer virus, accidentally forwarded via e-mail to an adversary, or lost when a cell phone is left in a taxi or rideshare.

In short, today's clients' confidential information is easily created, copied, accessed, and disseminated. This helps lawyers be productive and facilitates lawyer-client communication. But it also creates a risk that unauthorized persons will be able to access the clients' information and that attorneys will inadvertently forward confidential information to third parties.

In the information age, competently protecting confidential client information requires an understanding of technology and the risks associated with using it. According to Comment [8] to Model Rule 1.1, in order to maintain competence, lawyers must stay up-to-date about the benefits and risks of technology. Model Rule 1.6(c) provides that a lawyer shall make "reasonable efforts" to prevent inadvertent or unauthorized disclosure of or access to confidential client information. Comments [18] and [19] address "reasonable efforts" attorneys should take to protect confidentiality. The guidance is general, rather than specific. In short, the ABA explains that what is reasonable depends on the sensitivity of the client's information, the risk of disclosure absent additional security, and the financial and practical costs of implementing additional safeguards. Comment [19] also addresses an attorney's duties when transmitting communications. The comment explains that the lawyer's duty does not require the lawyer to use special security measures if the method of communication "affords a reasonable expectation of privacy."

Because technology is constantly changing, the risks and preventative measures are a moving target. Further, risk tolerance differs from client to client, even among the clients of a single firm. Some clients may need (or insist upon) additional measures to ensure their information is protected.

As a result, lawyers must be vigilant in assuring themselves that they understand their clients' needs and that they are taking appropriate steps to protect confidentiality. Simply handing the issue over to the firm's information technology person (or staff) is not enough. Attorneys must work with the technology experts to understand the vulnerabilities of client information, the range of actions possible to protect against unauthorized access and inadvertent disclosure, and the risks that remain despite such efforts. Cybersecurity experts encourage attorneys to develop data protection systems that include encryption, strong passwords, multi-factor authentication for remote access, anti-virus and anti-spyware software, and firewalls. Additional security for phones, tablets, and laptops can include limiting certain functionality (like printing) and adding the ability to wipe devices remotely if stolen. Firms can also protect client information by limiting who within the firm can access it and how it can be disseminated (such as by prohibiting flash drives and e-mails to and from non-firm e-mail accounts). Whichever methods are adopted, attorney and law firm staff training, periodic audits, and constant vigilance are essential.

Beyond protecting confidentiality generally, there are additional steps attorneys should take to protect against privilege and work product waiver (referred to collectively here as privilege waiver). This chapter has already highlighted the events that typically precipitate an attorney requesting a finding of privilege waiver: (1) intentional disclosure of privileged information by a party that comes to the attention of opposing counsel; and (2) inadvertent disclosure of privileged information by an attorney to opposing counsel.

Attorneys can lessen the risk of privilege waiver by attacking these specific issues. The first step is addressing party/client disclosures of privileged information. Today's clients live their lives online. They use e-mail, blogs, and social media to communicate with family, friends, customers, and acquaintances. This is not just individuals, but also clients that are business entities and governmental agencies. When clients share privileged or work product protected information in those forums, it is possible that an opposing party or attorney will learn about the disclosure and seek a waiver ruling. This is what happened in the *Lenz v. Universal Music Corporation* case. To address this issue, attorneys must educate their clients about privilege and how it is waived. Clients need to understand that their own disclosures are a major risk to the attorney-client privilege. To make the lesson memorable, attorneys should share concrete examples with their clients, perhaps telling them what happened in a case like *Lenz*.

The next step in reducing the privilege waiver risk is addressing inadvertent disclosure. Attorneys, not clients, are the primary cause of inadvertent disclosure and privilege waiver in litigation. Inadvertent disclosure should be attacked on two fronts: pre-production privilege review and clawback agreements and orders. In an ideal world, an attorney would detect and withhold every privileged document from a document production. But in litigation today, that is not always possible or practical. There are often so many documents (electronic, paper, or both) and such a tight discovery schedule and budget that it is not feasible for even careful attorneys to detect and withhold every privileged document.

Clawback agreements and orders can provide a client with protection in the event that privileged or work product documents slip through a document review and are disclosed to opposing counsel. A clawback agreement (which is ideally incorporated into a court order) describes the circumstances in which a privileged or work product document can be "clawed back" without waiving privilege or work product protection. Both Federal Rule of Civil Procedure 26 and Federal Rule of Evidence 502 contemplate clawback agreements (though the term "clawback" is only found in the comments and not in the text of these federal rules) as a way to protect against privilege waiver.

It is not enough simply to have a clawback agreement or order. The clawback must provide predictable protection against privilege waiver. For example, a clawback might provide that if a privileged document is disclosed the receiving attorney "must return it, must not disseminate it, and will not seek a waiver ruling based on the disclosure." More subjective clawback provisions often result in motion practice, with the receiving party asserting that privilege is waived because the disclosure was not "inadvertent," that the sending attorney did not "promptly" request the document's return, or arguing that some other provision of the clawback was not satisfied. *See, e.g., Mt. Hawley Insurance Company v. Felman Production, Inc.*, 271 F.R.D. 125, 133–36 (SD. W.Va. 2010) (as required by parties' clawback, the court analyzed whether producing party took "reasonable precautions" to avoid disclosure of privileged e-mail and ultimately determined the precautions were not reasonable and the privilege was waived).

Because avoiding cost and uncertainty is the goal, attorneys should strive to draft clawback provisions that provide predictable protection against waiver. For suggestions on drafting better clawback provisions and other tips for avoiding privilege waiver, see Paula Schaefer, *Technology's Triple Threat to the Attorney-Client Privilege*, 2013 J. PROF. LAW. 171, 191–93 (2013). In every case, an attorney should explain to the client the efforts that will be made to detect privileged documents pre-production, the protection the clawback will provide if documents are inadvertently produced, and the risks that will remain despite having a clawback in place. Because it is the client's privileged information that is at stake, the client should have the final word on how much risk is acceptable.

Profile of Attorney Professionalism. Loyalty to clients demands that attorneys protect the attorney-client privilege. This can be particularly difficult when a court orders the disclosure of information the attorney believes is privileged. This was the situation for attorney John Lawrence. Attorney Lawrence's former client, Jeffrey McDermott, was indicted for the murder of Elwood McKown. Prosecutors wanted to call Lawrence as a witness to testify about information McDermott told him when they were in an attorney-client relationship. The prosecution asserted this was proper because McDermott had waived the attorney-client privilege by telling a third party about the content of a discussion between McDermott and Lawrence. In a hearing on a motion to compel the attorney's testimony, the prosecution presented a witness (who happened to be John Lawrence's brother, Warren Lawrence) who testified that McDermott told him of a conversation with John Lawrence in which McDermott told John Lawrence he had killed Elwood McKown.

The court was not convinced that the privilege had been waived, noting that the prosecution had only presented the uncorroborated testimony of a single witness. Nonetheless, the court ordered attorney Lawrence to answer leading questions about the content of the conversation with McDermott. If attorney Lawrence admitted the content, then the court would find a waiver and expect Lawrence to testify further about the otherwise privileged information.

John Lawrence appeared with counsel and refused to answer any question about conversations he had with his client. The court found attorney Lawrence in criminal contempt of court, sentenced him to a thirty-day jail term, and imposed a $250 fine.

John Lawrence then appealed, arguing that without a prior finding that the privilege had been waived, an attorney cannot be compelled to disclose the content of a privileged conversation with his client. The appellate court agreed, finding the trial court abused its discretion. An attorney cannot be required to disclose privileged information so that a court can decide whether the client waived the privilege; the waiver decision must precede an order that the attorney testify. *State v. McDermott*, 598 N.E.2d 147, 148–50 (Ohio App. 1991).

SECTION 5

CONFLICTS OF INTEREST INVOLVING CURRENT CLIENTS

■ ■ ■

As part of the fiduciary duty of loyalty, the lawyer must, to the fullest lawful extent, elevate the client's interests over everyone else's interests, including the lawyer's own interests. Consistent with this legal duty to avoid conflicts of interest, professional conduct rules require the lawyer to either decline or withdraw from a representation affected by a conflict of interest. In some situations, the client may be able to waive a conflict of interest.

Chapter 16 focuses on conflicts of interests that will arise if a lawyer represents a client whose interests are directly adverse to the interests of another of the lawyer's clients. The chapter also addresses conflicts of interest that arise when the lawyer's representation of a client is materially limited by the lawyer's obligations to another. Chapter 17 focuses on situations in which a lawyer's own interests may conflict with those of a client. Both chapters consider when one lawyer's conflict of interest is imputed to other lawyers practicing in the same firm.

CHAPTER 16

CONFLICTS OF INTEREST

■ ■ ■

Chapter Hypothetical. Pearl is an attorney in a fifty-person law firm, Knox & Case, LLP. She works in the firm's torts litigation section. The questions in this chapter consider conflicts of interest questions that Pearl and some of her colleagues encounter at Knox & Case.

A. GENERAL PRINCIPLES

As a fiduciary, a lawyer owes a client a duty of loyalty. Part of the duty of loyalty is avoiding having (or representing someone who has) conflicting interests with your client. When a lawyer represents multiple clients and works in a firm that represents multiple clients, it can be challenging to identify, avoid, or otherwise resolve conflicts of interest between current clients. This is the focus of this chapter.

The fiduciary duty to avoid conflicts of interest is embodied in several professional conduct rules. This chapter will concentrate on Rules 1.7 and 1.10. Rule 1.7 prohibits a lawyer representing a client if (1) that client is directly adverse to another client or (2) if the lawyer's loyalty to that client would be materially limited by the lawyer's responsibility or loyalty to another (current client, former client, or third party), or by a personal interest of the lawyer. Such a conflict can be waived in certain circumstances.

Rule 1.10 provides that when lawyers work together in a law firm, all lawyers in the firm have a conflict if any one of them has a conflict. An exception to this rule relevant now is that if the conflict is personal to a lawyer and does not present a significant risk of materially limiting the representation by other lawyers in the firm, then the conflict is not imputed to the firm. And just as a conflict can be waived under Rule 1.7, an imputed conflict can be waived under Rule 1.10(c).

In order to identify conflicts of interest, law firms must adopt procedures to check for conflicts prior to providing advice in or accepting any matter—whether the matter is litigation or non-litigation. *See* Rule 1.7, Comment [3] (explaining that the conflict check procedures must be appropriate for the size and type of firm and practice). This generally requires the firm to maintain a database of current and former clients, as well as descriptions of their matters, so that the firm can determine if a prospective client's matter will create a conflict of interest. Law firms also send conflict checks to all attorneys in the firm listing information about new matters the firm is deciding whether to accept. It is important that all firm attorneys read these conflict checks in case any attorney is aware of a conflict that might not be revealed by a check of the firm database. For example, if the firm is considering taking a case adverse to your father, your conflict of interest may not be found through a check of the firm database. But you need to raise the issue so the firm is aware of your conflict.

If a law firm accepts a litigation matter despite a (possible) conflict of interest, the issue may be resolved by a party filing a motion seeking the firm's disqualification in the matter. In non-litigation matters, there is not a pending case in which to file a motion for disqualification. If the clients and attorney cannot resolve the matter, the client might file suit against the attorney based on a breach of the duty of loyalty. And, of course, a lawyer who has a conflict of interest and does not adequately address the problem is subject to professional discipline.

* * *

B. DIRECTLY ADVERSE CONFLICTS

Rule 1.7(a) provides that a lawyer shall not represent a client that is "directly adverse" to another client. The concept of "directly adverse" is more complex than it may appear at first blush. Of course, a single lawyer representing both the plaintiff and the defendant in the same lawsuit is an example of direct adversity. Rule 1.10 provides that if one lawyer in a firm has a conflict, the conflict is imputed to all lawyers in a firm. Thus, there is direct adversity (and a conflict of interest) if one firm lawyer represents the plaintiff while a different firm lawyer represents the defendant in the same case. These are two easy examples of prohibited conflicts of interest under Rule 1.7(a).

But that is not all. Clients would also directly adverse if the firm were to represent the plaintiff in a lawsuit against a defendant that the firm currently represents in a completely unrelated matter. Even though attorneys from the same firm are not on both sides of that case, there would still be direct adversity between two firm clients. So the defendant's law firm must turn down the opportunity to represent the plaintiff in that case. The defendant can rest assured that its lawyer (and its lawyer's law firm) will not be adverse to the defendant in any other matter as long as the lawyer and firm are representing it. Why should a lawyer be prohibited from representing both clients in this scenario? *See* Rule 1.7, Comment [6].

A few examples may help bring some clarity:

- If Law Firm advises Company A about tax matters, litigators in the firm cannot represent Company Z in a lawsuit against Company A (unless they seek and receive a conflict waiver from Company A). This is because the firm's clients would be directly adverse in that matter.

- It is also true that corporate attorneys at Law Firm cannot negotiate a contract on behalf of Company X against Company A as long as Company A is a tax client of the firm. Again, this is because two firm clients would be directly adverse in the negotiation.

- In summary, Rules 1.7(a) and 1.10(a) dictate that the firm will not take any matter adverse to Company A as long as Company A is a client.

The following problems will help you further develop your understanding of when there is a conflict of interest between two clients.

Problem 16.1. Pearl is one of a team of attorneys that currently represents the auto manufacturer Triad Motors in a number of products liability cases. Pearl's friend Denise was recently injured in a car accident in a Triad car in which the seatbelt may have malfunctioned. Refer to Rules 1.7 and 1.10 (and any helpful comments) as you analyze whether the following scenarios present a conflict of interest.

a. Can Pearl represent Denise in a lawsuit adverse to Triad?

b. Can Knox & Case attorney Johnelle, who has never represented Triad Motors in any case, represent Denise in a lawsuit adverse to Triad?

Problem 16.2. Pearl's mother Opal was hospitalized last year and is now engaged in a contentious billing dispute with Smoky Mountain Memorial Hospital. The hospital has referred the matter to an attorney and has threatened litigation. Opal asks Pearl if she will write a letter responding to the most recent litigation threat from the hospital's counsel. Opal thinks Pearl will have more luck dealing with the issue because she is a lawyer. Not wanting to disappoint her mom, Pearl uses Knox & Case letterhead to write a letter to Smoky Mountain Memorial Hospital's attorney.

Several days later, Erin, the section leader for the health law section at Knox & Case, calls Pearl. Erin tells Pearl that the firm represents Smoky Mountain Memorial Hospital in numerous matters and that Erin received an angry phone call this morning because the hospital received a letter from a Knox & Case attorney representing a client adverse to the hospital. Pearl realizes immediately that Erin is talking about her letter. But Pearl does not understand the problem—Knox & Case is not representing the hospital in the matter involving her mother. Analyze whether there is a conflict of interest in Pearl writing the letter on behalf of Opal in a dispute with the hospital.

Problem 16.3. Mervin, a partner in the corporate section at Knox & Case, has been approached by Venus Motors, which needs representation in merger discussions with Triad Motors. The only work the firm does for Triad Motors is the product liability work handled in the torts section. Rule 1.10(a) provides that if any firm attorney has a conflict, then it is imputed to all firm attorneys. Would a Knox & Case attorney's representation of Venus Motors in the merger negotiations be considered "directly adverse" to Triad Motors under Rule 1.7? Consider Comment [7].

* * *

Direct Adversity that Arises During a Representation. Direct adversity between clients can arise during the representation of a client or clients. For example, the acquisition or merger of corporate clients can result in a lawyer representing two clients that are adverse to one another—in the same or different matters.

Another scenario of adversity arising during a representation is when the lawyer's multiple clients who were in seeming alignment on an issue come to disagree. This could happen when a lawyer is representing co-parties in litigation (such as two plaintiffs or two defendants). It can also happen in a transactional matter, such as when a single lawyer is representing multiple parties who are trying to establish a relationship, such as a partnership. When a lawyer's multiple clients disagree, the lawyer ordinarily must withdraw from the representation of all of the clients. *See* Model Rule 1.7, Comments [29]–[33] (addressing special considerations in common representations).

Rule 1.8(g) addresses a corollary issue: when a lawyer represents two or more clients in a matter, the lawyer cannot make an aggregate settlement of claims of or against the clients (or in a criminal case, an aggregate agreement as to guilt or no contest pleas) absent each client's informed consent, confirmed in writing. To obtain informed consent, the lawyer must fully disclose the terms applicable to and participation of each client. *See* Model Rule 1.8, Comment [16] (explaining that to obtain informed consent to an aggregate settlement a lawyer "must inform each [client] about all the material terms of the settlement, including what the other clients will receive or pay if the settlement or plea offer is accepted.").

Problem 16.4. Knox & Case lawyer Miranda represents Venus Motors in litigation against Auto Distributors International, Inc. During the litigation, Auto Distributors International merges with a Knox & Case client, Grafton Distributing, Inc., to become the new company Grafton

Automotive Distributors, Inc. In light of the merger, Miranda is representing the plaintiff in litigation that is now directly adverse to a client of her law firm. How should she address the issue? *See* Model Rule 1.7, Comments [4] and [5].

* * *

C. MATERIAL LIMITATION CONFLICTS

Another reason a lawyer may be unable to loyally represent the interests of a client is if the lawyer feels a competing responsibility to someone else—another client (who is not directly adverse but nonetheless has an interest in the matter), a former client, a third party, or even the lawyer. Rule 1.7(a)(2) states that such competing responsibilities are a conflict of interest if "there is significant risk that the representation of the client will be materially limited" by those competing responsibilities. The following problems consider some material limitation conflicts.

Problem 16.5. Pearl is one of a team of attorneys that currently represents the auto manufacturer Triad Motors in a number of products liability cases. Pearl's friend Denise was recently injured in a car accident in a Triad car in which the seatbelt may have malfunctioned. Refer to Rules 1.7 and 1.10 (and any helpful comments) as you analyze whether the following scenarios present a conflict of interest.

    a. Denise hires an attorney at another firm to represent her in a lawsuit against Triad. Triad hires Krislyn at Knox & Case to represent Triad in Denise's case. Krislyn submits information about the case for a conflict check, and Pearl reads that the firm is considering taking a case adverse to her friend. Pearl thinks of Denise as a sister, and she knows she could never work on the case. Does Pearl have a conflict? Is it imputed to the firm under Rule 1.10?

    b. If the firm accepts Triad's case adverse to Denise, does the firm/Krislyn need to alert Triad to Pearl's conflict or seek Triad's consent? Should the firm take any measures to make sure that Pearl does not have any involvement in the case?

Problem 16.6. Mervin, a partner in the corporate section of Knox & Case, has been asked by Leo and Lynn to represent both of them in forming a partnership. Leo and Lynn seem to have a similar goal in forming the partnership to run their small business, but they disagree about several important issues that will need to be resolved. Are Leo and Lynn directly adverse such that Mervin cannot represent them both in forming the partnership? Is there a material limitation on Mervin's ability to represent both clients under Rule 1.7? Consider Comments [6]–[8] to Rule 1.7 as you analyze the possible conflict of interest.

* * *

Directly Adverse or Material Limitation for Two Clients? When you are analyzing the existence of a conflict of interest between two of a lawyer's current clients, you generally will not need to use the "material limitation" part of the rule. A lawyer cannot represent one client in a matter that will be adverse to the lawyer's other client (from a completely different matter) because the clients would be directly adverse. That situation is covered by Rule 1.7(a)(1).

Only look to Rule 1.7(a)(2) to determine if there is a material limitation conflict if you have already determined the two clients are not directly adverse in the matter. A material limitation would exist if there is something about the lawyer's relationship with one client that might adversely influence a lawyer's decision in the representation of another client. For example, if a lawyer would be inclined to settle a case for Client A rather than make bad precedent in a field that may negatively impact Client B, that is a material limitation conflict.

Practice your analysis of "directly adverse" or "material limitation" conflicts with two clients in the following problem.

Problem 16.7. Lonnie, a partner in Pearl's firm, represents Santa Fe Homes, a company that markets modular homes. Lonnie represents Santa Fe in business matters. Pearl is approached by Perma Windows, which would like Pearl to represent Perma Windows in a breach of contract case against Santa Fe Homes. With citation to authority, explain whether Pearl can represent Perma Windows in its litigation against Santa Fe Homes.

* * *

Positional Conflicts. A conflict of interest can arise when a lawyer (or another lawyer in the lawyer's firm) takes a position in one case that may adversely impact the interests of another client in another case. Comment [24] to Rule 1.7 explains that taking inconsistent positions in different cases does not create a conflict of interest except when there is a significant risk that a lawyer's work for one client "will materially limit the lawyer's effectiveness in representing another client in a different case." The comment gives the example of a precedent in one client's case seriously weakening the position of another client in a different case. The comment discusses factors relevant to whether clients must be informed of the risk, including the significance of the issue to the interests of the clients. The comment concludes that if there is a conflict of interest, the lawyer should consider the effectiveness of a conflict waiver, may refuse one representation, or may withdraw from one or both matters.

Problem 16.8. Knox & Case attorney Doree represents a doctor in a medical malpractice case in which she is arguing the claim is barred based on an interpretation of the state's notice statute. Meanwhile, Knox & Case attorney Carlee is representing a plaintiff in a different medical malpractice claim in which Doree's interpretation of the notice statute would harm the plaintiff. What factors will influence their determination of whether there is a conflict of interest in their clients' cases? If there is a conflict of interest, how should they resolve it?

* * *

A material limitation conflict can also arise because of a lawyer's relationship with an opposing attorney. This issue is addressed in the following problem and case.

Problem 16.9. Pearl has been asked to work on the case *McAllister v. Triad Motors*. When Pearl looks at the complaint, she sees that her boyfriend Chip represents McAllister in the case. Pearl thinks Chip is a good lawyer, but she thinks she is, too. She would kind of enjoy winning a case against Chip. Does Pearl have a conflict of interest that prevents her working on the case? Does Comment [11] help you decide? If this is a conflict, would the conflict be imputed to other attorneys in the firm?

The following case addresses a relationship between opposing counsel in the context of a criminal case. What remedy did the client seek upon learning about the undisclosed relationship? What other remedies might be available to the client? Is discipline also a possibility?

PEOPLE V. JACKSON
167 Cal.App.3d 829, 213 Cal.Rptr. 521 (1985)

PUGLIA, PRESIDING JUSTICE.

A jury convicted defendant of assault with intent to commit rape (Pen. Code, § 220), finding contemporaneous use of a deadly weapon (Pen. Code, § 12022, subd. (b)). Before sentencing, defendant discharged court-appointed trial counsel. Through retained counsel he moved for a new trial on grounds of ineffective assistance of counsel and prosecutorial misconduct. The crux of defendant's complaint was the existence of an ongoing "dating" relationship between trial counsel and the prosecutor. According to defendant's declaration in support of his motion for new trial, this relationship had not been disclosed to him. The record does not reveal when or in what manner the relationship ultimately became known to defendant. It is inferable, however, that defendant had no knowledge of it until after the conclusion of the trial.

Following an evidentiary hearing, the court denied the new trial motion. Imposition of sentence followed. On appeal, defendant renews his claims of ineffective assistance of counsel and prosecutorial misconduct. We shall reverse on the first ground.

I

The evidence at the new trial hearing establishes that defense counsel and the prosecutor began "dating" about eight months before defendant was charged. They continued to meet on "a regular basis" for movie and dinner dates, etc. throughout the duration of the criminal proceedings against defendant. During that time they appeared as counsel in directly adverse roles representing defendant and the People respectively at the preliminary examination, at pretrial settlement conferences, and at trial. They were never married nor engaged to each other nor did they ever live together.

Defense counsel and the prosecutor did not inform defendant or the court of their relationship. Defense counsel never divulged any confidential defense information to the prosecution. He testified he believed the situation created no possibility of conflict of interest and therefore did not require disclosure.

II

"It is settled that an indigent charged with committing a criminal offense is entitled to legal assistance unimpaired by the influence of conflicting interests." As guaranteed by section 15 of article I of the California Constitution, the right to effective assistance of counsel ". . . means more than mere competence. Lawyering may be deficient when conflict of interest deprives the client of undivided loyalty and effort." Under the California standard, appellate courts may not "indulge in nice calculations as to the amount of [resulting] prejudice" when a conviction is attacked on the ground that an appointed lawyer was influenced by conflict of interest. "[E]ven a potential conflict may require reversal if the record supports 'an informed speculation' that appellant's right to effective representation was prejudicially affected." "Proof of an 'actual conflict' is not required."

. . .

. . . "It is essential that the public have absolute confidence in the integrity and impartiality of our system of criminal justice. This requires that public officials not only in fact properly discharge their responsibilities but also that such officials avoid, as much as is possible, the appearance of impropriety." . . . As distinct from parties to casual social contacts, those who are involved in a sustained dating relationship over a period of months are normally perceived, if not in fact, as sharing a strong emotional or romantic bond. (*Cf.* Comment, *Ethical Concerns of Lawyers Who Are Related by Kinship or Marriage,* 60 OREGON L. REV. 399, 400 (1981).) Such an apparently close relationship between counsel directly opposing each other in a criminal prosecution naturally and reasonably gives rise to speculation that the professional judgment of counsel as well as the zealous representation to which an accused is entitled has been compromised. No matter how well intentioned defense counsel is in carrying out his responsibilities to the accused, he may be subject to subtle influences manifested, for example, in a reluctance to engage in abrasive confrontation with opposing counsel during settlement negotiations and trial advocacy.

A criminal defendant's "right to decide for himself who best can conduct the case must be respected wherever feasible." Accordingly, counsel involved in a potential conflict situation such as that disclosed by this record may not proceed with the defense without first explaining fully to the accused the nature of his relationship with opposing counsel and affording the accused the opportunity, if he so desires, to secure counsel unencumbered by potential divided loyalties.

Given the nature of the relationship shown here, the absence of disclosure inevitably fuels informed speculation as to the existence of a disabling conflict. Defendant is then left with no recourse but to impugn the loyalty and adequacy of his appointed counsel. Since the situation created by counsel's lack of disclosure defies its quantification, actual prejudice need not be shown by defendant as a condition to relief. A potential if not an actual conflict has been demonstrated and thus the appearance, at least, of impropriety. In these circumstances, we are foreclosed from "indulg[ing] in nice calculations as to the amount of [resulting] prejudice."

The judgment is reversed.

* * *

ABA Formal Ethics Opinion 494 (July 29, 2020). This formal ethics opinion is aimed at helping lawyers determine when a personal relationship with opposing counsel creates a material limitation conflict under Rule 1.7(a)(2) that prevents a representation or at least must be disclosed so that informed consent can be obtained. The opinion concludes that intimate relationships with opposing counsel and close friendships with opposing counsel create a material limitation conflict. Such conflicts must be disclosed and representation is permitted only if the lawyer obtains a client's informed consent. In contrast, other friendships and acquaintance relationships need not be disclosed.

The opinion explains that friendships are the most difficult issue to navigate. Some indicators of a close friendship that creates a material limitation conflict are: exchanging gifts on holidays, regularly socializing, routinely spending time in one another's homes, vacationing together, sharing confidences, or having a mentor-mentee relationship.

Sibling Relationships of Opposing Counsel and Material Limitation Conflicts in Criminal Cases. Does a conflict of interest exist when opposing parties are represented by a full-time county prosecutor and a criminal defense attorney who are siblings? The Supreme Court of Ohio Board of Commissioners on Grievances and Discipline considered this question and concluded that the situation "creates a conflict because the sibling relationship is a personal interest which could affect the lawyers' exercise of professional judgment on behalf of the clients." Supreme Court of Ohio Board of Commissioners on Grievances and Discipline Opinion Number 91–22. The opinion noted that state ethics opinions were somewhat split on this and similar issues, *see, e.g.*, Alabama State Bar General Counsel and Disciplinary Comm'n, Op. 85–74 (1985) (concluding that a lawyer or his law partner may represent a criminal defendant even though the lawyer's brother is assistant district attorney and may prosecute the same case), but concluded that, given the special role that prosecutors play and the need for the public to be confident that there is no conflict, the situation created an unwaivable conflict of interest. Do you agree with the approach taken by the Ohio ethics opinion?

* * *

D. CONSENT TO CONFLICTS

1. GENERALLY

Despite a conflict of interest, a lawyer may think it is possible to represent a client effectively and may seek the affected client's or clients' consent to the conflict of interest. This is also referred to as a conflict waiver. Model Rule 1.7(b) outlines the necessary elements of a conflict waiver. First, it is necessary that the attorney believes they can provide competent and diligent representation to each impacted client. Next, the representation cannot be one that is prohibited by law. Comment [16] reminds lawyers to refer to applicable law that may prohibit certain conflicting representations even with consent, such as representing more than one defendant in a capital case. Third, the conflict waiver cannot be for a litigation matter in which the lawyer or lawyers in a firm represent clients that are adverse in the same litigation. Finally, each impacted client must give informed consent and that consent must be confirmed in writing. The definition of "informed consent" (found in Model Rule 1.0) requires that a client agrees after a lawyer provides an explanation of the risks and alternatives to a proposed course of conduct. Comments [18] and [19] to Model Rule 1.7 provide additional detail about the disclosures that may be necessary in different conflict of interest scenarios.

Problem 16.10. Pearl has been asked to work on the case *McAllister v. Triad Motors*. When Pearl looks at the complaint, she sees that her boyfriend Chip represents McAllister in the case. Pearl thinks Chip is a good lawyer, but she thinks she is, too. She would kind of enjoy winning a case against Chip.

a. Assume that Pearl decides that it is a close call, but she has a possible conflict of interest that she should disclose to Triad. What information must Pearl disclose in order to seek informed consent to the conflict?

b. If Triad consents to Pearl's representation, does Chip also need to seek informed consent from his client, McAllister? If Chip's client does not like the idea, can McAllister seek the disqualification of Pearl, or is the only option to fire Chip?

* * *

2. ADVANCE CONFLICT WAIVERS

A law firm may be reluctant to represent a client if the firm fears that the representation will impact the firm's ability to represent other (perhaps more lucrative) clients in the future. In those situations, a lawyer may ask a new client to agree to waive future conflicts of interest. Rule 1.7(b)(4) requires that the client provide informed consent. How does one provide "informed consent" in the case of a conflict that does not yet exist? Comment [22] to Model Rule 1.7 explains the factors that impact the enforceability of an advance conflict waiver. As you read the following case, consider (1) why there was a conflict of interest, and (2) whether the advance waiver provided enough information to allow the affected client to provide informed consent.

SUPERCOOLER TECHNOLOGIES, INC. V. COCA-COLA CO.
2023 WL 5284850 (M.D. Fla. 2023)

ORDER

This cause comes before the Court for consideration on Defendant's, The Coca Cola Company ("Coca-Cola"), Motion to Disqualify The Paul Hastings Law Firm filed on April 12, 2023. Paul Hastings responded in opposition, not Plaintiff SuperCooler Technologies, Inc., ("SuperCooler").

I. INTRODUCTION

Coca-Cola's motion and Paul Hastings' opposition frame a particular conflict that is more likely to occur as law firms get bigger. Larger law firms aggregate more work and more clients. And as firms take on more clients, it is more likely that a law firm's advocacy for one client will rub up against the firm's duty of loyalty to another. In some cases, as here, the client and law firm find themselves on opposite sides in litigation.

Common sense may lead one to believe that a lawyer cannot sue a client on another client's behalf. But that is not so. The ethical rules governing the practice of law sometimes allow a lawyer to sue a client if the lawyer obtains informed consent from all involved. Here, Paul Hastings believed it obtained a waiver from Coca-Cola of any future litigation conflicts that might arise in an engagement letter endorsed by Coca-Cola's legal representative. And because it obtained informed consent from SuperCooler too, the law firm sees nothing wrong with hiring attorneys who have appeared in this case on SuperCooler's behalf. Coca-Cola has a different view and moves for the disqualification of SuperCooler's counsel and Paul Hastings.

II. BACKGROUND

A. Coca-Cola's Relationship With Paul Hastings

In 2021, Coca-Cola engaged Jonathan C. Drimmer ("Drimmer"), a partner at Paul Hastings, in connection with international human rights work in the Democratic Republic of Congo. Coca-Cola and Paul Hastings memorialized the terms of the engagement in a letter agreement, which was signed by Drimmer and one of Coca-Cola's in-house lawyers. The letter contains a provision titled "Waiver of Prospective Conflicts" that states:

> Because we represent a large number of clients in a wide variety of legal matters, it is possible that we will be asked to represent a client whose interests are actually or potentially adverse to your interests in matters that may include, without limitation, mergers, acquisitions, financing, restructuring, bankruptcy, litigation, or administrative, rulemaking or regulatory proceedings. We may also be asked to serve a subpoena or take other discovery of you on behalf of another client. In particular, the Firm has established relationships with clients engaged in a business in your industry or a related industry and may have represented such clients in connection with various aspects of their business, including, without limitation, mergers, acquisitions, financing, restructuring, bankruptcy, litigation, or administrative, rulemaking or regulatory proceedings.
>
> In any of these circumstances, we agree that we will not undertake any such representation if it is substantially related to a matter in which we have represented you. If the other representation is not substantially related to a matter in which we have represented you, however, then you agree to our accepting such representation and you waive any resulting actual or potential conflicts of interest that may arise, provided that (1) our effective representation of you and the discharge of our professional responsibilities to you are not prejudiced by our undertaking the other representation; (2) we protect your confidential information and implement ethical walls as necessary to screen the lawyers working on the other representation from involvement in your matters, and vice versa;

and (3) the other client has consented to and waived potential and actual conflicts of interest.

The first paragraph of this provision informs Coca-Cola of types of conflicts that may arise in the future if the company agrees to engage Paul Hastings as counsel. The second paragraph sets forth the terms of the agreed waiver and encourages Coca-Cola to "seek advice from independent counsel."

After the engagement letter was executed, Drimmer worked for Coca-Cola on other matters, but never executed another engagement letter or modified the original letter in writing.

B. Bondi, Wheatley, And Kats' Relationships With SuperCooler And Paul Hastings

In the summer of 2022, SuperCooler retained Bradley Bondi, Michael Weiss, Michael Wheatley, and Vitaliy Kats of Cahill Gordon & Reindel, LLP, to develop legal strategies and claims against Coca-Cola. After months of pre-litigation work on behalf of SuperCooler, the Cahill Gordon team, spearheaded by Bondi, filed a complaint on February 1, 2023.

About this time, Paul Hastings approached Bondi about potentially joining the firm. Those discussions progressed through late February or March 2023, when Paul Hastings asked Bondi to join it as a partner. Although Bondi accepted shortly after the offer was extended, he remained at Cahill Gordon throughout most of March. During this time, Bondi disclosed his intention to join Paul Hastings to SuperCooler. The Company decided to keep this matter with Bondi as he changed firms.

Wheatley and Katz joined Paul Hastings on March 21, 2023. They notified Coca-Cola's counsel via email on March 27 that they had changed law firm affiliations and filed a notice to that effect with the Court. On the evening of March 27, counsel for Coca-Cola responded via email and explained that they were not authorized to consent to Paul Hastings' representation of SuperCooler.

The next day, Jessica Lewis, in-house counsel for Coca-Cola, contacted Drimmer to discuss the conflicts issue with SuperCooler. In a series of calls, Drimmer eventually communicated Paul Hastings' General Counsel's view that the firm could represent SuperCooler in this matter based on the waiver in the firm's engagement letter.

Bondi joined Paul Hastings on April 3 and filed a notice with the Court on April 5.

C. Procedural History

SuperCooler launched this lawsuit against Coca-Cola in February 2023 and filed a Second Amended Complaint on July 7, 2023. The 187-page Second Amended Complaint asserts claims against Coca-Cola for breaches of contracts, breach of fiduciary duty, misappropriation of trade secrets under Florida law, "correction of inventorship" pursuant to 35 U.S.C. § 256, fraud in the inducement, unjust enrichment, promissory estoppel, a claim for declaratory relief, a violation of Florida Deceptive and Unfair Trade Practices Act ("FDUTPA"), and a Lanham Act violation.

Coca-Cola moved to disqualify SuperCooler's counsel and Paul Hastings on April 12, 2023.

III. LEGAL STANDARDS

The disqualification of counsel is an extraordinary remedy. *Gen. Cigar Holdings, Inc. v. Altadis*, S.A., 144 F. Supp. 2d 1334, 1337 (S.D. Fla. 2001) (citations omitted). Although "it is true that there is a constitutionally based right to counsel of choice, it is also well established that the right is not absolute." *In re BellSouth Corp.*, 334 F.3d 941, 955 (11th Cir. 2003). . . .

Disqualification "is a harsh sanction" that "should be resorted to sparingly." *Norton v. Tallahassee Mem'l Hosp.*, 689 F.2d 938, 941 n.4 (11th Cir. 1982). When considering a motion to disqualify counsel, a court must "be conscious of its responsibility to preserve a reasonable balance between the need to ensure ethical conduct on the part of lawyers appearing before it and other social interests, which include the litigant's right to freely chosen counsel." *Armor Screen Corp. v. Storm Catcher, Inc.*, 709 F. Supp. 2d 1309, 1317 (S.D. Fla. 2010) (quoting *Woods v. Covington Cnty. Bank*, 537 F.2d 804, 810 (5th Cir. 1976)).

The moving party bears the burden of proof. *In re BellSouth Corp.*, 334 F.3d at 961. "[T]he court may not simply rely on a general inherent power to admit and suspend attorneys," but must identify an ethical rule and find that counsel violated it. *Schlumberger Techs., Inc. v. Wiley*, 113 F.3d 1553, 1561 (11th Cir. 1997). Because a litigant is presumptively entitled to counsel of its choosing, only a compelling reason will justify disqualification. *In re BellSouth Corp.*, 334 F.3d at 961. And because a disqualification motion may be used to harass or for a tactical advantage, it should be viewed with caution. *Hermann v. GutterGuard, Inc.*, 199 F. App'x 745, 752 (11th Cir. 2006).

IV. ANALYSIS

This Order first addresses the sources of authority that govern the ethical issues raised in Coca-Cola's motion. It then discusses whether there is a conflict of interest under the applicable law and whether any such conflict has been waived with informed consent.

A. The Florida Rules Of Professional Conduct And Federal Common Law Apply.

. . .

In sum, the motion is governed by the Court's Local Rules, which incorporate the Florida Rules, and federal common law.

B. Paul Hastings' Representation Of SuperCooler Here Is A Conflict Of Interest Under Florida Rule 4–1.7(a).

Next, the Court considers whether Paul Hastings' representation of SuperCooler in this case is a conflict of interest under the Florida Rules of Professional Conduct. Florida Rule 4–1.7 "concerns conflicts of interests with current clients." *Young v. Acenbauch*, 136 S. 3d 575, 581 (Fla. 2014). Subsection (a) of that rule prohibits a lawyer from representing a client if the representation of one client will be directly adverse to another client or if there is a substantial risk that the representation of one client will be materially limited by the lawyer's responsibilities to another client. Fla. Rule 4–1.7(a)(1)–(2). The comments to the Florida Rule summarize the prohibition in broad terms: "a lawyer ordinarily may not act as advocate against a person the lawyer represents in some other matter, even if it is wholly unrelated." Fla. Rule 4–1.7, Cmt. ("Loyalty to a client").

Rule 4–1.7 is based on two principles. "First, a client is entitled to his lawyer's undivided loyalty as his advocate and champion." *Hilton v. Barnett Banks, Inc.*, No. 94–1036–CIV, 1994 WL 776971, at *3 (M.D. Fla. Dec. 30, 1994) (internal quotation marks omitted); *see also* Fla. Rule 4–1.7, Cmt. ("Loyalty to a client") ("Loyalty and independent judgment are essential elements in the lawyer's relationship to a client."). "Second, a lawyer should never place himself in a position where a conflicting interest may, even inadvertently, affect the obligations of an ongoing professional relationship." *Hilton*, 1994 WL 776971, at *3. So the Rule and the principles animating it reflect the commonsense notion that a lawyer should not sue a client on another client's behalf.

Coca-Cola argues that Rule 4–1.7 is unambiguous, and that Paul Hastings cannot represent SuperCooler in this matter because its interests are directly adverse to Coca-Cola—another Paul Hastings client. Coca-Cola points out that the Florida Rule is meant to "protect clients from lawyers seeking to benefit by playing both sides of the field for monetary or personal reasons." *Id.* (citing Rule 4–1.7 Cmt. ("The lawyer's own interests should not be permitted to have adverse effect on representation of a client.")). In response, Paul Hastings contends that it has not violated any Florida Rule and, among other arguments discussed below, that it can provide "competent and diligent representation" to both Coca-Cola and SuperCooler in their respective unrelated matters.

Coca-Cola is more persuasive here. Before the Court can determine whether Paul Hastings violated the Florida Rules, it must determine whether there is a conflict. Because it is undisputed that Coca-Cola is a current client of Paul Hastings, the Court finds that the firm's representation of SuperCooler here would violate Rule 4–1.7, if there is no effective and applicable waiver of future conflicts with informed consent.

C. Coca-Cola Waived This Specific Conflict Of Interest With Informed Consent.

Although Coca-Cola has shown there is a conflict of interest under Florida Rule 4–1.7(a), that conflict may be waived. First, this Order will review the guidance provided by the Florida Rules and the ABA on informed consent and waivers of future conflicts. Then, it will determine whether Coca-Cola gave informed consent when it agreed to waive future conflicts in the 2021 engagement letter.

i. Informed Consent And Waivers of Future Conflicts

Subsection (b) of Florida Rule 4.1–7 allows an attorney to represent a client even where there is an actual conflict of interest if: (1) counsel reasonably believe that they will be able to provide competent and diligent representation to each client; (2) the representation is not prohibited by law; (3) the representation does not involve the assertion of a position adverse to another client when the lawyer represents both clients in the same proceeding before a tribunal; and (4) each client gives informed consent.

The Florida Rules and ABA standards define informed consent as "denot[ing] the agreement by a person to a proposed course of conduct after the lawyer has communicated adequate information and explanation about the material risks of and reasonably available alternatives to the proposed course of conduct." Fla. R. Preamble, Terminology; ABA Model Rules of Prof'l Conduct R. 1.0(e). Under both the Florida Rules and the ABA standards, a client's waiver of future conflicts is valid when the client gives informed consent. These authorities and the comments associated with each outline several factors to consider in determining whether a client has given informed consent to waive future conflicts of interest.

The ABA standards expressly recognize that a lawyer may properly request a client to waive future conflicts, subject to the four-part test in Rule 1.7(b). ABA Model Rules of Prof'l Conduct R. 1.7, Cmt. 22. The ABA notes that the "effectiveness of such waivers is generally determined by the extent to which the client reasonably understands the material risks that the waiver entails." *Id.* The ABA explains that the more detail given about the types of future representations and the "actual and reasonably foreseeable adverse consequences of those representations, the greater the likelihood that the client will have the requisite understanding." *Id.* If the client is familiar with a particular type of conflict, according to the ABA, "then the consent ordinarily will be effective with regard to that type of conflict." *Id.* Although "general and open-ended" consent "ordinarily will be ineffective, because it is not reasonably likely that the client will have understood the material risks involved," such "consent is more likely to be effective" if the client is "an experienced user of legal services" and "reasonably informed regarding the risk that a conflict may arise." *Id.* This is particularly so, in the ABA's view, if the client is independently represented by counsel when it provides consent. *Id.*

Although Florida Rule 4–1.7(b) is identical to the ABA rule, the comments to the Florida Rule do not expressly recognize that a client may consent to a future conflict. Yet Florida incorporates the ABA's explanation and guidance for informed consent. The comments to the preamble of the Florida Rules explain that the process of obtaining informed consent varies depending on the rule and the circumstances. Fla. R. Preamble, Cmts. Ordinarily, this requires communication that includes a disclosure of the facts giving rise to the situation, any explanation reasonably necessary to inform the client or other person of the material advantages and disadvantages of the proposed course of conduct and a discussion of the client's or other person's options and alternatives. *Id.*; ABA Model Rules of Prof'l Conduct R. 1.0, Cmt. 6 (same). The more experienced the client is "in legal matters generally and in making decisions of the type involved," the less information and explanation is needed for consent to be informed. Fla. R. Preamble, Cmts.; ABA Model Rules of Prof'l Conduct R. 1.0, Cmt. 6 (same). And if a client is independently represented by other counsel, generally the client "should be assumed to have given informed consent." Fla. R. Preamble, Cmts.; ABA Model Rules of Prof'l Conduct R. 1.0 (same), Cmt. 6.

Thus, the relevant authorities underscore the fact-intensive nature of the informed consent inquiry. The effectiveness of a request to a client to waive future conflicts depends on what disclosure is needed to ensure that the client has reasonably adequate information to make an informed decision in view of the sophistication of the client and whether the client is represented by an independent lawyer.

ii. Did Coca-Cola Give Informed Consent?

Coca-Cola and Paul Hastings hotly dispute the effectiveness of the waiver of future conflicts found in the 2021 engagement letter. This dispute turns on whether Paul Hastings provided reasonably adequate information for Coca-Cola to understand the material risks of waiving future conflicts of interest. See Fla. R. Preamble, Cmts.; ABA Model Rules of Prof'l Conduct R. 1.0 (same), Cmt. 6. There are two parts of this inquiry. One, what information was provided, and two, was that information reasonably adequate for the client involved?

1. What Was The Disclosure?

Paul Hastings' disclosure is memorialized in the engagement letter. . . .

In short, the engagement letter includes a provision that gives Paul Hastings the freedom to represent a wide range of other clients in a wide range of matters, including litigation, that might conflict with the firm's duty of loyalty to Coca-Cola. Despite this, the letter contains an outer boundary—Paul Hastings will not represent other clients in matters substantially related to those in which it represents Coca-Cola or where the firm concludes any such representation would pose a "material risk."

Coca-Cola argues that the waiver provision is open-ended boilerplate that cannot be enforced. *First*, open-ended waivers are not per se unenforceable, as Coca-Cola suggests. *See* ABA Model Rules of Prof'l Conduct R. 1.7, Cmt. 22. *Second*, as determined above, the waiver provision is not open-ended. It is broad. The provision delineates an outer boundary and discloses the types of other clients Paul Hastings might represent, including those in Coca-Cola's "industry or a related industry," like SuperCooler.

. . .

2. Was The Disclosure Reasonably Adequate?

The second part of the informed consent analysis asks if the disclosure provided by Paul Hastings is reasonably adequate for a client like Coca-Cola. For its part, Coca-Cola generally ignores this half of the analysis. Paul Hastings does not.

The law firm points out that Coca-Cola is a sophisticated consumer of legal services that was represented by independent counsel when it gave its consent to future conflicts in the engagement letter. Coca-Cola's associate general counsel testified that he considers Coca-Cola to be "a sophisticated consumer of legal services." Coca-Cola employs between 150 and 200 in-house lawyers, depending on the entities counted, and spends "many millions of dollars" on legal services each year just on its in-house legal team. And in the last five years, it has retained more than 50—perhaps even more than 100—outside law firms, spending tens of millions of dollars. And it is undisputed that Coca-Cola was represented by an independent attorney who executed the agreement on Coca-Cola's behalf. On this record, I find that Coca-Cola is an experienced, frequent, and sophisticated consumer of legal services.

The question then is, given the disclosure in the engagement letter, was it reasonably foreseeable for Coca-Cola to understand that Paul Hastings may appear as counsel against it in litigation, considering Coca-Cola's experience with legal services and its familiarity with the conflicts that arise in litigation?

Think of it this way. A magician performing magic tricks is perceived differently by different people. A toddler in the audience might be surprised and delighted to see the magician pull a rabbit out of his hat. Teenagers and adults in the audience may respond differently based on the number and types of magic shows they have experienced. But the seasoned vaudeville actor lurking just off the stage won't be surprised.

Here, Coca-Cola is most like the jaundiced-eyed vaudeville actor. Coca-Cola knew what Paul Hastings is, what Paul Hastings does, and the types of clients Paul Hastings represents. Based on Coca-Cola's familiarity of the risks involved, its representation by independent counsel, and the disclosure provided, I find that Coca-Cola knowingly waived the specific conflict here—that is, it understood and consented to Paul Hastings serving as counsel to an opposing party in future litigation matters.

I also find that the requirements of Florida Rule 4.1–7(b) are satisfied and Paul Hastings' representation of SuperCooler does not violate Florida Rule 4–1.7.

V. CONCLUSION

For these reasons, and upon consideration of the applicable law, the parties' filings, and all evidence presented, Coca-Cola's Motion to Disqualify The Paul Hastings Law Firm (Dkt. 39) is DENIED.

* * *

Problem 16.11. Fiona is an attorney in the employment law section at Knox & Case. Orion Pharmaceuticals asks Fiona to represent the company in creating a new employee handbook. Fiona submits information for a conflict check and soon hears back from Shonda, the lead attorney in the firm's intellectual property section. Shonda explains that she cannot risk a conflict that would prevent the firm's IP lawyers being adverse to Orion Pharmaceuticals at some point in the future. She suggests that the firm should either decline to represent Orion Pharmaceuticals in the employment matter or should seek an advance conflict waiver. What information will Fiona need to provide to Orion Pharmaceuticals to seek its informed consent to the waiver of the future conflict?

Profile of Attorney Professionalism. In 2011, Richel Rivers and Mary Evelyn McNamara formed the law firm of Rivers McNamara PLLC in Austin, Texas, where they primarily practice family law. Family law can be challenging; as the firm's website points out, "Family law cases present some of the most complicated and emotional problems people face." The legal system can appear overwhelming to family law clients who are already facing personal difficulties, but McNamara and Rivers are committed to helping their clients navigate through the legal system and are known for offering legal guidance with compassion and understanding of their clients' experience. A particularly sensitive challenge in the family law practice area involves the lawyer's ability to manage the conduct of the case in compliance with legal rules of professional conduct and litigation practice that the client may find bewildering. The conflicts-of-interest rules of professional conduct present an early challenge to an attorney's decision to accept a family law client.

Prior to forming their new firm, Rivers and McNamara had been partners in a large, full-service law firm with several practice groups. In that setting, the broad scope of family law issues presented many potential conflicts of interest with former and current clients of attorneys in other practice areas. McNamara noted that if the Estate Planning Section prepared wills for both a husband and wife, then the Family Law Section could not represent either former client against the other in a subsequent divorce matter because substantially related issues of the character and extent of their estate were the subject of both the prior representation and the later divorce matter. Similarly, if the Business Section prepared business formation documents for a married couple, the Family Law Section could not represent either spouse in a subsequent divorce if the representation in reasonable probability would involve use of confidential information to the disadvantage of one of the former clients, or if issues presented in the prior business formation representation were substantially related to the divorce matter.

Conflicts arising from a firm's disparate practice areas became less common once Rivers and McNamara moved to their own firm, which is smaller and more specialized. Other types of conflicts, however, arise in large and small firms alike. One of the common issues involves consultations with prospective clients. Many initial consultations do not result in the prospective client hiring the firm, but the consultation itself still creates a conflict that is likely to prevent the firm from representing the consulting party's spouse in a related matter. This creates opportunities for troubling manipulation: a client aware of the conflicts rules could consult with several attorneys with the intent of creating a conflict that would preclude those attorneys from representing the other spouse. The *Model Rules* discourage this conduct by specifying that "a person who communicates with a lawyer for the purpose of disqualifying the lawyer is not a 'prospective client,'" and is therefore not entitled to the protections that prospective clients would ordinarily be afforded. *See* Model Rule 1.18, comment [2]. Some state-specific rules, such as in Texas, do not provide this explicit exception to the initial consultation conflict scenario. Furthermore, as McNamara explained, "it can be difficult to discern whether the multiple consultations are for the legitimate purposes of obtaining second opinions and gauging the capabilities of various lawyers or for the ethically suspect purpose of unfairly conflicting competent counsel from representing the opposing party." Attorneys therefore must treat every consultation carefully.

Robust intake procedures help ensure that potential conflicts are identified and managed from the beginning. Rivers explained that a conflicts-checking routine is undertaken when a prospective client first contacts the firm: "Our intake procedures require that the legal assistant identify the inquiring party immediately and perform a conflicts check against our listings of both prior clients and prior prospective client consultations." Only after the conflict check has been performed will an initial consultation be scheduled for the prospective client to meet with an attorney at the firm.

CHAPTER 17

CONFLICTS OF INTEREST BETWEEN LAWYER AND CLIENT

■ ■ ■

Chapter Hypothetical. You are a solo practitioner specializing in attorney professional conduct advice and litigation, including malpractice and disciplinary matters. You regularly provide law firms and attorneys with advice on complying with professional conduct rules and fulfilling legal duties to clients. In your practice, you are frequently asked about how to navigate transactions and interactions between attorneys and clients—everything from business transactions with clients to receiving gifts from clients. In these situations, the attorneys are often proponents of finding a way to make the transaction work, while you recognize there is a conflict of interest inherent in dealings between attorney and client. You want to help the attorneys avoid discipline and litigation in these conflict situations.

Lawyers are often in a position to benefit from their relationships with their clients and even take advantage of their clients' trust. But as a fiduciary, lawyers must put the interest of their clients ahead of their own personal interests. These benefits can take a number of forms that are discussed in this chapter—everything from a lucrative business transaction with a client to a sexual relationship with a client. The attorney may try to convince himself that the client entered into the relationship freely, but the law presumes that the lawyer took advantage of the client's trust. A client who later regrets a transaction with a lawyer—even a client who was happy at the time the transaction was entered—will be presumed to have been wrongfully influenced by the lawyer. Clients can undo such transactions based on the lawyer's abuse of the attorney-client relationship or seek liability based on the lawyer's breach of fiduciary duty.

A lawyer's interests can also be in conflict with a client's when the lawyer has an interest in the outcome of a client's matter. In those cases, the lawyer has an incentive to favor the lawyer's own interests over those of the client. And as a result, the lawyer may not provide the client the advice that is in the client's interests. As a fiduciary, an attorney should avoid these situations.

Rule 1.8 is based on these principles. It should serve as a reminder of the lawyer's fiduciary obligation to the client and the conflict of interest that can arise between lawyer and client. The rule prohibits lawyers from benefiting from the attorney-client relationship absent special protections of their clients' interests. When lawyers violate the provisions of Rule 1.8, they will not only face discipline but also possible liability for preferring their own interests over those of the client.

Imputation of Rule 1.8 Conflicts of Interest. The prohibitions contained in Rule 1.8 apply to all lawyers associated in a law firm, except for the prohibition contained in Rule 1.8(j). *See* Rule 1.8(k).

* * *

A. BUSINESS TRANSACTIONS WITH CLIENTS

Lawyers must proceed with caution when entering business transactions with clients. If the client later determines he or she is unhappy with the transaction, the client may sue the lawyer for breach of fiduciary duty, undue influence, or a similar cause of action. (Alternatively, if the lawyer sues the client over the transaction, the lawyer can expect the client to raise the lawyer's breach of fiduciary duty or undue influence as a defense.) Lawyers must remember that these are not arm's length transactions. Courts will presume the transaction is the product of attorney abuse of client trust and the attorney can only overcome that presumption by showing that attorney went to great lengths to protect the client. The first case that follows addresses this issue.

In an effort to guide attorneys in fulfilling their fiduciary duty, professional conduct rules provide detailed guidance regarding the steps attorneys should take prior to entering a transaction with a client. Under Rule 1.8(a), a lawyer entering a business transaction with a client must: (1) ensure that the transaction's terms are fair and reasonable and fully disclosed to the client in writing; (2) provide the client advice in writing that it is desirable for the client to obtain independent counsel; and (3) obtain informed, written consent of the client of the terms of the transaction including the lawyer's role in the transaction. The disciplinary consequences of failing to comply with such a professional conduct rule are addressed in the second case.

* * *

SECURITY FEDERAL SAV. & LOAN ASS'N V. RIVIERA, LTD.
856 S.W.2d 709 (Tenn. 1992)

CANTRELL, J.

[This case arose out of a failed business transaction between Tom Robinson, a business professional and engineer, and Mickey Ridings, who was a licensed attorney, as well as an accountant and former IRS auditor. Ridings advised Robinson's companies on pensions and benefits, and he also provided personal financial advice to Robinson. Additionally, Ridings co-owned Riviera, Ltd., which sold an apartment building to Robinson. Prior to the sale, Ridings advised Robinson about the value of the building and that Robinson would get favorable tax benefits from the transaction. After the transaction was completed, Robinson learned that the building was worth less than he had been told and that the tax benefit was not available.]

. . .

II.

We will address the fraud claim first. Mr. Robinson says that he was induced to enter into the transaction because of Mr. Ridings' fraudulent misrepresentations concerning the value of the property and the ability to take advantage of Riviera's 1987 losses. We think all the parties would concede that the representations concerning the tax benefits turned out to be false. Although the appellees assert that Mr. Robinson failed to prove the value of the property as of the date of the sale, the proof does fairly establish that the property was worth far less than the $2,500,000 to $2,700,000 represented by Mr. Ridings.

False representations alone, however, will not affect the validity of a transaction. The purchaser must have relied on the misrepresentations, and the reliance must have been reasonable under the circumstances.

If this were an arm's length transaction, we do not think Mr. Robinson could claim that his reliance on the representations about the property's value and the tax consequences was reasonable. He is a well-informed and sophisticated businessman accustomed to regarding such hyperbole with a jaundiced eye. Concerning the tax consequences of the sale, Mr. Robinson was actually warned . . . to obtain independent advice before signing the agreement. Moreover, the representations about the property's value had so little substantive underpinning that one much less astute than Mr. Robinson should have been suspicious.

Under these circumstances we do not think Mr. Robinson has made out a case on the basis of Mr. Ridings' fraudulent representations.

III.

A.

It is another matter, however, if the transaction was not at arm's length. As Justice Cardozo said in his famous quote in *Meinhard v. Salmon,* 249 N.Y. 458, 164 N.E. 545 (1928):

> Many forms of conduct permissible in a workaday world for those acting at arm's length, are forbidden to those bound by fiduciary ties. A trustee is held to something stricter than the morals of the market place. Not honesty alone, but the punctilio of an honor the most sensitive, is then the standard of behavior.

Id. at 464, 164 N.E. at 546.

It would be difficult to find a legal principle that enjoys a wider application. In *Turner v. Leathers,* 191 Tenn. 292, 232 S.W.2d 269 (1950), the Supreme Court of Tennessee quoted Pomeroy's *Equity Jurisprudence,* 5th Ed., Vol. 3, § 956, p. 792:

> Whenever two persons stand in such a relation that, while it continues, confidence is necessarily reposed by one, and the influence which naturally grows out of that confidence is possessed by the other, and this confidence is abused, or the influence is exerted to obtain an advantage at the expense of the confiding party, the person so availing himself of his position will not be permitted to retain the advantage, *although the transaction could not have been impeached if no confidential relation had existed.*

Id. at 298, 232 S.W.2d at 271 (emphasis in original).

This same principle applies to the whole reach of confidential and fiduciary relationships: trustee and beneficiary, attorney and client, confidential friend and adviser.

In *Bayliss v. Williams,* 46 Tenn. 440 (1869), the Supreme Court applied the same rule to a relationship founded on trust and confidence alone without any contractual obligations. The court said:

> Though Williams was not, by employment for compensation, their attorney or agent, he put himself in that relation by reason of friendship and gratuitous service proffered by him, and accepted by them, and of confidence upon and by them in him. . . .

Id. at 442.

B.

We think it is inescapable that Mr. Ridings was in a position of trust and confidence with respect to Mr. Robinson. Even the most astute business people are not experts on every aspect of their trade. They rely on the advice of skilled professionals—especially in the maze of regulations presided over by the IRS. Although Mr. Ridings seeks to avoid a finding of a fiduciary relationship by showing that he was not acting as Mr. Robinson's attorney at the time of the Riviera transaction, it is not necessary to show employment to perform services connected with the transaction. Nor is it necessary to show employment of any sort at the precise time of the transaction. Not many attorney-client relationships involve continuous day-to-day legal obligations, but the relationship of trust and confidence reaches across the gaps in actual employment and endures until it is clearly terminated.

In addition, Mr. Ridings overlooks the fact that the same principles of fiduciary duty apply to other relationships such as that of confidential friend and adviser. The proof clearly shows that as to his personal taxes, Mr. Robinson relied upon the advice of Mr. Ridings.

Considering all the evidence in this case we are of the opinion that the evidence preponderates against the chancellor's finding that no fiduciary relationship existed between Mr. Ridings and Mr. Robinson.

C.

Transactions between persons in a confidential relationship are not automatically invalid. The relationship of trust and confidence between persons in a fiduciary relationship, however, commands the close attention of the courts to the fairness of any transaction between them. The law raises a presumption that the transaction is invalid and the evidence required to overcome the presumption is determined by the circumstances of each case. The factors which are important in determining whether a transaction is fair include: (1) whether the fiduciary made a full and frank disclosure of all relevant information within his possession; (2) whether the consideration was adequate; and (3) whether the principal had independent advice before completing the transaction.

We are of the opinion that Mr. Ridings has failed to show that the transaction was fair. In fact, the proof demonstrates that the agreement was decidedly unfair to Mr. Robinson. Although Mr. Ridings maintains that he did not profit from the transaction, and the chancellor so found, we think the evidence clearly preponderates against that finding. Mr. Ridings got out from under the liability for the partnership debt, which in itself was a substantial benefit. By the terms of the agreement, he was also to receive $125,000 for his limited partnership interest which cost him nothing. The property was worth substantially less than the value represented to Mr. Robinson, and, when the plan to reap a tax benefit failed, most of the consideration for the transaction vanished.

* * *

IOWA SUPREME COURT ATTORNEY DISCIPLINARY BD. v. WINTROUB
745 N.W.2d 469 (Iowa 2008)

APPEL, J.

In this case, we consider the sanctions recommended by the Iowa Supreme Court Grievance Commission (Commission) against a previously suspended Iowa lawyer who allegedly engaged in improper business transactions with a client, neglected a client matter, and improperly retained an unearned fee. For the reasons expressed below, we reprimand the lawyer for his misconduct, but impose no further sanction in addition to his previously imposed two-year suspension. . . .

Bergman Matters

The undisputed facts reveal that Wintroub and Bergman were close personal friends for many years before the two entered into an attorney-client relationship. Over time, Bergman retained Wintroub to represent him on legal matters, usually involving litigation. Bergman frequently employed more than one attorney on the same matter, however, and Wintroub was not Bergman's attorney for business, corporate, or personal financial matters. The parties stipulated that Bergman believed that Wintroub was acting in his best interest at all times relevant to this disciplinary proceeding and that Bergman trusted Wintroub to do what was right.

In January 1994, Wintroub formed a Nebraska corporation called Takara Enterprises, Inc. for the purpose of buying, promoting, and selling artwork created by Seikichi Takara. In January 1999, at a time when Wintroub was representing Bergman in at least two lawsuits, Wintroub sold Bergman 22.5 shares of stock in Takara, Inc. for the sum of $150,000. Wintroub did not advise Bergman, a sophisticated investor, to seek independent counsel in connection with the transaction.

Shortly thereafter, Wintroub also procured a personal loan from Bergman. By May 25, 1999, loans totaling $275,000 from Bergman to Wintroub were memorialized in a promissory note drafted by Wintroub. The loan was unsecured and bore a rate of zero percent interest.

Prior to formalizing the loan, Wintroub made several disclosures to Bergman. He told Bergman that (1) he had monies owed to him from his principal client; (2) he had expanded his business in reliance on this client; (3) he had invested his personal financial resources to pay the expenses of his law practice; (4) he had exhausted his credit; (5) he had no other source of funds to keep his law practice in operation; (6) without the loan he might have to cut back his law practice, but would continue to represent Bergman; and (7) he had no idea when he would be able to repay the loan, but that it would certainly be a while. Wintroub did not advise Bergman to seek independent counsel to review the loan documents or transaction.

In 2000 and 2001, Bergman asked Wintroub to start paying on the promissory note, but Wintroub was unable to do so. In December 2000, Wintroub released John Sens, an associate, from his law firm. Sens had previously been assigned several of the Bergman matters. On February 21, 2001, Bergman terminated Wintroub's representation in a litigation matter adverse to James Moyer. Bergman then retained Sens as counsel. Sens sent Wintroub letters dated February 27, March 28, April 4, and June 13 asking Wintroub to deliver the Moyer file to him. Wintroub had conversations with Sens and Bergman in an attempt to persuade them to allow him to continue the representation. Among other things, Wintroub claimed that he intended the attorney's fees earned in the Moyer matter to be a source of repayment of the Bergman loan. Bergman, however, refused and, on September 12, 2001, filed a declaratory judgment action against Wintroub that, among other things, sought the return of the Moyer file. At this point, Wintroub returned the file. He also declared bankruptcy, thereby frustrating efforts by Bergman to collect on the loan.

Discussion

Business Relations with Client

Wintroub engaged in two business transactions with a client in which he and his client admittedly had conflicting interests. While there is no blanket prohibition on such transactions, our ethical rules in this area are very demanding. We have long held that when an attorney engages in business transactions with a client involving conflicting interests, the burden is on the attorney to show that he acted in good faith and made full disclosures. As a result of this burden, a record that fails to show affirmatively that a client was fully advised about the facts of a transaction or its legal consequences leads to an ethical violation.

We have further found that full disclosure means more than simply disclosing the material terms of a transaction. Full disclosure means the use of active diligence on the part of the attorney to "fully disclose every relevant fact and circumstance which the client should know to make an intelligent decision concerning the wisdom of entering the agreement." Further, the attorney must give the same kind of legal advice that the client would have received if the transaction involved a stranger and not the attorney. More recently, we emphasized that lawyers engaged in business transactions with clients involving conflicting interests " 'have a duty to explain carefully, clearly and cogently why independent legal advice is required.' "

Wintroub made significant material disclosures in connection with both of the Bergman transactions. In connection with the sale of stock in Takara, Inc., however, the stipulation upon which this case was tried did not show that Wintroub disclosed the financial performance of the company through financial statements, annual reports, or oral summaries for the period beginning in January 1994, when Wintroub formed Takara, until the time of Bergman's investment in January 1999. As a result, Wintroub has failed to meet his burden of showing full disclosure of every relevant fact and circumstance as required by our cases involving business relations with clients. Further, there is no record that Wintroub advised Bergman regarding the lack of liquidity ordinarily associated with minority interests in closely held corporations or the lack of control minority interests have over management. Finally, Wintroub admits that he did not advise Bergman of the need to obtain independent counsel in connection with the transaction. Because of Wintroub's failure to demonstrate full factual disclosure and his failure to urge Bergman to seek independent counsel, we conclude Wintroub violated DR 5–104(A) (a lawyer shall not enter into a business transaction with a client if they have differing interests therein and the client expects the lawyer to exercise professional judgment therein for the protection of the client unless the client has consented after full disclosure).

In connection with the personal loan, Wintroub made a robust disclosure of his own dire financial circumstances. Nevertheless, Wintroub committed an ethical violation when he failed to urge Bergman to seek independent counsel prior to entering into this substantial transaction and to explain why independent counsel was important. In connection with the loan transaction, competent independent counsel would have engaged in an interactive process that would have questioned the unsecured nature of the loan, the lack of interest or timetable for repayment, and possible contingencies that could arise, likely demonstrating why the unstructured nature of the loan was not in Bergman's best interests. While Wintroub may have fairly disclosed his financial circumstances, competent counsel would have explored Bergman's own financial needs and the potential for the unstructured loan transaction serving as a point of contention in the future. The record is devoid of evidence that Wintroub made any of these disclosures. We conclude that Wintroub violated DR 5–104(A) in connection with the loan transaction.

We reiterate, again, our statement that perhaps the safest and best course for an attorney is to decline to personally participate in business transactions where the attorney and the client have differing interests. The high standard of disclosure expected in these situations is difficult to meet. By insisting that the client obtain independent legal advice, the attorney may avoid any perception that his communications with his client have been colored or less than candid on the transaction in question, but even so, full disclosure of all relevant facts and circumstances is required.

* * *

Problem 17.1. Attorney Frank has been representing his client, Hill's Home Decor (HHD), in negotiations with a local landowner. HHD wants to build a new retail space that is five times larger than its current location. After eight months of negotiations, the landowner walked away from the potential deal with HHD. HHD's owner, Karen Hill, is very frustrated that the failed transaction will further delay her plan for constructing and opening a new location. Frank lets Karen know that he has an idea for another location. Frank and his two brothers own some land that might be appropriate for HHD's new store. Frank explains that the land is not currently on the market, but he is pretty sure that he and his brothers would be willing to sell to the right buyer. When Frank explains the land's location, Karen is excited about the possibility. She says, "Check with your brothers and let me know the price. I can't wait to make this happen."

Frank seeks your professional advice about how to navigate this situation. With reference to the cases discussed in this section and Rule 1.8(a), advise Frank about whether he should proceed with the deal. If you think the deal can be pursued, advise Frank about the steps he should take consistent with his legal and ethical obligations to his client HHD.

* * *

B. SEX WITH CLIENTS

The attorney-client relationship is built on trust. As a fiduciary, the lawyer is legally prohibited from taking advantage of that trust. A sexual relationship between attorney and client would be presumed to be an abuse of the attorney's influence. Model Rule 1.8(j) makes the issue simple for lawyers by prohibiting a lawyer having a sexual relationship with a client unless a consensual sexual relationship predated the attorney-client relationship. Comment [22] to the rule explains that the prohibition also applies when the lawyer is contemplating a sexual relationship with a constituent of an organizational client. If that constituent directs, supervises, or regularly consults with the lawyer on the client's matters, then a sexual relationship is forbidden. An additional reason supports this rule: as a fiduciary with a duty of loyalty to the client, the client is entitled to know that the lawyer's advice is guided by the best interests of the client and not the constituent who is having a sexual relationship with the client. As noted earlier, Model Rule 1.8(k) provides that the prohibition on sex with clients is not imputed to other lawyers in the attorney's firm.

Problem 17.2. Alex is one of a number of outside attorneys who provides legal advice to Pleasant Properties, L.P. Alex primarily interacts with and advises Helen, who is an executive vice president at Pleasant Properties. Alex and Helen are interested in dating. Analyze whether Alex's fiduciary duty to Pleasant Properties stands in the way of a possible romantic relationship with Helen. Please refer to Model Rule 1.8(j), and Comments [20]–[22] in your analysis.

Alternatively, assume that Alex's colleague at the law firm, Nat, who does not work for Pleasant Properties, wishes to date Helen. Analyze whether Rule 1.8(j) prohibits the possibility of a sexual relationship between Nat and Helen.

* * *

C. GIFTS FROM CLIENTS

Potential abuse of the fiduciary relationship is also the reason gifts between clients and attorneys are fraught. If a client gives a gift to a lawyer, the client (or the client's family) might later assert that the value of the gift must be returned because the gift was the product of the lawyer taking advantage of the special relationship with the client. An additional problem is introduced if the lawyer is representing the client in preparing the gift instrument—such as drafting the will in which a bequest to the lawyer is made—because there is a conflict of interest in that representation. In any litigation challenging a gift to a lawyer (whether the lawyer drafts the instrument or not), the presumption would be an abuse of the fiduciary relationship; the lawyer would have the burden of proving that the gift was not the product of the lawyer's undue influence.

The professional conduct rules provide some bright line rules for attorneys to follow to avoid gifts that are presumptively improper. First, Rule 1.8(c) prohibits a lawyer soliciting a substantial gift from a client. While the rule does not prohibit the lawyer accepting a substantial gift from a client that is not solicited, that does not mean accepting such a gift is advisable. Such a gift could still result in litigation against the attorney and a court would carefully scrutinize the attorney-client interaction to determine if undue influence was at play. *See* Model Rule 1.8, Comment [6] (explaining that while such a gift is not prohibited by the rules, it may be voided as the product of undue influence).

Second, the rule prohibits the lawyer from preparing an instrument giving the lawyer (or someone related to the lawyer) a substantial gift from the client. Rule 1.8(c) is designed to "eliminate the conflict of interest inherent in a lawyer's drafting a will from which he or she substantially benefits by banning the practice." *In re Kulig*, 282 A.3d 926, 935 (Vt. 2022). The text of the rule provides that this prohibition does not apply if the lawyer (or another recipient) is related to the client. Thus, the rule would allow a lawyer to prepare a will for the lawyer's grandparent, under which the lawyer receives a substantial gift. Again, despite the leeway provided by the rule, it would be prudent for a lawyer to avoid such a situation because it may raise questions about whether the attorney took advantage of the client/family member. This scenario is considered in Problem 17.3.

Problem 17.3. Lawyer Lora focuses primarily on estate planning. Lora's aunt, Jennifer, has asked Lora to draft a new will for Jennifer. Jennifer's estate is valued at approximately $5 million. Jennifer has two children, Sarah and Chris, who are to receive Jennifer's entire estate under her current will. Aunt Jennifer is now rethinking that plan. She feels her children have plenty of resources, and she wants to provide a significant gift to her favorite charities and a gift to recognize her special relationship with her niece (and attorney) Lora. Jennifer has asked Lora to prepare a new will in which Jennifer will give half of her estate to charity; give a lake house—which is valued at $500,000—to Lora; and give the $2 million remainder of the estate to her children. Analyze whether, consistent with professional conduct rules, Lora can draft the will. Next, advise Lora about possible legal consequences if she drafts the will and discuss steps she could take to lessen the risks.

* * *

D. AGREEMENTS REGARDING A LAWYER'S LIABILITY TO A CLIENT

As a fiduciary with a duty of competence to a client, a lawyer cannot negotiate with an unrepresented client to limit the lawyer's liability for malpractice or to settle a claim for such liability. Such a bargain contains an inherent conflict of interest—creating a benefit for the lawyer and a detriment for the client—when the lawyer is supposed to be acting on the client's behalf. Model Rule 1.8(h)(1) addresses the prohibition on prospectively limiting malpractice liability unless the client is independently represented in making the agreement. Model Rule 1.8(h)(2) prohibits the settlement of a malpractice claim with an unrepresented client unless the client is advised in writing and given a reasonable opportunity to consult with independent counsel about the matter. You will apply the latter part of the rule in the following problem.

Problem 17.4. Attorney Sarah belatedly realized that the statute of limitations expired on one of three claims she had agreed to file on behalf of her client, Gerbes Whole Foods, LLC. Sarah admits her error to her client's authorized constituent, but explains that this was the weakest of the three claims. Sarah is still optimistic that the company will recover its full damages through one of the other claims in the lawsuit (which she has now filed). The client's representative is upset, but is less so when Sarah offers to pay the client $5,000 to fully settle the claim. Sarah called you as she was drafting a settlement agreement. Advise her about what steps she should take prior to asking the client to enter the agreement.

* * *

E. USING INFORMATION TO THE DISADVANTAGE OF A CLIENT

Two important aspects of an attorney's fiduciary duty of loyalty are dealing honestly with the client and taking no advantage that arises from the attorney-client relationship in a matter that is adverse to the client. *Restatement (Third) of the Law Governing Lawyers* § 16(3). Model Rule 1.8(b) is a rule aimed at guiding attorneys in avoiding such a violation of fiduciary duty. The following problem, which is based on a real case, asks you to analyze whether a lawyer's conduct may run afoul of the duty of loyalty and the companion rule provision.

Problem 17.5. Attorney Richard Bowen hires you to respond to a bar disciplinary complaint. Richard was owed $11,000 by a former client that he had never been able to collect. Fortuitously (for Richard), a new client asked Richard to represent the client in negotiating a real estate purchase from Richard's former client.

Because the proceeds of the transaction (which would be paid to the former client) would substantially exceed $11,000, Richard decided that he would obtain the money he was owed through attachment of the proceeds. Richard filed a lawsuit to collect the unpaid bill and sought (and obtained) an *ex parte* writ of attachment on the former client's anticipated proceeds. When Richard's former client learned about the writ of attachment, he delayed the closing and threatened to walk away from the deal.

Richard's current client (the would-be purchaser) was upset to learn about the writ of attachment and Richard's role in potentially disrupting the sale. Ultimately, Richard was able to negotiate a payment of $5,000 from the former client, released the lien, and the current client closed on the purchase. The bar disciplinary complaint alleges that Richard violated Rule 1.8(b) by using information related to the representation of the client to the disadvantage of the client. Richard asserts that his client was not harmed in any way, because the sale ultimately closed. In your analysis, did Richard violate Rule 1.8(b) through his conduct or does the ultimate purchase of the property mean there was no violation? *See In re Bowen*, 252 A.3d 300 (Vt. 2021).

* * *

F. FINANCIAL ASSISTANCE AND GIFTS TO CLIENTS

Comment [10] to Model Rule 1.8(e) provides an explanation for why lawyers are prohibited from providing financial assistance or gifts to clients in connection with pending or contemplated litigation or administrative proceedings. The concern is that lawyers who subsidize lawsuits will encourage clients to pursue litigation that would not otherwise be brought and that "such assistance gives lawyers too great a financial stake in the litigation." Despite these concerns, the rule provides that some financial assistance and gifts from lawyer to client are permitted. Use the rule and Comment [11] as you answer problem 17.6, which implicates these issues.

Problem 17.6. You sometimes provide professional conduct advice to the law professor who directs your alma mater's Workers' Compensation Clinic. The Clinic's clients often need to appear at an administrative hearing, but many do not have the financial resources for appropriate attire or transportation to the hearing. Many of the clients and their families have food insecurity. The Clinic has some ability to raise funds that might be earmarked to support client financial needs during a case. Advise your client about what financial support the Clinic may and may not give clients and their families during a representation. Also provide advice on any limits on the Clinic's ability (such as through social media) to explain to the public about the financial support that may be provided to clients who retain the Clinic.

* * *

G. LITERARY AND MEDIA RIGHTS

In order to prevent a potential conflict of interest between attorney and client during the pendency of a matter (particularly one that is the subject of public interest), Rule 1.8(d) prohibits a lawyer from entering an agreement giving a lawyer literary or media rights in a portrayal of the representation. The concern is that such an agreement might cause the lawyer to take actions in the representation that would benefit the lawyer financially but that might not be in the client's interests. The rule is only a single sentence, but it is relatively complex. Carefully read the rule and Comment [9] to answer the following problem.

Problem 17.7. Attorney Allie represented a well-known celebrity in a high-profile trial. The matter is now concluded (there was no appeal and a full year has passed since the judgment), but the former client still has not paid over $100,000 in legal fees. The celebrity/former client has sold the story of her legal matter to a streaming service that is developing a movie based on the story. Advise Allie about whether, consistent with Rule 1.8(d), she may accept an interest in the celebrity's contract with the video streaming service in full satisfaction of the debt. Does entering into such an agreement with her former client implicate any other professional conduct rules?

* * *

H. RECEIVING PAYMENT FOR THE REPRESENTATION FROM A THIRD-PARTY

A conflict of interest can arise when a third-party pays the lawyer to represent a client. *See* Rule 1.7, Comment [13]; *see also* Rule 1.8(f), Comments [11] and [12]. There are a number of contexts in which a third party might pay the legal fees for another. For example, in a criminal representation, family members might pay for an attorney to represent the defendant. The following problem arises in such a case.

Problem 17.8. Dylan has a criminal law practice. Shawne contacted Dylan about a possible representation in a criminal matter. Shawne has been charged with first degree murder; the trial date is ten months away. Dylan told Shawne that her billing rate is $750 per hour and that for Shawne's case, Dylan would require a $500,000 retainer (from which the fees will be drawn as earned). Any unearned portion of the retainer would be returned, but Dylan fully expects the representation to cost at least $500,000. Shawne told Dylan that the only way she could provide a retainer of that size would be if her parents agreed to pay it. Shawne says her parents have the means to do so.

Dylan has asked your advice about whether she may accept the retainer if it is paid by Shawne's parents. Provide Dylan with your analysis of whether that is acceptable under the professional conduct rules and provide any additional advice about what Dylan must do to fulfill her professional conduct obligations.

* * *

Third-Party Payment and Insurance Defense. The area in which the issue of third-party payment of legal fees arises most often is in the area of insurance defense. Third-party payment of legal fees can get especially complicated in the insurance context. Most insurance liability contracts state that the insurance company will pay to defend the insured against certain lawsuits and will pay to indemnify the insured against judgments arising out of such suits. These contracts also allow the insurance company to choose and hire defense counsel. Usually, the interests of the insurer and insured will be aligned: both have an interest in asserting that the insured was not at fault in the incident, and both have an interest in minimizing the potential liability if the insured is found to be at fault. As you can imagine, however, conflicts often arise. Sometimes, there may be an allegation that the insured was engaging in activity not covered by the insurance policy. For example, some policies cover only the insured's negligent conduct, and will not cover the insured's intentional conduct. Thus, if there is evidence that the insured acted intentionally, the insurance company would benefit from that information—it wouldn't be liable to pay the ultimate judgment. The insured, however, would be disadvantaged by that information. In other cases, there might be particular categories of damages (commonly including punitive damages, for example) that would not be covered by insurance. Finally, another common conflict arises when potential liability under the policy could exceed the policy limit.

States take different approaches in how they handle the conflicts that can arise. One of the key questions, of course, is determining who the client is. Some states provide that defense counsel represents both the insured and the insurer as co-clients. Other states provide that counsel represents only the insured. In either case, however, separate counsel may be necessary when conflicts arise between the interests of the insured and the insurance company. In the following case, the court had to decide whether an insurance policy that required the insurer's "prior approval" of defense counsel services violated the rules of professional conduct.

IN THE MATTER OF THE RULES OF PROFESSIONAL CONDUCT AND INSURER IMPOSED BILLING RULES AND PROCEDURES
2 P.3d 806 (Mont. 2000)

LEAPHART, J.

In an original application for declaratory judgment, Petitioners assert that insurer-imposed billing rules and procedures violate the Rules of Professional Conduct.

. . .

Discussion

. . . . May an attorney licensed to practice law in Montana, or admitted *pro hac vice*, agree to abide by an insurer's billing and practice rules which impose conditions limiting or directing the scope and extent of the representation of his or her client, the insured? [The court stated there were several Rules of Professional Conduct that were relevant, including Rule 1.1 (Competence), Rule 2.1 (Advice), and Rule 1.8(f) (accepting compensation from one other than the client).]

In the present case, the parties do not dispute that insurers' billing and practice rules typically "impose conditions [upon an attorney appointed by an insurer to represent an insured] limiting or directing the scope and extent of the representation of his or her client." The Petitioners have focused on the requirement of prior approval in insurers' billing and practice rules. We therefore address that condition of representation while recognizing that other conditions limiting or directing the scope and extent of representation of a client may also implicate the Rules of Professional Conduct.

As a representative set of litigation guidelines, we briefly consider the guidelines submitted by the St. Paul Companies (hereafter, St. Paul). The declared policy of St. Paul's Litigation Management Plan (hereafter, the Plan) is to "[p]rovide a systematic and appropriate defense for St. Paul and its insureds, and to vigorously defend nonmeritorious claims and claims where the demands are excessive."...

[T]he Plan states that "[m]otion practice, discovery and research are items that have historically caused us some concern and which we plan to monitor closely. While we foresee very few differences of opinion, we require that defense counsel secure the consent of the claim professional prior to scheduling depositions, undertaking research, employing experts or preparing motions"....

Thus, the Plan expressly requires prior approval before a defense attorney may undertake to schedule depositions, conduct research, employ experts, or prepare motions. The Plan concludes that "[w]e understand that any conflicts between the St. Paul Litigation Management Plan and the exercise of your independent judgment to protect the interests of the insured must be resolved in favor of the insured. We expect, however, to be given an opportunity to resolve any such conflicts with you before you take any action that is in substantial contravention of the Plan."

A. Whether Montana has recognized the dual representation doctrine under the Montana Rules of Professional Conduct.

Petitioners assert that the insured is the sole client of a defense attorney appointed by an insurer to represent an insured pursuant to an insurance policy (hereafter, defense counsel) and that a requirement of prior approval in insurance billing and practice rules impermissibly interferes with a defense counsel's exercise of his independent judgment and his duty of undivided loyalty to his client. Petitioners argue that because the relationship of insurer and insured is permeated with potential conflicts, they cannot be co-clients of defense counsel.

Respondents argue that under Montana law, the rule is that in the absence of a real conflict, the insurer and insured are dual clients of defense counsel. From this fundamental premise, Respondents argue that as a co-client of defense counsel, the insurer may require pre-approval of attorney activities to assure adequate consultation. Respondents argue further that defense counsel must abide by a client's decisions about the objectives of representation and that defense counsel are obliged to consult with a client about the means for the objectives of representation. Respondents also argue that under Montana law, an insurer is vicariously liable for the conduct of defense counsel and that an insurer's control of litigation justifies holding an insurer vicariously liable for the conduct of defense counsel.

We conclude that Respondents have misconstrued our past decisions. This Court has not held that under the Rules of Professional Conduct, an insurer and an insured are co-clients of defense counsel....

.... None of these decisions addressed whether insurers and insureds are co-clients under the Rules of Professional Conduct, and none of them addressed whether defense counsels' compliance with insurance contracts that repose "absolute" control of litigation in insurers violated the Rules of Professional Conduct.

We note that Respondents argue that insurance contracts effectively place absolute control of litigation with insurers. However, Respondents' claim of absolute control of litigation cannot be reconciled with their insistence that whenever a conflict may arise between their litigation guidelines and an attorney's ethical obligations, the attorney is to follow the ethical course of action. Respondents' assertion that defense counsel are not only free to but must follow their independent judgment is inconsistent with their claim that insurers have absolute control of litigation.

B. Whether insurers and insureds are co-clients under Montana's Rules of Professional Conduct.

We turn to the question [of] whether an insurer is a client of defense counsel under the Rules of Professional Conduct. We note that some other courts have concluded that the insurer is not a client of defense counsel. In *Atlanta Int. Ins. Co. v. Bell* (1991), 438 Mich. 512, 475 N.W.2d 294, the court addressed whether defense counsel retained by an insurer to defend its insured may be sued by the insurer for professional malpractice. Recognizing the general rule that an attorney will only be held liable for negligence to his client, the court determined that "the relationship between the insurer and the retained defense counsel [is] less than a client-attorney relationship." *Bell*, 475 N.W.2d at 297. The court further determined, however, that although the insurer is not a client of defense counsel, the defense counsel nevertheless "occupies a fiduciary relationship to the insured, as well as to the insurance company." *Bell*, 475 N.W.2d at 297. Recognizing further that "the tripartite relationship between insured, insurer, and defense counsel contains rife possibility [sic] of conflict," *Bell*, 475 N.W.2d at 297, the court reasoned that "[t]o hold that an attorney-client relationship exists between insurer and defense counsel could indeed work mischief, yet to hold that a mere commercial relationship exists would work obfuscation and injustice." *Bell*, 475 N.W.2d at 297.

Nor is Michigan unique in concluding that the insured is the sole client of defense counsel....

Respondents argue vigorously that the interests of an insurer and an insured usually coincide and that most litigation is settled within an insured's coverage limits. These arguments gloss over the stark reality that the relationship between an insurer and insured is permeated with potential conflicts. *Compare* THOMAS D. MORGAN, WHAT INSURANCE SCHOLARS SHOULD KNOW ABOUT PROFESSIONAL RESPONSIBILITY, 4 CONN. INS. L. J. 1, 7–8, 1997 (concluding that designating insurer "a second client . . . would routinely create the potential for conflicts of interest"); Kent D. Syverud, *What Professional Responsibility Scholars Should Know About Insurance*, 4 CONN. INS. L. J. 17, 23–24 (1997) (recognizing "[b]oth insurance companies and insureds have important and meaningful stakes in the outcome [of] a lawsuit against the insureds, stakes that include not just the money that the insurance company must pay in defense and settlement, but also the uninsured liabilities of the insured, which include not just any judgment in excess of liability limits, but also the insured's reputation and other non-economic stakes. The history of liability insurance suggests that unbridled control of the defense of litigation by either the insurance company or the insured creates incentives for the party exercising that control to take advantage of the other"). *Compare also Restatement (Third) of the Law Governing Lawyers* § 215, Comment f(5) (Proposed Final Draft No. 2, 1998) . . . (recognizing "[m]aterial divergence[s] of interest might exist between a liability insurer and an insured. . . . Such occasions for conflict may exist at the outset of the representation or may be created by events that occur thereafter"). In cases where an insured's exposure exceeds his insurance coverage, where the insurer provides a defense subject to a reservation of rights, and where an insurer's obligation to indemnify its insured may be excused because of a policy defense, there are potential conflicts of interest.

We reject Respondents' implicit premise that the Rules of Professional Conduct need not apply when the interests of insurers and insureds coincide. The Rules of Professional Conduct have application in all cases involving attorneys and clients. Moreover, whether the interests of insurers and insureds coincide can best be determined with the perfect clarity of hindsight. Before the final resolution of any claim against an insured, there clearly exists the potential for conflicts of interest to arise. Further, we reject the suggestion that the contractual relationship between insurer and insured supersedes or waives defense counsels' obligations under the Rules of Professional Conduct. We decline to recognize a vast exception to the Rules of Professional Conduct that would sanction relationships colored with the appearance of impropriety in order to accommodate the asserted economic exigencies of the insurance market. . . . We hold that under the Rules of Professional Conduct, the insured is the sole client of defense counsel.

We caution, however, that this holding should not be construed to mean that defense counsel have a "blank check" to escalate litigation costs nor that defense counsel need not ever consult with insurers. Under Rule 1.5, M. R. Prof. Conduct, for example, an attorney must charge reasonable fees. *See* Rule 1.5, M. R. Prof. Conduct (providing in part that "[a] lawyer's fees shall be reasonable"). Nor, finally, should our holding be taken to signal that defense counsel cannot be held accountable for their work.

Respondents argue further, however, that even if an insurer is not a co-client of defense counsel, an insurer's control of litigation is necessary and appropriate. Respondents argue that the insurer must control the litigation in order to meet its duties to the insured to indemnify and to provide a defense. Further, Respondents argue that the insured has a good faith duty to cooperate with the insurer in defense of a claim that warrants an insurer's control of litigation, and that in any event insureds agree to insurers' control of litigation. Respondents also argue that insureds typically contract for a limited defense that does not protect their reputational interests and that they are not entitled to unlimited expenditures on their behalf. Further, Respondents assert that insurers and insureds have "aligned" interests in minimizing litigation costs and settlements.

None of these arguments is persuasive. Animating them is the deeply flawed premise that by contract insurers and insureds may dispense with the Rules of Professional Conduct. . . .

We conclude that whether the requirement of prior approval seldom results in denials of authorization for defense counsel to perform legal services begs the question whether the requirement of prior approval violates the Rules of Professional Conduct. Without reaching the issue here, moreover, we caution further that a mere requirement of consultation may be indistinguishable, in its interference with a defense counsel's exercise of independent judgment and ability to provide competent representation, from a requirement of prior approval. Further, the entitlement of insurers not to pay for overpriced or unnecessary services, which Petitioners do not dispute, also begs the question whether the requirement of prior approval violates the Rules of Professional Conduct.

Finally, Respondents argue that their billing and practice rules do not interfere with defense counsels' freedom of action. As previously discussed, they suggest that when an insurer denies approval for particular actions that defense counsel propose, nothing prevents defense counsel from exercising their independent judgment and doing the very thing for which the insurer has denied approval. We reject Respondents' underlying dubious premise that the threat of withholding payment does not interfere with the independent judgment of defense counsel. The very action taken by Petitioners in seeking declaratory relief in the present case is a blunt repudiation of that speculative premise. Further, if the threat of withholding payment were quite as toothless as Respondents suggest, we doubt that they would make such a threat, let alone that they would expressly incorporate it in their billing and practice rules.

C. Whether the requirement of prior approval violates the Rules of Professional Conduct.

Having concluded that the insured is the sole client of defense counsel, we turn to the fundamental issue whether the requirement of prior approval in billing and practice rules conflicts with defense counsels' duties under the Rules of Professional Conduct. The parties appear to agree that defense counsel may not abide by agreements limiting the scope of representation that interfere with their duties under the Rules of Professional Conduct. *Compare Annotated Model Rules of Professional Conduct* (Fourth ed. Center for Professional Responsibility American Bar Association) Rule 1.2, p. 12, Comment [4] (concluding "[t]he objectives or scope of services provided by a lawyer may be limited by agreement with the client or by the terms under which the lawyer's services are made available to the client. . . . [5] An agreement concerning the scope of representation must accord with the Rules of Professional Conduct and other law. Thus, the client may not be asked to agree to representation so limited in scope as to violate Rule 1.1").

We conclude that the requirement of prior approval fundamentally interferes with defense counsels' exercise of their independent judgment, as required by Rule 1.8(f), M. R. Prof. Conduct. Further, prior approval creates a substantial appearance of impropriety in its suggestion that it is insurers rather than defense counsel who control the day to day details of a defense.

Montana is not alone in rejecting arrangements that fetter lawyers' undivided duty of loyalty to their clients and their independence of professional judgment in representing their clients. In *Petition of Youngblood* (Tenn. 1995), 895 S.W.2d 322, the court determined that for inhouse attorney employees of an insurance company to represent insureds was not a per se ethical violation. However, the *Youngblood* court emphasized the loyalty that an attorney owes an insured and concluded that

> Some of the usual characteristics incident to [the employer-employee] relationship cannot exist between the insurer and the attorney representing an insured. The employer cannot control the details of the attorney's performance, dictate the strategy or tactics employed, or limit the attorney's professional discretion with regard to the representation. Any policy, arrangement or device which effectively limits, by design or operation, the attorney's professional judgment on behalf of or loyalty to the client is prohibited by the Code, and, undoubtedly, would not be consistent with public policy.

Youngblood, 895 S.W.2d at 328. The court went [on] to conclude that "[t]he same loyalty is owed the client whether the attorney is employed and paid by the client, is a salaried employee of the insurer, or is an independent contractor engaged by the insurer." *Youngblood*, 895 S.W.2d at 328....

We hold that defense counsel in Montana who submit to the requirement of prior approval violate their duties under the Rules of Professional Conduct to exercise their independent judgment and to give their undivided loyalty to insureds. Compare Rule 1.7(b) (providing "[a] lawyer shall not represent a client if the representation of that client may be materially limited by the lawyer's responsibility to another client or to a third person"); *Annotated Model Rules of Professional Conduct*, Comment [4] to Rule 1.7 (concluding "[t]he critical questions are the likelihood that a conflict will eventuate and, if it does, whether it will materially interfere with the lawyer's independent professional judgment in considering alternatives or foreclose courses of action that reasonably should be pursued on behalf of the client"); *State v. Jones* (1996), 278 Mont. 121, 125, 923 P.2d 560, 563 (concluding "[t]he duty of loyalty is 'perhaps the most basic of counsel's duties.' ")...

* * *

The Tripartite Relationship. Other courts have concluded that defense counsel in these situations represent both the insurer and the insured. *See, e.g., Nevada Yellow Cab Corp. v. Eighth Judicial Dist. Court*, 152 P.3d 737 (Nev. 2007).

Profile of Attorney Professionalism. While a student at Harvard Law School, Rehan Staton formed a strong community with the school's custodians, cafeteria workers, and security guards. As a former sanitation worker, Staton appreciated their hard work. He also knew that they could relate to his upbringing and experiences, including his perseverance through family financial hardships.

To show his appreciation to this community of workers, Staton used his own money to buy one hundred Amazon gift cards that he distributed with personal notes of thanks. Following the success of that effort, Staton co-founded a nonprofit organization, The Reciprocity Effect, to continue showing appreciation and thanks to the school's support staff. As of the spring of 2023, the organization had raised over $70,000. Sydney Page, *Former trash hauler enrolled at Harvard Law raises $70K for janitors, other workers there*, THE WASHINGTON POST (April 15, 2023).

Upon his graduation from Harvard Law School, Staton reflected upon his path, the difficulties he had faced, and the support of his family and community. In a post on LinkedIn, Staton said, "If I could talk to my younger self still living in poverty, I would tell him this: Regardless of what you lack, know that your resilience, hope, and the rich love and support you endlessly receive from your communities (no matter how big or small) will carry you through life's greatest challenges." Rehan Staton, Linkedin Post, available at https://www.linkedin.com/posts/rehan-staton-4204a9178_growing-up-we-often-didnt-have-heat-electricity-activity-7069674925468340224-uN3r?utm_source=share&utm_medium=member_desktop.

SECTION 6

CONTINUING DUTIES TO FORMER CLIENTS

■ ■ ■

Every client-lawyer relationship—both good and bad—will come to an end. Typically this occurs when the lawyer completes the representation. In other cases, the end may come because the client fires the lawyer or because the lawyer terminates the relationship. But the end of the attorney-client relationship does not mean that the lawyer is free from duties to a former client. Chapter 18 introduces some of the issues that can arise when the attorney-client relationship ends. Then, Chapter 19 addresses conflicts of interest that may arise between the interest of a current client and a former client.

CHAPTER 18

TERMINATION OF THE CLIENT-LAWYER RELATIONSHIP

■ ■ ■

Chapter Hypothetical. Lawyer Maria has a successful solo practice. But recently she has had disagreements with some of her clients. She fears that some of these relationships may be on the verge of ending.

The ending of a relationship is often messy. There may be disagreements as to who was to blame for the breakup and who owes what to whom once the relationship ends. The termination of the client-lawyer relationship raises its own set of potential issues. This chapter explores some of the issues associated with the termination of the client-lawyer relationship.

A. TERMINATION BY THE CLIENT

Model Rule 1.16(a)(3) lists one obvious way that an attorney-client relationship may terminate: when the client discharges the lawyer. It is well-established that a client has the absolute right to discharge a lawyer. Therefore, there is no breach of an attorney-client fee agreement when the client discharges the lawyer, regardless of whether the client had good cause to fire the lawyer. But at least in the case where a lawyer represents a client on a contingency fee basis, there may still be a question as to whether a lawyer can recover any fee after being discharged.

* * *

HUGHES AND COLEMAN, PLLC V. CHAMBERS
526 S.W.3d 70 (Ky. 2017)

Opinion of the Court by JUSTICE WRIGHT.

Personal-injury law firm Hughes & Coleman was hired by Travis Underwood after he was injured in a car crash. [Their agreement provided that the firm would be paid on a contingency-fee basis.] Underwood eventually became dissatisfied with the firm and fired them. [Underwood believed, incorrectly, that he was entitled to receive Personal Injury Protection (PIP)—or no-fault—payments from the escrow account that had been provided by his insurer. He fired the firm as a result of the firm's failure to disburse the funds.] Shortly after discharging Hughes & Coleman and hiring another attorney, Underwood agreed to a final settlement of his claims. This appeal asks whether Hughes & Coleman is entitled to be compensated for their services rendered before being fired. Our precedent entitles a discharged lawyer to receive, on a *quantum meruit* basis, a portion of a contingency fee on a former client's recovery—so long as the termination was not "for cause." Because Hughes & Coleman's firing was not for cause under this rule, the firm is entitled to *quantum meruit* compensation.

. . .

II. Analysis

With *Baker v. Shapero*, 203 S.W.3d 697 (Ky. 2006), this Court brought Kentucky in line with most other jurisdictions' treatment of a discharged attorney's entitlement to compensation on a former contingency-fee client's recovery. Before that, a Kentucky attorney whose client discharged her without cause was entitled to the agreed-upon contingency fee on her former client's final recovery (less the "reasonable cost" of the replacement attorney's services), despite having not completed the contracted-for work. *See LaBach v. Hampton*, 585 S.W.2d 434, 436 (Ky. App. 1979). This, the Court noted, was an "extreme minority position." So the Court overturned *LaBach* and held, instead, that "when an attorney employed under a contingency-fee contract is discharged without cause before completion of the contract, he or she is entitled to fee recovery on a *quantum meruit* basis only, and not on the terms of the contract." *Id.*

The term *quantum meruit*—literally meaning "as much as he has deserved"—refers generally to the "reasonable value of services." BLACK'S LAW DICTIONARY (10th ed. 2014). It is an equitable remedy entitling a person who has rendered services to recover payment for the reasonable value of those services. Its focus, then, is on the value of the benefit conferred to the other person—in the attorney-fee setting, *quantum meruit* recovery seeks to compensate the discharged attorney for the value of the services rendered before being fired. But the doctrine's equity roots limit its reach.

Baker v. Shapero's *quantum meruit* fee-recovery rule applies only when an attorney is discharged "without cause"—the negative implication being that an attorney forfeits any claim to a fee when validly discharged "for cause." But when exactly does a discharge amount to being "for cause"? That is an important question because, whatever it means, the *Baker v. Shapero* rule directs that an attorney who is discharged for cause recovers no fee at all—the lawyer, by doing whatever reprehensible thing or things that precipitated the for-cause firing, has lost her right to be compensated for the beneficial services she provided the client.

Since *Baker v. Shapero*, we have twice had occasion to address the related scenario of lawyers voluntarily withdrawing as counsel. Whether a withdrawn lawyer may recover a *quantum meruit* fee on his or her former client's ultimate recovery turns on whether the lawyer's reason for withdrawing constituted "good (or just) cause." *Lofton v. Fairmont Specialty Ins. Mgrs.*, 367 S.W.3d 593, 597–98 (Ky. 2012); *see also B. Dahlenburg Bonar, P.S.C. v. Waite, Schneider, Bayless & Chesley Co.*, 373 S.W.3d 419, 423 (Ky. 2012). In *Lofton*, we held that disagreeing with a client about the case's settlement value is not sufficient cause to allow a lawyer to withdraw and still receive a *quantum meruit* fee—because that simple conflict does not merit terminating the entire lawyer-client relationship, the lawyer's withdrawal forfeited the fee. Likewise, only two months later in *B. Dahlenburg Bonar*, we held that a lawyer forfeited her entitlement to a *quantum meruit* fee when she withdrew as co-counsel in a class action over worries that her clients' position jeopardized her relationships with other clients and colleagues.

Although those cases provide some guidance, they do not exactly provide the answer. Ending a lawyer-client relationship cancels the employment contract under which the client promised to pay the lawyer for his or her services. In this respect, situations where the lawyer ends the representation are different from those where the client does so.

When the lawyer withdraws, the ethical and contractual duties and obligations owed to the client are paramount to the analysis. Broadly speaking, attorneys must, among other things, competently represent and zealously advocate their clients' best interests. This Court rightly held in *Lofton* and *B. Dahlenburg Bonar*, respectively, that neither simple disagreements with clients over claim values, nor latent fears that the representation will somehow jeopardize the lawyer's relationships with third-parties, justify lawyers' casting aside their clients and the duties otherwise owed to them. Absent sufficient justification in the ilk of an irretrievable breakdown of the lawyer-client relationship, a lawyer who voluntarily withdraws from the representation will not be permitted to later insist on receiving a fee on the former client's ultimate recovery. Those prior cases rest largely on whether a lawyer's withdrawing was at odds with her ethical or contractual obligations to the client. It does not exactly translate to situations, as here, where it is the client who exercises his absolute prerogative to terminate the attorney-client relationship.

Where the client discharges the lawyer, different considerations are in play. As Maryland's highest court has explained, the *quantum meruit* rule seeks to "strike a balance between the client's absolute right to discharge his or her attorney and the attorney's right to fair compensation for services competently rendered prior to discharge." *First Union Nat'l Bank v. Meyer, Faller, Weisman & Rosenberg, P.C.*, 125 Md. App. 1, 723 A.2d 899, 910 (1999). Striking that balance requires recognizing a client's "basis" for discharging her attorney as distinct from "cause" justifying forfeiture of the attorney's compensation. *Somuah v. Flachs*, 352 Md. 241, 721 A.2d 680, 691 (1998).

A client may have a good-faith reason for being unhappy with her current lawyer that is not based on any sort of wrongful conduct by the lawyer. Although the client may feel that she had a good reason to discharge her attorney and hire a new one, that alone does not justify forfeiture of the discharged attorney's right to be paid for the services she provided before being fired. Consider *Lofton*'s facts, but flipped: lawyer and client disagree about settlement value, but instead of the lawyer withdrawing over the disagreement as in Lofton, the client fires the lawyer. Just as this simple disagreement is not sufficient cause for a withdrawing lawyer to later insist on being paid, it is not sufficient cause for a discharged lawyer to be barred from being fairly compensated for services rendered.

Instead, to justify fee forfeiture, the "cause" of the discharge must involve some sort of wrongful conduct by the attorney, resulting in an irreconcilable breakdown in the attorney-client relationship. It appears that most other jurisdictions also limit fee forfeitures by discharged attorneys in this way. *See, e.g., Somuah*, 721 A.2d at 688; *see also* 56 A.L.R. 5th 1, § 2[b] (orig. pub'd 1998) ("Generally, however, a complete forfeiture of attorney's fees will be warranted only when the attorney's 'clear' violation of a duty is found to have so destroyed the attorney-client relationship that the attorney is considered to no longer have a right to compensation for services rendered prior to the point of his or her discharge."). Thus, we now hold that an attorney's discharge should be deemed "for cause"—so as to bar the fired attorney from recovering a fee in *quantum meruit*—only where the reason for the discharge is some sort of culpable conduct by the attorney.

Applying that rule here, we surmise no cause justifying forfeiture of Hughes & Coleman's *quantum meruit* fee. While Underwood may have felt that he had good reason to be dissatisfied with his lawyers, the trial court was correct to rule that this dissatisfaction was not a sufficient cause to bar those lawyers from being paid for the work that they performed.

. . .

Perhaps Hughes & Coleman could have better explained [the PIP issue] to Underwood. Hindsight being what it is, it is tempting to criticize them for not being crystal clear about how PIP benefits work and what the firm's role would be exactly in helping to disburse them. Yet the trial court found that Hughes & Coleman's communications with Underwood were reasonable and adequate, emphasizing the fairly robust lines of communication with the Underwoods seen in the case-management records ... Given the voluminous records Hughes & Coleman kept documenting their correspondence with Underwood, that finding was supported by substantial evidence.

* * *

Good Cause Required? Some jurisdictions take the position that an attorney is entitled to a quantum meruit recovery for the reasonable value of the services rendered to the time of discharge regardless of whether the client had good cause to fire the attorney. *See Campbell v. Bozeman Investors of Duluth*, 964 P.2d 41 (Mont. 1998).

Reasonable Value of Services vs. Contract Price. The majority of courts hold that a lawyer fired without cause is entitled to recover the reasonable value of the services provided or the contingent fee amount, *whichever is less*. David Hricik, *Dear Lawyer: If You Decide It's Not Economical to Represent Me, You Can Fire Me as Your Contingent Fee Client, But I Agree I Will Still Owe You a Fee*, 64 MERCER L. REV. 363, 367 (2013). Section 40 of the *Restatement (Third) of the Law Governing Lawyers* takes the same position.

Problem 18.1. Client Angela had some questions about the fee agreement that she signed with Lawyer Maria. Angela sent several emails and left a couple of voicemail messages inquiring about the matter, none of which were returned by Maria. Angered by Maria's failure to communicate, Angela fired Maria and hired a new lawyer to pursue her lawsuit.

(a) Assume for purposes of this question that Angela lacked good cause to discharge Maria. Would Maria be entitled to recover on a *quantum meruit* basis if Angela hired a new lawyer and ended up recovering nothing from her lawsuit?

(b) Assume for purposes of this question that Angela ended up recovering $100,000 from her lawsuit after hiring a new lawyer. Did Angela have good cause to discharge Maria under the approach from *Hughes & Coleman*? What would the effect of your conclusion be on the ability of Maria to recover on a *quantum meruit* basis?

* * *

B. TERMINATION BY THE LAWYER

A lawyer who, without good cause, withdraws from the representation of a client prior to resolution of the matter forfeits the right to compensation under a contingency-fee contract. *See Augustson v. Linea Aerea Nacional-Chile S.A.*, 76 F.3d 658, 662 (5th Cir. 1996). Rule 1.16 describes a lawyer's professional responsibilities with respect to termination of the lawyer-client relationship.

1. MANDATORY WITHDRAWAL

Model Rule 1.16(a) was amended in 2023 to explicitly state that a lawyer has an obligation to "inquire into and assess the facts and circumstances of each representation" to determine whether the lawyer is required to withdraw (or not accept the representation). Rule 1.16(a) then lists four bases for mandatory withdrawal/declination of the representation. The first three were contained in the rule prior to the 2023 amendments:

(1) When the representation will result in violation of the rules of professional conduct or other law. An obvious example would be when the lawyer has a conflict of interest.

(2) When the lawyer's physical or mental condition materially impairs the lawyer's ability to represent the client. Note that a lawyer's physical or mental condition must *materially* impair the lawyer's ability to represent the client before withdrawal is mandatory under the second category.

(3) When the lawyer is discharged. The *Hughes & Coleman* case from above provides an example of this situation.

In 2023, a fourth enumerated basis for mandatory withdrawal was added to Model Rule 1.16(a):

(4) When the client seeks to use or persists in using the lawyer's services to commit or further a crime, despite the lawyer informing the client—pursuant to Rules 1.2(d) and 1.4(a)(5)—of the lawyer's inability to do so.

Taken together, the new introductory language (about investigating the facts) and the new subsection four are intended to remind lawyers of their obligations when representing a client that may be using the lawyer's services to commit a crime or fraud. A lawyer must investigate and ask questions to learn the nature of the client's conduct—there is no benefit to avoiding that information. It is in the client's and lawyer's interests for the lawyer to determine if the conduct is criminal or fraudulent so that the lawyer can advise against it and avoid participating in it.

In contrast, Rule 1.6(b)(2), which permits but does not require withdrawal, states that the lawyer "may" withdraw if the lawyer "reasonably believes" the client is using the lawyer's services to further criminal or fraudulent conduct. This subpart is not meant to encourage lawyers to avoid knowledge in order to participate in a possible crime or fraud. It instead permits a lawyer to withdraw even if the lawyer has not determined the conduct is criminal or fraudulent (but reasonably believes it is) and even if withdrawal will have material adverse effects on the interest of the client (which is required to withdraw under Rule 1.6(b)(1)).

Other bases for permissive withdrawal under Rule 1.6(b) are discussed in the following section.

* * *

2. PERMISSIVE WITHDRAWAL

Model Rule 1.6(b) lists seven situations in which a lawyer may, consistent with the lawyer's professional responsibilities, withdraw from the representation of a client—the first two were discussed in the last section. The decision below was decided prior to the adoption of the *Model Rules*. But consider which of the grounds listed in Rule 1.16(b) would be implicated today. The second decision considers two additional grounds for permissive withdrawal.

KRIEGSMAN V. KRIEGSMAN
150 N.J. Super. 474, 375 A.2d 1253 (App. Div. 1977)

MICHELS, J. A. D.

Appellants Messrs. Rose, Poley, Bromley and Landers (hereinafter "the Rose firm") appeal from an order of the Chancery Division denying their application to be relieved as attorneys for plaintiff Mary-Ann Kriegsman in this matrimonial action.

On December 22, 1975, plaintiff, who had been previously represented by other counsel, retained the Rose firm to represent her in a divorce action against her husband, defendant Bernard Kriegsman. The Rose firm requested and received consent to substitution of attorneys from plaintiff's former attorney. Plaintiff then paid an initial retainer of $1,000, plus $60 in court costs, with the understanding that she would be responsible for additional fees and expenses as litigation progressed. In March 1976, plaintiff paid the Rose firm another $1,000, plus $44 which was to be applied against costs.

During the 3½ months that the Rose firm represented plaintiff prior to its motion, the firm had made numerous court appearances and had engaged in extensive office work in plaintiff's behalf. The unusual amount of work required was necessitated in part by the fact that defendant appeared pro se, was completely uncooperative and had refused to comply with some of the orders entered by the court. As of April 5, 1976, the Rose firm alleged that it had spent 110 hours on plaintiff's case, billed at $7,354.50, and had incurred disbursements of approximately $242. Since, by then, plaintiff was on welfare and since she apparently did not have sufficient funds to pay the additional fees incurred, the Rose firm contended that they were entitled to be relieved from further representation. Plaintiff opposed the application before the court, pointing out:

> ... first of all, this case, I think, has accumulated a file this thick. I think at this point, for another attorney to step in, it would be very difficult to acquaint himself with every motion that has been brought up before this court. I feel that Mr. Koserowski (an associate in the Rose firm) has been with me, representing me, for four months, and when this case finally does go to trial, hopefully soon, he has all this knowledge at his fingertips. Whereas another attorney would have to, I don't know how they can, wade through all of this, and really become acquainted with it. That's the first thing. Secondly, when I first went to this law firm, I spoke to Mr. Rose, and he knew exactly my circumstances. He knew that there were very few assets in the marriage. He knew that I would have to borrow money from relatives to pay the thousand dollar retainer fee that they asked for. They knew that my husband was going to represent himself, which would be a difficult situation. They also knew that he had done certain bizarre things, such as sending letters to people, and doing strange things; so, therefore, we might expect a difficult case from him. Yet, they consented to take my case. Of course, I don't think any attorney can guess, when he consents to represent somebody, what might occur. I imagine some cases go to trial immediately things get resolved, and my case is probably the other extreme, where everything possible has happened. I think it's unfortunate, and I think they've done a very fine job of representing me. I feel they should continue.

Judge Cariddi in the Chancery Division agreed with plaintiff and denied the application of the Rose firm, but set the case down for trial within the month. The Rose firm appealed. . . .

When a firm accepts a retainer to conduct a legal proceeding, it impliedly agrees to prosecute the matter to a conclusion. The firm is not at liberty to abandon the case without justifiable or reasonable cause, or the consent of its client. We are firmly convinced that the Rose firm did not have cause to abandon plaintiff's case, and that the trial judge properly exercised his discretion when he denied the firm's application and scheduled an early trial date. It was to plaintiff's and the firm's advantage that the matter be heard and disposed of as expeditiously as possible. With trial imminent, it would be extremely difficult for plaintiff to obtain other representation, and therefore she clearly would be prejudiced by the Rose firm's withdrawal.

Since the Rose firm undertook to represent plaintiff and demanded and was paid a retainer of $2,000, they should continue to represent plaintiff through the completion of trial. The firm should not be relieved at this stage of the litigation merely because plaintiff is unable to pay to them all of the fees they have demanded. We are not unmindful of the fact that the Rose firm has performed substantial legal services for plaintiff and clearly is entitled to reasonable compensation therefor. Nevertheless, an attorney has certain obligations and duties to a client once representation is undertaken. These obligations do not evaporate because the case becomes more complicated or the work more arduous or the retainer not as profitable as first contemplated or imagined. Attorneys must never lose sight of the fact that "the profession is a branch of the administration of justice and not a mere money-getting trade." *Canons of Professional Ethics*, No. 12. As Canon 44 of the *Canons of Professional Ethics* so appropriately states: "The lawyer should not throw up the unfinished task to the detriment of his client except for reasons of honor or self-respect." Adherence to these strictures in no way violates the constitutional rights of the members of the firm.

Affirmed.

* * *

CUADRA V. UNIVISION COMMUNICATIONS, INC.
2012 WL 1150833 (D.N.J April 4, 2012)

[The client, Iris Cuadra, hired the firm Mark & Galusha to represent her in an employment discrimination suit alleging sexual harassment, among other claims. Cuadra also wished to pursue a second discrimination claim involving unlawful termination against the same employer but wanted to hire a different lawyer to represent her in this other matter. Over the course of several months, the attorney-client relationship devolved to the point that the firm sought leave to withdraw pursuant to Rule 1.16(b)(4) and (b)(7).]

Under Local Civil Rule 102.1, "[u]nless other counsel is substituted, no attorney may withdraw an appearance except by leave of Court." Also, under Local Civil Rule 103. 1, the New Jersey Rules of Professional Conduct (RPC) govern the conduct of attorneys before the District of New Jersey. The Court generally looks to New Jersey state court for interpretation of the RPCs and modifies as necessary by federal law.

Whether or not to grant withdrawal is within the discretion of a court. Consistent with RPC 1.16, the Court considers four criteria:

(1) the reasons why withdrawal is sought,

(2) the prejudice withdrawal may cause to litigants,

(3) the harm withdrawal might cause to the administration of justice and

(4) the degree to which withdrawal will delay resolution of the case.

. . .

Ms. Cuadra's counsel cites to an older version of subsection (b)(4), formerly (b)(3), that used to permit withdrawal if "(3) a client insists upon pursuing an objective that the lawyer considers repugnant **or imprudent**." RPC 1.16(b)(3) (2003) (emphasis added). Now, however, the rule states that withdrawal is permissive if "(4) the client insists upon taking action that the lawyer considers repugnant **or with which the lawyer has a fundamental disagreement**." RPC 1.16(b)(4) (emphasis added). The Pollock Commission, which recommended the adopted change to this rule, explained that:

> The rationale for the change is that allowing a lawyer to withdraw when the lawyer believes that the client's objectives or intended action is "imprudent" permits the lawyer to prevail in almost any dispute with a client by threatening to withdraw. That practice detracts from the client's ability to direct the course of the representation. Nevertheless, a lawyer should be permitted to withdraw when the disagreement over objectives or means is so fundamental that the disagreement threats the lawyer's autonomy. . . .

Under RPC 1.16(b)(4), the Court is unpersuaded that Ms. Cuadra is pursuing an objective that is either repugnant or the subject of a fundamental disagreement. Ms. Cuadra's counsel argues that "it would not be prudent" for his firm to continue representation given Ms. Cuadra's demeanor to counsel, her disagreement with his legal advice, and her decision to seek other counsel to pursue her second [discrimination] complaint. (Withdrawal Br. at 11; Mark Non-Privileged Decl. ¶¶ 2, 7–8.). As noted above, however, imprudence is no longer the standard. Moreover, this case illustrates the rationale that, if imprudence were the standard, an attorney could "prevail in almost any dispute with a client by threatening to withdraw" and thereby "detract[ ] from the client's ability to direct the course of the representation." Pollock Commission Cmt. to RPC 1.16. Ms. Cuadra made it clear at the hearing for this motion that it is very important to her to have her day in court, but that she did not want to pursue claims from her second [discrimination] complaint in this case. The record demonstrates that she raised this issue with her counsel at least as far back as March 2011. Her counsel disagrees with this course of action. But as RPC 1.2 makes clear, the client controls the scope and objectives of representation.

Although plaintiff's counsel does not appear to argue that plaintiff seeks a "repugnant" objective or course of action, the Court considers it for the sake of completeness. As noted above, the record before the Court demonstrates that Ms. Cuadra and her counsel have a dispute over the original scope of representation, but it does not conclusively demonstrate that she asked counsel to engage in an offensive course of action, nor does it demonstrate that she will be able to force counsel to violate an RPC in the future. And, obviously, there is nothing repugnant about Ms. Cuadra wanting to have her day in court, nor her exercise of her discretion to limit the scope of representation.

For related reasons, the Court does not find that there is a "fundamental disagreement" over the objectives or means such [that] it threatens counsel's autonomy. As discussed above, Ms. Cuadra's objective is to have her day in Court on her remaining claims, she has exercised her control over the scope of her claims, and she cannot force counsel to break his ethical code. Accordingly, the Court finds that, even though counsel may disagree with certain of Ms. Cuadra's decisions, counsel's autonomy perseveres.

Under RPC 1.16(b)(7), the Court is also unpersuaded that other good cause for withdrawal exists. Counsel argues that Ms. Cuadra treats him so poorly that "there is no reason why [he] should be forced to continue representing [her]. . . ." Counsel argues that she is disrespectful and no longer has confidence in his ability as a lawyer. Notably, counsel provides no case law to support his assertion that these reasons demonstrate good cause. Moreover, the Court has reviewed Ms. Cuadra's statements, and cannot find that they present good cause. Certainly, the statements presented to the Court do not demonstrate an ideal working relationship and some of them clearly signal Ms. Cuadra's periodic discontent with her counsel. But they are neither verbally abusive nor physically threatening. And as Ms. Cuadra made clear at the hearing for this motion, as she did during the December 13, 2011, hearing, she does not wish to terminate counsel from this case. This Court's observation in *Rusinow*, is instructive: "[a] sudden disenchantment with a client or a cause is no basis for withdrawal. Those who cannot live with risk, doubt and ingratitude should not be trial lawyers. A lawyer's duty to his or her client cannot be sacrificed to ambivalence." *Rusinow v. Kamara*, 920 F. Supp. 69, 72 (D.N.J. 1996). In short, RPC 1.16(b)(7) requires more than difficult client interactions before counsel may be relieved of his obligation to see a case through to resolution.

. . .

Even if counsel had provided good cause to withdraw, the other factors weigh against granting this motion. The prejudice that withdrawal would cause to the parties, the harm to the administration of justice, and delay of resolution of this case all demonstrate that the Court should exercise its discretion under RPC 1.16(c) to order Ms. Cuadra's counsel to continue representing her.

. . .

Relatedly, if the motion were granted, the Court does not find that Ms. Cuadra would be able to effectively proceed pro se, at least without further lengthy delay. This litigation has been ongoing for well over two years, involves an extensive factual and procedural history, and required substantial discovery. To require plaintiff, who has been relying on her counsel throughout that entire time, to stand in the shoes of her counsel at this very late date would, at a minimum, produce unmanageable delays and burden for the parties and the Court.

Similarly, the prospect of Ms. Cuadra obtaining new counsel at this time is remote at best. Her present counsel suggests that thirty days might be long enough for her to find replacement counsel, but the Court thinks that prediction rather unlikely. In the twelve months since Ms. Cuadra informed her counsel that he was not representing her on the termination claims, including the nearly three months since plaintiff's counsel first moved to withdraw, she has not found substitute counsel.

Even if plaintiff could find new counsel, the delay would be much longer, as new counsel would have to familiarize himself or herself with a factual and procedural background spanning nearly seven years. Moreover, this case has been litigated since 2009, and the current counsel is uniquely aware of the facts, documents, and legal issues of Ms. Cuadra's case. Thus, if the motion were granted, not only would Ms. Cuadra's objective to have her day in court be substantively thwarted, but the defendants would lose their right to have this matter resolved in a timely manner. . . .

Accordingly, even if withdrawal were appropriate, "other considerations must sometimes take precedence, such as maintaining fairness to litigants and preserving a court's resources and efficiency." *Haines v. Liggett Group*, Inc., 814 F. Supp. 414, 423 (D.N.J.1993). Thus, the Court also exercises its discretion under RPC 1.16(c) to order Ms. Cuadra's counsel to continue representing her notwithstanding any good cause he may have demonstrated.

* * *

Problem 18.2. Maria represents David, the plaintiff in a civil rights action. The court granted partial summary judgment in favor of the defendant on one of David's claims. Trial on the other claims is approaching. David has told Maria that, despite the court's ruling, he wants Maria to call witnesses in an effort to advance the legal theory that the court rejected on summary judgment. David explains that he wants to draw attention to the defendant's wrongful actions, even if he cannot prevail on this theory. Maria informs David that the testimony of these witnesses would be considered irrelevant since the court had already granted summary judgment on the issue to which they would testify. David tells Maria that if she does not call these witnesses and ask the questions he wants her to ask, he will sue her for legal malpractice. Maria is not sure she wants to continue to represent David in light of this. Does Maria have grounds to withdraw?

Problem 18.3. Maria represents Carlton. As part of the representation, Maria prepared a motion on Carlton's behalf. Carlton was displeased with the motion and has since told Maria that while he wants her to remain attorney of record, he will draft all future documents, including those to be filed with the court. Maria will simply sign any documents that need to be filed. As one might suppose, Maria is not pleased with Carlton's suggestion but has been unable to persuade Carlton to reconsider. Does Maria have grounds to withdraw?

Problem 18.4. Maria has been having difficulty with another client, Edith. Edith regularly changes her mind about what an acceptable settlement of her claim should be and whether she wants to take her case to trial, all of which Maria finds frustrating. Maria is also frustrated at Edith's delay in providing information that Maria needs to represent Edith and the fact that Edith sometimes comes by Maria's office without an appointment. For her part, Edith believes that Maria has been rude to her and says that she only comes by the office when Maria is late responding to her emails, text messages, or phone calls. (Maria disputes this.) Maria thinks that she and Edith have irreconcilable differences at this point. Does Maria have grounds to withdraw?

Unreasonable Financial Burden. At what point does the financial burden that a lawyer assumes become "unreasonable" for purposes of Rule 1.16(b)? What factors should be relevant in the determination? *See In re Franke*, 55 A.3d 713, 721 (Md. Ct. Spec. App. 2012) (granting motion to withdraw where solo practitioner was owed $120,000 and payment by client was uncertain).

The Duty of Confidentiality and Withdrawal from Representation. A lawyer's duty of confidentiality applies even when seeking permission from a court to withdraw. Therefore, a lawyer may only disclose such information as is reasonably necessary to permit the court to decide whether to permit withdrawal. *See State v. Jones*, 923 P.2d 560 (Mont. 1996) (finding lawyer violated Rule 1.6 when disclosing confidential communications to court).

Good Cause as a Prerequisite to Compensation. A lawyer in a contingent fee agreement must have good cause to withdraw before being entitled to any compensation for work performed. *See, e.g., Bell & Marra, PLLC v. Sullivan*, 6 P.3d 965, 970 (Mont. 2000); *see also* David Hricik, *Dear Lawyer: If You Decide It's Not Economical to Represent Me, You Can Fire Me as Your Contingent Fee Client, But I Agree I Will Still Owe You a Fee*, 64 MERCER L. REV. 363 (2013) ("As a matter of public policy, courts have generally held that a lawyer who is discharged with 'good cause' will receive only *quantum meruit* for work done, and an attorney who withdraws without 'just cause' will forfeit all right to compensation.").

Hybrid Fee Agreements and Termination. In an attempt to protect themselves from client decisions that adversely affect their right to compensation, some lawyers modify their contingent fee agreements to give themselves greater protection. "Generally, the provisions (a) either restrict the client's ability to terminate the lawyer, or expand the lawyer's right to withdraw from representing the client; (b) increase the compensation due if the client terminates the lawyer or the lawyer withdraws; or (c) a combination of those two approaches." David Hricik, *Dear Lawyer: If You Decide It's Not Economical to Represent Me, You Can Fire Me as Your Contingent Fee Client, But I Agree I Will Still Owe You a Fee*, 64 MERCER L. REV. 363, 364–65 (2013). In light of a client's absolute rights to terminate a relationship and to make certain decisions concerning the representation under Rule 1.2 (*e.g.*, whether to settle), should a lawyer be subject to discipline for including such a provision in a fee agreement? Several judicial decisions and ethics opinions have held that these types of agreements violate the rules of professional conduct and are unenforceable. *See* New York County Lawyers' Association Committee on Professional Ethics, Formal Opinion Number 736 (2006); *see also Compton v. Kittleson*, 171 P.3d 172, 174, 180 (Alaska 2007). *But see Gilbert v. Evan*, 822 So. 2d 42, 46 (La. Ct. App. 2002) (upholding agreement).

* * *

C. PROTECTING A CLIENT'S INTERESTS AND RESOLVING FEE DISPUTES UPON TERMINATION OF THE RELATIONSHIP

Sometimes the termination of a client-lawyer relationship results in animosity. Sometimes it results in confusion as to how much, if anything, the client owes the lawyer for the lawyer's services. The following section examines a lawyer's obligations as a fiduciary to protect a client's interests upon termination of the relationship and the steps lawyers may take to resolve their fee disputes.

* * *

1. PROTECTING A CLIENT'S INTERESTS UPON TERMINATION

Model Rule 1.16(d) requires that a lawyer take steps "to the extent reasonably practicable to protect a client's interests" upon termination of representation. The following case provides an example of the types of steps that may be required.

BOARD OF PROFESSIONAL RESPONSIBILITY V. PREWITT
647 S.W.3d 357 (Tenn. 2022)

[Beginning in 2012, lawyer Candes Vonniest Prewitt was involved in an "on-and-off romantic relationship" Demetrius Tucker that lasted for several years. In July 2015, Prewitt filed a complaint on behalf of Tucker and another individual, Harris, against their former employer involving a shooting at the nightclub where the two worked. In April 2018, the trial court granted the defendant's motion to exclude two of Tucker's expert witnesses.]

In late April 2018, the defendants moved for summary judgment, arguing that they did not owe a duty of care to the plaintiffs because the shooting was not foreseeable. Ms. Prewitt told neither Mr. Tucker nor Mr. Harris that summary judgment motions had been filed, and she did not prepare any response to the motions. Instead, in May 2018, she moved to withdraw from the case and postpone the summary judgment hearing. . . . As grounds for her motion to withdraw, Ms. Prewitt stated that "the communication between counsel and [the p]laintiffs ha[d] broken down." . . . Ms. Prewitt represented to the circuit court that her clients' interests would not be materially adversely affected by her withdrawal. Ms. Prewitt did not include her clients on the certificate of service for the motion to withdraw and did not send them copies of the motion. Ms. Prewitt claimed she told them both by telephone that she intended to withdraw from the case. On July 3, 2018, the circuit court entered an order allowing Ms. Prewitt to withdraw. The circuit court gave Mr. Tucker and Mr. Harris thirty days to obtain new counsel and continued the summary judgment hearing to August 10, 2018.

After Ms. Prewitt told Mr. Tucker she would no longer represent him, he consulted another attorney about taking over the case. The attorney asked Mr. Tucker to get him the case file and information about any lien Ms. Prewitt intended to assert for her work on the case. When Ms. Prewitt submitted a four-page document itemizing her work at $500 per hour, billed in quarter-hour increments and totaling $121,750, the attorney declined to represent Mr. Tucker. After some discussion with Mr. Tucker in an exchange of text messages, Ms. Prewitt agreed to release the lien in exchange for half of Mr. Tucker's recovery in the lawsuit. But when Ms. Prewitt turned over the case file to Mr. Tucker, she gave him an unconditional release of the lien. The attorney then agreed to take the case.

When Mr. Tucker's attorney reviewed the case file, he found that it was missing transcripts of the three depositions that had been taken, as well as a video recording of Mr. Tucker's shooting.[4] The attorney also

---

[4] Ms. Prewitt at first told the new attorney the file she turned over to Mr. Tucker contained everything she had pertaining to the case. Mr. Tucker had the name of the court reporter who had

learned that no depositions of medical or security experts had been taken, that the circuit court had excluded two expert witnesses, and that summary judgment motions were pending and set for hearing in less than thirty days. The attorney obtained a continuance of the hearing and filed a response to the summary judgment motions.

In October 2018, the circuit court heard the defendants' motions for summary judgment. In January 2019, the circuit court granted the motions for summary judgment. . . .

In January 2019, Mr. Tucker submitted a disciplinary complaint to the Board against Ms. Prewitt. . . .

Violation of Rule 1.16 (Declining or Terminating Representation)

The hearing panel determined that Ms. Prewitt violated Rule 1.16 when she withdrew from Mr. Tucker's case because her withdrawal could not be accomplished without a material adverse effect on the client's interest. This finding was based on Ms. Prewitt's delay in seeking to withdraw; the fact that summary judgment motions were pending and Ms. Prewitt did not inform future counsel about them; and her assertion of a substantial lien that could deter another lawyer from taking the case. The hearing panel also noted that Ms. Prewitt did not provide Mr. Tucker with a copy of the motion to withdraw, that she failed to inform him of the possible impact her withdrawal would have on the case, and that the timing of her withdrawal failed to give Mr. Tucker adequate time to hire other counsel.

Ms. Prewitt argues the hearing panel erred in concluding that her withdrawal from the case could not be accomplished without material adverse effect on the client, and thus was a violation of Rule 1.16. She points out that she withdrew for "good cause" which is allowed under Rule 1.16(b)(7). Even so, Rule 1.16 imposes additional requirements on a lawyer who withdraws from a case. The lawyer must, "to the extent reasonably practicable, take steps to protect the client's interests." Tenn. Sup. Ct. R. 8, RPC 1.16(d). This may include "(1) giving reasonable notice to the client; (2) allowing time for the employment of other counsel; (3) cooperating with any successor counsel engaged by the client; (4) promptly surrendering papers and property to which the client is entitled . . . ." *Id.* After withdrawal, "a lawyer must take all reasonable steps to mitigate the consequences to the client." Tenn. Sup. Ct. R. 8, RPC 1.16 Cmt. 9.

Even if Ms. Prewitt had good cause under Rule 1.16(b)(7) to withdraw, she violated Rule 1.16(d) when she did not give reasonable notice to her client. The timing of her motion to withdraw—after summary judgment motions had been pending for a month and were set for hearing—did not

---

transcribed the depositions, and he had to purchase additional copies of the missing transcripts. The video of the shooting was found in Mr. Harris's file.

allow adequate time for the employment of new counsel. The Board presented evidence that the lien Ms. Prewitt placed on the case was unreasonable, which further hindered Mr. Tucker's ability to retain new counsel. Additionally, Ms. Prewitt failed to cooperate with Mr. Tucker's subsequent attorney when she did not tell him about the pending summary judgment motions.[26] Ms. Prewitt's conduct did not show any effort to mitigate the consequences of her withdrawal.

* * *

2. IMPOSING ATTORNEYS' LIENS

Prewitt involved an attorney's lien. An attorney's lien is a device used to secure a lawyer's fee. A Pennsylvania ethics opinion describes the two common types of attorney liens:

> A retaining lien permits a lawyer to retain money, papers or other property in the lawyer's possession to secure payment of costs and fees from the client. Charging liens are divided into two sub-categories: equitable charging liens and legal charging liens. An equitable charging lien gives a lawyer a right to be paid out of a fund in the control or possession of the court, which fund resulted from the skill and labor of the lawyer, and such payment may be applied only to a particular case. A legal charging lien applies to funds of a client in the lawyer's possession and may be applied to all outstanding debts of the client owed to the lawyer.

Pennsylvania Bar Ass'n Committee on Legal Ethics & Prof'l Resp. Formal Op. No. 94–35 (1994).

The use of charging liens is common in contingent fee arrangements. The use of retaining liens is more controversial. As described in the Pennsylvania decision, the general or retaining lien gives a lawyer the right "to retain possession of documents, money or other property of his client coming into his hands by virtue of the professional relationship, until he has been paid for his services; or until he voluntarily surrenders possession of the property, with or without payment."

An attorney's assertion of a retaining lien potentially deprives a client or former client of property. This creates a certain amount of tension with Rule 1.16(d), which advises that upon termination of representation, "a lawyer shall take steps to the extent reasonably practicable to protect a client's interests, such as . . . surrendering papers and property to which the client is entitled." To some extent, this begs the question as to which

---

[26] Ms. Prewitt claims she did not have to cooperate with Mr. Tucker's new attorney because, when she spoke to the attorney, he had not yet been "engaged" but was still screening the case to decide whether he would take it. Black's Law Dictionary defines "engage" as "[t]o employ or involve oneself; to take part in; to embark on." Engage, Black's Law Dictionary (11th ed. 2019). The new attorney was involved in the case when he spoke with Ms. Prewitt as part of screening the case.

papers and property a client is entitled. Comment [9] to Rule 1.16 explains that an attorney may only employ a retaining lien "only to the extent permitted by law." *See* Rule 1.8(i)(1) (permitting a lawyer to acquire a lien authorized by law).

State ethics opinions and rules of professional conduct take a variety of approaches. Below are some examples:

- Montana Rules 1.8(j) & 1.16(d): "a lawyer may not acquire or assert a retaining lien to secure payment due for the lawyer's services against any client property, papers or materials other than those related to the matter for which payment has not been made."

- North Dakota Rule 1.19: "a lawyer may not assert a retaining lien against a client's 'files, papers, or property,' which includes '[a]ll pleadings, motions, discovery, memoranda, and other litigation materials which have been executed and served or filed' regardless of whether the client has paid the lawyer for drafting and serving and/or filing the document(s)."

- D.C. Rule 1.8(i): "a lawyer shall not impose a lien upon any part of a client's files, except upon the lawyer's own work product, and then only to the extent that the work product has not been paid for. This work product exception shall not apply when the client has become unable to pay, or when withholding the lawyer's work product would present a significant risk to the client of irreparable harm."

* * *

Problem 18.5. Frank, one of Maria's clients, fired Maria prior to completion of the representation and hired a new lawyer. Frank still owed Maria some fees under their agreement, so Maria refused to turn over Frank's file to his new lawyer, Phil, and asserted a retaining lien for her legal fees. As a result, Phil did not have any of the files, bills, pleadings, or other papers contained in the file that Phil needed in order to get up to speed on Frank's case. Look at the rules from Montana, North Dakota, and the District of Columbia above and analyze whether Maria's conduct would be permissible under each.

* * *

3. RETURNING CLIENT FILES

Rule 1.16(d) provides that upon termination of the relationship, a lawyer should surrender the papers and property to which the client is entitled but provides limited guidance as to which parts of the file a client is entitled. Below is an example of one state's attempt to define to which papers and property a client is entitled:

- Oregon State Bar Formal Op. No. 2005–125 (2005): "As a general proposition, and absent viable attorney liens, a lawyer is obligated to deliver a former client's entire file to the former client. By *entire file*, we mean papers and property that the client provided to the lawyer; litigation materials, including pleadings, memoranda, and discovery materials; all correspondence; all items that the lawyer has obtained from others, including expert opinions, medical or business records, and witness statements. The client file also includes the lawyer's notes or internal memoranda that may constitute 'attorney work-product.' "

To what extent can a lawyer charge a client for the costs associated with copying the file? The Oregon opinion above concludes that a lawyer cannot charge for copies "of original documents given by the client to the lawyer." A lawyer may charge for the copying costs of other material in the file in accordance with the fee agreement outlined in the retainer agreement. If, however, copying costs are not provided for in the agreement, the client is entitled to a copy of the file, free of charge. This would include the labor costs associated with copying the files. While this is a common approach to the issue of copying costs, some state rules permit copying costs to be borne by the former client. *See* Michigan State Bar Formal Op. R–19 (2000). Is Oregon's standard too onerous for attorneys, or does it best reflect the fiduciary nature of the attorney-client relationship?

* * *

4. ARBITRATING FEE DISPUTES

Lawyers have increasingly relied upon mandatory arbitration as a means of resolving fee disputes. ABA Ethics Opinion 02–425 (2002) concluded that a lawyer may permissibly "include in a retainer agreement with a client a provision that requires the binding arbitration of disputes concerning fees and malpractice claims, provided that the client has been fully apprised of the advantages and disadvantages of arbitration and has given her informed consent to the inclusion of the arbitration provision in the retainer agreement." Many bar associations now have fee arbitration programs that lawyers and clients may utilize.

Some states take a dimmer view of mandatory arbitration as a means of resolving fee disputes. *See* Ohio Op. No. 96–9 ("An engagement letter between a lawyer and an individual client should not contain language requiring a client to prospectively agree to arbitrate fee disputes."). When dealing with unsophisticated clients, the lawyer needs to be particularly careful about explaining the advantages and disadvantages of arbitration.

See *Marino v. Tagaris*, 480 N.E.2d 286 (Mass. 1985) (vacating arbitration award where client did not understand her rights as described in the material contained in bar-sponsored pamphlet explaining arbitration of fee agreements). Finally, arbitration agreements may be unenforceable on common law grounds (for example, the rules regarding unconscionability).

Profile of Attorney Professionalism. Following a $24.4 million verdict in favor of his client LBDS Holding Company, LLC, Texas lawyer Sanford E. Warren and his co-counsel received a Rule 11 Motion for Sanctions. In the motion, Defendants asserted that LBDS had falsified evidence it relied upon at trial and that its witnesses had testified falsely.

Attorney Warren immediately forwarded the motion to his client and set up a call with an LBDS principal—a person who also had been a fact witness in the case. That individual confirmed that the allegations in the Rule 11 motion were "essentially correct" and that a key contract offered as evidence at trial "was not authentic" because it contained forged schedules. He also admitted that LBDS employees had set up a fictitious domain name and sent emails from that fake domain that were introduced into evidence at trial.

Upon learning that he had offered false material evidence at trial, Warren attempted to persuade his client to correct or withdraw the evidence, which he was required to do under Texas Disciplinary Rules. *See* Texas Disciplinary Rule of Professional Conduct 3.03(b). When a client fails to act in that situation, the disciplinary rule requires that the attorney "take reasonable remedial measures, including disclosure of the true facts." *Id.*

Consistent with this authority, when LBDS failed to disclose its fraud to the court, Warren and his co-counsel informed the court. As part of this disclosure, the attorneys sought leave to withdraw as counsel to LBDS. They relied upon Texas Disciplinary Rule 1.15 (which is similar to Model Rule 1.16) to state grounds to withdraw as counsel. The LBDS attorneys explained that the client had used the law firm's services to perpetrate a fraud on the court, which is a basis to withdraw under Texas Disciplinary Rule of Professional Conduct 1.15(b)(3). They also noted that the disciplinary rule requires a lawyer to withdraw if the continued representation will result in the violation of professional conduct rules. *See* Texas Disciplinary Rule of Professional Conduct 1.15(a)(1). They then explained that the continuing representation would violate the disciplinary rule prohibiting a lawyer from furnishing testimony adverse to the lawyer's client if the lawyers were compelled to testify in the present matter or a related criminal matter. They also noted that the conflict of interest rule would be violated because the attorneys' representation of LBDS would be adversely limited by their own interests and obligations to follow the disciplinary rules. On these bases, the attorneys sought leave to withdraw. *See* Notice to Court Pursuant to Texas Disciplinary Rule of Professional Conduct 3.03 and Unopposed Motion to Withdraw as Counsel for Plaintiff, *LBDS Holding Company, LLC, v. ISOL Technology Inc. et al.*, No. 6:11–cv–00428–LED (E.D. Tex. filed May 21, 2014).

While it is difficult to disclose false testimony of a client and withdraw from a representation, Sanford Warren and his colleagues took the steps they determined necessary under Texas Disciplinary Rules.

CHAPTER 19

CONFLICTS OF INTEREST ARISING FROM PRIOR REPRESENTATION

■ ■ ■

Chapter Hypothetical. Larry and Lucy are partners in a two-person, general practice law firm. The two lawyers have handled a wide variety of cases over the past twenty-five years.

A. GENERAL PRINCIPLES

Once the attorney-client relationship ends, to what extent does the lawyer continue to owe the former client a duty to protect confidences and avoid conflicts of interest? How will any such duties affect the lawyer's freedom to undertake the representation of new clients whose interests are adverse to the interests of the former client?

Under Model Rule 1.9, a lawyer may represent a client adverse to a former client—without the need to seek the former client's consent—as long as the new matter is not the same representation or substantially related to the earlier representation.

A threshold issue is whether the representation of the original client has in fact terminated. A lawyer who wants to take on a lucrative new case against a client he or she has represented in the past will have an incentive to view the opposing party as a "former client" rather than a current client. Note, however, that the Rules generally characterize the relationship from the point of view of the client, not the attorney. *See* Rule 1.3, Comment [4].

In order to remove any doubt, a lawyer should communicate in writing when the attorney-client relationship has terminated. This writing should leave no question that the attorney has no continuing obligation to the client in the matter. And it clears the way for the client to be treated as a former client for purposes of conflicts of interest.

If an attorney's relationship with a client has terminated, then Rule 1.9 governs the attorney's analysis of whether a duty to the former client may preclude accepting representation of the new client. Note that under Rule 1.9, conflicts of interest can always be waived by the former client; there are no non-consentable conflicts under Rule 1.9. If the former client is willing to consent to the attorney's representation of the new client—

even in a substantially related matter—then Rule 1.9 will not prohibit the attorney from doing so.

Finally, however, it is important to note that Rule 1.7 may still regulate some aspects of a representation involving a former client. For example, an attorney's ongoing friendship with, or loyalty to, a former client may create a "material limitation" that interferes with the attorney's ability to diligently represent the new client's interests, especially where those interests might diverge with the former client's interests. In spite of the fact that the analysis involves a former client, this is a conflict governed by Rule 1.7.

* * *

Problem 19.1. Larry formerly represented Catrice. During the course of the representation, Larry became very close friends with Catrice. Now, their lawyer-client relationship is over they frequently spend time together and have even taken vacations together. Nora is a prospective client who wants Larry to represent her in a lawsuit against Catrice. Would Larry have a conflict of interest if he decides to represent Nora? If so, under which rule?

Problem 19.2. Lucy formerly represented Cara in a breach of contract matter. The representation concluded several months ago. Lucy has now agreed to represent Ollie in his unrelated personal injury action against Cara. Which conflict rule potentially applies to Lucy's representation of Ollie?

* * *

Note also that part of a lawyer's fiduciary duty towards a former client involves a duty of confidentiality. Rule 1.9(c) generally prohibits a lawyer from using information relating to the representation to the disadvantage of the former client. One exception to this rule is where the information in question is "generally known." When does information become generally known? *See* ABA Opinion No. 497.

Problem 19.3. In which of the following situations has information relating to the representation of a former client become "generally known" for purposes of Rule 1.9(c)?

(a) Facts that were disclosed in open court as part of a legal proceeding.

(b) Facts that are available in a public record.

(c) Facts that were widely reported in a local newspaper in the geographic area where a matter is pending.

(d) Facts relevant to a medical malpractice case that are widely known within the medical profession but not the general public.

* * *

B. CONFLICTS OF INTEREST BETWEEN CURRENT AND FORMER CLIENTS

1. MATERIAL ADVERSITY

A lawyer's fiduciary duty of loyalty is only implicated where the interests of a current client are materially adverse to those of a former client. Where the representation is not adverse, there are no real loyalty concerns. But where the interests of the current and former client are materially adverse, Rule 1.9 is implicated. In most cases, it is fairly easy to determine whether the parties' interests are materially adverse. For example, where a lawyer formerly represented a client and now represents the opposing party in the same or a substantially related matter, it is obvious that the interests of the opposing party are materially adverse to those of the former client. In other situations, it may not be quite so easy. Consider the following examples:

Problem 19.4. Putting aside the question of whether any of the matters below are the same or substantially related for purposes of Rule 1.9(a), which of the following scenarios would result in the firm representing a current client whose interests would be materially adverse to a former client?

(a) Larry used to do contract work for Jones Industries. He now does similar legal work on behalf of the Snyder Corporation, which happens to be Jones Industries' chief competitor.

(b) Larry previously helped Jones Industries obtain a patent for one of the company's products. Larry is now considering whether to represent Snyder Corporation in their attempts to challenge the validity of the same patent.

* * *

The "Hot Potato" Rule. A conflict that develops between two clients in unrelated cases could theoretically be solved by terminating representation of one client in favor of maintaining representation of the other. This creates a problematic incentive for lawyers to terminate their representation of clients when they are offered more lucrative opportunities to take cases adverse to their (now former) clients. In order to prevent this situation, courts apply a common law prohibition called the "hot potato" rule. *Picker Int'l., Inc. v. Varian Assoc., Inc.*, 670 F. Supp. 1363, 1365 (N.D. Ohio 1987) ("A firm may not drop a client like a hot potato, especially if it is in order to keep happy a far more lucrative client."). Permitting a firm to solve a conflict by dropping the less lucrative client would not only raise loyalty concerns, but would also undermine public confidence in the legal profession. This "hot potato doctrine" is now well established. If a conflict arises between adverse parties and both do not consent to the conflict, the presumption is that the affected law firm must withdraw from representing *both* parties in the matters.

One notable exception to this general rule is when a conflict is "thrust upon" a firm through no fault of its own. An ethics opinion from the Association of the Bar of the City of New York defined "thrust-upon" conflicts as:

> [C]onflicts between two clients that (1) did not exist at the time either representation commenced, but arose only during the ongoing representation of both clients, where (2) the conflict was not reasonably foreseeable at the outset of the representation, (3) the conflict arose through no fault of the lawyer, and (4) the conflict is of a type that is capable of being waived . . . but one of the clients will not consent to the dual representation.

Association of the Bar of the City of New York Formal Opinion No. 2005–05. While recognizing that law firms have a duty to consider potential conflicts at the outset of representation, the opinion concludes that a "flexible approach" that balances interests of the affected parties is appropriate in the case of "thrust upon" conflicts. *Id.*

* * *

2. SUBSTANTIALLY RELATED

The next requirement that must be met before a disqualifying conflict of interest exists is that the two matters are the same or substantially related. *See* Rule 1.9(a). A lawyer obviously may not quit work for a client and then go to work for the opposing party in the same matter. But the question of when two matters are "substantially related" is more complex. *See* Rule 1.9(a) Comment [3]. What factors should be relevant in making the determination? *See H.F. Ahmanson Co. v. Salomon Brothers*, 229 Cal App.3d 1445, 1455 (1991).

Problem 19.5. Lucy formerly defended AAA Motors in a patent infringement action involving the company's seatbelt. Lucy worked on the case for three years before the matter was finally resolved. Now, an individual has approached Lucy about the possibility of representing her in a products liability action against AAA Motors involving the company's allegedly defective design of the same seatbelt. The matters are obviously not the same. But are they "substantially related" for purposes of Rule 1.9(a)?

STATE EX REL. WAL-MART STORES, INC. V. KORTUM
559 N.W.2d 496 (Neb. 1997)

CONNOLLY, JUSTICE.

This is an original action for a peremptory writ of mandamus brought by relator, Wal-Mart Stores, Inc. (Wal-Mart). We are asked to determine whether a writ should issue disqualifying the law firm of Van Steenberg, Chaloupka, Mullin, Holyoke, Pahlke, Smith, Snyder, and Hofmeister, P.C. (Van Steenberg), from representing a party in an action against Wal-Mart because of the firm's prior representation of Wal-Mart in another case.

. . .

BACKGROUND

The factual statement of this case is taken largely from the findings of fact made by District Judge Donald E. Rowlands, II, who was appointed as special master by this court for the taking of evidence and for recommending findings of fact and conclusions of law. Additional facts were taken from the pleadings, the proceedings before the district court on the original motion to disqualify counsel, and various exhibits.

On July 21, 1994, Debra J. Holden filed suit against the Scottsbluff Wal-Mart store through her counsel, Leonard W. Shefren of Omaha, Nebraska. In her petition, Holden asserts that Wal-Mart was negligent in failing to properly maintain and/or warn of a hole in the store's parking lot and that this negligence caused her personal injury when she fell into the hole on July 1, 1992. Subsequent to Wal-Mart's filing an answer, Shefren withdrew as attorney of record. On or about September 7, 1995, Tylor Petitt, an attorney with Van Steenberg, entered an appearance as Holden's counsel.

Van Steenberg had previously defended Wal-Mart, through its partner Steve Smith, in four tort cases in the district court for Scotts Bluff County: *Ramirez v. Wal-Mart Stores, Inc.*, docket 34217; *Sanderson v. Wal-Mart Stores, Inc.*, docket 34218; *Pottorff v. Wal-Mart Stores, Inc.*, docket 38913; and *Nebarez v. Wal-Mart Stores, Inc.*, docket 41412.

The *Ramirez* and *Sanderson* cases involved claims of false arrest and malicious prosecution and ended in 1987 with summary judgments in favor of Wal-Mart. The *Pottorff* case involved claims that Wal-Mart was negligent in failing to properly maintain and/or warn of a dangerous condition in the floor of the store and that this negligence caused personal injury when the customer slipped and fell in an area that had previously been wet-mopped. The *Pottorff* case concluded in June 1993, with a jury verdict in favor of the plaintiff, approximately 1 year after Holden was injured but 2 years before Petitt entered an appearance as Holden's counsel. The *Nebarez* case involved claims by a customer who was injured in an assault inside the store and concluded in August 1994, with summary judgment in favor of Wal-Mart.

Wal-Mart does not have an outside claims administration firm or insurance agency that handles claims made against it. Instead, Wal-Mart relies on its staff of in-house attorneys to administer all claims and to hire legal counsel. A Wal-Mart attorney, Michelle Johnson, retained Smith to defend Wal-Mart in the aforementioned cases. In preparation for its defenses in those cases, Smith had complete access to the Scottsbluff Wal-Mart store and to its managers and staff.

While assisting Smith in preparation for Wal-Mart's defenses, Johnson related to Smith Wal-Mart's general defense strategy, internal policies, and the conduct of similar lawsuits in other parts of the country. In addition, Kern Radtke, manager of the Scottsbluff store, gave Smith complete access to procedure manuals, lists, and sales information. After Smith concluded his representation of Wal-Mart in the *Nebarez* case, he was informed by Wal-Mart that neither he nor Van Steenberg would represent Wal-Mart in any further matters.

The district court entered an order denying Wal-Mart's motion to disqualify Van Steenberg from further representation of Holden in her tort action against Wal-Mart. Wal-Mart brought this original action seeking a peremptory writ of mandamus from this court compelling the district court to vacate its order.

The special master appointed by this court found that during the time Wal-Mart was represented by Smith, the policies, procedures, and practices of which he was informed did not include any confidential information, trade secrets, or anything that was not discoverable. However, the special master recommended that a peremptory writ of mandamus be issued directing the district court to disqualify Petitt and Van Steenberg from further representation of Holden in her action against Wal-Mart. The special master reasoned that "the nexus between [the *Pottorff* case and the instant case], both in type and time of occurrence, is too close to avoid the appearance of impropriety, whether in the subjective eyes of Wal-Mart employees, or of the legally recognized reasonable person."

ANALYSIS

. . .

"Substantially Related" Test

Our first inquiry, and to a great extent the resolution of this action, involves a determination of what is meant by the phrase "substantially related subject matter." In *State ex rel. Freezer Servs., Inc. v. Mullen*, 235 Neb. 981, 987, 458 N.W.2d 245, 249–50 (1990), this court announced the rule that " '[a]n attorney, after receiving the confidence of a client, may not enter the service of others whose interests are adverse to such client, in the same subject-matter to which the confidence relates, or in matters so closely allied thereto as to be, in effect, a part thereof.' " In *State ex rel. FirsTier Bank v. Buckley*, 244 Neb. at 45, 503 N.W.2d at 844, this court expanded the rule announced in *State ex rel. Freezer Servs., Inc.*, by stating that:

> an attorney must avoid the present representation of a cause against a client of a law firm ... which he or she ... formerly [represented], and which cause involves a subject matter which is the same as or substantially related to that handled by the former firm while the present attorney was associated with that firm.
>
> ... However, this general rule arose, and has only been applied, in the context where an attorney or attorneys ceased working for a law firm that represented a particular client and then began working for another law firm in a position adversarial to that client.

In the instant case, no attorneys switched law firms. Instead, Smith of Van Steenberg formerly defended Wal-Mart, and Petitt of Van Steenberg is now suing Wal-Mart. Nonetheless, this court has made it patently clear that "confidences and secrets possessed by an attorney are presumptively possessed by other members of the attorney's firm." As such, an attorney or law firm must avoid the present representation of a cause against a client that the attorney or law firm formerly represented, and which cause involves a subject matter which is the same as or substantially related to that formerly handled by the attorney or law firm.

In *State ex rel. FirsTier Bank v. Buckley*, 244 Neb. at 44, 503 N.W.2d at 843, we stated that "[i]n defining 'substantially related,' the court looked at whether counsel may have received confidential information from the former client that could be used against it in the subsequent representation." However, it is now necessary to further define what constitutes a "substantially related subject matter."

In fashioning a "substantially related subject matter" test, a court must balance several competing considerations, including the privacy of the attorney-client relationship, the prerogative of a party to choose counsel, and the hardships that disqualification imposes on parties and the entire judicial process. However, the preservation of client confidences is given greater weight in that balancing.

Mindful of these competing interests, we determine that the subject matters of two causes are "substantially related" if the similarity of the factual and legal issues creates a genuine threat that the affected attorney may have received confidential information in the first cause that could be used against the former client in the present cause.

Simply stated, if the court determines that the unique factual and legal issues presented in both cases are so similar that there exists a genuine threat that confidential information may have been revealed in the previous case that could be used against the former client in the instant case, then disqualification must ensue.

A non-exhaustive list of the factors a court may consider in making this determination includes: whether the liability issues presented are similar; whether any scientific issues presented are similar; whether the nature of the evidence is similar; whether the lawyer had interviewed a witness who was a key in both causes; the lawyer's knowledge of the former client's trial strategies, negotiation strategies, legal theories, business practices, and trade secrets; the lapse of time between causes; the duration and intimacy of the lawyer's relationship with the clients; the functions being performed by the lawyer; the likelihood that actual conflict will arise; and the likely prejudice to the client if conflict does arise.

Clearly, the "appearance of impropriety" and attempted screening procedures . . . do not address whether two causes are "substantially related" and, thus, are not factors that may be considered in determining whether or not to disqualify an attorney or firm.

Whether Causes Are "Substantially Related"

. . . It is not disputed that Van Steenberg's interests are materially adverse to Wal-Mart's or that the information Smith acquired through his previous defenses of Wal-Mart is imputed to the entire Van Steenberg law firm. Thus, it is only left to be determined whether any of the previous cases in which Van Steenberg defended Wal-Mart are "substantially related" to the instant case against Wal-Mart.

Of the four cases in which Van Steenberg defended Wal-Mart, the case with factual and legal issues most closely related to the instant case is *Pottorff v. Wal-Mart Stores, Inc.*, Scotts Bluff County District Court, docket 38913. As such, we must determine whether the *Pottorff* case and the instant case are substantially related.

In the instant case, Holden asserts that Wal-Mart's negligence caused her to suffer a strained knee and sprained ankle when she fell into a hole located in the store's parking lot. Approximately 1 year after Holden was injured, but 2 years before Petitt entered an appearance as Holden's counsel, Van Steenberg concluded its defense of Wal-Mart in the *Pottorff* case. In the *Pottorff* case, the jury found that Wal-Mart's negligence caused Pottorff to suffer a bulging disk, an injured elbow, headaches, and leg pain when she slipped and fell in an area inside the store that had previously been wet-mopped.

Wal-Mart asserts that these cases are substantially related because in both cases a customer was injured in a fall on Wal-Mart's premises, the petitions alleged that Wal-Mart was negligent in failing to properly maintain its premises and in failing to warn of dangerous conditions, and Wal-Mart asserted contributory negligence and assumption of risk as defenses. Conversely, Van Steenberg, appearing amicus curiae, asserts that these cases are not substantially related because the *Pottorff* case involved a slip and fall on a slick floor, while the instant case involves a fall into a hole; the *Pottorff* case involved a floor, while the instant case involves a parking lot; and the accident in the *Pottorff* case happened inside the store, while the accident in the instant case happened outside the store.

Wal-Mart correctly asserts that the pleadings in these cases are similar. However, the mere fact that the pleadings are similar does not make the two cases substantially related. The differences in the factual and legal issues, where a plaintiff falls into a hole in a parking lot as opposed to where a plaintiff falls on a wet floor inside a store, are crucial and are not outweighed by the similarities.

We agree with the special master's findings that during the time Wal-Mart was represented by Smith, the policies, procedures, and practices Smith was told about did not include any trade secrets or anything that was not discoverable. Courts have recognized that defense strategies are confidential information that may be factored into the disqualification decision.... However, the defense strategies utilized in these types of relatively uncomplicated slip-and-fall actions are generally commonplace and routine. Wal-Mart did not assert that Van Steenberg became privy to any defense strategies that are unique, unexpected, unusual, or novel. Thus, we determine that an outside firm, with no prior association with Wal-Mart, would have the same or similar practical knowledge of how Wal-Mart would defend against this action and would have the same discovery opportunities.

Because Van Steenberg did not acquire any specialized knowledge of defense strategies or any other discovery advantages, we conclude that the similarity of the factual and legal issues does not create a genuine threat that Van Steenberg may have received confidential information from Wal-Mart that could be used against Wal-Mart in the instant case.

Because Wal-Mart failed to meet its burden of clearly showing that it has a legal right to the relief sought, we determine that the district court had no alternative but to deny Wal-Mart's motion to disqualify Van Steenberg. Since the district court did not have a clear legal duty to act at the time the writ was applied for, we decline to issue the requested writ.

* * *

Problem 19.6. Bob is suing Alice and her business, Alice's Auctions, Inc., for negligence and conversion. Bob had consigned a statue for auction to Alice's Auctions; however, due to a mistake, the high bidder was allowed to take the statue away after the auction without paying for it. Bob is now suing to recover the costs associated with retrieving the item. Ordinarily, individual shareholders of a corporation are not individually liable for the corporation's debts. In this case, however, Bob is attempting to "pierce the corporate veil" and hold Alice, the sole shareholder of Alice's Auctions, individually liable. Under the relevant law in the jurisdiction, if Bob is able to establish that Alice's Auctions "failed to follow corporate formalities, had nonfunctioning officers or directors, or failed to maintain corporate records," it would be appropriate for a court to pierce the corporate veil and allow Alice to be held individually liable. Alice has moved to disqualify Bob's attorneys, the Law Firm of Larry and Lucy, LLC. Twenty years ago, the firm helped Alice incorporate Alice's Auctions. Two years later, after conducting a "legal checkup" of the procedures being followed by Alice's Auctions, the firm sent Alice a letter reminding her of the need to maintain corporate records for the business to support its role as a separate entity and to help maintain a barrier against personal liability. The firm terminated representation of Alice after the legal checkup fifteen years ago. Should the court grant Alice's motion to disqualify Larry and Lucy?

Problem 19.7. Larry represents Jane in an employment discrimination case against Waking Universe Corporation. Larry had formerly served for ten years as an in-house attorney for Waking Universe. During that time, he helped craft the corporation's employment policies, advised company officials and managers how to act pursuant to those policies, how to make hiring and firing decisions, and was involved in nearly 600 employment-related matters. Some of the officials and managers he advised will be witnesses in Jane's case, and some of them were also involved in some of the prior employment matters. Should Larry be disqualified in the present matter?

* * *

C. MOBILE LAWYERS AND SCREENING

In 2009, the ABA amended Rule 1.10 to allow for screening in the case of an imputed conflict when lawyers moved from one firm to another. At the time the amendment to Model Rule 1.10 was adopted, the majority of jurisdictions did not permit screening absent the consent of the affected former client, although a significant number did allow for at least some forms of nonconsensual limited screening.

Not all states have adopted the screening rule. Model Rule 1.10 is more permissive in terms of screening in some respects than existing rules in many jurisdictions. In some jurisdictions, screening is not permitted when the personally prohibited lawyer played a substantial role in the same or a substantially related matter. *See, e.g.*, Ariz. Rules of Prof'l Conduct R. 1.10(d). At the same time, Model Rule 1.10 is more restrictive than the screening rules in some jurisdictions. For example, a handful of jurisdictions do not require (as does Model Rule 1.10) that the affected client be given notice that the firm is employing screening procedures. *See, e.g.,* Ill. Rules of Prof'l Conduct, R. 1.10(b). A few provide that screening is permitted, but impose no express requirement (like that found in Model Rule 1.10) that the screening be "timely." *Id.* However, Comment [4] to Model Rule 1.9(b) lists three policy considerations that it attempts to balance in the case of a lawyer making a lateral move. As you read the following materials, ask yourself whether the rule has succeeded in balancing these interests. Also, are there other policy interests that are implicated in the laterally-mobile lawyer situation and, if so, how should those be taken into account?

The following case addresses screening for a paralegal who has moved to a new firm. The case arises from a state that does not follow the Model Rule in allowing mobile attorneys to use screening as a means of avoiding imputation. Nonetheless, as you read the case you should analyze the arguments it makes in favor of allowing screening for a paralegal, and you should consider in what ways the issues might be similar or different for attorneys. You should also focus on the court's analysis of the procedures used for screening. In the states that do allow screening for mobile attorneys, compliance with these screening procedures is key to determining whether the firm can continue representation or whether the imputed conflict will lead to disqualification.

* * *

HODGE V. UFRA-SEXTON, LP
758 S.E.2d 314 (Ga. 2014)

HUNSTEIN, J.

We granted certiorari in this case to determine whether the Court of Appeals correctly held that a conflict of interest involving a nonlawyer can be remedied by implementing proper screening measures in order to avoid disqualification of the entire law firm. For the reasons set forth below, we hold that a nonlawyer's conflict of interest can be remedied by implementing proper screening measures so as to avoid disqualification of an entire law firm. In this particular case, we find that the screening measures implemented by the nonlawyer's new law firm were effective and appropriate to protect against the nonlawyer's disclosure of confidential information. However, we remand this case to the trial court for a hearing to determine whether the new law firm promptly disclosed the conflict.

On January 3, 2010, Monica Renee Williams was shot and killed at an apartment complex managed by Appellees UFRA-Sexton, LP and Signature Management Corporation (hereinafter "UFRA-Sexton").

Appellant Belinda Ann Hodge is the sister of Williams. Kristi Bussey had known Hodge for approximately ten years prior to Williams' death. Bussey assisted Hodge in obtaining her appointment as administratrix of Williams' estate and Hodge's appointment as the legal guardian for Williams' son.

Hodge retained attorney Craig Brookes of the law firm Hanks Brookes, LLC to pursue claims associated with the death of Williams. Bussey was a paralegal at Hanks Brookes and had worked there in that capacity since January 2007. Bussey was Hodge's primary contact with Hanks Brookes while she was employed at the firm. Bussey assisted with, and personally conducted, much of the investigation regarding Williams' death and the apartment complex where the death occurred. Bussey communicated regularly with Hodge about Hanks Brookes' investigation of the case, counsel's thoughts about the case, legal work being performed, and strategy for moving forward. Bussey participated in every face-to-face meeting Hodge had with Brookes while Bussey was employed with Hanks Brookes. Brookes spoke directly to Bussey about the status of her investigation, the results of his own investigation, his thoughts about the case, the strategies to be employed, and pertinent legal and factual considerations in the case.

Meanwhile, on March 29, 2010, UFRA-Sexton's insurer, Scottsdale Insurance Company, retained the firm of Insley & Race, LLC to represent UFRA-Sexton in the Williams matter. For the next six months, Insley & Race conducted a pre-suit investigation and evaluation of the incident, including numerous interviews, review of documents, and a detailed assessment.

In October 2010, Bussey left her position as a paralegal with Hanks Brookes and began working as a legal assistant at another law firm. In early 2011, Bussey applied for a paralegal position at Insley & Race. Brynda Rodriguez Insley personally called, and obtained a reference from, J.R. Hanks at Hanks Brookes. Hanks never disclosed any possible conflict with regard to Bussey or Hanks Brookes' work on the Williams case. Hanks was unaware that UFRA-Sexton was represented by Insley & Race in the Williams case.

Bussey began work as a paralegal at Insley & Race on March 15, 2011. At this time, neither Bussey nor Insley & Race was aware of any potential conflict regarding Bussey's work at Hanks Brookes, and Bussey did not know that Insley & Race was involved in a pre-suit investigation of Williams' death. Accordingly, Insley & Race did not employ any screening measures at that time.

On October 5, 2011, Bussey became aware of Insley & Race's involvement in the Williams case. Bussey immediately informed Insley & Race of her work with Hanks Brookes on the Williams case. Insley & Race immediately implemented screening measures, discussed more fully below, to protect against Bussey's disclosure of confidential information she had gained from working on the Williams case at Hanks Brookes.

Later that same evening, Insley sent an email to Brookes and other counsel for Hodge advising of the firm's representation of UFRA-Sexton and acknowledging the receipt of Hodge's demand letter. Insley did not mention any potential conflict involving Bussey.

On November 7, 2011, Hodge filed a complaint against UFRA-Sexton, and Insley & Race subsequently filed an answer on behalf of UFRA-Sexton. On December 6, 2011, counsel at Insley & Race disclosed Bussey's employment to Hodge's counsel. Hodge filed a motion to disqualify Insley & Race, requesting that Insley & Race voluntarily withdraw, and in the alternative, that the trial court issue an order disqualifying the firm from representing UFRA-Sexton in the Williams matter. UFRA-Sexton responded to Hodge's motion stating that Insley & Race was its counsel of choice and that it would not voluntarily withdraw.

The trial court denied Hodge's motion, finding that Insley & Race was UFRA-Sexton's counsel of choice, had developed specialized knowledge by working on the case for 18 months before learning of any potential conflict of interest, and had implemented appropriate and effective screening measures to protect against any disclosure of confidential information between Bussey and Insley & Race. Pursuant to Hodge's request, the trial court certified its order denying the motion to disqualify for immediate review. The Court of Appeals affirmed, finding that the trial court did not abuse its discretion in denying the motion to disqualify. We subsequently granted certiorari.

We review the trial court's ruling on a motion to disqualify for an abuse of discretion. We approach motions to disqualify with caution due to the consequences that could result if the motion is granted, such as the inevitable delay of the proceedings and the unique hardship on the client including the loss of time, money, choice of counsel, and specialized knowledge of the disqualified attorney. Additionally, we are mindful of counsel using motions to disqualify as a dilatory tactic. Accordingly, we view disqualification as an extraordinary remedy that should be granted sparingly.

It is well established that an attorney has a professional obligation to maintain client confidences and secrets. Ga. Rules of Prof'l Conduct, Rule 1.6(a). To protect this attorney-client relationship, the Georgia Rules of Professional Conduct provide that a "lawyer who has formerly represented a client in a matter shall not thereafter represent another person in the same or a substantially related matter in which that person's interests are materially adverse to the interests of the former client unless the former client gives informed consent, confirmed in writing." Rule 1.9(a). "When a lawyer has been directly involved in a specific transaction, subsequent representation of other clients with materially adverse interests in that transaction clearly is prohibited." *Id.*, Comment [2]. This Rule aims to protect former clients, avoid the appearance of any impropriety, and maintain public confidence in the integrity of our adversarial system.

Pursuant to Rule 1.10(a), " 'if one attorney in a firm has an actual conflict of interest, we impute that conflict to all the attorneys in the firm, subjecting the entire firm to disqualification.' " This Rule aims to give effect to the principle of loyalty to the client. Rule 1.10, Comment [6]. "Such situations can be considered from the premise that a firm of lawyers is essentially one lawyer for purposes of the rules governing loyalty to the client, or from the premise that each lawyer is vicariously bound by the obligation of loyalty owed by each lawyer with whom the lawyer is associated." *Id.*

Nonlawyers are also privy to confidential client information because it is often necessary for them to have access to this information to assist their attorney employers. However, our Rules do not regulate nonlawyers. Thus, the question presented here is how to protect the client's confidences, avoid impropriety, and maintain public confidence in the integrity of our adversarial system when nonlawyers change firms to work for opposing counsel.

There is a split of authority among the courts on this issue. The minority approach, which is what Hodge argues we should apply here, is to treat nonlawyers the same way we treat lawyers. Under this approach, when a nonlawyer moves to another firm to work for opposing counsel, the nonlawyer's conflict of interest is imputed to the rest of the firm, thereby disqualifying opposing counsel. UFRA-Sexton argues that we should adopt the majority approach and treat nonlawyers differently from lawyers. Under this approach, rather than automatic imputation and disqualification of the new firm, lawyers hiring the nonlawyer can implement screening measures to protect any client confidences that the nonlawyer gained from prior employment. After reviewing both approaches, we join today with "the majority of professional legal ethics commentators, ethics tribunals, and courts[, which] have concluded that nonlawyer screening is a permissible method to protect confidences held by nonlawyer employees who change employment."

We believe that screening measures are appropriate for nonlawyers, rather than imputed disqualification, for several reasons. First, nonlawyers generally have neither a financial interest in the outcome of a particular litigation nor a choice about which clients they serve, which reduces the appearance of impropriety. Second, nonlawyers have different training, responsibilities, and discovery and use of confidential information compared to lawyers. Third, as noted above, disqualification of the new firm would present a hardship to the new firm's client, such as delays, further expenses, and a loss of specialized knowledge.

Fourth, if imputation and disqualification were automatic, nonlawyers' employment mobility could be "unduly restricted." In recommending that screening measures be allowed for nonlawyers, the ABA Committee on Ethics and Professional Responsibility recognized that it was important for nonlawyers to "have as much mobility in employment opportunity as possible consistent with the protection of clients' interests." ABA Comm. on Ethics and Prof'l Responsibility, Informal Op. 88–1526, at 2. The ABA Committee noted that clients as well as the legal profession would be harmed by limiting nonlawyers' employment opportunities and requiring them to leave the careers for which they are trained. "A potential employer might well be reluctant to hire a particular nonlawyer if doing so would automatically disqualify the entire firm from ongoing litigation." Nonlawyers in sparsely populated towns or counties as well as nonlawyers previously employed by massive firms and involved in extensive litigation would be especially hard hit by the rule of imputed disqualification. "[A] lawyer may always practice his or her profession regardless of an affiliation to a law firm. Paralegals, legal secretaries, and other employees of attorneys do not have that option." If we were to impute the nonlawyer's conflict of interest to the entire firm, "employers could protect themselves against unanticipated disqualification risks only by refusing to hire experienced people." *Restatement (Third) of Law Governing Lawyers* § 123, Comment (f) (2000).

Fifth, our Rules recognize that screening is effective at protecting a client's confidences. Our Rules explicitly allow screening with regard to lawyers who are former judges and arbitrators or former public officers and employees. Rules 1.11, 1.12. The purpose of screening measures in Rules 1.11 and 1.12 is "to assure the affected parties that confidential information known by the personally disqualified lawyer remains protected." Rule 1.0, Comment [8]. The use of a screen for nonlawyers has the same purpose.

Finally, while our Rules do not regulate nonlawyers, they do regulate attorneys' conduct with regard to supervising non-attorneys. Our Rules require that (1) a lawyer who has supervisory authority over a nonlawyer must make reasonable efforts to ensure that the nonlawyer's conduct is compatible with the professional obligations of a lawyer; (2) a lawyer may not order or ratify a nonlawyer's conduct if it would violate the Rules; and (3) those with managerial authority over a nonlawyer must make reasonable efforts to ensure that the firm itself has measures in place to give reasonable assurance that the nonlawyer's conduct is compatible with the professional obligations of the lawyer. Rule 5.3(a), (b), (c). These professional obligations include protecting a client's confidences. See Rule 1.6(a). Thus, our Rules require that attorneys be held accountable for their nonlawyer employees' conduct, particularly where there is a threat to attorney-client confidentiality and the integrity of our judicial process. We are not suggesting that lawyers always have a duty to an opposing party to maintain that party's confidences in the absence of a prior attorney-client relationship. However, we are mindful that the former employee's attorney has no effective means of protecting against the nonlawyer's disclosure of the client's confidences once the nonlawyer leaves the attorney's employment. Therefore, the responsibility for protecting the confidentiality of attorney-client communications must fall to the new lawyer or firm hiring the nonlawyer and the implementation of screening measures.

Accordingly, as a matter of first impression, we set forth the following guidance for disqualification of a law firm based on a nonlawyer's conflict of interest. Once the new firm knows of the nonlawyer's conflict of interest, the new firm must give prompt written notice to any affected adversarial party or their counsel, stating the conflict and the screening measures utilized. *Cf.* Rule 1.11(a)(2) (regarding successive government and private employment, requiring that "written notice is duly given to the client and appropriate government entity"); Rule 1.12(c)(2) (regarding former judge or arbitrator, requiring that "written notice is promptly given to the appropriate tribunal"). The adversarial party may give written consent to the new firm's continued representation of its client with screening measures in place.

Absent written consent, the adversarial party may move to disqualify the new firm. The adversarial party must show that the nonlawyer actually worked on a same or substantially related matter involving the adversarial party while the nonlawyer was employed at the former firm. If the moving party can show this, it will be presumed that the nonlawyer learned confidential information about the matter. This prevents the nonlawyer from having to disclose the very information that should be protected.

Once this showing has been made, a rebuttable presumption arises that the nonlawyer has used or disclosed, or will use or disclose, the confidential information to the new firm. The new firm may rebut this by showing that it has properly taken effective screening measures to protect against the nonlawyer's disclosure of the former client's confidential information. If the new firm can sufficiently rebut the presumption and show that it promptly gave written notice of the nonlawyer's conflict, then disqualification is not required.

The specific screening measures that the new firm must implement will vary based on the particular circumstances in each case. *See* Rule 1.0, Comment [9] ("screening measures that are appropriate for the particular matter will depend on the circumstances"). Courts must evaluate whether the new firm took sufficient measures to reduce the potential for the breach of confidences by the nonlawyer. Courts may also consider the amount of time that has elapsed since the nonlawyer's work on the case in question at the previous firm, the size of the new and previous firms, and the number of individuals presumed to have confidential information.

At a minimum,

> [a] lawyer should give [nonlawyers] appropriate instruction and supervision concerning the ethical aspects of their employment, particularly regarding the obligation not to disclose information relating to representation of the client, and should be responsible for their work product. The measures employed in supervising nonlawyers should take account of the fact that they do not have legal training and are not subject to professional discipline.

Rule 5.3, Comment [1]. A lawyer should "screen" the nonlawyer, which our Rules define as isolating the nonlawyer "from any participation in a matter through the timely imposition of procedures within a firm that are reasonably adequate under the circumstances to protect information that the isolated [non]lawyer is obligated to protect under these Rules or other law." Rule 1.0(p).

> The personally disqualified [nonlawyer] should acknowledge the obligation not to communicate with any of the other lawyers in the firm with respect to the matter [and] other lawyers in the firm who are working on the matter should be informed that the screening is in place and that they may not communicate with the personally disqualified [nonlawyer] with respect to the matter.

Rule 1.0, Comment [9]. It may also be appropriate for the firm to institute procedures to prevent the nonlawyer from having contact with, or access to, any firm files or other materials relating to the matter. *Id.* It may also be prudent for the firm to present periodic reminders of the screen to the nonlawyer and all other firm personnel. *Id.* "In order to be effective, screening measures must be implemented as soon as practical after a [nonlawyer,] lawyer[,] or law firm knows or reasonably should know that there is a need for screening." *Id.* at Comment [10].

On the other hand, the new firm will be disqualified where (1) the nonlawyer has already revealed the confidential information to lawyers or other personnel in the new firm; (2) screening would be ineffective; or (3) "the nonlawyer necessarily would be required to work [or has actually worked at the new firm] on the other side of the same or a substantially related matter on which the nonlawyer [previously] worked." If these situations occur, the new firm must withdraw from representing its client because the confidentiality of the former client has been destroyed and the appearance of impropriety will result.

Having found that screening is appropriate for nonlawyers, we must now evaluate the measures used by Insley & Race in this particular case.

First, we begin by noting that Hodge has not waived the conflict of interest by giving written consent for Insley & Race to continue to represent UFRA-Sexton, and UFRA-Sexton has expressly requested that Insley & Race continue to represent it as [its] counsel of choice. Additionally, Bussey attests in her affidavit that she has neither discussed nor disclosed any confidential information that she obtained about the Williams matter during her employment with Hanks Brookes to any person at Insley & Race, and Bussey has not worked on the Williams case while at Insley & Race. Accordingly, automatic disqualification is not warranted.

Next, there is no dispute that Bussey worked on the Williams case while at Hanks Brookes, and therefore, it is presumed that Bussey learned confidential information about the Williams case. The burden now shifts to Insley & Race to rebut the presumption that Bussey used or disclosed, or will use or will disclose, confidential information about the Williams case to Insley & Race.

Bussey states in her affidavit that she was unaware of Insley & Race's involvement in the Williams case when she was hired on March 15, 2011, and Insley attests that the firm was unaware of any potential conflict in hiring Bussey. Bussey states that she did not learn of her new firm's involvement in the Williams case until October 5, 2011. Upon discovering that Insley & Race was counsel for UFRA-Sexton, Bussey immediately informed her co-workers, Insley, and the firm administrator. Insley immediately instructed Bussey not to be involved in the Williams case at Insley & Race in any way or to have any discussions with anyone about the case or her knowledge about it. Furthermore, Insley instructed Bussey that she would be restricted from any access to the electronic file and that Insley would make sure that appropriate screening measures were in place at Insley & Race. The firm administrator immediately implemented and confirmed electronic screening measures with Bussey, including taking steps to restrict Bussey's access to any information about the Williams case, implementing security measures to prevent Bussey from accessing any computerized information maintained by Insley & Race regarding the Williams case, and testing the security measures he implemented to ensure their success. Since October 5, Bussey has been unable to access the case management system used by Insley & Race for the Williams matter, including any calendar events, contact information, documents, and billing information for the Williams case. Additionally, the physical file was removed from the general file room and securely placed in the office of an associate.

Bussey and Insley state in their affidavits that Bussey will continue to fully abide by the screening and restrictive measures implemented at Insley & Race; Bussey will not have access to the electronic or physical file in the Williams case; and Bussey will not discuss or disclose any confidential information about the Williams case to anyone at Insley &

Race. Insley as well as the firm administrator attest that the screening and restrictive measures implemented on October 5, 2011, have and will remain in place throughout the duration of the case to prevent the disclosure of confidential information.

We find that in this particular case Insley & Race's screening measures were, and are, appropriate and effective to protect against Bussey's disclosure of confidential information she learned while working on the Williams case at Hanks Brookes. Insley & Race took sufficient screening measures to reduce the potential for the breach of confidences by Bussey, and therefore, Insley & Race has rebutted the presumption that Bussey used or disclosed, or will use or disclose, the confidential information.

Hodge contends that Insley & Race should be disqualified because the firm did not perform adequate conflict checks to detect whether Bussey had worked on the Williams case. Insley & Race responds that Hanks Brookes should have disclosed its involvement in the Williams case when Insley called Hanks to discuss hiring Bussey in March 2011. Although we agree that it would be prudent for a potential employer to conduct conflict checks before hiring a new nonlawyer, so as to implement appropriate screening measures and avoid the possibility of subsequent disqualification, in this case the potential conflict was missed, regardless of whether the blame rests with Insley & Race or Hanks Brookes. Importantly, Insley & Race implemented effective screening measures as soon as Bussey informed the firm of the conflict to ensure that Bussey would not disclose confidential information about the Williams case, and Bussey has not actually disclosed such confidential information.

Hodge also argues that Insley & Race did not timely disclose Bussey's conflict to Hanks Brookes on October 5, and instead waited until December 6 to do so. Hodge raised this argument before the trial court and the Court of Appeals, but neither court addressed this issue. Based on the guidelines we have established today, once Insley & Race knew of Bussey's conflict of interest, Insley & Race was required to give prompt written notice to Hodge or her counsel, stating the conflict and the screening measures implemented at Insley & Race. Therefore, we remand this case to the Court of Appeals to remand to the trial court for a hearing to determine whether Insley & Race gave prompt written notice to Hodge or her counsel.

Judgment vacated and case remanded with direction.

* * *

Screening Lawyers. *Hodge* dealt with a mobile paralegal. Under the Model Rule, a similar analysis would apply to mobile lawyers. Do you agree with the Model Rule position that screening should be allowed even for attorneys? Or do you agree with the court in *Hodge* that lawyers should be subject to a stricter rule?

Screening in Transactional Settings vs. Litigation. Some jurisdictions permit screening in transactional representation, but not in litigation. Tennessee's Rule 1.10(d) does not allow screening to be used to avoid imputed disqualification if "the lawyer's representation of the former client was in connection with an adjudicative proceeding that is directly adverse to the interests of a current client of the firm." Tenn. Rules of Prof'l Conduct R. 1.10(d). Is there a compelling reason to afford less protection in terms of confidentiality in transactional practice than is afforded in litigation?

Government Lawyers. The *Hodge* case discussed Rule 1.11. As Comment [3] to Rule 1.11 points out, a conflict exists where the lawyer now represents a private client whose interests are aligned with those of the lawyer's former government agency client. In other words, adversity between the old client and the new client is not required for disqualification. Does this make sense? Whose interests are being protected by this provision?

Judges. Compare Rule 1.11 with 1.12. What is the underlying purpose of Rule 1.12? Is it to facilitate judge mobility (*i.e.*, to ensure that judges are not unduly inhibited from moving back and forth from the bench to private practice)? If so, how does the rule effectuate this purpose? As amended by the ABA in 2002, Rule 1.12 also applies to mediators and other dispute resolution neutrals.

Rule 1.12(b) and Law Clerks. Rule 1.12(b) permits a law clerk for a judge to "negotiate for employment with a party or lawyer involved in a matter in which the clerk is participating personally and substantially, but only after the lawyer has notified the judge...." What purpose does notifying the judge serve here?

Duties of Lawyers Left Behind when Laterally Mobile Lawyers Leave a Firm and Take Clients with Them. What happens when a lawyer who leaves her former firm takes one or more of the firm's clients with her when she moves to a new firm? These clients become former clients of the lawyers who remain at the firm that had previously represented them. Under what circumstances can the lawyers left behind represent clients with interests adverse to the clients who followed the lawyer who left the firm? Re-read Rule 1.10(b) and consider the following problem:

Problem 19.8. Prior to partnering with Larry, Lucy was a partner in the Biggs Law Firm. She was primarily responsible for the representation of Farley Corporation in its antitrust suit against Harrison Company. Lucy supervised a team of several lawyers in this matter, including Cheyenne, who interviewed Farley Corporation company officials and reviewed confidential documents as part of the representation. Lucy eventually left the Biggs Law Firm to start her own firm with Larry and brought several clients (including Farley Corporation) with her. Cheyenne, the Biggs associate who had worked on the antitrust suit, decided not to leave the Biggs firm. Pappas Industries has now approached the Biggs Law Firm about the possibility of the firm representing Pappas against Farley Corporation in a matter that is substantially related to the Farley Corporation/Harrison Company antitrust dispute. Can the Biggs firm represent Pappas in this matter?

Problem 19.9. While Sierra was an associate at the Biggs Law Firm, she represented Charlotte Trucking in litigation against Charleston Food Distributors. Sierra was not the lead attorney, but did significant work in the case. While the case was still pending, Sierra was contacted by a search firm about whether she would be interested in interviewing for an associate attorney position at the Law Firm of Larry and Lucy, LLC, which happens to represent Charleston Food Distributors in the litigation in which Sierra represents Charlotte Trucking.

(a) Does Sierra have a conflict of interest that prevents her from interviewing for the job at Larry and Lucy's firm? Refer to Rule 1.9, Comment [7].

(b) Assume for purposes of this question that Sierra has received an offer from Larry and Lucy and that she plans to join the firm. With reference to Rule 1.9, analyze whether Larry and Lucy will have a conflict of interest in the *Charlotte Trucking v. Charleston Food Distributors* case and, if so, how the conflict can be resolved so that the firm can continue to represent Charleston Food Distributors.

Profile of Attorney Professionalism. Violette Neatley Anderson, born in 1882, was the first African-American woman admitted to practice before the United States Supreme Court. Before becoming a lawyer, Anderson worked as a court reporter for fifteen years (from 1905 to 1920). Her time in the courtroom developed her interest in trial practice, and she attended law school at the University of Chicago while continuing to work as a court reporter. In 1920, Anderson graduated from law school, passed the Illinois bar exam, and immediately began litigating cases as a solo practitioner. Anderson took both civil and criminal cases, and her career quickly skyrocketed. In 1922, Anderson gained media attention for successfully defending a woman accused of murdering a male lodger; Anderson persuaded the jury that her client had acted in self-defense. A Chicago newspaper reported that it was "to the credit of Attorney Anderson that her client was acquitted after a three days' battle before judge and jury." THE BROAD AX, July 29, 1922. Soon after her success at the highly publicized trial, Anderson was offered a position as an assistant prosecutor for the City of Chicago. She accepted the job in December of 1922, becoming the city's first female prosecutor as well as its first African-American prosecutor. In 1926, after Anderson had been licensed and in good standing for five years, she was admitted to practice before the United States Supreme Court.

In addition to her legal work, Anderson also engaged in political advocacy and community service. She served as president of the Friendly Big Sisters League of Chicago, vice-president of the Cook County Bar Association, and national president of the Zeta Phi Beta Sorority. Anderson worked to secure passage of the Bankhead-Jones Act, which authorized low-interest loans to enable sharecroppers and tenant farmers to buy land for themselves. In addition to personally lobbying the congressional representatives from Illinois, she also used her position as sorority president to organize a nationwide lobbying effort by sorority members. Anderson lived to see the bill signed into law in the summer of 1937 by President Franklin D. Roosevelt, but was struck ill with cancer shortly thereafter. In December of 1937, at 55 years of age, Anderson passed away.

PART 4

REPRESENTING CLIENTS

■ ■ ■

In Part 3, we examined the legal relationship between lawyer and client, highlighting the fiduciary duties and corresponding professional obligations owed to all clients. In this part of the book, the focus shifts to issues that arise in specific practice settings. The chapters in Part 4 explore both duties to clients and obligations to third parties in the context of litigation and transactional practice.

SECTION 1

LITIGATION PRACTICE

■ ■ ■

This section includes five chapters that focus on the legal duties and professional conduct obligations relevant to a lawyer engaged in litigation practice. Chapter 20 deals with pre-trial practice, while Chapter 21 addresses issues that arise during trial and appeal. Chapters 22 and 23 focus on criminal law practice, with Chapter 22 concentrating on prosecutors' ethical and legal obligations and Chapter 23 examining legal and ethical issues encountered by criminal defense lawyers. Finally, Chapter 24 addresses judicial conduct rules and other legal issues related to becoming and serving as a judge.

CHAPTER 20

PRE-TRIAL ADVOCACY

■ ■ ■

Chapter Hypothetical. The Lilith Corporation's president, Linus Coverdale, asks you to represent the company in a lawsuit filed by Necco Corporation. Necco manufactures and sells lift trucks and parts through authorized dealers. For many years, Lilith was an authorized Necco dealer but was terminated as a dealer in January of last year.

Necco sued Lilith for violation of the Computer Fraud and Abuse Act, computer trespass, misappropriation of trade secrets, and tortious interference with contract and business relations. Necco alleges that after Lilith was terminated as a dealer in January of last year, some of its employees gained unauthorized access to Necco's dealer website. According to Necco's complaint, the Lilith employees used a password obtained from Jane McLachlan, an employee of Hampstead Corporation. (Hampstead is an authorized Necco dealer.) Necco asserts that Lilith's unauthorized access only ceased when Necco deactivated and replaced Hampstead's password in February of this year.

Lilith was served with the Necco lawsuit on June 1 of this year. Lilith's president contacted you the next day. He tells you that he was not aware of the issues alleged in the case until he received the complaint.

A. INFORMAL FACT INVESTIGATION

Before a lawyer commences a civil action, brings criminal charges against a defendant, or begins work on a transactional matter on behalf of an organizational client, the lawyer may first need to conduct some investigation into the facts underlying the client's matter. Indeed, Comment [5] to Model Rule 1.1 (the rule regarding competence) explains that "[c]ompetent handling of a particular matter includes inquiry into and analysis of the *factual* and legal elements of the problem." (Emphasis added.) This investigation may bring the lawyer into contact with various individuals, some represented by counsel and some not. The following part of the chapter addresses some of the ethical issues involved when a lawyer engages in an informal investigation into the facts surrounding a matter.

* * *

1. SEEKING INFORMATION FROM INDIVIDUALS REPRESENTED BY COUNSEL

Model Rule 4.2 addresses a lawyer's ethical obligations when speaking to a party the lawyer knows to be represented by counsel. The rule is designed to effectuate the principle that a client can choose to interpose an attorney between herself and her adversary. ABA Formal Ethics Opinion 95–396 explains that such rules "provide protection of the represented person against overreaching by adverse counsel, safeguard the client-lawyer relationship from interference by adverse counsel, and reduce the likelihood that clients will disclose privileged or other information that might harm their interests." The rule also applies to contact with certain constituents of an organizational client that is represented by counsel. In contrast, Model Rule 3.4(f) speaks to a lawyer's ability to try to *prevent* an individual from speaking to a lawyer on the other side.

Use Rule 3.4(f) and Comment [7] to Rule 4.2 to answer the problem below.

* * *

Problem 20.1. Lilith Corporation's president, Linus Coverdale, tells you that Lilith employees who may have been involved in the unauthorized website access work in the company's Parts Group. They are Lora McDonald, Carlee Hixon, and Russell Marcus. Linus tells you that Dora Merigo was a member of the Parts Group until she was fired from Lilith in January of this year. She also may have been involved in accessing the Necco website. Finally, Linus notes that Jane McLachlan (the alleged source of the password) worked in the Lilith Parts Group for many years but left for Hampstead two years ago. Hampstead has not been named a party in the case and is not represented by counsel in the matter.

Consistent with Rule 4.2, which of these individuals may you interview at this time? Is Necco's counsel able to interview any of these individuals without violating Rule 4.2? Is it appropriate under the professional conduct rules for you to instruct any or all of these individuals that they should not talk to Necco's counsel if they receive a call or contact from her?

* * *

2. COMMUNICATING WITH UNREPRESENTED PERSONS, CLARIFYING YOUR PARTISAN ROLE, AND REFRAINING FROM RENDERING LEGAL ADVICE TO UNREPRESENTED PERSONS

Model Rule 4.3 discusses a lawyer's ethical obligations when communicating with a person who is not represented by a lawyer in a matter. The rule is designed to prevent a lawyer from taking advantage of an unrepresented person, possibly compromising that person's interests in the process. *See* Model Rule 4.3 Comments [1] and [2]. Use Rule 4.3 to help you answer the problem below.

* * *

Problem 20.2. You decide to contact Jane McLachlan, the alleged source of the password who now works at Hampstead (see the facts in Problem 20.1). You explain your role in the case as an attorney for Lilith. Jane admits that she was the source of the password for Lilith employees. She gave the password to Carlee Hixon and knew the Parts Group would use it to access the protected area of the Necco website. Jane asks you if you think Necco has a cause of action against her if it is revealed that she was the source of the password. What do you tell her?

* * *

B. PREPARING PLEADINGS, MOTIONS AND OTHER PAPERS

As a general rule, a lawyer owes no duty to exercise reasonable care on behalf of a non-client. So in most cases, the lawyer would not face malpractice liability to a non-client. However, a lawyer who files a frivolous claim or motion on behalf of a client could potentially face liability to a non-client. Further, a lawyer who files a frivolous claim or motion might also face sanctions or professional discipline.

* * *

1. TORT LIABILITY STEMMING FROM THE FILING OF FRIVOLOUS CLAIMS AND MOTIONS

Malicious Prosecution. One tort theory that might apply to the filing of a frivolous claim is malicious prosecution or wrongful initiation of civil proceedings. The party who has been forced to defend against a frivolous claim must prove (1) that the prior proceeding on the underlying matter terminated in the party's favor, (2) the absence of probable cause for those proceedings, and (3) "malice" on the part of the party who brought the underlying action. *Friedman v. Dozroc*, 312 N.W.2d 585 (Mich. 1981). The malice element is frequently defined to mean that the party had an improper purpose for bringing the action, *i.e.*, "a purpose other than that of securing the proper adjudication of the claim in which the proceedings are based." *Restatement (Second) of Torts* § 674. The key conflict in many malicious prosecution cases is the issue of probable cause, which the *Restatement (Second) of Torts* defines in this manner:

> One who takes an active part in the initiation, continuation or procurement of civil proceedings against another has probable

cause for doing so if he reasonably believes in the existence of the facts upon which the claim is based, and either

(a) correctly or reasonably believes that under those facts the claim may be valid under the applicable law, or

(b) believes to this effect in reliance upon the advice of counsel, sought in good faith and given after full disclosure of all relevant facts within his knowledge and information.

Restatement (Second) of Torts § 675.

Abuse of Process. The tort of abuse of process is a close cousin to the malicious prosecution or wrongful initiation tort. "For abuse of process to occur, there must be use of the process for an immediate purpose other than that for which it was designed and intended. The usual case of abuse of process is one of some form of extortion, using [a legal] process to put pressure upon [another] to compel him to pay a different debt or to take some other action or refrain from it." *Restatement (Second) of Torts* § 682 Comment [b].

Defamation. Where a lawyer makes false and defamatory statements about an individual, a defamation claim against the lawyer filing the complaint may be a possibility. However, the "litigator's privilege," which covers "communications preliminary to a proposed judicial proceeding, or in the institution of, or during the course and as a part of, a judicial proceeding" (provided the communication has some relation to the proceeding), should ordinarily protect the attorney who makes false and defamatory statements in a complaint or motion. *Restatement (Second) of Torts* § 586. In most jurisdictions, the privilege is absolute in nature. Thus, the fact the lawyer acted with knowledge that the statements were false is irrelevant. The privilege is absolute, the *Restatement (Second) of Torts* explains, so as not to deter lawyers from vigorously asserting their clients' rights. *See id.* § 586 Comment. [a].

Tortious Interference. Another possibility is a claim of tortious interference with contractual relations. For example, in *Mantia v. Hanson*, 79 P.3d 404, 406 (Or. Ct. App. 2003), the plaintiff sued one of its former employees on a tortious interference theory after the employee had filed allegedly frivolous claims against the plaintiff as part of an attempt to interfere with the plaintiff's business. In addition, the plaintiff sued the former employee's lawyers for asserting the allegedly frivolous claims on the employee's behalf. The court chose not to extend the litigator's privilege to interference claims. However, the court held that when an interference claim is based on the institution of legal proceedings, the plaintiff must establish that the lawyer employed "improper means" in interfering with the plaintiff's business relations with another. The court then defined the concept of "improper means" so that the definition tracked exactly the elements of a malicious prosecution or wrongful initiation claim. *Id.* at 414.

Thus, a plaintiff in such cases faces the same difficult burden faced in a malicious prosecution or wrongful initiation claim. *See* Alex B. Long, *Attorney Liability for Tortious Interference: Interference with Contractual Relations or Interference with the Practice of Law*, 18 GEO. J. LEGAL ETHICS 471 (2005) (discussing the use of interference claims resulting from litigation tactics).

* * *

2. SANCTIONS FOR FILING FRIVOLOUS CLAIMS AND MOTIONS

As you probably learned in Civil Procedure, under Rule 11 of the *Federal Rules of Civil Procedure*, by presenting a motion to a court, a lawyer certifies (among other things) that the motion is warranted by existing law (or by a non-frivolous argument for a change in the law) and that the motion is not being presented for an improper purpose. Model Rules 3.1 and 3.2 are the analogous rules of professional conduct. The following case explores a lawyer's obligations under these rules and the potential for a court to impose sanctions for the lawyer's failure to comply.

* * *

GARR V. U.S. HEALTHCARE, INC.
22 F.3d 1274 (3d Cir. 1994)

GREENBERG, CIRCUIT JUDGE.

I. INTRODUCTION

... This action arose in the aftermath of an article in the *Wall Street Journal* published on November 4, 1992, entitled "U.S. Healthcare Insiders Sold Stock Before Last Week's 17% Price Decline." The article recited that U.S. Healthcare, Inc. insiders, including Leonard Abramson, its chairman and president, had been heavy sellers of its stock before a 17% two-day drop in its price in the week before publication of the article. The article indicated the drop had been precipitated by disappointing earnings.

James R. Malone, Jr., a member of the Haverford, Pennsylvania law firm of Greenfield & Chimicles, who read the article on the morning it was published, was interested in its contents because his firm specialized in securities litigation. Indeed, ... Greenfield & Chimicles maintained a list of corporate stockholders available to become plaintiffs in securities litigation.[1] Robert K. Greenfield was on that list.[2] It is undisputed that after Malone read the article he examined a "representative sampling of

---

[1] This arrangement reverses the traditional regime which contemplates that the client start the steps towards formation of an attorney-client relationship by seeking legal representation.

[2] Robert K. Greenfield is not related to the Richard D. Greenfield of Greenfield & Chimicles.

stories relating to U.S. Healthcare," as well as a report on background information on the company. He also obtained considerable other information about U.S. Healthcare, including filings it had made with the Securities and Exchange Commission.

Malone does not contend that at the time that he was doing this research he had a client who had expressed any interest in the article to him. Rather, Malone was seeking to generate a lawsuit. Thus, in the pithy words of the district court, "[h]aving a case but no client," he called Greenfield, who lives in Florida, to discuss the U.S. Healthcare situation. Malone described the *Wall Street Journal* article to Greenfield and established that he owned stock in U.S. Healthcare. Malone asked Greenfield whether he would like Greenfield & Chimicles to file a suit on his behalf if the firm believed that there had been actionable wrongdoing, and Greenfield answered affirmatively. Within hours Malone determined that a certain class of U.S. Healthcare stockholders had "a legitimate and cognizable legal claim" stemming in part from the insiders' stock sales.

Events continued to unfold rapidly on November 4, 1992, for on that day Malone prepared and filed a class action complaint on behalf of Greenfield under section 10(b) of the Securities Exchange Act of 1934.... The gravamen of the complaint was that U.S. Healthcare and Abramson had issued false and misleading statements which were filed with the Securities and Exchange Commission and which caused Greenfield and the stockholder class to purchase U.S. Healthcare stock at artificially inflated prices. The complaint asserted controlling person liability against Abramson under section 20 of the Securities Exchange Act.... In the complaint, Malone recited that Greenfield fairly and adequately could represent the interest of the class of stockholders on whose behalf the action was being brought. Inasmuch as Malone mailed the complaint to Greenfield on November 4, 1992, Malone filed it before Greenfield received it. Obviously Malone did not think it important for Greenfield to see the complaint before it was filed even though Malone regards Greenfield as a distinguished retired corporate attorney.

On November 5, 1992, Malone on behalf of Allen Strunk filed a second class action against U.S. Healthcare and Abramson. The *Strunk* action repeated the allegations word for word from the Greenfield case except that the name of the plaintiff and the number of shares he owned were changed. Malone filed this action after Fred Taylor Isquith, an attorney in New York, contacted him and asked him to represent Strunk.

Malone and Strunk's New York lawyers were not the only attorneys interested in the U.S. Healthcare situation. On November 4, 1992, appellant Arnold Levin of the Philadelphia firm of Levin, Fishbein, Sedran & Berman, also read the *Wall Street Journal* article. Levin and his firm have what he characterized as "a long-standing professional relationship" with Greenfield & Chimicles, and Levin had a high regard for Greenfield & Chimicles' ethical standards and skill in handling federal securities law suits. On November 4, 1992, after Levin had read the article, Malone called him to discuss the merits of bringing a section 10(b) action against U.S. Healthcare and Abramson. Malone mentioned the *Wall Street Journal* article, and said he had done research into whether a section 10(b) action could be brought. Malone also told Levin that he had prepared such a complaint. Levin requested that Malone fax him a copy of the complaint, and Malone promptly did so. Levin then read the *Greenfield* complaint and reread the Wall Street Journal article and concluded, as he set forth in his affidavit, that "[b]ased upon my experience and understanding from the two documents," and in "reliance on the integrity of the pre-filing investigation of Greenfield & Chimicles," the section 10(b) action had merit.

There was even more interest in the U.S. Healthcare situation for on November 4, 1992, appellant Harris J. Sklar, a Philadelphia attorney in individual practice, also read the article. According to his affidavit, Sklar discussed the possibility of bringing an action against U.S. Healthcare with his client Scott Garr who was a U.S. Healthcare stockholder, and Garr authorized Sklar to bring the case on a class action basis. Sklar, however, saw the need to obtain co-counsel and consequently called Levin, as he had worked with him in the past. Levin then told Sklar of his dealings with Malone, and Levin and Sklar discussed the possibility of a suit. Sklar asked Levin to fax him a copy of the *Greenfield* complaint and Levin did so. Sklar then reviewed the complaint and, in his words as set forth in his affidavit, "[b]ased on my understanding of the securities laws and the facts as described in the *Wall Street Journal*," he determined that the complaint had merit. Sklar thus again spoke to Levin and indicated that Levin could file the class action on behalf of Scott Garr and Patricia Garr, his wife. On November 6, 1992, Levin and Sklar filed that complaint which replicated the *Greenfield* and *Strunk* complaints except that the names of the plaintiffs and the number of shares they owned were changed.

There was now an extraordinary development. On November 6, 1992, the same day that Levin and Sklar filed the *Garr* complaint, U.S. Healthcare and Abramson moved in the district court for the imposition of sanctions pursuant to Rule 11 in the *Greenfield*, *Strunk*, and *Garr* actions. This motion was a formidable document, as with attachments it exceeded 100 pages. At oral argument we asked U.S. Healthcare's attorney, Alan J. Davis, how it was possible that he filed this motion on the same day the *Garr* complaint was filed. He explained that he had anticipated that following the filing of the *Greenfield* complaint there would be additional complaints and accordingly his firm had a person waiting in the clerk's office to obtain copies of them when they were filed. . . .

In their brief, U.S. Healthcare and Abramson ... asserted that Malone, Levin, and Sklar failed to conduct "even the most cursory factual and legal investigation" of the case and that if they had done so they would have determined that the complaints had no basis in fact or law. The brief indicated that the three complaints demonstrated the "all too familiar pattern of an instant class action lawsuit based on newspaper reports followed by a covey of cut and paste copycat complaints."

As if what we have described is not remarkable enough, there was yet an additional extraordinary development in the *Greenfield* case. On November 8, 1992, Robert K. Greenfield finally read the complaint, and at that time came to the realization that he had made a mistake in bringing the action because he knew of no basis for it and because his son had substantial business dealings with U.S. Healthcare. Thus, he directed Malone to withdraw the complaint. When U.S. Healthcare and Abramson learned of Robert K. Greenfield's position, they supplemented their motion for Rule 11 sanctions to assert that Malone had failed to make a reasonable inquiry into whether Greenfield fairly and adequately could protect the interests of the plaintiff class.

... [T]he court found that Malone could not be sanctioned under Rule 11 with respect to the accuracy of the information on which he had predicated the *Greenfield* complaint because his inquiry into the underlying facts "was reasonable under the circumstances." ... However, the court found that Malone had violated Rule 11 with respect to the allegation in the complaint that Greenfield fairly and adequately could protect the interests of the class. ... But it also found that it could not say that Malone had made an inadequate inquiry into Strunk's ability fairly and adequately to protect the class. Accordingly, as Malone's factual inquiry into the merits of the case against U.S. Healthcare and Abramson had been reasonable, the court did not impose sanctions in the *Strunk* action.

The district court next discussed whether sanctions should be imposed on Levin and Sklar. ... The court rejected Levin's argument that he could rely on the integrity of the investigation by Greenfield & Chimicles, and it therefore ruled that Sklar could not rely on that investigation either. Ultimately the court held "that Levin and Sklar sought to act more quickly than fulfilling their duty would have allowed" and that "Levin['s] and Sklar's inquiry, or lack thereof, was unreasonable under the circumstances and a violation of Rule 11." ...

The court provided for the following sanctions. It required that Malone, Levin, and Sklar pay all of U.S. Healthcare's and Abramson's reasonable costs and attorney's fees incurred to that time, that the *Greenfield* and *Garr* complaints be dismissed without prejudice, and that the matter be referred to the Disciplinary Board of the Supreme Court of

Pennsylvania for an investigation into whether the conduct of Malone, Levin, and Sklar constituted a violation of the Pennsylvania Rules of Professional Conduct.... Of course, the court did not dismiss the *Strunk* action as there had been no Rule 11 violation in that case. Nevertheless, that case was dismissed without prejudice by stipulation on February 23, 1993. At oral argument, we were advised that none of the dismissed actions have been reinstituted.... Malone paid his sanction and did not thereafter appeal, but Levin and Sklar obtained stays and have appealed.

II. DISCUSSION

[The court quotes Fed. R. Civ. P. 11.]

... It is clear that the signer has a "personal, nondelegable responsibility" to comply with the requirements of Rule 11 before signing the document.

A signer's obligation personally to comply with the requirements of Rule 11 clearly does not preclude the signer from any reliance on information from other persons. For example, no one could argue fairly that it would be unreasonable for an attorney to rely on witnesses to an accident before bringing a personal injury action.... [A] determination of whether there has been " 'a reasonable inquiry may depend on ... whether [the signer] depended on forwarding counsel or another member of the bar.' " ... [I]nasmuch as the standard under Rule 11 is "fact specific," the court must consider all the material circumstances in evaluating the signer's conduct....

It is also important to observe that when the court examines the sufficiency of the inquiry into the facts and law, it must avoid drawing on the wisdom of hindsight and should test the signer's conduct by determining what was reasonable when the document was submitted. Thus, if under an objective standard, the signer made a reasonable inquiry both as to the fact and the law at the time a document was submitted, subsequent developments showing that the signer's position was incorrect will not subject the signer to Rule 11 sanctions for having submitted the document. On the other hand, a signer making an inadequate inquiry into the sufficiency of the facts and law underlying a document will not be saved from a Rule 11 sanction by the stroke of luck that the document happened to be justified. As the court indicated in *Vista Mfg., Inc. v. Trac-4 Inc.*, 131 F.R.D. 134, 138 (N.D. Ind. 1990), "A shot in the dark is a sanctionable event, even if it somehow hits the mark." The court in *Vista* correctly stated the law, for if a lucky shot could save the signer from sanctions, the purpose of Rule 11 "to deter baseless filings" would be frustrated. *Cooter & Gell v. Hartmarx Corp.*, 496 U.S. 384, 393 (1990).

There is also a temporal element in a determination of whether an inquiry was reasonable. Thus, we have recognized that a factor in ascertaining the reasonableness of the signer's inquiry is the amount of time available to investigate the facts and law involved. Accordingly, if a client comes into an attorney's office for an initial consultation concerning a possible case one day before the statute of limitations will run, the attorney might be justified in filing a complaint predicated on an inquiry which would be inadequate if the attorney had more time for investigation. On the other hand, an attorney with a great deal of time to file a document might be expected to make a more comprehensive inquiry than an attorney working under severe time constraints.

In reviewing a district court's Rule 11 determination, we use the abuse of discretion standard. . . .

Application of the foregoing principles requires us to affirm. . . . As Levin and Sklar explain in their brief: "Here, Levin acquired the knowledge from one whom he knew to be competent securities law counsel, Malone, coupled with the knowledge Levin obtained from the *Wall Street Journal*, and his experienced understanding of the securities laws. [sic] Levin passed this information on to Sklar so that he too could make the same certification." Brief at 17.

We do not doubt that sometimes it is difficult to reconcile the tension between the requirement that a signer personally discharge the Rule 11 obligations and the acknowledgment that a signer may rely on another party's inquiry in some cases. But this appeal presents no difficulties. Malone's declaration described the scope of his inquiry in great detail. He obtained a representative sampling of stories regarding U.S. Healthcare and a "disclo" report giving a great deal of financial information regarding U.S. Healthcare, including five-year figures showing sales, net income, earnings per share, and growth rate. He also considered financial ratios and examined forms filed with the Securities and Exchange Commission showing trading in U.S. Healthcare stock by insiders.[7] In fact, in the district court's view, Malone's inquiry was inadequate only as to Greenfield's status as the class representative.

On the other hand, Levin and Sklar relied only on the *Wall Street Journal* article, the *Greenfield* complaint, and Malone. They made no effort to examine the numerous materials Malone assembled, and they cannot justify their failure to have done so. They do not contend that Malone would not at their request have sent the materials to them. Alternatively, we see no reason why they could not have seen the materials by traveling the short distance from their offices in Philadelphia to Malone's office in Haverford, a Philadelphia suburb. We also point out that the documents on which Malone relied were all accessible to the public so that Levin and Sklar could have obtained them themselves.

---

[7] Malone obtained this information rapidly through the use of computer information retrieval services.

Furthermore, there were no time constraints requiring Levin and Sklar to file the *Garr* complaint on an expedited basis. The *Wall Street Journal* article was published on November 4, 1992, and Levin and Sklar filed the *Garr* complaint two days later. Levin and Sklar do not contend that they were confronted with a statute of limitations problem compelling immediate action. . . .

We also point out that Levin and Sklar have advanced no other reason why the *Garr* complaint had to have been filed within two days of the publication of the article. They do not contend, for example, that the Garrs needed emergency relief, nor do they suggest that U.S. Healthcare or Abramson might have evaded process or concealed assets if the suit had not been filed so quickly. . . .

At bottom, there is no escape from the conclusion that Levin and Sklar abdicated their own responsibilities and relied excessively on Malone contrary to Rule 11. . . . We recognize that it could be argued that it would have been pointless for Levin and Sklar to make an inquiry into the merits of the case sufficient to satisfy Rule 11 as Malone already had done so. Yet Rule 11 requires that an attorney signing a pleading must make a reasonable inquiry personally. The advantage of duplicate personal inquiries is manifest: while one attorney might find a complaint well founded in fact and warranted by the law, another, even after examining the materials available to the first attorney, could come to a contrary conclusion. Overall, we conclude that the Rule 11 violation in this case is so clear that even on a plenary review, we would uphold the sanctions imposed on Levin and Sklar. Accordingly, under the deferential abuse of discretion standard, we certainly must affirm the district court's determination that sanctions were required.

. . .

ROTH, CIRCUIT JUDGE, dissenting:

Although I share the majority's view that Levin and Sklar's conduct fell far short of the ideal, I do not share its belief that Rule 11 sanctions are appropriate in this situation. Instead, I believe that, when a court finds that an attorney has filed a meritorious complaint, the court should not go on to inquire whether the attorney conducted an adequate investigation prior to filing the complaint. I therefore respectfully dissent.

Except for changes in the named plaintiffs and the number of shares they owned, the complaint filed by Levin and Sklar on behalf of the Garrs was identical to the complaints filed by Malone on behalf of Greenfield and Strunk. As the majority notes, the district court did not dismiss the *Strunk* complaint, thereby implicitly finding that on its face it stated a valid claim. Presumably, had the district court not determined that Levin and Sklar violated Rule 11, it would not have dismissed the *Garr* complaint. Thus it is safe to assume that the district court believed that the *Garr* complaint on its face was meritorious.

In holding that the imposition of sanctions was appropriate in this case, the majority relies on the following statement in an opinion from a district court in another circuit: "A shot in the dark is a sanctionable event, even if it somehow hits the mark." *Vista Mfg., Inc. v. Trac-4, Inc.*, 131 F.R.D. 134, 138 (N.D. Ind. 1990). Though this statement has the virtue of being colorful, . . .the majority's conclusion that the *Vista* rule is necessary to further the purposes of Rule 11 is the product of an incomplete analysis of both the policies animating Rule 11 and the impact of that rule on the effectiveness of Rule 11. . . .

. . . The Supreme Court has stated that

> the central purpose of Rule 11 is to deter baseless filings in the District Court and thus, consistent with the Rule Enabling Act's grant of authority, streamline the administration and procedure of the federal courts. . . . Although the rule must be read in light of concerns that it will spawn satellite litigation and chill vigorous advocacy . . . any interpretation must give effect to the rule's central goal of deterrence.

Cooter & Gell v. Hartmarx Corp., 496 U.S. 384, 393 (1990). Similarly, the Advisory Committee indicated that the purpose of Rule 11 is "to discourage dilatory or abusive tactics and to help streamline the litigation process by lessening frivolous claims or defenses."

On the whole, the goals of deterring abuses of the system and streamlining litigation would be better served by the standard I advocate. Because the vast majority of "shots in the dark" will not hit their target, almost all of them will be subject to sanction. I find it difficult to believe that this slightly reduced probability of sanction will encourage lawyers to take blind shots. The deterrent function of Rule 11 to prevent baseless filings will not be undermined by not sanctioning when a complaint on its face does have merit. . . .

. . .

* * *

Problem 20.3. You also represented Lilith in an unrelated matter. The trial judge entered summary judgment in Lilith's favor. The plaintiff's claim was so lacking in detail and evidentiary support that you suspect the plaintiff's lawyer lacked probable cause to institute the action. Indeed, you believe that the plaintiff's lawyer simply relied on his client's version of events. You believe that had the plaintiff's lawyer conducted a reasonable investigation into the facts instead of relying solely on his client's version of events, he would have quickly realized that his client did not have a valid basis on which to pursue the claim against Lilith. You think the plaintiff's claim amounts to a "nuisance suit," filed simply to force Lilith to settle rather than incur the cost and aggravation of defending itself.

> (a) Assuming the plaintiff's lawyer simply took his client's word for the facts ultimately alleged in the complaint against Lilith, does Lilith have a valid malicious prosecution claim? *See Friedman v. Dozroc*, 312 N.W.2d 585 (Mich. 1981). At what point does a lawyer have an obligation to conduct an investigation into the facts beyond the account provided by a client?
>
> (b) Assuming the plaintiff's lawyer simply took his client's word for the facts ultimately alleged in the complaint against Lilith, is the lawyer subject to discipline under Rule 3.1? At what point does a lawyer have an obligation to conduct an investigation into the facts beyond the account provided by a client? *See generally* Rule 1.16, Comment [1].

* * *

Filing Time-Barred Claims. According to ABA Formal Ethics Opinion 94–387, knowingly filing a claim that is barred by the statute of limitations does not amount to either "the filing of a frivolous claim in violation of Rule 3.1, or a failure of candor toward the tribunal in violation of Rule 3.3." The ABA committee reasoned that the running of the statute of limitations is an affirmative defense that must be raised or it is waived. And the committee noted that "opposing counsel may fail to raise a limitations defense for any number of reasons, ranging from incompetence to a considered decision to forgo the defense in order to have a vindication on the merits or to assert some counterclaim." However, the committee also cautioned that "[t]he result ... might well be different if the limitations defect in the claim were jurisdictional, and thus affected the court's power to adjudicate this suit."

Do you agree that an attorney can ethically file a claim that she knows to be barred by the statute of limitations?

* * *

C. DISCOVERY

Model Rule 3.4 is entitled "Fairness to Opposing Party & Counsel." This obligation of fairness extends to all aspects of litigation, including the pre-trial discovery process. As you probably learned in Civil Procedure, the Federal Rules of Civil Procedure also have something to say about fairness in litigation. Rule 26 imposes upon the parties a duty to disclose, without awaiting a request, various forms of evidence. More generally, the rule attempts to ensure that the discovery process proceeds fairly. Rule 37 allows a court to impose sanctions for misconduct during the discovery process. The following part of the chapter explores some of the special ethical issues that may arise in the pre-trial discovery phase of litigation.

1. PRESERVATION AND SPOLIATION

When a client reasonably anticipates litigation (whether as a plaintiff or a defendant), the client has an obligation to preserve information that may be relevant to the case. Culpable destruction of such material is referred to as spoliation and may be punished by a court. In your civil procedure class, you likely studied the legal authorities that govern the range of sanctions for spoliation. Possible penalties include additional discovery, monetary sanctions, adverse inference instructions, and even dismissal or a default judgment.

In the information age, it is more challenging than ever for attorneys to guide their clients in preserving evidence. Because electronic information is stored in so many formats and in so many locations, attorneys must be skilled at asking the right questions of the right people to identify, collect, and preserve a client's information. Further, it can be tempting for clients who do not understand the consequences and the likelihood of detection to delete embarrassing or harmful information. Attorneys must educate their clients of the hazards of spoliation.

When attorneys do not competently guide their clients in preserving evidence, both client and attorney may face sanctions and other adverse consequences in the underlying case. Sanctions for discovery violations are on the rise in the e-discovery era, and sanctions for spoliation top the list of most frequently imposed sanctions. *See* Dan H. Willoughby, Jr., et al, *Sanctions for E-Discovery Violations: By the Numbers*, 60 DUKE L. J. 789, 803 (2010). Additionally, an attorney responsible for spoliation may also be disciplined for violating the jurisdiction's version of Model Rule 3.4(a) which prohibits an attorney unlawfully obstructing access to evidence or unlawfully altering, destroying, or concealing evidence (or counseling or assisting in such misconduct).

The following case is one of the best-known preservation cases from the dawn of the modern e-discovery era. Though the case is over two decades old now, it is still instructive about the complexity of an attorney's obligations in guiding clients in preservation.

* * *

ZUBULAKE V. UBS WARBURG LLC ("ZUBULAKE V")
229 F.R.D. 422 (S.D.N.Y. 2004)

SCHEINDLIN, J.

Commenting on the importance of speaking clearly and listening closely, Phillip Roth memorably quipped, "The English language is a form of communication! . . . Words aren't only bombs and bullets—no, they're little gifts, containing meanings!" What is true in love is equally true at law: Lawyers and their clients need to communicate clearly and effectively with one another to ensure that litigation proceeds efficiently. When communication between counsel and client breaks down, conversation becomes "just crossfire," and there are usually casualties.

I. INTRODUCTION

This is the fifth written opinion in this case, a relatively routine employment discrimination dispute in which discovery has now lasted over two years. Laura Zubulake is once again moving to sanction UBS for its failure to produce relevant information and for its tardy production of such material. In order to decide whether sanctions are warranted, the following question must be answered: Did UBS fail to preserve and timely produce relevant information and, if so, did it act negligently, recklessly, or willfully?

This decision addresses counsel's obligation to ensure that relevant information is preserved by giving clear instructions to the client to preserve such information and, perhaps more importantly, a client's obligation to heed those instructions. Early on in this litigation, UBS's counsel—both in-house and outside—instructed UBS personnel to retain relevant electronic information. Notwithstanding these instructions, certain UBS employees deleted relevant e-mails. Other employees never produced relevant information to counsel. As a result, many discoverable e-mails were not produced to Zubulake until recently, even though they were responsive to a document request propounded on June 3, 2002. In addition, a number of e-mails responsive to that document request were deleted and have been lost altogether.

Counsel, in turn, failed to request retained information from one key employee and to give the litigation hold instructions to another. They also failed to adequately communicate with another employee about how she maintained her computer files. Counsel also failed to safeguard backup tapes that might have contained some of the deleted e-mails, and which would have mitigated the damage done by UBS's destruction of those e-mails.

The conduct of both counsel and client thus calls to mind the now-famous words of the prison captain in Cool Hand Luke: "What we've got here is a failure to communicate." Because of this failure by both UBS and its counsel, Zubulake has been prejudiced. As a result, sanctions are warranted.

II. FACTS

The allegations at the heart of this lawsuit and the history of the parties' discovery disputes have been well-documented in the Court's prior decisions.... In short, Zubulake is an equities trader specializing in Asian securities who is suing her former employer for gender discrimination, failure to promote, and retaliation under federal, state, and city law.

A. Background

Zubulake filed an initial charge of gender discrimination with the EEOC on August 16, 2001. Well before that, however—as early as April 2001—UBS employees were on notice of Zubulake's impending court action.[7] After she received a right-to-sue letter from the EEOC, Zubulake filed this lawsuit on February 15, 2002.

Fully aware of their common law duty to preserve relevant evidence, UBS's in-house attorneys gave oral instructions in August 2001—immediately after Zubulake filed her EEOC charge—instructing employees not to destroy or delete material potentially relevant to Zubulake's claims, and in fact to segregate such material into separate files for the lawyers' eventual review. This warning pertained to both electronic and hard-copy files, but did not specifically pertain to so-called "backup tapes," maintained by UBS's information technology personnel. In particular, UBS's in-house counsel, Robert L. Salzberg, "advised relevant UBS employees to preserve and turn over to counsel all files, records or other written memoranda or documents concerning the allegations raised in the [EEOC] charge or any aspect of [Zubulake's] employment." Subsequently—but still in August 2001—UBS's outside counsel met with a number of the key players in the litigation and reiterated Mr. Salzberg's instructions, reminding them to preserve relevant documents, "including e-mails." Salzberg reduced these instructions to writing in e-mails dated February 22, 2002—immediately after Zubulake filed her complaint—and September 25, 2002. Finally, in August 2002, after Zubulake propounded a document request that specifically called for e-mails stored on backup tapes, UBS's outside counsel instructed UBS information technology personnel to stop recycling backup tapes. Every UBS employee mentioned in this Opinion (with the exception of Mike Davies) either personally spoke to UBS's outside counsel about the duty to preserve e-mails, or was a recipient of one of Salzberg's e-mails.

. . .

C. The Instant Dispute

The essence of the current dispute is that ... Zubulake has now presented evidence that UBS personnel deleted relevant e-mails, some of which were subsequently recovered from backup tapes (or elsewhere) and thus produced to Zubulake long after her initial document requests, and some of which were lost altogether. Zubulake has also presented evidence

---

[7] See *Zubulake IV*, 220 F.R.D. at 217 ("Thus, the relevant people at UBS anticipated litigation in April 2001. The duty to preserve attached at the time that litigation was reasonably anticipated.").

that some UBS personnel did not produce responsive documents to counsel until recently, depriving Zubulake of the documents for almost two years.

. . .

Zubulake now moves for sanctions as a result of UBS's purported discovery failings. In particular, she asks . . . that an adverse inference instruction be given to the jury that eventually hears this case.

III. LEGAL STANDARD

Spoliation is "the destruction or significant alteration of evidence, or the failure to preserve property for another's use as evidence in pending or reasonably foreseeable litigation." "The determination of an appropriate sanction for spoliation, if any, is confined to the sound discretion of the trial judge, and is assessed on a case-by-case basis." The authority to sanction litigants for spoliation arises jointly under the Federal Rules of Civil Procedure and the court's inherent powers.

. . . A party seeking an adverse inference instruction (or other sanctions) based on the spoliation of evidence must establish the following three elements: (1) that the party having control over the evidence had an obligation to preserve it at the time it was destroyed; (2) that the records were destroyed with a "culpable state of mind;" and (3) that the destroyed evidence was "relevant" to the party's claim or defense such that a reasonable trier of fact could find that it would support that claim or defense.

In this circuit, a "culpable state of mind" for purposes of a spoliation inference includes ordinary negligence. When evidence is destroyed in bad faith (*i.e.*, intentionally or willfully), that fact alone is sufficient to demonstrate relevance. By contrast, when the destruction is negligent, relevance must be proven by the party seeking the sanctions. In the context of a request for an adverse inference instruction, the concept of "relevance" encompasses not only the ordinary meaning of the term, but also that the destroyed evidence would have been favorable to the movant. . . . This is equally true in cases of gross negligence or recklessness; only in the case of willful spoliation does the degree of culpability give rise to a presumption of the relevance of the documents destroyed.

IV. DISCUSSION

In *Zubulake IV*, I held that UBS had a duty to preserve its employees' active files as early as April 2001, and certainly by August 2001, when Zubulake filed her EEOC charge. Zubulake has thus satisfied the first element of the adverse inference test. As noted, the central question implicated by this motion is whether UBS and its counsel took all necessary steps to guarantee that relevant data was both preserved and produced. If the answer is "no," then the next question is whether UBS acted willfully. . . . If UBS acted wilfully, this satisfies the mental culpability prong of the adverse inference test and also demonstrates that the deleted material was relevant. If UBS acted negligently or even recklessly, then Zubulake must show that the missing or late-produced information was relevant.

A. Counsel's Duty to Monitor Compliance

In *Zubulake IV*, I summarized a litigant's preservation obligations:

> Once a party reasonably anticipates litigation, it must suspend its routine document retention/destruction policy and put in place a "litigation hold" to ensure the preservation of relevant documents. As a general rule, that litigation hold does not apply to inaccessible backup tapes (e.g., those typically maintained solely for the purpose of disaster recovery), which may continue to be recycled on the schedule set forth in the company's policy. On the other hand, if backup tapes are accessible (i.e., actively used for information retrieval), then such tapes would likely be subject to the litigation hold.

A party's discovery obligations do not end with the implementation of a "litigation hold"—to the contrary, that's only the beginning. Counsel must oversee compliance with the litigation hold, monitoring the party's efforts to retain and produce the relevant documents. Proper communication between a party and her lawyer will ensure (1) that all relevant information (or at least all sources of relevant information) is discovered, (2) that relevant information is retained on a continuing basis, and (3) that relevant non-privileged material is produced to the opposing party.

1. Counsel's Duty to Locate Relevant Information

Once a "litigation hold" is in place, a party and her counsel must make certain that all sources of potentially relevant information are identified and placed "on hold," to the extent required in *Zubulake IV*. To do this, counsel must become fully familiar with her client's document retention policies, as well as the client's data retention architecture. This will invariably involve speaking with information technology personnel, who can explain system-wide backup procedures and the actual (as opposed to theoretical) implementation of the firm's recycling policy. It will also involve communicating with the "key players" in the litigation, in order to understand how they stored information. In this case, for example, some UBS employees created separate computer files pertaining to Zubulake, while others printed out relevant e-mails and retained them in hard copy only. Unless counsel interviews each employee, it is impossible to determine whether all potential sources of information have been inspected. A brief conversation with counsel, for example, might have revealed that [UBS employee] Tong maintained "archive" copies of e-mails concerning Zubulake, and that "archive" meant a separate on-line computer file, not a backup tape. Had that conversation taken place, Zubulake might have had relevant e-mails from that file two years ago.

To the extent that it may not be feasible for counsel to speak with every key player, given the size of a company or the scope of the lawsuit, counsel must be more creative. It may be possible to run a system-wide keyword search; counsel could then preserve a copy of each "hit." Although this sounds burdensome, it need not be. Counsel does not have to review these documents, only see that they are retained. For example, counsel could create a broad list of search terms, run a search for a limited time frame, and then segregate responsive documents. When the opposing party propounds its document requests, the parties could negotiate a list of search terms to be used in identifying responsive documents, and counsel would only be obliged to review documents that came up as "hits" on the second, more restrictive search. The initial broad cut merely guarantees that relevant documents are not lost.

In short, it is not sufficient to notify all employees of a litigation hold and expect that the party will then retain and produce all relevant information. Counsel must take affirmative steps to monitor compliance so that all sources of discoverable information are identified and searched. This is not to say that counsel will necessarily succeed in locating all such sources, or that the later discovery of new sources is evidence of a lack of effort. But counsel and client must take some reasonable steps to see that sources of relevant information are located.

2. Counsel's Continuing Duty to Ensure Preservation

Once a party and her counsel have identified all of the sources of potentially relevant information, they are under a duty to retain that information . . . and to produce information responsive to the opposing party's requests. Rule 26 creates a "duty to supplement" those responses. Although the Rule 26 duty to supplement is nominally the party's, it really falls on counsel. As the Advisory Committee explains,

> Although the party signs the answers, it is his lawyer who understands their significance and bears the responsibility to bring answers up to date. In a complex case all sorts of information reaches the party, who little understands its bearing on answers previously given to interrogatories. In practice, therefore, the lawyer under a continuing burden must periodically recheck all interrogatories and canvass all new information.

To ameliorate this burden, the Rules impose a continuing duty to supplement responses to discovery requests only when "a party[,] or more frequently his lawyer, obtains actual knowledge that a prior response is incorrect. This exception does not impose a duty to check the accuracy of prior responses, but it prevents knowing concealment by a party or attorney."

The continuing duty to supplement disclosures strongly suggests that parties also have a duty to make sure that discoverable information is not lost. Indeed, the notion of a "duty to preserve" connotes an ongoing obligation. Obviously, if information is lost or destroyed, it has not been preserved.

The tricky question is what that continuing duty entails. What must a lawyer do to make certain that relevant information—especially electronic information—is being retained? Is it sufficient if she periodically re-sends her initial "litigation hold" instructions? What if she communicates with the party's information technology personnel? Must she make occasional on-site inspections?

Above all, the requirement must be reasonable. A lawyer cannot be obliged to monitor her client like a parent watching a child. At some point, the client must bear responsibility for a failure to preserve. At the same time, counsel is more conscious of the contours of the preservation obligation; a party cannot reasonably be trusted to receive the "litigation hold" instruction once and to fully comply with it without the active supervision of counsel.

There are thus a number of steps that counsel should take to ensure compliance with the preservation obligation. While these precautions may not be enough (or may be too much) in some cases, they are designed to promote the continued preservation of potentially relevant information in the typical case.

First, counsel must issue a "litigation hold" at the outset of litigation or whenever litigation is reasonably anticipated. The litigation hold should be periodically re-issued so that new employees are aware of it, and so that it is fresh in the minds of all employees.

Second, counsel should communicate directly with the "key players" in the litigation, i.e., the people identified in a party's initial disclosure and any subsequent supplementation thereto. Because these "key players" are the "employees likely to have relevant information," it is particularly important that the preservation duty be communicated clearly to them. As with the litigation hold, the key players should be periodically reminded that the preservation duty is still in place.

Finally, counsel should instruct all employees to produce electronic copies of their relevant active files. Counsel must also make sure that all backup media which the party is required to retain is identified and stored in a safe place. In cases involving a small number of relevant backup tapes, counsel might be advised to take physical possession of backup tapes. In other cases, it might make sense for relevant backup tapes to be segregated and placed in storage. Regardless of what particular arrangement counsel chooses to employ, the point is to separate relevant backup tapes from others. One of the primary reasons that electronic data is lost is ineffective communication with information technology personnel. By taking possession of, or otherwise safeguarding, all potentially relevant backup tapes, counsel eliminates the possibility that such tapes will be inadvertently recycled....

. . .

a. UBS's Discovery Failings

UBS's counsel—both in-house and outside—repeatedly advised UBS of its discovery obligations. In fact, counsel came very close to taking the precautions laid out above. First, outside counsel issued a litigation hold in August 2001. The hold order was circulated to many of the key players in this litigation, and reiterated in e-mails in February 2002, when suit was filed, and again in September 2002. Outside counsel made clear that the hold order applied to backup tapes in August 2002, as soon as backup tapes became an issue in this case. Second, outside counsel communicated directly with many of the key players in August 2001 and attempted to impress upon them their preservation obligations. Third, and finally, counsel instructed UBS employees to produce copies of their active computer files....

b. Counsel's Failings

On the other hand, UBS's counsel are not entirely blameless. "While, of course, it is true that counsel need not supervise every step of the document production process and may rely on their clients in some respects," counsel is responsible for coordinating her client's discovery efforts. In this case, counsel failed to properly oversee UBS in a number of important ways, both in terms of its duty to locate relevant information and its duty to preserve and timely produce that information.

With respect to locating relevant information, counsel failed to adequately communicate with Tong about how she stored data....

With respect to making sure that relevant data was retained, counsel failed in a number of important respects. First, neither in-house nor outside counsel communicated the litigation hold instructions to Mike Davies, a senior human resources employee who was intimately involved in Zubulake's termination. Second, even though the litigation hold instructions were communicated to [UBS employee] Kim, no one ever asked her to produce her files. And third, counsel failed to protect relevant backup tapes; had they done so, Zubulake might have been able to recover some of the e-mails that UBS employees deleted.

. . .

c. Summary

Counsel failed to communicate the litigation hold order to all key players. They also failed to ascertain each of the key players' document management habits. By the same token, UBS employees—for unknown reasons—ignored many of the instructions that counsel gave. This case represents a failure of communication, and that failure falls on counsel and client alike.

. . .

I therefore conclude that UBS acted willfully in destroying potentially relevant information. . . . Because UBS's spoliation was willful, the lost information is presumed to be relevant.

B. Remedy

. . . I recognize that a major consideration in choosing an appropriate sanction—along with punishing UBS and deterring future misconduct—is to restore Zubulake to the position that she would have been in had UBS faithfully discharged its discovery obligations. That being so, I find that the following sanctions are warranted.

First, the jury empaneled to hear this case will be given an adverse inference instruction with respect to e-mails deleted after August 2001. . . .

Second, . . . UBS is ordered to pay the costs of any depositions or re-depositions required by the late production.

Third, UBS is ordered to pay the costs of this motion.

Finally, I note that UBS's belated production has resulted in a self-executing sanction. Not only was Zubulake unable to question UBS's witnesses using the newly produced e-mails, but UBS was unable to prepare those witnesses with the aid of those e-mails. Some of UBS's witnesses, not having seen these e-mails, have already given deposition testimony that seems to contradict the newly discovered evidence. . . .

. . .

VI. POSTSCRIPT

The subject of the discovery of electronically stored information is rapidly evolving. When this case began more than two years ago, there was little guidance from the judiciary, bar associations or the academy as to the governing standards. Much has changed in that time. There have been a flood of recent opinions—including a number from appellate courts—and there are now several treatises on the subject. In addition, professional groups such as the American Bar Association and the Sedona Conference have provided very useful guidance on thorny issues relating to the discovery of electronically stored information. Many courts have adopted, or are considering adopting, local rules addressing the subject. Most recently, the Standing Committee on Rules and Procedures has approved for publication and public comment a proposal for revisions to the Federal Rules of Civil Procedure designed to address many of the issues raised by the discovery of electronically stored information.

Now that the key issues have been addressed and national standards are developing, parties and their counsel are fully on notice of their responsibility to preserve and produce electronically stored information. The tedious and difficult fact finding encompassed in this opinion and others like it is a great burden on a court's limited resources. The time and effort spent by counsel to litigate these issues has also been time-consuming and distracting. This Court, for one, is optimistic that with the guidance now provided it will not be necessary to spend this amount of time again. It is hoped that counsel will heed the guidance provided by these resources and will work to ensure that preservation, production and spoliation issues are limited, if not eliminated.

* * *

Problem 20.4. When Linus Coverdale asked you to represent Lilith in the Necco case, you knew that electronic information would play a major role in the litigation. Using *Zubulake V* as a guide, what steps do you plan to take to ensure that information relevant to the case is preserved? Who would you like to meet with at Lilith in order to identify, collect, and preserve discoverable information?

* * *

2. MANIPULATING EVIDENCE

Model Rule 3.4 does more than simply require a lawyer to make reasonable efforts to ensure that potentially relevant evidence is not destroyed. The rule also affirmatively prohibits a lawyer from manipulating evidence, such as by falsifying evidence or counseling a witness to testify falsely. *See* Model Rule 3.4(b). The rule may be implicated in other ways. Comment [2] notes that applicable law may allow a lawyer to take temporary possession of physical evidence of client crimes for the purpose of conducting a limited examination. Any tests conducted, however, must not alter or destroy material characteristics of the evidence. Section 119 of the *Restatement (Third) of the Law Governing Lawyers* repeats this idea, noting that as long as the examination is "for the lawful purpose of assisting in the trial of criminal cases, . . . criminal laws that generally prohibit possession of contraband or other evidence of crimes are inapplicable to the lawyer." Once the examination is complete, however, criminal law may require that a defense lawyer turn the evidence over to law enforcement.

Note that Rule 3.4(a) applies not just to altering or obstructing access to tangible documents and electronic evidence, but also to procuring the absence of a witness. *In re Geisler*, 614 N.E.2d 939 (Ind. 1993) (involving lawyer who helped witness avoid service). This includes making threats against witnesses. *State ex rel. Bar Ass'n v. Cox*, 48 P.3d 780 (Okla. 2002) (involving lawyer who threatened to "dig up dirt" about potential witness if he testified).

* * *

3. FRIVOLOUS DISCOVERY REQUESTS AND OBJECTIONS AND DILATORY TACTICS

Model Rule 3.4 also speaks to a lawyer's ethical duties to comply with an obligation under the rules of a tribunal, refrain from making frivolous discovery requests, and to comply with discovery requests from the other side. Use Rule 3.4(c) and (d) to answer the problem below.

* * *

Problem 20.5. After several months of litigation, you work with Lilith employees to prepare "Lilith's Objections and Answers to Necco's Interrogatories." You provide a draft of the document to President Linus Coverdale, who is going to sign the document on behalf of Lilith. You ask him to review the answers and let you know if he has any questions or suggested changes. You receive the following email from Linus:

> Thanks for sending me the draft of "Lilith's Objections and Answers to Necco's Interrogatories." I see that you objected to producing information protected by the attorney-client privilege and there were a few spots where you objected that a word or phrase was ambiguous. But it looks like for the most part, you answered the questions.
>
> I have to tell you, I wish we could make this a little more difficult for Necco. I have worked with other lawyers in the past who could come up with a full page of objections for each and every interrogatory. Is there any reason why we don't want to do that in this case? Let me know what you think about trying that approach.—Linus

You do not think there are legitimate objections that you have not already asserted. You know that many attorneys would throw in a handful of objections just to be difficult, but you think that tends to hurt your relationship with opposing counsel and the court. It has been your experience that if you only object when there is a solid basis for doing so, opposing counsel is more likely to accept your objection as legitimate. And if opposing counsel files a motion to compel, the court is more likely to side with you when you have not objected to every interrogatory (or request for production) on questionable grounds. Further, you believe that you have more success in discovery when you do not make things unnecessarily difficult for opposing counsel. Opposing attorneys are more likely to provide information to you without a fight when you are doing the same in return.

In the end, you think your approach to discovery is much more cost effective, too.

In light of your views on these issues, draft a brief response to Linus's email. Explain why it is in the company's interest (and consistent with your legal and professional conduct obligations) for you to provide answers to interrogatories without asserting additional objections.

* * *

4. DISCLOSURE OF A CLIENT'S PERJURED TESTIMONY DURING A DEPOSITION

The next chapter explores a lawyer's dilemma when a client intends to commit or actually commits perjury at trial. But for now, note that Model Rule 3.3(a) requires a lawyer to take "reasonable remedial measures" if the lawyer comes to know that the client has offered material evidence that is false. This obligation extends to false testimony given in a deposition. *See* Model Rule 3.3, Comment [1]. Would it be a "reasonable remedial measure" for the lawyer in this situation to try to settle the case before it goes to trial so that the perjured testimony is never introduced at trial?

* * *

5. PROTECTING PRIVILEGE AND WORK PRODUCT AND ADDRESSING INADVERTENT DISCLOSURE

Recall that Chapter 15 discussed an attorney's obligation to protect privileged and work product protected information from disclosure in discovery. *See* Model Rule 1.6(c). The chapter also considered the obligations of a recipient of an inadvertent disclosure. *See* Model Rule 4.4(b). Review that material to complete the following problem.

* * *

Problem 20.6. You are reviewing "Necco's Objections and Responses to Lilith's First Requests for Production of Documents." As you begin to look at some of the documents, you come across a letter from Necco's litigation counsel addressed to Necco's general counsel. In the letter, Necco's attorney discusses how much the company should consider accepting to settle the Lilith litigation. With citation to authority, discuss the steps you will take next, including whether you will forward the letter to Lilith's president, Linus Coverdale.

Profile of Attorney Professionalism. When Judge Shira Scheindlin wrote the fifth *Zubulake* opinion in 2004 (excerpted earlier in this chapter), the concept of electronic discovery was brand new; she had little precedent to guide her. Judge Scheindlin had become interested in the intersection of technology and litigation procedure in the late 1990s, while serving as a member of the Advisory Committee on Civil Rules. By the time she authored the opinion in *Zubulake*, Judge Scheindlin had already given substantial thought to how discovery procedures could work with emerging technologies and the storage of electronic data. When the *Zubulake* decision was released, Judge Scheindlin's opinion in the case instantly became the leading guide for lawyers and companies trying to figure out how to deal with electronically stored information. Some of Judge Scheindlin's analysis from *Zubulake* was later incorporated into the Federal Rules of Civil Procedure.

In an interview for a podcast, Judge Scheindlin discussed the expense of discovery and the difficulties in litigating when one party has substantially greater financial resources than the other. She emphasized how the discovery rules interact with the lawyer's duties to the court and to the adversary, explaining that a party facing a burdensome discovery request has an obligation to handle it within the framework established by the rules:

> [T]hat's the key point. You can't use self-help. You either go for protection by coming to court or you comply. [You can't] just ignore it, put your head in the sand . . . and then say, "Well the reason I didn't do better is it was too expensive."

Podcast: Electronic Discovery and Law School Curriculums, ESI Bytes, (March 18, 2009).

CHAPTER 21

TRIAL AND APPELLATE ADVOCACY

■ ■ ■

Chapter Hypothetical. You serve as a law clerk to U.S. District Court Judge Martha Moore. Judge Moore has a busy docket that includes the matters discussed in the problems in this chapter.

Nowhere is the notion that a lawyer must zealously advocate on behalf of a client more deeply engrained than during trial. But a lawyer's duty in this regard is cabined by the requirement that the lawyer zealously advocate only "within the bounds of the law." ABA *Model Rules of Prof'l Conduct* Preamble ¶ 9. Thus, a lawyer's responsibilities to a client and to the legal system may sometimes be tension. Trials are, of course, governed by the law of evidence. But there are also rules of professional conduct that may impose additional limitations on a lawyer's advocacy on behalf of a client.

A. USING IRRELEVANT OR INADMISSIBLE INFORMATION

Model Rule 3.4(e) prohibits a lawyer from alluding "to any matter that the lawyer does not reasonably believe is relevant or that will not be supported by admissible evidence." A clear example of such conduct would be alluding in trial to the fact that a party is covered by insurance, evidence that is inadmissible under the Federal Rules of Evidence. *Falkowski v. Johnson*, 148 F.R.D. 132 (D. Del. 1993). In most instances, this type of misconduct is dealt with through objections by opposing parties, contempt citations, and new trials. However, professional discipline remains a possibility.

* * *

Problem 21.1. Judge Moore recently presided over the criminal trial of Carrie Anderson for the alleged murder of her child. During her opening statement, Anderson's attorney, Gloria Diaz, suggested to the jury that the child was not murdered but accidentally drowned in the family swimming pool. At trial, Anderson did not testify and no evidence was presented that the child drowned. Analyze whether Diaz violated Rule 3.4(e) through her opening statement.

B. LAWYER ACTING AS A WITNESS

The rules of professional conduct also seek to prevent lawyers from blurring the line between being an advocate for a client and being a witness. When a lawyer addresses a jury, the lawyer will, of course, attempt to present the facts in a persuasive manner. But Rule 3.4(e) limits the ability of a lawyer to assert personal knowledge of facts or to state personal opinions with regard to some matters. When it comes to witness testimony, a lawyer will, of course, examine witnesses in a manner that advances the client's objectives. But if an attorney actually testifies *as a witness* at trial, there are the concerns that "the attorney will not be a fully objective witness and . . . that the trier of fact will confuse the roles of advocate and witness and erroneously grant special weight to an attorney's arguments." *McElroy v. Gaffney*, 529 A.2d 889 (N.H. 1987). As you can see from Rule 3.7, there are situations in which a party may move to disqualify a lawyer from representing a client at trial based on these kinds of concerns. This raises a concern about the possibility that a client will be denied their choice of counsel.

Problem 21.2. Gloria was present when the police interviewed Carrie at the crime scene. At trial, one of the police officers who interviewed Carrie unexpectedly testified about the details of the crime scene in a manner that Gloria knew to be inconsistent with the facts.

(a) During closing argument, Gloria tells the jury, "I was present at the scene when the police officer interviewed Carrie, and I can tell you for a fact that he is lying." Read Model Rule 3.4(e). Is Gloria subject to professional discipline for this statement? Is discipline appropriate here, or should the justice system leave it to trial judges (like Judge Moore) to deal with such conduct? What should Judge Moore do in such a situation?

(b) Assume that Gloria knew in advance of trial what the substance of the officer's testimony would be and that the testimony would be harmful to her client's case. Read Model Rule 3.7. Can Gloria represent Carrie at trial? If not, could another lawyer in Gloria's firm do so?

* * *

C. COMMUNICATING WITH JURORS, THE JUDGE, AND COURT OFFICERS

Consistent with the goals of promoting impartial resolution of disputes (as well as the appearance of impartial resolution of disputes), Model Rule 3.5 places limits on the ability of lawyers to influence and communicate with judges, jurors, prospective jurors, and court officials. The rule prohibits a lawyer from seeking to influence such individuals through means prohibited by law. This would obviously include something along the lines of bribery. But it has also been held to cover such actions as providing gifts or making threats to a judge. *See In re Zeno*, 517 F. Supp. 2d 591 (D.P.R. 2007); *In re Garaas*, 652 N.W.2d 918 (N.D. 2002).

Rule 3.5 also prohibits a lawyer from communicating outside the presence of opposing counsel with judges, jurors, and prospective jurors during a proceeding. This prohibition on such *ex parte* communication applies regardless of whether the other individual or the lawyer initiates the communication. Given the concerns over lawyers being perceived as attempting to improperly influence such individuals, the rule has been rigorously applied. *See Fla. Bar v. Peterson*, 418 So. 2d 246 (Fla. 1982) (disciplining lawyer who allowed himself to be seated with jurors at lunch during a recess, which resulted in mistrial). Note that the prohibition on *ex parte* communications during a "proceeding" has been held to apply not just to communications during the course of a trial but to any step in the course of a legal dispute, from the filing of a claim to final disposition after appeal. *See Hancock v. Bd. of Prof. Responsibility of Supreme Court of Tenn.*, 447 S.W.3d 844 (Tenn. 2014).

* * *

Problem 21.3. During the course of jury selection in a personal injury case, lawyer Buddy Jarrett sends a "friend" request via social media to a potential juror in order to learn more about the individual. The individual reports Jarrett's actions to Judge Moore. Should Judge Moore report Jarrett's actions to disciplinary authorities for having violated Rule 3.5(b)?

Problem 21.4. Lawyer Bill Gulas was representing a client in a bitter divorce matter involving allegations of sexual abuse on the part of the other spouse. Judge Moore made several adverse rulings on Gulas' motions. In response, Gulas posted a "petition" on social media discussing the case, attacking Judge Moore for "protecting abusers," and asking readers to "sign the petition and reach out to Judge Moore to let her know that the law doesn't protect abusers." In response, dozens of people email and call Judge Moore's office to complain about her handling of the case. Has Gulas violated Rule 3.5? If so, what level of professional discipline is appropriate? Has he violated any other rules?

* * *

D. DISRUPTIVE AND DISCRIMINATORY CONDUCT

1. ENGAGING IN CONDUCT INTENDED TO DISRUPT A TRIBUNAL

Model Rule 3.5(d) prohibits a lawyer from engaging in conduct intended to disrupt a tribunal. Disruptive behavior in court is often addressed through a court's power to hold lawyers in contempt. But sometimes disruptive behavior in the courtroom has also resulted in professional discipline. Examples range from the dramatic to the childish. *See, e.g., Fla. Bar v. Martocci*, 791 So. 2d 1074 (Fla. 2001) (imposing discipline on lawyer who, *inter alia*, made faces and stuck out his tongue during proceeding). The rule has also been applied to conduct occurring outside the courtroom that was designed to disrupt the tribunal. *See People v. Maynard*, 238 P.3d 672 (Colo. 2009) (disciplining lawyer who filed multiple motions seeking the judge's recusal as a tactic to delay the proceeding).

* * *

Problem 21.5. Judge Moore is presiding over a wrongful death jury trial. The decedent, a twenty-eight year old mother of two, lost her life when a semi-truck driver fell asleep at the wheel and slammed into her car. During closing argument, the plaintiff's lawyer, Mitch Murphy, broke down and cried. At one point, he stopped speaking so that he could wipe his eyes with a handkerchief as he braced himself by holding onto the rail in front of the jury box. Judge Moore called both attorneys to the bench and asked Murphy if he needed a short break to collect himself. He said he was fine, but when he continued the closing, he started crying again.

Judge Moore believes the crying was an attempt by Murphy to disrupt the proceeding, to endear himself to the jury, and to influence the verdict. Advise Judge Moore about whether Murphy's crying amounts to professional misconduct under Rule 3.5(d) or any other professional conduct rule. Beyond referring Murphy to the bar for discipline, are there other steps Judge Moore can take to address what she perceives as misconduct in her courtroom?

* * *

2. DISCRIMINATORY COMMENTS AND ACTIONS

Model Rule 8.4(g) prohibits a lawyer from engaging in conduct that the lawyer knows or reasonably should know is harassment or discrimination on the basis of race, sex, and other characteristics in conduct related to the practice of law. While this would obviously include conduct occurring in the course of litigation, the rule expressly notes that the prohibition "does not preclude legitimate . . . advocacy consistent with these Rules." At what point does legitimate advocacy end and unethical discriminatory conduct begin? In an Indiana case, a lawyer made repeated references before the jury to the fact that the ex-wife (a white woman) of his client was living with "a black man" or "a black guy." *In re Thomsen*, 837 N.E.2d 1011 (Ind. 2005). Would this conduct amount to a violation of Rule 8.4(g)?

A number of jurisdictions have not adopted Rule 8.4(g). But Rule 8.4(d)'s prohibition on conduct prejudicial to the administration of justice might also reach discriminatory conduct occurring at trial. Discriminatory words or conduct manifesting bias on the basis of race and other characteristics have the potential to interfere with the proper administration of justice. Thus, courts and disciplinary authorities have applied this rule to improper statements at trial, *see In re Thomsen*, 837 N.E.2d 1011 (Ind. 2005) (disciplining lawyer who made repeated reference before the jury to the fact that the ex-wife (a white woman) of his client was living with "a black man" or "a black guy"), as well as discriminatory comments made to opposing counsel outside the courtroom. *See Fla. Bar v. Martocci*, 791 So.2d 1074 (2001) (disciplining lawyer who engaged in "sexist, racial, and ethnic insults" during depositions).

* * *

Problem 21.6. Lawyer Desean Monk represented a client in a personal injury action. As part of the case, Monk argued that the defendant's negligence had resulted in his client having a permanent limp. Monk's client expressed concern to Monk about the courtroom presence of Judge Moore's other law clerk, Justin, who uses a wheelchair for mobility and a respirator to help breathe. The client was concerned that the jury would compare his physical condition to that of Justin's and not award sufficient damages. So, during trial, Monk made an oral motion outside the presence of the jury, asking Judge Moore to not allow Justin to be in the courtroom during trial. Judge Moore denied the motion. Did Monk violate Rule 8.4(d) or (g)?

* * *

E. TRUTHFULNESS AND CANDOR

As an officer of the court, a lawyer owes special obligations to the legal system. One of these is the duty of candor owed to the tribunal. But, once again, this obligation may sometimes be in tension with the lawyer's responsibilities to the client.

1. DECEPTION AND TRICKERY AT TRIAL

One common narrative device in fictional courtroom dramas is for the hero/attorney to uncover the truth at trial through the use of a little bit of deception. So, sometime justice is achieved onscreen or in print through the use of trickery. But as covered in Chapter 3, Model Rule 8.4(c) prohibits a lawyer from engaging in "dishonesty, fraud, deceit, or misrepresentation." At what point does courtroom trickery cross the line from zealous advocacy into unethical conduct?

UNITED STATES V. THOREEN
653 F.2d 1332 (9th Cir. 1981)

EUGENE A. WRIGHT, CIRCUIT JUDGE:

I. INTRODUCTION

The issue before us is whether an attorney may be found in criminal contempt for pursuing a course of aggressive advocacy while representing his client in a criminal proceeding such that, without the court's permission or knowledge, he substitutes someone for his client at counsel table with the intent to cause a misidentification, resulting in the misleading of the court, counsel, and witnesses; a delay while the government reopened its case to identify the defendant; and violation of a court order and custom.

We affirm the district court's finding of criminal contempt. . . .

II. FACTS

. . .

In February 1980, [Attorney Thoreen] represented Sibbett, a commercial fisher, during Sibbett's non-jury trial before Judge Tanner for criminal contempt for three violations of a preliminary injunction against salmon fishing. In preparing for trial, Thoreen hoped that the government agent who had cited Sibbett could not identify him. He decided to test the witness's identification.

He placed next to him at counsel table Clark Mason, who resembled Sibbett and had Mason dressed in outdoor clothing denims, heavy shoes, a plaid shirt, and a jacket-vest. Sibbett wore a business suit, large round glasses, and sat behind the rail in a row normally reserved for the press. Thoreen neither asked the court's permission for, nor notified it or government counsel of, the substitution. On Thoreen's motion at the start of the trial, the court ordered all witnesses excluded from the courtroom. Mason remained at counsel table.

Throughout the trial, Thoreen made and allowed to go uncorrected numerous misrepresentations. He gestured to Mason as though he was his client and gave Mason a yellow legal pad on which to take notes. The two conferred. Thoreen did not correct the court when it expressly referred to Mason as the defendant and caused the record to show identification of Mason as Sibbett.

Because of the conduct, two government witnesses misidentified Mason as Sibbett. Following the government's case, Thoreen called Mason as a witness and disclosed the substitution. The court then called a recess. When the trial resumed, the government reopened and recalled the government agent who had cited Sibbett for two of the violations. He identified Sibbett, who was convicted of all three violations.

. . .

Judge Tanner found Thoreen in criminal contempt for the substitution because it was imposed on the court and counsel without permission or prior knowledge; the claimed identification issue did not exist; it disrupted the trial; it deceived the court and frustrated its responsibility to administer justice; and it violated a court custom. He found Mason's presence in the courtroom after giving the order excluding witnesses another ground for contempt because Thoreen planned that Mason would testify when the misidentification occurred. Judge Tanner held also that Thoreen's conduct conflicted with DR 1–102(A)(4)[4], DR 7–102(A)(6)[5], and DR 7–106(C)(5)[6] of the Washington Code of Professional Responsibility.

Thoreen's principal defense is that his conduct was a good faith tactic in aid of cross-examination and falls within the protected realm of zealous advocacy. He argues that as defense counsel he has no obligation to ascertain or present the truth and may seek to confuse witnesses with misleading questions, gestures, or appearances. . . .

. . .

1. Zealous Advocacy

. . .

Vigorous advocacy by defense counsel may properly entail impeaching or confusing a witness, even if counsel thinks the witness is truthful, and refraining from presenting evidence even if he knows the truth. . . . When we review this conduct and find that the line between vigorous advocacy and actual obstruction is close, our doubts should be resolved in favor of the former.

The latitude allowed an attorney is not unlimited. He must represent his client within the bounds of the law. As an officer of the court, he must "preserve and promote the efficient operation of our system of justice."

Thoreen's view of appropriate cross-examination, which encompasses his substitution, crossed over the line from zealous advocacy to actual obstruction . . . . Moreover, this conduct harms rather than enhances an

---

[4] "(A) A lawyer shall not: (4) Engage in conduct involving dishonesty, fraud, deceit, or misrepresentation."

[5] "(A) In his representation of a client, a lawyer shall not: (6) Participate in the creation or preservation of evidence when he knows or it is obvious that the evidence is false."

[6] "(C) In appearing in his professional capacity before a tribunal, a lawyer shall not: (5) Fail to comply with known local customs of courtesy or practice of the bar or a particular tribunal without giving to opposing counsel timely notice of his intent not to comply."

attorney's effectiveness as an advocate. It is fundamental that in relations with the court, defense counsel must be scrupulously candid and truthful in representations of any matter before the court. This is not only a basic ethical requirement, but it is essential if the lawyer is to be effective in the role of advocate, for if the lawyer's reputation for veracity is suspect, he or she will lack the confidence of the court when it is needed most to serve the client.

2. Criminal Contempt

18 U.S.C. § 401 (1976) provides

> A court of the United States shall have power to punish by fine or imprisonment, at its discretion, such contempt of its authority, and none other as
>
> (1) Misbehavior of any person in its presence or so near thereto as to obstruct the administration of justice; . . .
>
> (3) Disobedience or resistance to its lawful writ, process, order, rule, decree, or command.

. . . .

Because Thoreen's conduct was in the court's presence, our inquiry turns to whether it constituted contumacious misbehavior that obstructed the administration of justice.

. . . .

Contumacious misbehavior by an attorney includes disobeying a court's rulings or instructions, and deceiving the court. Examples of contumacious deceptive behavior are misrepresenting oneself as a practicing attorney, *Bowles v. United States*, 50 F.2d 848, 851 (4th Cir.), *cert. denied*, 284 U.S. 648 (1931); an attorney's swearing to and filing of admittedly false affidavits and supplemental complaint, plus the pursuit of meritless litigation, *Letts v. Icarian Development Co., S.A.*, No. 74 C 2252 (N.D. Ill., Sept. 15, 1980); and an attorney's presentation of false evidence, *United States v. Ford*, 9 F.2d 990, 991 (D. Mont. 1925).

Making misrepresentations to the court is also inappropriate and unprofessional behavior under ethical standards that guide attorneys' conduct. These guidelines, in effect in Washington and elsewhere, decree explicitly that an attorney's participation in the presentation or preservation of false evidence is unprofessional and subjects him to discipline.

Substituting a person for the defendant in a criminal case without a court's knowledge has been noted as an example of unethical behavior by the ABA Committee on Professional Ethics. *See* Informal Opinion No. 914, 2/24/66 (decided under the former ABA *Code of Professional Responsibility*).

Ethical standards establish the outermost limits of appropriate and sanctioned attorney conduct. While we acknowledge that a court's power to discipline or disbar an attorney " 'proceeds upon very different grounds' from those which support a court's power to punish for contempt," *Cammer v. United States*, 350 U.S. 399, 408 n.7 (1956), we consider and apply ethical benchmarks when determining whether an attorney's conduct is inappropriate to his role and thus constitutes contumacious misbehavior.

Counsel's conduct must cause an actual obstruction of justice before criminal contempt lies.

. . . .

Making misrepresentations to the fact finder is inherently obstructive because it frustrates the rational search for truth. It may also delay the proceedings. . . .

The record supports Judge Tanner's conclusion that Thoreen's substitution was misbehavior that obstructed justice. . . .

. . . .

To be held in criminal contempt, the contemnor must have the requisite intent. "[A]n attorney possesses the requisite intent only if he knows or reasonably should be aware in view of all the circumstances, especially the heat of the controversy, that he is exceeding the outermost limits of his proper role and hindering rather than facilitating the search for truth.". . . .

Thoreen admits he planned and intended the substitution, but defends by asserting that (1) it was a good faith effort to prove misidentification and attack the credibility of the government witnesses; (2) he never intended to misrepresent any facts to the court or to obstruct justice; and (3) he believed the court knew Sibbett's identity from the pretrial hearing.

The record shows that Sibbett's identification was not an issue, contradicting the need to attack credibility. The testimony about Sibbett's violations was thorough, credible, and not in conflict. Thoreen's alleged belief that the court would remember Sibbett from a pretrial proceeding is unrealistic because that hearing took place several months earlier and Sibbett was but one of many persons cited for violating the salmon fishing injunction.

His alleged lack of intent to deceive the court or to obstruct justice is irrelevant. Section 401(1) does not require specific intent. It suffices that he should have been aware that his conduct exceeded reasonable limits and hindered the search for truth.

IV. CONCLUSION

Thoreen's error in judgment was unfortunate. The court's ire and this criminal contempt conviction could have been avoided easily and the admirable goal of representing his client zealously preserved if only he had given the court and opposing counsel prior notice and sought the court's consent.[7]

We AFFIRM the contempt conviction. . . .

* * *

Thoreen's Conduct. At what point did Thoreen's conduct become zealous advocacy *outside* the bounds of the law? In your opinion, should Thoreen have been held in contempt? Which rules of professional conduct did he violate?

Permissible Deception and Trickery? When, if ever, is it acceptable for a lawyer to engage in deception or trickery at trial? For example, if the lawyer believes an adverse witness is lying, should the lawyer be permitted to imply that the lawyer has evidence that establishes that the adverse witness is lying (when the lawyer really does not have such evidence?)

* * *

2. CANDOR TOWARD THE TRIBUNAL

Comment 2 to Model Rule 3.3 explains that while "[a] lawyer acting as an advocate in an adjudicative proceeding has an obligation to present the client's case with persuasive force," that obligation is tempered by the lawyer's duty of candor toward the tribunal. Rule 3.3(a) prohibits a lawyer from making *any* false statement of fact or law (not just "material" ones) to a tribunal. This duty may arise in a number of situations.

* * *

a. Disclosure of Adverse Legal Authority

Part of presenting a client's case "with persuasive force" often means presenting existing precedent in the light most favorable to a client's position. But Model Rule 3.3(a)(2) requires more. The rule sometimes requires a lawyer to disclose precedent that is directly adverse to a client's position when not cited by the opposing side. The failure to do so amounts to a violation of the lawyer's duty of candor toward the tribunal. One of the principles underlying the duty is judicial efficiency: it would be a waste of judicial resources for a court to decide a matter without considering all of the relevant precedent, simply to have an appellate court reverse the decision on those grounds.

---

[7] While finding Thoreen's tactic misleading and obstructive of justice, we acknowledge that certain variations are acceptable. If identification is at issue, an attorney could test a witness's credibility by notifying the court and counsel that it is and by seeking the court's permission to (1) seat two or more persons at counsel table without identifying the defendant; *see* Duke v. State, 260 Ind. 638, 298 N.E.2d 453 (1973); (2) have no one at counsel table; (3) hold an in-court lineup.

***

Problem 21.7. Judge Moore has asked you to draft an order ruling on a motion for summary judgment. During your legal research, you notice that the lawyer for one of the parties not only misrepresented the facts in his brief, he failed to cite a state supreme court decision from within the controlling jurisdiction that is directly adverse to the client's position. You point this omission out to Judge Moore, who brings it up to the lawyer, William Cyrus, during a hearing. Cyrus admits he knew of the decision but argues that he was not obligated to cite it because the facts were distinguishable from the present case; thus, the prior decision was not controlling. Read Rule 3.3(a)(2) carefully. Is Cyrus' argument sound?

Zealous Advocacy? Doesn't it hurt your client's case to disclose adverse authority? The short answer is not necessarily, if done correctly. *See* Michael J. Higdon, *When the Case Gives You Lemons: Using Negative Authority in Persuasive Legal Writing*, 46 TENN. B.J. 14 (March 2010) (demonstrating that given the critical nature of the legal reader, including adverse case law in legal documents not only will help an attorney discharge her ethical obligation, but also make the document more persuasive, and offering specific suggestions on incorporating negative authority in a manner that enhances the strength of the advocate's argument.)

***

b. Disclosure of Adverse Facts

Generally speaking, a lawyer's duty of candor with respect to adverse facts is somewhat less stringent than the duty to disclose adverse legal authority. Indeed, absent any legal obligation to disclose facts (such as through the discovery process in civil litigation), a lawyer's duty of confidentiality under Rule 1.6 would ordinarily prohibit a lawyer from disclosing information that might be harmful to a client's case. But how far does this principle extend?

***

Problem 21.8. Following a criminal defendant's conviction, Judge Moore held a hearing to sentence the defendant. Due to a clerical error, Judge Moore was under the impression that the defendant had no prior criminal history. This was not accurate. The defendant actually had three prior convictions. Judge Moore announced that "in light of the fact that the defendant has no prior record, I'm not inclined to impose any jail time." Then, addressing the defendant's lawyer, Judge Moore asked, "Counselor, do you have anything further to add before I impose a sentence?" The lawyer knows of the client's prior convictions. How should the lawyer respond in light of Rules 1.6 and 3.3(a)(1)?

c. Protecting the Tribunal Against Perjury and Other False Evidence

Model Rule 3.3(a)(3) prohibits a lawyer from offering evidence the lawyer knows to be false. The rule also requires a lawyer to take "reasonable remedial measures" upon later learning that the lawyer has offered such evidence. The scope of these duties is complicated.

In *Nix v. Whiteside*, 475 U.S. 157 (1986), the U.S. Supreme Court held that a criminal defendant was not denied effective assistance of counsel when his appointed counsel threatened to withdraw because he believed his client was determined to commit perjury at his trial. The Court held that the lawyer's performance fell within the "range of reasonable professional assistance," as measured by "[p]revailing norms of practice as reflected in American Bar Association Standards and the like, . . ." There, the defendant, Whiteside, was charged with murder. Whiteside told his lawyer, Robinson, that he stabbed the victim because he believed the victim was reaching for a gun, although he had not actually seen a gun. Shortly before trial, he changed his story, telling Robinson that he had seen the victim reaching for something "metallic." Whiteside also insisted on testifying at his trial. Robinson told him that

> we could not allow him to [testify falsely] because that would be perjury, and as officers of the court we would be suborning perjury if we allowed him to do it; . . . I advised him that if he did do that it would be my duty to advise the Court of what he was doing and that I felt he was committing perjury; also, that I probably would be allowed to attempt to impeach that particular testimony.

The Court noted that "Robinson also indicated he would seek to withdraw from the representation if Whiteside insisted on committing perjury." Whiteside did take the stand but did not testify that he saw "something metallic." After he was convicted of murder, Whiteside alleged that Robinson had not provided effective assistance of counsel, due to his threats of disclosure and withdrawal if Whiteside testified to seeing "something metallic." The Court indicated its approval of Robinson's conduct:

> Although counsel must take all reasonable lawful means to attain the objectives of the client, counsel is precluded from taking steps or in any way assisting the client in presenting false evidence or otherwise violating the law. . . . Whether Robinson's conduct is seen as a successful attempt to dissuade his client from committing the crime of perjury, or whether seen as a "threat" to withdraw from representation and disclose the illegal scheme, Robinson's representation of Whiteside falls well within accepted

standards of professional conduct and the range of reasonable professional conduct . . . .

* * *

Knowledge of Intent to Commit Perjury. Model Rule 3.3(a)(3) prohibits a lawyer from offering evidence the lawyer knows to be false. But how often does a lawyer "know" in advance that a witness will testify falsely? Rule 1.0(f) defines the term "knows" as denoting actual knowledge. In *State v. McDowell*, 681 N.W.2d 500, 514 (Wis. 2004), the Wisconsin Supreme Court stated that "[a]bsent the most extraordinary circumstances, such knowledge must be based on the client's expressed admission of intent to testify untruthfully." Other courts have not gone so far as to require actual knowledge under these circumstances. *See* State v. Hischke, 639 N.W.2d 6, 10 (Iowa 2002) (holding that rule applies when a lawyer has "good cause to believe the defendant's proposed testimony would be deliberately untruthful"); United States ex rel. Wilcox v. Johnson, 555 F.2d 115, 122 (3d Cir.1977) (stating lawyer must have "firm factual basis" that client will testify falsely before lawyer is permitted to raise concerns with trial judge). Given the competing policy concerns, what standard should apply?

So What Do I Do? The *Nix* Court's discussion of Robinson's actions, coupled with a careful reading of Rule 3.3 and its Comments, yields a plausible sequence of responses to threatened or actual client perjury.

- If the client threatens to testify falsely, the lawyer must attempt to persuade the client not to do so.

- Following the lawyer's attempt to persuade the client, the lawyer's strategy depends upon whether her client is a criminal defendant or a party to a civil action. If a criminal defendant, the client must be permitted to testify unless the lawyer "knows" that she will commit perjury. *See* Rule 3.3(a)(3). If a civil party, and if the lawyer "reasonably believes" that she will commit perjury, the client may be permitted to testify or may be kept off the stand, at the lawyer's discretion.

- If, despite the lawyer's best efforts, the lawyer "knows" that the client has testified falsely, the lawyer must "remonstrate" with the client and attempt to persuade her to rectify the false testimony. Rule 3.3 Comment [10].

- If the client refuses to rectify the false testimony, the lawyer must first seek to withdraw from the representation, and if withdrawal is refused, "must make such disclosure to the tribunal as is reasonably necessary to remedy the situation, even if doing so requires the lawyer to reveal information that otherwise would be protected by Rule 1.6." Rule 3.3 Comment [10].

Narrative Testimony as an Alternative. *Nix* illustrates one approach to dealing with anticipated client perjury. Some jurisdictions permit an alternative approach. For example, in Florida, when a lawyer knows that a client charged with a crime intends to testify falsely,

> the lawyer's first duty is to attempt to persuade the client to testify truthfully. If the client still insists on committing perjury, the lawyer must threaten to disclose the client's intent to commit perjury to the judge. If the threat of disclosure does not successfully persuade the client to testify truthfully, the lawyer must disclose the fact that the client intends to lie to the tribunal and ... information sufficient to prevent the commission of the crime of perjury.

Amendment to the Rules Regulating The Florida Bar, 875 So.2d 448, 507–08 (Fla. 2004). If, at that point, the court does not permit the lawyer to withdraw, the lawyer must then allow the defendant to testify in a narrative fashion:

> [T]he defendant's attorney does not elicit the perjurious testimony by questioning nor argue the false testimony during closing argument. The attorney, of course, is not precluded from arguing sound, non-perjurious testimony or attacking the state's case. Under this procedure, a defendant is afforded his right to speak to the jury under oath and the constitutional right to assistance of counsel is preserved, but the defense attorney is protected from participating in the fraud. Under such a formula, the responsibility for committing or not committing fraud on the tribunal lies with the defendant, and not with his attorney, and the jury will decide whether the defendant's testimony is credible.

Sanborn v. State, 474 So.2d 309, 313 (Fla. App. 3 Dist. 1985).

* * *

Problem 21.9. In a bench trial pending before Judge Moore, the parties dispute whether a key document in the case is real or a forgery. The plaintiff testified that the document is authentic. You noticed, though, that her attorney relied entirely on other evidence (and never mentioned the controversial document) during closing argument. If the plaintiff's attorney believed that his client falsely testified about the document, has he undertaken the remedial measures contemplated by Rule 3.3(a)(3)?

* * *

Making a Truthful Witness Look Like a Perjurer. ABA Standard Relating to the Defense Function 4–7.6(b) provides that a criminal defense lawyer's "belief or knowledge that the witness is telling the truth does not preclude cross-examination." The parallel standard for prosecutors repeats this idea, but also adds the following: "A prosecutor should not use the power of cross-examination to discredit or undermine a witness if the prosecutor knows the witness is testifying truthfully." ABA Standard Relating to the Prosecution Function 3–5.7(b). Is there a good reason for the greater latitude given to criminal defense lawyers? Is it permissible to attempt to discredit a truthful witness in *civil* litigation, or would such conduct violate the rules listed above?

Nonadjudicative Proceedings. Note that a lawyer appearing as an advocate for a client in a nonadjudicative proceeding (such as before a legislative body) is under the same duty of candor outlined in Rule 3.3(a) as a lawyer acting as an advocate at trial. *See* ABA Model Rule 3.9.

* * *

F. TRIAL PUBLICITY

In *Gentile v. State Bar of Nevada*, 501 U.S. 1030 (1991), the Supreme Court held that a state can, consistent with the First Amendment, regulate an attorney's speech outside the courtroom that creates a "substantial likelihood of material prejudice" to a fair trial. The Court reasoned that this standard

> is designed to protect the integrity and fairness of a State's judicial system, and it imposes only narrow and necessary limitations on lawyers' speech. The limitations are aimed at two principal evils: (1) comments that are likely to influence the actual outcome of the trial, and (2) comments that are likely to prejudice the jury venire, even if an untainted panel can ultimately be found. Few, if any, interests under the Constitution are more fundamental than the right to a fair trial by "impartial" jurors, and an outcome affected by extrajudicial statements would violate that fundamental right. . . .

Justice O'Connor, concurring, noted, "Lawyers are officers of the court and, as such, may legitimately be subject to ethical precepts that keep them from engaging in what otherwise might be constitutionally protected speech."

Model Rule 3.6(a) reflects the holding in *Gentile* and articulates a general standard as to which extrajudicial statements are prohibited. Comment 5 lists six different subjects that can ordinarily be expected to present a substantial likelihood of material prejudice. Rule 3.6(b) identifies several subjects "about which a lawyer's statements would not ordinarily be considered to present a substantial likelihood of material prejudice." *Id.* cmt. 4.

Given the public attention that prosecutors can command, prosecutors are subject to additional restrictions concerning extrajudicial statements. Rule 3.8(f) generally prohibits a prosecutor "from making extrajudicial comments that have a substantial likelihood of heightening public condemnation of the accused." Prosecutors also must exercise reasonable care to prevent those who work with them from making such statements or statements that would violate Rule 3.6.

* * *

Problem 21.10. Following the arrest of Conner Anders, an alleged armed purse-snatcher, Anders' attorney held a press conference. He told the gathered media that Anders was wearing a leather jacket and boots at the time of arrest, but that "according to my police sources" the victim described the perpetrator as wearing a hooded sweatshirt and running shoes.

The prosecutor then issued a press release in which she stated, "I want to address the suggestion that we have the wrong person in custody. Despite Anders' attorney's assertion to the contrary, the victim never described the perpetrator as wearing a hooded sweatshirt and running shoes. She said he was wearing a leather jacket and boots. This is exactly what Conner Anders was wearing when he was arrested less than two blocks away from the crime scene. The public can rest assured that we have the right guy."

Assume that both attorneys believe that they have truthfully communicated facts through the media. Nonetheless, did Anders' attorney violate Rule 3.6? Did the prosecutor violate Rules 3.6 or 3.8(f)?

Application of the Litigation Privilege. Be careful what you say outside the court. Although lawyers enjoy a judicial privilege against civil liability for defamatory statements made in litigation, some cases have held that a communication of the same statements to a reporter and posttrial comments to the media about a case are not protected by the privilege. See *Bochetto v. Gibson*, 860 A.2d 67 (Pa. Sup. Ct. 2004) and *Brown v. Gatti*, 99 P.3d 299 (Or. App. 2004).

* * *

G. FRIVOLOUS APPEALS

Federal Rule of Appellate Procedure 38 provides that if an appellate court determines that an appeal is frivolous "it may, after a separately filed motion or notice from the court and reasonable opportunity to respond, award just damages and single or double costs to the appellee."

According to the Seventh Circuit Court of Appeals, "An appeal is frivolous within the meaning of Rule 38, when it 'was prosecuted with no reasonable expectation of altering the district court's judgment and for purposes of delay or harassment or out of sheer obstinacy.'" *Flexible Manufacturing Systems, Inc. v. Super Prods. Corp.*, 86 F.3d 96 (7th Cir. 1996).

In *Nagle v. Alspach*, 8 F.3d 141 (3d Cir. 1993), the trial court granted summary judgment to the defendant based upon four separate grounds. The defendant appealed on only two of those grounds. Thus, even had the appellate court reversed on those two grounds, the two unchallenged grounds would have supported the trial court's judgment. Because the appeal was "doomed to failure from the moment the plaintiff-appellants' brief was filed in this court," the Third Circuit held that the appeal was "frivolous" under Fed. R. App. P. 38. The Court explained:

> The purpose of Rule 38 damages is to compensate appellees who are forced to defend judgments awarded them in the trial court from appeals that are wholly without merit, and to "preserve the appellate court calendar for cases worthy of consideration." Another important purpose is to discourage litigants from unnecessarily wasting their opponents' time and resources.). Moreover, even though an appellee makes no request for Rule 38 damages, the court may raise the issue *sua sponte*.
>
> Damages under Rule 38 are appropriate when an appeal is "wholly without merit." [citations omitted]. Our inquiry is an objective one, focusing "on the merits of the appeal regardless of good or bad faith." . . .
>
> . . . .
>
> We are well aware that injudicious awards of Rule 38 damages may have the potential to chill the zeal for pursuing novel questions and difficult appeals. . . .[S]ometimes a questionable appeal may be due to mere overzealousness or inexperience of counsel, and it is sometimes difficult to draw the line "between the tenuously arguable and the frivolous." Hence, we move with caution and will not label an appeal frivolous unless it lacks colorable support or is wholly without merit. Here, however, there was no possibility of success, and it is patently unfair to allow appellees who have been damaged financially by a frivolous appeal to go uncompensated. We see no chilling effect whatsoever in requiring an attorney, once a proper decision to appeal has been made, to be professional and diligent in prosecuting it. Indeed, any other rule would prejudice the very clients whose interests the attorney is duty-bound to protect, and who properly rely on their attorneys to zealously advocate their causes.
>
> We also believe it is appropriate to impose the burden for payment of these damages upon appellants' counsel rather than on the

appellants. . . . . [T]he burden for payment of Rule 38 damages may be imposed upon counsel for appellant when the frivolous appeal stems from counsel's professional error. Appellants' counsel has offered no reason to show that the fault for the frivolous appeal lies anywhere but with him. Moreover, it is inconceivable that appellants would request that their attorney not challenge alleged errors when the failure to do so would result in a certain loss. In [a previous case], we set the standard that

> attorneys have an affirmative obligation to research the law and to determine if a claim on appeal is utterly without merit and may be deemed frivolous. We conclude that if counsel ignore or fail in this obligation to their client, they do so at their peril and may become personally liable to satisfy a Rule 38 award. The test is whether, following a thorough analysis of the record and careful research of the law, a reasonable attorney would conclude that the appeal is frivolous.

Appellants' counsel should have known that unless all four conclusions reached by the district court in support of its summary judgment were challenged, the appeal he filed had no chance whatsoever of success. It is manifestly evident that the responsibility for paying these damages rests squarely upon counsel.

Id. at 145–46.

Compare the standards for attorney conduct under Federal Rule of Civil Procedure 11 and Federal Rule of Appellate Procedure 38. Which rule provides more guidance for attorneys? Which rule is easier to comply with? As discussed in an earlier chapter, clients are generally in charge of the objectives of the representation, while lawyers are generally in charge of the means of achieving the client's objectives. How does that division of authority apply in the decision whether to file an appeal?

Profile of Attorney Professionalism. Lawyers sometimes use the phrase "the best trial lawyer I've ever seen" to describe another lawyer. Sometimes the phrase is used about lawyers who have achieved substantial public fame and notoriety. But sometimes the phrase is used to refer to lawyers who have built impressive reputations among their colleagues but are not household names. An example of this type of lawyer is Joseph A. Ball. Ball was born in 1902 in Stuart, Iowa, a town of 900. Unable to afford to go to medical school, Ball wound up going to law school instead. He started his career in the Los Angeles district attorney's office before eventually establishing a wide-ranging practice. Ball tried over 500 jury cases in his seventy-five year career. According to one account, "[b]efore a jury, Ball had a friendly, conversational manner. He seemed to be confiding in each juror. He did not preach, rant, or shout. He quietly reasoned with jurors, using plain, simple words, like a chat with a neighbor over the back fence. He liked people and they liked him."

Ball was president of the California State Bar during the communist scare of the 1950s. He spoke out about the need for lawyers to represent unpopular clients who had been the victims of McCarthyism. He was also senior counsel to the Warren Commission, which investigated President John F. Kennedy's assassination. Until a few months before his death at the age of 97, Ball was studying quantum mechanics and string theory in physics. Ball referred to himself as a simple country lawyer. The founder and chancellor of the American College of Trial Lawyers called Ball "the best trial lawyer I've ever seen." ROGER K. NEWMAN, THE YALE BIOGRAPHICAL DICTIONARY OF AMERICAN LAW 26 (2009).

CHAPTER 22

CRIMINAL PROSECUTION PRACTICE

■ ■ ■

Chapter Hypothetical. Edward is the district attorney for the town of Pleasant Hill. He and two of his assistant district attorneys are facing controversy surrounding some of their actions.

"The prosecutor has more control over life, liberty, and reputation than any other person in America."

—Robert H. Jackson, *The Federal Prosecutor*, 24 J. AM. JUD. SOC'Y 18 (1940).[1]

* * *

BERGER V. UNITED STATES
295 U.S. 78 (1935)

. . . . [The prosecutor] is the representative not of an ordinary party to a controversy, but of a sovereignty whose obligation to govern impartially is as compelling as its obligation to govern at all; and whose interest, therefore, in a criminal prosecution is not that it shall win a case, but that justice shall be done. As such, he is in a peculiar and very definite sense the servant of the law, the twofold aim of which is that guilt shall not escape or innocence suffer. He may prosecute with earnestness and vigor—indeed he should do so. But, while he may strike hard blows, he is not at liberty to strike foul ones. It is as much his duty to refrain from improper methods calculated to produce a wrongful conviction as it is to use every legitimate means to bring about a just one. . . .

* * *

While prosecutors are subject to all of the generally applicable rules of professional conduct that other lawyers are, Model Rule 3.8 recognizes several special ethical obligations on the part of prosecutors. The rule singles out prosecutors for special treatment because of the special role that

---

[1] Jackson served as United States Solicitor General, United States Attorney General, and Associate Justice of the Supreme Court, the only person to hold all three offices. In 1945, Jackson took a leave from the Court to serve as U.S. Chief of Counsel for the prosecution of Nazi war criminals at the Nuremberg Trials.

prosecutors play. As comment 1 observes, "[a] prosecutor has the responsibility of a minister of justice and not simply that of an advocate." This chapter explores the special responsibilities and ethical obligations of a prosecutor.

* * *

A. THE INVESTIGATIVE FUNCTION OF PROSECUTORS

Prosecutors often work closely with police in the investigation of alleged criminal acts. Standard 1.3 of the *ABA Standards for Criminal Justice: Prosecutorial Investigations* advises that a prosecutor "should take steps to promote compliance by law enforcement agents with relevant legal rules" and "should not seek to circumvent ethical rules by instructing or recommending that others use means that the prosecutor is ethically prohibited from using." One situation in which a prosecutor's ethical obligations may come into tension with the investigative work of law enforcement is in the case of communication with a represented person.

* * *

STATE OF MINNESOTA V. CLARK
738 N.W.2d 316 (Minn. 2007)

ANDERSON, PAUL H., JUSTICE.

Courtney Bernard Clark was convicted in Ramsey County for murdering Rodney Foster and attempting to murder Foster's girlfriend, B.B., while committing or attempting to commit aggravated robbery, kidnapping, and criminal sexual conduct. [During an interview prior to his arraignment and another after his arraignment, Clark denied involvement with the crimes. During a third interview, however, Clark admitted his involvement in the crimes.] At Clark's trial, the state introduced over Clark's objection ... [the recorded interview in which] Clark admitted tying up Foster and B.B. and robbing Foster ... and stated that Foster died "by accident." ... On appeal, Clark argues that the district court erred on several grounds when it admitted the recorded interviews .... We affirm.

The third interview was conducted on August 3 at the request of Clark [after Clark had been arraigned]. There was disputed testimony about how and when the public defender's office had been notified about the planned interview. The parties had difficulty establishing a time when Clark's lawyer could be present during police questioning, and assistant district attorney Charles Balck prevented the police from speaking with Clark outside the presence of his lawyer on several occasions prior to August 3. Shortly after 8:40 p.m. on August 3, however, [Balck left a voicemail message at the public defender's office, indicating that Clark had requested to speak to the police and that "there would be contact with the police as a result of the defendant's contact." No one from the public defender's office was present when the third interview began shortly after 9 p.m.]

We now turn to Clark's claims regarding violations of his Sixth Amendment right to counsel and Minn. R. Prof. Conduct 4.2 . . . In his brief, Clark . . . asserted that "part of" an accused person's right to counsel "is based on" Rule 4.2. But at oral argument, Clark conceded that a Sixth Amendment claim is analytically distinct from a Rule 4.2 claim and that each is governed by a different body of law. Having made this distinction, Clark focused his argument on the state's alleged violation of Rule 4.2. It is not clear whether Clark's comments at oral argument constituted an implicit withdrawal of his Sixth Amendment claim. Accordingly, we first address whether the state violated Clark's Sixth Amendment right to counsel, and second, whether the state violated Rule 4.2. . . .

Sixth Amendment Right to Counsel

The Sixth Amendment to the U.S. Constitution guarantees that "[i]n all criminal prosecutions, the accused shall enjoy the right to * * * have the assistance of counsel for his defence." U.S. Const. amend. VI. This right attaches as soon as the accused person is subject to adverse judicial proceedings, including arraignments. *See, e.g., United States v. Gouveia*, 467 U.S. 180, 187–88 (1984). An accused person can waive his Sixth Amendment right to counsel, but the government bears the burden of proving that the person "understood that he had a right to have counsel present during an interrogation and that he intentionally relinquished or abandoned that known right." *Giddings v. State*, 290 N.W.2d 595, 597 (Minn.1980). In deciding whether the government has met its burden, courts consider the circumstances of each case, including the age, experience, and background of the defendant. *Giddings*, 290 N.W.2d at 597.

In this case, the district court concluded that the state met its burden of proving that Clark "voluntarily, knowingly, and intelligently abandoned or relinquished" his known right to counsel during his post-arraignment interviews. . . .

Minnesota Rule of Professional Conduct 4.2

Minnesota Rule of Professional Conduct 4.2 provides:

> In representing a client, a lawyer shall not communicate about the subject of the representation with a person the lawyer knows to be represented by another lawyer in the matter, unless the lawyer has the consent of the other lawyer or is authorized to do so by law or a court order.

"[O]ur case law clearly establishes that [Rule] 4.2 applies to prosecutors involved in custodial interviews of a charged suspect." *State v. Miller*, 600 N.W.2d 457, 464 (Minn.1999). Moreover, police contact with a suspect may be attributed to a prosecutor when the prosecutor orders or ratifies the police contact, as apparently happened in this case. *Id.* The purpose of Rule 4.2 is to protect the represented individual "from the supposed imbalance of legal skill and acumen between the lawyer and the party litigant." *Id.* at 463 (quotation marks omitted).

In this case, the district court admitted Clark's statements from the post-arraignment interviews after finding that Clark's lawyer had notice of the interviews and an opportunity to be present. Clark essentially argues that the district court misconstrued what Rule 4.2 requires, and that the state violated the rule by failing to obtain his lawyer's consent before conducting the interviews. The state argues that the court properly construed and applied Rule 4.2, and further, that suppression of Clark's statements would be unwarranted even if the state did violate the rule. In light of these arguments, we first consider what steps the state must take when Rule 4.2 applies before interviewing a represented criminal defendant outside the presence of the defendant's lawyer. We then decide whether the state took those steps here, and if not, whether the state's violation of Rule 4.2 warrants suppression of Clark's statements.

Rule 4.2 Requirements

Precisely what Rule 4.2 requires of the state in the context of a criminal case is a question of law we review de novo. *See Lennartson v. Anoka-Hennepin Indep. Sch. Dist. No. 11*, 662 N.W.2d 125, 129 (Minn.2003). In *Miller*, we described the scope of Rule 4.2 as follows:

> [Rule] 4.2 protects the right of counsel to be present during any communication between the counsel's client and opposing counsel. The focus of [Rule] 4.2 is on the obligation of attorneys to respect the relationship of the adverse party and the party's attorney. * * * [T]he party cannot waive the application of [Rule 4.2]-only the party's attorney can approve the direct contact and only the party's attorney can waive the attorney's right to be present during a communication between the attorney's client and opposing counsel.

600 N.W.2d at 464 (citing *United States v. Lopez*, 4 F.3d 1455, 1462 (9th Cir.1993)).... Based on the passage above and the plain language of Rule 4.2, we agree with Clark that a lawyer representing a criminal defendant is owed more than notice and an opportunity to be present before the state interviews the defendant about the subject of the representation. We also agree that the operative word in Rule 4.2 is "consent."

The more difficult question is precisely what the defendant's lawyer must consent to before the state may permissibly communicate with the defendant. Our language in *Miller* could support an interpretation of Rule 4.2 requiring the state to obtain the lawyer's consent before communicating with the defendant outside the lawyer's presence. Under this interpretation, the state could interview a defendant who insists on speaking to the police over his lawyer's objection, as long as the lawyer is present during the interview. This interpretation denies the defense lawyer "veto power" over a defendant's decision to speak with the police, while arguably helping to achieve the Rule's purpose-protecting the defendant from being "taken advantage of." *See Miller*, 600 N.W.2d at 463 (quotation marks omitted).

An alternative interpretation of Rule 4.2 is that the state must obtain consent from the defendant's lawyer before engaging in any communication with the defendant, even when the defendant has requested contact with the police after being counseled against such contact and the defendant's lawyer is present. This interpretation is troubling in that it substantially infringes on a defendant's autonomy in favor of his lawyer's beliefs as to the defendant's best interests. *See* Carl A. Pierce, *Variations on a Basic Theme: Revisiting the ABA's Revision of Model Rule 4.2 (Part III)*, 70 TENN. L. REV. 643, 648 (2003) ("[T]he no-contact rule * * * is simply too paternalistic and does not accord sufficient respect for the client's autonomy or the client's freedom to speak without the prior consent of [his] lawyer."); John Leubsdorf, *Communicating with Another Lawyer's Client: The Lawyer's Veto and the Client's Interests*, 127 U. PA. L. REV. 683, 689 (1979) ("A legal system valuing informed personal choice should not assume that a client aided by his lawyer cannot make a sound decision whether to communicate with opposing counsel."). Such an infringement on personal autonomy is arguably unnecessary in the criminal law context, given the protections that the Constitution and case law provide to criminal defendants against government overreaching. As previously stated, these protections are entirely independent of Rule 4.2.

Notwithstanding the concerns set forth above, we conclude that when a government attorney is involved in a matter such that Minn. R. Prof. Conduct 4.2 applies, the state may not have any communication with a represented criminal defendant about the subject of the representation unless (1) the state first obtains the lawyer's consent; (2) the communication is "authorized by law" as discussed below; or (3) the state obtains a court order authorizing the communication. We reach our conclusion on the plain and unambiguous language of the rule as currently written.[10] Accordingly, to the extent that any of our past cases suggest that

---

[10] We recognize that one undesirable consequence of our interpretation of Rule 4.2 may be that the police-in order to avoid a potential obstacle to admissibility of a statement under the Rule-will be less likely to obtain legal advice before proceeding to interview a represented defendant who has expressed the desire to speak with them. In light of this possible consequence and the other concerns we have articulated in this opinion, we invite a review by the appropriate

the state can meet the requirements of Rule 4.2 by providing the defendant's lawyer notice and an opportunity to be present, those cases are no longer good law.

Whether the State Violated Rule 4.2

With the foregoing principles in mind, we must now decide whether the state violated Rule 4.2 when officers Frazer and Doran conducted the post-arraignment interviews with Clark. There was no court order authorizing the interviews; accordingly, the state must establish either that Clark's lawyer consented to the interviews or that the interviews were authorized by law. The record contains no evidence that Clark's lawyer consented to the August 3 interview between Clark and the police. . . .

We also conclude that the post-arraignment interviews of Clark were not communications "authorized by law" for the purposes of Rule 4.2. The comments following Rule 4.2 provide examples of communications authorized by law, including

> communications by a lawyer on behalf of a client who is exercising a constitutional or other legal right to communicate with the government. Communications authorized by law may also include investigative activities of lawyers representing governmental entities, directly or through investigative agents, *prior to the commencement of criminal or civil enforcement proceedings.*

Minn. R. Prof. Conduct 4.2 cmt. 5 (emphasis added). There is no dispute in this case that the . . . August 3 interview took place after criminal proceedings were commenced against Clark. Further, we do not conclude that Clark was "exercising a constitutional or other legal right" when he communicated with the police during these interviews. Finally, we discern no other basis on which to conclude that the interviews in this case were authorized by law.

For all of the foregoing reasons, we conclude that the state violated Rule 4.2 by conducting the post-arraignment interviews with Clark.

Whether Suppression is Warranted

Having concluded that the state violated Rule 4.2, we must determine whether the sanction that Clark seeks in this appeal-that is, suppression of the post-arraignment interview statements-is warranted. As a preliminary matter, we note that Rule 4.2 is a rule of professional conduct, not a constitutional or statutory provision. "The rules are designed to provide guidance to lawyers and to provide a structure for regulating conduct through disciplinary agencies." Minn. R. Prof. Conduct, Scope cmt. 20. Accordingly, a rule violation is "a basis for invoking the disciplinary

---

committee(s) of Rule 4.2 as it relates to government lawyers' contact with represented criminal defendants.

process," *id.* cmt. 19, and "does not necessarily warrant any * * * nondisciplinary remedy," *Id.* cmt. 20.

Based on analogous principles underlying their own rules of professional conduct, "nearly every court that has ruled on [a no-contact rule violation in a criminal law context] has found that suppression of a [statement] is an inappropriate remedy for a lawyer's ethical violation." *State v. McCarthy*, 819 A.2d 335, 341 (Me. 2003) (footnote omitted); *see, e.g., State v. Johnson*, 318 N.W.2d 417, 437 (Iowa 1982) (concluding that suppression of a defendant's statements is not an appropriate remedy for the government's violation of the no-contact rule) . . . .

Unlike these jurisdictions, we have not adopted a per se rule placing suppression of defendant's statements outside the ambit of possible sanctions for a violation of Rule 4.2. Rather, we have taken a case-by-case approach to determining whether the state's conduct is so egregious as to compromise the fair administration of justice. *See State v. Ford*, 539 N.W.2d 214, 224–25 (Minn. 1995). In cases where the state's conduct is sufficiently egregious, we may determine that suppression is warranted.

One such case is *State v. Lefthand*, 488 N.W.2d 799 (Minn.1992). We had not yet articulated the egregiousness standard when we decided Lefthand, a case that references Rule 4.2 indirectly in the broader context of constitutional protections against self-incrimination. *Id.* at 801 n.6. Nonetheless, we concluded that suppression of Lefthand's inculpatory statement was warranted regardless of his apparent waiver of constitutional protections given the circumstances under which the police obtained the statement. *Id.* at 801–02; *see also Ford*, 539 N.W.2d at 224 (noting that Lefthand was advised of and waived his constitutional rights). Specifically, the police interviewed Lefthand with permission from the prosecutor assigned to the case but without notification to the defendant's lawyer. *Lefthand*, 488 N.W.2d at 800. At the time of the interview, Lefthand, who had made his first court appearance in connection with two alleged homicides, was in custody pending a court-ordered Rule 20 mental competency examination. *Id.* We did not indicate in *Lefthand* how the interview came to occur, but we noted in a subsequent case that *Lefthand* initiated contact with the police. *Ford*, 539 N.W.2d at 224.

. . . .

[W]hen we consider all the evidence in the record, we do not perceive Balck's actions as evidencing the bad faith or blatant disregard of professional obligations that we have previously associated with the phrase "egregious conduct." . . . Balck tried to reach Clark's lawyer on August 2 and refused to allow a police interview to occur because Balck was unable to "get [a] message through." We see no basis to discount as unreliable Frazer's sworn testimony that after Balck made several unsuccessful attempts to reach Clark's lawyer on August 2, Balck told Frazer that "we're just going to have to wait until we get this thing ironed out" and "[i]t isn't going to happen today." Moreover, Frazer indicated that Balck expressed his intention that the state "take the high road" with respect to Clark's case.

. . . .

At a minimum, the record supports a conclusion that there was poor communication between both offices that may have led to frustration on both sides; this frustration may have led to Balck's lapse in judgment when he did not attempt to prevent the 9 p.m. interview on August 3. [W]e conclude that in light of all the testimony before the district court, Balck's failure to prevent the August 3 interview to proceed is more appropriately characterized as a lapse of professional judgment under frustrating circumstances [than a flagrant display of professional misconduct.]

. . .

For all of the foregoing reasons, we conclude that the district court did not err when it denied Clark's motion to suppress the statements Clark made to the police during the post-arraignment interviews on July 26 and August 3.

* * *

Problem 22.1. Francis was convicted of murder and is on death row. While doing some additional investigation into Francis' case, Francis' lawyers learned that Gary, one of the assistant district attorneys in Edward's office, had spoken to Francis outside the presence of and without the consent of her court-appointed lawyer about her case following her arraignment. Francis had requested the meeting in order to discuss the possibility of a plea deal and voluntarily consented to the interview outside the presence of her lawyer. At trial, the prosecution introduced statements made by Francis during the interviews that it claimed cast doubt on her veracity.

(a) Is Gary subject to discipline under Model Rule 4.2?

(b) If so, should his violation result in a new trial?

* * *

Conflicts of Interest. "The prosecutor's client is the public, not particular government agencies or victims." *ABA Standards for Criminal Justice: Prosecutorial Investigations*, Standard 1.2. Without the work of police officers, prosecutors would not be able to obtain convictions. In short, prosecutors rely heavily on the police. Given this reality, does a prosecutor have a disqualifying conflict of interest under Rule 1.7(a)(2) when called upon to prosecute police officers who have allegedly engaged in criminal behavior? *See* Kate Levine, *Who Shouldn't Prosecute the Police*, 101 IOWA L. REV. 1447 (2016).

Subpoenas to Lawyers. One common way for a prosecutor to uncover relevant facts is through the issuance of a subpoena. But Rule 3.8(e) provides that a prosecutor may not subpoena a lawyer in a grand jury or other criminal proceeding to present evidence about a past or present client except under exceptional circumstances. Why are prosecutors prohibited from doing this?

* * *

B. THE DECISION TO CHARGE

Model Rule 3.8(a) requires that a prosecutor have probable cause before prosecuting a criminal charge. This parallels the constitutional requirement that a prosecutor must have probable cause to believe that the accused committed the charged offense. *Bordenkircher v. Hayes*, 434 U.S. 357, 363 (1978). Prosecutors have discretion when it comes to the decision to charge an individual with a crime. They are not required to file all criminal charges that might be supported by the evidence. *See ABA Criminal Justice Standards: The Prosecution Function*, Standard 3–4.4. This may include the discretion not to pursue criminal charges in appropriate circumstances. *Id.* Standard 3–1.2. Prosecutors also have considerable discretion when it comes to plea bargains. Thus, for example, the Supreme Court has held that it is constitutionally permissible for a prosecutor to make good on a threat made during plea negotiations to reindict a defendant on more serious charges if the defendant fails to plead guilty to the crime he was originally charged with, provided probable cause exists to believe the defendant committed the other crime. *See Bordenkircher*, 434 U.S. at 364 (1978). The *ABA Criminal Justice Standards* advise that a prosecutor should avoid bias, prejudice, and other improper considerations when exercising prosecutorial discretion. *Id.* Standard 3–1.6.

* * *

Problem 22.2. The state legislature recently passed a measure requiring businesses open to the public to post a sign if they let transgender people use multi-person bathrooms. The failure to post such a sign subjects the business to criminal penalties.

(A) Assume that police charge a local business owner with a violation of the law, and Edward, the district attorney of Pleasant Hill, declines to prosecute the case. Which of the following would be a legitimate consideration in Edward's exercise of discretion?

(1) While there is a probable cause to believe a particular business has violated the law, Edward does not believe his office will be able to obtain a conviction;

(2) There are limited resources within the prosecutor's office;

(3) Edward believes enforcing the measure would adversely impact his chances for re-election; and

(4) Edward believes the law is discriminatory and likely unconstitutional.

(B) Assume instead that Edward announces that his office will not prosecute *any* cases brought under this law. Should Edward's discretion as a prosecutor give him the authority not to prosecute such cases?

* * *

What remedy does a criminal defendant have against a prosecutor if the prosecutor lacked probable cause to bring charges against the defendant, or (worse still) the prosecutor framed the defendant? In theory, a tort claim of malicious prosecution might be one possibility. However, a public prosecutor enjoys absolute immunity in such cases, provided the prosecutor acts in his or her official capacity. *Restatement (Second) of Torts* § 656. Another possibility might be a constitutional tort claim under 42 U.S.C. § 1983. However, as alluded to above in conjunction with the *Brady* decision below, prosecutors had long enjoyed absolute immunity in § 1983 actions for their actions occurring *during* trial. This includes knowingly presenting false evidence at trial. *See Imbler v. Pachtman*, 424 US 409 (1976). However, there is currently a circuit split on the question of whether prosecutors who *prepare* false evidence prior to trial are also entitled to immunity. *Compare Michaels v. New Jersey*, 222 F.3d 118 (3d Cir. 2000) (yes) *with McGhee v. Pottawattamie Cnty.*, 547 F.3d 922 (8th Cir. 2008) (no).

* * *

C. PROVIDING EXCULPATORY EVIDENCE TO THE DEFENSE

BRADY V. MARYLAND
373 U.S. 83 (1963)

Opinion of the Court by MR. JUSTICE DOUGLAS, announced by MR. JUSTICE BRENNAN.

Petitioner and a companion, Boblit, were found guilty of murder in the first degree and were sentenced to death, their convictions being affirmed by the Court of Appeals of Maryland. Their trials were separate, petitioner being tried first. At his trial Brady took the stand and admitted his participation in the crime, but he claimed that Boblit did the actual killing. And, in his summation to the jury, Brady's counsel conceded that Brady was guilty of murder in the first degree, asking only that the jury return that verdict "without capital punishment." Prior to the trial petitioner's counsel had requested the prosecution to allow him to examine Boblit's extrajudicial statements. Several of those statements were shown to him; but one dated July 9, 1958, in which Boblit admitted the actual homicide, was withheld by the prosecution and did not come to petitioner's notice until after he had been tried, convicted, and sentenced, and after his conviction had been affirmed.

Petitioner moved the trial court for a new trial based on the newly discovered evidence that had been suppressed by the prosecution. Petitioner's appeal from a denial of that motion was dismissed by the Court of Appeals without prejudice to relief under the Maryland Post Conviction Procedure Act. The petition for post-conviction relief was dismissed by the trial court; and on appeal the Court of Appeals held that suppression of the evidence by the prosecution denied petitioner due process of law and remanded the case for a retrial of the question of punishment, not the question of guilt. The case is here on certiorari.

. . . .

We agree with the Court of Appeals that suppression of this confession was a violation of the Due Process Clause of the Fourteenth Amendment. The Court of Appeals relied in the main on two decisions from the Third Circuit Court of Appeals—*United States ex rel. Almeida v. Baldi*, 195 F.2d 815, and *United States ex rel. Thompson v. Dye*, 221 F.2d 763—which, we agree, state the correct constitutional rule.

This ruling is an extension of *Mooney v. Holohan*, 294 U.S. 103, 112, where the Court ruled on what nondisclosure by a prosecutor violates due process:

> It is a requirement that cannot be deemed to be satisfied by mere notice and hearing if a state has contrived a conviction through the pretense of a trial which in truth is but used as a means of depriving a defendant of liberty through a deliberate deception of court and jury by the presentation of testimony known to be perjured. Such a contrivance by a state to procure the conviction and imprisonment of a defendant is as inconsistent with the rudimentary demands of justice as is the obtaining of a like result by intimidation.

In *Pyle v. Kansas*, 317 U.S. 213, 215–216 we phrased the rule in broader terms:

> Petitioner's papers are inexpertly drawn, but they do set forth allegations that his imprisonment resulted from perjured testimony, knowingly used by the State authorities to obtain his conviction, and from the deliberate suppression by those same authorities of evidence favorable to him. These allegations sufficiently charge a deprivation of rights guaranteed by the

Federal Constitution, and, if proven, would entitle petitioner to release from his present custody. *Mooney v. Holohan*, 294 U.S. 103.

The Third Circuit in the *Baldi* case construed that statement in *Pyle v. Kansas* to mean that the "suppression of evidence favorable" to the accused was itself sufficient to amount to a denial of due process. 195 F.2d at 820. In *Napue v. Illinois*, 360 U.S. 264, 269, we extended the test formulated in *Mooney v. Holohan* when we said: "The same result obtains when the State, although not soliciting false evidence, allows it to go uncorrected when it appears." . . .

We now hold that the suppression by the prosecution of evidence favorable to an accused upon request violates due process where the evidence is material either to guilt or to punishment, irrespective of the good faith or bad faith of the prosecution.

The principle of *Mooney v. Holohan* is not punishment of society for misdeeds of a prosecutor but avoidance of an unfair trial to the accused. Society wins not only when the guilty are convicted but when criminal trials are fair; our system of the administration of justice suffers when any accused is treated unfairly. An inscription on the walls of the Department of Justice states the proposition candidly for the federal domain: "The United States wins its point whenever justice is done its citizens in the courts." A prosecution that withholds evidence on demand of an accused which, if made available, would tend to exculpate him or reduce the penalty helps shape a trial that bears heavily on the defendant. That casts the prosecutor in the role of an architect of a proceeding that does not comport with standards of justice, even though, as in the present case, his action is not "the result of guile," to use the words of the Court of Appeals.

* * *

Extending *Brady*. Subsequent decisions have established that a prosecutor has a duty under *Brady* to disclose not only evidence that the prosecutor personally knows of, but also "any favorable evidence known to the others acting on the government's behalf in the case, including the police." Kyles v. Whitley, 514 U.S. 419, 437 (1995). In *Giglio v. U.S.,* 405 U.S. 150 (1972), the United States Supreme Court held that the prosecution's failure to turn over evidence that could be used to impeach a prosecution witness may warrant a new trial under the *Brady* rationale.

Brady held "that the suppression by the prosecution of evidence favorable to an accused upon request violates due process where the evidence is material either to guilt or to punishment." Model Rule 3.8(d) articulates an ethical obligation on the part of prosecutors that is similar to the legal duty owed under *Brady*. The rule requires a prosecutor "to make timely disclosure to the defense of all evidence or information known to the prosecutor that tends to negate the guilt of the accused or mitigates the offense."

***Brady* vs. Rule 3.8(d).** Read Rule 3.8(d) carefully. How does a prosecutor's obligation under the rule differ, if at all, from the constitutional obligation under *Brady*? Or are the obligations co-extensive? *Compare In re Riek*, 834 N.W.2d 384, 391 (Wis. 2013) ("Prosecutors should not be subjected to disciplinary proceedings for complying with legal disclosure obligations. We thus construe the ethical mandate of SCR 20:3.8(f)(1) in a manner consistent with the scope of disclosure required by the United States Constitution, federal or Wisconsin statutes, and court rules of procedure.") *with* ABA Formal Op. No. 09–454 ("[T]he ethical obligations established by Rule 3.8(d) are not coextensive with the prosecutor's constitutional duties of disclosure.").

* * *

Problem 22.3. Cole was on trial for first-degree murder. At trial, the prosecution's key witness, Agatha, testified that Cole had confessed to the murder. A few days later and while the trial was still ongoing, the assistant prosecutor handling the case, Ben, informed Cole's lawyer, Denise, that, before trial, Agatha had cut a deal with the district attorney, Edward, under which pending charges against Agatha for writing bad checks would be dropped in exchange for her testimony against Cole. Ben explained to Denise that he had only learned of this information that same day. He explained that the district attorney, Edward, was overseeing the prosecution of Agatha but had failed to inform Ben of the deal.

(a) Has there been a violation of Cole's constitutional rights due to the failure to disclose the prosecution's deal with Agatha?

(b) Is Ben subject to discipline under Model Rule 3.8(d)?

* * *

Explanations for *Brady* Violations. In *Connick v. Thompson*, 563 U.S. 51 (2011), a prisoner was on death row for 14 years before his legal team uncovered exculpatory blood evidence. Lawyers within the District Attorney's office had known of this blood evidence but failed to turn it over to the prisoner's lawyers. Why would the prosecutors fail to turn over this evidence? Because they didn't understand the law? Because their biases caused them to make incorrect assessments of the exculpatory nature of evidence? Some other reason? *See generally* Alafair S. Burke, *Improving Prosecutorial Decision Making: Some Lessons of Cognitive Science*, 47 WM. & MARY L. REV. 1587 (2007).*

* * *

---

* One of the prosecutors in this case was Gerry Deegan, the prosecutor from *In re Riehlmann* from an earlier chapter who told his friend that he had suppressed blood evidence.

D. TRIAL PUBLICITY

The rules of professional conduct also single out prosecutors for special treatment when it comes to trial publicity. Rule 3.6(a) prohibits *all* lawyers who are participating or have participated in the investigation or litigation of a matter from making extrajudicial statements that the lawyer knows or reasonably should know will be disseminated by means of public communication and will have a substantial likelihood of materially prejudicing an adjudicative proceeding in the matter. Comment 5 to the rule lists some examples of such statements, several of which involve statements made in the criminal context. Rule 3.6(b) goes on to list several types of statements that a lawyer may make, notwithstanding this restriction in paragraph (a).

Reflecting the power prosecutors have to shape public opinion, Rule 3.8(f) also generally prohibits prosecutors in particular from making "extrajudicial comments that have a substantial likelihood of heightening public condemnation of the accused." These rules attempt to strike a balance between the public's legitimate interest in receiving information concerning the judicial process (particularly where the criminal law is concerned) and the equally strong interest in preserving fairness in the trial process (again, particularly in the criminal context).

* * *

Problem 22.4. Denise was Cole's lawyer. When she learned that Edward's office had initially failed to disclose information about the deal between Agatha and Ben, she announced that she would be seeking a mistrial. When Ben was asked at a press conference about whether the incident might impact the public's opinion as to Cole's guilt, Ben responded, "I doubt many members of the public would doubt Cole's guilt if they had seen the DNA test results that I have." Is Ben subject to discipline for his statements to the press?

The *Gentile* Decision. In *Gentile v. State Bar*, 501 U.S. 1030 (1991), the United States Supreme Court held that, as a constitutional matter, a state need not demonstrate that extrajudicial statements by a lawyer during the pendency of a trial present a "clear and present danger" of prejudice to the trial before they may be restricted. Instead, given the heightened dangers associated with extrajudicial statements occurring during the pendency of a trial, states may constitutionally prohibit statements having a substantial likelihood of prejudicing the proceeding. ABA Model Rule 3.6 now reflects this standard.

* * *

E. REMEDYING WRONGFUL CONVICTIONS

Rule 3.8(g) is a recent addition to the *Model Rules*, which speaks to a prosecutor's duty to do justice. Upon learning of "new, credible and material evidence creating a reasonable likelihood that a convicted defendant did not commit an offense of which the defendant was convicted," a prosecutor is required to take steps to address the matter, including perhaps conducting additional investigation. Upon learning of clear and convincing evidence that an individual in the prosecutor's jurisdiction was wrongly convicted, Rule 3.8(h) requires that the prosecutor seek to remedy the conviction.

* * *

Problem 22.5. Recall from earlier that Francis had been convicted of murder and was on death row. During their investigation into her case, Francis' lawyers uncovered a bombshell: DNA evidence that was known to the assistant district attorney trying Francis' case but that was never disclosed to Francis' lawyer, which strongly pointed to another individual as being the actual murderer. The attorneys take the new evidence to Edward, the district attorney in Pleasant Hill where Francis was convicted. What is Edward's ethical responsibility at this point?

***Brady* and Post-Conviction Proceedings.** At least one court has held that a prosecutor's duty under Rule 3.8(d) to disclose exculpatory evidence applies to post-conviction proceedings. *See Attorney Grievance Comm'n of Maryland v. Cassilly*, 262 A.3d 272 (Md. Ct. App. 2021).

Prosecutorial Misconduct Leading to Wrongful Convictions. According to information released by the Death Penalty Information Center in March, 2021, of the 185 death-row exonerations that have occurred since 1973, 69.2% involved police or prosecutorial misconduct. Death Penalty Information Center, *DPIC Special Report: The Innocence Epidemic* 4 (2021). Official misconduct contributed to the wrongful convictions of 58.2% of white exonerees compared to 78.8% of Black exonerees and 68.8% of Latinx exonerees. What accounts for these numbers? What can be done to address the problem?

Profile of Attorney Professionalism. Norm Maleng served as Prosecutor for King County, Washington for 28 years. In that capacity, he created Washington's first Special Assault Unit, which "became a national leader in developing innovative techniques to make the criminal-justice system more humane and less terrifying to vulnerable victims." Judge Robert S. Lasnik & David Boerner, *The Legacy of Norm Maleng*, 84 WASH. L. REV. 3, 5 (2009).

According to a judge, "Although he was the lawyer for county government and its elected officials, Norm never lost sight of the fact that he and his deputies represented the people of King County. If elected officials violated that trust, they could not expect the King County Prosecutor to cover up or defend that dereliction of duty. Norm Maleng's client was always the people of his community." *Id.* at 7.

Maleng became a state and national leader in prosecutorial circles. But he is probably most famous for his actions with respect to the death penalty. As a prosecutor, Maleng sought the death penalty. However, "he never delegated these decisions, recognizing that the people had entrusted this responsibility to him personally. He approached each case knowing that his responsibility was to arrive at a just decision, sensitive to the victim, the community, and the defendant." *Id.* at 9–10.

Maleng oversaw the prosecution of the Green River Killer, a serial killer in Washington and California who pled guilty to the murders of 49 women. Maleng chose not to seek the death penalty in the case "in return for a plea of guilty and the killer's cooperation in recovering bodies and closing cases where families were unsure what had happened to their loved ones." *Id.* at 10. Reflecting upon Maleng's death years later, a judge made the following observation:

> Dr. Martin Luther King, another of Norm's personal heroes, once observed:
>
>> On some positions, cowardice asks the question, Is it expedient? And then expedience comes along and asks the question, Is it politic? Vanity asks the question, Is it popular? Conscience asks the question, Is it right? There comes a time when one must take the position that is neither safe nor politic nor popular, but he must do it because conscience tells him it is right.
>
> His decision on the Green River case was not safe, politic, or popular. But once Norm determined that the decision was right, he had all he needed to go forward.
>
> Norm was respected by all, and he was loved by many. Love is not an emotion one commonly associates with a prosecutor, but Norm's unique nature earned him this love. In Justice Jackson's words, he tempered zeal with kindness, sought truth and not victims, served the law and not factions. He exercised the power the people gave him with humility and wisdom. Norm's legacy lives in all of us he inspired.

Id.

CHAPTER 23

CRIMINAL DEFENSE PRACTICE

■ ■ ■

Chapter Hypothetical. Kevin was convicted of murder and sentenced to death. His conviction was affirmed on appeal. He was represented at trial by Lucas. Kevin is now represented by Abby in his efforts to obtain post-conviction relief. He is also considering filing a legal malpractice action and disciplinary charges against Lucas.

Criminal defense work poses its own set of professional challenges. The primary goal of the law governing criminal defense lawyers is to ensure competent representation of criminal defendants. There are three main bodies of law—constitutional law, tort law, and the rules of professional conduct—that, in theory, work together to advance this goal.

A. CONSTITUTIONAL LAW: INEFFECTIVE ASSISTANCE OF COUNSEL

Allegations of lawyer incompetence may arise as convicted felons seek to have their convictions overturned because of their counsel's alleged ineffective assistance during their trial or sentencing. These claims are based on the Sixth Amendment right to counsel and the Supreme Court's holdings that the right to counsel is the right to the *effective* assistance of counsel. The issue can also arise under similar provisions of state constitutions.

STRICKLAND V. WASHINGTON
466 U.S. 668 (1984)

JUSTICE O'CONNOR delivered the opinion of the Court.

This case requires us to consider the proper standards for judging a criminal defendant's contention that the Constitution requires a conviction or death sentence to be set aside because counsel's assistance at the trial or sentencing was ineffective.

I

A

During a 10-day period in September 1976, respondent planned and committed three groups of crimes, which included three brutal stabbing murders, torture, kidnaping, severe assaults, attempted murders, attempted extortion, and theft. After his two accomplices were arrested, respondent surrendered to police and voluntarily gave a lengthy statement confessing to the third of the criminal episodes. The State of Florida indicted respondent for kidnaping and murder and appointed an experienced criminal lawyer to represent him.

Counsel actively pursued pretrial motions and discovery. He cut his efforts short, however, and he experienced a sense of hopelessness about the case, when he learned that, against his specific advice, respondent had also confessed to the first two murders. By the date set for trial, respondent was subject to indictment for three counts of first-degree murder and multiple counts of robbery, kidnaping for ransom, breaking and entering and assault, attempted murder, and conspiracy to commit robbery. Respondent waived his right to a jury trial, again acting against counsel's advice, and pleaded guilty to all charges, including the three capital murder charges.

In the plea colloquy, respondent told the trial judge that, although he had committed a string of burglaries, he had no significant prior criminal record and that at the time of his criminal spree he was under extreme stress caused by his inability to support his family. He also stated, however, that he accepted responsibility for the crimes. The trial judge told respondent that he had "a great deal of respect for people who are willing to step forward and admit their responsibility" but that he was making no statement at all about his likely sentencing decision.

. . .

In preparing for the sentencing hearing, counsel spoke with respondent about his background. He also spoke on the telephone with respondent's wife and mother, though he did not follow up on the one unsuccessful effort to meet with them. He did not otherwise seek out character witnesses for respondent. Nor did he request a psychiatric examination, since his conversations with his client gave no indication that respondent had psychological problems.

Counsel decided not to present and hence not to look further for evidence concerning respondent's character and emotional state. That decision reflected trial counsel's sense of hopelessness about overcoming the evidentiary effect of respondent's confessions to the gruesome crimes. It also reflected the judgment that it was advisable to rely on the plea colloquy for evidence about respondent's background and about his claim of emotional stress: the plea colloquy communicated sufficient information about these subjects, and by forgoing the opportunity to present new evidence on these subjects, counsel prevented the State from cross-examining respondent on his claim and from putting on psychiatric evidence of its own.

. . .

[T]he trial judge found numerous aggravating circumstances and no (or a single comparatively insignificant) mitigating circumstance. With respect to each of the three convictions for capital murder, the trial judge concluded: "A careful consideration of all matters presented to the court impels the conclusion that there are insufficient mitigating circumstances . . . to outweigh the aggravating circumstances." He therefore sentenced respondent to death on each of the three counts of murder and to prison terms for the other crimes. The Florida Supreme Court upheld the convictions and sentences on direct appeal.

B

Respondent subsequently sought collateral relief in state court on numerous grounds, among them that counsel had rendered ineffective assistance at the sentencing proceeding. . . .

Applying the standard for ineffectiveness claims articulated by the Florida Supreme Court in *Knight v. State*, 394 So.2d 997 (1981), the trial court concluded that respondent had not shown that counsel's assistance reflected any substantial and serious deficiency measurably below that of competent counsel that was likely to have affected the outcome of the sentencing proceeding. The court specifically found: "[A]s a matter of law, the record affirmatively demonstrates beyond any doubt that even if [counsel] had done each of the . . . things [that respondent alleged counsel had failed to do] at the time of sentencing, there is not even the remotest chance that the outcome would have been any different. The plain fact is that the aggravating circumstances proved in this case were completely overwhelming. . . ."

The Florida Supreme Court affirmed the denial of relief.

C

Respondent next filed a petition for a writ of habeas corpus in the United States District Court for the Southern District of Florida. . . .

[T]he District Court concluded that "there does not appear to be a likelihood, or even a significant possibility," that any errors of trial counsel had affected the outcome of the sentencing proceeding. . . . The court accordingly denied the petition for a writ of habeas corpus. [The Fifth Circuit Court of Appeals reversed the judgment of the District Court and remanded the case.] Petitioners, who are officials of the State of Florida, filed a petition for a writ of certiorari seeking review of the decision of the Court of Appeals.

II

In a long line of cases . . . this Court has recognized that the Sixth Amendment right to counsel exists, and is needed, in order to protect the fundamental right to a fair trial. The Constitution guarantees a fair trial through the Due Process Clauses, but it defines the basic elements of a fair trial largely through the several provisions of the Sixth Amendment, including the Counsel Clause:

"In all criminal prosecutions, the accused shall enjoy the right to a speedy and public trial, by an impartial jury of the State and district wherein the crime shall have been committed, which district shall have been previously ascertained by law, and to be informed of the nature and cause of the accusation; to be confronted with the witnesses against him; to have compulsory process for obtaining witnesses in his favor, and to have the Assistance of Counsel for his defence."

Thus, a fair trial is one in which evidence subject to adversarial testing is presented to an impartial tribunal for resolution of issues defined in advance of the proceeding. The right to counsel plays a crucial role in the adversarial system embodied in the Sixth Amendment, since access to counsel's skill and knowledge is necessary to accord defendants the "ample opportunity to meet the case of the prosecution" to which they are entitled. Adams v. United States ex rel. McCann, 317 U.S. 269, 275, 276, 63 S.Ct. 236, 240, 87 L.Ed. 268 (1942); *see* Powell v. Alabama, supra, 287 U.S. at 68–69, 53 S.Ct. 63–64.

Because of the vital importance of counsel's assistance, this Court has held that, with certain exceptions, a person accused of a federal or state crime has the right to have counsel appointed if retained counsel cannot be obtained. That a person who happens to be a lawyer is present at trial alongside the accused, however, is not enough to satisfy the constitutional command. The Sixth Amendment recognizes the right to the assistance of counsel because it envisions counsel's playing a role that is critical to the ability of the adversarial system to produce just results. An accused is entitled to be assisted by an attorney, whether retained or appointed, who plays the role necessary to ensure that the trial is fair.

For that reason, the Court has recognized that "the right to counsel is the right to the effective assistance of counsel." McMann v. Richardson, 397 U.S. 759, 771, n. 14, 90 S.Ct. 1441, 1449, n. 14, 25 L.Ed.2d 763 (1970). Government violates the right to effective assistance when it interferes in certain ways with the ability of counsel to make independent decisions about how to conduct the defense. *See, e.g.*, Geders v. United States, 425 U.S. 80, 96 S. Ct. 1330, 47 L.Ed.2d 592 (1976) (bar on attorney-client consultation during overnight recess). Counsel, however, can also deprive a defendant of the right to effective assistance, simply by failing to render "adequate legal assistance," *Cuyler v. Sullivan*, 446 U.S., at 344, 100 S.Ct., at 1716. Id., at 345–350, 100 S.Ct., at 1716–1719 (actual conflict of interest adversely affecting lawyer's performance renders assistance ineffective).

The Court has not elaborated on the meaning of the constitutional requirement of effective assistance in the latter class of cases—that is, those presenting claims of "actual ineffectiveness." In giving meaning to the requirement, however, we must take its purpose—to ensure a fair trial—as the guide. The benchmark for judging any claim of ineffectiveness must be whether counsel's conduct so undermined the proper functioning of the adversarial process that the trial cannot be relied on as having produced a just result. . . .

III

A convicted defendant's claim that counsel's assistance was so defective as to require reversal of a conviction or death sentence has two components. First, the defendant must show that counsel's performance was deficient. This requires showing that counsel made errors so serious that counsel was not functioning as the "counsel" guaranteed the defendant by the Sixth Amendment. Second, the defendant must show that the deficient performance prejudiced the defense. This requires showing that counsel's errors were so serious as to deprive the defendant of a fair trial, a trial whose result is reliable. Unless a defendant makes both showings, it cannot be said that the conviction or death sentence resulted from a breakdown in the adversary process that renders the result unreliable.

A

. . . In any case presenting an ineffectiveness claim, the performance inquiry must be whether counsel's assistance was reasonable considering all the circumstances. Prevailing norms of practice as reflected in American Bar Association standards and the like, *e.g.*, ABA Standards for Criminal Justice 4–1.1 to 4–8.6 (2d ed. 1980) ("The Defense Function"), are guides to determining what is reasonable, but they are only guides. No particular set of detailed rules for counsel's conduct can satisfactorily take account of the variety of circumstances faced by defense counsel or the range of legitimate decisions regarding how best to represent a criminal defendant. Any such set of rules would interfere with the constitutionally protected independence of counsel and restrict the wide latitude counsel must have in making tactical decisions. Indeed, the existence of detailed guidelines for representation could distract counsel from the overriding mission of vigorous advocacy of the defendant's cause. Moreover, the purpose of the effective assistance guarantee of the Sixth Amendment is not to improve the quality of legal representation, although that is a goal of considerable importance to the legal system. The purpose is simply to ensure that criminal defendants receive a fair trial.

Judicial scrutiny of counsel's performance must be highly deferential. It is all too tempting for a defendant to second-guess counsel's assistance after conviction or adverse sentence, and it is all too easy for a court, examining counsel's defense after it has proved unsuccessful, to conclude that a particular act or omission of counsel was unreasonable. A fair assessment of attorney performance requires that every effort be made to eliminate the distorting effects of hindsight, to reconstruct the circumstances of counsel's challenged conduct, and to evaluate the conduct from counsel's perspective at the time. Because of the difficulties inherent in making the evaluation, a court must indulge a strong presumption that counsel's conduct falls within the wide range of reasonable professional assistance; that is, the defendant must overcome the presumption that, under the circumstances, the challenged action "might be considered sound trial strategy." There are countless ways to provide effective assistance in any given case. Even the best criminal defense attorneys would not defend a particular client in the same way.

The availability of intrusive post-trial inquiry into attorney performance or of detailed guidelines for its evaluation would encourage the proliferation of ineffectiveness challenges. Criminal trials resolved unfavorably to the defendant would increasingly come to be followed by a second trial, this one of counsel's unsuccessful defense. Counsel's performance and even willingness to serve could be adversely affected. Intensive scrutiny of counsel and rigid requirements for acceptable assistance could dampen the ardor and impair the independence of defense counsel, discourage the acceptance of assigned cases, and undermine the trust between attorney and client.

Thus, a court deciding an actual ineffectiveness claim must judge the reasonableness of counsel's challenged conduct on the facts of the particular case, viewed as of the time of counsel's conduct. A convicted defendant making a claim of ineffective assistance must identify the acts or omissions of counsel that are alleged not to have been the result of reasonable professional judgment. The court must then determine whether, in light of all the circumstances, the identified acts or omissions were outside the wide range of professionally competent assistance. In making that determination, the court should keep in mind that counsel's function, as elaborated in prevailing professional norms, is to make the adversarial testing process work in the particular case. At the same time, the court should recognize that counsel is strongly presumed to have rendered adequate assistance and made all significant decisions in the exercise of reasonable professional judgment.

These standards require no special amplification in order to define counsel's duty to investigate, the duty at issue in this case. As the Court of Appeals concluded, strategic choices made after thorough investigation of law and facts relevant to plausible options are virtually unchallengeable;

and strategic choices made after less than complete investigation are reasonable precisely to the extent that reasonable professional judgments support the limitations on investigation. In other words, counsel has a duty to make reasonable investigations or to make a reasonable decision that makes particular investigations unnecessary. In any ineffectiveness case, a particular decision not to investigate must be directly assessed for reasonableness in all the circumstances, applying a heavy measure of deference to counsel's judgments.

The reasonableness of counsel's actions may be determined or substantially influenced by the defendant's own statements or actions. Counsel's actions are usually based, quite properly, on informed strategic choices made by the defendant and on information supplied by the defendant. In particular, what investigation decisions are reasonable depends critically on such information. For example, when the facts that support a certain potential line of defense are generally known to counsel because of what the defendant has said, the need for further investigation may be considerably diminished or eliminated altogether. And when a defendant has given counsel reason to believe that pursuing certain investigations would be fruitless or even harmful, counsel's failure to pursue those investigations may not later be challenged as unreasonable. In short, inquiry into counsel's conversations with the defendant may be critical to a proper assessment of counsel's investigation decisions, just as it may be critical to a proper assessment of counsel's other litigation decisions.

B

An error by counsel, even if professionally unreasonable, does not warrant setting aside the judgment of a criminal proceeding if the error had no effect on the judgment. The purpose of the Sixth Amendment guarantee of counsel is to ensure that a defendant has the assistance necessary to justify reliance on the outcome of the proceeding. Accordingly, any deficiencies in counsel's performance must be prejudicial to the defense in order to constitute ineffective assistance under the Constitution.

In certain Sixth Amendment contexts, prejudice is presumed. Actual or constructive denial of the assistance of counsel altogether is legally presumed to result in prejudice. So are various kinds of state interference with counsel's assistance. Prejudice in these circumstances is so likely that case-by-case inquiry into prejudice is not worth the cost. . . .

[A]ctual ineffectiveness claims alleging a deficiency in attorney performance are subject to a general requirement that the defendant affirmatively prove prejudice. . . . Even if a defendant shows that particular errors of counsel were unreasonable, therefore, the defendant must show that they actually had an adverse effect on the defense.

It is not enough for the defendant to show that the errors had some conceivable effect on the outcome of the proceeding. Virtually every act or omission of counsel would meet that test, and not every error that conceivably could have influenced the outcome undermines the reliability of the result of the proceeding. . . .

[W]e believe that a defendant need not show that counsel's deficient conduct more likely than not altered the outcome in the case. . . .

. . . The result of a proceeding can be rendered unreliable, and hence the proceeding itself unfair, even if the errors of counsel cannot be shown by a preponderance of the evidence to have determined the outcome.

Accordingly, the appropriate test for prejudice finds its roots in the test for materiality of exculpatory information not disclosed to the defense by the prosecution, and in the test for materiality of testimony made unavailable to the defense by Government deportation of a witness. The defendant must show that there is a reasonable probability that, but for counsel's unprofessional errors, the result of the proceeding would have been different. A reasonable probability is a probability sufficient to undermine confidence in the outcome.

. . .

The governing legal standard plays a critical role in defining the question to be asked in assessing the prejudice from counsel's errors. When a defendant challenges a conviction, the question is whether there is a reasonable probability that, absent the errors, the factfinder would have had a reasonable doubt respecting guilt. When a defendant challenges a death sentence such as the one at issue in this case, the question is whether there is a reasonable probability that, absent the errors, the sentencer—including an appellate court, to the extent it independently reweighs the evidence—would have concluded that the balance of aggravating and mitigating circumstances did not warrant death.

V

. . .

With respect to the performance component, the record shows that respondent's counsel made a strategic choice to argue for the extreme emotional distress mitigating circumstance and to rely as fully as possible on respondent's acceptance of responsibility for his crimes. . . . Counsel's strategy choice was well within the range of professionally reasonable judgments, and the decision not to seek more character or psychological evidence than was already in hand was likewise reasonable.

The trial judge's views on the importance of owning up to one's crimes were well known to counsel. The aggravating circumstances were utterly overwhelming. Trial counsel could reasonably surmise from his conversations with respondent that character and psychological evidence would be of little help. Respondent had already been able to mention at the plea colloquy the substance of what there was to know about his financial and emotional troubles. Restricting testimony on respondent's character to what had come in at the plea colloquy ensured that contrary character and psychological evidence and respondent's criminal history, which counsel had successfully moved to exclude, would not come in. On these facts, there can be little question, even without application of the presumption of adequate performance, that trial counsel's defense, though unsuccessful, was the result of reasonable professional judgment.

With respect to the prejudice component, the lack of merit of respondent's claim is even more stark. The evidence that respondent says his trial counsel should have offered at the sentencing hearing would barely have altered the sentencing profile presented to the sentencing judge. As the state courts and District Court found, at most this evidence shows that numerous people who knew respondent thought he was generally a good person and that a psychiatrist and a psychologist believed he was under considerable emotional stress that did not rise to the level of extreme disturbance. Given the overwhelming aggravating factors, there is no reasonable probability that the omitted evidence would have changed the conclusion that the aggravating circumstances outweighed the mitigating circumstances and, hence, the sentence imposed. Indeed, admission of the evidence respondent now offers might even have been harmful to his case: his "rap sheet" would probably have been admitted into evidence, and the psychological reports would have directly contradicted respondent's claim that the mitigating circumstance of extreme emotional disturbance applied to his case.

. . .

Failure to make the required showing of either deficient performance or sufficient prejudice defeats the ineffectiveness claim. Here there is a double failure. More generally, respondent has made no showing that the justice of his sentence was rendered unreliable by a breakdown in the adversary process caused by deficiencies in counsel's assistance. Respondent's sentencing proceeding was not fundamentally unfair.

We conclude, therefore, that the District Court properly declined to issue a writ of habeas corpus. The judgment of the Court of Appeals is accordingly

Reversed.

* * *

***Strickland* in Practice.** It is notoriously difficult to prevail on an ineffective assistance of counsel claim. *See* Stephanos Bibas, *The Psychology of Hindsight and After-the-Fact Review of Ineffective Assistance* *of Counsel*, 2004 UTAH L. REV. 1, 1 (2004) ("Courts rarely reverse convictions for ineffective assistance of counsel, even if the defendant's lawyer was asleep, drunk, unprepared, or unknowledgeable."). First, the *Strickland* decision itself establishes a formidable burden for those seeking post-conviction relief. In addition, such claims also rely on the cooperation of the lawyer accused of providing ineffective assistance of counsel. As one author explains, "[a] successful claim often inquires into defense counsel's conversations and interactions with the defendant. Therefore, it is unlikely to be successful without the cooperation of the criminal defense attorney about whom the defendant is complaining." Meredith J. Duncan, *The (So-Called) Liability of Criminal Defense Attorneys, A System in Need of Reform*, 2002 BYU L. REV. 1, 27 (2002). As one might imagine, some criminal defense lawyers are not particularly interested in participating in such claims.

Confirmation Bias. Some have suggested that confirmation bias—the tendency of individuals to interpret new evidence so as to confirm their initial judgments—may play a role in ineffective assistance of counsel claims. If, for example, a judge is inclined to believe that most defendants are guilty, a judge "might discount alleged attorney errors, regarding them as tactical decisions or irrelevant to the foreordained outcome." Stephanos Bibas, *The Psychology of Hindsight and After-the-Fact Review of Ineffective Assistance of Counsel*, 2004 UTAH L. REV. 1, 1 (2004).

Problem 23.1. It is standard practice in the relevant jurisdiction in a capital case like Kevin's for an attorney to prepare a "social history" of the criminal defendant. This social history involves a detailed investigation into the defendant's upbringing and background that may serve to mitigate the defendant's punishment upon a finding of guilt. Lucas, acting as Kevin's attorney at trial, failed to prepare a social history. Lucas was aware of some of Kevin's childhood history but he did not possess the sort of detailed knowledge he would have acquired had he conducted a full social history. Instead, Lucas made a tactical choice to devote his time, energy, and money to establishing that Kevin was not guilty of the murder for which he was ultimately convicted. Had Lucas conducted a social history, he would have found that Kevin had suffered horrific physical and sexual abuse from the time he was a young child up until he ran away from a foster home at age 16. None of this information was presented to the jury during the sentencing phase of the trial. Kevin was sentenced to death. Did Lucas render ineffective assistance of counsel as defined in *Strickland*? What arguments must Abby make on Kevin's behalf?

* * *

Another way a criminal defense lawyer may fail to provide effective assistance of counsel is where the lawyer has a conflict of interest. The normal conflict of interest rules apply in these cases. But the fact that a criminal defense lawyer has a conflict of interest raises special concerns.

* * *

Problem 23.2. In a matter unrelated to Kevin's case, Lawyer Lucas represents Lettley, a criminal defendant charged with first-degree murder. Lucas also happens to represent another criminal defendant in an unrelated matter. The other client confesses to Lucas (in confidence) that he actually committed the murder of which Lettley is accused. Is there a conflict under Rule 1.7(a)(2) and, if so, why?

* * *

Assume in the problem above that Lucas seeks permission from the court to withdraw as counsel, that the court refuses to allow him to withdraw, and that Lettley is convicted. Should Lettley's conviction be overturned on the grounds of ineffective assistance of counsel in violation of the Sixth Amendment to the United States Constitution?

In *Cuyler v. Sullivan*, 446 U.S. 335 (1980), the Supreme Court held that "[in] order to establish a violation of the Sixth Amendment, a defendant who raised no objection at trial must demonstrate that an actual conflict of interest adversely affected his lawyer's performance." Thus, the mere "possibility of conflict is insufficient to impugn a criminal conviction. In order to demonstrate a violation of his Sixth Amendment rights, a defendant must establish that an actual conflict of interest adversely affected his lawyer's performance." This standard applies regardless of whether the defense attorney is appointed or privately retained.

But what if the criminal defendant, through counsel, does advise the court about the possibility of a conflict? Courts have held under these circumstances that if the trial court fails to take "adequate steps to ascertain whether the risk was too remote to warrant separate counsel," *Holloway v. Arkansas*, 435 U.S. 475, 484 (1978), or improperly requires joint or dual representation, then reversal is automatic, without a showing of prejudice, or adverse effect upon the representation. *Lettley v. State*, 746 A.2d 392 (Md. 2000).

One situation in which a conflict of interest might arise is where a criminal defense lawyer jointly represents co-defendants. A comment to Model Rule 1.7 observes that "[t]he potential for conflict of interest in representing multiple defendants in a criminal case is so grave that ordinarily a lawyer should decline to represent more than one codefendant." Model Rule 1.7 cmt. [23]. Some states actually establish a presumption that joint representations of co-defendants in a criminal matter is improper and require a defense lawyer to show that a conflict does not exist or is unlikely to arise before the lawyer may jointly represent the co-defendants. *See* Tenn. R. Prof'l Conduct Rule 1.7 cmt. [35].

Conflicts of interest pose a special concern in the case of a public defender. Ordinarily, if one lawyer in a firm has a conflict, that conflict is imputed to the other members of the firm under Model Rule 1.10(a). But a comment to Rule 1.11 explains that this imputed disqualification rule does not apply in the case of a government lawyer. *See* Rule 1.11 cmt. [2]. Why should this be the rule in the case of a public defender?

* * *

B. TORT LAW: LEGAL MALPRACTICE

Another way the law regulates the conduct of criminal defense lawyers is through tort law, most notably legal malpractice claims. The basic elements of a legal malpractice claim against a criminal defense lawyer are the same as they are in other contexts. But the malpractice plaintiff faces special challenges in this context. For example, the majority of courts to consider the issue have concluded that *Strickland*'s ineffective assistance of counsel standard articulates the standard of care for purposes of legal malpractice claim. Thus, a finding that that a lawyer's representation was not constitutionally defective operates as collateral estoppel on the breach of duty element in a malpractice claim. Meredith J. Duncan, *The (So-Called) Liability of Criminal Defense Attorneys, A System in Need of Reform*, 2002 BYU L. REV. 1, 35 (2002).

In addition, the majority of courts have adopted special causation requirements—based on policy concerns—in these cases that impose a substantial hurdle for plaintiffs. The following decision surveys the different approaches courts have adopted in these cases.

BARKER V. CAPOTOSTO
875 N.W.2d 157 (Iowa 2016)

MANSFIELD, JUSTICE.

[In 2006, Robert Barker entered a plea of guilty to the charge of solicitation of a minor. Barker was placed on probation but was later imprisoned for violation of the terms of his probation.]

[In 2009,] Barker filed an application for postconviction relief from his conviction for solicitation of a minor. His application alleged that his prior counsel had committed ineffective assistance of counsel because there was no factual basis for his guilty plea to solicitation of a minor to engage in a sex act. In a written ruling, the district court granted the application on February 28, 2011.

On March 1, 2013, Barker filed a petition alleging that Magee and Capotosto committed legal malpractice by advising him to plead guilty to an offense for which there was no factual basis. Thereafter, Capotosto filed a motion for summary judgment, which Magee joined. They argued Barker could not establish that he was factually innocent in the underlying criminal case. They urged that the Iowa courts should require a plaintiff to prove actual innocence in order to maintain a suit for legal malpractice occurring in the course of criminal representation. They also argued that, as a matter of law, their alleged malpractice did not cause Barker's damages. [The district court granted the motion on the first ground. Barker appealed.]

A party seeking to establish a prima facie claim of legal malpractice must show the following: (1) a duty arising from the established existence of an attorney-client relationship; (2) the attorney breached that duty; (3) the attorney's breach was the proximate cause of injury to the client; and (4) the client suffered actual damage, injury, or loss. Ruden v. Jenk, 543 N.W.2d 605, 610 (Iowa 1996). Additionally, we have held that a criminal defendant must "achieve relief from a conviction before advancing a legal malpractice action against his former attorney." *Trobaugh v. Sondag*, 668 N.W.2d 577, 583 (Iowa 2003).

In *Trobaugh,* we noted that some courts had also required proof of actual innocence before allowing recovery but declined to reach the issue. . . . Barker's case squarely presents the issue reserved in *Trobaugh*—whether proof of actual innocence is required in a "criminal malpractice" suit. We are not the first court to confront this question. Other jurisdictions have addressed whether to require actual innocence in a criminal malpractice action. We consider three of the approaches taken elsewhere and their supporting reasoning.

Of those jurisdictions to have considered the issue, a majority have adopted an "actual innocence" requirement. . . .

[*Ang v. Martin*, 154 Wash.2d 477, 114 P.3d 637 (2005)] from Washington exemplifies the reasoning of those courts that have adopted an actual innocence requirement. The Angs, a married couple who owned a medical examination company, became the target of a social security fraud investigation. They were eventually indicted on eighteen criminal counts, including bank and tax fraud. Their counsel attempted to negotiate a plea bargain, but the Angs rejected the proposed agreement. The case went to trial, but just before the close of the prosecution's case, the Angs' attorneys recommended they accept a plea—one the Angs considered less attractive than previous offers. The Angs agreed to plead guilty to two counts but allegedly only after Dr. Ang was told that his wife might be sexually assaulted in prison.

Upon retaining new counsel, the Angs successfully moved to withdraw their pleas. The case went to trial again, and the Angs were acquitted of all eighteen counts. The Angs then filed a legal malpractice action against their original attorneys. The jury in the malpractice action was instructed that the Angs had to prove they were innocent of the underlying criminal charges by a preponderance of the evidence. The Angs lost their malpractice case and assigned error to the instruction on appeal.

The Washington Supreme Court upheld the instruction, deciding that actual innocence—as well as relief from the underlying criminal charges—was a necessary component of a plaintiff's suit for criminal malpractice. The court noted the Angs may have been legally innocent, as evidenced by the successful withdrawal of their guilty pleas and their subsequent acquittal of all charges, but that did not necessarily mean they were actually innocent of the criminal conduct they had been accused of in the prior proceedings. In the court's view, actual innocence was "essential" to proving causation, both proximate and but-for causation. Additionally, the court found that requiring criminal malpractice plaintiffs to prove their actual innocence

> will prohibit criminals from benefiting from their own bad acts, maintain respect for our criminal justice systems procedural protections, remove the harmful chilling effect on the defense bar, prevent suits from criminals who may be guilty, [but] could have gotten a better deal, and prevent a flood of nuisance litigation.

As *Ang* illustrates, courts adopting the actual innocence element in criminal malpractice actions have been motivated by public policy concerns. Principal among these concerns is that "it would violate public policy to allow a person to profit from participating in an illegal act."

Another rationale is that actual innocence prevents the former criminal defendant from shifting the responsibility for his or her conviction. If a plaintiff committed the crimes he or she was accused of, then he or she "alone should bear full responsibility for the consequences of [his or her] acts, including imprisonment. Any subsequent negligent conduct by a plaintiff's attorney is superseded by the greater culpability of the plaintiff's criminal conduct."

Also, courts have found that constitutional protections, such as postconviction relief for ineffectiveness of counsel, provide a sufficient remedy for guilty defendants. Moreover, courts have noted a substantial interest in preserving the availability of representation to criminal defendants. Criminal defense counsel is often working for reduced fees or has been appointed at public expense, and "[t]he public has a strong interest in encouraging the representation of criminal defendants, particularly those who are ruled to be indigent." In declining to require criminal malpractice plaintiffs to prove actual innocence, courts might be "[s]etting the standard at a lower level [which] may well dampen counsels' willingness to enter the criminal defense arena." *Mahoney*, 727 A.2d at 1000. And further, the differing burdens of proof in criminal and malpractice actions could create confusion for the jury.

Additionally, these courts commonly focus on the causation element of a malpractice case in their reasoning. Many of them have asserted in some form that the plaintiff's criminal behavior—rather than the attorney's conduct—led to the plaintiff's predicament. Judge Posner perhaps best voiced this consideration in *Levine v. Kling,* 123 F.3d 580 (7th Cir. 1997), a case in which the United States Court of Appeals for the Seventh Circuit determined that Illinois law required a criminal malpractice plaintiff to establish innocence, either by postconviction relief or other means.

> On [the plaintiff's] view there would be cases in which a defendant guilty in fact of the crime with which he had been charged, and duly convicted and imprisoned (perhaps after a retrial in which he was represented by competent counsel), would nevertheless obtain substantial damages to compensate him for the loss of his liberty during the period of his rightful imprisonment.
>
> Not only would this be a paradoxical result, depreciating and in some cases wholly offsetting the plaintiff's criminal punishment, but it would be contrary to fundamental principles of both tort and criminal law. Tort law provides damages only for harms to the plaintiff's legally protected interests, *Restatement (Second) of Torts,* § 1 comment d, § 7(1) (1965), and the liberty of a guilty criminal is not one of them. The guilty criminal may be able to obtain an acquittal if he is skillfully represented, but he has no right to that result . . . and the law provides no relief if the "right" is denied him.

Alaska has adopted a somewhat different approach. Instead of requiring the former criminal defendant to establish actual innocence, this approach allows the criminal defense attorney to raise actual guilt as an affirmative defense to the malpractice suit. *See* [*Shaw v. State,* 861 P.2d 566, 572 (Alaska 1993)]. The attorney must prove her or his former client's guilt by a preponderance of the evidence, but in doing so, the attorney is not limited to the evidence admissible on the criminal charge. In placing this burden on the defendant, the Alaska Supreme Court noted the plaintiff still must obtain postconviction relief before bringing the malpractice claim. The court also cited the similarity between an actual guilt defense and other affirmative defenses in tort such as comparative negligence and assumption of the risk.

As a third alternative, some courts have rejected an actual innocence requirement entirely.

The Kansas Supreme Court recently considered, and declined to adopt, an actual innocence requirement. *See* [*Mashaney v. Bd. of Indigents' Def. Servs.,* 302 Kan. 625, 355 P.3d 667, 687 (2015).] The case involved an individual charged with one count of aggravated criminal sodomy and one count of aggravated indecent liberties with a child. After the first trial ended in a mistrial, the individual was convicted in a second jury trial and sentenced to 442 months in prison. Years later, Mashaney successfully moved to vacate or set aside his sentence, and his case was set for a new trial. At that point, the defendant agreed to enter an *Alford* plea to two counts of attempted aggravated battery and one count of aggravated endangerment of a child in return for the State dropping the original charges. The court sentenced Mashaney to seventy-two months in prison, and he was released for time served.

Mashaney subsequently filed a malpractice suit against his former trial counsel, his former appellate counsel, and the state board of indigent defense services. He sought damages for the nearly eight years he spent in prison. The court dismissed Mashaney's claim against the state board and granted judgment on the pleadings to the attorneys. On appeal, the Kansas Court of Appeals held that a plaintiff as a threshold matter must prove actual innocence to pursue a criminal malpractice action.

The Kansas Supreme Court reversed. First, the court disagreed with the broad notion that public policy supports the actual innocence rule. It indicated that the justifications for the rule were too simplistic and "no match for the complexities of a case such as this." Next, the court stated that requiring actual innocence produced inequitable results in that former defendants who received "lengthy prison sentences as a direct result of their lawyers' negligence will be deprived of any tort remedy for that malpractice and some lawyers representing criminal defendants will escape liability when their civil counterparts would not." The court added that actual innocence was based on a flawed conception of causation in tort law because if counsel "fails to demonstrate the State's inability to prove guilt beyond a reasonable doubt when a competent lawyer could have and would have done so, the client has been legally injured by being convicted and imprisoned," regardless of innocence. Moreover, the court found the notion that actual innocence furthers the availability of criminal defense representation supported by judicial speculation rather than empirical evidence.

Lastly, the Kansas Supreme Court noted that in a prior decision, it had adopted the "exoneration rule," under which the criminal malpractice plaintiff had to obtain relief from her or his conviction before bringing any claim. It indicated that this requirement effectively precluded the bringing of frivolous malpractice claims by criminal defendants.

This recent Kansas decision mirrors the recommendation of the *Restatement of the Law Governing Lawyers*. Regarding actions for malpractice by a criminal defendant, the *Restatement* concludes that "it is not necessary to prove that the convicted defendant was in fact innocent," although it notes that "most jurisdictions addressing the issue have stricter rules." *Restatement (Third) of the Law Governing Lawyers* § 53 cmt. d, at 392 (Am. Law Inst.2000) [hereinafter *Restatement*]. The *Restatement* adds,

> As required by most jurisdictions addressing the issue, a convicted defendant seeking damages for malpractice causing a conviction must have had that conviction set aside when process for that relief on the grounds asserted in the malpractice action is available.

Thus, this aspect of the *Restatement* is consistent with our holding in *Trobaugh*.

We often look to the *Restatements* for guidance.

We find the approach taken by the *Restatement* and like-minded jurisdictions to be persuasive. The prerequisite that the malpractice plaintiff obtain judicial relief from her or his conviction, which the *Restatement* endorses and which we adopted in *Trobaugh* after "considering all of the issues presented and the wealth of commentary on this issue," serves as an important screen against unwarranted claims and "preserves key principles of judicial economy and comity." But we do not think an additional actual innocence screen is appropriate. Such a prerequisite goes beyond respecting the criminal process—i.e., "judicial economy and comity"—and interposes an additional barrier to recovery that other malpractice plaintiffs do not have to overcome.

Furthermore, a criminal defendant already "must prove both that the lawyer failed to act properly and that, but for that failure, the result would have been different." *Restatement* § 53 cmt. d, at 392; *see also Vossoughi*, 859 N.W.2d at 649 (noting that to establish a prima facie claim of legal malpractice, the plaintiff must produce evidence showing the attorney's breach of duty caused actual injury). Often, the innocence or guilt of the client will enter into the causation inquiry that is part of the plaintiff's prima facie case. For example, if Barker's counsel had refused to let him plead guilty to the nonexistent crime of soliciting a minor to commit a sex act, would the State have pursued the original charges, assuming it could have done so? What would have been the outcome of those charges? Would Barker have been incarcerated anyway? A criminal defendant who was factually guilty of the crime for which he or she was convicted—or at least guilty of a related crime or a crime with which he or she was originally charged—will likely confront significant causation issues in his legal malpractice action. We see no reason why such issues cannot be resolved, as they generally are in malpractice actions, by the fact finder.

Thus, we think the causation determination will frequently take into account the guilt or innocence of the client. And ultimately, we are not persuaded by the remaining public policy concerns other than causation. For example, while the notion that an individual should not "profit from participating in an illegal act" is a good general principle, it is too general to describe how our legal system actually operates. We do not bar criminal defendants who are guilty of their crimes from recovering overpayments from their criminal defense counsel, suing for clearly illegal searches, or suing the medical staff in the prison for medical malpractice. By analogy, a criminal defendant who is convicted of a crime due to legal malpractice, and gets that conviction set aside, should not be categorically barred from suing his or her former attorney just because the defendant may have been guilty of some lesser charge that would have resulted in a lower sentence.

. . .

Additionally, while we wholeheartedly agree that "[t]he public has a strong interest in encouraging the representation of criminal defendants, particularly those who are ruled to be indigent," *Glenn*, 569 N.E.2d at 788, it also has an interest in encouraging competent representation. Attorneys who serve indigent persons in other contexts, such as legal aid attorneys, are not exempt from potential malpractice claims.

Finally, we are not persuaded that an actual innocence requirement is needed to prevent a proliferation of nuisance suits. A criminal malpractice plaintiff still must obtain relief from the conviction. And unless the plaintiff's claim is based on standards of care and professionalism understood and expected by laypersons, the plaintiff will have to retain an expert to go forward. Furthermore, attorneys will still be able to avail themselves of traditional malpractice defenses.

. . . .

Hence, for the reasons stated, we conclude that a client's showing of actual innocence is not a prerequisite to bringing a legal malpractice claim against a former criminal defense attorney.

* * *

Competing Approaches. Tort law is designed to provide compensation for injury as well as to deter misconduct (or to encourage desirable conduct). Which of the rules discussed in *Barker* best furthers those goals? Is a special rule needed at all in these kinds of cases? Why not just apply traditional malpractice principles to these cases?

Other Scenarios? Should a client have a malpractice claim where the client committed the crime but, due to the negligence of the lawyer, spent more time in prison than the law allows?

* * *

C. RULES OF PROFESSIONAL CONDUCT

Problem 23.3. Review the facts from Problem 23.1. What rules of professional conduct did Lucas violate in his representation of Kevin?

* * *

Finally, the rules of professional conduct may also help encourage competent representation of criminal defendants. One common reason for the incompetent representation of criminal defendants is excessive caseloads on the part of defense attorneys. Excessive caseloads are a particular problem at many public defenders' offices. Any lawyer who accepts a case "that results in a caseload so high that it impairs her ability to provide competent representation, to act with reasonable diligence and to keep the client reasonably informed" violates the rules of professional conduct. *State ex rel. Missouri Public Defender Commission v. Waters*, 370 S.W.3d 592, 607 (Mo. 2012) (en banc). Excessive caseloads also make it more likely that a lawyer's representation of one or more clients will be materially limited by the lawyer's responsibilities to other clients under Rule 1.7(a)(2). These ethical rules apply to public defenders as they do to any lawyer; there is no exception for public defenders or criminal defense attorneys more generally. *See* ABA Standing Committee on Ethics and Professional Responsibility issued Formal Opinion 06–411

Constitutional and tort law relating to the work of criminal defense attorneys may also work in conjunction with the rules of professional conduct to define the scope of a criminal defense attorney's professional obligations. As the Missouri Supreme Court has explained, "while the ethical rules do not supplant a trial judge's obligation to protect [a] defendant's Sixth Amendment rights, they do 'run [ ] parallel to' that duty and, therefore, can assist both judges and public defenders in ensuring that constitutional rights are protected when appointments are made." *Waters*, 370 S.W.3d at 608. For example, in *Waters*, the Missouri Supreme Court considered the interplay between a defendant's Sixth Amendment right to counsel and a public defender's ethical obligation not to accept work that the defender does not believe he or she can perform competently. In *Waters*, the trial court said it believed it "had no choice" but to appoint a public defender, "regardless of the public defender's ability to provide competent and effective representation in another case, because to do otherwise would have violated the defendant's Sixth Amendment right to counsel, as the court could identify no other realistic mechanism by which to provide other counsel." *Id.* at 597. The Missouri Supreme Court rejected this idea and held that "the Sixth Amendment and this Court's ethics rules require that a court consider the issue of counsel's competency, and that counsel consider whether accepting an appointment will cause counsel to violate the Sixth Amendment and ethical rules, before determining whether to accept or challenge an appointment." *Id.* at 609.

* * *

Problem 23.4. Patty is a public defender. Patty's caseload currently exceeds what is considered reasonable by lawyers within the field. One day,

Safir, Patty's boss, informs Patty that the local court has appointed the public defender's office to represent several indigent defendants and that Patty is being assigned several of the new cases. Patty reasonably believes that there is no way she can competently represent her current clients as well as her newly-appointed clients. Thinking back to the rules discussed so far throughout this course, what should Patty do?

Problem 23.5. Assume for purposes of this question that Patty agrees to represent the new clients and that, as a result of pre-existing obligations to other clients, she ends up providing incompetent representation for the new clients. A disciplinary hearing panel finds that Patty violated Rules 1.1, 1.3, and 1.4 in several of the cases. Should the fact that Patty is a public defender who was assigned more cases than she could realistically handle be treated as a mitigating factor when the panel considers what form of discipline to impose?

Profile of Attorney Professionalism. "Born in Delaware in 1959, Bryan Stevenson grew up in a poor rural community where he developed a sense that 'there was this break in the world, and if you grew up on one side of that crack, it was definitely different than if you grew up on the other side of it.' . . . He entered law school with no clear idea of what kind of law he wanted to practice—or even if he wanted to practice law at all—but going to Georgia to work with the Southern Prisoners Defense Committee (now the Southern Center for Human Rights) exposed him to people desperately needing legal assistance and whose cases revealed a stark bias against the poor and people of color. That experience moved him in the direction of the kind of litigation and advocacy to which he now devotes his professional life." Gruber Foundation, Yale University, https://gruber.yale.edu/justice/bryan-stevenson.

After graduation from law school, Stevenson worked as a staff attorney for the Southern Center for Human Rights in Atlanta (1985) and then as executive director of the Alabama Capital Representation Resource Center (1989–95). In 1995, he founded the Equal Justice Initiative (EJI), a private, nonprofit organization that provides legal representation to indigent defendants and prisoners who have been denied fair and just treatment in the legal system. "Based in Montgomery, Alabama, EJI litigates on behalf of juvenile offenders, poor people denied effective representation, minority defendants whose trials are marked by racial bias or prosecutorial misconduct, and others against whom the justice system may be stacked. Working with EJI, Stevenson has largely been responsible for reversals and reduced sentences in more than 75 death penalty cases and has provided an effective training and consulting resource for counsel representing death row inmates." Gruber Foundation, Yale University, https://gruber.yale.edu/justice/bryan-stevenson His best-selling book, *Just*

Mercy, describes the work of the EJI and was eventually turned into a motion picture.

CHAPTER 24

SERVING AS A JUDGE

■ ■ ■

Chapter Hypothetical. Ida Ione was a lawyer who ran for local judicial office in New Dakota against the incumbent, Judge Robert Lloyd. Based on the strength of some negative advertising her campaign ran against Judge Lloyd, Ida Ione was elected. Now that she is on the bench, Judge Ione is facing professional discipline for statements she made about Judge Lloyd during the campaign as well as for the negative campaign ads. Judge Ione is also facing several motions from litigants asking that she disqualify herself from serving as a judge in several matters.

Being a judge is potentially a pretty good gig. Your work can be intellectually stimulating, your decisions may have a dramatic impact on the lives of those who appear before you, and the jokes you tell at bar association meetings and among lawyers are funnier than when you were a practicing lawyer. The pay—although a bone of contention for many judges—is not too bad. In 2023, the salary for federal district judges was over $223,000 and the salary for federal appellate judges was close to $246,000. Being a judge also carries with it at least some job security. The term of office for many state judges extends over a period of several years. Federal judges have life tenure during good behavior. Perhaps it is no surprise that many lawyers aspire to the bench. Even if you have no judicial aspirations, you will probably have to deal with judges on occasion during your career. Moreover, you will be impacted by the judicial selection process at the state and federal level, at least in a professional capacity. Therefore, it is important that lawyers understand the ethical rules pertaining to judges.

The judicial disciplinary process operates in much the same as the lawyer disciplinary process. State judicial conduct rules are based on the ABA's *Model Code of Judicial Conduct* (CJC). There is a judicial conduct organization in every state that handles complaints of judicial misconduct. At the state level, discipline for a violation of the rules can range from admonition to removal. At the federal level, the Judicial Conduct and Disability Act establishes a similar process. Article III federal judges can only be removed from the bench through the impeachment process.

* * *

A. BECOMING A JUDGE

1. THE JUDICIAL SELECTION PROCESS

Judicial selection methods vary widely. Federal judges are appointed by the President with the advice and consent of the Senate. Article III of the federal Constitution provides that federal judges "shall hold their Offices during good Behaviour." In contrast, judicial elections are common at the state level. According to one estimate, 87% of state judges are selected or retained on the basis of popular election. Judith L. Maute, *Selecting Justice in State Courts: The Ballot Box or the Backroom?*, 41 S. TEX. L. REV. 1197, 1203 (2000).

Merit selection combines elements of appoitive and elective systems while (proponents argue) reducing some of the harmful effects of both. Under a merit selection plan (sometimes also called the "Missouri Plan" for the state from which it originated), judges are typically appointed by the governor, who chooses from a list of applicants screened and prepared by a merit selection commission. After the initial appointment, the judge must then stand for a retention election on annual basis. Voters simply vote "yes" or "no" on the question of whether the judge should be retained in office. Thus, in theory, judges and judicial candidates are spared some of the problems associated with running in a contested election while still being subject to the will of the voters.

Today, the majority of states employ either partisan or non-partisan elections to select some or all of their appellate and/or general jurisdiction trial court judges. Only a handful retain a system of pure gubernatorial or legislative appointment. The rest rely upon some sort of merit selection. Judith L. Maute, *Selecting Justice in State Courts: The Ballot Box or the Backroom?*, 41 S. TEX. L. REV. 1197, 1203 (2000).

Regardless of which type of selection process is at issue, there are concerns with judicial candidates being dragged into the political process. A candidate for judicial office might be perceived as being too partisan or beholden to special interests, for example. In order for the public to have trust in the judiciary, judges must be perceived to have at least some measure of independence from the other branches of government.

* * *

The popular election of judges raises special concerns. Canon 4 of the ABA *Model Code of Judicial Conduct* places limits on the political activities of candidates for judicial office. Read Rules 4.1A(1)–(12) & (B) and 4.2B & (C). As these rules demonstrate, the ethical rules governing judges impose limitations not just on conduct related to a judicial but on campaign *speech* as well. As the case below also illustrates, these limitations on speech are subject to the First Amendment.

***

2. LIMITATION ON CAMPAIGN ACTIVITIES AND FREE SPEECH CONCERNS

REPUBLICAN PARTY OF MINNESOTA V. WHITE
536 U.S. 765 (2002)

SCALIA, J., delivered the opinion of the Court.

The question presented in this case is whether the First Amendment permits the Minnesota Supreme Court to prohibit candidates for judicial election in that State from announcing their views on disputed legal and political issues.

[At the time, Minnesota had a rule of conduct that provided that a "candidate for a judicial office, including an incumbent judge," shall not "announce his or her views on disputed legal or political issues." Gregory Wersal, a potential candidate for judicial office, filed suit, seeking a declaration that this "announce clause" violated the First Amendment. The Eighth Circuit held that the announce clause did not violate the First Amendment.]

As the Court of Appeals recognized, the announce clause both prohibits speech on the basis of its content and burdens a category of speech that is "at the core of our First Amendment freedoms"—speech about the qualifications of candidates for public office. 247 F.3d at 861, 863. The Court of Appeals concluded that the proper test to be applied to determine the constitutionality of such a restriction is what our cases have called strict scrutiny, *id.*, 247 F.3d at 864; the parties do not dispute that this is correct. Under the strict-scrutiny test, respondents have the burden to prove that the announce clause is (1) narrowly tailored, to serve (2) a compelling state interest. In order for respondents to show that the announce clause is narrowly tailored, they must demonstrate that it does not "unnecessarily circumscribe protected expression." *Brown* v. *Hartlage,* 456 U.S. 45, 54, 71 L. Ed. 2d 732, 102 S. Ct. 1523 (1982).

The Court of Appeals concluded that respondents had established two interests as sufficiently compelling to justify the announce clause: preserving the impartiality of the state judiciary and preserving the appearance of the impartiality of the state judiciary. . . .

A

One meaning of "impartiality" in the judicial context—and of course its root meaning—is the lack of bias for or against either *party* to the proceeding. Impartiality in this sense assures equal application of the law. That is, it guarantees a party that the judge who hears his case will apply the law to him in the same way he applies it to any other party. This is the traditional sense in which the term is used. . . .

We think it plain that the announce clause is not narrowly tailored to serve impartiality (or the appearance of impartiality) in this sense. Indeed, the clause is barely tailored to serve that interest *at all*, inasmuch as it does not restrict speech for or against particular *parties*, but rather speech for or against particular *issues*. To be sure, when a case arises that turns on a legal issue on which the judge (as a candidate) had taken a particular stand, the party taking the opposite stand is likely to lose. But not because of any bias against that party, or favoritism toward the other party. *Any* party taking that position is just as likely to lose. The judge is applying the law (as he sees it) evenhandedly.

B

It is perhaps possible to use the term "impartiality" in the judicial context (though this is certainly not a common usage) to mean lack of preconception in favor of or against a particular *legal view*. . . . Impartiality in this sense may well be an interest served by the announce clause, but it is not a *compelling* state interest, as strict scrutiny requires. A judge's lack of predisposition regarding the relevant legal issues in a case has never been thought a necessary component of equal justice, and with good reason. For one thing, it is virtually impossible to find a judge who does not have preconceptions about the law. As then-Justice Rehnquist observed of our own Court: "Since most Justices come to this bench no earlier than their middle years, it would be unusual if they had not by that time formulated at least some tentative notions that would influence them in their interpretation of the sweeping clauses of the Constitution and their interaction with one another. It would be not merely unusual, but extraordinary, if they had not at least given opinions as to constitutional issues in their previous legal careers." *Laird* v. *Tatum*, 409 U.S. 824, 835, 34 L. Ed. 2d 50, 93 S. Ct. 7 (1972) (memorandum opinion). Indeed, even if it were possible to select judges who did not have preconceived views on legal issues, it would hardly be desirable to do so. "Proof that a Justice's mind at the time he joined the Court was a complete *tabula rasa* in the area of constitutional adjudication would be evidence of lack of qualification, not lack of bias." *Ibid.* . . . And since avoiding judicial preconceptions on legal issues is neither possible nor desirable, pretending otherwise by attempting to preserve the "appearance" of that type of impartiality can hardly be a compelling state interest either.

C

A third possible meaning of "impartiality" (again not a common one) might be described as open-mindedness. This quality in a judge demands, not that he have no preconceptions on legal issues, but that he be willing to consider views that oppose his preconceptions, and remain open to persuasion, when the issues arise in a pending case. This sort of impartiality seeks to guarantee each litigant, not an *equal* chance to win the legal points in the case, but at least *some* chance of doing so. It may well be that impartiality in this sense, and the appearance of it, are desirable in the judiciary, but we need not pursue that inquiry, since we do not believe the Minnesota Supreme Court adopted the announce clause for that purpose.

Respondents argue that the announce clause serves the interest in open-mindedness, or at least in the appearance of open-mindedness, because it relieves a judge from pressure to rule a certain way in order to maintain consistency with statements the judge has previously made. The problem is, however, that statements in election campaigns are such an infinitesimal portion of the public commitments to legal positions that judges (or judges-to-be) undertake, that this object of the prohibition is implausible. Before they arrive on the bench (whether by election or otherwise) judges have often committed themselves on legal issues that they must later rule upon. More common still is a judge's confronting a legal issue on which he has expressed an opinion while on the bench. Most frequently, of course, that prior expression will have occurred in ruling on an earlier case. But judges often state their views on disputed legal issues outside the context of adjudication-in classes that they conduct, and in books and speeches. Like the ABA Codes of Judicial Conduct, the Minnesota Code not only permits but encourages this. *See* Minn. Code of Judicial Conduct, Canon 4(B) (2002) ("A judge may write, lecture, teach, speak and participate in other extra-judicial activities concerning the law . . ."); Minn. Code of Judicial Conduct, Canon 4(B), Comment. (2002) ("To the extent that time permits, a judge is encouraged to do so . . ."). That is quite incompatible with the notion that the need for open-mindedness (or for the appearance of open-mindedness) lies behind the prohibition at issue here.

The short of the matter is this: In Minnesota, a candidate for judicial office may not say "I think it is constitutional for the legislature to prohibit same-sex marriages." He may say the very same thing, however, up until the very day before he declares himself a candidate, and may say it repeatedly (until litigation is pending) after he is elected. As a means of pursuing the objective of open-mindedness that respondents now articulate, the announce clause is so woefully underinclusive as to render belief in that purpose a challenge to the credulous . . .

IV

. . . The Minnesota Supreme Court's canon of judicial conduct prohibiting candidates for judicial election from announcing their views on disputed legal and political issues violates the First Amendment.

Accordingly, we reverse the grant of summary judgment to respondents and remand the case for proceedings consistent with this opinion.

It is so ordered.

* * *

Impartiality. Following *White*, the terminology section of the CJC was amended to define the term "impartiality" in terms of the absence of bias concerning a party or class of parties as well as "maintenance of an open mind in considering issues that may come before a judge."

Restrictions on Campaign Speech. The "announce clause" at issue in *White* originally appeared in the 1972 version of the ABA's Code of Judicial Conduct. By 1990, the ABA had dropped the "announce" language from the CJC, but some jurisdictions (like Minnesota) continued to use it. Regarding the issue in *White*, CJC Rule 4.1(A)(13) now prohibits judges and candidates for elected judicial office from making "pledges, promises, or commitments that are inconsistent with the impartial performance of the adjudicative duties of judicial office" in connection with "cases, controversies, or issues that are likely to come before the court." Similarly, Rule 4.1(A)(12) prohibits judicial candidates from making statements that might affect the outcome or otherwise impair the fairness of pending or impending cases.

Problem 24.1. On the eve of her election, Ida Ione ran a television ad that contained the following lines: "For too long, Judge Robert Lloyd has been giving the benefit of the doubt to criminal defendants in his courtroom. Isn't it time we had a judge who trusts law enforcement officers to do their job and gives *them* the benefit of the doubt? Vote for Ida Ione." Following his defeat, Robert Lloyd filed disciplinary charges against Judge Ione concerning this ad. Is Judge Ione subject to discipline under Rule 4.1(A)(13) for the statements in her advertisement?

Restrictions on the Criticism of Judges. Some judicial campaigns over the past few decades have been decidedly nasty. Model Rule 8.2(a) prohibits a lawyer from making a statement that the lawyer knows to be false or with reckless disregard as to its truth or falsity concerning the qualifications or integrity of a judge. This rule would apply in the campaign context as well as more generally. Similarly, CJC Rule 4.1(A)(11) prohibits a candidate for judicial office from knowingly, or with reckless disregard for the truth, making a false or misleading statement.

Problem 24.2. During some of her campaign speeches, Ida Ione told audiences that "Judge Lloyd is a radical who pushes a radical agenda by legislating from the bench." Following his defeat, Robert Lloyd filed disciplinary charges against Judge Ione concerning this statement. Is Judge Ione subject to discipline for this statement under either of the rules discussed above?

Soliciting Campaign Contributions. In *Williams-Yulee v. Florida Bar*, 575 U.S. 433 (2015), the Supreme Court considered the constitutionality of a Florida rule of judicial conduct that, like CJC Rule 4.1(A)(8), prohibited a judge from personally soliciting campaign funds. The Court held that the rule satisfied strict scrutiny review. According to the Court, a state has a compelling interest protecting the integrity of the judiciary and in maintaining the public's confidence in an impartial judiciary. Florida's rule was narrowly tailored insofar as it only restricted a narrow slice of speech ("give me money") and still permitted a candidate's campaign committee to solicit donations.

Problem 24.3. Read CJC Rules 4.1(A) and 4.2(B). During the campaign, Ida Ione approached Adam Trusty, a wealthy business owner who was known for his dislike of Judge Lloyd, and asked Adam to publicly endorse Ida's campaign.

(a) Is Ida Ione subject to discipline for her communications with Adam soliciting his support?

(b) Regardless of your answer above, should candidates for judicial office be permitted to personally seek such endorsements?

* * *

B. STANDARDS OF CONDUCT FOR JUDGES

Canon 1 of the CJC articulates a broad standard of conduct for judges. Not only must judges comply with the law (Rule 1.1), they must, at *all times*, act in a manner that promotes public confidence in the independence, integrity, and impartiality of the judiciary. *See* In re Removal of a Chief Judge, 592 So.2d 1025 (Fla. 1992) (removing judge from office after judge made racially insensitive remarks during a newspaper interview because his comments "eroded public confidence in the judiciary and cast doubt on his impartiality"). Moreover, they must avoid even the *appearance* of impropriety. (Rule 1.2) In addition, judges may not abuse the prestige of judicial office to advance their own interests or the interests of others, nor may they allow others to do so. (Rule 1.3) The CJC also articulates a host of other, more specific rules governing the conduct of judges on and off the bench.

Problem 24.4. After it became clear to Judge Lloyd on election night that he had lost the election, he drowned his sorrows with a few drinks and drove home. He was arrested on his way home for driving under the influence. Is Judge Lloyd subject to discipline for his DUI arrest?

* * *

1. ASSURING THE QUALITY OF JUSTICE

The Model Code includes numerous rules addressing a judge's responsibilities with respect to assuring the quality of justice. Judges must be competent and diligent (Rule 2.5), and they must perform their duties without bias or prejudice. (Rule 2.3). They must require order and decorum in the courtroom and must be "patient, dignified, and courteous" to individuals in the courtroom. (Rule 2.8). *See Spruance v. Commission On Judicial Qualifications*, 532 P.2d 1209 (Cal. 1975) (disciplining judge who, *inter alia*, made a "raspberry" during defendant's testimony and gave "the finger" to a party in court).

* * *

2. PERSONAL AND EXTRAJUDICIAL ACTIVITIES

a. Restrictions on Personal and Civic Activities

Given the concern that a judge's activities off of the bench might raise concerns about the judge's impartiality, independence, or integrity, the CJC also places limits on a judge's ability to engage in various civic activities. For example, Rule 3.6 prohibits a judge from holding membership in an organization that practices invidious discrimination on the basis of race, sex, and other characteristics.

Problem 24.5. Read CJC Rules 3.1–3.4 and then consider whether Judge Ione would be subject to professional discipline in each of the following instances:

(a) The judge voluntarily testifies before a legislature about the need to increase judicial salaries.

(b) The judge suggests to a former law clerk that the judge testify as a character witness at the criminal trial of the former clerk and then voluntarily testifies on the clerk's behalf.

(c) The judge posts racist and misogynistic statements on social media from the judge's personal computer.

(d) The judge accepts an appointment by the governor to chair a special committee on improving access to justice.

* * *

b. Restrictions on Professional Engagements and Extrajudicial Moneymaking Activities

In an attempt to limit concerns that a judge may use the judicial office to obtain other benefits, run the risk of creating conflicts of interest, or engage in ventures that distract the judge from the performance of judicial

CH. 24   SERVING AS A JUDGE   507

duties, the CJC places limits on a judge's professional engagements and moneymaking activities.

Problem 24.6. Read CJC Rules 3.8–3.12, 3.14, and 3.15 and then consider whether Judge Ione would be subject to professional discipline in each of the following instances:

(a) After giving a lecture at a law school, the judge's travel expenses are paid for by the law school.

(b) After giving a lecture at a law school, the judge accepts a gift from the law school of a baseball cap and coffee mug.

(c) The judge, without receiving compensation, acts as a lawyer for her mother in a breach of contract claim in small claims court in a different jurisdiction than the one in which the judge sits.

(d) On weekends, the judge participates in running a family-owned bait and tackle store at the lake.

* * *

c. Restrictions on Accepting Gifts and Loans

The CJC also seeks to limit concerns over impartiality and the appearance of impropriety by placing limits on the ability of judges to accept gifts and loans. Rule 3.13(A) generally prohibits a judge from accepting gifts, loans, or other things of value that "would appear to a reasonable person to undermine the judge's independence, integrity, or impartiality."

Problem 24.7. Read Rules 3.13(B) and 3.15 and then consider whether Judge Ione could accept the gift or loan offered in each of the following instances:

(a) A $50,000 interest-free loan from her best friend, who happens to be a lawyer in the judge's jurisdiction.

(b) A home loan from a bank that is offered on terms offered to other members of the public.

(c) A pair of tickets to a professional football game offered by a lawyer in a local law firm.

(d) Free registration and hotel costs for Ione and her spouse, offered by a law reform organization, to attend a legal conference sponsored by the organization.

* * *

Judicial Conduct Rules for Federal Judges. Federal judges at the District Court and Circuit Court levels are bound by the *Code of Conduct for United States Judges*, which is similar to the ABA's *Model Code of*

Judicial Conduct. Importantly, this Code does not apply to justices of the United States Supreme Court.

In November 2023, after a series of news stories involving justices and their family members who went on trips/vacations and received loans/financial benefits from others generated public controversy, the Court adopted a Code of Conduct to "gather in one place the ethics rules and principles that guide the conduct of the Members of the Court." Many of the specific provisions parallel those found in the ABA's *Code of Judicial Conduct*.

Federal judges are also subject to the Judicial Conference Regulations on Gifts, which address "the giving, solicitation, or acceptance of certain gifts by officers and employees of the judicial branch."

* * *

C. REGULATING THE INTERACTION BETWEEN LAWYERS AND JUDGES

1. MOTIONS FOR RECUSAL

CJC Rule 2.11(A) requires the disqualification of a judge when the judge's impartiality might reasonably be questioned. Federal judges are subject to the same standard. *See* 28 U.S.C. § 455(a). Both rules then go on to provide a non-exhaustive list of when a judge's impartiality might reasonably be questioned. The most obvious example is when a judge has a personal bias or prejudice concerning a party.

* * *

CHENEY V. U.S. DIST. COURT FOR DIST. OF COLUMBIA
541 U.S. 913 (2004)

Memorandum of JUSTICE SCALIA.

[The Sierra Club made a motion seeking Justice Scalia's recusal in a pending case in which the group sought records relating to the participation of energy industry officials in a federal energy task force headed up by Vice President Dick Cheney. The suit named Vice President Cheney and other members of the Bush Administration as defendants. The motion stemmed from a duck-hunting trip that Vice President Cheney and Justice Scalia went on with others that was hosted by an individual who owned a company that provided services and equipment rental to oil rigs in the Gulf of Mexico. Cheney and Scalia flew together on a government plane. The two hunted separately from each other and were never alone during the trip. They flew back separately and, according to Scalia, never discussed the pending case.]

Let me respond, at the outset, to Sierra Club's suggestion that I should "resolve any doubts in favor of recusal." That might be sound advice if I were sitting on a Court of Appeals. There, my place would be taken by another judge, and the case would proceed normally. On the Supreme Court, however, the consequence is different: The Court proceeds with eight Justices, raising the possibility that, by reason of a tie vote, it will find itself unable to resolve the significant legal issue presented by the case.... Moreover, granting the motion is (insofar as the outcome of the particular case is concerned) effectively the same as casting a vote against the petitioner. The petitioner needs five votes to overturn the judgment below, and it makes no difference whether the needed fifth vote is missing because it has been cast for the other side, or because it has not been cast at all....

My recusal is required if, by reason of the actions described above, my "impartiality might reasonably be questioned." 28 U.S.C. § 455(a). Why would that result follow from my being in a sizable group of persons, in a hunting camp with the Vice President, where I never hunted with him in the same blind or had other opportunity for private conversation? The only possibility is that it would suggest I am a friend of his. But while friendship is a ground for recusal of a Justice where the personal fortune or the personal freedom of the friend is at issue, it has traditionally not been a ground for recusal where official action is at issue, no matter how important the official action was to the ambitions or the reputation of the Government officer.

A rule that required Members of this Court to remove themselves from cases in which the official actions of friends were at issue would be utterly disabling. Many Justices have reached this Court precisely because they were friends of the incumbent President or other senior officials-and from the earliest days down to modern times Justices have had close personal relationships with the President and other officers of the Executive. [Justice Scalia listed numerous examples.]

It is said, however, that this case is different because the federal officer (Vice President Cheney) is actually a named party. That is by no means a rarity. At the beginning of the current Term, there were before the Court (excluding habeas actions) no fewer than 83 cases in which high-level federal Executive officers were named in their official capacity—more than 1 in every 10 federal civil cases then pending. That an officer is named has traditionally made no difference to the proposition that friendship is not considered to affect impartiality in official-action suits....

Richard Cheney's name appears in this suit only because he was the head of a Government committee that allegedly did not comply with the Federal Advisory Committee Act (FACA), 5 U.S.C. App. § 2, p. 1, and because he may, by reason of his office, have custody of some or all of the Government documents that the plaintiffs seek. . . .

In sum, I see nothing about this case which takes it out of the category of normal official-action litigation, where my friendship, or the appearance of my friendship, with one of the named officers does not require recusal. . . .

As the newspaper editorials appended to the motion make clear, I have received a good deal of embarrassing criticism and adverse publicity in connection with the matters at issue here-even to the point of becoming (as the motion cruelly but accurately states) "fodder for late-night comedians." Motion to Recuse 6. If I could have done so in good conscience, I would have been pleased to demonstrate my integrity, and immediately silence the criticism, by getting off the case. Since I believe there is no basis for recusal, I cannot. The motion is Denied.

* * *

The Fox Guarding the Henhouse? Although 28 U.S.C. § 455(a) applies to Supreme Court justices, there is a rather gaping hole in the law. As Professor Caprice L. Roberts has observed,

> [T]he recusal decision is left up to the individual Justice and there is no formal procedure for Court review of the [recusal] decision of a Justice in an individual case. In other words, when any one Justice weighs the perilous issue of whether recusal is proper, there is no review mechanism, no opinion or public reasoning required, no legal accountability, and no mechanism to handle replacement when recusal occurs.

Caprice L. Roberts, *The Fox Guarding the Henhouse?: Recusal and the Procedural Void in the Court of Last Resort*, 57 RUTGERS L. REV. 107, 109 (2004) (quotations omitted).

* * *

Problem 24.8. Judge Ione is facing several recusal motions on the basis of personal bias. In which of the following situations is her disqualification required?

(a) A lawyer who represents a party in a matter pending before Judge Ione posted a picture on Facebook of the lawyer and the judge together at a college football game.

(b) A party in a matter pending before Judge Ione is a former client of the judge.

(c) A criminal defendant in a matter pending before Judge Ione has previously been held in contempt of court by Judge Ione in another matter.

CH. 24 SERVING AS A JUDGE 511

(d) The publisher of a book written by Judge Ione that generated substantial royalties for the judge has a copyright infringement matter pending before the judge.

* * *

Rule 2.11(A) lists other situations in which a judge's impartiality might reasonably be questioned. This includes where a close family member of the judge is acting as a lawyer in a proceeding before the judge, has an economic interest in the subject matter or controversy, or has more than a *de minimis* interest that could be substantially affected by the outcome of the case.

* * *

Problem 24.9. Judge Ione has been assigned to a case in which a cell phone company is suing another cell phone company in a multi-billion dollar lawsuit for patent infringement concerning the second company's major product. The first company has moved to disqualify Judge Ione on the grounds that her spouse owns stock in the second company valued at $70,000. Judge Ione was stunned to learn of her spouse's investment.

(a) Is the judge's disqualification required under Rule 2.11(A)?

(b) Is the judge otherwise subject to discipline under Rule 2.11(B)?

* * *

Recall that Rule 4.1(A)(13) prohibits judges and candidates for elected judicial office from making "pledges, promises, or commitments that are inconsistent with the impartial performance of the adjudicative duties of judicial office" in connection with "cases, controversies, or issues that are likely to come before the court." Even if a judge stops short of pledging or promising to rule a certain way, a judge's statements concerning a matter may lead to disqualification. CJC Rule 2.11(A)(5) addresses the situation in which a candidate or judge makes public statements that do not necessarily pledge or promise a particular result, but that may *appear* to commit the candidate or judge to rule a certain way. Rather than prohibiting such statements, Rule 2.11(A)(5) requires the speaker to recuse himself or herself in the matter in question based on the fact that the judge's impartiality (in the sense of open-mindedness) may reasonably be questioned.

Problem 24.10. Recall from earlier that while still a judicial candidate, Ida Ione ran an advertisement that contained the following lines: "For too long, Judge Robert Lloyd has been giving the benefit of the doubt to criminal defendants in his courtroom. Isn't it time we had a judge who trusts law enforcement officers to do their job and gives *them* the benefit of the doubt? Vote for Ida Ione." A criminal defendant facing charges in a case before Judge Ione that will involve testimony from a police officer has moved to disqualify the judge. Is Judge Ione's disqualification required under Rule 2.11(A)(5)?

* * *

Another possible ground for disqualification is that a party or a party's lawyer made substantial contributions to a judge's campaign. *See* CJC Rule 2.11(A)(4). Campaign contributions to a judge may also raise constitutional issues.

* * *

CAPERTON V. A.T. MASSEY COAL CO., INC.
556 U.S. 868 (2009)

JUSTICE KENNEDY delivered the opinion of the Court.

In this case the Supreme Court of Appeals of West Virginia reversed a trial court judgment, which had entered a jury verdict of $50 million. Five justices heard the case, and the vote to reverse was 3 to 2. The question presented is whether the Due Process Clause of the Fourteenth Amendment was violated when one of the justices in the majority denied a recusal motion. The basis for the motion was that the justice had received campaign contributions in an extraordinary amount from, and through the efforts of, the board chairman and principal officer of the corporation found liable for the damages.

Under our precedents there are objective standards that require recusal when "the probability of actual bias on the part of the judge or decisionmaker is too high to be constitutionally tolerable." *Withrow v. Larkin*, 421 U.S. 35, 47, 95 S. Ct. 1456, 43 L.Ed.2d 712 (1975). Applying those precedents, we find that, in all the circumstances of this case, due process requires recusal.

I

In August 2002 a West Virginia jury returned a verdict that found respondents A.T. Massey Coal Co. and its affiliates (hereinafter Massey) liable for fraudulent misrepresentation, concealment, and tortious interference with existing contractual relations. The jury awarded petitioners Hugh Caperton, Harman Development Corp., Harman Mining Corp., and Sovereign Coal Sales (hereinafter Caperton) the sum of $50 million in compensatory and punitive damages.

In June 2004 the state trial court denied Massey's post-trial motions challenging the verdict and the damages award . . .

Don Blankenship is Massey's chairman, chief executive officer, and president. After the verdict but before the appeal, West Virginia held its

2004 judicial elections. Knowing the Supreme Court of Appeals of West Virginia would consider the appeal in the case, Blankenship decided to support an attorney who sought to replace Justice McGraw. Justice McGraw was a candidate for reelection to that court. The attorney who sought to replace him was Brent Benjamin.

In addition to contributing the $1,000 statutory maximum to Benjamin's campaign committee, Blankenship donated almost $2.5 million to "And For The Sake Of The Kids," a political organization formed under 26 U.S.C. § 527. The § 527 organization opposed McGraw and supported Benjamin. Blankenship's donations accounted for more than two-thirds of the total funds it raised. This was not all Blankenship spent, in addition, just over $500,000 on independent expenditures-for direct mailings and letters soliciting donations as well as television and newspaper advertisements-" 'to support . . . Brent Benjamin.' "

To provide some perspective, Blankenship's $3 million in contributions were more than the total amount spent by all other Benjamin supporters and three times the amount spent by Benjamin's own committee. Caperton contends that Blankenship spent $1 million more than the total amount spent by the campaign committees of both candidates combined.

Benjamin won. He received 382,036 votes (53.3%), and McGraw received 334,301 votes (46.7%).

In October 2005, before Massey filed its petition for appeal in West Virginia's highest court, Caperton moved to disqualify now-Justice Benjamin under the Due Process Clause and the West Virginia Code of Judicial Conduct, based on the conflict caused by Blankenship's campaign involvement. Justice Benjamin denied the motion in April 2006. He indicated that he "carefully considered the bases and accompanying exhibits proffered by the movants." But he found "no objective information . . . to show that this Justice has a bias for or against any litigant, that this Justice has prejudged the matters which comprise this litigation, or that this Justice will be anything but fair and impartial." In December 2006 Massey filed its petition for appeal to challenge the adverse jury verdict. The West Virginia Supreme Court of Appeals granted review.

In November 2007 that court reversed the $50 million verdict against Massey [in a 3–2 decision]. . . .

[Caperton sought rehearing and moved for Benjamin's disqualification, but Benjamin refused to withdraw. The court again reversed the jury verdict. Caperton then filed a petition for writ of certiorari, alleging that Benjamin's refusal to disqualify himself violated the Due Process Clause.]

It is axiomatic that "[a] fair trial in a fair tribunal is a basic requirement of due process." *Murchison, supra*, at 136, 75 S.Ct. 623. As the

Court has recognized, however, "most matters relating to judicial disqualification [do] not rise to a constitutional level." *FTC v. Cement Institute*, 333 U.S. 683, 702, 68 S. Ct. 793, 92 L. Ed. 1010 (1948). The early and leading case on the subject is *Tumey v. Ohio*, 273 U.S. 510, 47 S. Ct. 437, 71 L. Ed. 749 (1927). There, the Court stated that "matters of kinship, personal bias, state policy, remoteness of interest, would seem generally to be matters merely of legislative discretion." *Id.*, at 523, 47 S. Ct. 437....

As new problems have emerged that were not discussed at common law, however, the Court has identified additional instances which, as an objective matter, require recusal. These are circumstances "in which experience teaches that the probability of actual bias on the part of the judge or decisionmaker is too high to be constitutionally tolerable." *Withrow*, 421 U.S., at 47, 95 S. Ct. 1456....

The difficulties of inquiring into actual bias, and the fact that the inquiry is often a private one, simply underscore the need for objective rules. Otherwise there may be no adequate protection against a judge who simply misreads or misapprehends the real motives at work in deciding the case. The judge's own inquiry into actual bias, then, is not one that the law can easily superintend or review, though actual bias, if disclosed, no doubt would be grounds for appropriate relief. In lieu of exclusive reliance on that personal inquiry, or on appellate review of the judge's determination respecting actual bias, the Due Process Clause has been implemented by objective standards that do not require proof of actual bias. *See Tumey*, 273 U.S. at 532, 47 S. Ct. 437; *Mayberry*, 400 U.S. at 465–466, 91 S. Ct. 499; *Lavoie*, 475 U.S., at 825, 106 S. Ct. 1580. In defining these standards the Court has asked whether, "under a realistic appraisal of psychological tendencies and human weakness," the interest "poses such a risk of actual bias or prejudgment that the practice must be forbidden if the guarantee of due process is to be adequately implemented." *Withrow*, 421 U.S. at 47, 95 S. Ct. 1456.

We turn to the influence at issue in this case. Not every campaign contribution by a litigant or attorney creates a probability of bias that requires a judge's recusal, but this is an exceptional case.... We conclude that there is a serious risk of actual bias—based on objective and reasonable perceptions—when a person with a personal stake in a particular case had a significant and disproportionate influence in placing the judge on the case by raising funds or directing the judge's election campaign when the case was pending or imminent. The inquiry centers on the contribution's relative size in comparison to the total amount of money contributed to the campaign, the total amount spent in the election, and the apparent effect such contribution had on the outcome of the election.

Applying this principle, we conclude that Blankenship's campaign efforts had a significant and disproportionate influence in placing Justice

Benjamin on the case. Blankenship contributed some $3 million to unseat the incumbent and replace him with Benjamin. His contributions eclipsed the total amount spent by all other Benjamin supporters and exceeded by 300% the amount spent by Benjamin's campaign committee. Caperton claims Blankenship spent $1 million more than the total amount spent by the campaign committees of both candidates combined. . . .

The judgment of the Supreme Court of Appeals of West Virginia is reversed, and the case is remanded for further proceedings not inconsistent with this opinion.

* * *

Problem 24.11. On the eve of trial, the plaintiff in a civil case assigned to Judge Ione learned that the defendant, Adam Trusty—who had previously publicly endorsed Judge Ione in her campaign against Judge Lloyd—had donated $25,000 to Judge Ione's campaign, the maximum amount allowed by law and 25% of the total contributions Judge Ione received. The plaintiff then moved to disqualify Judge Ione in the matter.

(a) Is Judge Ione's disqualification required under Rule 2.11(A)?

(b) If Judge Ione refuses to disqualify herself, would this offend due process?

* * *

Procedure for Disqualification Motions. Rule 2.11(C) of the Code of Judicial Conduct explains the procedure through which the lawyers for the parties may waive a judge's disqualification. The judge is supposed to disclose the basis for his or her disqualification on the record and give the parties and their lawyers the opportunity (outside the presence of the judge) to decide whether to waive the disqualification. The one basis for disqualification that the parties cannot waive, however, is bias concerning a party or lawyer or personal knowledge of facts in dispute in the proceeding under Rule 2.11(A).

* * *

2. INTERACTIONS BETWEEN LAWYERS AND JUDGES

a. Ex Parte Communication

CJC Rule 2.9(A) generally prohibits a judge from having a conversation outside the presence of the parties or their lawyers, concerning a pending or impending matter. Lawyers are likewise prohibited from having such conversations with a judge. *See* Model Rule 3.5(a) & (b). The obvious concerns are preserving the appearance of impartiality and protecting the adversarial nature of proceeding. As an extreme example, in one case, a trial judge was publicly reprimanded for initiating a phone conversation with a prosecuting attorney outside the presence of defense counsel in which the judge provided advice as to how the prosecuting attorney should try the case. *Matter of Starcher*, 457 S.E.2d 147 (W. Va. 1995). An exception exists for scheduling, administrative, or emergency purposes that do not address substantive matters. CJC Rule 2.9(A)(1).

* * *

b. A Judge's Duty to Report Lawyer and Judicial Misconduct to Disciplinary Authorities

Just like a lawyer, a judge who knows that a lawyer has committed a violation of the rules of professional conduct that raises a substantial question concerning the lawyer's honesty, trustworthiness, or fitness to practice law in other respects must inform the appropriate disciplinary authority. *See* Rule 2.15(B). One author notes that "the conventional wisdom suggests that this is still a duty that is largely ignored." Arthur F. Greenbaum, *Judicial Reporting of Lawyer Misconduct*, 77 UMKC L. REV. 537, 539–40 (2009). For example, in one year, the Utah Office of Professional Conduct reported that only 0.5 percent of all disciplinary referrals came from judges. *Id.* at 540 n.9. Assuming the conventional wisdom is accurate, why don't judges report lawyer misconduct?

Judges also owe duties with respect to misconduct on the part of other judges. Again, they must report another judge's misconduct that raises a substantial question concerning the lawyer's honesty, trustworthiness, or fitness to practice law in other respects must inform the appropriate disciplinary authority. *See* Rule 2.15(A). But they also must take "appropriate action" when they have merely a "reasonable belief" that the performance of a lawyer or another judge is impaired by drugs or alcohol, or by a mental, emotional, or physical condition. *See* Rule 2.14.

* * *

c. A Lawyer's Duty to Report Judicial Misconduct to Disciplinary Authorities

Lawyers have their own reporting obligation concerning judicial misconduct. Read Rule 8.3(b) of the *Model Rules of Professional Conduct* and CJC Rule 2.16(B) and then consider the problem below:

Problem 24.12. Lawyer Ronnie and his opposing counsel, Neil, have both noticed some erratic behavior from Judge Ione during trial. On one occasion, the judge fell asleep during trial. On another, the judge's speech was slurred. There are rumors around the courthouse that the judge is sometimes drunk on the bench and Ronnie thinks he caught a whiff of alcohol coming from the judge when he passed her in the hallway. Both lawyers are concerned about Judge Ione's behavior but fear retribution if they report their concerns. Are Ronnie and Neil obligated to report the judge's conduct to the state's judicial conduct organization?

* * *

d. Avoiding Complicity in Judicial Misconduct

Finally, lawyers have a professional responsibility to not knowingly assist a judge in conduct that is a violation of applicable rules of judicial conduct. *See* Model Rule 8.4(f). So, for example, the lawyer who makes a loan to a judge that is prohibited by the CJC may violate Model Rule 8.4(f). *See Lisi v. Several Att'ys*, 596 A.2d 313 (R.I. 1991). And the lawyer who contributes money to a judge's campaign after the judge improperly personally solicits the lawyer's contribution may also be subject to discipline. *See In re LeBlanc*, 972 So.2d 315 (La. 2007).

Profile of Attorney Professionalism. Judge Robert R. Merhige, Jr. was appointed to the federal bench in Richmond, Virginia in 1967. Merhige was in private practice as a trial lawyer for over twenty years when he was appointed. Said one longtime Richmond lawyer, "I remember being very enthusiastic about him going on the bench because everybody felt he was pretty much the best lawyer in town." Bill Lohman, *A Judge's Legacy*, UNIVERSITY OF RICHMOND SCHOOL OF LAW ALUMNI MAGAZINE, pp. 15-17 (Summer 2005), available at https://issuu.com/urscholarship/docs/summer2005/12.

Merhige was known as a stickler for courtroom decorum and once expelled his own father from court for falling asleep on the front row. *Id.* at 17. Only 5% of his decisions were reversed on appeal. Over the course of his career, he oversaw numerous high-profile cases, including the bankruptcy reorganization of A.H. Robins, the manufacturer of the Dalkon Shield. He also ordered the University of Virginia to admit women in 1970. *Id.* at 15.

But Merhige was perhaps most famous for having ordered the desegregation of dozens of Virginia school systems. His decisions in this area provoked considerable public scorn. According to his obituary in the *Washington Post*, "He was widely considered the most hated man in Richmond in the early 1970s and required 24-hour protection by U.S. marshals. Segregationists threatened his family, spat in his face and shot his dog to death after tying its legs. Protesters held weekly parades outside his home. A guest cottage on his property, where his mother-in-law lived, was burned to the ground. Said one local lawyer, "He was doing, in my mind, exactly what the law required him to do." Patricia Sullivan, *Federal Judge Robert R. Merhige Dies*, THE WASHINGTON POST (Feb. 20, 2005).

Merhige retired from the bench in 1998. Looking back on the desegregation cases, he observed, "If I had gotten off (the bench), the kooks would have said they won." "I wouldn't give them the satisfaction." Lohnman, *supra* at 16.

SECTION 2

TRANSACTIONAL PRACTICE AND THE REPRESENTATION OF ORGANIZATIONAL CLIENTS

■ ■ ■

The core ethical and fiduciary duties a lawyer owes to an organizational client are no different from the duties owed to an individual client. A lawyer must act competently and diligently in pursuing the client's objectives, the lawyer must protect client confidences and avoid conflicts of interest. But the nature of representing an organizational client poses some special challenges. For example, with whom in the organization should the lawyer address concerns that someone in the company is engaged in illegal conduct?

In a transactional practice, there are unique attorney challenges, too. For example, outside of a litigation setting, the transactional lawyer is dealing with *future* client conduct. If that conduct—that the lawyer helps facilitate in a transaction—is later determined to amount to a crime or fraud, both lawyer and client could face serious liability. In this non-litigation setting, it is a competent lawyer's job to advise against such conduct so the client can be protected.

These legal and ethical issues, and others, are addressed in Chapter 25, regarding transactional practice, and in Chapter 26, regarding representing organizational clients.

CHAPTER 25

TRANSACTIONAL PRACTICE

■ ■ ■

Chapter Hypothetical. You work in a five-person law firm in the town where you grew up. Most of your clients are small- to medium-sized business owners. You have a transactional law practice, handling matters that include forming partnerships, limited liability companies, and corporations; negotiating leases, real estate purchases, and various contracts; and advising clients about a variety of legal issues that arise in their businesses. You do not handle any litigation; there are other attorneys in your office you refer your clients to if they need to file or defend a lawsuit. Each problem in this chapter is related to your work for a different client.

A. CONFLICTS OF INTEREST IN TRANSACTIONAL MATTERS

Multiple individuals sometimes ask a single lawyer to represent them in a non-litigation matter. For example, individuals starting a new business venture together may want a lawyer to help them select and form a business entity, such as a corporation, partnership, or limited liability company. The prospective clients may believe that they want the same thing and conclude it will be fine for them to be represented by the same lawyer.

After a lawyer represents multiple individuals in forming a business organization, the lawyer (or a different lawyer in the same firm) may be asked to represent the organization itself in various legal matters. In some situations, the representation of the organizational client may create a conflict with one or more of the former clients—the individuals whom the lawyer represented when the company was formed.

An attorney who has an ongoing attorney-client relationship with a corporate client may be asked to serve on the company's board of directors.

In all of these situations and more, lawyers must carefully analyze whether the scenario presents a conflict of interest. The fact that the representation does not have the adverseness of litigation does not answer the question of whether there is a conflict. If there is a conflict, the attorney must determine whether it is appropriate to seek informed consent to the representation under Rule 1.7(b). Use the conflicts of interest professional conduct rules (and associated comments) contained in Rules 1.7, 1.9, and 1.10 to answer the following questions.

Problem 25.1. Josephine Bishop is preparing to retire and move to Florida. For over thirty years, she has been the sole owner of a successful photography business, Framed Tots. For the past five years, she has worked with a young photographer, Paul Flowers. Josephine and Paul have agreed that Josephine will sell the business to Paul "for a fair price." They ask you to represent them in working out the terms of the deal and preparing a contract for the sale. Analyze whether you should accept the matter. Assuming that you do accept the matter, analyze whether you should seek informed consent under Rule 1.7(b); and discuss what you should tell Josephine and Paul about the confidentiality of their discussions with you.

Problem 25.2. Over the past decade, you have represented your friend and neighbor Jake Johnson in various real estate contract negotiations. You are not currently representing Jake in any matter when you get a call from Kris Springer. Kris asks you to represent him in the purchases of real estate from Jake.

First, analyze whether you may accept the matter. Which facts will influence whether you may represent Kris in the negotiation. If you are inclined to accept the matter, determine whether it is advisable to seek informed consent to a conflict and from whom.

Second, assume that you decide you should not represent Kris as a client because it would be impossible for you not to use confidential information about Jake's business model and contract negotiation strategy that you have learned from your prior representations. Under these facts, analyze whether you may refer Kris to another attorney in your firm to avoid the conflict.

Problem 25.3. Five years ago, three individuals—Max, Emma, and Leah—hired you to help them form a general partnership. Since then, you have represented the partnership in numerous matters. Max and Leah now come to you with a concern that Emma is competing with the partnership in violation of the partnership agreement. As the partnership's attorney, may you write a letter to Emma insisting that she comply with the terms of the partnership agreement?

Problem 25.4. For many years, you have represented the Taylor Corporation. You frequently advise the company and represent it in contract negotiations with suppliers. Other lawyers in your firm represent the corporation in employment, intellectual property, and business litigation matters. The company's CEO asks if you would consider serving on the corporation's board of directors. What are the possible adverse consequences of taking a seat on the board?

Problem 25.5. Assume that you represented both Stacy and John in forming a Limited Liability Company (LLC). Eighteen months after they hired you, Stacy is unhappy with the LLC Agreement; she thinks that you drafted the document in a way that gives John a disproportionate amount of power in the management of the business. With citation to specific provisions of the *Restatement (Third) of the Law Governing Lawyers*, describe the causes of action Stacy could assert against you in a lawsuit.

* * *

B. REPRESENTING CLIENTS IN NON-LITIGATION MATTERS

In litigation, a lawyer is presented with a factual scenario that occurred in the past: a contract may have been breached, an employee may have been discriminated against, or a tort may have been committed. It is litigation counsel's job to zealously advocate on the client's behalf, making the most persuasive arguments under the law and facts that the subject conduct should (in the case of plaintiff's counsel) or should not (in the case of defense counsel) result in liability. Assuming that litigation counsel was not involved in the underlying conduct, there is no chance that counsel will be found liable for the conduct that is the subject of the litigation.

An attorney's role is somewhat different in non-litigation matters. In a transactional practice, an attorney typically is addressing a client's future conduct. Rather than making the best of facts that have occurred in the past (as litigation counsel must do), the transactional attorney has the opportunity—and the obligation—to competently advise the client about how to comply with legal obligations and avoid liability in the future. The client needs this information in order to decide how to proceed. But this may mean giving the client advice that he or she does not want.

In these representations, the transactional lawyer faces a risk that is not an issue for litigation counsel. Because the transactional lawyer may be a participant in the client's conduct, it is possible for the lawyer to face criminal and civil liability for the lawyer's actions. *See Restatement (Third) of the Law Governing Lawyers*, §§ 8, 56, 57 (2000). In the transactional setting, fraud is a typical basis of liability for both lawyer and client in civil litigation and criminal prosecutions.

As a fiduciary, the lawyer must act competently, diligently, and loyally in the interest of the client. *See* R*estatement (Third) of the Law Governing Lawyers*, §§ 16, 52(1) (2000). Professional conduct rules provide some (but not a great deal of) guidance to attorneys concerning meeting these duties to clients in non-litigation settings. *See, e.g.,* Model Rules 1.1, 2.1. Other rules remind lawyers that they cannot participate in client crime and fraud. *See, e.g.,* Model Rules 1.2(d), 1.4(a)(5), 4.1(b), 1.16(a). Following these rules should result in both lawyer and client avoiding serious forms of misconduct and liability.

The following four Parts address these legal and professional conduct issues in transactional lawyering. Part 1 addresses the legal and ethical issues surrounding advising clients. Then, Part 2 considers professional conduct rules that govern attorney conduct in negotiations and other interactions with third parties. Thereafter, Part 3 discusses tools the lawyer may use to avoid participating in client misconduct when the client insists upon a course of conduct the lawyer has advised against. Finally, Part 4 looks at the consequences lawyers may suffer when they become participants in client misconduct.

* * *

1. ADVISING CLIENTS

Clients—even sophisticated business clients—often see the law in black and white terms. They understand the law as a line that they cannot cross. They want their lawyers to tell them if a proposed course of conduct is "legal" or "illegal."

Most legal issues that our clients face are not so simple. While a client's planned conduct may not be "illegal" it may certainly lead to substantial liability and should be avoided. This is the type of advice that competent lawyers must provide to clients. Clients cannot make an informed decision about how to proceed if lawyers only provide technical advice about black and white violations of the law.

Instead, lawyers must explain how a prosecutor may view an issue and why a client's plan may lead to a criminal prosecution. A lawyer must explain that silence may amount to fraud if a client has a duty to share information and is concealing information in an attempt to mislead another party. Lawyers must help clients understand the breadth of the law and the consequences of viewing it in a narrow or technical way.

Model Rule 2.1 provides some guidance in this regard. The rule encourages lawyers to "exercise independent professional judgment" and "render candid advice." Comment [1] notes that lawyers may have to tell the client things that the client does not want to hear. Highlighting the relationship between unethical conduct and legal liability, Comment [2] provides that, "moral and ethical considerations impinge upon most legal questions and may decisively influence how the law will be applied."

Other rules remind lawyers that they need to make a judgment call and not participate in conduct that may amount to a crime or fraud. Rule 1.2(d) prohibits counseling a client to engage in or assisting a client in conduct the lawyer knows is criminal or fraudulent. Comments [9]–[13] elaborate upon this rule. Rule 1.4(a)(5) requires the lawyer to explain to the client that the lawyer cannot provide such assistance. Rules that will be discussed later in this chapter (Rules 4.1, 1.6(b), and 1.16) provide additional guidance for lawyers who believe they are being asked to participate in (or have already participated in) criminal or fraudulent conduct. Lawyers read such rules narrowly at their own and their client's peril. Neither lawyer nor client should be inclined to play fast and loose with the possibility of engaging in criminal and/or fraudulent conduct. Civil liability is also possibility for the lawyer who counsels or assists a client to engage in wrongful conduct that violates the rights of a third person. *Restatement (Third) of the Law Governing Lawyers* § 94.

* * *

Problem 25.6. You represent a small family-owned corporation, The Good Egg, Inc. Father and son owners Jim Dale Coster and Jim Dan Coster are engaged in the day-to-day operations of the company. Recently, Jim Dan mentioned to you that changes in egg safety rules have made it more difficult than ever to get eggs approved for shipment by USDA egg inspectors. Jim Dan explained, "The risk of salmonella is actually quite low. But after other foodborne illness outbreaks in the US in recent years, the feds are watching us more closely than ever. It's killing us." You asked, "Is there anything I can do to help?" Jim Dan responded, "I think Dad has it covered for now. He's found an inspector who doesn't mind making an extra buck once in a while. I guess it's just the new cost of doing business."

You understood Jim Dan's comment to mean that Jim Dale is bribing a USDA egg inspector to allow shipments of bad eggs. You know that the company and the Costers will face criminal penalties if their eggs cause a salmonella outbreak under the circumstances. Beyond that, plaintiffs will line up to sue if a salmonella outbreak is traced to The Good Egg.

How would you advise The Good Egg in these circumstances? Should you ask additional questions to determine if bribes are being paid or defer to Jim Dan's assessment that this is the "new cost of doing business?"

Problem 25.7. Your client, the Peanut Company of America (PCA), has asked you for advice about a planned tax position PCA is considering. PCA has made some recent expenditures that it wants to deduct as expenses. After researching the issue, you conclude that if the Internal Revenue Service (IRS) challenges this deduction, PCA's position is unlikely to prevail. Indeed, you are unable to find any substantial authority in support of PCA's position. That concerns you because you know that the Internal Revenue Code imposes a penalty on a taxpayer for substantial understatement of tax liability that can be avoided if the taxpayer had substantial authority for the position taken. Nonetheless, you believe that PCA's position is actually warranted under a literal reading of the relevant position of the Code, even if it is unlikely to withstand IRS review. Can you advise PCA that it can take the deduction? If so, what will you say when you provide this advice?

* * *

2. HONESTY IN NEGOTIATIONS AND OTHER INTERACTIONS WITH THIRD PARTIES

Because a lawyer is an agent of the client, a client faces liability for fraudulent misrepresentations that a lawyer makes on the client's behalf. Further, the lawyer faces personal liability for his or her fraudulent misrepresentations even if they were made in the context of representing a client.

If a lawyer abides by Rule 4.1, the lawyer can avoid this liability for client and self. The rule prohibits the lawyer from making a false statement to a third party or failing to disclose a material fact when disclosure is necessary to avoid assisting in a crime or fraud, unless disclosure is prohibited by Rule 1.6. (As you will see in Part 3, the exceptions to Rule 1.6 allow disclosure to prevent a client from committing a crime or fraud under these circumstances.)

As you read the following case, note all of the parties that Wright sued and the basis for Wright's claims against them. If Pennamped had followed Rule 4.1, would this case have been avoided?

WRIGHT V. PENNAMPED
657 N.E.2d 1223 (Ind. App. 1995)

SHARPNACK, CHIEF JUDGE.

Donald H. Wright appeals the trial court's order of summary judgment in favor of the defendant-appellees, Bruce M. Pennamped and his law firm, Lowe Gray Steele & Hoffman ("the Appellees"). Wright is seeking damages arising from the Appellees' alleged deceptive and fraudulent conduct during a commercial loan transaction. Wright raises four issues for our review, which we consolidate and restate as whether the trial court erred in granting summary judgment. We affirm in part and reverse in part.

Facts

[Wright was a self-employed general contractor and real estate developer who was looking to refinance the apartment complex he owned, the Diplomat Apartments, in the amount of $500,000.00. On May 29, 1991, Ray Krebs, the vice president of mortgage banking at SCI Financial Corporation ("SCI"), submitted a proposal of financing to Wright. Wright accepted the proposal on June 3, 1991. The proposal contained a prepayment provision that Wright did not understand, but he anticipated that he would have his attorney, Richard L. Brown, explain any provisions he did not understand when Brown received the proposed loan documents prior to closing. After signing the proposal, Wright provided Brown's name, address, and telephone number to Krebs. Krebs then relayed this information to Pennamped. Pennamped, a partner in the law firm of Lowe Gray Steele & Hoffman, became involved in the loan transaction on July 2, 1991, when he had a luncheon meeting with Krebs. SCI retained Pennamped and the firm to represent its interests and to prepare the necessary loan documents. Pennamped drafted the loan documents on July 31, 1991, and forwarded copies marked "DRAFT DATED 7-31-91" to Krebs and Brown. The draft contained a prepayment provision.

On Friday, August 2, 1991, Brown reviewed the draft documents and discussed them with Wright. Brown and Wright discussed the prepayment provision as well as additional terms in the draft documents. Wright did not indicate to Brown that the prepayment provision in the draft note was any different than the one in the proposal for financing. Based on their discussion, both Wright and Brown accepted and approved the form and substance of the draft documents. In the meantime, Don Wilson, Senior Vice President of the funding bank, Kentland Bank, reviewed the draft and requested of Krebs that changes be made to the prepayment penalty provision. On August 5th, Pennamped and Wright's attorney, Brown, discussed the loan agreement. Pennamped never mentioned any changes to the document. Pennamped asked Brown if he had any problems with the proposed loan documents, and Brown responded that he did not. Brown informed Pennamped he had two cases set for the following morning and he would be unable to attend the closing set for 9:00 a.m the next day. Pennamped completed the changes to the loan documents that Wilson had requested on the afternoon of August 5, 1991. No one informed Brown or Wright about the changes, although Pennamped told Krebs that he should speak to Wright and explain the changes. Krebs said he would do so, but never did. Pennamped never made any further inquiry regarding the matter.

Because Brown was in court, Wright attended the closing alone. No one ever informed him about the changes to the agreement. Wright executed the documents. Wright learned of the new prepayment provision when he attempted to pay off the loan. Under the terms of the original agreement, Wright's prepayment penalty would have been $4,931.49. Under the terms as modified, the prepayment penalty was $97,504.38.]

... On July 18, 1993, Wright filed a complaint for damages against Kentland Bank, Krebs, SCI, Pennamped, and Lowe Gray Steele & Hoffman. Wright sought recovery from the defendants based on fraud, constructive fraud and breach of fiduciary relationship, obtaining money and property by false pretenses, deception, criminal mischief, conversion and theft, and forgery. Wright subsequently amended his complaint to include a count based on breach of implied contract.

On September 8, 1993, the Appellees filed their motion for summary judgment. On December 1, 1993, Wright filed his opposition to the motion for summary judgment. Following a hearing on December 21, 1993, the trial court took the motion under advisement. On March 4, 1994, the trial court issued its order granting the Appellees' motion for summary judgment. The trial court found that an essential element of each of Wright's non-contractual theories is the intent to deceive and that Wright failed to come forward with any evidence supporting an inference of fraud. The court held that the Appellees had no contractual duty to Wright and therefore, Wright's breach of implied contract claim must fail. The trial held there was no just cause for delay and ordered the entry of final judgment in favor of the Appellees. Wright appeals this judgment.

Discussion

. . .

I. Quasi-Contract

[Court's discussion omitted]

II. Actual Fraud

The elements of actual fraud are: (1) the fraud feasor must have made at least one representation of past or existing fact; (2) which was false; (3) which the fraud feasor knew to be false or made with reckless disregard as to its truth or falsity; (4) upon which the plaintiff reasonably relied; (5) and which harmed the plaintiff. *Scott v. Bodor*, 571 N.E.2d 313, 319 (1991). An intent to deceive, or "scienter," is an element of actual fraud, whether classified as a knowing or reckless misrepresentation or as an additional element to a knowing or reckless misrepresentation. . . . Fraud may be proven by circumstantial evidence, provided there are facts from which the existence of all of the elements can be reasonably inferred. . . .

[The court agreed with Wright that there was sufficient evidence of actual fraud to survive summary judgment.]

We conclude, therefore, that the trial court erred in granting summary judgment on Wright's claim for actual fraud.

III. Constructive Fraud

The elements of constructive fraud include:

" '1. a duty owing by the party to be charged to the complaining party due to their relationship,

2. violation of that duty by the making of deceptive material misrepresentations of past or existing facts or remaining silent when a duty to speak exists,

3. reliance thereon by the complaining party,

4. injury to the complaining party as a proximate result thereof, and

5. the gaining of an advantage by the party to be charged at the expense of the complaining party.'"

... Contrary to the trial court's ruling in the present case, intent to deceive is not an element of constructive fraud.... Instead, the law infers fraud from the relationship of the parties and the surrounding circumstances. The Appellees contend that the trial court nonetheless properly entered summary judgment in their favor on Wright's claim for constructive fraud because there is an absence of the type of relationship which may form a basis of a claim for constructive fraud. Furthermore, Appellees contend this relationship did not give rise to a legal duty to disclose....

As we have observed previously, however, "Defendants are mistaken in arguing that constructive fraud can *only* exist where there is a confidential or fiduciary relationship. In Indiana, the term constructive fraud encompasses several related theories. All of these theories are premised on the understanding that there are situations which might not amount to actual fraud, but which are so likely to result in injustice that the law will find a fraud despite the absence of fraudulent intent. Defendants are correct in asserting that a constructive fraud may be found where one party takes unconscionable advantage of his dominant position in a confidential or fiduciary relationship. This is not, however, the exclusive basis for the theory of constructive fraud. In Indiana, constructive fraud also includes what other jurisdictions have termed 'legal fraud' or 'fraud in law.' *This species of constructive fraud recognizes that certain conduct should be prohibited because it is inherently likely to create an injustice....*" Scott, 571 N.E.2d at 323–24 (emphasis added).....

Considering the facts in the light most favorable to Wright and contrary to the Appellees' contentions on appeal, this case is amenable to the application of the doctrine of constructive fraud. The facts as alleged by Wright suggest a situation that is so likely to result in injustice that the law will find a fraud despite the absence of fraudulent intent. *See Scott*, 571 N.E.2d at 323–24. The material alteration of loan documents after the review and approval of those documents by opposing counsel and the presentation of the revised documents for execution with no indication that changes have been made is the sort of conduct which "should be prohibited because it is inherently likely to create an injustice...." *Id.* at 324.

In the alternative, Appellees contend this relationship did not give rise to a legal duty. Appellees claim that Pennamped did not owe Wright a duty to disclose the changes made to the loan documents. Furthermore,

Appellees argue that even if Pennamped did have a duty, Pennamped satisfied this duty by delegating the performance to Krebs. We disagree.

A party to a contract has a duty to the other party to disclose changes. *Peoples Trust & Savings Bank v. Humphrey,* Ind. App., 451 N.E.2d 1104, 1112 (1983). The Appellees argue that although Pennamped altered the contract, he did not owe a duty to Wright because Pennamped was not a party to the contract.

Contrary to Appellees' contention, as discussed previously, we find that Pennamped had a duty to disclose. As the drafting attorney, Pennamped assumed a duty to inform Wright of any changes to the loan documents prior to their execution. . . . In opposing the motion for summary judgment, Wright submitted the affidavit of Richard L. Johnson, the senior partner in the law firm of Johnson Smith Densborn Wright & Heath. The significance of this affidavit was to establish the customs and practices of financing transactions. Johnson commenced the practice of law in 1972 and has concentrated his practice in the areas of banking law, real estate law, and commercial law. After setting forth his qualifications and extensive experience as lender's counsel and in drafting or preparing documents to be used in lending transactions, Johnson's affidavit states:

> Based upon my experience as lender's counsel, I believe the following to be the customs and practices in the industry in relation to real estate and/or commercial financing transactions:
>
> (a) At any time changes or revisions are made to draft or proposed loan documents by the attorney charged with the responsibility of drafting such documents—no matter how trivial or seemingly insignificant such changes or revisions may be—it is expected and understood by all other attorneys involved in the transaction that the drafting attorney will take whatever steps are necessary and/or appropriate to fully disclose and identify all such document changes and revisions to other attorneys involved in the transaction.
>
> (b) Typically, when any changes or revisions are made to proposed or draft loan documents, the drafting attorney will circulate, in writing, a "red-lined" copy or some other written materials which will highlight and/or more particularly identify and/or describe the changes and revisions that have been or are contemplated to be made.
>
> (c) At the very least, the drafting attorney is responsible to verbally disclose to all other attorneys involved in the transaction—prior to execution of final documents—any and all changes and revisions that the drafting attorney has made to previously-distributed draft documents.

(d) Any changes or revisions to the substance or form of documents which have been previously circulated to the participating attorneys should be fully disclosed to such other attorneys.

(e) The closing of the transaction should not occur until final revisions to the loan documents have been fully disclosed to and approved by all parties and their respective counsel.

Based on this relationship, Wright could expect that Pennamped would inform him of any changes in the loan documents. Therefore, Pennamped had a duty to disclose material information to Wright concerning the loan documents.

Furthermore, Appellees' argument is in contradiction with Rule 4.1(b) of the Rules of Professional Conduct which states, "[i]n the course of representing a client a lawyer shall not knowingly . . . (b) fail to disclose that which is required by law to be revealed." Ind. Professional Conduct, Rule 4.1(b). As previously stated, the drafting attorney assumes a duty to disclose any changes in the documents prior to execution to the other parties. *See id.*

Courts hold attorneys to a separate and more demanding standard than the attorneys' clients. *Fire Insurance Exchange v. Bell*, 643 N.E.2d 310, 312 (1994). Pennamped may have assisted his client, Krebs, in the commission of constructive fraud by failing to disclose to Wright that Pennamped changed the loan documents. Since Pennamped knew the documents were altered, he had a duty to disclose.

Lastly, we address whether Pennamped delegated his duty to Krebs. Pennamped may have created an agency relationship where he was the principal and Krebs was his agent within this narrow scope of disclosing changes to Wright. Therefore, Pennamped may have discharged his duty by delegating it to Krebs. However, this raises a question of whether Pennamped actually instructed Krebs to inform Wright of the changes. The existence of an agency is a question of fact, therefore this issue should be decided by a trier of fact and not decided upon summary judgment. *Bryan Mfg. Co. v. Harris* (1984), Ind. App. 459 N.E.2d 1199, 1204.

We conclude, therefore, that the trial court erred in granting summary judgment on Wright's claim for constructive fraud.

To sum up, while we affirm the trial court's entry of summary judgment for the defendant on the theory of quasi-contract, we reverse summary judgment on the theories of actual and constructive fraud. The case is remanded to the trial court for further proceedings consistent with this opinion.

* * *

Problem 25.8. Mick Stirts hired you to represent him in negotiations with Cost-Mart Big Box Stores. Cost-Mart is interested in purchasing a lot that Mick owns and has been unable to sell for ten years. (Mick told you that the site was once home to a gas station, which is why he has had trouble selling the lot.) Cost-Mart is in the process of purchasing several adjoining lots where it will build a Cost-Mart Wholesale Club, which will include a gas station on the lot currently owned by Mick. You successfully negotiated a "conditional agreement" in which Cost-Mart agreed to pay Mick $50,000 for the lot, conditioned on its purchase of the adjoining lots within ninety days. Mick was thrilled with the price. The last offer he had received for the land was for $7,000—and that was three years ago.

This morning, Mick tells you that he needs you to take care of one last detail. He says that he "technically co-owns the lot with a former business partner" named Ginny Sampson. Mick would like you to offer Ginny $5,000 for her interest in the land. He feels certain she will take the offer. Legally, you know that Mick owes his co-owner and business partner a duty to disclose the $50,000 conditional agreement with Cost-Mart. You tell him this. But Mick insists, "You need to keep the deal quiet. At this point, it is conditional and even that wouldn't have happened without me. Why should I share that with Ginny? Just work out a deal with her for $5,000."

Under applicable professional conduct rules, can you negotiate the $5,000 deal with Ginny without revealing the conditional agreement? What are the possible legal consequences for you personally if you handle the negotiations with Ginny as Mick has suggested? What are the possible legal consequences for Mick?

* * *

3. TOOLS LAWYERS CAN USE TO AVOID LIABILITY FOR PARTICIPATING IN CLIENT MISCONDUCT

Even though clients may choose to engage in misconduct against the lawyer's advice, the lawyer cannot participate in that misconduct. Professional conduct rules require a lawyer to withdraw if the representation "will result in violation of the rules of professional conduct or other law." Model Rule 1.16(a)(1). Even if the lawyer is not certain that conduct will violate law or professional conduct rules, a lawyer is nonetheless permitted to withdraw if the lawyer "reasonably believes" the client is using the lawyer's services to perpetrate a crime or fraud. Model Rule 1.16(b)(2).

Other rules allow a lawyer who has been engaged in a client's fraudulent misconduct to make a disclosure to prevent or mitigate damages to a third party. Rule 1.6(b)(2) permits disclosure to prevent a client from committing a crime or fraud likely to cause substantial injury to a third party, while Rule 1.6(b)(3) allows disclosure to "prevent, mitigate, or rectify" financial injury caused by a client's crime or fraud. In both cases, it is necessary that the client used the lawyer's services to commit the crime or fraud. "In extreme cases," Rule 4.1(b) might require a lawyer to disclose a fact when substantive law equates the failure to do so as assisting the client's crime or fraud. Model Rule 4.1(b) & Comment [3].

These rules effectively give the lawyer an avenue to protect himself or herself from liability for fraud. But they may also lead clients to change course. Explaining what the lawyer plans to do under the authority of professional conduct rules may cause a client to re-think a plan that would have resulted in liability for the client.

Finally, lawyers should note that organizational clients do not have the same autonomy as clients that are natural persons when it comes to questions of engaging in misconduct. Chapter 25 addresses the need for the organizational client's lawyer to take additional steps to protect the client from constituent misconduct.

* * *

Problem 25.9. Refer to the facts in Problem 25.8. Assume for purposes of this problem that you told Mick that you would not negotiate the purchase of Ginny's interest in the property without revealing the Cost-Mart conditional agreement to her. Mick responded, "That's fine. I'll negotiate the deal myself. I will just need your help drafting the contract. Leave the purchase amount blank and I'll fill it in after I work out the price with her." Under applicable professional conduct rules, what steps are you permitted or required to take at this point? What would you do?

* * *

4. LAWYER CRIMINAL AND CIVIL LIABILITY FOR PARTICIPATING IN CLIENT MISCONDUCT

This chapter has noted that a lawyer may face civil or criminal liability for conduct undertaken on a client's behalf. In limited circumstances, defenses and exceptions to liability apply because of the lawyer's role. *See Restatement (Third) of the Law Governing Lawyers* § 8 (explaining that the "traditional and appropriate activities" of the lawyer representing a client should be considered in determining the propriety of a lawyer's conduct under the criminal law); § 57 (defining limited exceptions and defenses to civil liability for conduct undertaken on a client's behalf). Otherwise, a lawyer can expect to face liability to the same extent and on the same basis as a non-lawyer. *See Restatement (Third) of the Law Governing Lawyers* § 8 (except as noted, a lawyer is "guilty of a [criminal] offense for an act committed in the course of representing a client to the same extent and on the same basis as would a non-lawyer acting similarly."); § 56 (unless an exception or defense applies, "a lawyer is subject to liability . . . when a nonlawyer would be in similar circumstances"); § 95 (a lawyer counseling or assisting a client in conduct that violates the rights of a third person is subject to liability unless an exception or defense applies).

The following case concerns lawyer Joseph Collins' criminal conviction for participating in a corporate client's fraudulent scheme. During the years of fraud described in the case, attorney Collins was a partner in the global law firm Mayer Brown. When the fraud was revealed, client Refco, Inc. had no choice but to file for bankruptcy. Several company executives were tried and convicted for the roles they played in the fraudulent scheme.

* * *

UNITED STATES V. COLLINS
581 Fed. Appx. 59 (2d Cir. Oct. 22, 2014)

Present DENNIS JACOBS, GUIDO CALABRESI and CHRISTOPHER F. DRONEY, CIRCUIT JUDGES.

SUMMARY ORDER

Joseph Collins appeals from a judgment of the United States District Court for the Southern District of New York (Preska, Ch. J.), sentencing Collins principally to one year and one day imprisonment after a jury convicted him of conspiracy, securities fraud, false filings with the Securities and Exchange Commission, and wire fraud. We assume the parties' familiarity with the underlying facts, the procedural history, and the issues presented for review.

Collins was outside counsel for Refco, Inc., from as early as 1997 until revelations of accounting fraud in 2005 forced the corporation into bankruptcy. The government eventually charged Collins with supporting Refco executives' scheme to conceal large amounts of intercompany debt. The scheme was based on a series of artfully timed loans, euphemistically called "short-term financings," which bounced the debt back and forth between a Refco subsidiary and Refco's parent company immediately before and after audits. The short-term financings kept the growing intercompany debt hidden from auditors, banks, customers, and regulators throughout a 2004 leveraged buyout of Refco and throughout a 2005 initial public offering.

Collins prepared documents for many of the individual transactions that, in aggregate, effected the short-term financings. However, Collins claimed in his defense that he did not know of the fraud scheme motivating these transactions. The government's showing that Collins was aware (or consciously avoided awareness) of the fraud included: Collins' work in drafting a Proceeds Participation Agreement ("PPA") in 2002, which revealed Refco's desperate capital shortage and buried the intercompany debt in a side letter; Collins' failure to disclose the PPA in the 2004 leveraged buyout, when the terms of the PPA might have raised the buyers' suspicions; Collins' ready willingness to opine in 2002 that Refco's $700 million in intercompany debt was enforceable and collectable; and conversations with another attorney in 2004, negotiating a sale of Refco stock, in which Collins was explicitly confronted about the existence of $1.1 billion of debt.

In 2013, after a five-week trial, a jury convicted Collins of seven counts related to the fraud. Collins now appeals his conviction, challenging the district court's exclusion of opinion testimony and the delivery of a jury instruction on conscious avoidance. Neither decision represents prejudicial error.

1. The district court excluded the opinion testimony of two lawyers. This Court "review[s] a district court's evidentiary rulings for manifest error." *Raskin v. Wyatt Co.*, 125 F.3d 55, 65–66 (2d Cir. 1997). Opinion testimony is inadmissible if it is not "helpful to . . . determining a fact in issue." Fed. R. Evid. 701(b); *see id.* R. 702(a). An opinion is unhelpful and therefore may not be received in evidence if, for example, the testimony would merely recapitulate aspects of the evidence that the jury can already perceive on its own, *see Cameron v. City of New York*, 598 F.3d 50, 62 (2d Cir. 2010); the testimony "would merely tell the jury what result to reach," *United States v. Rea*, 958 F.2d 1206, 1215 (2d Cir. 1992) (quoting Fed. R. Evid. 704 Advisory Committee Note); or an expert's testimony would deal with matters within "the ken of the average juror," *United States v. Castillo*, 924 F.2d 1227, 1232 (2d Cir. 1991).

Collins' counsel sought to elicit opinions from one lay witness and one expert regarding the materiality of the PPA during the 2004 leveraged buyout. According to Collins' proffer, both witnesses would have testified that the PPA would have appeared immaterial to the leveraged buyout in the eyes of a lawyer unaware of Refco's fraud. The expert, a mergers and acquisitions lawyer, would also have testified generally about the work of transactional lawyers. The district court rejected both proffers on the grounds that the testimony would not be helpful to the jury, that the opinions depicting the PPA as immaterial would be conclusory, that Collins could alternatively establish immateriality through cross-examination of government witnesses, that a "war of experts" should be avoided, and that the materiality vel non of the PPA was within the competence of a jury unassisted by opinion testimony. As it transpired, fact witnesses proved sufficient for Collins' counsel to present the defense view of the PPA's materiality, including testimony that rights under the PPA were "extinguished" before the leveraged buyout closed. The district court's evidentiary rulings were valid exercises of its discretion.

2. The district court delivered a conscious avoidance charge over Collins' objection. When the parties in a trial dispute the element of

knowledge, a conscious avoidance charge is appropriate if "the evidence would permit a rational juror to conclude beyond a reasonable doubt that the defendant was aware of a high probability of the fact in dispute and consciously avoided confirming that fact." *United States v. Cuti*, 720 F.3d 453, 463 (2d Cir. 2013) (quotation marks omitted). This test is satisfied "where[ ] a defendant's involvement in the criminal offense may have been so overwhelmingly suspicious that the defendant's failure to question the suspicious circumstances establishes the defendant's purposeful contrivance to avoid guilty knowledge." *United States v. Svoboda*, 347 F.3d 471, 480 (2d Cir. 2003) (internal quotation marks and alteration omitted); *see United States v. Goffer*, 721 F.3d 113, 127–28 (2d Cir. 2013). The evidence supporting that overwhelming suspiciousness is often the same evidence used to demonstrate actual knowledge. *See Svoboda*, 347 F.3d at 480.

Collins argues on appeal that the government introduced insufficient evidence to support a conscious avoidance charge.[1] This argument is untenable in view of the government's evidence that Collins provided a 2002 legal opinion regarding $700 million in intercompany debt, at a time when Refco's public filings reported only $179 million in intercompany debt. Further undercutting Collins' argument is the trial evidence that another lawyer told him in 2004 that Refco's CEO had revealed the existence of a $1.1 billion debt while negotiating the price of an equity sale. This evidence was sufficient to support the district court's conscious avoidance charge.

For the foregoing reasons, and finding no merit in Collins' other arguments, we hereby AFFIRM the judgment of the district court.

* * *

Problem 25.10. Consider the first time when Refco executives asked Joseph Collins to prepare the documentation for the short-term financings that were part of the fraudulent scheme. Of course, company executives did not say, "This is part of a fraudulent scheme." Instead, they described the need to document a short-term loan that had no purpose other than to remove debt from the company's books for a short period of time. With citation to authorities referenced throughout this chapter, describe the steps Collins should have taken to gather information, advise his client, and withdraw from the representation if necessary.

---

[1] Collins further argues that the district court's instruction misstated the legal standard for conscious avoidance, but he concedes that controlling precedent of this Court supports the district court's instruction. *See Goffer*, 721 F.3d at 128. Given that precedent, we see no fault in the content of the conscious avoidance instruction.

Profile of Attorney Professionalism. Tamar Frankel, a professor at Boston University School of Law, focuses her teaching and writing on issues of fiduciary law, corporate governance, mutual funds, securitization, and financial system regulation. Her book titles include TRUST AND HONESTY, AMERICA'S BUSINESS CULTURE AT A CROSSROAD (2006), FIDUCIARY LAW (2010), and THE PONZI SCHEME PUZZLE (2012). Professor Frankel wants to help lawyers and the public at large understand that "[l]aw is not the enemy of business. It is the enemy of crooked business." Tina Spee, *Conversations with Tamar Frankel*, Law Dragon (Feb. 22, 2007), https://tamarfrankel.com/conversations/.

Professor Frankel's work in the area of fiduciary duty law has been recognized by the Institute for the Fiduciary Standard's establishment of the "Frankel Fiduciary Prize" to honor individuals who advance fiduciary principles.

Since beginning her legal career in 1948, Frankel has practiced law in both her native Israel and in the U.S. Her experiences have ranged from being an attorney in the legal department of the Israeli Department of Justice to designing the corporate structure of the Internet Corporation for Names and Numbers (ICANN). She has been a visiting scholar at the Securities and Exchange Commission and has lectured at schools including Oxford University, Tokyo University, and Harvard Law School.

Professor Frankel has been a trailblazer for women teaching corporate law. She began her law-teaching career at Boston University School of Law in 1967. She was one of only twelve women teaching corporations law at a U.S. law school prior to 1980 who went on to become tenured, full professors. Margaret V. Sachs, *Women in Corporate Law Teaching: A Tale of Two Generations*, 65 MD. L. REV. 666, 666–67 (2006). In discussing her approach to teaching, Professor Frankel has said it is important "not to get stuck in your own generation." She combats that by "listen[ing] to the new generation" and "[trying] to understand a very different world." Tina Spee, *Conversations with Tamar Frankel*, Law Dragon (Feb. 22, 2007), https://tamarfrankel.com/conversations/.

CHAPTER 26

REPRESENTING ORGANIZATIONAL CLIENTS

■ ■ ■

Chapter Hypothetical. The attorneys in this chapter's problems represent Trucker's Fuel Stop, Inc. ("TFS"). TFS is the country's second largest truck stop chain, with locations in forty-eight states.

TFS is a privately held company. Members of the Hanson family own approximately 70% of the company's stock. All Hanson family members who own company stock are also members of the board, with one exception—family matriarch Patty Hanson owns company stock but is no longer a board member. TFS employees own the remaining 30% of company shares. Company stock is not available for purchase by the general public.

When a client is an organization, such as a partnership, limited liability company, corporation, or governmental body, a lawyer owes the client all of the same legal and ethical duties discussed in other chapters of this book. However, this chapter looks at the unique challenges of representing a client that cannot speak for itself. The organizational client must speak through its agents (referred to as "constituents" in the *Model Rules*). While this may seem like a minor matter, it significantly complicates the lawyer's job in a number of ways.

First, what should the lawyer do when the agents of the company are engaged in conduct that may result in substantial liability to the organization—such as criminal penalties, civil liability for fraud, or breach of fiduciary duty? Certainly, a competent lawyer has a duty to advise any client (whether an individual or organization) about the risks of engaging in such misconduct and the lawyer cannot participate in such misconduct. Does the attorney for an organizational client have any additional duties to protect the organization from liability?

Second, when the client is an organization, which communications between employees and attorneys are privileged? To whom within the organization can the lawyer disclose confidential information without risking breach of attorney-client privilege? During internal investigations, what should the company's lawyer explain to employees about privilege, client identity, and the prospect of privilege waiver?

Third, lawyers must be especially mindful of conflicts of interest when they represent organizational clients. In the course of representing these clients, when can the lawyer also represent agents of the organization? When can the attorney represent the organization in matters adverse to agents of the organization, and when should the attorney refuse to do so? In what circumstances can the company lawyer represent management in a derivative suit brought by shareholders?

All of these questions turn on the issue of loyalty: what does it mean to be loyal to a client that is an entity and not a person? Rule 1.13(a) makes clear that when a lawyer is retained by an organization, the lawyer's client is the organization itself. Therefore, the lawyer owes the duty of loyalty to the entity. Loyalty to an entity can be confusing, because the organization's lawyer necessarily deals with people who speak on the organization's behalf. *See* Model Rule 1.13(a) and Comment [1] (organizations act through their authorized constituents). Understandably, the lawyer may sometimes think of these people as the client even though they are not, or may feel loyalty to these individuals more than to the actual client. This chapter is aimed at providing a framework for addressing these issues in practice.

* * *

A. PROTECTING ORGANIZATIONAL CLIENTS FROM CONSTITUENT MISCONDUCT

In 2002, Congress passed the Sarbanes-Oxley Act in response to accounting fraud in publicly traded companies, including Enron and WorldCom. The fraudulent conduct by the companies' own executives ultimately destroyed these companies and caused company stockholders to lose their investments. The Sarbanes-Oxley Act was aimed at protecting companies—and their investors—from future fraud. Among its numerous provisions, section 307 of the Act addresses the role that lawyers should play in preventing corporate fraud. That section required the Securities and Exchange Commission (SEC) to adopt attorney conduct rules that would guide attorneys in reporting violations of law to higher authorities in the company so that the company could appropriately address the misconduct.

In response to this directive, in 2003, the SEC adopted "Standards of Professional Conduct for Attorneys Appearing and Practicing Before the Commission in the Representation of an Issuer," codified at 17 C.F.R. Part 205. These rules provide detailed direction to attorneys for publicly traded companies concerning their obligation to report violations of law "up-the-ladder" within the corporation. Another provision of the SEC rule gives an attorney permission to disclose confidential client information to the SEC if doing so will protect the company or its investors from substantial injury.

The latter type of rule is sometimes described as a "loyal disclosure" rule because it permits disclosure of client confidences out of loyalty to the organizational client. In short, the disclosure is allowed for the purpose of protecting the client from the negative consequences of agent misconduct.

In 2002, the ABA formed the Task Force on Corporate Responsibility to consider rule amendments to address the same issues of corporate fraud. In 2003, the ABA strengthened its up-the-ladder reporting rule (Model Rule 1.13(b)) and adopted a loyal disclosure rule (Model Rule 1.13(c)) similar to those that had just been adopted by the SEC. Numerous states followed the ABA's lead and incorporated such provisions into their professional conduct rules. The ABA and SEC rules will be discussed in greater detail in the following sections.

At the outset, it may be helpful to briefly consider how these rules fit within the legal and ethical framework discussed in previous chapters. Recall that attorneys have an ethical and legal obligation to competently advise their clients about the legal consequences of proposed conduct. Nonetheless, a client that is a natural person can choose to engage in conduct that is contrary to the attorney's advice. If the conduct could result in liability for the lawyer, he or she should withdraw (Model Rule 1.16(a), (b)), and may be permitted (Model Rule 1.6(b)) or required (Model Rule 4.1(b)) to disclose confidential information to avoid assisting in client misconduct. But the attorney need not protect the individual client from himself or herself.

Organizational clients are different though. Such clients act through agents who may be engaged in conduct that: (1) is in the agent's personal interest but harms the organization, or (2) that is part of a misguided plan that will ultimately result in liability for the organization. The *Model Rules* recognize that an organization's agents usually speak for it, but that the lawyer should stop listening when the lawyer determines the agents are engaged in such misconduct. *See* Model Rule 1.13(b) and Comment [3]. The up-the-ladder reporting and loyal disclosure rules are intended to prompt lawyers to take further steps to protect an organizational client from agents who may harm it through misconduct. This is consistent with a lawyer's fiduciary duty of loyalty to the client: the lawyer must put the interests of the client before the interests of any third party, including an agent.

* * *

1. UP-THE-LADDER REPORTING

The ABA's up-the-ladder reporting rule applies to all organizational clients, not just companies with registered securities. Though the text is slightly more complex than this summary, Model Rule 1.13(b) essentially provides that the organization's attorney should alert higher authorities in the organization (including the organization's highest authority) when a constituent of the organization is engaged in: (1) a violation of a legal obligation to the organization; or (2) a violation of law that, if imputed to the organization, would result in substantial injury to the organization.

The SEC's up-the-ladder reporting rule requires attorneys appearing and practicing before the SEC in the representation of an issuer (a company with registered securities) to report "evidence of a material violation" to higher authorities of the corporation. A "material violation" is defined as a "material violation of an applicable United States federal or state securities law, a material breach of fiduciary duty arising under United States federal or state law, or a similar material violation of any United States federal or state law." 17 C.F.R. § 205.2(i).

Section 205.3(b) requires that an attorney report to the corporation's chief legal officer (or both the chief legal officer and the chief executive officer). 17 C.F.R. § 205.3(b)(1). The attorney then must determine if he or she has received an "appropriate response," defined as a response that causes the attorney to believe: (1) there is no material violation; (2) the company has adopted appropriate remedial measures; or (3) the company has retained an attorney to review the material violation and either (i) has implemented that attorney's remedial recommendations; or (ii) has been advised that the attorney may assert a "colorable defense" on behalf of the company. 17 C.F.R. § 205.2(b).

If the attorney reasonably believes that he or she has not received an "appropriate response," then the attorney must report the evidence to the audit committee, or a committee of directors who are not employees of the company (if there is no audit committee), or to the full board of directors (if there is no committee of directors not employed by the company). 17 C.F.R. § 205.3(b)(3). As an alternative to reporting up-the-ladder under section 205.3(b), the attorney may instead report evidence of a material violation to the corporation's qualified legal compliance committee. 17 C.F.R. § 205.3(c).

* * *

Problem 26.1. Doug Michaels, an attorney in TFS's general counsel's office, works primarily on negotiating and drafting TFS contracts. For the past year, Doug has worked with TFS Vice President Hank Silvers on all new rebate contracts with TFS customers. These contracts provide customers a rebate based on numerous factors, including the volume of fuel purchased each quarter. The rebate contracts are an important part of TFS's business model because the rebates encourage customers to purchase all of their fuel from TFS.

Hank and Doug were recently negotiating a rebate contract between TFS and Missouri Trucklines. As the negotiations were drawing to a close,

Doug had a troubling conversation with TFS customer billing supervisor Charlene Mills. Doug called Charlene to ask her to estimate the rebate Missouri Trucklines could expect given certain assumptions about their quarterly purchases. He asked Charlene to run the numbers by applying the rebate formula contained in most of TFS's rebate contracts. Doug wanted the information so he could provide Missouri Trucklines with an estimate of the rebates they should expect if they signed the contract.

Charlene responded, "Do you want to know how the rebate formula actually works or how it is supposed to work?"

"Isn't that the same thing?" Doug asked.

Charlene then explained that for the past two years, at the direction of Hank Silvers, the customer billing department has been adjusting rebate numbers by applying a secondary formula. She then described why the secondary formula is unlikely to be detected by customers. With a laugh she noted, "No one has caught on yet." Charlene concluded by telling Doug that the secondary formula has saved the company approximately $12.5 million over the past two years.

As a fiduciary, what legal obligation does Doug owe TFS as he addresses the rebate issue? Analyze whether Doug has an up-the-ladder reporting obligation in light of the information provided by Charlene. (Note on applicable professional conduct rules: The state where Doug practices has adopted a professional conduct rule identical to Model Rule 1.13(b). You should assume that SEC attorney conduct rules do not apply to Doug because TFS is not an "issuer.")

* * *

2. LOYAL DISCLOSURE

Loyal disclosure is only permitted under Model Rule 1.13(c) when up-the-ladder reporting fails, i.e., when the highest authority capable of acting either insists upon or fails to timely and appropriately address "an action or a refusal to act that is clearly a violation of law." Then, the attorney may disclose confidential information if the attorney "reasonably believes" the conduct (that is clearly a violation of law) "is reasonably certain to result in substantial injury to the organization," but such disclosure is allowed "only if and to the extent the lawyer reasonably believes necessary to prevent substantial injury to the organization." The rule does not define who can (or cannot) be the recipient of such disclosure. *Id.* The ABA rule does not permit disclosure by an attorney investigating the alleged violation of law or defending the organization or any of its constituents against a claim arising out of an alleged violation of law. Model Rule 1.13(d).

The SEC's loyal disclosure rule allows an attorney to disclose confidential client information to the SEC "to the extent the attorney reasonably believes necessary" to prevent the client's commission of a "material violation" that is "likely to cause substantial injury" to the issuer client. 17 C.F.R. § 205.3(d)(2)(i).[1] The rule also allows disclosure to the extent the attorney reasonably believes necessary "to rectify the consequences of a material violation" (when the attorney's services were used in furtherance of the violation) that "caused or may cause substantial injury" to the financial interest or property of the issuer client. 17 C.F.R. § 205.3(d)(2)(iii). Though not explicitly stated in the text of the SEC rule, it is implicit that disclosure outside the corporation can occur only after "reporting up" efforts have failed—the rule only permits disclosure "to the extent" necessary.

It can be hard for attorneys to envision that it might be in the client's interest to disclose information that the client is involved in illegal conduct. Attorneys may even rationalize that if the conduct is unlikely to be discovered and is actually profitable to the company, it would not be in the company's interest to disclose it. These loyal disclosure rules recognize, though, that it is not in the company's long-term interest to be engaged in misconduct for which the company could suffer substantial financial harm. Prior professional conduct rules gave attorneys no mechanism to encourage legal compliance in the case of financial fraud: an attorney's only option was to withdraw from the representation under the prior Model Rule 1.13(b). Under loyal disclosure rules, though, the attorney can explain that he or she has the power to protect the organization through disclosure if management chooses to do nothing. Even if loyal disclosure itself is rare, perhaps the possibility of it will discourage financial fraud.

What happens if a lawyer reports all the way up the corporate ladder, makes a loyal disclosure, and then is discharged by the organizational client? Rule 1.13(e) provides that if the lawyer reasonably believes that the discharge resulted from either of these actions, the lawyer "shall proceed as the lawyer reasonably believes necessary to assure that the organization's highest authority is informed of the lawyer's discharge or withdrawal."

* * *

Problem 26.2. Assume that Doug discussed the rebate issue (discussed in Problem 26.1) with Frank Silvers, then with TFS general counsel Jane Harmon, and ultimately with the TFS board of directors. Everyone Doug has met with insists that the rebate plan is profitable and

---

[1] Another provision of the rule—section 205.3(d)(2)(ii)—is not a loyal disclosure provision because it is not aimed at protecting the company but rather its purpose is to allow disclosure to prevent an issuer from committing or suborning perjury or perpetrating a fraud on the SEC. This provision is more akin to Model Rule 3.3 than to Model Rule 1.13(c).

unlikely to be detected, so there is no reason to change what the company is doing.

Doug is now considering whether he has a legal and professional conduct obligation of "loyal disclosure." (Note on applicable professional conduct rules: The state where Doug practices has adopted a professional conduct rule identical to Model Rule 1.13(c). Recall that SEC rules do not apply because TFS is not an "issuer.")

Which factors weigh in favor of loyal disclosure? Against loyal disclosure? If Doug determines that loyal disclosure is appropriate, to whom should Doug disclose the information?

* * *

B. ORGANIZATIONAL CLIENTS AND ATTORNEY-CLIENT PRIVILEGE

1. COMMON ORGANIZATIONAL CLIENT ATTORNEY-CLIENT PRIVILEGE ISSUES

Whether a client is an organization or an individual, the same attorney-client privilege applies. For a communication to be privileged, it must be made in confidence, between attorney and client, for the purpose of seeking or giving legal advice. *Restatement (Third) of the Law Governing Lawyers* § 73.

But even though the privilege is the same, the nature of the organizational entity can complicate the privilege analysis. One issue is who can speak on behalf of the corporation to create a privileged communication. As discussed in an earlier chapter, courts follow different approaches to determine which of a corporation's agents can have privileged conversations with counsel. In federal court, *Upjohn v. United States*, 101 S. Ct. 677 (1981), guides the corporate privilege analysis. States are not bound by *Upjohn*, so some take a different approach to determining which agents' communications with counsel are protected by privilege. *See, e.g., Consolidation Coal Co. v. Bucyrus-Erie Co.*, 432 N.E.2d 250, 257–58 (Ill. 1982) (adopting a modified control group test). *See also Restatement (Third) of the Law Governing Lawyers* § 73(2) and Comment [d]. Because of the differences in approach, research is necessary in each case to determine the contours of the privilege.

Whether legal advice was the purpose of a communication between company and lawyer is another hurdle in analyzing organizational attorney-client privilege. In-house attorneys for organizations often wear two hats, sometimes addressing business concerns and other times advising about legal matters. If the communication is not for the purpose of seeking or giving legal advice, it will not be protected by privilege. In

Higgins v. Eichler, the court determined that numerous documents evidencing communications with in-house counsel, Glenn Madere, were not privileged. In several instances, the court explained the documents did not reflect that Madere (who was also a corporate officer) was acting "in his capacity as counsel" or that he was "giving, sharing, or receiving legal advice." *Higgins v. Eichler*, 1998 WL 181825, *1–4 (E.D. Pa. 1998).

When there is a mixed purpose of both business advice and legal advice for the communication with counsel, courts have applied different tests to determine whether the communication is privileged. *Compare In re Grand Jury*, 23 F.4th 1088 (9th Cir. 2021) (holding that "the primary purpose standard test applies to attorney-client privilege claims for dual-purpose communications.") *with In re Kellogg Brown & Root, Inc.*, 756 F.3d 754 (D.C. Cir. 2014) (holding that "[i]n the context of an organization's internal investigation, if one of the significant purposes of the internal investigation was to obtain or provide legal advice, the privilege will apply."). In 2023, the U.S. Supreme Court appeared poised to answer the question of when such dual-purpose communications should be protected by the privilege, but ultimately dismissed the case after oral argument without a decision. *In re Grand Jury*, 143 S. Ct. 543 (2023) (dismissing the writ of certiorari as improvidently granted).

A related problem is that constituents of the organization may forward documents to counsel or copy counsel on email under the mistaken belief that an attorney's involvement creates a privileged communication. *See, e.g., Simon v. G.D. Searle & Co.*, 816 F.2d 397 (8th Cir. 1987) (noting that business documents sent to the company's attorneys "do not become privileged automatically"); *In re Vioxx Products Liability Litigation*, 501 F.Supp.2d 789, 800–01 (E.D. La. 2007) (explaining that despite extensive regulation of its industry, a corporation cannot assume that everything sent to the legal department will be protected by the attorney-client privilege). It is important for the organization's personnel to understand that they must be seeking legal advice in order for the privilege to attach.

An organization's attorney-client privilege can also be put at risk through a lack of confidentiality. Even though an organization may have many employees, not every employee needs to know the content of communications with counsel. Because confidentiality is a necessary component of privilege, organizational clients can jeopardize the privilege by forwarding privileged communications beyond those persons within the company who need to know. *See, e.g., In re Grand Jury Subpoenas*, 561 F.Supp.1247, 1258–59 (E.D.N.Y. 1982) (finding documents not privileged because they were forwarded to a constituent of the company who did not need to know the information); *Restatement (Third) of the Law Governing Lawyers* § 73(4). The lawyer's professional conduct obligation in regard to confidentiality is similar. Comment [2] to the organizational client professional conduct rule (Rule 1.13) notes that lawyers cannot disclose confidential client information to agents of the organization except when authorized to carry out the representation.

* * *

Problem 26.3. TFS has been sued by Fanny's Pie Factory for breach of contract. Maureen Albright, an attorney at the firm Spinner, Ahern & Albright, was hired by TFS to represent TFS in the case. In discovery, Fanny's Pie Factory has requested that TFS produce all communications by TFS employees during a defined time period that "refer or relate to the TFS contract with Fanny's Pie Factory and/or Fanny's Pie Factory product quality." Analyze whether Maureen will be successful in asserting that the following documents are privileged.

Assume that state law (and not federal law) is applicable and that the state follows the *Upjohn* approach regarding which agents of the company may have privileged communications with counsel. You may also rely upon cases cited in this part of the text and the *Restatement* as you answer the following questions.

   a. An email from TFS accounts payable supervisor Bif Allington to in-house attorney Doug Michaels. Bif noted that he recalls that Doug negotiated the TFS contract with Fanny's. Bif asked Doug for advice about whether, under the terms of the contract, TFS should refuse to pay Fanny's for approximately $500 worth of product that was past its sell-by date when it was received by TFS. Bif suggested that alternatively he can pay the full invoiced amount and seek a refund from Fanny's.

   b. An email from TFS employee Kitty Blair to TFS employees Herb Strobel, Annika Overhoffer, and Benton Tucker. All of these employees manage various TFS truck stops. Kitty stated, "I just wonder if other people have had problems with the Fanny's pies lately. We keep receiving pies that are already expired, meaning they arrive after their 'sell-by-this-date' sticker." She included a "cc" of the email to Regional Vice President Harley Crandall. Harley then forwarded the email to in-house attorney Doug Michaels with a note, "What should we do about this?"

   c. A memo from Doug Michaels to TFS Regional Managers. Doug asked for the managers' opinion regarding whether the Fanny's Pies contract should be renegotiated when it expires or if there is another supplier that the company would like to consider. Also in the memo, Doug noted reports of product inconsistency as a reason to think about a new supplier.

* * *

2. ORGANIZATIONAL ATTORNEY-CLIENT PRIVILEGE AND INTERNAL INVESTIGATIONS

Another privilege issue unique to organizational clients arises when attorneys receive information from company agents in an investigation. This information may reveal a possible basis for criminal or civil liability of the agent, the organization, or both. Even though attorneys want to encourage company employees to be candid in these discussions, the promise of privilege could be confusing. While it is true the conversations may be protected by privilege, the privilege belongs to the organization and not to the individual providing information. The organization may later wish to waive privilege, even though it is against the interests of the individual who disclosed the information.

Professional conduct rules and case law address what a company's lawyer should communicate to company employees in this situation. Model Rule 1.13(f) provides that a lawyer should explain the client's identity—that it is the organization and not the individual—in dealings with company agents, if the agent's interests are adverse to the organization. Comments [10] and [11] elaborate that in a situation of adversity between organizational client and constituent, the lawyer should explain whom the lawyer represents and the impact on attorney-client privilege.

Alerting a client's employees of such issues at the outset of an internal investigation is often referred to as providing an "*Upjohn* warning" or "corporate *Miranda* warning." This warning should include notice to the employee of the following: (1) the lawyer represents the organization and not the individual; (2) the privilege belongs to the organization and not the individual; (3) the organization may later choose to waive the privilege; (4) the individual should keep the conversation confidential; and (5) the individual may wish to consult his or her own attorney. To avoid any uncertainty about the content of these warnings to employees, lawyers are encouraged to put them in writing.

Without this warning, the client's agent might reasonably believe he or she has an attorney-client relationship with the lawyer. This misapprehension could harm the corporate client who might be prohibited from disclosing the information from the agent's interview, even though it is in the corporate client's interest to do so. Further, such a misapprehension could result in the lawyer violating fiduciary duties to the agent/client, as well as professional conduct obligations prohibiting conflicts of interest (the dual representation of parties with adverse interests) and disclosure of client confidences (if the lawyer disclosed information at the corporate client's direction but against the wishes of the agent). The following case considers the sufficiency of counsel's *Upjohn* warning to constituents of AOL Time Warner.

IN RE GRAND JURY SUBPOENA: UNDER SEAL
415 F.3d 333 (4th Cir. 2005).

WILSON, DISTRICT JUDGE.

This is an appeal by three former employees of AOL Time Warner ("AOL") from the decision of the district court denying their motions to quash a grand jury subpoena for documents related to an internal investigation by AOL. Appellants in the district court [asserted] that the subpoenaed documents were protected by the attorney-client privilege. Because the district court concluded that the privilege was AOL's alone and because AOL had expressly waived its privilege, the court denied the appellants' motion. We affirm.

I.

In March of 2001, AOL began an internal investigation into its relationship with PurchasePro, Inc. AOL retained the law firm of Wilmer, Cutler & Pickering ("Wilmer Cutler") to assist in the investigation. Over the next several months, AOL's general counsel and counsel from Wilmer Cutler (collectively referred to herein as "AOL's attorneys" or the "investigating attorneys") interviewed appellants, AOL employees Kent Wakeford, John Doe 1, and John Doe 2.[2]

The investigating attorneys interviewed Wakeford, a manager in the company's Business Affairs division, on six occasions. At their third interview, and the first one in which Wilmer Cutler attorneys were present, Randall Boe, AOL's General Counsel, informed Wakeford, "We represent the company. These conversations are privileged, but the privilege belongs to the company and the company decides whether to waive it. If there is a conflict, the attorney-client privilege belongs to the company." Memoranda from that meeting also indicate that the attorneys explained to Wakeford that they represented AOL but that they "could" represent him as well, "as long as no conflict appear[ed]." The attorneys interviewed Wakeford again three days later and, at the beginning of the interview, reiterated that they represented AOL, that the privilege belonged to AOL, and that Wakeford could retain personal counsel at company expense.

The investigating attorneys interviewed John Doe 1 three times. Before the first interview, Boe told him, "We represent the company. These conversations are privileged, but the privilege belongs to the company and the company decides whether to waive it. You are free to consult with your own lawyer at any time." Memoranda from that interview indicate that the attorneys also told him, "We can represent [you] until such time as there appears to be a conflict of interest, [but] . . . the attorney-client privilege belongs to AOL and AOL can decide whether to keep it or waive it." At the end of the interview, John Doe 1 asked if he needed personal counsel. A

---

[2] Because the grand jury has indicted Wakeford, we refer to him by name.

Wilmer Cutler attorney responded that he did not recommend it, but that he would tell the company not to be concerned if Doe retained counsel.

AOL's attorneys interviewed John Doe 2 twice and followed essentially the same protocol they had followed with the other appellants. They noted, "We represent AOL, and can represent [you] too if there is not a conflict." In addition, the attorneys told him that, "the attorney-client privilege is AOL's and AOL can choose to waive it."

In November, 2001, the Securities and Exchange Commission ("SEC") began to investigate AOL's relationship with PurchasePro. In December 2001, AOL and Wakeford, through counsel, entered into an oral "common interest agreement," which they memorialized in writing in January 2002. The attorneys acknowledged that, "representation of [their] respective clients raise[d] issues of common interest to [their] respective clients and that the sharing of certain documents, information, ... and communications with clients" would be mutually beneficial. As a result, the attorneys agreed to share access to information relating to their representation of Wakeford and AOL, noting that "the oral or written disclosure of Common Interest Materials ... [would] not diminish in any way the confidentiality of such Materials and [would] not constitute a waiver of any applicable privilege."

Wakeford testified before the SEC on February 14, 2002, represented by his personal counsel. Laura Jehl, AOL's general counsel, and F. Whitten Peters of Williams & Connolly, whom AOL had retained in November 2001 in connection with the PurchasePro investigation, were also present, and both stated that they represented Wakeford "for purposes of [the] deposition." During the deposition, the SEC investigators questioned Wakeford about his discussions with AOL's attorneys. When Wakeford's attorney asserted the attorney-client privilege, the SEC investigators followed up with several questions to determine whether the privilege was applicable to the investigating attorneys' March–June 2001 interviews with Wakeford. Wakeford told them he believed, at the time of the interviews, that the investigating attorneys represented him and the company.

John Doe 1 testified before the SEC on February 27, 2002, represented by personal counsel. No representatives of AOL were present. When SEC investigators questioned Doe about the March–June 2001 internal investigation, his counsel asserted that the information was protected and directed Doe not to answer any questions about the internal investigation "in respect to the company's privilege." He stated that Doe's response could be considered a waiver of the privilege and that, "if the AOL lawyers were [present], they could make a judgment, with respect to the company's privilege, about whether or not the answer would constitute a waiver."

On February 26, 2004, a grand jury in the Eastern District of Virginia issued a subpoena commanding AOL to provide "written memoranda and other written records reflecting interviews conducted by attorneys for [AOL]" of the appellants between March 15 and June 30, 2001. While AOL agreed to waive the attorney-client privilege and produce the subpoenaed documents, counsel for the appellants moved to quash the subpoena on the grounds that each appellant had an individual attorney-client relationship with the investigating attorneys, that his interviews were individually privileged, and that he had not waived the privilege. Wakeford also claimed that the information he disclosed to the investigating attorneys was privileged under the common interest doctrine.

The district court denied John Doe 1's and John Doe 2's motions because it found they failed to prove they were clients of the investigating attorneys who interviewed them. The court based its conclusion on its findings that: (1) the investigating attorneys told them that they represented the company; (2) the investigating attorneys told them, "we *can* represent you," which is distinct from "we *do* represent you"; (3) they could not show that the investigating attorneys agreed to represent them; and (4) the investigating attorneys told them that the attorney-client privilege belonged to the company and the company could choose to waive it.

The court initially granted Wakeford's motion to quash because it found that his communications with the investigating attorneys were privileged under the common interest agreement between counsel for Wakeford and counsel for AOL. Following a motion for reconsideration, the court reversed its earlier ruling and held that the subpoenaed documents relating to Wakeford's interviews were not privileged because it found that Wakeford's common interest agreement with AOL postdated the March–June 2001 interviews. In addition, the court held that Wakeford failed to prove that he was a client of the investigating attorneys at the time the interviews took place. The court based its conclusion on its findings that: (1) none of the investigating attorneys understood that Wakeford was seeking personal legal advice; (2) the investigating attorneys did not provide any personal legal advice to him; and (3) the investigating attorneys believed they represented AOL and not Wakeford. This appeal followed.

II.

Appellants argue that because they believed that the investigating attorneys who conducted the interviews were representing them personally, their communications are privileged. However, we agree with the district court that essential touchstones for the formation of an attorney-client relationship between the investigating attorneys and the appellants were missing at the time of the interviews. There is no evidence of an objectively reasonable, mutual understanding that the appellants were seeking legal advice from the investigating attorneys or that the investigating attorneys were rendering personal legal advice. Nor, in light of the investigating attorneys' disclosure that they represented AOL and that the privilege and the right to waive it were AOL's alone, do we find investigating counsel's hypothetical pronouncement that they *could* represent appellants sufficient to establish the reasonable understanding that they *were* representing appellants. Accordingly, we find no fault with the district court's opinion that no individual attorney-client privilege attached to the appellants' communications with AOL's attorneys.[3]

We apply a two-fold standard of review in this case. We give deference to the district court's determination of the underlying facts, and review those findings for clear error. *In re Grand Jury Subpoena v. Under Seal,* 341 F.3d 331, 334 (4th Cir.2003); *see also In re Allen et al.,* 106 F.3d 582, 601 (4th Cir.1997) (noting the two-fold standard of review). A finding of fact is clearly erroneous, despite the presence of evidence to support it, when the reviewing court, after carefully examining all the evidence, is "left with the definite and firm conviction that a mistake has been committed." *Anderson v. City of Bessemer City,* 470 U.S. 564, 573, 105 S. Ct. 1504, 84 L.Ed.2d 518 (1985). We review the application of legal principles *de novo*. *In re Grand Jury Subpoena,* 341 F.3d at 334.

"The attorney-client privilege is the oldest of the privileges for confidential communications known to the common law." *Upjohn v. United States,* 449 U.S. 383, 389, 101 S. Ct. 677, 66 L. Ed. 2d 584 (1981). "[W]hen the privilege applies, it affords confidential communications between lawyer and client complete protection from disclosure." *Hawkins v. Stables,* 148 F.3d 379, 383 (4th Cir.1998). Because its application interferes with "the truth seeking mission of the legal process," *United States v. Tedder,* 801 F.2d 1437, 1441 (4th Cir.1986), however, we must narrowly construe the privilege, and recognize it "only to the very limited extent that . . . excluding relevant evidence has a public good transcending the normally predominant principle of utilizing all rational means for ascertaining the truth." *Trammel v. United States,* 445 U.S. 40, 50, 100 S. Ct. 906, 63 L. Ed. 2d 186 (1980). Accordingly, the privilege applies only to "[c]onfidential disclosures by a client to an attorney made in order to obtain legal assistance." *Fisher v. United States,* 425 U.S. 391, 403, 96 S. Ct. 1569, 48

---

[3] The grand jury's return of an indictment against Wakeford does not moot his appeal because the government continues to seek records from the March–June 2001 interviews for trial as to Wakeford and through a second grand jury as to others. Given this high probability of reoccurrence, our opinion is in no way advisory. *See In re Grand Jury Proceedings,* 33 F.3d 342, 347 (4th Cir.1994) (applying the "capable of repetition, yet evading review" exception to the mootness doctrine in the context of expired grand jury).

L. Ed. 2d 39 (1976).[4] "The burden is on the proponent of the attorney-client privilege to demonstrate its applicability." *Jones*, 696 F.2d at 1072.

The person seeking to invoke the attorney-client privilege must prove that he is a client or that he affirmatively sought to become a client. "The professional relationship ... hinges upon the client's belief that he is consulting a lawyer in that capacity and his manifested intention to seek professional legal advice." *United States v. Evans*, 113 F.3d 1457, 1465 (7th Cir. 1997). An individual's subjective belief that he is represented is not alone sufficient to create an attorney-client relationship. *See United States v. Keplinger*, 776 F.2d 678, 701 (7th Cir. 1985)("We think no individual attorney-client relationship can be inferred without some finding that the potential client's subjective belief is minimally reasonable"); *see also, In re Grand Jury Subpoena Duces Tecum*, 112 F.3d 910, 923 (8th Cir. 1997) ("[W]e know of no authority ... holding that a client's beliefs, subjective or objective, about the law of privilege can transform an otherwise unprivileged conversation into a privileged one."). Rather, the putative client must show that his subjective belief that an attorney-client relationship existed was reasonable under the circumstances.[5]

With these precepts in mind, we conclude that appellants could not have reasonably believed that the investigating attorneys represented them personally during the time frame covered by the subpoena. First, there is no evidence that the investigating attorneys told the appellants that they represented them, nor is there evidence that the appellants asked the investigating attorneys to represent them. To the contrary, there is evidence that the investigating attorneys relayed to Wakeford the company's offer to retain personal counsel for him at the company's expense, and that they told John Doe 1 that he was free to retain personal counsel. Second, there is no evidence that the appellants ever sought personal legal advice from the investigating attorneys, nor is there any evidence that the investigating attorneys rendered personal legal advice.

---

[4] This circuit has adopted the classic test to determine whether the attorney-client privilege applies to certain communications or documents. The privilege applies only if (1) the asserted holder of the privilege is or sought to become a client; (2) the person to whom the communication was made (a) is a member of the bar of a court, or his subordinate and (b) in connection with this communication is acting as a lawyer; (3) the communication relates to a fact of which the attorney was informed (a) by his client (b) without the presence of strangers (c) for the purpose of securing primarily either (i) an opinion on law or (ii) legal services or (iii) assistance in some legal proceeding, and not (d) for the purpose of committing a crime or tort; and (4) the privilege has been (a) claimed and (b) not waived by the client. *United States v. Jones*, 696 F.2d 1069, 1072 (4th Cir. 1982).

[5] This court addressed the question of whether a corporate employee could personally assert the attorney-client privilege for communications with corporate counsel conducting an internal investigation in *United States v. Aramony*, 88 F.3d 1369 (4th Cir. 1996). In *Aramony*, this court affirmed the finding of the district court that Aramony was not the client of internal investigation counsel. The court noted that Aramony did not seek legal advice; Aramony could not have reasonably believed that the information he disclosed would be kept confidential; and internal investigation counsel told Aramony that they were retained to represent the company. *Id.* at 1390–92.

Third, when the appellants spoke with the investigating attorneys, they were fully apprised that the information they were giving could be disclosed at the company's discretion. Under these circumstances, appellants could not have reasonably believed that the investigating attorneys represented them personally.[6] Therefore, the district court's finding that appellants had no attorney-client relationship with the investigating attorneys is not clearly erroneous.[7]

The appellants argue that the phrase "we *can* represent you as long as no conflict appears," manifested an agreement by the investigating attorneys to represent them. They claim that, "it is hard to imagine a more straightforward assurance of an attorney-client relationship than 'we can represent you.' " We disagree. As the district court noted, "we *can* represent you" is distinct from "we *do* represent you." If there was any evidence that the investigating attorneys had said, "we *do* represent you," then the outcome of this appeal might be different. Furthermore, the statement actually made, "we *can* represent you," must be interpreted within the context of the entire warning. The investigating attorneys' statements to the appellants, read in their entirety, demonstrate that the attorneys' loyalty was to the company. That loyalty was never implicitly or explicitly divided. In addition to noting at the outset that they had been retained to represent AOL, the investigating attorneys warned the appellants that the content of their communications during the interview "belonged" to AOL. This protocol put the appellants on notice that, while their communications with the attorneys were considered confidential, the company could choose to reveal the content of those communications at any time, without the appellants' consent.

We note, however, that our opinion should not be read as an implicit acceptance of the watered-down "*Upjohn* warnings" the investigating attorneys gave the appellants. It is a potential legal and ethical mine field. Had the investigating attorneys, in fact, entered into an attorney-client relationship with appellants, as their statements to the appellants professed they could, they would not have been free to waive the appellants' privilege when a conflict arose. It should have seemed obvious that they could not have jettisoned one client in favor of another. Rather, they would have had to withdraw from all representation and to maintain all confidences. Indeed, the court would be hard pressed to identify how

---

[6] The district court made no finding as to whether the appellants, in fact, believed that the investigating attorneys represented them personally.

[7] Appellants maintain the district court improperly relied on *In re Bevill, Bresler, & Schulman Asset Mgmt. Corp.*, 805 F.2d 120, 123 (3d Cir. 1986), in determining that appellants did not have an attorney-client relationship with the investigating attorneys. They contend that *Bevill* creates a litmus test this circuit has not adopted for determining whether there is an attorney-client relationship between corporate employees and corporate counsel. It is unnecessary to decide whether we find *Bevill* fully consistent with our views on this matter because based on the circumstances we have identified, it would not have been objectively reasonable for appellants to believe that the investigating attorneys represented them personally.

investigating counsel could robustly investigate and report to management or the board of directors of a publicly-traded corporation with the necessary candor if counsel were constrained by ethical obligations to individual employees. However, because we agree with the district court that the appellants never entered into an attorney-client relationship with the investigating attorneys, they averted these troubling issues.

III.

[The court determined there was no evidence that Wakeford and AOL shared a common interest before December 2001 and found no error in the district court's conclusion that Wakeford had no joint defense privilege before that time].

IV.

After review of the district court's factual findings and legal conclusions, we find no clear error. . . . The district court therefore properly denied the appellants' motions.

AFFIRMED

* * *

Problem 26.4. Doug Michaels approached the TFS board a second time with his concerns about rebate fraud. This time, the board agreed that the company should hire a law firm to conduct an investigation to determine if TFS is engaged in illegal conduct. The company hired Loretta Sawyer from the firm Sawyer & Bernstein to conduct the investigation and prepare a report on her findings.

Loretta worked with in-house attorney Doug to create a list of individuals who are knowledgeable about the rebate issue. She has decided to interview TFS Vice President Hank Silvers first. Draft an *Upjohn* warning that Loretta can present to Hank at the beginning of his interview. If you complete additional research to prepare your *Upjohn* warning, please make a note of the source or sources that you find most useful.

* * *

C. ORGANIZATIONAL CLIENTS, CONSTITUENTS, AND CONFLICTS OF INTEREST

Professional conduct rules acknowledge that, subject to the conflict of interest rules, an attorney may simultaneously represent an organizational client and its officers, employees, directors, and other constituents. Model Rule 1.13(g). Accordingly, there is no conflict if: (1) organization and constituent are not directly adverse, (2) there is not a significant risk that the representation of the organization would materially limit the representation of the constituent and vice versa, and

(3) there is not a significant risk that the representation of either will be materially limited by lawyer's responsibility to another (current client, former client, or third party) or the lawyer's own personal interest. Model Rule 1.7(a). Even if there is a conflict or potential conflict in representing the organization and individual, the lawyer may still proceed with the representation if the lawyer believes he or she can competently and diligently represent both, they will not assert claims against one another, and both provide informed consent. Model Rule 1.7(b). Apply these rules as you consider the proposed simultaneous representation in Problem 26.5.

Another possible conflict can arise when a lawyer is asked to represent the company in a matter adverse to one of the company's agents—perhaps even an agent the lawyer has worked with closely in the past on matters for the company. The lawyer should consider several factors when determining whether there is a conflict of interest in accepting the representation. Obviously, if the agent is a current client of the lawyer or the lawyer's firm—even in a completely unrelated matter—the representation is prohibited. Model Rule 1.7(a)(1). Also, if the lawyer's personal relationship with the agent will limit the lawyer's ability to represent the organization, the lawyer should refuse to accept the case. Model Rule 1.7(a)(2).

Further, if the agent is a former client of the lawyer or the lawyer's firm, the representation also is problematic if the new matter for the organization is substantially related to the former representation of the agent. Model Rule 1.9(a). This is the issue that was raised in Problem 24.3 in the Transactional Practice chapter.

Finally, another possible conflict scenario arises with a derivative suit. A derivative suit is a lawsuit filed by a shareholder (or other owner) on behalf of the company. *See, e.g.,* Fed. R. Civ. P. 23.1 (explaining procedural requirements for a derivative suit in federal court). Company managers may seek representation in the matter from the lawyers who currently represent the company in other matters or that have represented the company in the past. Even though the derivative lawsuit is brought in the name of the company, the *Model Rules* recognize that it is not necessarily a conflict for counsel to represent management. Comments [13] and [14] to Model Rule 1.13 address this issue. Refer to these comments, as well as Model Rule 1.7, when you answer Problem 26.6.

* * *

Problem 26.5. Last month, the IRS and FBI raided the corporate offices of TFS; their search warrant allowed them to collect evidence of the rebate fraud scheme. It now appears imminent that the U.S. Attorney will pursue criminal charges (mail fraud, wire fraud, and perhaps others) against TFS and Hank Silvers. TFS has retained attorney Maggie Haynes to represent TFS during the criminal investigation and in any future criminal prosecution. TFS's board has asked Maggie to consider also representing Hank Silvers. The board's thinking is that the company's interests are aligned with Hank's in that both deny that fraudulent conduct occurred and both want to avoid a conviction. Analyze the appropriateness of Maggie representing both TFS and Hank Silvers.

Problem 26.6. TFS's employee shareholders (who own approximately 30% of company stock) have filed a derivative suit on behalf of the company against the current board. The lawsuit alleges that the board intentionally and affirmatively encouraged the rebate fraud, in breach of the board's fiduciary duties of care and loyalty to TFS. The board has reached out to Loretta Sawyer from the law firm Sawyer & Bernstein to represent the board in the matter. (Recall that Loretta is the attorney who conducted the internal investigation on behalf of the company in Problem 26.4.) Should Loretta represent the board in this case?

Profile of Attorney Professionalism. Roger Balla was employed as in-house counsel of Gambro, Inc., a distributor of kidney dialysis equipment. In July 1985, he learned that Gambro's German affiliate planned to ship to Gambro kidney dialyzers that did not comply with regulations of the U.S. Food and Drug Administration (FDA). Specifically, the German affiliate advised Gambro:

> For acute patients risk is that acute uremic situation will not be improved in spite of the treatment.... The chronic patient may note the effect as a slow progression of the uremic situation and depending on the interval between medical check-ups the medical risk may not be overlooked.

Balla informed Gambro's president that the dialyzers must be rejected because of their failure to meet FDA requirements. Initially, the president followed Balla's advice and notified the German affiliate that the dialyzers would not be accepted. Later, though, the president alerted the German affiliate that Gambro would accept and re-sell the dialyzers.

When Balla learned of this decision, he again approached Gambro's president with his concern that the company was engaging in illegal conduct. This time, Balla said he would do "whatever is necessary" to stop the sale of the dialyzers. Shortly thereafter, Gambro's president fired Balla.

As an Illinois-licensed attorney, Balla consulted Illinois' professional conduct rules and concluded that he was required to disclose information about the dialyzers. At the time, Illinois's Rule 1.6(b) provided, "A lawyer shall reveal information about a client to the extent it appears necessary to prevent the client from committing an act that would result in death or serious bodily injury." Following the rule's mandate, Balla disclosed information about the non-compliant dialyzers to the FDA. Relying on this information, the FDA seized the shipment of dialyzers.

Chapter 6 of this text includes a note about Balla's litigation against Gambro. The Illinois Supreme Court refused to allow him to pursue a cause of action for retaliatory discharge against his employer. The facts in this profile are contained in the court's decision. *Balla v. Gambro*, 584 N.E.2d 104 (Ill. 1991).

Beyond its significance as a retaliatory discharge case, Balla's case provides important insight about the challenges faced by corporate counsel. Balla took concerns of illegal conduct up-the-ladder of the corporation in an effort to protect both the company and future users of the non-compliant dialyzers. When his advice was ignored, he persisted in voicing his concerns and lost his job as a result. Ultimately, Balla took additional steps to prevent the sale of the dialyzers because he was required to do so under applicable professional conduct rules. While some attorneys may have deferred to the president, Balla took the more difficult path required of an attorney.

PART 5

ATTORNEY WELL-BEING AND LEGACY

■ ■ ■

This book is organized around the theme of the professional life of a lawyer. These final chapters invite you to plan for your well-being—in all its dimensions—throughout your career and to give thought to how you define a successful career. Chapter 27 focuses on attorney well-being. Beyond discussing well-being planning and practices, the chapter asks you to consider the legal and ethical implications of the attorney well-being movement. Finally, Chapter 28 considers the legacy of a number of impressive lawyers and judges and asks you to give thought to what you want your legacy to be.

CHAPTER 27

ATTORNEY WELL-BEING

■ ■ ■

As you know by now, law school can be challenging for your well-being. There is a heavy work load. Students who have been successful throughout their prior studies may find law school their first difficult academic experience. Some feel pressure to outperform classmates. For others, the greatest stress is the uncertainty—whether they are studying enough, taking the right classes, and pursuing the right opportunities. There is also the financial pressure of foregoing employment while investing money into legal education, in the hopes that the investment will be worthwhile in the long run. Law students with family responsibilities or other outside obligations may feel even greater time pressure to get everything done. Students with disabilities that impact their ability to study the law have an additional challenge to address. You can probably add your own unique challenges to this list.

The law school experience can lead law students to neglect the people (family, friends, communities), activities (exercise, travel, reading for pleasure, to name a few examples), and practices (faith, meditation, etc.) that bring joy and happiness. The stress and uncertainty of the experience can cause or exacerbate mental health concerns, such as depression and anxiety. For some, this leads to problematic coping mechanisms such as unhealthy eating, drinking, or drug use. While many law students seek and benefit from counseling, medical assistance, and other support for their well-being, others may not seek out those resources for a myriad of reasons, including stigma and concern that treatment may have to be revealed during bar admission.

Similar issues—and new ones—can present wellness challenges for attorneys. Attorneys are responsible for helping clients navigate legal problems that will impact their finances, mental health, and perhaps even their liberty. This responsibility can be stressful and may even result in secondary trauma for the lawyer. Mark Rabil *et. al.*, *Secondary Trauma in Lawyering: Stories, Studies, and Strategies*, 56 WAKE FOREST L. REV. 825 (2021). Further, the profession is demanding, with clients and employers often expecting a lawyers to work around the clock. For many lawyers, it is a struggle to find the right balance between work and life outside of the law. And just like law students, some lawyers may cope in unhealthy ways and may neglect getting help for mental health and other struggles.

But do law student and lawyers have greater well-being challenges than the rest of the population? Is the legal profession in crisis because of a lack of attorney well-being? This chapter considers those issues, as well as the proposition that there is a connection between attorney well-being and the ethical practice of law. This chapter will prompt you to think about if and when bar officials, lawyer assistance programs, firms, and colleagues should intervene to address a concern about attorney well-being. Finally, the chapter asks you to think about some of the tools that may help you thrive in law school and beyond.

Instead of presenting a single hypothetical question in this chapter, the problems in this chapter ask you to consider a variety of hypotheticals related to wellness, attorney ethics, and tools for your personal well-being.

A. THE ATTORNEY WELL-BEING MOVEMENT: AN ISSUE OF ATTORNEY ETHICS AND CLIENT PROTECTION?

In 2017, the National Task Force on Lawyer Well-Being released its report *The Path to Lawyer Well-Being: Practical Recommendations for Positive Change* ("Task Force Report"). The ABA Commission on Lawyer Assistance Programs (CoLAP), the National Organization of Bar Counsel, and the Association of Professional Responsibility Professors are given credit for conceptualizing the Task Force.

The Task Force opines, "To be a good lawyer, one has to be a healthy lawyer. Sadly, our profession is falling short when it comes to well-being." The Report relies upon two CoLAP-sponsored reports, one about lawyers' self-reported mental health and substance use disorders and another that surveyed law students about their well-being. From these studies, the Task Force concludes that "too many" law students and lawyers experience high rates of substance use and depression.

The Task Force Report asserts that "troubled lawyers can struggle with even minimum competence" and cites an author who "suggests" that 40 to 70 percent of discipline and malpractice claims involve substance abuse, depression, or both. The Task Force Report calls well-being "part of a lawyer's ethical duty of competence." One of the five core recommendations of the report is to emphasize the well-being-competence connection. Section 20.2 of the Report recommends revising Rule 1.1 and/or its comments to "clearly includes lawyers' well-being in the definition of 'competence.'" One option, according to the Report, is to define competence as including the "mental, emotional, and physical ability reasonably necessary to the representation," while another option is to amend the rule's comment to clarify that "professional competence requires an ability to comply with all of the Court's essential eligibility requirements." The discussion concludes with a note that a lawyer should not be disciplined for failing to meet the well-being requirement. The well-being rule amendments are not meant to serve as a discipline threat, but instead to underscore the importance of well-being in representing clients.

Many view the Task Force Report as heralding in a new emphasis on attorney well-being. Most states now have a lawyer committee focused on issues of wellness, providing continuing legal education programs on wellness topics, and making recommendations—such as to amend professional conduct rules. *See* Institute for Well-Being In the Law's interactive map, available at https://lawyerwellbeing.net. The American Bar Association's accreditation standards were revised in February 2022 to require law schools to provide students with substantial opportunities for development of "professional identity" which is defined as including the study of "well-being practices considered foundational to successful legal practice." ABA Standard 303(b)(3), Interpretation 303–5. The ABA also adopted Standard 508(b) requiring law schools to provide students information about well-being resources. Interpretation 508–1 explains that well-being resources may include information on services related to mental health, substance abuse, counseling, food pantries, and emergency assistance funds.

As this book goes to press, the ABA and several states are considering adding language about well-being to their competence professional conduct rule and/or associated comments. California, New Mexico, Utah, and Vermont already have amended comments associated with their competence rules to address attorney well-being. For example, Utah's new comment to its competence rule provides, "Lawyers should be aware that their mental, emotional, and physical well-being may impact their ability to represent clients and, as such, is an important aspect of maintaining competence to practice law and compliance with the standards of professionalism and civility. Resources supporting lawyer well-being are available through the Utah State Bar." In approving this comment, Utah explained that the comment's guidance is not meant to be "punitive or impose additional requirements or burdens on lawyers. Rather, it is intended to be educational and to point lawyers to the importance of prioritizing their well-being."

The new emphasis on attorney well-being—and the suggestion that well-being is an aspect of attorney competence—appropriately have been the subject of scrutiny by experts in the field. Nicholas Lawson has noted problems with the validity of the two main studies relied upon by the Task Force, has disputed the well-being challenges faced by lawyers are more pronounced than in other segments of the population, and points out the lack of empirical evidence that attorney addiction and mental health issues have any causal relationship with attorney malpractice and discipline.

Nicholas D. Lawson, *"To Be a Good Lawyer, One Has to be a Healthy Lawyer": Lawyer Well-Being, Discrimination, and Discretionary Systems of Discipline,* 34 GEO. J. LEGAL ETHICS 65 (2021).

Lawson also raises concerns about the Task Force's suggestion that Rule 1.1 should be amended to make well-being a component of competence, arguing that this improperly shifts the competence inquiry from attorney performance to attorney health, running afoul of the Americans with Disabilities Act. The proposed rule change also increases the risk that legal employers will discriminate against individuals with mental health and substance abuse disorders, falsely believing the conditions are linked to incompetence. *Id.* at 93. Lawson has also questioned the role of Lawyer Assistance Programs (LAPs) in promoting the well-being movement and in asserting that LAP well-being interventions are effective. He concludes,

> Irrespective of treatment effectiveness, LAPs pose a problem to the profession by disseminating and perpetuating inaccurate information about lawyers and mental health disorders and disabilities. Whether these LAP practices have something to do with strong personal opinions among LAP staff about particular treatments, conflicts of interest, or the fact that LAPs and those associated with LAPS generally operate with near-absolute civil immunity is less important than recognizing the fact of these repeated misleading claims and their potential negative impact.

Id. at 92.

In the following excerpt from his 2022 article, Alex Long explains the hazards of stigma and discrimination that can arise from the Task Force and state bars associating attorney well-being with competence to practice law.

WHAT THE LAWYER WELL-BEING MOVEMENT COULD LEARN FROM THE AMERICANS WITH DISABILITIES ACT

Alex B. Long
William & Mary Law Review Online, Vol. 63, No. 4 (2022)

Whether in formal ethics opinions dealing with the issue of lawyers with disabilities or reports such as the National Task Force's report *The Path to Lawyer Well-Being*, the lawyer well-being movement has sometimes perpetuated harmful stereotypes concerning disability. This Article suggests that in order to effectively improve lawyer well-being, the organized bar should look more carefully at the text of the Americans with Disabilities Act (ADA), as well as the policies that underlie it.

THE STIGMATIZING EFFECT OF THE ABA NATIONAL TASK FORCE'S REPORT

There are several problems with the *Path to Lawyer Well-Being Report*'s premises and proposals. The report explains that its suggestion that Rule 1.1 be amended to explicitly link competence with well-being is designed "to reduce stigma associated with mental health disorders." Yet, in the same breath, the National Task Force tells lawyers with mental health disorders (as well as other members of the profession) that the absence of a mental health disorder is a predicate to fitness to practice law. In other words, one cannot be a good lawyer if one has some type of mental health disorder. It is difficult to imagine a more stigmatizing comment in a document intended to help reduce the stigma concerning mental health disorders.

The notion that freedom from substance use and mental health disorders is an indispensable predicate to fitness to practice is not only stigmatizing, but also simply wrong. To be sure, we want everyone—including lawyers—to be free from substance abuse and mental health disorders. And the fact that a lawyer is, for example, actively abusing alcohol or experiencing depression undoubtedly makes it more likely on average that client representation is adversely impacted. But it should be equally obvious that there are also many outstanding lawyers who are actively abusing alcohol or experiencing depression.

Indeed, there is little empirical evidence that the existence of a mental impairment places a lawyer at a significantly greater risk of legal malpractice, incompetence, and other rule violations, or is even significantly predictive of such conduct. In several instances, individual plaintiffs have challenged the legality of questions related to mental health and treatment in the professional licensing context. In some instances, when challenged on the issue of whether past mental health treatment was a reliable predictor of future professional misbehavior, states were unable to offer credible evidence in support of their position that it is. The ABA itself has previously noted that "[r]esearch in the health field and clinical experience demonstrate that neither diagnosis nor the fact of having undergone treatment support any inferences about a person's ability to carry out professional responsibilities or to act with integrity, competence, or honor."

Of course, a lawyer who is presently experiencing the debilitating effects of depression or untreated bipolar disorder would logically be more likely to have difficulty providing competent representation than a lawyer not experiencing these conditions. It might even be true that these types of conditions—if not properly treated—are more likely to result in incompetent representation of clients than many physical impairments. But if one of the primary goals of the National Task Force Report is to end the stigma that discourages lawyers from seeking help, it is counterproductive for the report to make sweeping generalizations about the fitness of a lawyer based merely on the diagnosis or existence of a mental impairment.

WHAT THE LAWYER WELL-BEING MOVEMENT COULD LEARN FROM THE ADA

Ultimately, what is perhaps most noteworthy about the National Task Force Report and the ethics opinions involving lawyers with mental impairments is how little the ADA seems to have influenced them. The ADA is unquestionably the single most important statute on disabilities and disability discrimination. Yet, there is not a single mention of the law in the entire seventy-two pages of the National Task Force Report. While a few ethics opinions reference the ADA, they typically do so only in passing or with the observation that a fuller discussion of the law is beyond the scope of the opinion. Yet, it is impossible to discuss issues related to the employment of individuals with mental impairments in any sort of meaningful way without taking the ADA into consideration. Therefore, the failure of the report or the ethics opinions to do so is quite remarkable. The following sections discuss the various ways that consideration of the underlying policies and specifics of the ADA might better inform the lawyer well-being movement.

A. Underlying Policies of the ADA

The ADA defines "disability" as a physical or mental impairment that substantially limits a major life activity. One also has a disability for purposes of the ADA when one has "a record of such an impairment" or when a defendant takes a prohibited action against that individual based on the perception that the individual has a physical or mental impairment. The decision to define the concept of disability in terms of impairments that are actually substantially limiting or that cause an employer to subject an individual to adverse treatment is significant.

This definition reflects a deliberate shift from the so-called "medical model" of disability. The medical model tended to reduce the idea of disability to an individual's underlying medical conditions, rather than involving societal responses to these conditions. Defining disability in terms of underlying medical conditions tended to prevent any inquiry into an individual's actual abilities. As one author put it, this view of disability treated disability "as a medically determined category that is inconsistent with work." Under this view, the existence of a physical or mental impairment was inherently limiting, and the individual "afflicted" with the impairment was in need of a medical cure. The effect was to label and stigmatize the individual "with a status of physiological inferiority."

The ADA took a different approach. The ADA's multi-pronged definition of disability recognizes that not all physical or mental impairments are substantially limiting, and sometimes the limitation may stem from others' reactions to an impairment. In short, the ADA recognizes that stereotypical assumptions about what an individual can or cannot do based simply on a medical diagnosis can be as limiting as an impairment itself.

In the employment context, the ultimate inquiry under the ADA is not whether an individual has a physical or mental impairment but whether the individual with a disability is qualified for the position in question. This requires an individualized assessment. An individual with a disability is qualified for a position when the individual can perform the essential functions of a position with or without a reasonable accommodation. In addition to recognizing that not all impairments are disqualifying, the ADA recognizes that some individuals with physical or mental impairments are perfectly capable of performing the essential functions of their jobs with relatively inexpensive or minor adjustments to the way the job is normally performed.

The ADA has helped reshape the way individuals, employers, and courts think about disability. Yet, the National Task Force Report never references the ADA, and the term "disability" appears only infrequently. Instead, the authors employ a medical model of disability that largely views mental impairments or mental health issues as disqualifying. The report regularly discusses "impairments" and the steps other lawyers should take to prevent a lawyer with an impairment from causing harm. But rarely is there any suggestion that not all impairments pose a significant risk of harm to a client or are even always significantly limiting.

The ethics opinions on the subject of lawyers with mental impairments take a similar approach. The opinions tend to dwell not on the issues raised when a lawyer has a mental impairment that substantially limits the ability of the lawyer to competently represent clients, but on the supposed issues raised by the mere fact that a lawyer has a mental impairment. As a result, the opinions usually bypass any discussion of the fact that a lawyer with a mental impairment may be perfectly qualified to perform the essential functions of a lawyer.

If ethics committees truly wish to reduce the stigma associated with mental impairments, the opinions could begin by incorporating the ADA's terminology and concepts. Rather than treating mental impairments as inherently limiting, ethics opinions should discuss impairments in terms of whether they are substantially limiting for a particular attorney, in other words, whether they amount to disabilities. As such, ethics opinions should focus on whether an individual lawyer with a disability can perform the essential functions of a position, with or without a reasonable accommodation.

In doing so, leaders in the legal profession may come to find that the Rules of Professional Conduct and legal rules of the ADA coexist quite nicely. For example, the ADA defines the essential functions of a position as the "fundamental job duties" an employee must be able to perform. Equal Employment Opportunity Commission (EEOC) guidance on the issue of lawyers with disabilities has listed several duties that are essential functions for many attorney positions, including conducting legal research, writing motions and briefs, counseling clients, drafting opinion letters, presenting an argument before an appellate court, and conducting depositions and trials. Of course, the essential functions of a tax lawyer position are likely to be different than the essential functions of a public defender position. But the Rules of Professional Conduct make clear that whatever specific function a lawyer must perform, the lawyer must be able to do so competently and diligently. In short, a lawyer who cannot perform the essential functions of a job in a manner that complies with the Rules of Professional Conduct is not qualified for the position in question.

Ethics opinions may also look to the ADA's reasonable accommodation requirement when discussing a lawyer's supervisory duties under Rule 5.1. In fact, ABA Formal Opinion 03–429 is one of the only ethics opinions to address this requirement in the context of a lawyers' ethical obligations under Rule 5.1. When discussing the obligation of a partner or lawyer with similar managerial authority to make reasonable efforts to adopt measures to prevent an impaired lawyer from violating the Rules of Professional Conduct, the opinion observes that "[s]ome impairments may be accommodated." The opinion suggests that if, due to an impairment, a lawyer is unable to perform the essential functions of a job as the job is currently constituted, a supervisory lawyer may be able to satisfy the lawyer's obligations under Rule 5.1 by seeking to alter the manner in which those duties are performed or perhaps by reassigning the lawyer to a position involving duties the lawyer can perform. In doing so, the supervisory lawyer may fulfill the lawyer's legal obligations under the ADA as well as the lawyer's ethical obligations under Rule 5.1.

CONCLUSION

As one of the chief Senate sponsors of the ADA noted, the chief "thesis" of the ADA is that "people with disabilities ought to be judged on the basis of their abilities; they should not be judged nor discriminated against based on unfounded fear, prejudice, ignorance, or mythologies; people ought to be judged based upon the relevant medical evidence and the abilities they have." The National Task Force's report deserves praise for bringing increased attention to the issue of well-being in the legal profession and for some of its recommendations. But the fact that the report fails to incorporate the basic principles and substance of the ADA represents a glaring shortcoming. As a result, the report perpetuates some of the unfounded fear, prejudice, ignorance, and myths the ADA was designed to combat. The ethics opinions concerning lawyers with mental impairments largely suffer from the same flaws. In the process, the opinions provide advice that might create a risk of legal liability.

If and when there is a second edition of the National Task Force Report, the authors should strive to communicate the basic thesis of the ADA when addressing the issue of lawyer well-being. Currently, the words "Americans with Disabilities Act" do not even appear in the report, and the term "disability" itself is mentioned only in passing. The report provides an opportunity to help educate lawyers about the nature of disability as it applies to well-being. The only way the authors can truly educate lawyers on the subject is by articulating the values of the ADA. The authors of ethics opinions have a similar opportunity to explain to lawyers how their ethical obligations are consistent with their legal obligations under the ADA.

* * *

Problem 27.1. Considering the Task Force Report and the articles cited above, analyze the advantages and disadvantages of amending Rule 1.1 to include lawyer well-being in the definition of attorney competence. If the inclusion of well-being in Rule 1.1 is not intended to be a threat or a basis for discipline, what is the purpose of a rule change? Would such a change be effective in accomplishing that purpose?

* * *

B. WHEN SHOULD THE BAR, EMPLOYERS, AND COLLEAGUES INTERVENE TO ADDRESS CONCERNS ABOUT ATTORNEY WELL-BEING?

1. BAR ADMISSION HURDLES FOR APPLICANTS WITH ALCOHOL- AND DRUG-RELATED INCIDENTS IN THEIR PAST

One way the bar attempts to address well-being issues is through the bar admission process. For example, in Tennessee, a court rule gives the Tennessee Board of Law Examiners (TBLE) authority to investigate and make a determination of the character and fitness of each bar applicant to become a licensed attorney. Tenn. Sup. Ct. R. 7, Article 6. Although the Tennessee Lawyers Assistance Program (TLAP) promotes itself as a confidential resource for law students, TLAP plays a different role when the TBLE refers a bar applicant to TLAP for an evaluation related to fitness to practice. Tenn. Sup. Ct. R. 7, 6.04(d). In that case, TLAP completes an evaluation, makes recommendations (such as that the applicant should have a monitoring agreement), and, when there is a monitoring agreement, issues progress reports to the disciplinary authority about compliance or noncompliance. Tenn. Sup. Ct. R. 33.05(E)(3), 33.07. If a bar applicant does not submit to an evaluation by TLAP, that fact is sufficient basis to deny bar admission. Tenn. Sup. Ct. R. 7, Sec. 6.04(d).

TLAP's recommendation of a monitoring agreement typically will cause the TBLE to exercise its authority to order "conditional admission." The conditional admission rule allows the TBLE to condition admission on the applicant's compliance with requirements (such as those in a monitoring agreement) "tailored to detect and deter conduct, conditions or behavior which could render an applicant unfit to practice law or pose a risk to clients or the public and to encourage continued abstinence, treatment, remediation, counseling, or other support" and that are based on "clinical or other appropriate evaluations," "take into consideration the recommendations of qualified professionals, when appropriate," and protect the applicant's privacy. Tenn. Sup. Ct. R. 7, sec. 10.05(a), (c). The bar applicant is responsible for any cost of investigation, testing, and monitoring. Tenn. Sup. Ct. R. 7, sec. 10.05(g). Conditional admission can be required for up to 60 months. Tenn. Sup. Ct. R. 7, sec. 10.05(e).

A recent bar applicant's experience provides a concrete example of how these rules impact bar applicants. This individual wants to share his story in hopes that it might be helpful to future bar applicants and may even lead to change in the current system.

MY BAR ADMISSION EXPERIENCE

By Anonymous (2023)

Law school was the first academic experience that clicked for me. It was a natural fit. I was engaged in my classes. In fact, I only missed three classes in law school—two for job interviews and one for a funeral. And I remember coming into school the day after the funeral to talk to the professor about the material I had missed. I developed friendships with classmates and formed close relationships with several professors. I finished at the top of my class. I accepted an associate position at a great law firm that I worked for while I was in law school.

Once I found a sense of purpose in law school, I became a different person than I had been in undergrad. Back then, I was abusing alcohol and smoking weed because I wasn't secure in who I was. I wanted to present a fun, alpha-male social appearance. It was never that I couldn't stop drinking or using marijuana. My issues were related to my personal identity.

When I was nineteen and a sophomore in college, I had three arrests that were all later expunged. The first was for underage consumption and public intoxication. While out with friends that night, I was relieving myself under a bridge near campus. The second was also for underage consumption and public intoxication. I had been walking home on campus, wearing a sports jersey, when a car drove by and shouted some profanity about my team. I responded, yelling back. A police officer happened to hear this and then stopped me. Both of these arrests were resolved with community service and an alcohol course. The arrests were subsequently expunged from my record. My third arrest was related to a party I attended in my home town. Someone had called in a noise complaint. When the police arrived, they did an illegal search of our cars. When the police found a small amount of marijuana in my car, I was cited for simple possession. Because the search was determined to be illegal, the prosecutor did not pursue charges. I also had that expunged.

At the age of twenty-five, when I finished law school, I don't think anyone in the building who spent time with me would say that they had any concerns about me. They might have worried that I'd be a workaholic. But no one who knew me was concerned that I had a substance abuse problem. I drank socially, but I also went long stretches without drinking at all, particularly in the weeks prior to final exams. I received a referral to student conduct after being written up for carrying an airplane size bottle of alcohol into a football game during law school. I immediately disclosed that to the law school's dean of students and admitted my mistake.

As part of my bar application, I disclosed the three expunged arrests and the student conduct matter. Like all Tennessee bar applicants, I had a character and fitness interview with a member of the bar. I remember thinking that it went really well. I had a good conversation with the attorney. My impression was that everything was good. I think that my interviewer saw that I had fully disclosed prior conduct, I was contrite, I had a strong academic record, and I had reformed myself.

I heard from the [Tennessee Board of Law Examiners ("TBLE")] a day or two after bar results came out. It was a weekend when I was still really excited about passing the bar exam. But the notice said that I was subject to additional character and fitness investigation. I was referred to [Tennessee Lawyers Assistance Program ("TLAP")] for additional evaluation.

I felt distraught and downtrodden. Even though I had changed my life in law school, it felt like that didn't matter. The arrests from when I was nineteen were still the focus. At this point, I had a feeling in my gut that things weren't going to go well. But I had no idea what was going to happen.

When I met with the director of TLAP, he got me to trust him pretty quickly. I told him my story. I shared that my father, uncle, and grandfather were alcoholics. I told him that as a way of acknowledging that I know what alcoholism looks like. I see how someone might have a concern about me, but that fails to take into consideration who I am as a person. I thought of the TLAP director as a counselor who was trying to help me.

Based on what he said, I thought he was going to act as my intermediary. He would go with me before the TBLE to get them to sign off on my admission to the bar. When I left that meeting, I thought he was going to help me.

I quickly realized that I was wrong. I later came to think of him as my judge, jury, bailiff, and psychologist. It was as if full authority had been delegated to him and that whatever he told the TBLE was going to seal my fate. Shortly after our meeting, he put in writing that I needed to complete an evaluation at a treatment facility. He gave me a list of options. There were only two that were nearby. I chose the one that would be the least expensive—approximately $8,000.

I was evaluated at a treatment facility for 72 hours. I was surrounded by people who appeared to be in bad condition. There was a pilot whose hands were shaking so much he couldn't eat his lunch. I was assigned a treatment center patient/resident who was about my age. He was supposed to show me the bathroom and where to eat—and monitor me. He told me that he entered the facility after regularly drinking 18 beers a night for months.

As part of the evaluation, they took my hair, blood, and urine. They only found evidence of alcohol use. I filled out a bunch of questionnaires. They asked about which substances I had used. I had to write out everything about the arrests and my family history. They talked to my firm's managing partner, as well as my girlfriend, mother, and one of my law professors. I had sit-down, one-on-one meetings with two psychiatrists. One was trying to be my best friend and get me to open up; the other doctor was stone cold, showed no emotions, and was completely factual.

On the afternoon of the final day, the stone-cold doctor said something along the lines of, "You had problems in the past, but I think you're in remission." The other doctor opined that I needed a monitoring agreement and that I would need to be sober for a year. We got onto a call with TLAP's director. As soon as the doctor made that recommendation about monitoring, TLAP's director started coordinating the logistics. I thought I was doomed.

I thought about pleading with the TLAP director. I thought about suing. I talked to several lawyers I trust. All of them threw their hands in the air and said "I think you have to do this." I understood I would not get my license if I didn't do it. So I signed the monitoring agreement so that I could be conditionally admitted.

My one-year monitoring agreement provides that its purpose is "diagnostic monitoring to rule out substance use disorders." (Consistent with this, the facility's assessment report does *not* diagnose me with any substance use disorder. The report says that I "may benefit from a period of diagnostic monitoring with TLAP to demonstrate that [I do] not have a problem with either alcohol or drugs.") Among other things, the monitoring agreement required me to be abstinent from alcohol and substance use, participate in daily check-ins by phone app, and participate in random drug and alcohol screenings within six hours of notification. Additionally, under the monitoring agreement, I was required to meet with a peer monitor every Friday for the entire year, meet with TLAP four times during the year, and participate in therapy during the year.

I had to inform my firm about the monitoring agreement, because the terms of the agreement would sometimes require me to be late for work to submit to drug testing. I passed all of the drug tests because I was abstinent—as required by the agreement—for the entire year. I had to pay for both the tests and the therapy required by the monitoring agreement. I estimate that in the course of the year, I spent approximately $4,000. This means my total cost of assessment and monitoring was approximately $12,000. I appreciate that I was able to afford this because I had a job that paid me well. I do not know how someone with a lower-paying position would be able to pay for this without loans or other resources.

I am telling my story because I would like to help future bar applicants who are in this situation. I would encourage them to talk to their trusted advisors if they find themselves dealing with these issues. I think there are problems with the current system—that I hope are apparent from my story—that need to be addressed.

* * *

Problem 27.2. Do you think it was necessary for public protection for Anonymous to have a one-year "diagnostic" monitoring agreement to rule out substance abuse? Regardless of your answer, do you think it is appropriate for Anonymous and other bar applicants to bear the cost of assessment and monitoring? What changes, if any, would you recommend in the bar admission process (including the lawyer assistance program's role) for applicants with alcohol- or drug-related arrests or charges in their past, including ones that have been expunged?

Problem 27.3. The Task Force Report recommends that law schools and others should ally themselves with lawyer assistance programs to provide treatment and other services to law students and lawyers. Task Force Report, p. 14. After reading about Anonymous' bar admission experience, would you have any concern about your law school recommending that you utilize services of your state lawyer assistance program prior to bar admission, particularly if you had any alcohol- or drug-related arrests or charges in your past?

* * *

2. PROVIDING RESOURCES AND SUPPORT FOR LAWYERS

Another way bar authorities and legal employers might address well-being issues is to offer confidential resources and support to members of the profession who are struggling but not engaged in professional misconduct. Outside of the bar admission and discipline processes (when applicants and attorneys may be referred there for *non-confidential* services), lawyer assistance programs can provide a confidential resource for law students, lawyers, and judges seeking help to address stress, mental health concerns, and substance abuse. This can include referrals to therapists, treatment centers, support groups, and other resources.

The Task Force Report offers several suggestions for how legal employers can support lawyer well-being. ABA Model Rule 5.1(a) requires law firm partners and others with similar managerial authority to make reasonable efforts to develop internal policies and practices—or "ethical infrastructures"—that further competent representation. Similarly, the Report suggests that legal employers establish infrastructures designed to promote well-being. For example, the Report suggests that law firms establish a Wellness Committee or a Wellness Advocate with responsibility for "evaluating the work environment, identifying and addressing policies and procedures that create the greatest mental distress among employees, identifying how best to promote a positive state of well-being, and tracking progress of well-being strategies." Task Force Report, p. 31. This could include developing policies and practices that allow for meaningful vacations, discourage excessive work, and "protect time for lawyers to recover from work demands by regulating work-related calls and emails during evenings, weekends, and vacations." *Id.* Appendix D.

Partners, managers, and supervisors can also contribute to lawyer well-being by engaging with lawyers who may be experiencing addiction or mental health issues in a constructive manner. In discussing a supervisor's responsibilities under Model Rule 5.1, some legal ethics opinions suggest an almost confrontational approach when a supervisor suspects that another lawyer is experiencing a well-being issue. Some opinions recommend that the supervisor "confront the impaired lawyer with the facts of his impairment" and "forcefully urg[e]," "insist," or "require" that the lawyer "seek appropriate assistance, counseling, therapy, or treatment." *See* Alex B. Long, *What the Lawyer Well-Being Movement Could Learn from the Americans with Disabilities Act*, WM. & MARY L. REV. ONLINE 63, 85 (2022) (quoting opinions). However, the Americans with Disabilities Act places limits on employer's ability to ask questions that are likely to elicit information about a disability or to require that an employee undergo a medical exam or treatment based on general assumptions about an employee's condition. Instead, there must be specific evidence that would cause a reasonable person to question the employee's ability to perform the job before such action is permitted. Rather than *confronting* an individual who might be experiencing an issue, a better approach—and one more consistent with the letter and spirit of the ADA—might be for a supervisor to engage in a cooperative and nonconfrontational, interactive process with the lawyer that is designed to help the parties exchange information in an effort to determine an appropriate accommodation or means of addressing the lawyer's issues.

* * *

Problem 27.4. Read the Task Force Report's Recommendations for Lawyer Assistance Programs, which is available at https://lawyerwellbeing.net/wp-content/uploads/2017/11/Lawyer-Wellbeing-Report.pdf. In your opinion, which of the specific recommendations are most likely to be beneficial for the legal profession as a whole, as well as individual lawyers? Read the Task Force Report's Recommendations for Legal Employers, including Appendix D. Which of the specific recommendations are most likely to contribute to a healthy organizational culture? What are some of the possible impediments to implementing these recommendations?

* * *

3. WHEN CLIENTS ARE HARMED BY AN ATTORNEY'S SUBSTANCE ABUSE

The previous sections highlighted the dangers of the bar, lawyer assistance programs, and colleagues imposing unnecessary burdens upon or even discriminating against attorneys who may or may not have a substance use disorder or mental health diagnosis. But when an impaired lawyer harms a client, the analysis changes. The following case addresses this issue.

IN THE MATTER OF JUSTIN K. HOLSTIN, RESPONDENT
413 P.3d 447 (Kan. 2018)

In a letter signed March 14, 2018, addressed to the Clerk of the Appellate Courts, respondent Justin K. Holstin, an attorney admitted to practice law in the state of Kansas, voluntarily surrendered his license to practice law in Kansas, pursuant to Supreme Court Rule 217.

At the time the respondent surrendered his license, four disciplinary complaints were pending, alleging that the respondent violated the Kansas Rules of Professional Conduct 1.15 (safekeeping property) and 8.4(g) (professional misconduct that reflects adversely on the lawyer's fitness to practice law).

On February 8, 2018, at 9:45 a.m. a hearing panel of the Kansas Board for Discipline of Attorneys convened a hearing on the formal complaint.

During the hearing, the hearing panel became concerned that the respondent was under the influence of alcohol. The hearing panel recessed the hearing, made arrangements for alcohol testing, and requested the respondent submit to testing to determine the presence of the alcohol. The respondent agreed to submit to the testing. A representative from the Kansas Lawyers Assistance Program along with a representative from the Disciplinary Administrator's office transported the respondent to a facility for the alcohol testing. The respondent's breath alcohol concentration at 11:17 a.m. was .185. To validate its accuracy, a second test was administered at 11:33 a.m. indicating a breath alcohol concentration level of .200. Also on February 8, 2018, the Disciplinary Administrator filed a motion for temporary suspension requesting that the court issue an order to the respondent to show cause why his license should not be temporarily suspended. On February 13, 2018, the court issued an order to show cause and scheduled the matter for argument on March 6, 2018. On March 6, 2018, Kimberly L. Knoll, Deputy Disciplinary Administrator, and the respondent appeared before the court and argued the motion for temporary suspension. For good cause shown, on March 7, 2018, the court granted the motion and ordered the temporary suspension of the respondent's license to practice law.

This court finds that the surrender of the respondent's license should be accepted and that the respondent should be disbarred.

IT IS THEREFORE ORDERED that Justin K. Holstin be and he is hereby disbarred from the practice of law in Kansas, and his license and privilege to practice law are hereby revoked.

* * *

Problem 27.5. While the *Holstin* case does not reveal the specifics of how clients were harmed by the attorney's conduct, we can see that there were four ethics complaints against Holstin, with at least one alleging violations related to safekeeping of client property, in addition to allegations of misconduct that reflects adversely on the lawyer's fitness to practice law. Do you think that client harm should be a prerequisite to the bar disciplining an attorney struggling with substance abuse? Or would it be appropriate for an attorney to be disciplined because colleagues report that the attorney has a substance use disorder that reflects adversely on the lawyer's fitness but has not yet specifically caused harm? What are the benefits and risks of each approach?

* * *

4. IDENTIFYING AND ADDRESSING THE WARNING SIGNS OF AN ATTORNEY IN DISTRESS

The following article was written by attorney Joanna Litt following the suicide of her attorney-husband, Gabe Litt. As you read this piece, consider the factors that contributed to Gabe Litt's deteriorating mental state, the reasons his colleagues and firm might have overlooked signs of distress or chosen not to act, and whether the attorney well-being movement discussed in this chapter may have a positive impact on preventing lawyer suicide in the future.

'BIG LAW KILLED MY HUSBAND': AN OPEN LETTER FROM A SIDLEY PARTNER'S WIDOW[1]

Joanna Litt
The American Lawyer (Nov. 12, 2018)

My husband took his life—our life—on Sunday, October 14, one month to the day before our 10-year wedding anniversary. We had been planning a trip for over a year in anticipation of celebrating.

I'm beyond lost and I don't know how I'm going to get through the rest of my life. Gabe was my best friend, my partner, my lover, and my constant. I turned to him for everything, and he was always there with the most perfect advice and words. He was my world, and after losing him, I can absolutely say, my better half. . . . And now he's gone. He saw no other choice or path.

I never thought in a million years that he could or would do that. And I keep going back to one thought: "Big Law" killed my husband.

We met on our first day of law school (he graduated third in our class). We had every class together and sat next to each other for two bars because of our last names. He was the smartest person I had ever met. He was also the kindest, most selfless person I've ever met.

I know in my heart that overall, more than anything, we were happy. I would find myself during the day thinking how lucky I was to have him and our life. No one made me feel more special and loved—everything he did, he did for us. And that's why I have this overwhelming need to tell our story, his story. I don't want anyone else to experience the utter shock and pain I am in.

Gabe and I worked hard at our marriage. Marriage isn't easy and I would never pretend it was. Our most serious problem revolved around

---

[1] Full article available at: www.law.com/americanlawyer/2018/11/12/big-law-killed-my-husband-an-open-letter-from-a-sidley-partners-widow/. This excerpt reprinted with permission from the 2018 edition of The American Lawyer © 2018 ALM Global Properties, LLC. All rights reserved. Further duplication without permission is prohibited, contact 877-256-2472 or asset-and-logo-licensing@alm.com.

Gabe's struggle with binge drinking. It wasn't on a daily basis, but maybe three or four times a year there would be some event or function where he drank too much.... I didn't have much compassion or realize his drinking was masking a deeper pain and I made him feel very guilty....

He saw someone professionally a few times, but that was it.

Then there were a series of ill-fated events at work. First, his mentor and confidant suddenly announced he was leaving the firm. This had a huge impact on Gabe personally. It also caused a big shake up at the firm, and another of his treasured partners left to take early retirement.

Gabe, thrust suddenly into an important leadership role, was told in no uncertain terms that the firm was not going to hire any lateral support. Shortly thereafter, the last partner who was senior to Gabe decided to leave, and an associate whom Gabe spent a lot of time mentoring also left....

It was also during this time that Gabe was asked to chair the summer associate program. [The firm's] position in some rankings had fallen and Gabe poured his heart and soul into that program. I know there were many others that helped him, but he passionately assumed responsibility for all 13 candidates, wanting to make sure they had the professional summer experience of a lifetime and wouldn't hesitate to accept an offer from the firm. The success of the program was overwhelming and he didn't even tell me. I found out from someone after he died that the associate reviews were glowing.

Finally, Gabe started working on the Mattress Firm case—a huge bankruptcy. It was a little over a month away from filing a Chapter 11 petition, and I had never seen him so stressed out and anxious. He was trying not to burden me with what was going on, but he wasn't sleeping, I hadn't seen him smile in weeks, and most everything he said was negative.

He told me he had experienced stress during cases before, but it had never been this bad. I didn't know what to do....

The Sunday before leaving to file in Delaware, he spent all day at the office. When I finally called him that evening, it was clear he was in distress and had been working himself to exhaustion. He told me his body was failing him. I picked him up and we decided he should go to the emergency room. He actually said to me on the way there, "You know, if we go, this is the end of my career."

I've never felt so helpless in my life. I didn't know whom to reach out to or to tell my husband was in crisis. I called his closest colleague and asked if she had noticed anything unusual with his behavior at work. She said he was working more with his door closed, and then she said something I'll never forget: She said his sense of humor had been gone for a while. I asked her to keep an eye on him at work and then I just brought him home. I tried to make sure he slept and was rehydrating and eating so he could make the trip to Delaware.

About a week later Mattress Firm publicly filed. I sent an article announcing the bankruptcy to my mom and a couple of close friends with the exact words, "This is the case that is killing my husband."

Gabe came home from Delaware late Tuesday evening. I was hoping the worst was over, but he wasn't any better. I convinced him to skip a conference in Los Angeles that he was supposed to attend that Wednesday and Thursday and we stayed home together. I thought this would do him some good, but what I found out later was that he had stopped responding to work emails. And when he told me he was going into work that Friday, he instead spent the day at his biological father's grave—a man he never met—a couple of hours away from our home.

During this terrible spiral, I told him to quit. I told him we could sell our beautiful house and move to Mammoth, our happy place, and snowboard all winter and then figure it out. He said he couldn't quit in the middle of a case. The irony is not lost on me that he found it easier to kill himself. . . .

Suicide has now become my new world and I am desperately searching for answers. Though it's only the beginning stages of trying to figure out why this happened, I came across a concept, maladaptive perfectionism, that combines unrealistic standards of achievement with hypercriticism of failing to meet them.

Gabe displayed most if not all of the characteristics. Simply put, he would rather die than live with the consequences of people thinking he was a failure.

Looking back on the things Gabe confided in me, I now know I missed a lot of signs. He told me he felt like he was doing the work of three people—and I think that's being generous. He told me the deal to resolve the bankruptcy kept changing. He also felt that while a senior partner in Chicago was heading the case, a lot of pressure fell directly on him. . . . He said he felt like a phony who had everyone fooled about his abilities as a lawyer, and thought after this case was over, he was going to be fired—despite having won honors for his work.

On the morning he killed himself, he said he got an email and had to go into work to put something together. I wanted to ask if I could go with him and just sit there, but instead, I simply offered to make him a sandwich for lunch. And without any hesitation, he said, "No baby, I'll be fine—I won't be long." I'll be haunted by those words forever. . . .

And then he left, taking his gun with him, and shot himself in the head in the sterile, concrete parking structure of his high-rise office building.

I feel like I lost my husband so quickly—within the course of a month—but I'm now starting to realize how hard he must have been on himself all the time. The constant striving to be perfect at work, to be the perfect husband, son, uncle, brother and friend. And then living with this deep unbearable shame that he wasn't performing to the impossibly high standards he set for himself. He said a few times how he couldn't turn off his head, but again, I didn't understand the severity of that statement.

. . .

[At a memorial service at the firm], I heard story after story about Gabe's encouraging nature and how he made people feel like they could succeed at anything they put their mind to. One close colleague said she wished "Gabe had his own Gabe."

Gabe lived his life with integrity and treated those around him with sincerity, kindness, and a genuine sense of presence. Unfortunately, I know my husband died not knowing the impact he had on so many people. I believe he died feeling overworked, inferior and undervalued. And I know he died with a lot of shame.

So as I write our story and think about it more and more, I know "Big Law" didn't directly kill my husband—because he had a deep, hereditary mental health disorder and lacked essential coping mechanisms. But these influences, coupled with a high-pressure job and a culture where it's shameful to ask for help, shameful to be vulnerable, and shameful not to be perfect, created a perfect storm.

I don't have any immediate solutions, but for the sake of retaining people like Gabe in these important professions, something needs to change. . . .

* * *

Problem 27.6. Suicide & Crisis Lifeline. If you or someone in your life is thinking about suicide, the Suicide and Crisis Lifeline is available 24 hours a day by texting or calling 988. For more information, including stories of hope and recovery, the 988 Suicide & Crisis Lifeline's website is https://988lifeline.org.

Problem 27.7. Your Reflections on Joanna and Gabe Litt's Story. Do you agree with Joanna Litt's assessment about the factors that created the "perfect storm" that contributed to Gabe Litt's suicide? Are there specific recommendations you would make to law firms to prevent or lessen the risk of attorney suicide? What actions would you have taken if you had been Gabe Litt's colleague?

* * *

C. THRIVING AS LAW STUDENTS AND LAWYERS: MAKING CHOICES AND DEVELOPING TOOLS TO SUPPORT YOUR WELL-BEING

Margaret Swarbrick is credited with developing a framework for understanding the dimensions of wellness and their connection to increased life satisfaction. She explains that with her approach, "People are given an active role and responsibilities to self-monitor their own health behaviors and increase activity in the dimension where they perceive there is an imbalance." Margaret Swarbrick, *A Wellness Approach*, PSYCHIATRIC REHABILITATION JOURNAL, Vol 29, n. 4, 311–4 (Spring 2006).

While there are different conceptualizations of the dimensions of wellness, Swarbrick and her co-author Jay Yudof describe wellness in eight dimensions:

- Emotional
- Financial
- Social
- Spiritual
- Occupational
- Physical
- Intellectual
- Environmental

Swarbrick and Yudof have created an online guide that provides additional detail about opportunities to enhance each wellness dimension. Peggy Swarbick & Jay Yudof, *8 Dimensions of Wellness*, Collaborative Support Networks of NJ (2015), available at https://www.center4healthandsdc.org/uploads/7/1/1/4/71142589/wellness_in_8_dimensions_booklet_with_daily_plan.pdf.

The following discussion highlights how some of these aspects of wellness can be improved through thoughtful selection of where you practice law, as well as the well-being practices you adopt as an attorney. This discussion is not meant to be all-encompassing. Rather, each section is intended to give you some concrete suggestions to consider in developing a plan to thrive as a lawyer.

1. CONSIDERATIONS IN SELECTING YOUR EMPLOYERS THROUGH THE YEARS

Given the interconnectedness of the dimensions of well-being, your workplace will undoubtedly have an impact on your personal wellness. Your first post-graduation job is one step in a career that will likely include several job changes. Early-career legal jobs may not be a perfect match for you and that is okay. In these first positions, you are developing your competencies and learning about the type of workplace setting you enjoy. It is also helpful to recognize that your ideal work environment may change over time. What fits for you five years after graduation may not work for you five years later. You have the freedom to make job changes and completely reinvent yourself throughout your career. A law degree provides you a great deal of flexibility to pivot and change.

Many high-paying legal jobs can be all-consuming, taking time and energy away from other aspects of a rewarding life. And while there may be benefits that justify you accepting such a position (the opportunity to work on interesting legal issues, learning from great lawyers, salary to pay off student loans, etc.), you should also consider the costs, as well as whether you see a long-term future there. (For example, are there more senior attorneys who are living the life you hope to live in the years ahead?) Female lawyers are often told that motherhood may stand in the way of them succeeding in some law firms. The narrative is that women typically take primary responsibility for raising children, so when female attorneys become mothers, they often leave the firm to keep up with their self-imposed parenting responsibility. This misleading narrative allows firms to dodge responsibility for losing a disproportionate number of female lawyers. After all, firms have no control over motherhood and women's choices of how to parent.

But lawyers should reframe the question as this: is it possible to succeed at the firm if the lawyer wants or needs to spend time on things outside of the practice of law? On the issue of parenthood, lawyers should ask if it is possible for a lawyer with young or school-age children to succeed in the firm if the lawyer is a single parent or has a spouse that works outside of the home. While firms would never say "we rely upon the unpaid labor of our attorneys' spouses," in some firms, the only attorneys who can meet the firm's time demands (particularly after parenthood) are ones with a stay-at-home spouse who cares for all of the family's needs, including the lawyer's needs. This has a disproportionate impact on female attorneys whose spouses are more likely to work outside the home.

The good news is that many legal employers make it possible for lawyers to be single parents or part of a two-career family while actively participating in parenting and other activities outside of work. Most women who leave a firm after having children do not leave the legal workforce; they move on to a legal employer that is a better fit for their priorities. *See* Paula Schaefer, *On Balance: Leading by Leaving*, 83 TENN. L. REV. 931 (2016).

In recent years, a number of researchers have turned their focus to the question of what a lawyer should look for in a legal workplace that will lead to happiness, motivation, and an overall sense of well-being. Lawrence Krieger and Kennon Sheldon use self-determination theory as a guide for their research into lawyer happiness. Self-determination theory posits that people feel a greater sense of motivation at work when three psychological needs are met: (1) they feel competent in their work; (2) they have a sense of autonomy and authenticity; and (3) they experience a sense of relatedness/connectedness to their colleagues.

Krieger and Sheldon's recent research involved a survey completed by over 6,000 lawyers in four states. The survey data supported Krieger and Sheldon's hypothesis that there is a strong correlation between competence, autonomy, and relatedness for lawyer well-being. The researchers concluded that the correlations "indicate that well-being co-occurs with these factors so robustly that it may not be possible to experience thriving without relative satisfaction of all of these needs." Krieger and Sheldon also concluded from their study that some of the external factors thought to have an impact on happiness (prestige, earnings) were not as important as internal motivation. Among their findings: lawyers with prestigious jobs are less happy than "service" lawyers that typically received the lowest pay; as lawyer income increased, well-being decreased; and billable hours were the strongest negative predictor of well-being. Lawrence S. Krieger & Kennon M. Sheldon, *What Makes Lawyers Happy?: A Data-Driven Prescription to Redefine Professional Success*, 83 GEO. WASH. L. REV. 554 (2015).

* * *

Problem 27.8. Despite research like Krieger and Sheldon's, many lawyers (at least initially) are drawn to large firms that pay high salaries. Do you perceive that your classmates place a higher value on such jobs? If so, what factors (such as salary) or messages—from professors, alumni, career services, family, or others—contribute to this perception? Can and should law schools work to change that perception?

* * *

2. YOUR MINDSET MATTERS: FRAME STRESSFUL SITUATIONS AS EXCITING AND EMBRACE YOUR ABILITY TO GROW

Anne Brafford draws on her background as a lawyer and a student of positive psychology in her book *Positive Professionals: Creating High-Performing Profitable Firms through the Science of Engagement* (ABA Law Practice Div. 2017). Much of Brafford's book is focused on how law firm leadership can enhance engagement among lawyers and create positive environments in law firms. But she also provides science-backed suggestions that law students and new attorneys can apply to change their mindset to improve their performance.

Research reveals that a "positive stress mindset" leads to better performance. Relying upon findings of prior research studies, Brafford offers a positive stress mindset checklist. It provides that when encountering a stressful situation (such as arguing a motion in court or making a presentation), a person should (1) acknowledge the stress; and (2) frame it as a positive thing ("I'm jittery because this is important and I care about doing well."). The person should next (3) label the feelings as excitement rather than focusing on calming down; (4) reflect upon the person's strengths and previous successes; (5) think about (or write down) the person's values; and (6) picture the support of loved ones.

Supporting the "excitement" element of the checklist, Brafford discusses a 2014 study by Alison Brooks in which participants were asked to perform one of three stressful tasks. Participants were divided into four groups and assigned a statement to say or think before completing the task: (1) "I am excited." (2) "I am anxious." (3) "I am calm." The fourth group was not asked to think or say anything. The participants' anxiety wasn't lessened regardless of group, but the "excited" group performed best on the three tasks. Brafford explains, "If we interpret jittery feelings as excitement rather than anxiety, our stress response can be a powerful resource.... [O]ur body surges with a chemical cocktail of endorphins, adrenaline, cortisol, testosterone, and dopamine. Our breath deepens..., senses sharpen, and the brain focuses." *Id.* at 113.

Also in her book, Brafford discusses the advantages of attorneys adopting a "growth mindset." The leading growth mindset researcher is Carol Dweck who has been doing work in this area for decades. Dweck has concluded that the difference between people who succeed and equally talented people who do not is their mindset. Dweck explains that those with a fixed mindset believe that intelligence and abilities are set, while those with a growth mindset believe that effort and engagement can result in improved performance. In short, people with a growth mindset believe that they are in control and have the ability to improve their performance. Legendary Tennessee women's basketball coach Pat Summitt undoubtedly had a growth mindset. If you search for her most famous quotes, many are focused on the importance of hard work—rather than ability—in creating success. For example, Coach Summitt famously said, "Here's how I'm going to beat you: I'm going to outwork you. That's it. That's all there is to it."

Brafford explains that that a growth mindset is supported by science: the brain has the ability to grow and change throughout adulthood. She also describes the negative impact that a fixed mindset can have on performance. Those who believe their abilities are fixed can be harmed by their lack of effort and negative self-talk in areas where they do not believe they are talented. Those with a growth mindset have an enhanced ability to learn and grow.

* * *

Problem 27.9. Watch the talk *Growth Mindset Introduction: What it is, How it Works, and Why it Matters* at https:/m.youtube.com/watch?v=75GFzikmRY0. At the 4:30 minute mark, the talk turns to how a growth mindset influences our ability to learn. Listen to the discussion of the four key ingredients to growth: effort, challenges, mistakes, and feedback. In your own words, how does someone with a fixed mindset deal with these issues? What about a person with a growth mindset? In thinking about these differences, do you now recognize that there are areas of study in law school in which you have had a fixed mindset, believing that others had a natural talent that you lacked? Does understanding the science and power of a growth mindset make you want to approach that area in a new way in the future?

* * *

3. ADOPT A GRATITUDE PRACTICE

Researchers have found a connection between gratitude and mental health. For example, one study asked students who were seeking mental health counseling to also write a weekly letter of gratitude to someone. (The control group in this study only received counseling and another group received counseling and was asked to write about negative experiences rather than gratitude). At four and twelve weeks after the exercise, students who wrote the gratitude letters reported better mental health than those who had only received counseling or who received counseling and wrote about negative experiences. The results also reflected that benefits gradually accrued over time. Y. Joel Wong, *et. al, Does Gratitude Writing Improve the Mental Health of Psychotherapy Clients? Evidence from a Randomized Controlled Trial*, PSYCHOTHERAPY RESEARCH, Vol. 28, No. 2, 192–202 (2018).

UC Davis Psychology Professor Robert Emmons, known as the leading expert on the science of gratitude, explains that the research reveals physical (lower blood pressure), psychological (more positive emotions, joy, pleasure, optimism, and happiness), and social (less lonely and more helpful, forgiving, and outgoing) benefits of having a regular gratitude practice.

A gratitude practice could take one of several forms. Some people devote the end of each day to write three things for which they are grateful. Others mentally reflect upon or pray about moments of gratitude each day. Another approach is to write a letter of gratitude, as mentioned in the Wong study discussed above. Significantly, that study found that it is unnecessary to mail the letter—the key is writing it. In whatever form, gratitude has two key components (according to Dr. Robert Emmons): it affirms there are good things in the world and it recognizes that goodness in our lives comes from others.

In a blog post titled *Why Gratitude is Good* (available at greatergood.berkeley.edu), Dr. Emmons explains some of the reasons a gratitude practice causes a shift. First, he explains that being grateful reminds us to appreciate and celebrate life, rather than taking things for granted. He explains that gratitude causes us to "notice the positives more, and that magnifies the pleasures you get from life. Instead of adapting to goodness, we celebrate goodness." Second, he notes that practicing gratitude blocks our ability to express negative emotions like envy, resentment, and regret which are inconsistent with gratitude. Third, gratitude provides a positive framework or perspective that contributes to resilience following adversity. Finally, those who practice gratitude have a greater sense of self-worth. Dr. Emmons explains, "I think that's because when you're grateful, you have the sense that someone else is looking out for you . . . or you notice a network . . . of people who are responsible for helping you get to where you are right now."

* * *

4. INTEGRATE MINDFULNESS INTO YOUR DAY

There is a growing body of research that having a mindfulness practice is just as important as physical exercise to our health. Mindfulness—defined as a nonjudgmental present moment awareness—can be cultivated through daily meditative practice. The ability to be more present can help you be less reactive to stressful situations. Your present awareness of self can also interrupt patterns of worrying and ruminating. This new habit can break the cycle of chronic stress and its harm to our physical health.

An easy introduction to mindfulness can be found in free online videos and audio recordings. If you search for "box breathing," you will find a number of videos and websites explaining how to do this simple breathing exercise to help reset your breathing, relieve stress and anxiety (by reducing levels of the stress hormone cortisol), and improve concentration. While sitting comfortably or lying down, breathe in deeply for four seconds, hold for four seconds, breath out for four seconds, and hold for four seconds. Try using box breathing for five to ten minutes a couple of times each day. While it can be employed when you feel yourself getting stressed, it can also be helpful to use it on a schedule—such as while sitting in your car for a few quiet minutes before walking into school or work.

Downloading an app (some require a paid subscription) is an option to add more structure to your mindfulness practice. Some currently available apps include Insight Timer, Headspace, and Calm. If you are interested in taking a mindfulness class (usually running over the course of several weeks), you will find numerous online and in-person options in most communities. One well-known course is Mindfulness-Based Stress Reduction or MBSR which was developed in the 1970s by Dr. Jon Kabat-Zinn at the University of Massachusetts Memorial Medical Center. Another class that may be of interest to law students and lawyers is mPEAK (which stands for Mindfulness, Performance Enhancement, Awareness & Knowledge). It was developed to help elite athletes perform at their top level, but can help any professional who wants to use mindfulness to break out of negative patterns of thinking to enhance their performance.

A recent study revealed numerous positive effects for law students who took a mindfulness class—with benefits that will serve them well in practice. Students at Georgia State University School of Law agreed to participate in a research study that measured the impact of mindfulness training on their well-being. One theme that emerged from interviews with students was that the mindfulness breathing exercises introduced in the class helped students manage stress. ("I found the breathing exercises valuable because I noticed that it helped reduce my anxiety in high-stress situations" and "When I had trouble focusing on my homework I would do a breathing meditation and found it easier to complete.")

Based on their review of survey instruments completed by students before and after taking a mindfulness class, the study's authors concluded mindfulness training resulted in the following for students: (1) lowered perceived stress and improved stress management; (2) development in the area of "reappraisal" or the ability to reframe a challenging situation in a more positive way, which reflects resilience; (3) recognition of automatic habits (such as harsh self-criticism) and developing a nonreactive response; (4) increases in self-compassion; and (5) improvements in self-acceptance (accepts and acknowledges good and bad qualities of self) and perception of self as growing, expanding, and open to new experiences. The researchers connected each of these benefits to skills that will help these future lawyers engage in the practice of law. Charity Scott & Paul Verhaeghen, *Calming Down and Waking Up: An Empirical Study of the Effects of Mindfulness Training on Law Students*, 21 NEV. L.J. 277, 302–16 (2020).

* * *

Problem 27.10. Loving Kindness Meditation. In the mindfulness study discussed above, the authors discuss surprise at students' positive reaction to a "loving kindness meditation." They feared that students would find this meditation—in which compassion and positive wishes are offered to oneself—might be viewed as too touchy-feely. But it turned out that students ranked it among their favorite parts of the mindfulness class. If you want to try this meditation, search the web for "loving kindness meditation" and you will find several video and audio options.

* * *

5. SEEK CONFIDENTIAL PROFESSIONAL SUPPORT WHEN YOU STRUGGLE

In particularly stressful times at school or work, we can neglect habits that are good for our health (regular exercise, healthy eating, restorative sleep, etc.) and slip into negative coping strategies. Alcohol and substance abuse, overeating, and disordered sleep can make things worse—especially for those with a heavy workload and/or whose work involves conflict over a prolonged period of time. This can be a warning sign of deteriorating mental health. In short, if your work causes stress and anxiety, the long-term coping mechanism should not be ones that take a further toll on your physical and mental health.

We can sometimes fail to recognize that we are neglecting healthy practices or relying on unhealthy ones. There are tools that can help a person see when things are off course—and motivate the adoption of positive behaviors. Using a fitness tracker can help a person see daily exercise, steps taken, and hours of sleep. Many trackers can be set to remind the wearer to get up and move every hour and go to bed at a set time.

While prior generations once viewed the act of seeking therapy or medical care for mental health or substance abuse as a sign of weakness, much of that stigma is a relic of the past. Today, we recognize that seeking help is necessary to navigate the challenges of modern life, including life in the law.

* * *

Problem 27.11. SMART Goals. A useful approach to creating a plan for achieving a goal is to make it "SMART": Specific, Measurable, Achievable, Relevant, and Time-Bound. For example, a SMART goal related to gratitude is the following: "Before bed each day for the rest of the semester, I will write three things I am grateful for in my journal. I think this will help me appreciate the good things in my life." Using the suggestions from this chapter, consider making a SMART goal that you will focus on this month or semester.

Profile of Attorney Professionalism. Candice Reed drew upon her years of experience as a lawyer and her Masters in Applied Positive Psychology when she designed the course *Thriving as a Lawyer*. Since

2019, she has been teaching the course to rave reviews at her alma mater, the University of Tennessee College of Law.

Reed described the course and some key takeaways from the first class meeting in this 2023 post on LinkedIn:

> I designed the course [*Thriving as a Lawyer*] to introduce law students to the scientific principles of positive psychology and how they may be applied to foster greater wellbeing among law students, attorneys and the legal profession at large. We meet primarily over two weekends during the spring semester, and this year's cohort met for the first time this past weekend. Spending three full days in one law school class is likely no one's ideal way to spend a weekend, but these students energized and inspired me with their enthusiasm, thoughtfulness and engagement with the material and one another. Here are some of my key takeaways from our first weekend together:
>
> - Attorney wellbeing is no longer a taboo subject. These law students recognize that the practice of law is stressful and are yearning for the guidance and skills that will help them successfully navigate around the likely wellbeing pitfalls of the profession.
> - Today's law students are comfortable discussing mental health and are not squeamish or reluctant to raise their hands and seek help when they need it.
> - Law students are considering employers' culture of wellbeing (or lack thereof) when considering job offers. They are looking beyond employers' marketing and talking points and inquiring about flexible work arrangements (and schedules), mental health benefits and insurance coverage, leave policies, etc.
> - Diversity, Equity, Inclusion & Belonging policies and practices are key to cultivating a culture of wellbeing.
> - Law students are not settling. They understand better than prior generations how to protect and bolster their personal wellbeing, and they are not willing to sacrifice that wellbeing for a big(ger) paycheck—at least not indefinitely.
> - Today's law students are plugged in (often literally) and keenly aware of what is going on in the world. They expect positive change and group the adults in the room into two categories; we're either (1) helping or (2) in the way. And they have no problem asking you to step aside if you're not helping. They will (respectfully) check their

leaders, their bosses, their professors, because frankly they're not all that impressed with the mess we've made of things.

- They're also ready to have the tough conversations. They're aware of the landmines, but yearning for real talk about complicated issues—the kind of conversation that connects and unites and ultimately moves mountains.

I appreciate how they wrestle with their conflicting (or is it complimentary?) notions of pragmatism and idealism, empathy and disdain, anxiety and optimism. It's inspiring and real and so very relatable. Two more months to go with this cohort of students, and I'm learning from them every day.

Candice Reed, LinkedIn Post, available at https://www.linkedin.com/posts/candicelreed_positivepsychology-attorneywellbeing-wellbeing-activity-7026598929899159552-7k1w?utm_source=share&utm_medium=member_desktop.

CHAPTER 28

REFLECTIONS ON A REWARDING CAREER AS A LAWYER

■ ■ ■

Chapter Hypothetical. After many years of practicing law, you are ready to retire and enjoy the good life. As you start to look back on your life as a lawyer, how do you hope you will be remembered? How will you judge whether you have been successful in your legal career?

There are a few rules of professional conduct that have particular application for a lawyer approaching the end of their career. For example, a lawyer or law firm that is thinking about selling the firm must comply with the requirements of Rule 1.17, including notifying clients about the proposed sale. As lawyers near retirement, they need to consider how any unresolved client matters will be taken care of upon retirement. Even younger lawyers for whom the thoughts of retirement are not in the front of their minds need to plan for the unfortunate possibility of an untimely death. Thus, a solo practitioner's duty of diligence may require that the attorney prepare a plan that designates another lawyer to review client files and take appropriate protective action in the event of the solo practitioner's death or disability. *See* Model Rule 1.3, Comment. 5.

But as a lawyer's professional life comes to a close, the more relevant issues for most lawyers will be related to satisfaction and success. A lawyer cannot know at the beginning of their career what the future holds. As some of the decisions in the book illustrate, some lawyers serve as cautionary tales for others. Yet, this book has also included numerous examples of lawyers whose careers serve as models for future lawyers. More examples follow in this chapter. What is it that accounts for the different paths that some lawyers' professional lives take?

A group of researchers on the subject of effective leadership identified four components of enduring success: happiness (feelings of pleasure and contentment); achievement (accomplishments that compare favorably against similar goals others have strived for); significance (the sense that you've made a positive impact on people you care about); and legacy (a way to establish your values or accomplishments so as to help others find future success). Laura Nash & Howard Stevenson, *Success That Lasts*, HARV. BUS. REV., Feb. 2004, at 104. As Professor Deborah Rhode notes, "The challenge for leaders is setting priorities that strike a balance among all four goals." Deborah L. Rhode, *What Lawyers Lack: Leadership*, 9 U. ST. THOMAS L.J. 471, 495 (2011).

"Successful" lawyers may follow different paths to attain their success. Some reflect on their careers and feel a sense of accomplishment and significance in having made a positive impact on the lives of their clients. Others leave behind a legacy of serving as a leader within their law offices or the organized bar. Others derive a sense of happiness and achievement by serving as mentors or role models.

Other lawyers may derive satisfaction from serving as leaders within the broader community. When Thomas Jefferson designed the first law school curriculum at the College of William & Mary in 1780, he did so with the idea that newly-trained lawyers would help preserve America's constitutional republican government and so would need to be "virtuous leaders who would place the public interest above their own private interest . . . [and be] well positioned to provide direction and leadership to the new nation." Davison M. Douglas, *The Jeffersonian Vision of Legal Education*, 51 J. LEGAL EDUC. 185, 185 (2001). In order to receive their degrees, aspiring lawyers were required to study a host of "non-legal" subjects (philosophy, rhetoric, the law of nations, etc.) so that aspiring lawyers could "assume positions of leadership in the secular world." *Id.* at 196.

As you read the following article discussing the career of Tennessee Supreme Court Justice Sharon Lee at the time of her retirement from the court, reflect upon the ways in which you would regard her career as a success.

A PASSION FOR JUSTICE: SHARON G. LEE

T Law News, A Digital Newsletter of the
University of Tennessee College of Law, September 2023

Tennessee Supreme Court Justice Sharon G. Lee retired in 2023 after serving on the state's highest court for 15 years. In her wake, she leaves a celebrated legacy of fair decision-making and a desire to ensure justice for every citizen.

Childhood in the Courtroom

Growing up in Madisonville, Tennessee, Lee walked to the Monroe County Courthouse after school every day. Her mother served there as clerk of the chancery court and her uncle, nationally-known plaintiffs' lawyer J.D. Lee, had a law office across the street. "I watched a lot of trials and spent time in my uncle's office," Lee recalls—but she did not envision a career in law. "There were not any women lawyers at that time. I never saw anyone who looked like me, so I didn't see it in my future."

Still, early exposure to the courtroom sparked Lee's interest. After initially pursuing education in the medical field, she turned to business, earning a degree in accounting from the Haslam College of Business in 1975. While she enjoyed her studies and graduated with high honors, Lee didn't think a career in public accounting was for her. "Law school seemed the only option," she says. Despite the continued scarcity of female lawyers, Lee began researching law schools with her uncle's encouragement. "He advised me to go to UT College of Law because I'd get a great education and make connections that would serve me for the rest of my career. And he was right."

Broad Range of Experience

Lee went to work for her uncle after graduation. A year later, she was ready to build her own practice. For the next 26 years, she worked as a general practitioner in Madisonville, handling a wide variety of work from boundary line disputes to custody cases, wills, personal injury cases, partnership dissolutions, and even a capital murder case. "I ran the gauntlet in the cases I handled and enjoyed every bit of that experience," Lee says. She loved getting to know her clients and making a positive difference in their lives. "That personal connection that you make with clients in a small town is what stands out to me. Many people can't afford to pay, but in a small town, you do pro bono work without hesitation."

During her tenure in Monroe County, Lee also served as county attorney and city attorney for two of the four cities in the county, and as city judge for Madisonville. Those experiences convinced her she would enjoy being a judge. When there was an opening on the Tennessee Court of Appeals, two judges approached Lee to suggest she apply. "I initially said no, but they planted the seed and encouraged me," Lee says. Finally, deciding she had nothing to lose, Lee worked hard to let the selection commission know who she was and why she was qualified. She was appointed by Gov. Phil Bredesen in 2004, the first woman to serve on the Eastern Section of the court in its nearly eight-decade history.

Focus on the People

Lee's new role as a judge prompted a change of pace in her work life. In private practice, she had a heavy case load and needed to work quickly and efficiently. "When I became a Court of Appeals judge, I had to slow myself down, become more thoughtful and deliberate—and realize I didn't always have to reach an instant decision."

In 2008, Lee was appointed to fill a vacancy on the Tennessee Supreme Court. Her time in general practice gave her experience in many types of criminal and civil cases, and she brought that understanding to the Supreme Court. "Most importantly, I knew the effect a court's decision has on individuals, families, and businesses," she says. "No matter what the case is, there is always a person on the other end."

With that understanding, Lee sought to view every case through the lens of lawyer and client. "I try to state the ruling so that lawyers and judges can understand and apply it—but also so the party involved can understand my reasoning, know they were heard, and see that I did my best to be fair and just."

Rodd Barckhoff, adjunct professor and interim director of the Center for Advocacy and Dispute Resolution at the College of Law, worked with Lee for almost 15 years when he served as a staff attorney for the Tennessee Supreme Court. "I can attest to her legendary work ethic, intelligence, and preparation," Barckhoff says. "Her writing as a jurist is unmistakably her voice. Read any of her majority or dissenting opinions and you'll hear equal measures of common sense, vision, and wisdom—and above all else, a concern for fairness."

Leadership and Community Investment

During her term as Chief Justice of the Tennessee Supreme Court from 2014–2016, Lee proposed the Davidson County Business Court Pilot Project to increase the justice system's efficiency in handling complex business cases. The project saw remarkable success, resolving many important complex business cases in a relatively short time. "This was an important way for the Court to respond to a need," Lee says, "and a great way to encourage businesses to locate in Tennessee and stay here."

Outside her career in law, Lee has invested time in her family and community, raising two daughters and now spending time with her three grandchildren. She's also served as a board member of the YWCA of Knoxville and the Tennessee Valley Authority, the YWCA Foundation, the Monroe County Boys and Girls Club, and the East Tennessee Historical Society, and contributed to the College of Law through presentations and council appointments. "Justice Lee has been an invaluable supporter and resource for me during my first year as dean of the College of Law," Dean Lonnie T. Brown, Jr. says. "She is a person of great integrity, conviction, and courage. I am so proud and thankful that we can claim her as one of our own, and that our students have such a wonderful role model to inspire them."

Passion and Purpose

From start to finish, Lee is motivated by a firm belief in justice. "I really believe everyone should be treated fairly, with dignity and respect," she says. "No one is above or beneath the law."

A few years ago, Lee was checking out at a local grocery store when the cashier suddenly thanked her. "You represented me and helped me get custody of my granddaughter," the woman told Lee. "Now she is graduating from high school and starting college."

Lee didn't remember the case, but in that moment, she realized how a routine part of her day many years ago had affected this woman and her family in a significant way. "My daughter was home that weekend studying for the bar," Lee recalls. "I told her the story and said, 'This is why we are lawyers.' Using your talents, skills, and education to help people who find themselves in difficult circumstances—that's what it's all about."

* * *

Another example of a lawyer who used his legal training to serve as a leader within his community is Mahatma Gandhi. Before returning to India to help lead India's independence movement, Gandhi was a lawyer in South Africa for twenty years. As described by Professor Charles DiSalvo in his book *M.K. Gandhi, Attorney at Law: The Man Before the Mahatma* (2013), Gandhi developed a successful commercial law practice by representing Indian merchants in South Africa. Upon arriving in South Africa, he found that European colonists were seeking to deny Indians their civil and economic liberties. Having become a respected figure in South Africa's Indian community, Gandhi's merchant clients turned to him for assistance. In this capacity, "Gandhi acted as the community's political organizer, not as the community's lawyer." Charles R. DiSalvo, *Attorney Gandhi's Questions*, W. VA. LAWYER (Jan–Mar. 2014), at 37. In his time outside of his practice, Gandhi helped organize citizens and sought to bring the denial of Indian civil rights to the attention of government officials.

DiSalvo describes the second phase of Gandhi's legal career: "When the attacks on Indian rights nevertheless continued, Gandhi altered the shape of his practice and his life. In this second phase, Gandhi began to devote some of his professional work and time to defending his community. When the colonial government, for example, attempted to drive Indians out of businesses by denying them the necessary operating licenses, Gandhi and a colleague went to court to fight this effort. . . . Gandhi performed this work while continuing to operate, and indeed expand, his commercial law practice. Alongside his community work, he continued his business practice. The two aspects of his practice operated parallel with, but separate from, each other." *Id.*

Eventually, when the attacks on Indian civil liberties continued, many Indians engaged in civil disobedience. "When his Indian compatriots resisted the law and found themselves prosecuted in criminal court by the government, it was Gandhi who was at their side. In this portion of his life, Gandhi dedicated his entire practice to defense work. The needs of his clients and his community commanded his complete professional attention and entirely defined his practice." *Id.*

* * *

At the end of your life, what do you want your legacy to be? What will a eulogist say of you at your memorial service? It is hard to imagine living a more meaningful or remarkable life than Pamela L. Reeves, who served as Chief Judge of the U.S. District Court for the Eastern District of Tennessee.

Born in 1954, Reeves grew up in a loving family in the mountains of Southwest Virginia. She did not have indoor plumbing until she was twelve years old. In her own words, "I came from very humble beginnings. I did not have a lot to inspire or motivate me as a child."

She was the first member of her family to attend college. She attended the University of Tennessee where she was involved in student government. She went on to attend law school at the University of Tennessee College of Law. While in law school, one of her most memorable and significant achievements was her work on the case *Tennessee Valley Authority v. Hill*, 437 U.S. 153 (1978). In the case, the U.S. Supreme Court held that the Endangered Species Act prohibited the Tennessee Valley Authority's completion of a dam project that would impact the survival of the endangered snail darter.

After law school, Reeves married Charles Swanson, her law school classmate. They had two children, Reedy and Amanda. In her legal career, Reeves specialized in sexual harassment law—one of the first attorneys in Tennessee with this specialty. She also became involved in bar association service. "I learned that when you serve on committees and you're willing to do the grunt work, you learn about the organization from the bottom up," Reeves explained. "And then when the time comes when you might be in a position to become a leader, people respect you because they know you've paid your dues." She would go on to be the first female president of the Tennessee Bar Association. Later, she would become the first female judge to serve on the U.S. District Court for the Eastern District of Tennessee. *Pamela Reeves Obituary*, KNOXVILLE NEWS SENTINEL, (September 11–13, 2020); *Pamela Reeves Interview*, UT Law's Institute for Professional Leadership's Six Pack Series, available at https://youtu.be/2fg_yJKitXI.

In 2020, Judge Reeves died after a battle with cancer. Swanson sent a message to her close friends on the day she passed away. He has given us permission to share that message with you.

Email to Friends Regarding the Passing of Pamela Reeves

From Charles Swanson (Sept. 10, 2020)

I am very sad to say this will be our final Pam Report. We lost our Pam at 11:45 a.m. today.

Over the past few weeks, Pam has been the recipient of many, many visits by those who were led to see her a last time and to share with her heartfelt appreciation for the person she has been and the amazing impact she has had on her friends (all of us!), persons she mentored, counseled and advised, her profession, her community, and the hearts and minds of all who were fortunate enough to have our path through this world brightened by the power and love of Comet Pam. What a privilege it has been to watch and listen as so many came to say thank you in such emotionally heartfelt ways.

So many, as well, took time in these last days to write, text, call, email, and send recorded messages of love, devotion, gratitude and admiration. These messages were received with the humble "Who, me?" attitude those who knew her so well have come to expect. But they were all so real, so marked by wonder, love, and gratitude that when it became necessary to read them to her—because she could not focus herself—I could barely do it without having to stop every paragraph to gather my emotions.

Here is a small sample of hundreds of messages sent in the past few days: "I would never have pushed myself to do the things I have done without your encouragement." "You were not cut from the same cloth as the rest of us. . . . Choosing to find the best in everyone. . . above petty conflicts, ignoring personal affronts. . . you have an inner compass that has never failed you." "Thank you for being a wonderful example of how to be a strong, professional woman." "New to the area, I had not heard of you when you assumed the bench. . . , yet, to this day, NEVER have I heard an unflattering word. . . . . You are fair, firm, respected and care about the people who come before you." "What a positive impact you have had on my life." "When we think of you, we smile." "You are the one who cleared out my fridge when my mother-in-law died." "You are a very strong and special lady. . . such an inspiration." "You are always giving a damn when it is not your turn to give a damn!" "Thank you for being an amazing role model. . . . You overcame every hurdle and helped others overcome their hurdles. . . passionate, caring, fearless, and determined. . . ." "Your professional and personal impact on our state has been so significant. . . . You have led, mentored, and inspired so many."

This is just a sample. You can't tell which of these was a next door neighbor child, which was a law school dean, and which was a Supreme Court Justice. Neither could she.

I always end these reports with a statement of gratitude. While this may be my last Pam Report for a while, this one can be no different. Thank you. Thank you for loving her, thank you for being a major part of our lives, thank you for your endless and overwhelming kindnesses you have extended to us throughout this journey. She taught us how to love and how to treat each other and how to hold one another close through good times and bad. Thank you to each and every one of you from the bottom of my currently aching heart. She taught us in her life and in her death how much we need each other and that will be no less true tomorrow than it is today.

Let us together honor her life, her love and her legacy by staying close and by loving each other from the bottom of our hearts. I have started my part of that pledge already.

Much, much love,

Charles

———

Profile of Attorney Professionalism. Throughout this book, you have read Profiles of Attorney Professionalism. These profiles have highlighted trailblazers, community leaders, new attorneys pursuing a passion and serving others, distinguished judges who made a mark, and seasoned attorneys who made an impact for their clients and their communities. If you were to be included in the next edition of this book, what would you want us to say about you as a law student? What do you hope would be written about your career fifty years from today?

INDEX

References are to Pages

ADMISSION TO THE BAR
See Bar Admission, this index

ADVERTISING
See Marketing of Legal Services, this index

AMERICAN BAR ASSOCIATION (ABA)
Bar examination
    See Bar Admission, this index
    Generally, 15
    Multi-State Professional Responsibility Examination (MPRE), 14–15
Law school accreditation, 45, 52, 116, 601

AMERICANS WITH DISABILITIES ACT (ADA)
Bar exam, 31
Law offices, 114–15
Representing Clients, 242, 245, 602

APPELLATE PRACTICE
Decision to appeal, 456
Frivolous appeals, 456–58

ATTORNEY-CLIENT PRIVILEGE
Clawback agreements, 313
Definition, 293–95
Disclosure and waiver, 312–13
Educating clients to protect privilege, 316
Exceptions, 304–05
Organizational clients, 545–47
Reducing the risk of privilege waiver, 314–17
Waiver through intentional conduct, 304–12
Work Product Doctrine
    See Work Product Doctrine, this index

ATTORNEY-CLIENT RELATIONSHIP
Authority and power to obligate the client, 239–40
Client wrongdoing
    Avoiding complicity in client misconduct, 523–25
    Client crime and fraud, 282–83
    Preventing and rectifying consequences of client crime and fraud, 282–83
Client's rights & responsibilities
    Allocation of decision-making authority, 233–38
    Lawyers' power to obligate clients, 239–40
Court appointments, 83–90, 193–94
Declining cases, 193–94
Safekeeping client funds & property
    See Client Funds & Property, this index
Scope of relationship
    Generally, 185–93
    Limited scope representation, 186
    Unbundled legal services, 192
Termination of attorney-client relationship
    See Termination of Client-Lawyer Relationship, this index
When relationship is formed, 179–85

AUTHORITY AND POWER TO OBLIGATE CLIENT
See Attorney-Client Relationship, this index

BAR ADMISSION
Character & fitness
    Generally, 15–33
    Candor, 32–33
    Criminal history, 30
    Financial responsibility, 30–31
    Mental health, 31–32
    References, 44
    Substance abuse, 32
Examination, 15
General requirements, 14–15
Multi-jurisdictional practice
    See Multi-Jurisdictional Practice, this index

BAR ASSOCIATIONS
American Bar Association (ABA)
    See American Bar Association, this index

BILLING THE CLIENT
See Fees, this index

CANDOR
Bar admission, 32–33
Duty of candor toward a tribunal, 450–55

CHARACTER & FITNESS
See Bar Admission, this index

CLIENT FUNDS & PROPERTY
Generally, 225–27
Interest on Lawyer's Trust Accounts (IOLTA), 226
Returning papers, property, and client advances for fees not earned, 380
Third party claims, 226
Trust accounts, 225–26

CLIENT-LAWYER RELATIONSHIP
See Attorney-Client Relationship, this index

COMPETENCE
Agreements prospectively limited a lawyer's liability, 353
Constitutionally ineffective assistance of counsel, 477–88
Disciplinary rules, 251–53
Malpractice
    See Malpractice, this index
Preserving confidentiality competently, 314–17

CONFIDENTIALITY
Attorney-client privilege
    See Attorney-Client Privilege, this index
Competently preserving confidentiality, 314–17
Disclosure
    See Disclosure, this index
Duty of confidentiality, 276–80
Duty to resist disclosure, 320
Exceptions to confidentiality, 281–90
    Client crime or fraud, 282–84
    Complying with court order or law, 285–89
    Detecting conflicts of interest, 289–90
    Establishing claim or defense, 284–85
    Preventing death or substantial bodily harm, 281–82
    Securing legal advice, 284
Former clients
    See Former Client Conflicts, this index
General principles, 389–91
Lawyer's relationship with others, 327–30
Organizational clients
    See Organizational Clients, this index

CONFLICTS OF INTEREST
Conflicts of Interest
    Consent, 330–39
    Directly adverse conflicts, 322–25
    General principles, 321–22
    Imputed or Vicarious Conflicts, 321
    Material limitation conflicts, 325–30
Conflicts of Interest Between Lawyer and Client
    See Conflicts of Interest Between Lawyer and Client, this index
Criminal defense, 486–88
Disclosure to detect conflicts of interest, 289–90
Former clients
    See Former Client Conflicts, this index
Organizational clients
    See Organizational Clients, this index
Positional conflicts, 326
Pro bono
    See Pro Bono Service, this index
Transactional representation, 521–23

CONFLICTS OF INTEREST BETWEEN LAWYER AND CLIENT
Agreements regarding a lawyer's liability to a client, 353
Business transactions with clients, 344–51
Financial assistance and gifts to clients, 354–55
Gifts from clients, 352–53
Insurance and client conflicts, 356–63
Lawyer's relationship with others, 327–30
Literary rights of clients, 355
Receiving payments for the representation from a third person, 356–63
Sex with clients, 351–52
Using information to the disadvantage of a client, 354

CONTINGENT FEES
Generally, 197
Prohibited contingent fees
    Criminal cases, 207–08
    Domestic relations, 207–08

CORPORATIONS
See Organizational Clients, this index

COURT APPOINTMENTS
See Pro Bono Service, this index

CRIMINAL DEFENSE PRACTICE
Conflicts of interest, 487–88
Constitutionally ineffective assistance of counsel, 477–88
Legal malpractice, 488–94
Prosecutors
    See Criminal Prosecution Practice, this index
Rules of professional conduct, 494–96

DEFAMATION
Generally, 418, 456

DEPOSITIONS
See Pre-Trial Advocacy, this index

DILIGENCE
Generally, 252–53
Agreements prospectively limiting a lawyer's liability, 353
Disciplinary rules, 252–53

DIMINISHED CAPACITY OF CLIENTS
Guardian ad litem, 243–44

Representing clients with diminished capacity, 242–45

DISCIPLINE
ABA Model Rules for Lawyer Disciplinary Enforcement, 36
ABA Standards for Imposing Lawyer Sanctions, 52
Hierarchy of discipline, 52
Reciprocal discipline, 36
Self-Incrimination, 36

DISCLOSURE
Adverse legal authority, 450–51
Authorized disclosures
    Exceptions to the lawyer's duty of confidentiality, 281–90
    Impliedly-authorized, 276–77
Former client information
    See Former Client Conflicts, this index
Generally, 390–91
Inadvertent disclosure, 312–14
Lack of malpractice insurance, 270
Perjury, 452–55
Work product disclosure
    See Work Product Doctrine, this index

DISCOVERY
See Litigation, this index

DUTIES
Care, 4
Competence and diligence, 4, 251–68
Fiduciary duties
    See Fiduciary Duty, this index
Former Clients
    See Former Client Conflicts, this index
Loyalty
    Generally, 4
Prospective clients, 181–85
Third parties
    See Third Parties, this index

EX PARTE COMMUNICATION
See Judges, this index

FEES
Contingent fees
    See Contingent Fees, this index
Expenses, 206
Fee-sharing arrangements, 212
Hourly fees and flat fees, 197
Liens, 383–84
Non-refundable retainers, 208–12
Prohibited contingent fees, 207–08
Reasonableness, 198–207

FIDUCIARY DUTY
Generally, 4–5, 275–80
Civil liability for breach of fiduciary duty, 4–5, 275

Client Funds and Property, Safekeeping
    See Client Funds & Property, this index
Confidentiality
    See Confidentiality, this index
Conflicts of Interest
    See Conflicts of Interest, this index

FORMER CLIENT CONFLICTS
Conflicts of interest, 389–410
Material Adversity, 391–92
Playbook information, 393–98
Screening, 398–409
Substantially related, 392–98

INTEREST ON LAWYERS' TRUST ACCOUNTS (IOLTA)
See Client Funds and Property, this index

JUDGES
Communicating with judges ex parte, 515–16
Criticizing judges, 504
Judicial misconduct
    Avoiding complicity, 517
    Lawyer monitoring, 565
    Reporting, 516–17
Personal and extrajudicial activities of judges, 506–08
Political and campaign activities, 500–05
Recusal, 508–15
Standards of Conduct, 505–08

LAW FIRMS
Discrimination, Diversity, and Inclusion, 113–17
Law firm names, 144
Law-Related Services, 62
Leaving a firm, 117–23
    Wrongful discharge, 113
Non-competition agreements, 122–23
Non-lawyer ownership of law firms, 93–94
Organizational structure, 104
Partners, managers, & supervisory lawyers, 104–10
Sale of Law Practice, 65
Subordinate lawyers, 110–13
Supervisory lawyers, 109

LITIGATION
Adverse legal authority disclosure, 450–51
Appeals, 456–58
Communicating with jurors, the judge, and court officers, 442–43
Criminal defense practice
    See Criminal Defense Practice, this index
Cross-examinations, 454–55
Deception and trickery, 445–50
Disclosure of adverse legal authority
    See Disclosure, this index
Discovery, 427–39
    Depositions and perjury, 439

Frivolous discovery requests and
objections, 438–39
Inadvertent disclosure, 312–13, 439
Manipulating evidence, 437–38
Preservation and spoliation, 428–37
Protecting privilege and work
product, 314–17, 439
Discriminatory comments and actions,
444–45
Disruptive and disrespectful behavior, 444–45
Frivolous claims and motions, 419–27
Irrelevant or inadmissible information, 441
Lawyer acting as a witness, 442
Manipulating evidence, 437–38
Perjury, 452–55
Pre-trial advocacy, 415–40
Preservation and spoliation, 428–38
Prosecutors
See Prosecutors, this index
Time-barred claims, 427
Trial publicity, 455–56, 474
Truthfulness & candor, 445–55

MALPRACTICE
Civil liability for malpractice
Generally, 4, 253–70
Causation and damages, 269–70
Duty and breach, 253–68
Informed judgment/Judgmental
immunity rule, 257–68
Malpractice insurance
Generally, 270–71
Disclosure of lack of insurance, 270
Filing claims, 271
Mandatory insurance, 270
Notification of claims, 271
Settling claims, 353

MARKETING OF LEGAL SERVICES
Advertising, 123–44
Constitutional landscape, 125–36
False or misleading communications,
136–37
Law firm names, 144
Online marketing, 137–43
Regulatory landscape, 136–45
Specializations, 143
Client referrals
Generally, 144
Legal services plans and lawyer
referral services, 145
Reciprocal fee agreements, 145
Solicitation
Live person-to-person contact, 148–61
Other restrictions on lawyer
solicitation, 162–73
Websites, 137

MISCONDUCT
Attempt to violate a rule, 38
Conduct prejudicial to the administration
of justice, 40–41
Criminal acts, 38–39

Dishonest conduct, 39–40
Harassing or discriminatory conduct, 41
Reporting misconduct, 42–52

MULTI-JURISDICTIONAL PRACTICE
Attorney licensure in multiple
jurisdictions, 64–65
Choice of law, 74–75
Remote practice, 73
Temporary practice in a state where not
licensed, 66–73
Pro hac vice admission, 66–67
Unauthorized practice of law, 67–74

NEGOTIATION
Honesty, 526–32

ORGANIZATIONAL CLIENTS
Attorney-client privilege, 545–55
Authorized Agents, 241–42, 545
Conflicts of interest, 555–57
Derivative litigation, 540, 556
Internal investigations, 548–55
Loyal disclosure, 543–45
Protecting organizational clients from
constituent misconduct, 540–45
Serving as director of organizational
clients, 522–23
Up-the-ladder reporting, 541–43

PLEA BARGAINING
See Prosecutors, this index

PRE-TRIAL ADVOCACY
See Litigation, this index

PRO BONO SERVICE
Access to justice problem
Generally, 77–78
Use of non-lawyer to address, 90–94
Use of technology to address, 90, 94–98
Attorney Pro Bono, 81–82
Bar admission requirement, 79–81
Conflicts of interest, 83
Court appointments, 83–90
Law Student Pro Bono, 78–79
Mandatory pro bono, 94
Accepting court appointments, 98–105
Promoting pro bono, 92–93
Reporting, 81–82
State rules, 81

PROSECUTORS
Brady duties, 470–73
Conflicts of interest, 468
Decision to charge
Generally, 469–70
Prosecutor's liability, 470
Defense counsel
See Criminal Defense Practice, this
index
Exculpatory evidence, 470–73
Investigative function, 462–69

Newly-Discovered Evidence, 475
Plea bargaining, 469
Remedying wrongful convictions, 475
Role of prosecutors, 461–62
Subpoenas to lawyers, 469
Trial publicity
    See Litigation, this index

RECUSALS
See Judges, this index

REFERRALS
See Marketing of Legal Services, this index

REGULATION OF LEGAL PROFESSION
Discipline
    Generally, 35–37
    Disciplinary process, 36–37
    Imposing disciplinary sanctions, 52–55
    Model Rules for Lawyer Disciplinary Enforcement, 36–37
Model Rules of Professional Conduct, 35–36
Other consequences of attorney misconduct, 55
Reporting professional misconduct, 42–52
Voluntary compliance with model rules, 37

RETALIATORY OR WRONGFUL DISCHARGE
See Law Firms, this index

SARBANES-OXLEY ACT
Generally, 540
Reporting misconduct, 540–45

SCREENING
Former clients, 398–409
Government lawyers, 408
Judges, 408
Law clerks, 408
Litigation, 408
Transactions, 408

SOLICITATION
See Marketing of Legal Services, this index

TERMINATION OF CLIENT-LAWYER RELATIONSHIP
Former clients
    See Former Client Conflicts, this index
Hybrid fee agreements and public policy, 380
Liens, 383–84
Returning client property and unearned fees, 384–85
Termination by client
    Generally, 367–71
    Effect on lawyer's compensation, 371
    Discharge without cause, 371
Termination by lawyer
    Generally, 371–80
    Mandatory withdrawal, 372–73
    Permissive withdrawal, 373–80
Wrongful discharge claims, 113

THIRD PARTIES
Insurance defense and the tripartite relationship, 356–63
Third party payment of fees, 356

TRANSACTIONAL PRACTICE
Advising clients, 524–26
Avoiding complicity in client misconduct, 524–26, 532
Competently representing clients in non-litigation matters, 523–24
Conflicts of interest, 521–23
Liability for participating in client misconduct, 533–36
Loyal disclosure, 543–45
Negotiation honesty, 526–32
Protecting organizational clients from constituent misconduct, 540–45
Up-the-ladder reporting, 541–43

UNAUTHORIZED PRACTICE OF LAW
Generally, 57–64

WEBSITES
See Marketing of Legal Services, this index

WELL-BEING
    Generally, 563–88
Bar admission, 569–73
Client harm, 575–76
Ethics issues, 562–69
Resources and support, 574
Thriving as law students and lawyers, 581–88
Warning signs of attorney distress, 577–81

WORK PRODUCT DOCTRINE
Clawback agreements and orders, 313
Defined, 302–03
Exceptions, 304–05
Inadvertent disclosure and waiver, 312–13
Organizational clients, 545–55
Waiver through intentional conduct, 304–12